MANUFACTURING OPERATIONS STRATEGY
THIRD EDITION

ALEX HILL & TERRY HILL

palgrave
macmillan

Previously published as *Manufacturing Strategy: Text and Cases* in 1995 and 2000
This edition published 2009 by
PALGRAVE MACMILLAN

Palgrave Macmillan in the UK is an imprint of Macmillan Publishers Limited, registered in England, company number 785998, of Houndmills, Basingstoke, Hampshire RG21 6XS.

Palgrave Macmillan in the US is a division of St Martin's Press LLC, 175 Fifth Avenue, New York, NY 10010.

Palgrave Macmillan is the global academic imprint of the above companies and has companies and representatives throughout the world.

Palgrave® and Macmillan® are registered trademarks in the United States, the United Kingdom, Europe and other countries.

ISBN-13: 978–0–230–52091–2
ISBN-10: 0–230–52091–X

This book is printed on paper suitable for recycling and made from fully managed and sustained forest sources. Logging, pulping and manufacturing processes are expected to conform to the environmental regulations of the country of origin.

A catalogue record for this book is available from the British Library.

Short Contents

Chapter

Case Studies

Long Contents

7 FOCUS: PRINCIPLES AND CONCEPTS — 205

8 FOCUS: METHODOLOGY — 225

CASE STUDIES   373

Preface to the Third Edition

Currently in many industrial companies, strategic developments are predominantly based on marketing decisions at the front end of the debate, with operations being forced to react to these at the back end of the process. Since operations managers come late into these discussions, it is difficult for them to successfully influence corporate decisions. The outcome is the loss of the sizable and key operations perspectives and understanding of markets and customers and sometimes the formulation and later development of strategies which operations is unable to successfully support. This is not to say that this happens for lack of trying; the work ethic is strong in the operations culture. However, if the basic link between the operations processes and infrastructure (that is, operations strategy) and the market is not strategically sound, then – by definition – the business will suffer.

The many reasons why this happens are addressed in the book. Significant among them is that typically the attention of operations managers primarily focuses upon the day-to-day part of their task. It concerns operational detail and is output-oriented, while in strategic terms their role is seen as being reactive.

The purpose of this book is twofold. First, it is to help operations executives to recognize and undertake the strategic dimension of their task. It is intended to help them think, analyse and discuss corporate issues and to formulate a functional strategy in line with the needs of a firm's markets.

Second, it is to provide the wherewithal for executives in other functions to relate to, understand and discuss operations' strategic role and contribution to supporting a company's agreed markets. The way in which the book fulfils this purpose is to introduce and explain the concepts, ideas and language that underpin the emerging subject area of operations strategy.

In this way it helps to provide insights and evaluates operations' corporate contribution through strategic perspectives, rather than just through short-term performance. It not only helps operations managers to develop and provide appropriate corporate-level inputs, but also enables other executives to recognize and appreciate the strategic perspectives which emanate from operations and which need to be given due consideration within the business debate.

The strategic perspective of operations forms the basis on which the book is written, but the approach places these issues within the rightful context of the business whole. Thus, it recognizes that in today's world, the majority of companies will be unable to sustain success over a long period of time if their strategy is based upon a limited view of what is important. The book, therefore, emphasizes the essential requirement to link operations strategy to those of marketing and other functions in order to determine the best strategies for the business as a whole. In summary, the book is written as an attempt to:

1   Close the gap between operations and marketing in terms of strategy formulation.

2   Provide a set of principles and concepts which are pragmatic in nature and designed to be applied to each different part of a business.

3   Offer an analytical approach to the development of operations strategy rather than advocate a set of prescriptive solutions. Each business and each part of each business is different. The resolution of strategy through prescription is, therefore, by definition inappropriate. Furthermore, the complexity in operations is such that it encourages companies to take strategic short cuts. As a consequence, prescriptive approaches seem doubly attractive. The book argues strongly against such approaches. In suggesting a means of developing an operations strategy and raising essential issues throughout, it provides a way of coping with this complexity. The principles and concepts outlined provide a basis for placing operational detail in an essential strategic framework.

Outlined in the book is a basic approach to developing an operations strategy which has been used successfully in many companies throughout the world. It provides a logical, practical and effective way for operations to interface with marketing and other functions in formulating business strategy. In so doing, it ensures that the 'front-end' debate concerns not just the outward-looking stance of marketing, but the outward-looking stance of the business as a whole. This thereby reduces the number of situations in which marketing-led strategies may be adopted which – in overall terms – will be harmful to the business. It does this by emphasizing the consequences for the total business of different decisions – a technique which is a prerequisite for developing sound strategic direction.

Many executives shy away from discussions of operations because they see it as an area of technology and/or complex detail. This is because, traditionally, operations is presented in this form. The approach in this book is to group together relevant operational detail into key strategic issues, and to provide an understanding of how these apply in companies. The development of a strategic language also gives the opportunity to move away from what often constitutes current practice – a discussion of operational problems. This is not only an inappropriate operations contribution at the executive level, but also has the effect of dulling the interest of other functions in examining the operations issues involved. Strategic language, on the other hand, helps to orient and maintain the debate at the appropriate level. It stimulates executive interest and enables others to address the complexity by creating a manageable number of operations variables.

The book comprises eleven chapters, followed by a number of case studies. Chapter 1 sets the scene by drawing some important international comparisons at national, industry and plant levels. The exhibits embody a growing awareness of the fact that those countries which clearly emphasize the importance of operations' contribution to business success have consistently outperformed other developed countries with a sound industrial tradition.

The core of the book is in the nine central chapters. The headings highlight some key developments within operations strategy. Together they form the substance of the language development as well as the methodologies to be used in its formulation. Chapters 2, 3 and 4 provide the context and content on the approach to be adopted when developing an operations strategy and detail what needs to be undertaken at each step. They include some illustrations to help with this explanation. Chapter 5 deals exclusively with the choice of process, the basis for that choice and the business implications that follow. Chapter 6 introduces the concept of 'product profiling', which provides companies with a methodology for testing the current or anticipated future level of fit between the characteristics of their markets and those of their operations processes and infrastructure. Chapters 7 and 8 deal with the concept of focus and the need to assign plants or parts of a plant to a defined set of tasks. The latter provides a detailed methodology statement on how to undertake this development. Chapter 9 examines the implications behind supply chain decisions. Companies need to address where they should position themselves on the process spectrum, while realizing that both in-house and suppliers' processes fall within the remit of a firm's operations strategy as both will impact how well a company can meet the needs of its markets.

Although at first sight these last three chapters appear to concern solely operations process decisions, it is important to recognize that they are also a critical part of infrastructure formulation, since the size and shape of plants are significant factors in what constitutes an appropriate infrastructure, the subject of Chapter 10. This chapter introduces some important concepts as a way of providing a business with the insights necessary to formulate developments in the wide range of functions within operations. This approach will enable these important, expensive and time-consuming tasks to be designed in order to support the requirements of a company's markets. It will enable them to be given strategic shape and direction rather than emanating from specialized perspectives.

The final chapter concerns the area of accounting, finance and performance measurement which is important because it provides some of the essential basic data used in the formulation of strategic decisions and its measurement. As with Chapter 10, it is not intended to be a comprehensive statement of the area, but only to represent some operations management views of serious shortcomings in this essential information provision. The professional accountant may find the approach in the front end of the chapter provocative; it is intended, however, to be more constructive than that. The issues raised aim to challenge current practice and ideas as a way to stimulate improvement.

The second part of the book contains a number of case studies developed from the research and consulting activities of the authors. They have been chosen to provide, for executives and students alike, learning vehicles that, through the analysis of actual business situations, address and illustrate the concepts and approaches explored in the preceding chapters.

Finally, we trust that all who use the book will find it helpful. It is vital that operations takes its full part in strategic formulation if industrial companies are to prosper in the face of increasing world competition.

Alex Hill

Terry Hill

To
PM and HH
LK and DT
JB, SA and OJ

Summary

- Global competition increased significantly in the 1980s and has accelerated ever since.

- Over the past 30 years, the manufacturing output of countries such as the UK and US has declined in comparison to others such as Germany, Japan and France.

- Emerging nations in East and Southeast Asia are prospering from the development of their manufacturing industry.

- A nation's prosperity depends on its comparative productivity with other countries. Emerging nations are successfully challenging Western economies and, for the first time in its history, the US may see a fall in living standards over the next 20 years.

- Asian automobile companies are significantly more productive than those in the more established manufacturing nations of North America and Europe.

- Successive UK governments have seen overseas competition as necessary for developing a strong domestic manufacturing base, but the UK manufacturing industry has been slow to respond.

- High-volume UK industries such as motorcycles, automobiles, trucks and shipbuilding have been lost to emerging nations.

- Many North American and European countries have failed to recognize the size of the competitive challenge they face and the impact of increasing world manufacturing capacity. There is still too little research and development investment. Senior managers lack operations experience and do not involve operations managers in strategic discussions.

- Operations managers must become less obsessed with meeting short-term performance targets and start thinking strategically. Managers striving to overcome competitors work and think differently to those simply meeting operational targets.

- Operations managers must take the initiative, change their role and think and act more strategically.

High levels of industrial competition created a stark new reality in the 1980s. Manufacturing companies in most industrial nations struggled to survive by restructuring and downsizing their activities. This signalled an economic change that continued into the 1990s and has even increased pace into the new millennium.

Despite this new challenge, most Western companies still believe operations should focus on short-term issues and leave strategy to the marketing and finance functions. However, this book argues that an operations strategy is essential for companies to compete in domestic and world markets. Without one, it will not be able to survive, let alone grow its market share.

This chapter compares the performance of nations and businesses over the past 30 years. It shows that newer ones are outperforming those with strong industrial traditions by using different operations management approaches. This has further increased the level of competition and the need to use operations as a strategic force both within businesses and between nations.

Manufacturing output

Performance trends in a nation's wealth-creating sectors reflect the overall prosperity of the country. For most countries, manufacturing is the most significant wealth-creating activity and its level of output gives a clear insight into a country's general wellbeing.

Comparative figures on balance of payments of goods over the past 47 years reveal the mixed fortunes of major industrial nations. Some countries of manufacturing repute have lost ground, while others (for example Germany and Ireland) have maintained sound growth throughout (see *Exhibit 1.1*).

Country	1960	1970	1980	1990	2000	2002	2007
Germany	n/a	17,995	11,010	90,741	96	213,235	326,719
China	n/a	n/a	4,249	9,165	34,474	44,167	217,746
Ireland	n/a	n/a	n/a	4,827	43,279	56,257	36,314
Korea	n/a	n/a	−4,613	−2,461	16,954	14,777	29,409
Indonesia	n/a	n/a	7	5	25	24	30
Japan	n/a	n/a	0	0	0	0	0
Canada	0	0	0	0	0	0	0
Italy	n/a	n/a	n/a	0	0	0	0
US	0	0	0	0	0	0	−1
Australia	−225	441	1,187	452	−7,828	−9,601	−20,327
France	n/a	n/a	n/a	n/a	−5,684	12,641	−60,498
India	−943	−408	−7,600	−7,808	−16,496	−9,556	−61,504
UK	−808	−36	2,658	−37,414	−65,952	−95,410	−175,298

NOTE: Indonesia 1980 is 1981 and 2007 is 2006; Japan 1980 is 1985; Germany 1970 is 1971; China 1980 is 1982 and 2007 is 2006.
SOURCE: OECD, Main Economic Indicators, April 2008

EXHIBIT 1.1 Comparative balance of payments on goods for selected countries, 1960–2007 ($millions)

Of equal concern to these nations is how well they fare within the increasingly competitive markets they serve. *Exhibit 1.2* shows percentage share of world trade in manufactured goods for selected countries from 1980 to 1996. The yearly performances of these different countries vary noticeably. The US's strong export position after losing ground in the 1980s strengthened in the 1990s to reach a period high in 1996. Germany and Japan, while declining in the period, were still major performers in terms of world trade. The UK was the world's number one manufacturing nation at the start of the 1900s but now only contributes to 5 per cent of world trade. Meanwhile, several European countries have steadily improved and set an important benchmark as the major economic blocs of North America, Asia Pacific and Europe took shape in the 1990s and strengthened into the 21st century.

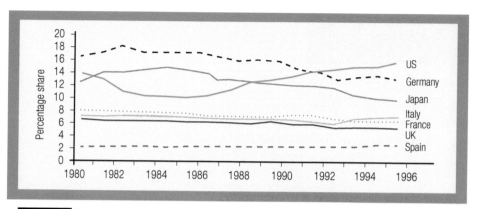

EXHIBIT 1.2 Percentage share of world trade in manufactured goods for selected countries, 1980–96

SOURCE: OECD and UK Department of Trade and Industry for relevant years

Several emerging nations are effectively competing in export markets and improving their trade balances. As a result, the world competitive position of the US and Europe has worsened. This is shown in *Exhibits 1.3, 1.4* and *1.5*. The export–import trade ratios in *Exhibit 1.3* show the relative trading performances of main manufacturing nations, while *Exhibit 1.4* provides the same export–import ratio for North America and the European Union. *Exhibit 1.5* shows the trade balance for electronic products, an increasingly important manufacturing sector.

Country	Aerospace		Electronic industry		Office machinery and computers		Pharmaceutical		Total		
	1984	1995	1984	1995	1984	1995	1984	1995	1972	1984	1995
Japan	0.10	0.26	10.55	3.07	5.61	1.97	0.27	0.40	2.82	2.78	1.74
Italy	1.09	0.99	1.19	0.64	0.74	0.81	0.97	0.97	1.31	1.24	1.30
Germany	1.05	1.08	1.45	0.93	0.87	0.59	1.74	1.51	1.53	1.42	1.28
France	2.21	2.35	1.12	0.97	0.69	0.68	1.93	1.25	1.10	1.11	1.08
Canada	0.65	1.34	0.47	0.47	0.40	0.59	0.34	0.30	n/a	1.01	1.01
UK	1.43	1.53	0.73	0.87	0.73	0.97	2.14	1.74	1.09	0.81	0.90
US	2.98	3.20	0.52	0.65	1.83	0.59	1.70	1.12	0.84	0.63	0.73
Australia	0.11	0.38	0.07	0.17	0.04	0.27	0.34	0.46	n/a	0.54	0.51

SOURCE: OECD, Main Science and Technology Indicators, 1974, 1984 and 1998

EXHIBIT 1.3 Export–import ratio for selected sectors (1984 and 1995) and total manufacturing (1972, 1984 and 1995)

Region	Total manufacturing	
	1990	1995
European Union	1.10	1.25
North America	0.71	0.69

SOURCE: OECD, Main Science and Technology Indicators, 1998

EXHIBIT 1.4 Total manufacturing export–import ratio by region

Country	1985	1993	1998
	$bn		
Japan	37.1	75.2	58.9
Singapore	1.1	11.4	22.5
Korea	2.0	11.3	17.1
Malaysia	0.7	9.0	16.9
Hong Kong	1.3	2.1	(0.5)
France	(1.5)	(4.1)	(3.9)
UK	(3.0)	(6.0)	(4.4)
Germany	(0.7)	(7.1)	(4.4)
Australia	(2.6)	(4.6)	(7.7)
Italy	(2.1)	(4.3)	(9.4)
Canada	(6.7)	(7.5)	(11.4)
Total Europe	(10.7)	(32.2)	(27.0)
US	(14.5)	(29.1)	(50.4)

NOTES
1 Electronic equipment includes electronic data processing, office equipment, controls and instruments, medical, industrial, military, communications, consumer and telecommunications. Components comprise active, passive and other.
2 These trade balances are calculated by subtracting the value of imports from the value of exports. Figures in brackets indicate an unfavourable balance.

SOURCE: *Yearbook of World Electronics Data*, 1988 and 1993, Vols 1 and 2 (Elsevier Advanced Technology, Oxford) and 1999, Vols 1 and 2 (Reed Electronics Research, Sutton)

EXHIBIT 1.5 Trade balance for electronic equipment and components for selected countries by value ($bn) for 1985, 1993 and 1998

The growing prosperity of emerging nations is built on the development of wealth-creating sectors such as manufacturing. Successive UK governments ignored this and acted on the often-painful premise that exposure to overseas competition is necessary for developing a strong domestic manufacturing base. Of deeper concern, however, was manufacturing industry's slow response to this exposure. Many UK firms complained about 'unfair' external competition and focused on domestic rather than overseas competitors. They adopted inadequate reactive strategies without appreciating the consequences of these decisions. Excess capacity tended to be filled by chasing sales, increasing variety and reducing order sizes. All this gave overseas higher volume competitors a substantial advantage and UK industries such as motorcycles, automobiles, trucks and shipbuilding have been lost. The same is true in the US and *Exhibit 1.6* shows how their car plants have had to close while Japanese companies are setting them up just down the road.

Many businesses recognized too late that competition had increased and markets had subsequently changed. They spent most of the past 25–30 years trying to catch up with their competitors and are still struggling to compete. While nations such as the US, the UK and others with long manufacturing traditions have suffered from this surge in competition, countries such as Japan and Singapore move from strength to strength. Of deep concern are the facts underlying these trends, especially that of comparative productivity between nations.

Implants			Closures		
Firm	Location	Capacity (000s cars)	Firm	Location	Capacity (000s cars)
Honda	Marysville	360	General Motors	Leeds	250
	East Liberty	150		Norwood	250
	Alliston	100		Detroit	212
				Pontiac	100
NUMMI	Fremont	100	Chrysler	Kenosha	300
Toyota	Georgetown	240	General Motors	Framington	200
	Cambridge	50		Lakewood	200
Nissan	Smyrna	480		Pontiac	54
Mazda	Flat Rock	240	Chrysler	Detroit	21
Total implant capacity		1,720	Total closure capacity		1,817

NOTE: NUMMI – New United Motor Manufacturing Inc., a joint venture between General Motors and Toyota.

EXHIBIT 1.6 The challenge of world competition: the North American auto lesson in the 1990s

Productivity: national comparisons

A nation's prosperity depends on its comparative productivity. The past three decades of increasing competition have brought this sharply into focus. Although not a precise measure, it allows performance of individual countries to be compared and ranked against each other. There are two important dimensions of a productivity slowdown for any nation. The first is the rate of the slowdown itself; the second is the cumulative effect of the slowdown on the comparative level of productivity between a country and its competitors.

When a nation's growth rate lags substantially behind that of other industrialized countries for a protracted period, its standard of living declines and companies find themselves at a serious competitive disadvantage. As this condition continues, recovery becomes increasingly difficult. For the first time in its history, the next US generation may fail to enjoy an improvement in living standards and may even experience a decline.

Productivity measures the relationship between outputs (in the form of goods and services produced) and inputs (in the form of labour, capital, material and other resources). Two types of productivity measurement are commonly used: labour productivity and total factor or multifactor productivity. Labour productivity measures output in terms of hours worked or paid for. Total factor or multifactor productivity not only includes the labour input but also all or some of the plant, equipment, energy and material input. However, a change in productivity must not be attributed to a single input. All inputs are interrelated and combine to create change. For example, production methods, capital investment, process technology, labour force, managerial performance, capacity utilization, material input/usage rates, capacity scale and product mix are all potential contributors to productivity improvements. Furthermore, the relative importance of these will vary from nation to nation, industrial sector to industrial sector, company to company, plant to plant and time period to time period.

Although it may be difficult to gain a consensus on the quantitative dimensions of productivity measurement, the qualitative conclusions on the differing levels and trends within nations are clearly shown in *Exhibits 1.7* and *1.8*. There is significant growth in countries such as Korea, Taiwan and Sweden over the past 40 years, but the comparative slowdown in the US signals that its lead is shrinking, living standards are levelling off and its competitive position is declining.

Country	1960	1970	1980	1990	1995	2000	2006
Korea	n/a	6	29	88	131	192	287
Sweden	28	53	74	95	122	177	247
Taiwan	n/a	13	45	91	113	149	199
US	53	62	94	98	115	147	198
France	23	46	71	99	114	144	175
Netherlands	20	39	70	99	120	139	167
Germany	29	52	77	99	111	132	165
Japan	14	38	64	95	109	131	161
UK	30	43	54	89	107	117	152
Belgium	18	33	65	97	109	126	148
Canada	41	59	75	95	108	134	139
Italy	20	37	44	93	114	116	111

SOURCE: Monthly Labor Review, Bureau of Labor Statistics, US Department of Labor, www.bls.gov, Feb 2007

EXHIBIT 1.7 Trends in manufacturing output per hour for selected countries, 1960–2006 (1992 = 100)

Country	Annual growth in output per hour (% per year)				
	1970–80	1980–90	1990–2000	2000–6	1970–2006
Korea	2	6	4	16	8
Sweden	2	2	3	14	6
Taiwan	3	5	2	8	5
US	3	0	2	9	4
France	3	3	2	5	4
Japan	3	3	1	5	3
Germany	3	2	1	6	3
UK	1	4	2	6	3

NOTE: Analysis is based on figures in Exhibit 1.7.

EXHIBIT 1.8 Annual percentage growth in output per hour 1970–2006

Productivity: plant-level comparisons

In the 1990s, competition significantly increased in most North American, Asia Pacific and European markets as strong 'domestic' companies were challenged by global companies. This trend has continued and relative performance against market needs will determine which companies gain ground and market share.

The automotive industry is one example of the fierce fighting taking place. This sector is core to many industrial economies due to the combined size of its manufacturing, assembly and supply chain activities. *Exhibit 1.6* showed how Japan is winning market share in the US automotive industry. Regional and global overcapacity means competition will remain high and productivity will continue to be key to an organization's success. To succeed in the future, auto companies must increase efficiency to compete against new rivals and fresh benchmarks. *Exhibit 1.9* illustrates the current productivity differences between organizations. For some, the gap is enormous and clearly shows the challenge from Japan and Korea. Furthermore, *Exhibit 1.10* shows that these differences are related to companies rather than locations by presenting the data given in *Exhibit 1.9* by location for both the parent company and manufacturing plant. The best and worst productivity figures again highlight the marked contrasts provided by Asia Pacific and the more established manufacturing nations of North America and Europe.

Auto maker and location			Vehicles (000s) produced	Vehicles per employee	
			1998	1997	1998
Canada	Toyota	Cambridge	172	n/a	83
	GM	Oshawa	459	57	57
Czech Republic	Skoda	Mlada Boleslav	288	31	35
France	Renault	Douai	385	61	68
	PSA	Aulnay	262	52	58
	PSA	Sochaux	237	26	31
Germany	GM	Eisenach	175	77	76
	Ford	Saarlouis	290	59	59
	VW	Emden	330	28	37
Italy	Fiat	Melfi	383	70	73
	Fiat	Mirafiori	416	54	61
Japan	Mitsubishi	Mizushuma	521	147	163
	Nissan	Kyushu	430	99	119
	Honda	Suzuka	568	123	116
	Honda	Sayama	485	112	114
	Mitsubishi	Okazaki	173	111	113
	Toyota	Takaota	450	122	103
Korea	Daewoo	Changwon	248	165	165
	Hyundai	Ulsan #2	157	62	65
Spain	VW	Navarra	311	70	76
	SEAT	Martorell	499	69	69
	Renault	Valladolid	214	59	64
UK	Nissan	Sunderland	289	98	105
	Toyota	Burnaston	172	58	72
	Honda	Swindon	112	62	64
	Ford	Dagenham	250	62	61
	Rover	Longbridge	282	34	31

cont'd

Auto maker and location		Vehicles (000s) produced	Vehicles per employee	
		1998	1997	1998
US	Toyota/GM NUMMI	362	87	87
	Honda East Liberty	239	85	87
	Honda Marysville	456	82	88
	Ford Atlanta	257	75	84
	Toyota Georgetown	475	78	83
	Ford Chicago	255	69	81
	Ford Wayne	227	79	72
	Nissan Smyrna	309	72	56
	GM Doraville	257	n/a	51

NOTE: GM's Oshawa figures are for two car plants.
SOURCE: *Motor Business Europe* (Q4, 1999), *Motor Business International* (Q4, 1999) and *Motor Business Japan* (Q4, 1999). The Economist Intelligence Unit (UK) 1999

EXHIBIT 1.9 Productivity in some of the world's auto plants, 1997 and 1998

Regional location		Vehicles per employee (1998)	
Parent company	Manufacturing plant	Best	Worst
European	Europe	76	31
Japanese	Japan	163	103
	Europe	105	64
	North America	88	56
North American	Europe	76	59
	North America	84	51
Korean	Korea	165	65

EXHIBIT 1.10 Best and worst productivity levels by auto maker and regional location (1998)

Why has this happened?

The reasons for this are many and varied, and are discussed below. Some are unsubstantiated opinions whereas others are supported by fact. Some are more relevant to certain nations, sectors and companies and others less so. However, learning from past failures is a step towards determining how to build a more successful competitive future.

Failure to recognize the size of the competitive challenge

Consciously or otherwise, industries and societies have failed to recognize the size of the competitive challenge, the impact it has had and will have on our very way of life and the subsequent need to change. The significant loss of smokestack industries since the 1950s in major industrial nations is the most vivid example. They misunderstood the size of the competitive challenge. And the challenge will continue. In the shadow of Japan, there are now many other competitors eager to take a larger share in world manufacturing output. *Exhibit 1.11* provides one such example.

Country	1985	1990	1995	2001	2005	2005 (1990 = 100)
China	n/a	645	1,242	2,929	2,548	395
Taiwan	381	737	1,266	1,825	2,736	371
South Korea	248	669	695	897	2,320	347
Netherlands	50	106	95	413	338	319
US	3,668	2,660	3,520	3,185	4,099	154
Italy	1,535	2,889	2,537	4,163	3,912	135
Germany	4,401	6,872	5,579	7,560	7,882	115
Spain	350	800	506	932	904	113
Japan	7,399	8,629	6,992	10,481	9,381	109
Denmark	58	67	61	62	67	100
Belgium	130	224	189	245	209	93
France	695	920	601	861	730	79
UK	1,010	1,179	753	846	577	49

NOTE: Up to 1990, the data for Germany includes the former DDR.
SOURCE: *CECIMO Statistical Overview of the Machine Tool Industry 1985–2005* (2006)

EXHIBIT 1.11 Production of machine tools without parts and accessories for selected countries (millions)

Failure to appreciate the impact of increasing manufacturing capacity

World manufacturing capacity up to the mid-1960s was, by and large, less than demand; in this period companies sold all they could make. With the rebuilding of some industrial nations and the emergence of others, output in both traditional and new industrial nations began to outstrip total demand. At first, the more traditional sectors (such as shipbuilding and steel) were caught in the bind of overcapacity. Since then, this has spread into other sectors such as automobiles and semiconductors. The most significant and consistent outcome has been the impact on competition. Overcapacity has contributed to the competitive nature of markets. The results have added to the dynamic nature of current markets both in terms of the form that competition takes and the timescales of change experienced.

Lack of research and development investment

The pressure to market more and better products has heightened in recent years because of increasing competition and shorter product life cycles. Companies must meet this need by investing in research and development (R&D). *Exhibit 1.12* shows the clear commitment of major manufacturing nations. By 1989, Japan headed the list for the first time (the detail is not included in *Exhibit 1.12* but was 2.98 per cent compared with the US at 2.88 per cent for 1989) and it continues to do so. The Korean figures also show a real commitment to technical development on which Korea is building an increasingly competitive economy. *Exhibit 1.13* shows the outcome of this approach in the international trade balance for highly intensive R&D-based industries. Both Korea and Japan export significantly more electronics products than they import. By contrast, the US has a huge deficit in electronics, office machinery and computers.

Country	1981	1985	1992	1995	1997	2002	2005
Japan	2.32	2.77	2.95	2.98	2.83	3.17	3.33
Korea	n/a	n/a	2.08	2.68	2.79	2.53	2.78
US	2.45	2.93	2.74	2.61	2.64	2.66	2.62
Germany	2.45	2.72	2.48	2.30	2.39	2.49	2.48
France	2.01	2.25	2.42	2.34	2.26	2.23	2.13
Canada	1.23	1.44	1.55	1.62	1.64	2.04	1.98
UK	2.42	2.31	2.13	2.02	1.94	1.83	1.78
Total EU	n/a	n/a	1.92	1.84	1.84	1.76	1.73
Australia	n/a	1.27	1.59	1.62	1.68	1.69	n/a
Italy	1.01	1.13	1.20	1.01	1.05	1.13	1.10

NOTE: 1995 figure for Australia is for 1994;1997 figures for Australia, Japan, South Korea, UK and Total EU are for 1996 respectively.
SOURCE: OECD, Main Science and Technology Indicators for relevant years

EXHIBIT 1.12 Gross domestic expenditure on R&D as a percentage of gross domestic product (GDP)

Country	Aerospace	Electronic industry	Office machinery and computers	Pharmaceutical	Instruments	Total
Korea	(1,188)	34,222	10,710	(1,488)	(1,284)	40,972
Japan	(5,117)	39,370	(3,264)	(4,987)	14,941	40,943
Ireland	(2,408)	1,564	6,015	18,031	6,204	29,406
Switzerland	(272)	(2,131)	(3,930)	13,713	13,964	21,344
Germany	20	(3,564)	(8,599)	7,580	19,661	15,098
France	13,261	(2,737)	(10,680)	4,282	(910)	3,216
UK	5,460	(319)	(9,688)	5,405	(801)	57
Italy	498	(7,791)	(7,240)	(1,099)	(1,519)	(17,151)
Canada	2,799	(5,809)	(8,378)	(4,767)	(5,237)	(21,392)
Australia	(2,454)	(6,600)	(5,706)	(3,213)	(3,056)	(21,029)
US	38,635	(53,476)	(53,651)	(14,879)	3,477	(79,894)

EXHIBIT 1.13 International trade balance for highly intensive R&D industries in 2005 ($ millions)

Top management's lack of operations experience

Top management's lack of operations experience has further ramifications for a business. Since operations accounts for some 60–70 per cent of assets, expenditure and people, operations managers must be more involved in strategic decisions and senior executives must fully appreciate their arguments. Once a company has made large investments, rarely does it invest a second time to correct any mistakes. There is no such lack of experience in Japan and Germany, where a full and perceptive insight into operations is a prerequisite for top management.

However, the consequences of this knowledge gap do not stop here. As Wickham Skinner observes:

> To many executives, manufacturing and the production function is a necessary nuisance – it soaks up capital in facilities and inventories, it resists changes in products and schedules, its quality is never as good as it should be, and its people are unsophisticated, tedious, detail-oriented and unexciting. This makes for an unreceptive climate for major innovations in factory technology and contributes to the blind spot syndrome.[1]

And this brings with it many important consequences. One is that senior executives do not perceive the strategic potential of operations. Typically it is seen in its traditional productivity-efficiency mode with the added need to respond to the strategic overtures of marketing and finance. The result is that operations concentrates its effort and attention on the short term, while adopting its classic, reactive posture towards the long-term strategic issues of the business.

Operations managers' obsession with short-term performance

The emphasis within the operations manager's role has, in turn, been directed towards short-term issues and tasks. The overriding pressures to meet day-to-day targets and the highly quantifiable nature of the role and the output measures have reinforced the tendency of operations executives to concern themselves with this feature to the exclusion of the important long term. The skills of operations managers are high on short-term tasks such as scheduling, maintaining efficiency levels, controls and resolving labour problems.

Skinner rightly observed this 20 years ago when he commented:

> Most factories were not managed very differently in the 1970s than in the 1940s and 1950s. Manufacturing management was dominated by engineering and a technical point of view. This may have been adequate when production management issues centred largely on efficiency and productivity and the answers came from industrial engineering and process engineering. But the problems of operations managers in the 1970s had moved far beyond mere physical efficiency.[2]

This trend has continued in line with the fast-changing nature of markets. By the turn of the century, the operations job had changed from one that concerned maintaining the steady state operations by sound day-to-day husbandry to one that is now multidimensional. It is increasingly concerned with managing greater complexity in product range, product mix, volume changes, process flexibility, inventory, cost and financial controls and employee awareness because of the more intensive level of domestic and international competition.

This is the nature of the new task in the new millennium. No longer are the key issues solely confined to operational control and fine-tuning the system. The need is for broad, business-oriented operations managers, but companies have produced too few of them. The use of specialists as the way to control our businesses has increasingly led to a reduction in the breadth of a line manager's responsibilities, which has narrowed the experience base. Furthermore, many operations managers, outgunned by the specialist argument, have found themselves unable to cope with the variety of demands placed on them. The response by many has been to revert increasingly to their strengths. This has, therefore, reinforced their short-term role and their inherently reactive stance to corporate strategic resolution.

Operations executives do not, on the whole, explain the important, conceptual aspects of operations to others in the organization. Seldom do they evaluate and expose the implications for operations of corporate decisions so that alternatives can be considered and more soundly based decisions can be reached. This is partly because of a lack of developed language to help explain the corporate operations issues involved. Lacking in the strategic dimension, therefore, operations has often been forced into piecemeal change, achieving what it can as and when it has been able. The result has been a series of intermittent responses lacking corporate coordination.

Operations strategy

In the past two decades, countries such as Japan, Germany and Italy, as well as emerging industrial nations such as South Korea and Taiwan, have gained competitive advantage through operations, with India and China next in line. The Japanese, in particular, have

OPERATIONS MANAGERS **MUST** BECOME STRATEGIC

FUNCTIONS IMPLEMENT STRATEGY

Corporate strategy provides **opportunities** and **options**

gone for existing markets and provided better goods with few, if any, inherent benefits derived from material and energy resources. The earlier examples serve to illustrate this.

One of the keys to this achievement through operations has been the integration of these functional perspectives into corporate strategy debate, and it is appropriate now to explain what this embodies and how it differs from the conventional approaches to the management of operations. In broad terms, there are two important roles that operations can offer as part of the strategic strengths of a company.

The first is to provide operations processes that give the business a distinct advantage in the marketplace. In this way, operations will provide a market edge through unique technological developments in its process and operations that competitors are unable to match. This is quite rare and examples are hard to find. One such is Pilkington's float-glass process.[3]

The second is to provide coordinated operations support for the essential ways in which products win orders in the marketplace that is better than such support provided by the operations functions of its competitors. Operations must choose its process and design its infrastructure (for example controls, procedures, systems and structures) that are consistent with the existing way(s) by which products win orders, while being able to reflect future developments in line with changing business needs. Most companies share access to the same processes, and thus technology is not inherently different. Similarly, the systems, structures and other elements of infrastructure are equally universal. What is different is the degree to which operations matches process and infrastructure to those criteria that win orders. In this way, operations constitutes a coordinated response to the business needs that embraces all those aspects of a company for which operations is responsible.

To do this effectively, operations needs to be involved throughout the whole of the corporate strategy debate to explain, in business terms, the implications of corporate marketing proposals and, as a result, be able to influence strategy decisions for the good of the business as a whole. Too often in the past, operations has been too late in this procedure. Corporate executives have tended to assume that competitive strategies are more to do with, and often in fact are one and the same as, marketing initiatives. Implicit, if not explicit, in this view are two important assumptions. The first is that operations' role is to respond to these changes rather than to make inputs into them. The second is that operations has the capability to respond flexibly and positively to these changing demands. The result has been operations' inability to influence decisions, which has led to a posture that appears to be a function that is forever complaining about the unrealistic demands placed upon it.

The need for an operations strategy to be developed and shared by the business is not only to do with the critical nature of operations within corporate strategy but also a realization that many of the decisions are structural in nature. This means that they are hard to change. If the business does not fully appreciate the issues and consequences, it can be locked into a number of operations decisions that will take years to change. These can range from process investments on the one hand to human resource management practices and controls on the other. Decisions not in line with the needs of the business can contribute significantly to a lack of corporate success. To change them is costly and time-consuming. But even more significant, they will come too late. The development of a corporate policy consisting of a coordinated set of main function inputs will mean that a business would be able to go in one consistent, coherent direction based on a well-argued, well-understood and well-formed strategy. This is achieved, in part, by moving away from argument, disagreement, misunderstanding and short-term, parochial moves based on interfunctional perspectives to the resolution of these differences at the corporate level. Currently, marketing-led strategies leave the aftermath to be resolved by operations, which, without adequate appropriate guidance or discussion and agreement at the corporate level, resolves the issues as best it can largely from its unilateral view of what is best for the business as a whole.

In the majority of cases, operations is simply not geared to a business's corporate objectives. The result is an operations system, good in itself, but not designed to meet market needs. Operations left in the wake of business decisions is often at best a neutral force, and even sometimes inadvertently pulls in the opposite direction. Seen as being concerned solely with efficiency, the question of operations' strategic contribution is seldom part of the corporate consciousness.

What does all this mean for operations managers? One clear consequence is the need to change from a reactive to a proactive stance. The long-term inflexible nature of operations means that the key issues, and there are many of them, involved in process choice and infrastructure development need to be reflected in business decisions, with the business being made aware of the implications for operations of proposed corporate changes. When this is achieved, the strategy decisions that are then taken reflect what is best for the business as a whole. So, operations management's attention must increasingly be towards strategy. This does not mean that day-to-day operations are unimportant, but time must also be spent developing and implementing strategy. Top management have, by and large, perceived improvements as coming from corporate activities such as acquisitions, mergers and new product or market development. However, strategies must also be developed and implemented at a functional level. In successful businesses, operations develop the capability to support current and future market requirements within a well-chosen, well-argued and well-understood business strategy.

Reflections

There is a growing and consistent awareness that the emphasis in successfully managed operations function is increasingly towards issues of strategy. Early evidence was provided in the Advisory Council for Applied Research and Development's 1983 booklet entitled *New Opportunities in Manufacturing: The Managements of Technology*. This specifically recommended that 'companies in manufacturing should review the balance of their senior management (team) and ensure that the role of a suitably qualified board member includes responsibility for manufacturing strategy'.[4] In the 21st century, this board-level contribution is even more crucial to the continued success and growth of companies.

Top management needs to pay a great deal more than lip service to the task of ensuring that operations' input into the strategic debate is comprehensive and that the agreed corporate decisions fully reflect the complex issues involved. Much determination will need to be exercised to ensure that the more superficial approaches to incorporating the wide-ranging aspects of operations into business decisions are avoided. The rewards for this are substantial.

Operations executives must begin to think and act in a more strategic manner. In an environment traditionally geared to meeting output targets, the pressure on operations has been to manage reactively and to be operationally efficient rather than strategically effective. It has been more concerned with doing things right (efficiency) than doing the right things (effectiveness). Over the years, this has been seen as the appropriate operations task and contribution. Furthermore, it has given rise to the related assumption that any other posture would imply negative attitudes, with operations appearing to be putting obstacles in the way of achieving key business objectives. At times, this puts operations in the vicious circle of business demands on operations, operations' best response, a recriminating business appraisal of that response, new business demands for improved operations performance and so on. The purpose of this book is to help to avoid the all-too-common corporate approach to operations by providing a set of concepts and approaches that together create a platform from which operations can make a positive contribution to developing powerful competitive strategies. But, operations executives must first accept that they need to manage their own activities strategically and this is almost as much a change in management attitude as it is an analytical process.

The purpose of thinking and managing strategically is not just to improve operational performance or to defend market share. It is to gain competitive advantage and it implies an attempt to mobilize operations' capability to help to gain this competitive edge. Kenichi Ohmae, a leading Japanese consultant with McKinsey,[5] suggests that when managers are striving to achieve or maintain a position of relative superiority over competitors, their minds work very differently from when the objective is to make operational improvements against, often arbitrarily set, internal objectives.

This chapter has highlighted operations' tendency to emphasize operational efficiency more than competitive advantage. The danger for the business is that operations gets so used to absorbing and responding to demands that reacting becomes the norm. Each crisis is viewed as a temporary situation that often militates against recognizing the need to review strategies fundamentally. By the time this need becomes obvious, the business is often at a serious competitive disadvantage.

The aims of this book are to help operations reverse its reactive tendencies and change its short-term perspective; that is, to explain operations from a strategic perspective by identifying the managerial and corporate issues that need to be addressed to establish competitive advantage.

There is much evidence that in many traditional manufacturing nations the capability exists to turn domestic manufacturing around and to challenge and beat overseas competition in both home and world markets. There are already examples of that turnaround in competitive performance, but the key ingredients include tough, professional management, combining strategic analysis of key issues with the intuitive, creative flair that for so long has been directed primarily towards solving operational problems.

It is imperative that operations managers take the initiative. For some organizations or functions within a business, the status quo even suits them. In those same organizations, operations is played off against a forever changing set of objectives and targets, and it hurts. If operations waits for other corporate initiatives, they will not come soon enough. The lack of empathy and understanding by top management towards operations often means that, when difficulties arise, the preferred course of action is to get rid of the problem by selling off the business or buying in from outside. The causes of the problem are seldom addressed. Companies should realize that there are no long-term profits to be made in easy manufacturing tasks – anyone can provide these. It is in the difficult areas where profits are to be made. Furthermore, selling off inherent infrastructure can lead to an inability to compete effectively in future markets. The critical task facing operations managers is to explain the essential nature of operations in business terms, and this must embrace both process technology and infrastructure development.

Discussion questions

1   Comment on the comparative balance of payments on goods (1960–2007) for selected countries shown in Exhibit 1.1. Why do these differences exist? What is the impact of these trends on the economies of the countries involved?

2   Comment on the varying trends in manufacturing output per hour for selected countries shown in Exhibit 1.7. What are the causes of these variations? What is the impact of these trends on the economies of the countries involved?

3   Comment on the level of production of machine tools without parts and accessories for selected countries shown in Exhibit 1.11. Why do these differences exist? What is the impact of these trends on the economies of the countries involved?

4   What has been the policy of the UK government to the UK manufacturing industry over the past 30 years? Why do you think it has taken this stance? What do you believe has been the impact of this?

5   What would be the long-term impact of the trends shown in Exhibits 1.1, 1.7 and 1.11? How can these trends be reversed?

Notes and references

1   Skinner, W. (1983) 'Operations technology: blind spot in strategic management', Harvard Business School working paper 83–5, p. 11.

2   Skinner, 'Operations technology', p. 6. These views are also confirmed by Skinner in his book *Operations Management, Strategic Context and Managerial Analysis* (2000) Basingstoke: Macmillan Business.

3   The development of the float-glass process in the 1950s by Pilkington, a UK glass manufacturer, was a remarkable step forward in the technology of float-glass making. The costly grinding and polishing operations in the conventional manufacture of glass were eliminated and the result was plate glass production at a fraction of the cost.

4   Advisory Council for Applied Research and Development (1983) *New Opportunities in Manufacturing: The Management of Technology*, London: HMSO Cabinet Office, October, p. 48.

5   Ohmae, K. (1982) *The Mind of the Strategist*, New York: McGraw-Hill, pp. 36–7.

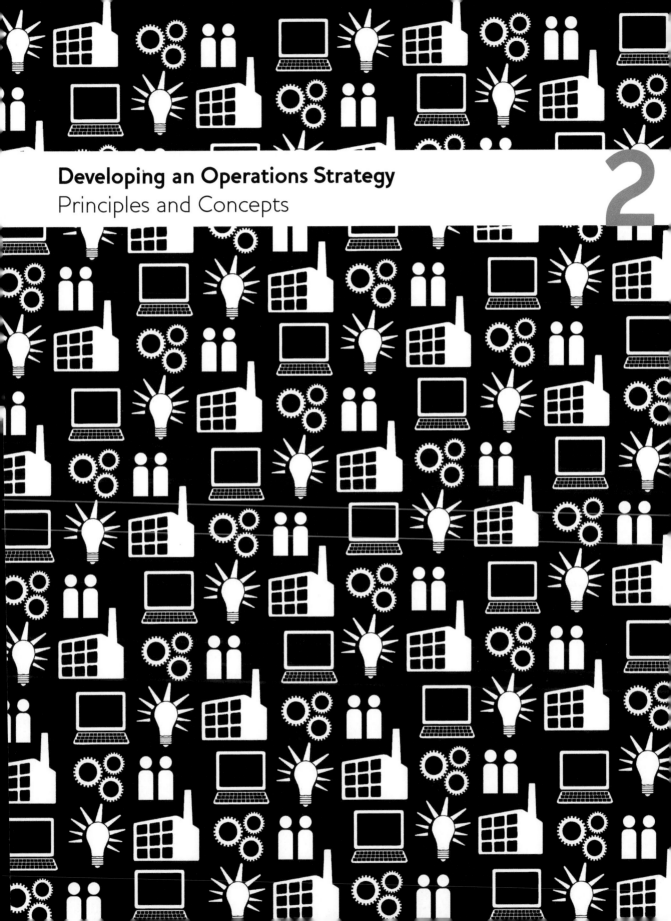

Developing an Operations Strategy

Principles and Concepts

2

Summary

Faced with the pressures of increasing competition, businesses need to coordinate the activities of their principal functions within a coherent strategy. All functional contributions and insights are essential to understand, resolve and agree strategic direction. Within manufacturing companies, operations strategic as well as operational roles are essential to the wellbeing of the business. Given the size of operations investments, getting it right is critical as reinvestment is sizable and takes a long time to effect. This chapter addresses the following:

- Functional strategies within the context of a firm – strategy is at different levels, from corporate through business unit to functional, while the interface between them is essential.

- Executive roles – an executive's role comprises content (both day to day and strategic) and style (the task of managing people). The emphasis in this chapter concerns the strategic role of the operations executive.

- Business unit strategy – concerns determining how it competes in its different markets and the mix of market-driven and market-driving scenarios.

- Developing an operations strategy – operations executives need to be proactive rather than reactive in strategy formulation. As with other functional strategies, markets set the agenda and link business objectives through to functional strategies.

- Order-winners and qualifiers – a key dimension in better understanding markets is to distinguish between the role of qualifiers (necessary to get onto and remain on a customer's list of potential suppliers) and order-winners (those criteria that win business from other qualified, potential suppliers).

- Outputs of operations strategy – developing a strategy concerns closing the gap in terms of how well operations supports the needs of customers for which it is responsible.

Companies invest in a wide range of functions and capabilities in order to design, make and sell products at a profit. Consequently, the degree to which a company's functions are aligned to the needs of its markets will significantly affect its overall growth in sales and profits. Appropriate investment in processes and infrastructure in operations is fundamental to this success, whereas a lack of fit between these key investments and a company's markets will lead to a business being well wide of the mark. If a firm could change its operations investments without incurring penalties such as long delays and large reinvestments, then the strategic decisions within operations would be of little concern or consequence. However, nothing could be further from the truth. Many executives are still unaware

> that what appear to be routine operations decisions frequently come to limit the corporation's strategic options, binding it with facilities, equipment, personnel, basic controls and policies to a non-competitive posture, which may take years to turn round.[1]

The compelling reasons to ensure fit are tied to the invariably large and fixed nature of operations process and infrastructure investments. They are large in terms of the size of the investment (£s) and fixed in that it takes a long time to agree, sanction and implement these decisions in the first instance and even longer to agree to change them. It is similar to the oil tanker captain who, on being asked to change direction, would respond: 'you should have asked me 20 kilometres ago.'

Having invested inappropriately, companies invariably cannot afford to put things right, both in terms of the size of the reinvestment and the time to implement the changes. The financial implications, systems development, training requirements and time to make the changes would leave the company, at best, seriously disadvantaged. To avoid this, companies need to be aware of how well operations can support the marketplace and be conscious of the investments and time dimensions involved in changing current positions into future proposals.

Functional strategies within the context of a firm

For most businesses, strategy needs to be developed at three levels – corporate, business unit and functional. How this comes about relates to the increasing corporate complexity that comes with size. As companies grow, they become more complex, and the way they handle this complexity is to break the business into parts called 'functions'. This allows specialisms to develop and makes managing the whole easier. One further outcome of this restructuring is the need to develop strategy at both the level of the business and the level of the function. As successful companies continue to grow, they find it increasingly difficult to manage the whole as one business and so break the total into parts that are typically called 'business units'. From a strategy viewpoint, the outcome is the additional need for strategy development at the corporate level, as outlined in *Exhibit 2.1*.

Level of strategy	Distinctive tasks
Corporate	Strategic activity at the corporate level concerns the direction of the total business and addresses issues such as where to invest and/or divest, and priorities in terms of sales revenue growth Implementation concerns the allocation of investment funds in line with these priorities
Business unit	Business units comprise different parts of a total business. For each business unit, strategic direction concerns identifying the markets in which it competes, agreeing where it intends to grow (including new markets), the nature of competition and the relevant competitive criteria in its current and future markets, in terms of maintaining and growing share Implementation concerns discussing and agreeing how and where to invest, in terms of functional tasks and alternative approaches
Functional	Each business unit will comprise a number of functions such as research and development, sales and marketing, operations and engineering that make up the total activities within a business unit. The strategic role of each function is to support those competitive dimensions within a market for which it is wholly or partly responsible. In this way, the market comprises the agenda for functional strategies and becomes the mechanism for determining development and investment priorities Implementation concerns consistently meeting the competitive norms involved and selecting from alternative approaches to attain the improvement goals laid down

SOURCE: Adapted from Hill, T. (2005) *Operations Management*, 2nd edn, Basingstoke, Palgrave Macmillan

EXHIBIT 2.1 Levels of strategy and their distinctive tasks

The three levels of strategy are:

- **Corporate-level strategy** – this concerns the market sectors in which a company, as a whole, decides to compete, the degree of importance it attaches to each sector in terms of future revenue and profit growth and the priority given to each sector in terms of investment and other allocations of resources.

- **Business unit-level strategy** – companies often comprise several businesses and the inherent diversity leads to the need for an increasing level of independence between the parts that make up the corporate whole. Business unit strategies, therefore, concern identifying the markets in which this part of the whole business competes, the dimensions of competition involved and the competitive criteria to fulfil in order to enable it to retain and grow market share.

- **Functional-level strategy** – having determined the competitive factors within each market in which a business competes, functions are tasked with fulfilling these requirements. Functional strategies, therefore, concern investing in and developing the necessary capabilities to provide those competitive factors in a business unit's markets for which it is solely or jointly responsible.

This book concerns strategy at the business unit level and the role and development of an operations strategy within a company. It is about how to develop operations strategies to support (with the other relevant functions in a business) agreed markets. However, this requires coordination on the horizontal dimension (across functions) and the vertical dimension (linking functional strategies with the business level).

Functional executives: strategy versus other roles

Executives have several sets of responsibilities. These tasks concern:

1 **Content of the operations management task** – the responsibilities involve:
   - **the day-to-day or operational role** that involves managing and controlling the various aspects of the operations functions effectively (capably and productively) and efficiently (within the cost and budget parameters agreed)
   - **the strategic role** that concerns supporting the competitive drivers within a company's markets for which operations is solely or jointly responsible, for example quality conformance (making a product to specification) and delivering a customer order on time and in full.

2 **Style** – managing people:
   - **internally** involving the people within the operations function itself and also the people interface between operations and other functions within the organization so as to meet people's own personal needs, the needs of the operations function and those of the overall business
   - **externally** involving the people interface outside the organization at both the supplier and customer ends of the supply chain.

Whereas the day-to-day and managing people tasks are invariably recognized as being an integral and central part of an operations manager's role, the strategic dimension is not. In part this is due to a failure to separate the tasks, so that while the operational or day-to-day role forms part of the corporate and executive's own expectations, the strategy role does not. While both are essential, the lack of expectation by the business and the typically low contribution made by operations in the strategy development process result in operations executives underperforming on this key dimension of their role. But given the significant contribution made by operations in securing the second sale, as illustrated in *Exhibit 2.2*, operations' involvement in deciding which markets and customers to target and understanding the requirements of customers when an order is placed in terms of the operations delivery system's ability to meet those needs are the components of the strategic process. While the prime responsibility for the initial sale often resides within the sales and marketing function, customers come back mainly due to how their requirements have been met. In this way, operations, being primarily responsible for the fulfilment of the first order, secures (or fails to secure), by proxy, the second sale. Developing the capability to meet customers' needs is the outcome of functional strategies. Most, and often all, of these needs fall within the strategic responsibility of operations.

Functions' contributions in gaining initial and repeat orders		
Gaining the first sale	Fulfilling the order or contract	Securing the second sale
Sales and marketing	Operations	Operations

EXHIBIT 2.2 Operations, by proxy, secures the second sale

Business unit strategy

Functional strategies interface with the business units of which they are part and, in that way, these two levels of strategy need to be linked. While this chapter concerns developing an operations strategy, before addressing this, let's first look at how a business unit strategy should be developed compared to how it often is.

As discussed earlier, organizations use functions to cope with the complexity that comes with size and manage the task involved. However, businesses are not a number of different parts or functions, but are wholes. An essential task, therefore, is to rebuild the parts back into a whole and nowhere is this more critical than at the strategic level within a firm. Also, as *Exhibit 2.3* illustrates, the heads of functions will appropriately form part of the strategy development group as these parts form the whole business.

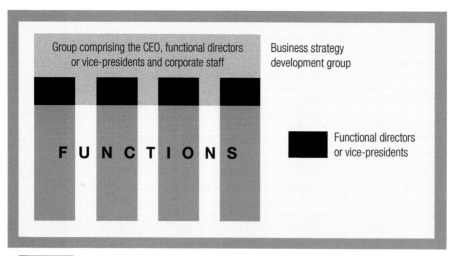

Group comprising the CEO, functional directors or vice-presidents and corporate staff

Business strategy development group

F U N C T I O N S

Functional directors or vice-presidents

EXHIBIT 2.3 Composition of the business unit strategy-making group

SOURCE: Hill, T. (2005) *Operations Management*, 2nd edn, Basingstoke, Palgrave Macmillan

Discussion and agreement about current and future markets have already been high-lighted as an integral part of strategy development. This step requires functions to discuss their views on markets, address and resolve differences and agree on what is best for the business overall. Similarly, the outcomes of this debate would be major inputs into developing a strategy at the business unit level, with the desired process being in line with that shown in *Exhibit 2.4*. Functions would debate current and future markets, and highlight constraints and opportunities as part of their input into developing a strategy for the firm, thus providing both a market-driven and market-driving orientation. Similarly, opportunities and strategic initiatives would be signalled at the business unit level and form part of the essential debate and strategic outcome.

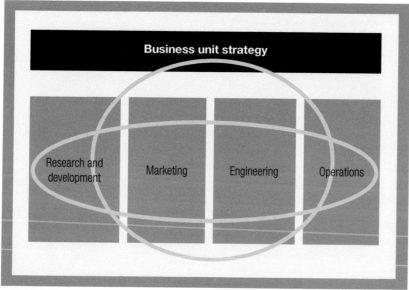

EXHIBIT 2.4 Ideal business unit strategy-making process

SOURCE: Hill, T. (2005) *Operations Management*, 2nd edn, Basingstoke, Palgrave Macmillan

Reality is far from this:

> In many firms, business unit strategy is developed as a series of independent statements. Lacking essential integration, the result is a compilation of distinct, functional strategies that sit side by side, layer on layer in the same corporate binder. Integration is not provided if, in fact, it was ever intended.[2]

The outcome, rather than being similar to that represented by *Exhibit 2.4*, is more like that shown in *Exhibit 2.5*.

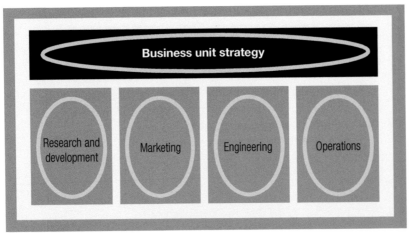

EXHIBIT 2.5 Real-life business strategy-making process

SOURCE: Hill, T. (2005) *Operations Management,* 2nd edn, Basingstoke, Palgrave Macmillan

Charged with developing strategies for their own parts of a business, functions such as research and development, marketing, operations and engineering prepare such statements independently. The result is a comprehensive list of functional statements that are then put together as the strategy for the corporate whole. However, company-wide debate rarely concerns how these fit together or assesses their support of agreed markets. Congruence is assumed and is given credence by the use of broad descriptions of strategy that, instead of providing clarity and the means of testing fit, wash over the debate in generalities.

Through debate and challenge, functional strategies must be developed that support agreed markets with consistency between the various parts of a business. Only in this way can coherent strategies be forged that align all functions to support customer needs. Thus, business unit strategy is the outcome of functional strategies and can only be achieved by integration across the functional boundaries; business unit strategy, then, is both the binding mechanism for and the end result of this process, as *Exhibit 2.4* illustrates. Thus, all the functions within a firm need to be party to agreeing the blueprint of strategy. They are then party to the debate and its resolution that facilitates the identification of the individual strategies necessary to support the agreed direction and for which each function takes responsibility.

Market-driven

Being market-driven concerns providing the competitive criteria in a market to the required levels, for example meeting the delivery lead times that customers require or expect, or reducing costs to enable price in a market to be matched or bettered.

Market-driving

On the other hand, market-driving concerns proactively seeking ways to change the competitive norms and hence create a situation where a company can influence its market position vis-à-vis its competitors. In this way, an organization can improve on current, required levels of a given driver to gain a competitive edge. The way to do this can be either a market-based or a resource-based approach,[3] as explained below and summarized in *Exhibit 2.6*:

- **Market-based** – here companies proactively identify where market advantage could be gained by outperforming the current norms on one or more relevant market drivers and then allocating resources to this end.

- **Resource-based** – continuing the theme of being more proactive in arriving at appropriate strategies has seen the emergence of resource-based competition. Again the emphasis is to be knowingly proactive in seeking ways to change the competitive norms for market advantage. The orientation here is to exploit the potential of existing internal resources and capabilities in order to outperform current norms on one or more competitive drivers. However, it is also essential to ensure that the competitive advantages that result by consciously looking to exploit existing resources or create synergies within the organization are, in fact, what customers need and are willing to pay for should additional costs be involved.

The strategic mix	Market-driven		Strategy based on understanding current and future markets and recognizing how the competitive drivers are time- and market-specific. Will differ depending on whether it concerns maintaining share, growing share or entering new markets
	Market-driving	Market-based	Proactive approach to identify where advantage can be gained by outperforming current norms in one or more drivers and then investing in appropriate resources and capabilities
		Resource-based	Exploit the potential of existing resources and capabilities to outperform current norms on one or more competitive drivers

SOURCE: Hill, T. (2005) *Operations Management*, 2nd edn, Basingstoke, Palgrave Macmillan

EXHIBIT 2.6 Market-driven and market-driving strategies

The market-driven and market-driving strategic mix

For most companies, their current and future markets will comprise a mix of both market-driven and market-driving strategies. Much of what a company sells, the customers it sells to, the markets in which it competes and how it competes within these today will be similar to yesterday and the same for tomorrow. But, being aware of the need to proactively seek ways to drive markets and exploit resource-based opportunities is an essential element of the strategic task in times when markets are increasingly different and competitive. For this reason, most companies will need to have a strategy that is a mix of the market-driven and market-driving approaches, as illustrated in *Exhibit 2.6.*

Strategies versus philosophies

Strategies concern supporting markets. Therefore, those functions that have the principal or shared responsibility for providing the needs of markets have to develop a strategy to undertake those tasks. Many companies, however, have failed to recognize this link. Consequently, all functions (irrespective of whether or not they have responsibility for directly supporting a company's markets) have been asked to provide strategic statements as an input into the overall strategy of the firm. The source of this misunderstanding stems from companies' failure to distinguish between strategies (actions to directly support markets) and philosophies (preferred ways of accomplishing tasks or approaches to elements of the overall management task).

This mixing of philosophies in with strategies has added to the confusion inherent in strategy development. For example, R&D's strategic inputs may concern issues such as product design and material substitution; marketing's issues may include branding, pricing and customer relations; operations' may include delivery reliability and quality conformance; and engineering's may include process development and technical support. However, other functions typically do not have a strategic role per se.

Human resources, accounting and finance, for example, provide essential inputs to a business but, invariably, they have neither the principal nor shared responsibility for any factors in a company's markets. Consequently, they would not have a strategic role; however, that is not to say that their role is insignificant. On the contrary, their inputs are essential and far-reaching. They are, though, in the form of philosophical statements about approaches that enhance the overall ability of a company to undertake and fulfil its operational and strategic tasks.

Why argue for this distinction? The reason is to increase a company's awareness of what strategy is, which functions are responsible for providing the relevant dimensions and the key role of other functions to help in this task. Until companies sharpen their awareness of the necessity to understand markets, identify the functions with prime responsibility for providing relevant market needs and harness the support of the whole organization in that provision, they will continue to be disadvantaged in a world where the level of competition continues to increase. Without this, strategy will continue to be expressed and explained in a broad, generic manner, fail to provide direction and give functions no option other than do what they think best. Motherhood and apple pie have good attributes in themselves but are not necessarily strategic in their origins or orientation.

A recap on functional strategy development

At this point, let's pause and reflect. This book concerns the development of an operations strategy. As a key function within a business, one role of operations (as with other functions) is to contribute to meeting the corporate objectives set by a business and, in so doing, needs to be party to their agreement in order to exploit available opportunities while recognizing the timescales and constraints involved. As *Exhibit 2.7* shows, strategy development is an interactive process linking all parts of a business with one another and with the objectives set within a given period. And, the core to this is the markets (recognizing the market-driven and market-driving dimensions referred to earlier) in which a company competes. Note that the separation of the operations strategy in *Exhibit 2.7* from the other functional strategy elements is merely to reflect the orientation of this book. It is important to remember that what needs to dominate strategy development is the business itself and not one functional view.

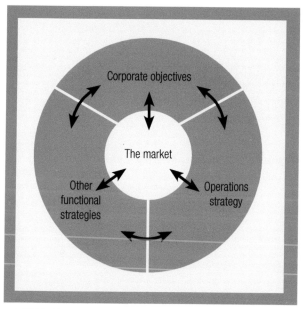

EXHIBIT 2.7 Markets at the centre of strategy development
SOURCE: Hill, T. (2005) *Operations Management*, 2nd edn, Basingstoke, Palgrave Macmillan

Operations strategy in action

To maintain profitable growth over time requires sound direction, with the relevant functions providing support for the needs of agreed markets, because it is functions and not the business that implement strategy. The business brings together the parts and it is at this level that agreement on where to retain and grow share, the competitive factors that underpin this, the functional strategies that need to be fulfilled and the commitment of the resources enable this to happen. But making it happen is the task of functions and operations is being recognized as a major, often dominant, player in determining and securing competitive advantage.

Functional dominance within corporate strategy

In broad terms, the changing world demand/capacity balance has brought with it a change in the fortunes of different functions. Up to the mid-1960s, many industries had enjoyed a capacity/demand relationship that favoured operations' position in the sphere of strategic influence. This, together with postwar growth, helped to create the dominance of the operations function in many corporations. As the demand/capacity balance began to even out and selling into existing and new markets became more difficult, the power base of corporate influence began to swing away from operations, heralding the rise of marketing. Then by the mid-1970s, the impact of recessions and energy crises had, in turn, opened the door to the influence of accounting and finance. These varying fortunes, however, rarely seemed to be based on what was best for the total good of the business, but more on which functional perspective appeared to provide the key to corporate success or salvation. As a result, those functions, out in the cold themselves, were left without due corporate influence.

These events reinforced the functional bias within the business unit strategy debate explained above. The independent formulation of functional strategies and the failure to cross-relate them continues to be the order of the day. This failure to debate strategy has led to the essential perspectives and contributions of key functions being left out of strategic outcomes.

However, the existence of increasing world competition, overcapacity in many industries within the manufacturing sector, increasing scarcity of key resources and decreasing product life cycles make it all the more logical for businesses to incorporate the key functional perspectives when determining policy decisions. Why, then, does this not happen? In many organizations, operations adopts, or is required to take, a reactive stance in strategy discussions. Yet how can the perspectives of the function that controls such a large slice of the assets, expenditure and people, and is so influential in customer retention, thus underpinning the very welfare of a company, be omitted?

Reasons for operations' reactive role in business unit strategy formulation

The importance of operations' contribution to the success of a business is readily acknowledged. The prosperous nations of today owe their success to their wealth-creating sectors, of which operations is a key part. Why then do operations executives typically adopt a reactive role within strategic debate? And why does this situation not improve?

How operations executives see their role

A prime reason why operations' strategic contribution is reactive is that this is how operations executives view their strategic role. They define their role as requiring them to react as well as possible to all that is asked of the operations system. They feel they must:

*   exercise skill and experience in effectively coping with the exacting and varying demands placed on operations

- reconcile the trade-offs inherent in these demands as best they can.

Rarely do they see as an integral part of their role the need to contribute appropriately to business unit decisions that will impact the demands on operations and its ability to provide the necessary market support.

They do not explain the different sets of operations implications created by alternative policy decisions and changes in direction. By not contributing at this level, they fail to help the company to arrive at decisions that embrace all the important business perspectives.

How companies see operations' strategic contribution

Companies themselves often reinforce operations executives' emphasis on the short-term operational aspects of their overall task. They too see their principal, if not whole, role as involving the day-to-day management of operations and signal this orientation through discussion, integration and required contributions.

Companies also reinforce this orientation by the way in which they develop managers within operations. Many companies typically promote operators to supervisors, supervisors to managers, and managers to executives, with scant regard for the change in emphasis that needs to take place. They provide little help to make this transition a success.

The outcome is that the short-term, 'minding the store' role is reinforced by corporate expectations. Thus, the accepted and required contribution of operations executives tends to be confined to the day to day, and the reactive role in strategy decision-making continues to be the reality.

Too late in the corporate debate to effectively influence strategic outcomes

Operations executives typically are not involved, or do not involve themselves, in strategy decisions until these decisions have started to take shape. Before long, this point of entry into the strategy debate becomes the norm. The result is that operations has less opportunity to contribute and less chance to influence outcomes. As a consequence, operations managers always appear to be complaining about the unrealistic demands made of them and the problems that invariably ensue.

Failure to say 'no' when strategically appropriate

The 'can't say no' syndrome is still the hallmark of the operations culture. But this is unhelpful. Operations executives tend to respond to corporate needs and difficulties without evaluating the consequences or alternatives and then explaining these to others. Any senior executive, including those in operations, must be able to say 'no' from a total business perspective and with sound corporate-related arguments. In typical situations, operations managers accept the current and future demands placed on the systems and capacities they control, and then work to resolve them. In this way, they decide between corporate alternatives, but only from a narrow functional perspective of what they believe to be best for the business. This ill serves a company. Resolving corporate-related issues in a unilateral way is not the most effective method to resolve the complex alternatives at hand. This resolution needs corporate-wide debate to ensure that the relevant factors and options are taken into account so that an appropriate business decision can be concluded.

Strategic decisions need to encompass the important trade-offs embodied in alternatives that have their roots in the process and infrastructure investments associated with operations and are reflected in the high proportion of assets and expenditures under its control.

Lack of language to explain, and concepts to underpin, operations strategy

On the whole, operations managers do not have a history of explaining their functions clearly and effectively to others in the organization. This is particularly so on strategy issues and the consequences that will arise from the business decisions under discussion. On the other hand, marketing and finance executives are able to explain their function in a more straightforward and intelligible manner. By talking about how strategic alternatives will affect the business, they can capture the attention of others regarding the issues at hand and their strategic outcomes.

However, the reasons for this difference in perspective and presentation are not solely attributable to operations executives themselves. The knowledge base, concepts and language essential to highlighting corporate relevance and arresting attention have not been developed to the same level within operations as within other key functions. Consequently, shared perspectives within operations, let alone between functions, are not held, which contributes to the lack of interfunctional understanding.

For evidence of this last point, compare the number of books and articles written and postgraduate and postexperience courses provided in the area of operations strategy to those for the other major functions of marketing and accounting/finance. Relatively few contributors address this fundamental area. The result is that operations executives are less able to explain their essential perspectives. Hence, executives from other functions are less attuned to the ideas and perspectives that form the basis for understanding operations' strategic contribution.

Functional goals versus business needs

In many organizations, the managers of different functions are measured by the efficiency of that function (an operational perspective) and not by overall effectiveness (a business perspective). Furthermore, their career prospects are governed by their performance within the functional value system. As a consequence, managers may often take actions that score on how the function is measured but which may be suboptimal for the business as a whole.

Competing in different values systems, being measured against different performance criteria and gaining prominence and promotion through different functional perspectives of what is key to the success of a business have contributed to the functional silo problems that characterize many businesses. This has created a situation where shared perspectives and overlapping views are left to individual accomplishment and endeavour rather than in response to clear corporate direction.

Exhibit 2.8 illustrates this dichotomy. An accountant or salesperson, when receiving a customer order, will typically look at one figure as being the most significant measure of business relevance – the total value ($s, £s, €s) of the order placed.

Given the same document, operations managers will look at the order make-up. For them, the business relevance of an order is not its value, but the product mix, volumes and delivery requirements it embodies. This aspect determines the ease with which an order can be made in terms of the process configurations already laid down and the process lead times involved. It will reflect operations' ability to meet the cost base and delivery schedule of the product(s) ordered, and hence the profit margin and delivery performance that will result.

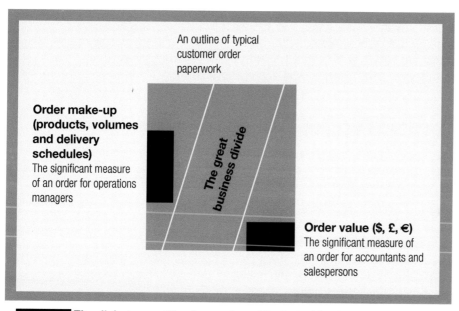

EXHIBIT 2.8 The dichotomy of business views illustrated by the different figures included on typical customer order paperwork

Where marketing is measured by the level of sales revenue achieved, each $, £, € of sales in their value system will carry the same weight as any other $, £, € of sales. Hence all sales are deemed equal. In reality, all orders are never the same value to a business. The higher the level of fit between product mix and anticipated volumes and actual sales, the more that target level will normally be met. Product costs based on one level of volumes or process configurations based on a given product mix are rarely, if ever, realigned with incremental volume and mix changes. Even the costings that underpin initial forecasts are rarely, if ever, adjusted each time the market picture alters. A great business divide, therefore, separates the two realities of marketing and operations. The simplistic measure of total sales value disguises those market characteristics so essential to operations' ability to sustain cost and profit margin structures in a business and provide the order-winners and qualifiers that create long-term growth.

Length of tenure

In the past 20–30 years, there has been a growing practice to reduce the length of tenure for job incumbents. Introduced under the umbrella of 'executive development', it has been seen as a way of broadening perspectives and signalling the company's level of regard for an executive's future within the corporation. However, the significant drawbacks of this trend have largely gone unnoticed. Managerially and strategically, short job tenure invariably goes against the overall corporate good. It militates against executives developing the areas of responsibility within their control and contributing to the essential long-term strategic requirements of a business. Without the necessary level of continuity to see through developments and without sufficient understanding of the essential functional perspectives within the strategic debate, executives are discouraged from taking the longer term corporate perspective. In fact, to start developments in key areas without the time frame to see their completion is arguably irresponsible.

The result is a tendency to maintain the status quo and meet functional goals above all else. In times of change, neither of these promotes the corporate good. Instead, managers will make decisions that are based on how they will affect themselves politically in the future rather than how they will affect the business's competitive position.

Top management's view of strategy

The authors of business plans and marketing reviews look outwards from the business. Top executives associate themselves with these activities, seeing them as essential components in developing business strategy. The result is that they give adequate and appropriate attention to the external environment in which the business operates.

Operations' plans typically address stated business needs and are based on internal dimensions such as capability, capacity and costs and top executives are unlikely to take part in developing these. The result is that executives see operations as not having an external dimension and assume, therefore, that the business strategy debate need not embrace these perspectives. Rather, they focus on operations outcomes of strategic alternatives such as capacity and costs.

But, as highlighted earlier, operations plays a vital role in supporting a company's chosen markets. Assessing the investment and time required for such support and which markets to grow is fundamental to strategic debate and agreed outcomes. In many companies, however, top management has abdicated the key task in strategy of linking markets and operations or is not even aware that such a linkage should be made and maintained.

The content of business unit strategy

The failure of companies to incorporate functional perspectives into their strategy debate stems in part from the approaches to strategy development as advocated by leading researchers and writers in the field. The training of both executives charged with strategy development and specialists who provide relevant support reinforces such failure. This problem is apparent in the content of strategy statements and manifests itself in a number of ways.

Strategy statements are general in nature

Since strategy is general in nature, using all-encompassing statements to convey it is deemed appropriate. The result is that expressions of strategy typically use words with more than one meaning. This broadbrush manner assumes that these general perspectives are universal in both nature and relevance. But what typifies markets today is difference not similarity. Thus general statements are inappropriate, inaccurate and misleading. By ignoring the differences that exist within markets, functional strategies in turn become general in nature and are driven by their own rather than a business perspective.

General statements may underpin theory and provide broad overviews of potential scenarios. But companies compete in their own markets in which specific order-winners and qualifiers will prevail. Thus strategy, like management, is an applied field where specific and not generalized reviews are required. The key to understanding a business is to determine the ways in which it competes in all its different segments. And you can be sure, segments will require functional strategies to reflect these differences.

Strategy debate and formulation stops at the interface

Functional strategies are typically not linked to one another. Most companies require each function to provide a strategic statement but fail to integrate them. The result is that strategy debate stops at the interface between functions.

In many large corporations, this approach is also re-enacted at the next level. Often, multinationals seem unable or unwilling to incorporate individual company statements into a strategy for the whole group. This failure to link, either by default or intent, is a consistent and comprehensive weakness in strategy formulation. The result is that in times of increasingly dynamic and competitive markets, companies systematically fail to realize their strategic potential and consequently are outperformed.

Furthermore, this apparent lack of need to integrate strategies is paralleled in the literature. A review of books on strategic marketing and corporate strategy will confirm that the link between the marketing-related dimensions of strategy and those of operations is not made. The implication is, therefore, that it is not a necessary part of strategy development; or, if it is deemed necessary, its impact is of insufficient consequence to be an integral part of the review process.

Thus strategy formulation as advocated and undertaken by leading researchers in the fields of corporate and marketing strategy also stops at the interface. Methodologies are put forward that lead companies into making major decisions and commit a business for many years ahead without requiring the essential interface between corporate and business unit strategy and between the functions that make up the firm, as illustrated in *Exhibit 2.9*.

The consequences are enormous. First, the risks associated with such approaches in today's markets are substantial. The source of risk is not a result of the uncertainty of future markets and the unknown moves of competitors but of the process of internal strategy formulation. Second, such approaches consistently result in a failure to create the type of strategic advantage that comes directly from embracing key functional perspectives and arriving at commonly agreed and understood corporate directions.

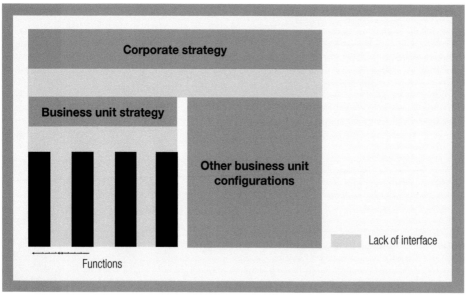

Corporate strategy

Business unit strategy

Other business unit
configurations

Lack of interface

Functions

EXHIBIT 2.9 The lack of interface between the different levels of strategy

Whole versus parts

The underlying rationale for these advocated and adopted methodologies appears to be based on the assumption that corporate improvement can be accomplished by working solely on the corporate whole. Although reshaping the whole is an important facet of strategic resolution, the necessary links to constituent parts and the role of those parts in bringing about agreed direction and change are fundamental. Unless companies forge these links when choosing what is best for the business and agreeing on directions to pursue, they are unlikely to arrive at appropriate decisions essential for their growth and prosperity over time.

Typical outcomes

The results of this lack of integration are documents and statements that have the trappings, but not the essence, of business debate. With functional strategies independently derived, the nearest they get to being integrated is that they sit side by side in the same binder. For most companies, the title 'business strategy' is a misnomer. In reality, the strategy is no more than a compilation of functional strategies separated, as in the binder, one from another.

Furthermore, even a function's presentation of its strategy is not intended to, and does not, in fact, spark business-based discussion. Those companies that justify this procedure on the grounds that it requires its executives to engage in rigorous, functionally oriented debate are not only guilty of false rationalization but also are missing the point. In today's markets, companies that fail to harness the resources of all facets of their business will be seriously disadvantaged. Not only will they miss out, they may well be in danger of missing out altogether.

Developing an operations strategy

Companies require a strategy not based solely on marketing, operations or any other function, but one that embraces the interface between markets and functions. Thus, what should and must be the link between functional strategies is the markets a business serves or intends to serve. One critical link is that between marketing and operations. Both functions must have a common understanding and agreement about a company's markets. Only then can the degree of fit between the proposed marketing strategy and operations' ability to support it be known at the business level and objectively resolved within corporate perspectives and constraints.

For this to take place, relevant internal information explaining the company's operations capabilities needs to be available within a business, as well as the traditional marketing information that is primarily concerned with the customer and market opportunities associated with a company's products. It is not sufficient that such information should be available – and often it is not. To be effective, the ownership of its use must be vested in top management. As with other functions, operations strategy is not owned by operations. It requires corporate ownership.

Senior executives need to understand all the strategic inputs in the corporate debate, because without this understanding, the resolution between conflicting or non-matching functional perspectives cannot be fully investigated and resolved. Without this, individual functions must themselves handle the trade-offs involved as best they can.

Typically, top executives inappropriately delegate this task. Developing and agreeing strategy is top management's key task. In fact, it is the one task that cannot be delegated. If it is, top executives will find themselves only able to exercise control over decisions taken in a global, after-the-event way.

Linking business objectives and functional strategies through markets

Functional strategies concern investing and developing in ways that support the needs of markets in terms of being both market-driven and market-driving. As *Exhibit 2.7* showed earlier, the role of functional strategies is to contribute to meeting agreed business objectives. The form and size of contribution will vary from market to market but the strategic development process for all functions is similar:

- **Phase 1 – understand markets**, ensuring both a market-driven and market-driving approach while maintaining an ongoing, rigorous review throughout this first critical step.

- **Phase 2 – translate** these reviews into strategic tasks. For example, if price is a competitive driver, the task is to reduce costs; if on-time delivery is a competitive factor, improving the reliability of meeting customer due dates is the task.

- **Phase 3 – check** that what is currently provided matches what is required in a market-driven scenario or the new level in a market-driving scenario.

- **Phase 4 – develop a strategy** (the prioritizing of investments and developments) to close the gap where the level of provision falls short of the requirement or achieve the new level of performance in a market-driving scenario.

1 Corporate objectives[2]	**2** Marketing strategy
Growth	Product markets and segments
Survival	Range
Profit	Mix
Return on investment	Volumes
Other financial measures	Standardization versus customization
	Level of innovation
	Leader versus follower alternatives

Exhibit 2.10

Framework for linking corporate objectives and operations and marketing strategy development[1]

3 How do products qualify and win orders in the marketplace?[3]	**Operations strategy**	
	4 Process choice	**5** Infrastructure
Price	Choice of alternative processes	Function support
Quality conformance	Trade-offs embodied in the process choice	Operations planning and control systems
Delivery – speed – reliability	Role of inventory in the process configuration	Quality assurance and control
Demand increases	Make or buy	Operations systems engineering
Colour range	Capacity – size – timing – location	Clerical procedures
Product range		Compensation agreements
Design		Work structuring
Brand name		Organization
Technical support		
After-sales support		

NOTES

1 Although the steps to be followed are given as finite points in a stated procedure, in reality the process will involve statement and restatement as several of these aspects will impinge on each other.

2 Here, corporate objectives are set at the level of the business unit.

3 The basis for establishing the qualifiers and order-winners in a market will either be the product(s) they sell to all customers or the specific needs of customers (see later detail in the text).

- **Phase 5 – implement** the necessary investment and development priorities.

In this way, companies are better able to coordinate functional contributions, with markets appropriately providing the common agenda for all. Invariably, two functions that are central to this task are operations and marketing, as the next section reflects.

The framework given in *Exhibit 2.10* is intended to help explain what currently happens as well as what needs to take place so that the link between corporate objectives and marketing and operations strategy decisions can be made. The exhibit shows that the framework has five columns, each representing a step. These are, in one sense, classic steps in business planning. The problem is that most corporate planners treat the first two as interactive with 'feedback loops' and the last two as linear and deterministic. While each step has substance in its own right, each impacts the others – hence the involved nature of strategy formulation. This is further exacerbated by the inherent complexity of operations and the general failure to take account of the essential interaction between marketing and operations strategies. What is required, therefore, is an approach that recognizes these features and yet provides an ordered, analytical way forward. The suggested approach to link operations with marketing decisions is schematically outlined in *Exhibit 2.10*.

A glance at *Exhibit 2.10* reveals a gap between columns 2 and 3. This is to indicate the corporate objectives/marketing strategy interface that typically takes place as part of a firm's corporate planning procedure and often as a separate business exercise. Column 3 highlights the need for companies to understand their markets (the criteria listed here are typical of some that may relate to a firm's various markets) as this forms the basis for defining operations', as well as other functions', task to support the needs of agreed markets. And just as there are typically different markets, there will be different tasks that call for different strategies.

The approach provides the key to stimulating corporate debate about the business so as to enable operations to assess how it needs to and the degree to which it can support products and/or customers in the marketplace and to identify the developments and investments it needs to undertake as part of its strategic role. This approach has been researched and tested successfully in many industries and businesses of different sizes.

How it works

How to use the methodology outlined in *Exhibit 2.10* will be covered in two sections of the book. The following sections will overview the basic steps. Chapter 3 will cover the methodology to be followed when undertaking these types of analyses. Specifically, it will:

- provide background for analysing the cases included in this text by explaining what data are reviewed and why

- give an approach for students to follow if their course requires an in-plant review

- help executives to undertake reviews of this kind within their own businesses.

The objective of using this framework is to develop an operations strategy (steps 4 and 5 below) as part of the set of functional strategies tasked to deliver the objectives set by the business. As previously highlighted in *Exhibit 2.7* and illustrated by column 3 in the framework in *Exhibit 2.10*, markets are at the centre of this development process. In all instances, the review will need to look forward, as operations will have to support products throughout their life cycles, anticipate planned new product introductions, recognize that competition within markets may change existing competitive drivers, the needs of current customers may similarly change over time and the needs of new customers may vary.

However, to get to steps 4 and 5, the three earlier steps need to be taken. With some understanding of what is to be achieved in an operations strategy statement, it is now opportune to go through each step in turn and then to explain how the necessary interrelations between these parts come together as a whole to form a strategy for a business. Note that the corporate objectives of step 1 relate to the level of the business unit.

Step 1 Corporate objectives

Typically, executives establish the future objectives of a business as the first step in the strategy development process. In so doing, it provides the basis for establishing a clear, strategic direction for a business and demonstrates both the strategic awareness and strategic willingness essential to corporate success. In addition, it defines the boundaries and marks the parameters against which the various inputs can be measured and consistency established, thus providing the hallmarks of a coherent corporate plan.

For each company, the objectives will be different in essence and emphasis. They will reflect the nature of the economy, markets, opportunities and preferences of those involved. The important issues here, however, are that they need to be well thought through, hold logically together and provide the necessary direction for the business. Typical measures concern profit in relation to sales and investment, together with targets for both absolute growth and market share growth. Businesses may also wish to include employee policies and environmental issues as part of their overall sets of objectives.

Step 2 Marketing strategy

The next step taken by most companies is for marketing to assess future markets in terms of both known and potential customers, products and competitors. From this, sales forecasts will be established that provide the basis for calculating revenue and profits. As part of this phase, the outcomes of the marketing plans will be measured against the desired business objectives. As you would expect, statement and restatement form part of the iterative process that typifies these initial steps in the strategy development process, as illustrated in *Exhibit 2.11*.

In most companies, however, the gap depicted between steps 1 and 2 and steps 4 and 5 is the way that strategy development proceeds. While checking that overall there is sufficient capacity available and running the accounting numbers using standard costs as the basis for converting sales forecasts into revenue and profit outcomes, the assumption is that actual and sales forecasts will be the same in terms of mix, order size, frequency and range of customer needs, and that operations can meet these forecasts by fulfilling what are typically an unspecified range of different customer needs.

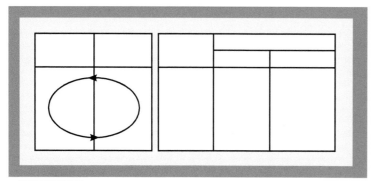

EXHIBIT 2.11 The iterative link between corporate objectives and marketing strategy

For operations, the high level nature of such assumptions results in insufficient detail in terms of varying customer needs such as order size, lead times and level of price sensitivity and its impact on margins, which, in turn, are essential in making decisions around sales forecasts.

So, how do you improve the strategy development process such that it provides sufficient insights on customer needs for operations to understand what is required and hence develop an appropriate strategy. The way forward is to analyse the market in more detail.

Step 3 How do products qualify and win orders in the marketplace?

Operations' strategic task is to meet the qualifiers (competitive criteria that get and keep companies in markets but do not win orders) for which it is responsible and to provide, better than the operations functions of competitors, those criteria that enable the products to win orders in the marketplace (as will be shown later, the basis for analysing markets may be customers rather than products) against competitors that have also qualified. The debate initiated by this methodology is iterative in nature. This is both appropriate for and fundamental to strategic resolution. Thus the company as a whole needs to agree on the markets and segments within these markets in which it decides to compete.

These critical decisions cannot be the responsibility or prerogative of a single function. Typically, however, most companies develop strategy through a marketing perspective (see steps 1 and 2). Although the marketing debate is pre-eminent in corporate strategy procedures, the problem is that this is often where the debate ends. As a function, marketing will have an important and essential view, but it is not the only view and it should not be allowed to dominate corporate strategy resolution. Functional dominance, of whatever origin, is detrimental to developing an appropriate business strategy.

Markets provide the agenda for all functional strategies. As such, clarity and insight are essential. Part of improving this provision is to recognize that market reviews need to be undertaken using a 360° format. Functions have different perspectives on what details and insights need to be provided as part of the outcome of a market debate and, in part, this is driven by a need for clarification on those competitive dimensions that they are responsible for providing. Marketing's views will be part of this, but so will the views and insights of other functions. Part of providing these essential insights is the task of establishing the competitive criteria involved and, in turn, which of these are qualifiers and which order-winners. Then, functional strategies entail investing in and developing the capabilities to provide those qualifiers and order-winners for which they are solely or jointly responsible. In our context, it is those qualifiers and order-winners that are the task of operations to provide that form the basis for where operations spends its time and money on process and infrastructure investment and development (steps 4 and 5 of *Exhibit 2.10*) and as illustrated in *Exhibit 2.12*.

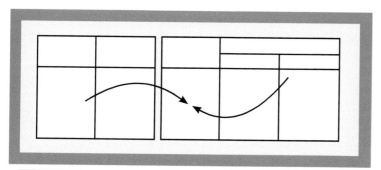

EXHIBIT 2.12 How defining relevant qualifiers and order-winners links corporate objectives with marketing and operations strategies

The procedure is, in reality, to ask questions about the market that require operations' answers. This step, therefore, links corporate objectives with marketing proposals and commitments and with the operations processes and infrastructure necessary to support these to ensure fit (see *Exhibit 2.12*).

Step 4 Process choice

Operations can choose from a number of alternative processes to make particular products. The key to this choice is volume and associated order-winners. Each choice, therefore, needs to reflect the current and future trade-offs involved for the various products and customers. The issues embodied in these trade-offs are both extensive and important. Chapter 5 has been devoted to process choice and will examine in detail the implications of this fundamental decision.

Step 5 Infrastructure

Operations infrastructure consists of the non-process features within production. It encompasses the procedures, systems, controls, compensation packages, work-structuring alternatives, organizational issues and so on within operations. Chapter 10 discusses and illustrates some of the major areas involved.

Although the five steps discussed above comprise the elements of operations strategy development, the first two steps are treated in a somewhat superficial way in this text, as they are dealt with rigorously in other textbooks. The purpose of including them is to demonstrate the integral nature of strategy formulation and reinforce the interactive nature of the procedures involved. Steps 3–5 are dealt with extensively in later chapters. Step 3, which concerns the order-winners and qualifiers of different products, is now discussed in general terms. A more detailed review is provided in Chapter 3.

Understanding markets: the reality

Let us start by restating the important distinction made earlier in the chapter. Markets and marketing are not the same thing. Whereas markets constitute the business itself, marketing is a function. As there will typically be several markets served by a business, the relevant criteria to retain and grow existing market share, change the rules (become market-driving) and enter new markets will differ from market to market as well as from each other. The strategic role of functions (including marketing and operations) is to debate and agree the markets in which to compete and support those criteria for which they are solely or jointly responsible. In that way, the company becomes market-driven – as opposed to marketing-driven.

The cornerstone in all this is understanding markets. Markets are the essence of a business, the very reason for its existence and, consequently, you can never know too much about them. Identifying differences, supporting these insights with clear explanations and descriptions and verifying them with supporting data would, therefore, be reasonable to expect. The reality is, however, that the necessary clarity is usually not provided. Instead, current approaches to business strategy development typically fail to provide sufficiently adequate insights on which to build functional strategies. One outcome of this is that without adequate clarity, each function's investment and development priorities are in line with what they think are the best aspects to improve. The essential link between market needs and functional strategies is not provided.

Current approaches to market reviews usually embody a number of characteristics that contribute to the general nature of the outcomes and the provision of statements that lack essential meaning. This results in descriptions of markets that imply a similarity that does not exist. For example:

- Markets are usually only looked at and described from a marketing point of view. Segment descriptions are typically based on factors such as geographical regions (for example Europe and North America) and sectors in which customers operate (for example food and financial services) or service/product clusters. While this has a sound rationale from a sales and marketing viewpoint, for example in terms of arranging promotional and sales activities and the orientation of technical literature and support, the assumption is carried forward (as it is implied) that each segment is coherent in terms of the way a company needs to compete. A pause for reflection will lead to the recognition that this is both an unreal and inaccurate inference to draw. Although from the viewpoint of marketing, Europe/North America or food/financial services are coherent segments, from an operations point of view, there will be different sets of demands from groups of customers within these marketing segments and hence these will constitute different markets.

- Views of markets are positioned at too high a level in the strategy process. As emphasized throughout, with growing competition, markets are becoming increasingly different rather than increasingly similar as competitors seek to gain customers by changing the offering. The only way to uncover this essential difference is to dig deep. Current approaches fail to do this and result in statements about markets that are broadbrush in nature and inadequate in terms of the insights they provide.

- The inadequacy of the outputs that result is further compounded by the use of general phrases to provide market descriptions. Words and phrases such as 'customer service' and 'delivery' are examples of this. Each can be defined in more than one way, and once there is more than one meaning, misunderstanding and a failure to clarify will follow. The result is that general descriptions are used in analysing markets that in themselves embody more than one segment. One dimension compounds the other, with the result that generalities mask critical and essential insights and necessary clarity is replaced by unhelpful ambiguity.

The result is that the key, first step of clarifying and agreeing markets, the basis on which to link corporate direction and relevant functional support, is not provided. As a consequence, the failure to coordinate strategic direction continues, interfunctional rivalries are reinforced and the approaches used to develop business strategy do not deliver what is required or intended.

Given the increasingly dynamic, competitive and fast-changing nature of markets, it is of paramount importance that companies improve the way they develop strategy and particularly the need to forge the link between marketing and operations.

In summary, what typically happens now is that:

- Market descriptions are limited to the views of marketing. While these views give essential insights from a marketing perspective, they fail to yield the key differences and provide essential insights into markets from the view of other functions, particularly that of operations.

- The words and phrases used to describe markets are not sufficiently precise to provide the clarity needed to yield essential insights.

- The procedures used are not sufficiently exacting to expose and challenge these critical deficiencies, and inadequate outcomes result.

Given the pivotal role of market understanding to strategy development, how does a company improve its approach in this key phase of the process? This question is answered in the following section.

Understanding markets: the approach to follow

Clarity about markets is essential. Companies are in multiple markets and the outcome of the debate on markets should identify, and provide a clear understanding of, the differences that exist. The steps to secure these insights are as follows:

1 **Avoid general words and phrases** – as markets are at the core of a business, using general words and phrases needs to be consciously and rigorously avoided. Each dimension should be expressed on its own and a single definition needs to be associated with each word or phrase used. In this way, each competitive dimension put forward as being relevant can be discussed separately and its relevance assessed. One classic example of this is the phrase 'customer service'. While a desirable objective, the answer to the question 'what does it mean' is not self-evident as it embodies a number of potential meanings. Using 'customer service' to describe the competitive nature of a market thus confuses rather than clarifies.

   Two further illustrations are the words 'quality' and 'delivery'. It is essential, for example, to separate the dimension of design from that of quality conformance. Whereas the former concerns creating the specification for a product, the latter describes the task of meeting the given specification. While the perspectives are interrelated, the tasks are not only different but also form part of different functional strategies, with the former the task of the design function, while the latter is part of the strategic task of operations.

   Similarly, take the aspect of 'delivery'. Separating the issue of 'on time' from that of 'speed' (that is, short lead times) is an essential part of understanding the key dimensions of a market. Describing both under the one word 'delivery' fails to distinguish essential insights.

2 **Long lists denote poor strategy process** – the outcome of the discussion on how a company competes in its markets is typically a long list. The intention seems to be to cover all aspects. Nothing could be further from the truth. This phase of the strategy process concerns distilling the very essence of how a company has to compete. In this way essential clarity is provided.

3 **Separate out order-winners and qualifiers** – a further step to improve a company's understanding of its markets is to separate relevant competitive criteria into:
   - **Qualifiers** – these criteria get a product into a marketplace or onto a customer's shortlist and keep it there. They do not in themselves win orders but provide the opportunity to compete. The failure to provide qualifiers at appropriate levels will lead to a loss of orders. Consequently, qualifiers are order-losing in nature, as a failure to provide a qualifier results in not being on the list as the opportunity to compete is not in place. In such situations, competitors do not win orders from a rival, rather the rival loses orders to its competitors.
   - **Order-winners** – having gained entry to a market is only the first step. The task then is to know how to win orders against competitors who have also qualified to be in the same market. With qualifiers, you need to match customers' requirements (as do competitors), whereas with order-winners, you need to provide them at a level better than your competitors.

Finally, when applying this concept, there are some key points to remember:

- Qualifiers are not less important than order-winners, they are different. Both are essential. With qualifiers, a company needs to qualify and requalify at all times to stay on a customer's shortlist. If you are not on the list, you cannot compete.
- Order-winners and qualifiers are time- and market-specific – they will be different from market to market and will change over time within a market.
- The relevance and importance of order-winners and qualifiers will typically be different to retain market share, grow share in existing markets and enter new markets.
- The relative importance of qualifiers and order-winners will change when moving from being market-driven to being market-driving.
- As highlighted earlier, not all criteria will be either a qualifier or an order-winner. Some criteria do not relate to some markets.

4   **Weight qualifiers and order-winners** – to improve clarity still further, it is essential to weight qualifiers and order-winners in the following way:

- **Qualifiers** – it is adequate and appropriate to limit the classification of qualifiers into two categories – qualifiers (denoted by a Q) and order-losing sensitive qualifiers (denoted by QQ). The latter is intended to alert a company to the fact that failure to provide criteria which are considered to be 'order-losing sensitive' will lead to a rapid loss of business.
- **Order-winners** – the appropriate step here is to allocate 100 points across all the order-winners within a market. This forces the different levels of relevance to be exposed and provides an essential step in distilling out importance. It is essential to avoid procedures where, for example, stars are allocated as a way of indicating importance or phrases such as 'more important' or 'less important' are used, as these approaches avoid confronting and resolving the key step of determining the relative importance of one criteria with another. Such approaches bypass the need to discriminate between the relative importance of one criterion vis-à-vis another, as any level of importance can be attributed to any criteria.

The outcome of using this method of weighting is illustrated later in the chapter.

The procedure for establishing order-winners and qualifiers

To create the essential interface between marketing and operations, a business must understand its markets from the viewpoints of both these functions. Classically, companies fail to distinguish clearly between the market (business) and marketing (functional) perspectives. This lack of clarity shows itself in several ways. In many companies, the strategy debate typically ends when steps 1 and 2 of the framework in *Exhibit 2.10* have been accomplished. The assumption is that marketing's view of the market is how the market is. The key nature of step 3 lies in facilitating the important distinction between the function and the business by undertaking a 360° review of the market, which involves asking market-oriented questions requiring operations answers. These questions ask how different products or customers qualify and win orders in their respective markets.

In developing an operations strategy, the identification of relevant order-winners and qualifiers for different products or customers is a key step. This helps companies to move from what is often a vague understanding of its many markets to a new and essential level of awareness. Too often, companies describe their business as composed of relatively large segments and, in so doing, make the assumption that all products or customers within a segment have similar qualifiers and order-winners because they have similar names, or belong to the same segment from the viewpoint of marketing. Until the company recognizes these differences, it will not achieve the level of clarity essential to increasing business understanding and on which to base strategic decisions.

The procedure used to gain these insights is now outlined:

- Marketing is requested to separate the business into different segments as it perceives them. The procedure, as with other aspects of strategy debate, is iterative in nature. Thus marketing's separation of the business is requested to provide relevant insights and market distinctions as the initial inputs into the debate that follows. These are then considered as explained below and very often revised as the strategy formulation progresses.

- To focus discussion, marketing selects products and/or customers that represent these market segments, together with two future time periods for each segment. Note that the selected periods may differ as they are chosen to reflect the characteristics of each segment. This step serves three purposes. First, it helps to test whether the chosen segments are sufficient to distinguish the market differences that exist. Second, it enables the debate to be oriented towards the particular rather than the general. Third, it allows specific data to be collected and analyses to be completed on the representative sample of products or customers chosen for each segment, a later step in the procedure.

- Then, actual and forecast sales volumes/revenue for chosen representative products or customers are provided to help identify the relative importance of each segment and the expected future growth or decline.

- Based on the representative sample of products or customers, the executives in the strategy-making group (see *Exhibit 2.3*) determine the relevant order-winners, qualifiers and weightings. A good starting point is to ask the executives to independently record their own views, including the use of the weighting system for order-winners and assigning Qs or QQs for qualifiers, as described earlier. Listing the views of individual executives highlights the level of difference initially involved. This will often be sizable and, where this is so, the iterative nature of strategy discussion kicks in.

- When agreement on the order-winners, order-winners' weightings and qualifiers has been reached, a final, essential check is made. This concerns analysing data from actual representative customer orders to verify the order-winners and qualifiers and their respective weightings.

  For example:
  - If price is considered to be a heavily weighted order-winner, this should result in low margins (for these analyses, it is recommended that contributions – invoiced price less variable cost – are used); if price is considered a qualifier, margins should be high and so on.
  - Similarly, a check on delivery speed can be made by calculating actual lead times (the date an order was placed compared to the requested delivery date).

- Checks on on-time delivery, making products to specification (quality conformance) and other relevant competitive criteria would follow a similar pattern by checking actual performance and comparing it with the order-winner/qualifier category and the respective weightings used by executives.

Such analyses provide several advantages, including:

1 Allows the strategy-making group to check their initial views one with another.

2 Necessitates differences to be reconciled, many of which may result from different interpretations as well as different points of view. This highlights the fact that different views exist and the failure of executives to discuss markets in depth results in these differences not being exposed, evaluated and reconciled, without agreement being reached on different segments and the relative importance of order-winners and qualifiers within and between segments.

3 Provides a check on whether the outcome of the analysis of representative orders (the way customers behave) differs from the reconciled views of the strategy-making group. This serves to emphasize the need to always check opinion with data analysis. As *Exhibit 2.13* illustrates, whereas customer contracts are agreed towards the top of the supplier and customer organizations, actual customer requirements are embodied in the orders that customers subsequently place. It is only by analysing orders that customer requirements (their behaviours) can be identified.

4 Highlights that the essential task of the strategy-making group is to understand the markets in which the company competes and what it will take for the company to retain and grow market share today and in the future.

5 Underscores the fact that market reviews form the agenda for all the functional strategies. Without this, functions will lack guidance and have no alternative but to pursue strategies they believe to be appropriate. The outcome of the business debate sets the agenda. The functional role is then to implement and fulfil the strategy agreed by the strategy-making group.

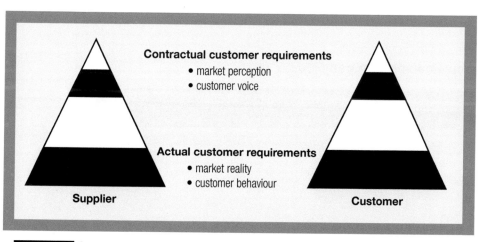

EXHIBIT 2.13 Contractual versus actual customer requirements

Examples of the eventual outcomes are provided as *Exhibits 2.14*, *2.15* and *2.16*, with a brief outline of each to illustrate the insights provided by this approach.

US graphics company (Exhibit 2.14)

Customer A represented the relationship this company sought to develop with all its customers. The distinguishing competitive approach by the company was to support its customers with high-level design and R&D capability, which would not only provide development help in meeting the ink needs of customers but also, as part of the sale, provide fast, technical support in the field. To provide this level of technical expertise and support, high margin sales were necessary. To its customers, while ink was a relatively small percentage of their total costs, having printing presses not making saleable products due to ink problems impacted both costs and their ability to deliver on time.

Criteria		Customer A			Customer B		
		CY	CY + 1	CY + 2	CY	CY + 1	CY + 2
Design (product specification)		40	40	40	30	40	50
Price		Q	Q	Q	40	20	Q
Delivery	– reliability	QQ	QQ	QQ	QQ	QQ	QQ
	– speed	30	20	Q	30	20	Q
Quality conformance		QQ	QQ	QQ	QQ	QQ	QQ
R&D support services		30	40	60	–	20	50

NOTE: Q denotes qualifier, QQ denotes an order-losing sensitive qualifier, CY denotes current year.

EXHIBIT 2.14 US graphics company: order-winners and qualifiers for two customers

Customer B, on the other hand, typified customers who were price sensitive. The strategy for this company was to convert Customer B into a Customer A-type relationship. Where this failed, the company would proactively decide not to continue supplying such customers in the future.

European cable-making company (Exhibit 2.15)

Criteria		Product: Marine (1/50)			Product: Mining (8/25)		
		CY	CY + 2	CY + 4	CY	CY + 2	CY + 4
Design		45	35	25	50	45	40
Quality conformance		Q	Q	Q	30	20	Q
Delivery	– reliability	QQ	QQ	QQ	QQ	QQ	QQ
	– speed	40	35	30	20	20	20
Price		15	30	45	Q	15	40

NOTE: Q denotes qualifier, QQ denotes an order-losing sensitive qualifier, CY denotes current year.

EXHIBIT 2.15 European cable-making company: order-winners and qualifiers for two products

The level of price sensitivity was not high for either its marine or mining sectors. Design and delivery speed were key factors in gaining contracts. However, more pressure on price was anticipated because the design capability would become a less significant order-winner as competitors entered these two more specialized cable sectors.

European engineered sealing system company (Exhibit 2.16)

This example shows the different mix of order-winners, qualifiers and weightings for three different customers for similar technical products and systems. A review of these illustrates the importance for companies to work at this level of detail in order to adequately understand their markets and the different sets of customers' behaviours and requirements. In this way, the needs of customers and segments become clearer. This in turn allows the strategy-making group of a company to determine where resources and attention should be placed in terms of retaining and growing market share and the relative importance of products and customers to the company's current and future performance.

Criteria		Customer A (France)		Customer B (UK)		Customer C (Germany)	
		CY	CY + 3	CY	CY + 3	CY	CY + 3
Price		25	40	50	60	Q	20
Delivery	– reliability	QQ	QQ	QQ	QQ	Q	QQ
	– speed	35	40	20	20	15	25
Quality conformance		QQ	QQ	QQ	QQ	QQ	QQ
Design		Q	Q	Q	Q	30	25
Technical support		25	20	30	20	30	15
Brand name		15	Q	Q	Q	25	15

NOTE: Q denotes qualifier, QQ denotes an order-losing sensitive qualifier, CY denotes current year.

EXHIBIT 2.16 European engineered sealing systems company: order-winners and qualifiers for three customers

Understanding the criteria chosen and their relative weightings

As a starting point, marketing is asked to determine the weightings for each relevant order-winner. This involves allocating percentage points to each criterion for both current and future time periods. In this part of the procedure, the discussion concerns not only the individual weights but also the reasons why any changes in emphasis are anticipated in the future.

Where changes do occur, the business must support the full range of criteria together with the changes in emphasis involved. As explained earlier, whereas some of these will be non-operations features, the major thrust will in fact be from operations. Certainly, the provision of any significant changes in emphasis anticipated in the future will typically be operations based, and the need to reconcile the process and infrastructure investments appropriate to meet the change in requirements will have to be fully discussed, understood and eventually agreed on by all concerned.

A final word concerns the order-winner weightings initially proposed. When this procedure is first adopted, there is a distinct tendency to include a host of criteria and, as a result of not distinguishing between their relative importance, the percentage points will often be spread across all the criteria, so failing to identify the critical order-winning feature(s). Understanding the criteria and weightings selected is necessary to ensure that this situation does not arise. Marketing's view of how orders are won is a most useful first step in developing an appropriate strategy. As explained earlier, this debate is then fuelled by the views of other functions and the collection of relevant data. The company will achieve the necessary level of understanding and essential insights only if such rigorous debate is maintained throughout the strategy-making process.

Invariably, the challenge to marketing's views made by other functional perspectives and the data collected for representative products and customers will change the initial view of the market. The need to verify and understand the criteria and respective weightings continues to be a task at the very core of the strategy process. This rigorous approach provides essential insights and involvement in these debates and outcomes results in functions gaining an essential understanding of the company's markets and their strategic role in supporting them.

Identifying qualifiers with the potential to become order-winners

An integral part of the procedure is to identify any qualifiers associated with the different sets of products or customers with the potential to become order-winners. Once a company identifies such criteria, it must decide whether to invest to initiate this change. The impact it would have on market share, the time it would take for competitors to catch up and the investments involved in bringing about this change would be some of the issues to be addressed in this market-driving strategy decision.

Identifying qualifiers that are order-losing sensitive

Identifying any qualifiers that are order-losing sensitive has already been mentioned. It is highlighted here because of the potential impact on customer retention and overall sales revenue. Operations must be fully aware of any qualifier that if it failed to provide might quickly result in lost orders. Where these are identified, the discussion that follows is aimed at determining the degree of order-losing sensitivity and the degree of risk the business is prepared to take. The company can make appropriate decisions once it understands the trade-offs between associated costs, investments and sales revenue.

The iterative nature of strategy development

The key to developing business unit and functional strategies is to recognize the iterative nature of their development. And key to this is the need for regular and frequent discussions based on analysis of customer data. Customer reviews based on order-winners and qualifiers and checked by the analysis of representative orders are an essential element of this process.

Too often strategy is infrequently undertaken and is characterized by discussion based on the opinions of executives that are typically functional in orientation and insight. While contributing views is a key element of strategy debate, the role of opinion is to serve as a pointer to the relevant data that need to be analysed to check whether or not the view is correct.

Markets are difficult to understand, so regular and frequent discussions underpinned by relevant data are critical to gaining essential insights. Meeting regularly (monthly should be the maximum time gap) and reviewing part of the total market (manageable slices is key here) makes this difficult but fundamental task manageable. Furthermore, regular customer-based discussions and functional reviews help to overcome the inherent sensitivity that typically characterizes the challenging question and fact-based approach so essential to strategy formulation.

The outputs of operations strategy

Some possible order-winners and qualifiers	Some typical areas for review and improvement
Price	Reduce costs in all areas particularly regarding materials and overheads which typically make up some 70–90 per cent of total costs
Quality conformance	Make products to specification. Build quality into the process and delivery system rather than checking conformance after the event. Also, improvements here impact costs
Delivery reliability	Assess on-time delivery performance by product and customer. Review current approaches to meeting orders – involves discussions on the extent to which products can be or are made to order and the role of activities and investments such as scheduling and inventory in meeting these requirements
Delivery speed	Review the elements of the operations process with the purpose of reducing the lead time in the various steps comprising the operations process
Product range	Review the process capability and skill base in relation to current and future product range requirements. Identify and supplement capabilities in line with proposed needs
Demand spikes	Assess current capacity provision in terms of the ability to rapidly increase in line with known or anticipated changes in demand. Approaches include short-term capacity and inventory-holding alternatives
New products – time to market	Identify the elements of lead time within the new product development process for which operations is responsible. Assess the work involved and opportunity to reduce the task content, current start times in relation to the overall procedures and opportunities to complete part or all of the task in parallel (rather than in sequence) with other elements of the process
Meeting specific customer needs	Assess current approaches to identify how standard products can be modified in line with specific customer requirements and the impact on costs, lead times, quality conformance and the overall schedule

SOURCE: Adapted from Hill, T. (2005) *Operations Management*, 2nd edn, Basingstoke, Palgrave Macmillan

EXHIBIT 2.17 Some possible order-winners and qualifiers and some typical areas for review and improvement

Three basic outputs accrue from using this approach and these are now discussed.

1 Setting the strategic task for operations

As emphasized earlier, the market/customer needs set the agenda for all functions. *Exhibit 2.17* lists some of the order-winners and qualifiers that fall within the remit of operations and some typical areas for review and improvement that will form part of operations' strategic task. As highlighted earlier, prioritizing where operations spends its time and money will be provided by the order-winners, qualifiers and weightings that make up a market or market segment. As the adage goes – it is not about doing things right but doing the right things.

2 Assessing operations' alignment with product/customer needs

This concerns a review of the implications for operations processes and infrastructure support of selling products in current and future markets and/or supporting the provision of customer needs today and in the future, as depicted in *Exhibit 2.18*. It involves assessing the degree of match between what exists in operations and those processes and infrastructure features needed to provide the order-winners and qualifiers of a company's markets.

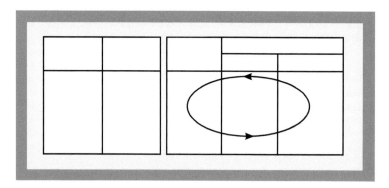

EXHIBIT 2.18 Assessing the implications for operations processes and infrastructure of order-winners

This check should also be done for all future product proposals or new customer agreements. The essential regular review should be used to pick up any volume or order-winner/qualifier changes, which may be significant as measured against the relevant base year. By checking on and assessing competitors' moves and actions and reviewing customer behaviour changes and trends, the relative levels of match and mismatch are monitored, thus detecting incremental market changes that have occurred over time, which often otherwise go unnoticed. Only by reviewing current and future requirements against the original decisions can the full change be assessed.

3 Operations' input into the business strategy debate

Once determined, the operations strategy and the necessary investments and time period for change form part of the business strategy debate, as illustrated in *Exhibit 2.19*.

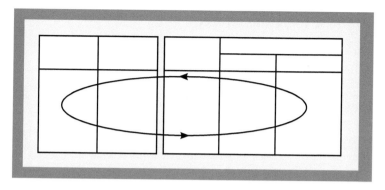

EXHIBIT 2.19 Operations' input into the business strategy debate

As a consequence, the company as a whole is now required to review the business in both marketing and operations terms. It changes the style and substance of business decisions from functionally based arguments and perspectives to ones that address functional differences by resolving the trade-offs involved at the business level. This business-level resolution, therefore, leads to an agreed understanding of the business objectives, marketing strategy and operations strategy. In reality, it will lead to one of five positions based on the degree of fit between the marketing and strategic interface:

1   Where the interface is sufficiently close and requires little, if any, adjustment.

2   Where the interface is not sufficiently close, but the business decision is not to invest the required time and money to bring it closer to 1 above.

3   Where the interface is not sufficiently close, and the decision is to change the marketing strategy to reduce the mismatch and move towards 1 above.

4   Where the interface is not sufficiently close and the decision is to allocate the time and investment to enable operations to bring its processes and infrastructure to that required to support the marketing strategy and so move towards 1 above.

5   A combination of alternatives 3 and 4 to move towards position 1.

In situations 3 and 4, the company decides to reposition marketing and operations, respectively, to bring about the position described in 1. In the case of 2, it is essential that the reality of the mismatch is translated into operations targets and budgets to present a manageable, achievable and hence controllable task. In this way, the inadequacies of operations' performance against budget are separated from the consequences of the business strategy decision to accept the mismatch involved. The business is, therefore, able to learn the extent of the consequences resulting from the operations/marketing interface mismatch and use this vital information in its future strategic decisions.

Chapter 4 discusses the outputs described here and provides examples of different strategy applications.

Operations typically develops more than one strategy

As markets are different, the order-winners and qualifiers relating to these markets will also be different. Consequently, operations (as well as other functions) will need to develop different strategies to support these different sets of market needs.

Typically in the past this has neither been recognized nor provided. The failure of business strategy approaches to identify difference has led to general strategic approaches being adopted by operations. This, in turn, has fuelled the trend for operations to fulfil its strategic role by introducing solutions in the form of panaceas. If markets are deemed to be the same, generic support for these makes sense. Rarely is this so.

Business debate needs to direct its attention to highlighting the differences inherent in markets. Clarity of meaning and distinguishing between order-winners and qualifiers are both part of achieving this. As markets are the key to the continued success and growth of companies, no effort should be spared in rooting out these essential differences. Operations' task is, then, to develop the different strategic responses required to support a company's different markets.

Reflections

To be effective, strategies must display the following characteristics that are central to the procedure and the outcomes:

- **Congruence of purpose and function** – As illustrated in *Exhibit 2.7*, the markets in which a company competes should link business objectives and functional strategies. Otherwise functions will base strategies on their own perspectives and understanding, which disrupts the essential gains of coherent direction of the parts and the whole. Congruence of purpose and function, therefore, is an essential ingredient of strategy formulation and implementation.

- **A focus on key priorities** – The coherent direction in which functional strategies need to be formed will lead to an agreement on which developments and investments are the most important for supporting given markets. Priorities for timescales and costs are agreed on and functions base subsequent actions and activities on these outcomes. This prioritizing mechanism is a key characteristic of effective strategies. It gives essential context, orients actions, keeps the list of tasks small and manageable, focuses attention on what is critical and promotes coordination and cooperation between the different functions in the core task of being competitive within agreed markets.

- **Commitment through understanding** – Knowing where the company is going and why is essential if strategies are to be effective. In addition, knowing where and why builds commitment among participants. An understanding of the rationale underpinning the strategies to be taken and the priorities to be pursued gives essential and appropriate direction in the short term, while providing the basis for strategic rethinking that the future will undoubtedly demand.

- **Regular reviews and revisions** – Strategy development is an essential executive task. It is unique to this level within a business and cannot be delegated in terms of

STRATEGY CONCERNS **DIRECTION** AND **COORDINATION**

DON'T SEND IN THE CHARIOTS **BEFORE** FIRING ANY ARROWS

Functions **must** fight the same battle

insight, review and direction. An integral part of successfully undertaking these developments is the frequency and nature of the discussion. Regular and frequent reviews on one part of the market at a time make the task manageable and keep it in the forefront of everyone's mind. Underpinning these difficult debates with data on products and customers provides the insights necessary to create sufficient understanding to give appropriate direction and the knowing commitment of the scarce resources of money and time.

- **Routine performance measurement** – Strategy leads to appropriate direction, the pursuit of priorities and the essential commitment to see them through. As part of the continuous reappraisal of strategy decisions, performance needs to be monitored on a regular basis. Routine checks are vital in themselves. Adherence to and progress towards agreed strategies is essential for all developments and close and continuous monitoring of performance is integral to a successful strategy. Furthermore, strategy is not a once-and-for-all development that remains unaddressed between one review time and the next. Continuous reassessment needs to be undertaken and the routine measurement of performance is an integral part of this procedure.

Market- or marketing-led?

Many companies do not keep in sharp focus the critical differences between being market-led and being marketing-led.[4] To substitute the business (market) perspective with a functional (marketing) perspective will invariably lead to distorted strategies and eventually to corporate disadvantage. Checking the characteristic of a strategy based on the perspectives of a single function against those listed above clearly underscores these essential differences. Furthermore, in many businesses, this way of handling market reviews and strategy formulation is made worse by the fact that marketing is becoming increasingly characterized by the perceived role of creating ideas. Generating ideas often becomes an end in itself, with the rigour of testing business fit left to others. Many businesses, however, fail to appreciate that the most significant orders are the ones to which a company says 'no'. For this marks the boundaries of the markets in which it competes and defines the context in which operations' strategic response needs to be made. To be able to say 'no' means that a company has agreed and understands the markets in which it competes, and this can only be resolved through rigorous corporate debate.

Operations strategy

In the past, companies have seen operations' role as being the provider of corporate requests. Business strategy debate has stopped short of discussing the implications of decisions for operations. This behaviour has been based on two incorrect assumptions:

1 Within a given technology, operations is able to do everything.

2 Operations' contribution solely concerns the achievement of efficiency rather than also including the effective support of market needs.

The result for many companies is that not only have the profit margins they once enjoyed been eroded, but also the base on which to build a sound and prosperous business in the future is no longer available. A company is exposed and vulnerable without the frequent operations strategy checks necessary to evaluate the fit between the business and operations' ability to provide the necessary order-winners and qualifiers of its various products and customers. In times of increased world competition, being left behind can be sudden and fatal. In many instances, averting the end is the only option left. Turning the business around, however, will only be achieved by switching from an operational to a strategic mode, which will require a corporate review of the marketing and operations perspectives and of the financial implications of the proposals.

Operations strategy comprises a series of decisions concerning process and infrastructure investment, which, over time, provide the necessary support for the relevant order-winners and qualifiers of the different market segments of a company. It is built on keeping the strategic developments relevant to the business, that is, it must reflect the aspects of operations' performance critical to those segments of the firm under review. Identifying the pertinent aspects, and setting aside those that are not, provides for a strategy that is oriented to the market and the simplicity and clarity of direction this affords.

On the other hand, operations strategy is not:

- A list of all aspects typically comprising an operations function and an attempt to develop a strategic statement about each. Differentiating the important from the less important aspects in terms of market needs is a key feature of sound strategy development.

- A list of potential operations improvements such as flexible, lean and agile. Although sound investments to make, they are not by rights strategic in orientation. Such arguments are not strategic (that is, related to market needs) in origin, and imply that this is, in essence, operations' strategic task. Essential difference is now excluded and operations' contribution to strategic discussion is limited.

- An exhortation that the strategic perspectives of the operations function should be paramount.

Operations' strategic task is to transform, over time, support for a company's markets into an appropriate collection of facilities, structures, controls, procedures and people. This chapter has provided essential insights into the principles and concepts that underpin this task. Chapter 3 looks in some depth at order-winners and qualifiers and Chapter 4 at the procedures to follow.

Discussion questions

1 How do functional strategies interface with the business as a whole?
2 What is the difference between being market-driven and market-driving within the context of strategy development?
3 Do all functions necessarily have a strategic role? Explain.
4 Give three key reasons for operations' reactive role in strategy development. Explain the reasons for your choice.

5   What are the steps in developing a functional strategy? Use operations as the example in your answer.

6   Outline the steps linking corporate objectives with marketing and operations strategies. Why does this often not work in reality?

7   What is the essential difference between order-winners and qualifiers? Could a competitive criterion be an order-winner in one market and a qualifier in another market? Explain.

8   Why is it recommended to weight order-winners using percentages?

9   What are the principal outputs of an operations strategy?

Notes and references

1   Skinner, W. (1969) 'Manufacturing: missing link in corporate strategy,' *Harvard Business Review*, May–June, p. 13.

2   Hill, T. (1998) *The Strategy Quest*, Bristol: AMD Publishing, p vii. Copies are available from the publisher, whose address is 'Albedo', Dousland, Devon, PL20 6NE.

3   Hill, T. (2005) *Operations Management*, Basingstoke: Palgrave Macmillan.

4   See Hill, T. (1993) *The Essence of Operations Management*, Englewood Cliffs, NJ: Prentice Hall, p. 25.

Exploring further

Bozarth, E. and McDermott, C. (1998) 'Configurations in marketing strategy: a review and directions for future research', *Journal of Operations Management*, 16(4): 427–39.

Dell, M. and Fredman, C. (1999) *Direct from Dell*, London: HarperCollins.

Hayes, R.H. and Upton, D.M. (1998) 'Operations-based strategy', *California Management Review*, 40(4): 8–24.

Menda, R. and Dilts, D. (1997) 'The manufacturing strategy formulation process: linking up multifunctional view points', *Journal of Operations Management*, 14: 315–31.

Ward, P.T. and Duray, R. (2000) 'Manufacturing strategy in context: environment, competitive strategy and manufacturing strategy', *Journal of Operations Management*, 18(2): 123–38.

Order-winners and Qualifiers

3

Summary

The rationale behind the perspectives and characteristics of order-winners and qualifiers was introduced in the last chapter. Understanding these fully and reviewing operations' alternative ways of supporting them is now provided:

- Strategic scenarios and approaches – strategy formulation tends to be expressed in general terms. It is essential when developing strategy that clarity in terms of priorities and direction is provided.

- Today's markets – today's markets are characterized by increasing difference (rather than increasing similarity) and speed of change. This requires executives to gain clarity and insight and continuously discuss markets so as to improve clarity and identify changes early.

- Trade-offs – the ongoing debate about trade-offs has raised questions concerning whether they can be eliminated or not. In reality, trade-offs need to be addressed at five different levels from decisions concerning which business unit should be allocated some or all of the available funds through which market, which order-winner or qualifier, which function and which investment.

- Order-winners and qualifiers – the market provides the agenda for all functional strategies. Consequently, some are operations related and operations specific, while others are not part of operations' provision.

- Benchmarking – the role and attributes of using benchmarking allows companies to make performance comparisons within their own group of companies, within their own sector and against other companies in unrelated sectors. It is part of the way to achieve superior performance within one's own markets.

The last chapter introduced the concept of order-winners and qualifiers, discussed the rationale behind these perspectives and outlined their distinguishing characteristics. This chapter examines these dimensions more fully, explaining specific criteria in some detail.

The essence of strategy stems from the need for companies to gain a detailed understanding of their current and future markets. Functions are then required to develop strategies based on supporting the requirements of those markets in which the business decides it wishes to retain and/or grow share. Operations strategy (as with other functional strategies), therefore, consists of the investments, developments and actions undertaken to support the order-winners and/or qualifiers in agreed markets and for which operations is solely or jointly responsible. The pattern of decisions that results constitutes the strategy of the function.

In reality, strategies often comprise a mix of decisions, not all of which will be in line with their strategic task(s), either by default (a result of either not being conscious of the inconsistency between the decisions taken and strategic requirements, or failing to meet the need even though adequate resources and time had been provided) or by design (there will invariably be instances where companies decide not to invest adequately for pragmatic reasons). Regarding the latter, such instances do not constitute 'poor strategy', because 'good strategy' is not a result of making the right decisions but is the outcome of a company knowing what it is doing and adjusting corporate expectations in line with reality.

In summary, the key elements of functional strategy development are:

1 Being party to the decisions and agreements on current and future markets
2 Identifying and agreeing relevant order-winners and qualifiers whether in a market-driven or market-driving scenario
3 Assessing how well these order-winners and qualifiers are currently supported
4 Agreeing a pattern of decisions and actions to maintain or improve existing levels of support
5 Being aware of the extent of current and future fit, any timescales involved in point 4 and adjusting corporate expectations in line with reality
6 Implementing the components of strategy.

Throughout, functions need to be proactive in strategic discussions while explaining their perspectives so that the rest of the business understands them. In this way, functional perspectives form part of both the discussion and decision.

Markets and market segments

In the last chapter, the terms 'market', 'market segments', 'products' and 'customers' were used as ways of describing markets. For operations, a market is a cluster of one or more customers for whom the order-winners, qualifiers and weightings are similar. Such a group represents a similar strategic task in terms of what operations needs to provide in order to retain and grow share. Consequently, the term 'market' and 'market segments' are deemed interchangeable.

Strategic scenarios and approaches

As highlighted in Chapter 2, strategic formulation tends to be expressed in general terms. Key reasons include:

- Since strategy implies a broad review, companies also perceive the underlying characteristic of strategic outputs to be broad.

- Companies appear to seek strategies that are uniform in nature. This offers apparent clarity in the form of consistent strategic statements that are easy to express, explain and address. Uniformity is inherently attractive no matter what the company's size.

It is not surprising then that typical expressions of corporate strategy include general terms such as 'customer service', 'responsiveness', 'meeting customers' needs' and 'delighting the customer'. Furthermore, researchers, writers and advisers have proffered generic statements concerning corporate strategy formulation with expressions such as 'low cost', 'differentiation', 'critical success factors' and 'core competence'. The use of general terms similar to these brings two major drawbacks. First, difference is not brought into focus but remains blurred. Second, decisions concerning the nature of the market segments in which a company competes or wishes to compete are not resolved at the strategic level. A company may not recognize that orders for products, often within the same market segment, are won in different ways. This lack of clarity brings conflicting demands on operations, which reinforces its tendency to be reactive in strategic formulation and disperses the essential coherence necessary to provide strategic direction, guidance and advantage.

As markets are characterized by increasing difference not increasing similarity, the need for clarity becomes ever more essential. Ask chief executive officers whether the markets served by the group of companies under their control are similar in nature and the answer would be 'no'. Ask if the markets served by a typical company are the same and the answer would again be 'no'. How is it then that companies expect or believe that operations' strategic task (in terms of process and infrastructure investments) in support of these would be common? As this is not so, why do companies apply the same operations approaches to support their different markets not only in one plant but in all their different plants?

The strategic process, therefore, needs to be based on a deep understanding of differences in markets and within a market. All too often, companies debate strategy in general terms and undertake strategy using general courses of action. Invariably and increasingly, this leads to a lack of fit between functional strategies and market requirements. Where this happens, companies will find themselves seriously disadvantaged.

Before moving on to the characteristics of today's markets, let us review what typically happens to firms in the absence of clear, well-defined strategic debate.

Strategic vacuum

The absence of a conscious operations strategy development process within a business typically leads to a strategic vacuum into which a raft of solutions – panaceas or flavour-of-the-month initiatives – continues to be drawn.

This type of response is underpinned by a basic logic. Executives recognize that operations, as a significant part of the company both in size and its contribution to retaining and growing market share, should be making and needs to be making a significant contribution to the overall success of the business. There is, therefore, due pressure on operations to respond to these corporate demands and expectations. Without strategic context, operations traditionally responds by introducing currently popular solutions. In this way, companies seek to achieve parity by modelling operations on best practice. However, although a particular solution may be good in itself, its application to a specific problem may not be appropriate. Given operations' reactive nature and the existence of corporate initiatives, it is easy to see why most companies have invested regularly and significantly over the years in responses that, by and large, are eventually discarded. The cause of their abandonment is principally their lack of relevance to the solution.

Characteristics of today's markets: difference and speed of change

As emphasized in Chapter 2, whereas past markets were characterized by similarity and stability, current markets are characterized by difference and rapid change.

The market characteristics of today place a greater need on understanding than in the past, and one theme throughout is the need to attain this necessary level of understanding. The last chapter outlined a framework for gaining more detailed market insights. A wide range of methodologies has been put forward by academics, consultants and other advisers specifying approaches that would lead to strategic insights and appropriate answers. Driven by a need for generic solutions, the approaches advocated too often set aside the overriding difference that exists in companies in order to offer a universal way of developing strategy that typically overarches a very different range of businesses. Failing to recognize and cope with difference and avoiding the essential interface between corporate, business unit and functional strategies and between functions themselves has resulted in approaches that appear complete but which, when applied, are unable to cope with the complex nature of today's businesses and their markets. Strategy development is not that easy.

All that is common for companies is that current and future markets are the essence of strategy and provide the agenda on which to base functional strategic responses. Companies will be unable to arrive at successful and workable strategic decisions unless they adequately understand their markets. Only then will they be able to identify the strategic alternatives to meet the needs of their different markets and thus move away from prescriptive approaches. The solutions developed by academics and consultants are most attractive in what they offer. However, the all-embracing and solution-oriented characteristics of these approaches do not provide executives with the insights necessary to cope with their complex businesses nor warn them that the approach has limitations and that strategy development will be ongoing, difficult, time-consuming and necessitate many months of exacting work. Furthermore, the approaches invariably fail to start with sufficient emphasis on understanding markets. As a result, executives are impeded by their failure to complete this fundamental task. Also, as with most aspects of management, an essential ingredient in doing a task well is hard work. Understanding today's varied and fast-changing markets is no exception. As *Exhibit 3.1* highlights, the problem – understanding market requirements – is difficult. The solution – identifying the action to take, such as reducing cost where price is a significant order-winner – is easy. Finally, implementation – in this example, undertaking the necessary investments, decisions and actions to reduce cost – is difficult. Too much of the time, both executives and academics/other advisers focus on the solution phase.

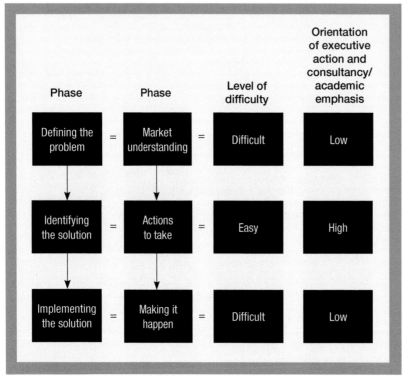

EXHIBIT 3.1 Phases and characteristics of strategy development and implementation

Trade-offs

The trend towards increasingly competitive markets brings with it the question of whether it is possible to improve on all competitive fronts at the same time or whether companies need to recognize and choose between the trade-offs inherent in investments.

The concept of trade-offs has received much interest since the late 1960s when Skinner put the issue at the centre of the operations strategy paradigm.[1] In the 40 years since, significantly different positions are still taken by researchers on the existence[2] as well as the implications of trade-offs for a business and the relevance of these issues for operations strategy and the company as a whole.

The concern with the proposition that trade-offs can be set aside, reduced to a level that no longer restricts options or strategic direction, or even that they are somehow manageable now and in the future ignores the fact that trade-offs are an integral feature of business.

The investment of time and money to change, develop or improve elements of the delivery system or infrastructure within operations always involves choices, and with choices there are trade-offs – relevant performance dimensions that are better served by one approach compared to another. Compromise is inherent in choice and so to put forward a view of operations' business contribution that is in denial of this introduces a premise that is unsustainable or misleading in several ways:

- operations' inputs into strategic discussion need not include the issue of choice nor an explanation of the constraints that follow

- similarly, the rest of the company may assume that operations' contribution to meeting the competitive needs of a company's markets is neither constrained nor limited such that these must be taken into account

- consequently, the compromises that are inherent in choice and that need to be fully understood by a business when making strategic decisions are taken out of the corporate arena and are, in fact, made at the functional rather than business level within the organization.

However, nothing could be further from the truth. Where a company allocates resources and how these investments are spent will impact what offerings a business can provide and how well it can provide them. When addressing these issues, companies, whether consciously or not, make choices at several levels. Some concern direction, others concern means but, as the next section explains, all embody trade-offs. Although, for ease of explanation, these choices have been separated into discrete statements at different levels, they are part of a whole that would require iterative discussion as part of the mechanism of selection.

Level 1: Which business unit?
Where companies are of a size that makes splitting the whole into two, or more, business units, the investment decision at the corporate level concerns to which business the resources should be allocated. These decisions around investment (and similarly divestment) concern critical issues about future sales revenue and profit growth.

Level 2: Which market?
As businesses are typically in two or more markets, prioritizing the investments made by functions such as operations needs to reflect the corporate importance of the market choices involved.

Level 3: Which order-winner or qualifier?

The competitive drivers in markets typically differ. Thus having made choices at level 2, the next set of choices concerns which order-winner(s)/qualifier(s) in the chosen market(s) is the priority in terms of where investments will be made.

Level 4: Which function?

To improve the company's ability to better provide a chosen order-winner or qualifier, the next choice is how to achieve this most effectively. The first step is to determine how this will be provided in terms of the two or more functions that often can contribute to improving support for a competitive driver in a company's market(s). To illustrate these options, let's overview the contribution that different functions could make to two competitive dimensions: price and delivery speed.

Price

Where price is an order-winner, the strategic task of relevant functions is to reduce cost in terms of the product specification itself, or the operations processes used in its provision. The trade-off decision facing a business at this level includes deciding which function or functions are best able to contribute to this requirement in terms of investment (time and money) and return. For example:

1   The **design function** could be required to simplify the current design in order to:
    - take out material cost, for example by reducing the material content, or substituting a lower cost material, while still meeting the required product specification
    - reduce the labour cost involved by, for example, reducing the number of parts of the product and thus the time needed to make and assemble it.

2   The **operations function** could be required to improve the existing process so as to:
    - reduce waste, for example reducing the number of rejects or the level of process waste
    - reduce the time to make the product by increasing process speed while maintaining quality conformance levels.

3   The **engineering function** could invest in modifying, or retrofitting, the existing process in order to:
    - increase throughput speed
    - reduce the number of people to run the process
    - reduce the level of rejects or process waste.

Delivery speed

Where delivery speed is an order-winner, the strategic task concerns reducing the operations lead time involved. Again the trade-off decisions concern which function or functions would best be able to contribute to this requirement in terms of investment (time and money) and return. For example:

- operations could invest to reduce lead time through a better production planning and control system, or through improved integration with suppliers

- operations could trade lead time for inventory and move from, say, a make-to-order to an assemble-to-order position

- design could modify the product structure and increase modularization, thus allowing a change from a make-to-order to an assemble-to-order position with little or no increase in inventory.

At this point, it is worth recalling that trade-offs at different levels are not independent of one another. The above examples do not affect the selection of which market, or which order-winners/qualifiers; these are still open options. For example, when addressing the need to improve delivery speed, there is the option to redefine the business so as to, say, reduce the available range of offerings and move to a make-to-stock policy with zero delivery lead times.

Level 5: Which investment?

The evaluation of alternative investments has to take into account not only the trade-offs inherent in the investment itself but also a comparison between these investments and alternatives. Let's explain. Investing in advanced manufacturing system (AMS) is a way to meet a wider range of products and the high- and low-volume demands that would be involved. One trade-off discussion, however, that this proposal ignores is to asses the outcome of spending this money in other ways. For example, spending $3m on an AMS would enable a company to meet the range offering on hand. An alternative is to spend part of this investment on a process to meet the high-volume products within the company's range while continuing to make other products on existing processes. The benefits of increased capacity and lower unit costs would enable the company to compete more effectively in this part of the market.

It is clear that investing in processes that can meet the demands and volumes of a range of products will bring one set of trade-offs. Investing part or all of the same funds in the high- or low-volume segment of a total market will bring another set of trade-offs. Here again, choice brings alternatives and issues of compromises that highlight the trade-offs on hand and the alternative decisions to be taken.

Investment for strategic vis-à-vis operational reasons

Investments and developments can be made to meet either strategic or operational goals and some illustrations are given in *Exhibit 3.2*. Both are clearly sound decisions but are undertaken for different purposes and to deliver different outcomes. Part of the operations executive task is to ensure that these differences are understood and form the basis of the executive decision process. As already emphasized, the executive task is to ensure that time and money are spent on the 'right things'.

Order-winners and qualifiers: basic characteristics

Identifying relevant order-winners and qualifiers, and the relative weightings to be attached to them, helps companies to achieve these critical insights. The following sections describe what these criteria are and how they work. This first section provides some important background for the discussion of specific criteria that follows. When discussing markets, a company should keep in mind the following:

Activity
Cost reduction
Inventory reduction
Change from make-to-stock to make-to-order position
Improve quality conformance levels

Exhibit 3.2
Examples of the different strategic and operational outcomes that may result from activities

Strategic dimensions	Operational dimensions
Lower costs lower the price	Lower costs increase profits
Could increase operations lead time	Improves cash flow
Increases operations lead time	Improves cash flow
Right first time	Lower costs increase profits

- General statements about markets embody imprecise meanings. As a result, executives take away from strategy discussions their own understandings that are typically based on their own functional perspectives. Thus, a prerequisite for sound strategy development (that is, agreement by all on what markets the company is and should be in and the competitive characteristics of those markets) is missing.

- Order-winners and qualifiers are market-specific. The criteria relating to one market will carry different order-winners, qualifiers and weightings than another market. It follows, therefore, that there are few general rules.

- When developing order-winners and qualifiers, companies must distinguish the level of importance for individual criteria for each market. To do this, they weight order-winners by allocating a total of 100 points; for qualifiers, a distinction is made between a qualifier and an order-losing sensitive qualifier (that is, one that will cause a business to lose customers' orders quickly). Examples of these dimensions were given earlier in *Exhibits 2.14*, *2.15* and *2.16* together with supporting text.

- Order-winners and qualifiers and their relative weightings will change over time. To assess these potential changes, a company must weight each criterion for the current period and two future periods. The latter will need to reflect the nature of the market; for example, for a printing company, the future time periods may be next year and the year after, but for an aerospace company, they would need to be several years ahead so reflecting the product life cycles involved. Again, *Exhibits 2.14*, *2.15* and *2.16* illustrate these points.

- Differences typically exist between the criteria and their weightings necessary to retain existing market share, those necessary to increase market share and those to gain new customers. These differences need to be reflected in the relevant order-winners and qualifiers and their respective weightings.

- Similarly, the criteria that relate to winning orders for a primary supplier will differ from those for secondary or other supplier categories. Although customers tend to infer that the criteria are the same, common sense challenges that logic. The large percentage share of demand that typically goes to a primary supplier creates very different contractual demands and opportunities than those for other suppliers. The way in which secondary or other suppliers win their part of the contract needs to reflect this.

- Not all order-winners and qualifiers relate to operations. However, over time, operations-related criteria will often come to the fore, for example price, on-time delivery and quality conformance.

Order-winners and qualifiers: specific dimensions

There is a range of order-winners and qualifiers, and, as highlighted above, not all of them form part of operations' strategic task. Consequently, this section separates the different categories and reviews typical criteria within each category. As stressed earlier, strategy is market- and time-specific and, therefore, not all order-winners and qualifiers will relate to, or be of the same importance to, all companies.

Operations-related and operations-specific criteria

This category concerns those order-winners and qualifiers that are specific to operations and will, where relevant, form part of operations' strategic role.

Price

In many markets, and particularly in the growth, maturity and saturation phases of a product life cycle (see *Exhibit 3.3*), price typically becomes an increasingly important order-winner. When this is so, operations' task is to provide the low costs necessary to support the price sensitivity of the market, so creating the level of profit margin necessary to support the business investment involved and create opportunity for the future. As in many of the pertinent analyses in operations, highlighting the pockets of significant cost will give direction to the areas where resource allocation should be made and management attention given.

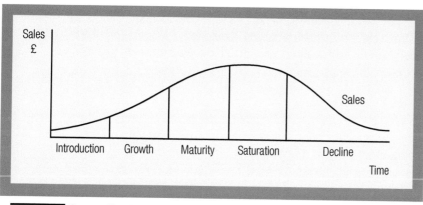

EXHIBIT 3.3 Generalized product life cycle

In most manufacturing companies in North America, Europe and other developed industrial nations, direct labour is typically only a small part of total costs. Materials followed by overheads are usually the two main cost areas, a fact that should be reflected in the provision of information, allocation of resources and frequency of review.

Since price is an omnipresent factor in most markets, companies are reticent to consider that it may not be a relevant order-winner. This misunderstanding often stems from the fact that price comparisons with alternatives will typically form part of a customer's evaluation. However, where price is an order-winner, margins will be low. Only then will cost reduction be a priority. Where margins are high, price is not an order-winner but a qualifier. In such markets, customers will compare one price to another, not to seek the lowest price but to check that the quoted price is within an acceptable range. Therefore, companies need to recognize the key difference between being price competitive (a qualifier) and competing on price (an order-winner).

Such an evaluation is not unique to the aspect of price. Customers will typically cross-check all relevant criteria. In the case of qualifiers, this is to ensure a ballpark fit, whereas for order-winners, customers will typically be looking for a 'better than' performance.

As explained earlier, qualifiers get a company into and maintain it within a market. As such, they do not win orders but are essential prerequisites for a company to be considered as a potential supplier. Where price is a qualifier, a company cannot simply charge whatever it wishes. The company must price the product according to what the market will bear, keeping exploitation within sensible bounds. Failure to do so will result in lost orders to competitors that are more price competitive. In such situations, a company will have turned a qualifier (that is, a product highly priced within acceptable limits) into an order-losing criterion (the price has become too high).

Where price is an order-winner, low (or anticipated low) margins give operations the clear task of reducing costs in order to maintain or improve available margins. Where companies decide to reduce price significantly thus altering its role (qualifier to an order-winner) or its importance as an order-winner, they must similarly change related elements of operations strategy. Companies electing to alter the role of price would need to assess the lead times involved to bring this about, any associated investments and their cost-reducing potential. Deciding to reduce price without assessing these factors will invariably lead to inappropriate strategies. While the decision to reduce price, although difficult to evaluate, is easy to make, cost reduction, on the other hand, is easy to evaluate but difficult to achieve.

Cost reduction

When price is an order-winner, a strategic role for operations is to reduce costs. To this end, companies need to concentrate their efforts in those areas where costs are greatest. Since materials and overheads typically account for some 80–90 per cent of the total, these will be the areas that should yield the best results and should receive the pro rata attention they deserve. Companies need to ensure that the emphasis on controlling and reducing direct labour costs as the principal source of cost reduction has not been carried forward from the past. Too often this traditional orientation unduly influences the direction of cost reduction initiatives.

Lean operations

The drive towards reducing waste within operations is encapsulated by the term 'lean operations'.[3] As it implies, the aim is to seek out and eliminate waste in all its forms including the elimination of non-value-added activities and inventory reduction.

Many organizations have undertaken continuous improvement efforts to increase productivity. The key areas for re-evaluation, however, are broadly based as they reflect the more significant areas of expense and cost reduction opportunity within each company. Typical lists include eliminating waste (for example doing necessary tasks wrong the first time and doing unnecessary tasks; the estimated costs associated with these non-value activities range from 20 to 30 per cent and 10 to 20 per cent respectively), product design, quality at source, process redesign, just-in-time (JIT) production control systems, set-up reduction, overhead reduction and the involvement of people. The outcomes create significant improvements and separate out the high performers. Examples of this are increasingly common. One study investigated the relative importance of 18 automotive component plants, 9 in Japan and 9 in the UK. *Exhibit 3.4* shows the difference between those plants categorized by the report as being 'world class' (note that all world-class plants were Japanese but not all Japanese plants were world class) and the remainder of the sample.

Dimension	Relative plant performance	
	World class	Other
Units per (100 = best)		
I hour	95	54
I square metre of floor space	89	64
Level of rework (% direct labour time)	1.5	4.1
Hours of inventory	11	75

EXHIBIT 3.4 Relative average performance of world-class and other plants against selective dimensions

A key factor in the approach to driving out costs is to avoid concentrating on one aspect of cost rather than total cost as this can lead to missed opportunities. For example, Heinz, the US-based food company, introduced a labour cost reduction plan at its Starkist tuna factories in Puerto Rico and American Samoa. With increasing competition from low labour cost areas, this policy seemed to make sense. But a study revealed that the workers were so overworked that each day they were leaving tonnes of meat on the bone. Adding workers, slowing down production lines, increasing supervision and retraining increased costs by $5m but cut waste by $15m with a $10m saving each year. A similar example is provided by a Dutch-based food preparation company. The growing importance of high-volume demand from large supermarket chains in Europe had brought an increased emphasis on price as an order-winner. The company's response was to seek direct labour productivity improvements. But this diverted attention from controlling costs elsewhere. Further reviews revealed high levels of waste in preparation. For example, lettuce loss was four times higher than the standards set. Additional training and close monitoring of actual performance compared to standards soon got waste down to acceptable levels and, with it, associated costs.

Continuous improvement

Going hand in hand with the drive to cut costs and reduce waste is the recognition that improvement should not only be the result of business-level activity led by specialists (and resulting in stepped changes and significant breakthroughs) but should also be continuously sought by all involved. Continuous improvement[4] describes the ongoing drive to seek improvements (no matter what their size) in all aspects of a business and for this to be set within the domain of the staff undertaking the work involved. In this way, improvement becomes an integral part of a person's job and is ongoing in nature. The success of this approach has been clearly demonstrated in Japanese automobile companies over several decades. Known as 'kaizen', a Japanese term meaning 'continuous improvement', the benefits were clearly demonstrated and maintained over time. Increasingly, Western companies have adopted this approach with significant results. While typically the changes that result are small leading to incremental improvements, the wealth of ideas leads to sizable results overall with immediate and identifiable benefits. Toyota, for example, typically implements an average of 30 ideas per employee per year, generating significant savings. In 2002, Boardroom Inc., a US publishing company, received an average of 100 ideas per employee. Similar levels of ideas were also recorded by Milliken Inc., a US-based textile and chemicals company, while Wainwright Industries, an aerospace and automotive group, implemented an average of 65 ideas per employee in 2003.

Continuous improvement also signals a change in management style, where responsibility and authority to seek out and implement changes is pushed down the organization. Undertaking these improvement activities is built into the job, with appropriate training and development being provided and time set aside to carry out these tasks.

Experience curves

Evidence clearly shows that as experience accumulates, performance improves, and the experience curve is the quantification of this improvement. The basic phenomenon of the experience curve is that the cost of manufacturing a given item falls in a regular and predictable way as the total quantity produced increases. The purpose of this section is to draw attention to this relationship and its role in the formulation of operations strategy. It is helpful to note that while the cost/volume relationship is the pertinent corporate issue, some of the examples will, in fact, relate price to volume because the information, not being company derived, uses average industry price as a convenient substitute.

The price of a new product almost always declines after its initial introduction and as it becomes more widely accepted and available. However, it is not so commonly recognized that over a wide range of products, costs also follow a remarkably consistent decline. The characteristic pattern is that the cost declines (in constant $s, €s or £s) by a consistent percentage each time cumulative unit production is doubled. The effects of learning curves on labour costs have been recognized and reported over the past 60 years, beginning with studies on airframe production in the United States prior to the Second World War. However, experience curves are distinctly different from this. The real source of the experience effect is derived from organizational improvement. Although learning by individuals is important, it is only one of many improvements that accrue from experience. Investment in operations processes, changes in production methods, product design and improvements in all functions in a business account for some part of the significant experience-related gains.

The experience curve is normally drawn by taking each doubling of cumulative unit production and expressing the unit cost or price as a percentage of the cost or price before doubling. So an 80 per cent experience curve would mean that the cost or price of the one-hundredth unit of a product is 80 per cent of that of the fiftieth; of the two-hundredth, 80 per cent of that of the one-hundredth and so on. *Exhibit 3.5* shows the experience curve for colour film produced by Japanese companies.[5] *Exhibit 3.6* also illustrates the basic features of these curves, explained as follows:[6]

- The horizontal axis measures the cumulative quantity produced on a logarithmic scale. *Exhibit 3.6a* and *b* show the same information plotted on a linear and logarithmic scale, respectively. The information on *Exhibit 3.6a* reveals a smooth curve and the implied regularity of the relationship between unit cost and total volume. However, *Exhibit 3.6b* shows the same information plotted on double logarithmic scales. This presentation shows percentage changes as a constant distance, along either axis. The straight line on the log–log scale in *Exhibit 3.6b* means that a given percentage change in one factor has resulted in a corresponding percentage change in the other. The nature of that relationship determines the slope of the line that can be read off a log–log grid.

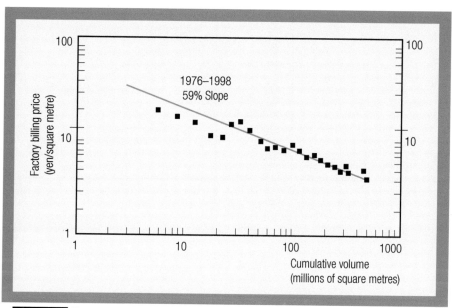

EXHIBIT 3.5 Experience curve for colour film produced by Japanese companies, 1976–98

SOURCE: *Photo Electric News* and *Japanese Economic Journal*

- Returning to *Exhibit 3.5*, the logarithmic scale shows that many doublings of production can be achieved early on, but later vastly larger quantities are needed to double the cumulative unit volumes then involved. This implies, as one would expect, that movement down the experience curve slows with time. Initially, additional growth in annual volumes can offset this, but the levelling in demand associated with the mature stage in a product life cycle and the eventual saturation and later decline through technical obsolescence will slow the rate of progress down the curve.

- The vertical axis of an experience curve is usually cost or price per unit and is also expressed logarithmically. However, the cost or price per unit must be adjusted for inflation to allow comparisons to be drawn over time; *Exhibit 3.5* shows that improvements further down the curve become, in absolute terms, quite small. Thus, as progress is made down the curve, each incremental movement will both take longer and yield less.

The characteristic decline in cost or price per unit was established by the Boston Consulting Group's (BCG) work in the 1960s and early 1970s as between 20 and 30 per cent for each doubling of cumulative production. Although the BCG claims that this can go on (in constant $s, €s or £s) without limit and despite the rate of experience growth, in reality, this tends not to happen for the reasons given earlier.

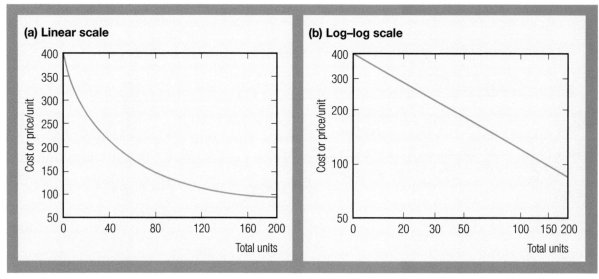

EXHIBIT 3.6 Cost/volume or price/volume relationship

Furthermore, it is important to stress that the experience curve characteristics are phenomenological in nature. They portray a relationship between cost or price and volume that can, but does not necessarily, exist. Consequently, the BCG concludes that:

> these observed or inferred reductions in costs as volume increases are not necessarily automatic. They depend crucially on a competent management that seeks ways to force down costs as volume expands. Production costs are most likely to decline under this internal pressure. Yet in the long run the average combined cost of all elements should decline under the pressure for the company to remain as profitable as possible. To this extent the relationship is of normal potential rather than one of certainty.[7]

Delivery reliability or on-time delivery

Delivery reliability or on-time delivery (OTD) means supplying the products ordered in full and on the agreed due date. It is, therefore, a major task of the operations function. In many businesses, this criterion now constitutes a qualifier. Very often, in fact, it is order-losing sensitive, in that if companies miss due dates, customers will quickly respond by reducing the amount of business they allocate to them or even take them off the potential supplier list altogether. As companies seek to reduce inventory levels, certainty of suppliers meeting agreed delivery dates is paramount. The role of OTD as a qualifier (Q) or often an order-losing sensitive qualifier (QQ) is a consequence of the improvements made by suppliers in this regard and in response to increasing pressure from customers. OTD performance is now an important prerequisite, and its measurement by customer, sector and overall is a key factor in most businesses. The need to identify different OTD expectations is a critical step here as with other order-winners and qualifiers.

For the operations function, this involves consideration of capacity, scheduling and inventory, particularly regarding work-in-progress and finished goods. Such checks need to be supplemented by regular reviews of those dimensions affecting a company's record on delivery reliability, such as completed line item reviews (product mix made as measured against the production plan) and checks on lead time performance throughout the total process.

The exactness of the due date can vary from an appointed hour on a given day to delivery of the agreed quantity starting, and finishing, in an agreed week. The level of data collection and the timing and proactive nature of the feedback to customers will need to form part of this decision. As a rule, the more exact the delivery, the more proactive a supplier should be in the data collection and the more regular the performance summaries and feedback to customers should be.

These data are the source of information about the size of 'call-offs' (what a customer actually wants rather than the total quantities expressed in any contract or agreement) and the lead times associated with deliveries. The former concerns the issues of costs and price agreements, the latter leads into the criterion of delivery speed.

Delivery speed

A company may win orders through its ability to deliver more quickly than competitors or to meet the delivery date required when only some or even none of the competitors can do so. Products that compete in this way need an operations process that can respond to this delivery speed requirement. The key measurement here is to compare a customer's lead time (the time between the order or call-off being placed and required delivery date) with the operations lead time (OLT). As shown in *Exhibit 3.7*, the OLT is a combination of the material lead time (MLT – the time taken for a supplier to deliver) or order backlog (OBL – the number of orders already accepted and waiting to be made) whichever is the greater plus the process lead time (PLT – the length of time it takes to make the order). Note that here a further possible element of lead time is delivering the order to a customer's premises. This would need to form part of these calculations and is addressed in a later section but has been omitted here to simplify the discussion. Such comparisons, as shown in *Exhibit 3.8*, can result in the customer lead time (CLT) being shorter than the OLT (Situation 1) or the reverse (Situation 2).

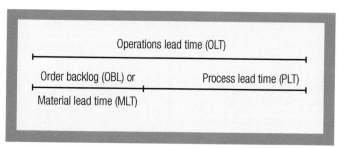

EXHIBIT 3.7 The components of operations lead time

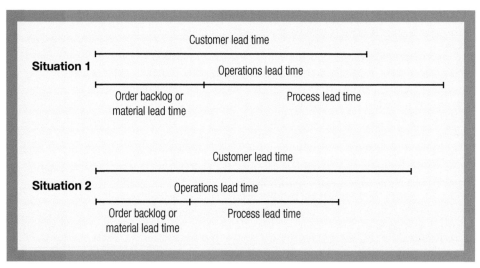

NOTE: The lead times presented are illustrative.

EXHIBIT 3.8 Customer lead time and operations lead time comparisons

Situation 1

In Situation 1, where an order is accepted, then to meet the agreed due date, operations will need to select from a number of options so as to shorten its lead time norms in line with the promised delivery date. These include:

- increasing short-term capacity by overtime working

- change customer priorities in the existing order backlog queue or jobs going through the operations process.

Where such situations are infrequent, short-term responses such as these will often suffice, with the former increasing costs and the latter increasing the scheduling pressures within operations. However, where Situation 1 represents an increasing trend, such short-term options become unsustainable and will need to be replaced by a strategic solution that will move the business back to the position where Situation 2 is the norm.

Such a trend would, in turn, be reflected in the order-winner weighting allocated to delivery speed in the regular review of markets and allow the strategy-making group (see *Exhibit 2.3*) to select from a range of options based on the investment required, the timescales involved and the benefits provided. (Note that the options below do not include reducing the company's existing PLT, as it is assumed that this would already form part of operations' ongoing activities) These include:

- Increase capacity either on a permanent (an additional shift or the purchase of additional equipment) or semi-permanent (for example a move to increased daily working hours for a given period) basis and hence reduce PLT.

- Hold selected materials in stock and hence reduce the MLT element of the OLT.

- Move from a make-to-order position to either an assemble-to-order (and associated work-in-progress inventory) or make-to-stock (and associated finished goods inventory) position and hence reduce the PLT.

- Contract with suppliers to guarantee providing a given number of orders at all times and with it the facility to choose how to use the associated capacity allocation, hence reducing the OBL element of a supplier's own OLT.

- Similarly, arrange for a supplier to hold selected material inventory (with guarantees of usage or compensation) and hence reduce the MLT element of a supplier's own OLT.

Exhibit 3.9 helps explain the last two options: it shows how the same elements make up a supplier's OLT (which, in turn, form the MLT of the company) as those in the company's own OLT. What the latter two options offer is a way of helping a supplier to reduce the OBL or MLT (respectively) of its own OLT and hence reduce the MLT element of the company's own OLT.

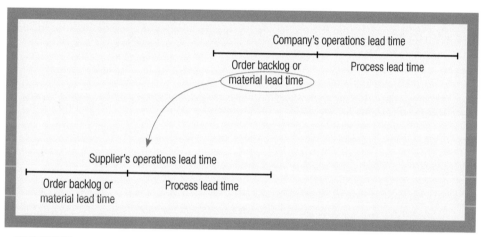

EXHIBIT 3.9 The elements making up a supplier's operations lead time that constitute the company's own material lead time

Situation 2

In Situation 2, there is no delivery speed element with such customers. The task in operations is to schedule customer orders to meet the promised due dates.

A market-driving option

Falling within a company's market debate in such situations should be a discussion around reducing its own existing OLT by a range of alternatives where it is considered that customers would value shorter lead times, or to change the accepted current market norms on suppliers' lead times to disadvantage competitors and in that way increase market share. The market-driving nature of such an alternative should form part of a company's strategic options.

An organization's response to reducing lead times needs to be corporate wide, and often the lead times associated with operations before and after the actual manufacturing activity can be a substantial part of the time it takes from order entry to customer delivery. (Lead time reduction in product development is addressed under the section on design covered later in the chapter.) From the moment an order reaches the factory, all elements of lead time need to be reviewed, with the aim of reducing each component involved in the total process. To succeed, companies must transform themselves and simply break the paradigms that hold current procedures and norms in place.[8]

Companies can knowingly offer short lead times to customers by holding, for example, excess capacity, maintaining low or zero order backlogs or holding inventory at any or all stages in the process. As highlighted earlier, such decisions would fall within the domain of the business strategy-making group, with operations' role to implement and maintain the chosen alternatives.

With customers typically reducing their own lead times, many companies are finding that the element of delivery speed is becoming an increasing factor in their markets (Situation 1, *Exhibit 3.8*). As discussed earlier, a company's response to delivery speed, as with all criteria, can be either reactive or proactive. Possible scenarios from which a company may select (and from which a company may choose different positions for different customers/products) are outlined in *Exhibit 3.10*.

Initial positions	Length of lead times
1 *Design to order* – new product response where companies design and manufacture a product to meet the specific needs of a customer	Long
2 *Engineer to order* – changes to standard products are offered to customers and only made to order. Such changes would be substantial in nature and customer specific. Lead times include the relevant elements of design, engineering and all operations	
3 *Make to order*[1] – concerns manufacturing a standard product (any customization is nominal and does not increase total lead times) only on receipt of a customer order or against agreed schedules or call-offs	
4 *Assemble to order* – components and subassemblies have been made to stock. On receipt of an order (or against an agreed schedule or call-off), the required parts are drawn from work-in-progress/component inventory and assembled to order	
5 *Make to stock* – finished goods are made ahead of demand in line with sales forecasts. Customers' orders are met from inventory	Short

NOTE

1 Some customers require companies to make to print (that is, make a product in line with a given drawing). In such markets, lead times only include raw materials purchase/supply and manufacturing. They do not include design, but some customer-induced redesign during the process will often be involved.

EXHIBIT 3.10 Alternative responses to markets and their lead time implications

Exhibit 3.10 sets out a series of time-related alternatives and firms need to determine their current and preferred position by market as the first step to establishing a strategic response. Companies' potential opportunity to reduce lead times will depend on the nature of their markets (for example whether they sell standard or special products and offer a design-and-manufacturing or manufacturing-only capability) and their decisions to hold different levels of raw materials/components, work-in-progress and finished goods inventory. As a company moves (or is able to move) from point 1 to 5 in *Exhibit 3.10*, overall lead times will reduce. However, as explained above, any repositioning is a corporate decision directly affecting the element of delivery speed. Adjusting its position on this continuum so as to eliminate or reduce the impact of delivery speed would need to be supported by shortening each element of lead time within the overall process. Stalk and Hout argue that time-based management has a further, significant advantage. Compared with the more traditional, bureaucratic or entrepreneurial approaches, it leads to reductions in overhead costs, as shown in *Exhibit 3.11*.

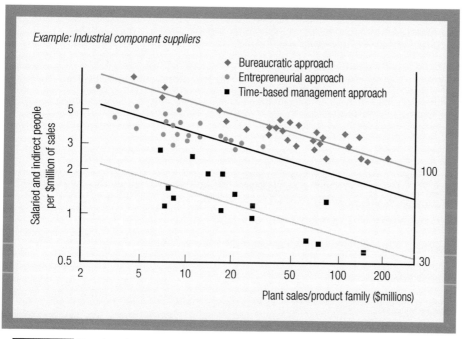

Example: Industrial component suppliers

◆ Bureaucratic approach
● Entrepreneurial approach
■ Time-based management approach

Salaried and indirect people per $million of sales

Plant sales/product family ($millions)

EXHIBIT 3.11 Overhead costs incurred in time-based management approaches compared with those involved in classic structures: industrial component suppliers

SOURCE: Based on Stalk, G.S. Jr and Hout, T.M. (1990) *Competing Against Time: How Time-based Competition is Reshaping Global Markets*, New York, Free Press

Quality conformance

Quality conformance (making products to specification) as a competitive criterion has been thrust centre stage since the late 1970s. Although its importance has been recognized throughout this period, many companies were slow to respond to the new quality conformance levels provided by competitors. In part this was not helped by the lack of definition of the word 'quality' that has been broadened to encompass many dimensions. The lack of clarity that followed contributed to the subsequent failure to recognize the size of the competitive threat. This new, sustained level of quality conformance represented a stepped change in performance that, in some sectors, redefined the role of quality conformance from a qualifier into an order-winner.

The spearhead for this change came predominantly from Japanese manufacturing companies. In the immediate postwar period, the need to address the poor image for quality enjoyed by most of Japan's manufacturing sector became a national as well as corporate priority. The outcome of the investment and development initiatives changed the image and raised the threshold in both the national and international arenas. The results were instrumental in changing customers' expectations and access to the large and growing markets of Western economies followed. Now, in many sectors, including automobiles, motorcycles and electrical and electronic products, Japanese companies have a significant share of these major markets.

At the business level, the strategy-making group needs first to recognize the different dimensions that fall under the quality umbrella and then the function(s) with prime responsibility for providing each of these (see *Exhibit 3.12*). Once the role and importance of a dimension within a market for a customer has been established, the current level of provision and the gap between requirement and current performance creates the task. With strategic direction provided, appropriate resources can be allocated, so ensuring that a company can match competitors (market-driven) or create new norms (market-driving), whichever approach the business decides appropriate.

Dimensions of quality		Function(s) with prime responsibility for provision
Performance	A product's primary operating characteristics	Design
Features	Secondary characteristics, the 'bells and whistles'	Design
Reliability	The probability of a product malfunctioning within a given period	Design
Aesthetics	How the final product looks	Design
Durability	A measure of a product's life in terms of both its technical and economic dimensions	Design
Conformance	The degree to which a product is manufactured to the agreed specification	Operations
Serviceability	The ease of servicing (planned or breakdown) to include the speed and provision of after-sales service	Design and after-sales
Perceived quality	How a customer views the product	Marketing and design

SOURCE: Based on Garvin, D.A. (1987) 'Competing on the eight dimensions of quality', *Harvard Business Review*, November–December, pp. 101–19

EXHIBIT 3.12 The dimensions of quality and the functions typically responsible for their provision

In the context of this section, the aspect of quality that principally concerns operations is conformance – making a product to specification. Linked closely to design (which determines the specification itself; see *Exhibit 3.12*), quality within this definition is a key operations task. Its role in most markets is now or has reverted (see earlier) to that of a qualifier (customers expect a product to meet the specification) and the order-losing characteristics of such dimensions enable newcomers to enter markets and take share from established players.

One example of this is provided by the automobile sector. The growth in Japanese companies' share within the volume and luxury sectors of this market has been outstanding. This is partly due to the continued high levels of quality conformance achieved compared to their principal competitors. Link this to their superior productivity performance, as shown in *Exhibits 1.9* and *1.10*, and the reasons for their success begin to emerge. Toyota becoming the world's number one car maker in 2008 endorses these points.

The recent attention attracted by quality-based approaches in management has further emphasized the advantages of completing tasks correctly the first time. This, in part, has been an extension of the improvements in the quality conformance of products and the significant benefits that have been secured. Much has been written on the approaches that have underpinned success.[9]

Demand increases

In some markets, a company's ability to respond to increases in demand is an important factor in winning orders. These sales may reflect the high seasonality of customers' requirements or be of a spasmodic or one-off nature. The factors here include the level of predictability surrounding demand itself, a product's shelf life and the frequency of product modifications in line with market requirements. All will affect operations' response.

Knowing the pattern of seasonal demand makes it possible to reach agreement between supplier, manufacturer, distributor and customer about inventory holdings throughout, process capacity and planned increases in labour (for example overtime working or additional shifts). With one-off or spot business (for example during an influenza epidemic when demand is for the same product that may have a short shelf life, thus limiting viable inventory levels, or where a product is customer specified at some point in the process and, therefore, cannot be made ahead of demand, or a significant order for a product over and above agreed call-off quantities or simply an unexpected, sizable order for a given product), holding materials or forms of capacity, arranging short-term increases in labour capacity (for example through overtime), rearranging priorities or some combination of these will typically be a supplier's response.

The phenomena described here provide another example of the way that a lack of essential clarity can lead to serious levels of corporate misunderstanding. The generalized discussion surrounding these key aspects of a business typically involves words such as 'flexibility'.[10] However, the extent to which a company intends to respond to such significant increases in demand is an important strategic decision. To allow each function to respond according to its own interpretation invariably reduces the benefits of corporate cooperation on the one hand and leads to mismatches on the other.

Product range

As highlighted earlier, markets are increasingly characterized by difference, not similarity. However, the balance between levels of customization and the volume base for repetitive operations has to be addressed by the business as a whole. That markets are increasingly segmenting is a given. Operations' role is to continue to develop processes that can cope with product range differences and provide low costs. It needs to be able to bridge these essential differences in order to retain the volume base so essential to efficient operations.

Where product ranges are widening, process developments need to reflect the broadening nature of the product base and the lower volume implications that tend to go hand in hand with these trends. While the former needs to be recognized at the time that process investments are made, the latter is reflected in reduced set-up times, whether manual or automated (for example a numerically controlled facility), so enabling companies to cope with the lower volume nature of such changes while retaining the necessary levels of cost.

Examples of these trends are seen in the automobile industry. The pressure on car makers at the lower end of the volume scale is to continue to differentiate their products as a way of competing not only with their traditional competitors but with makers at the higher end of the volume scale as well. BMW's 7 Series offers a marked uplift in customization, more akin to the very low-volume luxury car makers such as Rolls-Royce and Aston Martin. Handcrafted leather interiors and its 'any colour' option are examples of this. Competition based on increasing the product and option range is also coming from traditional, high-volume car companies. Several Japanese car makers (for example Toyota) have been and are continuing to develop a production system capable of responding to individual customer requirements. As a result, to support increases in product range options successfully, operations needs to develop its processes to provide these in a cost- and time-efficient way.

Operations-related but not operations-specific criteria

Although businesses separate clusters of activities into different functions, in reality they are, and need to form, part of the same whole. Thus, many functions within a company will directly support operations or will undertake tasks that link or directly affect operations strategic and operational (day-to-day) roles.

Design

The links between design, operations and markets are the very essence of a business. The way that these interrelate, therefore, is fundamental to sound strategy development and implementation. Both design and operations' aim is to provide products according to their technical and business specifications. In addition, these two functions combine to provide the product development phase that comes before the ongoing selling/operations activity that forms the commercial substance of companies. Three of the more important dimensions involved are addressed in this section and have been chosen because they are fundamental to this basic corporate activity.[11]

Low cost

Design is increasingly important in providing essential support for several criteria relevant to today's markets. Products have to be designed both with process characteristics and cost reduction in mind. Design not only concerns functionality but has a critical impact on product costs and with direct materials typically accounting for some 40–60 per cent of the total, the opportunities to reduce costs at source are substantial. In addition, this essential link reinforces the need to meet the design for operations requirements in terms of labour cost reduction through increased automation and other labour-saving approaches. For many years, corporate appeals by Western firms to design for operations have been more exhortation than accomplishment, a view confirmed by a committee of the National Research Council in the early 1990s.[12] It found the overall quality of engineering design – the process of turning a concept into a finished product or determining how to make a new toaster, dress or computer as efficiently as possible – to be poor. Long before a product reaches the store, 70 per cent or more of its cost is determined by its design. However, responses to these issues have been spasmodic.

Any third-rate engineer can design complexity. The emphasis on making designs simple needs to be part of the designer's make-up and the corporate demands placed on this function. In the new millennium, pressure on price has continued and will continue to be an important competitive factor in many segments. Thus, design's role in the total corporate response is fundamental in more ways than one.

Product range

The increasing level of product diversification has already been recognized as an important factor in today's competitive markets and central to this provision is the design function. The pressure on design will vary from market to market and the interpretation and execution of these requirements are central to a company's ability to remain competitive. The tendency for Western designers to be more interested in functionality than the commercial facets of design is in marked contrast to competitors, particularly the Japanese. As Hiroyuki Yoshida, head of Toyota's design centre, reflected:

> Whatever the merits of a design, it has to be robust enough to go through our engineering and manufacturing system. The commercial point of design has not been lost. We are in the business to make low-cost, high-quality cars for a mass market. We are making cars, not art.[13]

Within this context, markets are increasingly segmenting. Design needs to be able to meet these changes and to recognize, certainly in terms of attitude and speed of response, that change is a fundamental characteristic of today's markets.

It is now the age of diversification and those companies unable to keep pace with this growth of diversity will decline. Many companies are directing much more attention to incorporating the perspectives and preferences of customers into future designs. A classic example of this is provided by Toyota and Mazda. Both have built complexes in Tokyo that incorporate vehicle design studios in which the visitors are invited to 'design' their own cars. Thus ideas on what constitutes a potential customer's ideal vehicle are included as inputs into future designs.

However, the demand for styling and product features has to be reconciled with other pressures. Environmentally friendly products are not only a growing concern of customers but also high on the agenda of legislative bodies. For example, clean air legislation in the US and the EU is at the forefront of changing pressures on vehicle design. Their requirements for minimum percentage sales of low-emission vehicles and ultra-low-emission vehicles have been an added stimulus for improvements on all car emission standards. The targets for the next five years will mean that unless there is a major breakthrough in existing engine technology, companies will have to develop a viable electric car in the next 10 years. The advent of hybrid cars introduced by many of the major auto companies in the past five years is the first step to meeting these demands.

Lead times

The reduction of lead times within the operations process has already been highlighted as an increasingly important order-winner. Similarly, speed to market with new product designs and developments has become a significant competitive factor. The increasing priority of speed is based on a recognition that it can simply negate the competition. The results of such improvements, as shown in *Exhibit 3.13*, speak for themselves. In addition, companies receive a number of distinct advantages from reducing product design and development lead times, including the following:

1. **Benefits of double gain:** Being first in the market brings advantages of both higher volumes and higher margins – the opportunity for double gain. These advantages are:
   - **Product life cycles are extended** – If a product is introduced sooner, rarely will it become obsolete sooner. This advantage accrues even more so where customers incur high switching costs. The usual outcome of early product introduction is to gain more customers who, in turn, stay longer (see *Exhibit 3.14*).
   - **Increased market share** – The first producer will, in the beginning, command 100 per cent market share. Thus, the earlier a product appears, the more likely the prospect of obtaining a large market share. Link this to the previous factor and the impact on total life cycle volumes is marked.
   - **Higher profit margins** – A company will naturally enjoy a higher level of pricing freedom in the early stages of a product's life cycle. This will provide higher margins in the early stages, with the opportunity for operations to provide lower costs in light of the volume advantages highlighted above (see *Exhibit 3.15* and also the earlier section on experience curves).
   - **Double gain** – The first three factors combine to give a situation of double gain – companies gain higher sales and also achieve a higher margin on each sale.

Company	Product	Development time (months)	
		Old	New
AT&T	Telephones	24	12
Hewlett-Packard	Computer printers	54	21
Honeywell	Thermostats	48	12
Ingersoll Rand	Air-powered grinders	42	14
Warner Electric	Clutches and brakes	36	9

EXHIBIT 3.13 Examples of reduction in product development lead time

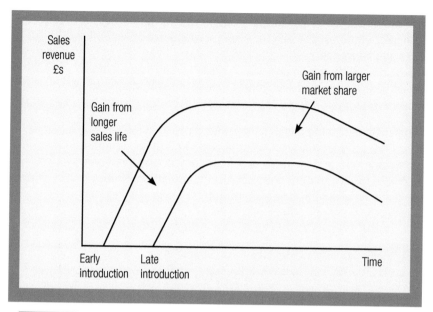

EXHIBIT 3.14 Increased sales revenue element of the benefits of double gain

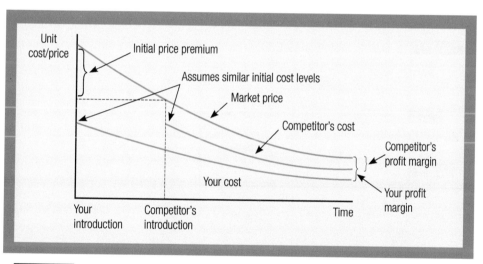

EXHIBIT 3.15 The higher profit margin element of the benefits of double gain

2 **Technology, consumer preference and corporate image:** Reductions in product development lead times also provide opportunities for companies to sustain technology leadership and corporate image:

  • **Exploiting technology opportunities** – Where organizations develop products quickly, they are more able to synchronize product developments with the latest technologies and thus exploit these opportunities fully.

- **Matching consumer change** – Short product development lead times help a business to match market changes, thereby tracking more closely changes in consumer preferences and demands.
- **Corporate image** – Developing products more quickly will help a firm to maintain its corporate image of being a progressive frontrunner in developments and technology excellence.

3   **Reduction in design costs:** Compressing development lead times also results in a reduction in design costs. This is achieved in part by increased levels of cooperation, which reduces misunderstandings and ensures the incorporation of functional perspectives throughout. In addition, the changed role and contribution of design within the process also leads to less time being spent in the design stages, with associated reductions in cost.

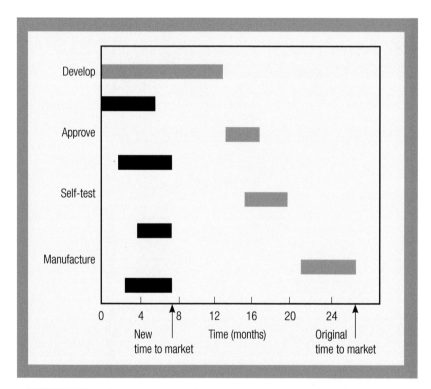

EXHIBIT 3.16 Digital Equipment Company's reduced completion time for a new product development

SOURCE: Reeve, R. (1992) 'Profiting from teamwork', *Manufacturing Breakthrough*, January–February, p. 22 (with permission)

Exhibit 3.13 provided examples of what can be achieved, while *Exhibit 3.16* shows how this is accomplished. A glance at the latter shows a two-pronged approach to reducing lead times:

- shorten the total time to complete the steps in the process

- start the steps earlier, running some in parallel.

Although some steps in the revised approach are much shorter, the gain is more cumulative in nature and a combination of the two elements above, as clearly shown in *Exhibit 3.17*. This compares approaches to product development by Japanese, North American and European car makers. A close look at the details illustrates the two-pronged approach, and reflects the different approaches and values of those involved, as explained below:

Development phase	Japanese			United States			European		
	Begin	End	Stage length	Begin	End	Stage length	Begin	End	Stage length
Concept study	42	34	8	62	44	18	62	47	15
Product planning	38	29	9	57	39	18	57	40	17
Advanced engineering	42	27	15	56	30	26	52	39	13
Product engineering	30	6	24	40	12	28	39	16	23
Process engineering	28	6	22	32	6	26	38	8	30
Pilot run	7	3	4	9	3	6	9	3	6
Total	–	–	82	–	–	122	–	–	104

NOTE: Data in months before start of production; figures have been rounded. Sample sizes are Japan, 12; United States, 6; and Europe, 10.
SOURCE: Clark, B. and Fujimoto, T. (1989) 'Overlapping problem-solving in product development', in Ferdows, K. (ed.) *Managing International Manufacturing*, Amsterdam: Elsevier Science

EXHIBIT 3.17 Average project lead times and stage length in Japanese, US and European car makers

- Western designers typically expect to develop products that require little or no modification. As perfection is rarely, if ever, achieved, any necessary changes are identified and made in later phases. However, part of the typical design function's attitude is a resistance to change since, given the perfection syndrome, a need for change implies failure. The result is long first-phase lead times, which are subsequently further increased because of the inherent resistance to change.

- The Japanese alternative is based on a different set of expectations. Knowing that perfection is impossible, designers conclude their proposals much more quickly than their Western counterparts and, ready to accept change, respond to the demands of the modification stages with appropriate expectations and corresponding speed. The result is a significant overall reduction in development lead times.

A look back at the examples of product development lead time reduction clearly illustrates the shared responsibility for two or more functions to provide this criterion, as highlighted in *Exhibit 3.18*.

Competing on time is a key aspect in many markets and has several dimensions. Delivery speed and product development lead times have been highlighted. Another aspect is also emerging: plant start-ups. A *Business Week* article[14] highlighted the gap between

Japanese and North American car makers in terms of the length of time needed to change over a factory to produce a new model. *Exhibit 3.19* shows the significant differences, part of which comes from the insistence by Japanese car makers that their engineers adapt designs to a plant's existing capabilities.

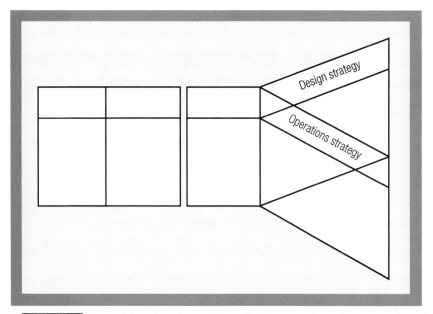

EXHIBIT 3.18 Shared functional provision of relevant order-winners and qualifiers

Plant	Car model	Elapsed times (days)
North American		
Oshawa, Ontario	Chevy Lumina	87
Kansas City	Ford Contour/Mercury Mystique	60
Japanese		
Georgetown, Kentucky	Toyota Camry	18
Marysville, Ohio	Honda Accord	3

EXHIBIT 3.19 Comparative changeover times to produce a new model, North American and Japanese car makers

Distribution

Distribution's role in quick and reliable delivery has been mentioned earlier. As part of the total process, distribution plays an essential role in delivery. In addition, the costs of this facet of overall provision (including those of storage, warehouse administration and movement) typically have been rising both in themselves and as a percentage of the total. Highlighting the potential source of cost reduction inherent in distribution-related activities has not, however, received the attention that other supply chain activities have.

Non-operations-related criteria

It is not unusual for companies to be in markets whose relevant order-winners are not directly related to operations. In these types of markets, operations will be required to support one or more qualifiers. Some of the more important criteria that frequently characterize markets are now briefly discussed. In all instances, each function responsible for the criterion reviewed would have the task of providing and maintaining the required level of support.

Design leadership

The role of design and its relationship to competitive issues such as product development lead times and product costs have already been discussed. However, one of the design function's principal roles concerns the development of products in terms of features, aesthetics, perceived levels of design specification and reliability (including costs) while in service (see *Exhibit 3.12* above). Furthermore, where frequent design introductions offer a competitive edge, this requirement will be at the forefront of the function's strategic priorities. Linked to the need for shorter product development lead times, this criterion is increasingly emerging as a major competitive factor in today's markets.

For example, responding to the challenge from Yamaha, Honda almost doubled its range of motorcycle models in less than two years, eliminating Yamaha's short-lived advantage. Liz Claiborne, a designer/manufacturer of separates and sportswear, introduced two additional clothing seasons to reflect more clearly consumer buying patterns; Zara, a Spanish-based clothes designer and manufacturer, typically gives products a six-week shelf life. Seiko has increased its dominant role in the watch market with a highly automated factory capable of producing new models each day. In semiconductors, the competitive factor is largely the speed with which new product technologies can be applied to chips.

The importance of product design has always been recognized. Markets can be dominated by this dimension and unique design, particularly in the past, has been considered the principal order-winning provision of this function. However, companies are increasingly recognizing the other contributions that the design function can make in winning orders, the key elements of which have been discussed in earlier sections.

Being an existing supplier

Where a company is an existing supplier, it may continue to win orders in part or solely because of this factor. The criterion tends to be relevant to both low-volume and spares markets. In the former, operations needs to continue to support the relevant order-winners and qualifiers. In the latter, it needs to recognize the impact that its performance on relevant criteria will have on orders for any new or existing products in the future.

Marketing and sales

The marketing and sales functions' principal orientation is towards the marketplace. Its important links to customers and its insights into the characteristics of relevant market segments – including issues of pricing, competitive threats, growth and/or decline of existing segments and identification of new opportunities – is an essential part of a company's strategic provision.

Brand name

Through a variety of activities, including design, advertising and increasing or maintaining market share, companies seek to establish brand names for their products. Where this has been achieved and maintained, companies will win orders partly due to the image its products have in the markets in which they compete.

Technical liaison and support

In certain markets, customers will seek technical liaison from suppliers during the precontract phase and technical support thereafter. The quality and extent of a supplier's in-house technical capability to support product development, particularly towards its introduction in the early stages of its manufacture, will be an important criterion in these markets.

After-sales support

Companies may look for ways of differentiating their total product by offering, for instance, a high level of customer support (see *Exhibit 3.13*). One example is BMW. The company has a fleet of cars funded jointly with its dealers and strategically placed throughout the UK. The purpose is to go to the support of any BMW that has broken down by the roadside. The company's aim is to maintain the level of this standby fleet so that it can deal with the 80 per cent of BMW breakdowns in the UK that can actually be solved at the roadside.

A further example of after-sales is the motor repairs sector. Compact discs enable a mechanic to call up information on any component or car by typing in the relevant part or the vehicle's chassis number. In repair procedure terms, the mechanic can find out which faults cause which problems and what procedures should be followed. Service sales staff are similarly able to investigate customer details and vehicle records to help in their service support provision. Companies already using these customer support systems include Volkswagen, BMW, Opel, PSA (Peugeot and Citroen), General Motors and Toyota.

Benchmarking

The failure of a company to assess and monitor its competitors is at best a mark of corporate complacency and at worst a sign of strategic naivety. For a company, such a monitoring process comprises:

- A continuous updating of the level and dimensions of competition within its markets.

- Seeking proactively to improve its own business performance by learning from other companies about what can be done and how to do things better.

Benchmarking[15] is an approach that was identified and highlighted in the mid-1980s and since that time many companies have used this as one of the ways to enhance their competitive position. Its contribution is to redirect the corporate spotlight from assessing internal performance (typically using internal measures) to checking externally how its performance compares with best practice. In this way, it reinforces the clear need to identify market requirements, to differentiate importance and to establish the level of performance that needs to be achieved within each competitive dimension.

As shown in the earlier section on experience curves, all companies tend to learn and improve through time, but the key question is whether the rate of improvement is adequate to become and/or remain competitive. Benchmarking forces companies to look outwards and recognize this external perspective as the way to identify the levels of performance that need to become their new targets. Furthermore, checking against performance in other businesses (and particularly in unrelated sectors) leads to further distinct advantages:

- It describes the 'what' rather than the 'how', presenting companies with targets and not solutions. This increases the ownership aspect and reinforces the inappropriateness of solution-oriented approaches.

- Having targets helps to create a uniform response from all parts of a business – when goals are common, improvement becomes a shared task.

- It reinforces the executive role, rather than that of support staff, as the key element to bring about sustained performance improvements.

- External, and particularly ex-sector, comparisons are often perceived as being more objectively derived and therefore more readily accepted.

- It opens up new improvement horizons that frequently represent a stepped change in performance. In so doing, it gives the opportunity to leapfrog competitors in selected and relevant dimensions of performance.

Benchmarking is concerned with the search for best practices, whatever their source, in order to achieve superior performance. It involves continuously measuring a company's products, services and practices both against competitors and the leaders in any business sector. It is not an end in itself, but a means to help to achieve levels of competitiveness. In this way, it offers an important dimension within the domain of order-winners by ensuring that corporate performance against relevant criteria is measured against externally derived, best practice norms. Benchmarking moves a company from having an inward bias to incorporating external perspectives, which invariably introduces a stepped change in terms of performance. These external antennae help a company to assess what is going on and also to manage itself within its own environment.

The first step in implementing benchmarking is to determine the key functions within a business that need to be reviewed. When the relevant performance variables to measure these functions have been agreed, identifying best-in-class performances sets the target. What follows is the task of assessing the action programmes to bring corporate performance into line with and then to surpass best-in-class companies.

For benchmarking to be successfully implemented, key elements need to be in place. These include:

- **Rigour:** Companies need to ensure that the targets to be achieved are set high enough, with targets derived from knowledge, not intuition.

- **Overcoming disbelief:** In the initial phases of this process, companies need to convince themselves that not only can they do better but they can meet the daunting tasks that benchmarking reviews typically identify.

- **Accountability:** Benchmarking represents an ongoing procedure for measuring performance and ensuring improvement. A prerequisite is to instill in everyone the responsibility and authority for identifying, checking and implementing the changes necessary to achieve this improvement.

- **Culture change:** Managers typically spend most of their time on internal issues. Reorienting companies to be externally rather than internally focused is essential to the successful introduction and ongoing development of this approach and associated improvements.

Best-in-class exemplars

Companies need to assess themselves against externally derived standards and these can be identified from a number of different company classifications, including:

- Other parts of the same company – internal benchmarking[16]

- Direct competitors

- Companies in the same industrial sector but not direct competitors

- Latent competitors

- Companies outside the industry.

Recognizing the different categories enables a firm to identify a broader range of potential best-in-class sources, thereby improving the quality and representative nature within this critical phase. An example that illustrates the advantages of using best-in-class exemplars is afforded by *Exhibit 3.20*, which shows how IBM's use of perspectives outside its own industry helped it to identify its future targets.

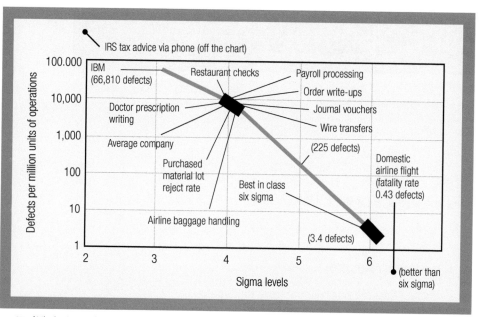

NOTE: At the beginning of 1990, IBM admitted its overall defect rate was around 3 sigma, or 66,810 defects per million operations.

EXHIBIT 3.20 Benchmarking quality helped IBM identify its best-in-class, six sigma target

SOURCE: Rayner, B.C.P. (1990) 'Market-driven quality: IBM six-sigma crusade', *Electronic Business*, 15 October, p. 28 (with permission)

Ways to close the gap then surpass exemplars

Improving performance results from a number of coordinated actions across key functions. But there are different levels of achievement and these need to be part of the targets set:

- **Try harder** – A classic approach that, if adopted, implies a failure to recognize the principles underpinning benchmarking.

- **Emulate** – Involves setting achievement targets on a par with competitors and/or best-in-class exemplars.

- **Leapfrog** – Setting targets higher than existing exemplar norms.

- **Change the rules of the game** – Entails setting the pace in driving the order-winners and qualifiers in relevant markets.

These constitute target levels of change but at the beginning the difficulty many companies face is identifying the different levels of achievement. Many find that looking outside helps to identify more clearly the levels of higher achievement, as shown in *Exhibit 3.21*.

Exemplar	Level of achievement	
	Emulate	Change the rules of the game
Internal benchmarking	80	20
Direct competitors		
Industry sector but not competitor	↓	↓
Latent competitor		
Outside the industry	20	80

EXHIBIT 3.21 Source and levels of targeted achievement

Competitors are moving targets

That order-winners and qualifiers change over time was highlighted earlier. This is because markets are dynamic and competitors are moving targets. Companies that set their sights without taking these dimensions into account may fall further behind. Failing to identify the rate of improvement of competitors may lead to companies setting targets only to find that the goalposts have moved. At best they will have closed the gap but more often they will find themselves even further behind and less able to catch up.

Reflections

In today's markets, it is less likely that companies will have a sustainable competitive advantage. To compete effectively and continue to be successful, firms need to fully understand their markets in order to consciously and frequently assess competitors and identify what it will take to retain and grow market share. But strategy debate has been and continues to be general in nature. Typical outcomes are general descriptions that foster independent responses from functions. Unless individual functions are able, and are required, to develop strategies that directly support their markets, these firms will lose substantial and essential advantage. Companies that fail to provide coherent strategies will continue to lose out.

Identifying and weighting order-winners and qualifiers forms a key element of this strategic provision. Without such insights, agreement on what constitutes markets is replaced by individual views grounded in the biases and preferences of different functions. This leads to unsophisticated responses and allows, even encourages, unrelated functional initiatives to be developed.

For operations, investments in both processes and infrastructure are expensive and fixed. Once commitments have been made, it is difficult and sometimes impossible to make changes, certainly within the allowable timeframes of current commercial environments. The overall effect on corporate performance will be significant. In the short term, it can lead to substantial disparity in performance, while in the long term, it can be at the root of corporate success or failure.

CUSTOMER
IS ONLY RIGHT
AFTER THE
ORDER/CONTRACT
IS AGREED

TIME SPENT IN
RECONNAISSANCE IS
SELDOM WASTED
Sir MacPherson Robertston
(1860–1945)

Supplying
company decides
whether or not to
accept the business.
AFTERWARDS, the
customer **IS**
right

Determining order-winners and qualifiers

It takes time for companies to gain an understanding of their markets. In fact, strategy debate has a calendar time base that cannot be circumvented. The characteristics of markets and the perspectives of functions must be allowed adequate time, both in their explanation and reception. Going away for a corporate strategy weekend or arranging one-off discussions will lead to generalized statements but little insight.

The strategy facet of order-winners and qualifiers is similarly bound by these characteristics. Seeking to clarify and understand these key insights will take time and requires soundings from the following different sources:

- **Functional perspectives: a 360° review** – The internal perspectives of those functions that are engaged in the provision of products or that interface with the marketplace hold important insights into customer requirements. It needs to be a 360° review. Too often companies limit this internal review to the marketing function. In part, this is based on the historical perception that marketing's view of the market represents the market, but other functions have added to this position by failing to assess customers and markets from their own perspectives. As a result, they contribute little to the market debate and fail to improve the insights on markets. One consequence has been that companies have given undue weight to marketing's view, which typically emphasizes the need to respond to customers' actual or perceived wishes and demands. Checking the impact on a business has not usually been part of a firm's overall assessment of a market, segment or customer.

  When developing strategy, the roles and expectations of a company and customer differ before and after the point at which an order/contract is placed, as shown in *Exhibit 3.22*. Up to that point, a company is in control of whether it takes on an order/contract and, equally, a customer is in control of with whom an order/contract is placed. After that point, a customer is right to expect the promise to be fulfilled. Such discussions are often not easy and need to take account of current and future opportunities, relationships, market share and similar issues.

Player	Before		After
Customer	Selects which supplier	Order/contract placed	Is right
Supplying company	Decides, as a business, whether to take on the order	Order/contract accepted	Must meet the promise

EXHIBIT 3.22 The roles of a company and customer before and after an order/contract is placed

- **Customers' views** – Checking with customers on what they believe they require can invariably lead to a distorted view of reality. Setting aside the aspect of self-interest, customers place orders on suppliers in one system and make demands on supplier's plants in another. Furthermore, customers are unlikely to acknowledge that the business they offer to a supplier is anything other than favourable. Equally, they typically fail to make distinctions concerning different criteria – it is safer to ask for everything at the highest level of provision.

Most times, those involved in agreeing contracts do not know the critical dimensions of the contracts being discussed. Few have attempted to find out. All present their business in its best light. To seek the views of customers can only be one part of an assessment of a company's market.

- **Actual orders** – The real demands on a supplier are embodied in the characteristics of the individual orders, call-offs, and/or scheduled deliveries placed by customers. Tracing the volumes, lead times, margins and other relevant aspects of these will bring an essential perspective when evaluating opinion. Analysing the key data that are an inherent by-product of their systems will show the characteristics of the commercial transactions that represent the very nature of their markets.

- **Customer reviews** – Working with customers is essential to maintain and grow sales. Discussion with customers is a key component of this process. However, seeking customers' views is typically restricted to the sales and marketing function and is characterized by the criticisms listed above. This traditional approach needs to be replaced. Reviews of customers should be undertaken by executives from sales/marketing, operations and other relevant functions, be based on data that analyse the real demands of customers and be ongoing in nature and frequent in occurrence.

The purpose of such reviews is to highlight the nature of the actual demands made by customers, to discuss ways to improve customer support (including possible changes in a customer's own activities and procedures), to proactively develop customer relationships that are business rather than functionally based, and to agree the improvement priorities for functions that would now form part of a coordinated corporate approach.

The capsizing effect

The need for companies to be proactively alert stems from the nature of today's markets. Whereas companies in the past could recover from being outperformed and strategically outmanoeuvred, this is increasingly less likely. A growing phenomenon of the current competitive environment is the capsizing effect. Companies find that one day they are confident, secure and well directed and the next capsized, bottom up and sinking. The capsizing effect is often due to a lack of corporate awareness of competitive performance. Not being alert to the dimensions and extent of competitive performance leaves a company vulnerable to significant reversals of fortune and hence irretrievably disadvantaged.

To avoid being competitively outmanoeuvred (or sinking altogether), a company must understand its markets with sufficient insight and undertake this task on an ongoing basis. This not only provides understanding of sufficient adequacy on which to base corporate strategic directions but gives the essential inputs from which coordinated functional strategic outputs are formed.

Hitting singles versus home runs

One essential feature of management that is singularly omitted from its many descriptions is hard work. Clearly identifying markets, establishing functional strategies to support these and implementing the outcomes is a demanding role. One characteristic essential for completing these necessary parts is persistence. Winning teams build on hitting singles and do not rely on home runs.

Little is new, even less is complex

Earlier it was pointed out that any third-rate engineer can design complexity. The same holds true for strategy. Moving from what is complex and uncertain to what is understood and clear is the result of hard work – the same as required of a designer to get from the initial complex design to the simple.

Sound foundations for strategy are built on understanding; to respond to changing markets, a company must know where it is. In the past, companies have tolerated an inadequate understanding of their markets, with the result that they have been unable to respond and lost market share or even lost out all together. Complexity is an inherent feature of most aspects of business and none more so than markets. But it need not be so.

Similarly, nothing is new. The issues and criteria (even the aspect of time) discussed in this chapter are not revolutionary. For example, 80 years ago, Henry Ford highlighted the 'meaning of time' as an essential and integral competitive factor in all stages of his business from raw materials to distribution.[17] With ore extraction to sold product lead times at a little over four days and average shipping times between factory and branches of just over six days, the meaning of time was well understood and exercised as long ago as the 1920s. What is new is the need to identify markets in terms of what wins orders and then to develop functional strategies to support these. Every long journey begins with a first step – in strategy this first step is understanding your markets.

Discussion questions

1   What are the key elements when developing a functional strategy?
2   What constitutes a market from an operations perspective?
3   What is the result when an operations strategy development process is not in place?
4   What is a trade-off? Select two levels within an organization where trade-off choices will need to be made and discuss the issues involved.
5   What are the basic characteristics of order-winners and qualifiers?
6   Select two operations-related and operations-specific criteria and explain, using illustrations, some of the issues involved.
7   What is the difference between operations-related and operations-specific and operations-related but not operations-related criteria? Illustrate your answer.

Notes and references

1 Skinner, W. (1969) 'Manufacturing: missing link in corporate strategy', *Harvard Business Review*, May–June, pp. 136–144.

2 For example, Schonberger, R.J. (1982) *Japanese Manufacturing Techniques: Nine Hidden Lessons of Simplicity*, New York: Free Press and Womack, J.P., Jones, D.T. and Roos, D. (1990) *The Machine that Changed the World*, New York: Rawson Associates question the existence of trade-offs, while Ferdows, K. and De Meyer, A. (1990) 'Lasting improvements on manufacturing performance', *Journal of Operations Management* 9(2): 168–84; New, C.C. (1992) 'World class manufacturing versus trade-offs', *International Journal of Operations & Production Management*, 12(6): 19–31; Corbett, C. and Van Wassenhove, L. (1993) 'Trade-offs? What trade-offs? Competence and competitiveness in manufacturing strategy', *California Management Review*, Summer, pp. 107–121; Hayes, R.H. and Pisano, G.P. (1996) 'Manufacturing strategy: at the intersection of two paradigm shifts', *Production and Operations Management Journal*, 5(1): 25–41; and Clark, K.B. (1996) 'Competing through manufacturing and the new manufacturing paradigm; is manufacturing strategy passé?', *Production and Operations Management Journal*, 5(1): 42–58 take the view that it is possible to overcome trade-offs.

3 These are many books and articles addressing the area of lean manufacturing. References to some are provided here: Womack, J.P. and Jones, D.T. (1996) *Lean Thinking: Banish Waste and Create Wealth in your Corporation*, New York: Simon & Schuster; Womack, J.P., Jones, D.T. and Roos, D. (1990) *The Machine that Changed the World*, New York: Rawson Associates; Hines, P., Bicheno, J. and Rich, N. (2000) *End to End Lean*, Portland, OR: Productivity Press; Hines, P., Lamming, R.C., Jones, D.T. et al. (eds) (2000) *Value Stream Management: The Development of Lean Supply Chains*, London: FT/Prentice Hall; Taylor, D. and Brunt, D. (eds) (2001) *Manufacturing Operations and Supply Chain Management: the Lean Approach*, London: Thomson Learning.

4 There are many articles and books on continuous improvement and references to some are provided here: Beattie, J. (2007) 'Staying competitive through continuous improvement', *Business Information Review*, 24(2): 262–74; Redman, J. and Bessant, J. (2007) 'What advantages lie ahead for improvement programmes in the UK?: lessons from the CINet Continuous Improvement Survey 2000', *International Journal of Technology Management*, 37(3/4): 290–303; Vasilash, G.S. (2007) '08 Honda Accord: continuous improvement in action', *Automotive Design and Production*, 119(9): 38–42.

5 Other examples of experience curves in the public domain include those for the crushed-bone and limestone industry, 1925 to 1971, Henderson, B. (1974) 'The experience curve reviewed v. price stability', in Boston Consulting Group, *Perspectives* 149; 'The Model T Ford, 1909 to 1923', in Abernathy, W.J. and Wayne, K. (1974) 'Limits of the learning curve', *Harvard Business Review*, 52(5): 109–19; and random access memory (RAM) components, 1976 to 1984, in Ghemawat, P. (1985) 'Building strategy on the experience curve', *Harvard Business Review*, 42: 143–9.

6 The computation of an experience curve is clearly detailed in 'Experience and cost: some implications for manufacturing policy', Harvard Business School paper, 9–675–228 (revised July 1975). Other relevant articles include Hall, G. and Howell, S. (1985) 'The experience curve from the economist's perspective', *Strategic Management Journal*, 6(3): 197–213; Amit, R. (1986) 'Cost leadership strategy and experience curves', *Strategic Management Journal*, 7(30): 281–93; Sallenave, J.-P. (1985) 'The uses and abuses of experience curves', *Long Range Planning*, 18(1): 64–72.

7 Boston Consulting Group (1972) *Perspectives in Experience*, Boston, MA, p. 12.

8 Further details and approaches are to be found in Stalk, G.S. Jnr and Hout, T.M. (1990) *Competing Against Time: How Time-based Competition is Reshaping Global Markets*, New York: Free Press; Schmenner, R.W. (1988) 'The merit of making things fast', *Sloan Management Review*, Fall, pp. 1–17; Blackburn, J.D. (1991) *Time-based Competition; The Next Battleground in American Manufacturing*, Homewood, IL: Business One Irwin; Chung, C.H. (1999) 'Balancing the two dimensions of time for time-based competition, *Journal of Managerial Issues*, 11(3): 299–312; Jayaram, J., Vickery, S.K. and Droge, C.

(1999) 'An empirical study of time-based competition in the North American automotive suppliers industry, *International Journal of Operations & Production Management*, **19**(10): 1010–24; Abdinnour-Helm, S. (2000) Time-based competition through better customer service', *Production and Inventory Management Journal*, **41**(1): 24–9; De Toni, A. and Meneghetti, A. (2000) 'Traditional and innovative paths towards time-based competition', *International Journal of Production Economics*, **66**(3): 255–71; Lee, C.-Y., Rittisakdanon, N. and Zhou, X. (2001) 'Re-engineering for time-based competition: reducing time to market by re-engineering', *International Journal of Management*, **18**(1): 33–48; Hillman Willis, T. and Jurkus, A.F. (2001) 'Product development and essential ingredients of time-based competition', *Review of Business*, **22**(1/2): 22–8.

9   Books or articles that specifically address approaches to quality conformance include: Juran, J.M. (1974) *Quality Control Handbook*, Maidenhead: McGraw-Hill; Crosby, P.B. (1979) *Quality is Free*, Maidenhead: McGraw-Hill; Juran, J.M. and Gryna, F.M. (1980) *Quality Planning and Analysis*, New York: McGraw-Hill; Deming, W.E. (1982) *Quality, Productivity and Competitive Position*, Cambridge, MA: MIT Press; Feigenbaum, A.V. (1983) *Total Quality Control: Engineering and Management*, 3rd edn, Maidenhead: McGraw-Hill; Taguchi, G. (1986) *Introduction to Quality Engineering: Designing Quality into Products and Processes*, Tokyo: Asian Productivity Organization.

10 The basic misunderstandings surrounding the word 'flexibility' are highlighted in Hill, T.J. and Chambers, S.H. (1991) 'Flexibility: a manufacturing conundrum', *International Journal of Operations & Production Management*, **11**(2): 5–13.

11 The dimensions of quality listed in Exhibit 3.12 that relate to design function are addressed in a later section.

12 Hoover, C.W. Jnr co-chaired the committee that studied engineering design in the United States. The critical findings were embodied in his article, 'US products designed to fail', *Chicago Tribune*, 6 July 1991, p. 15.

13 Quoted in Leadbetter, C. (1991) 'Toyota's conundrum: creating a global car for a niche market', *Financial Times*, 17 July, p. 16.

14 Treece, J.B. (1994) 'Motown's struggle to shift on the fly', *Business Week*, 11 July, p. 103.

15 Readings on benchmarking include Osterhoff, R., Locander, W.B. and Bounds, G.M. (1991) 'Competitive benchmarking at Xerox', in Stahl, M.J. and Bounds, G.M. (eds) *Competing Globally Through Customer Value*, New York: Quorum Books, pp. 788–98; McNair, C.J. and Leibfried, K.A. (1992) *Benchmarking: A Tool for Continuous Improvement*, New York: HarperCollins; Zairi, M. (1998) *Benchmarking for Best Practice: Continuous Learning Through Sustainable Innovation*, Oxford: Butterworth-Heinemann; Francis, G. and Holloway, J. (2007) 'What have we learned? Themes from the literature on best practice benchmarking', *International Journal of Management Review*, **9**(3): 171–86; Walleck, A.S., O'Halloran, J.D. and Leader, C.A. (1991) 'Word-class manufacturing: benchmarking world-class performance', *The McKinsey Quarterly*, 1 November, pp. 3–24.

16 Internal benchmarking is an idea based on identifying the best in class within one's own total company in terms of concepts, usefulness and speed of introduction.

17 Ford, H. ([1926]1998) *Today and Tomorrow*, Cambridge, MA: Productivity Press, particularly Chapter 10, 'The meaning of time'.

Exploring further

Adler, P.S., Goldoftas, B. and Levine, D.I. (1999) 'Flexibility versus efficiency? A case study of model changeovers in the Toyota production system', *Organisation Science*, **10**(1): January–February.

Ahlstrom, P. and Westbrook, R. (1999) 'Implications of mass customization for operations management – an exploratory survey', *International Journal of Operations & Production Management*, **19**(3): 262–74.

Beach, R., Muhlemann, A.P., Price, D.H.R., Paterson, A. and Sharp, J.A. (2000) 'A review of manufacturing flexibility', *European Journal of Operations Research*, **122**: 41–57.

Bicheno, J. (2004) *The New Lean Toolbox: Towards Faster Flexible Flow*, Buckingham: Picsie Books.

Brown, S. and Bessant, J. (2003) 'The manufacturing strategy – capabilities links in mass customization and agile manufacturing – an exploratory study', *International Journal of Operations & Production Management*, **23**(7): 707–30.

Chamber, S. and Johnston, R. (2000) 'Experience curves in services: macro- and micro-level approaches', *International Journal of Operations & Production Management*, **20**(7): 842–60.

Cooney, R. (2002) 'Is "lean" a universal production system?', *International Journal of Operations and Production Management*, **22**(10): 1130–47.

Deming, W.E. (1981) 'Improvement of quality and productivity through action by management', *National Productivity Review*, **1**: 12–22. Francis, J. (2008) 'Benchmarking: get the gain without the pain', *Supply Chain Management Review*, **12**(4): 23–4.

Gunasekaran, A. and Yusuf, Y.Y. (2002) 'Agile manufacturing: a taxonomy of strategic and technical imperatives', *International Journal of Production Research*, **40**(6): 1357–85.

Gupta, D. and Benjaafar, S. (2004) 'Make-to-order, make-to-stock or delay product differentiation? A common framework for modeling and analysis', *IIE Transactions*, **36**(6): 529–46.

Hopp, W.J. and Spearman, M.L. (2000) *Factory Physics*, 2nd edn, Singapore: McGraw-Hill.

Juran, J.M. (2004) *Architects of Quality*, New York: McGraw-Hill.

de Koster, M.B.M. and Balk, B.M. (2008) 'Benchmarking and monitoring international warehouse operations in Europe', *Production Operations Management*, **17**(2): 175–84.

Narasimhan, R., Swink, M. and Soo, W.K. (2006) 'Disentangling leanness from agility: an empirical investigation', *Journal of Operations Management*, **24**: 440–57.

Ohno, T. (1988) *The Toyota Production System: Beyond Large-scale Production*, Portland, OR: Productivity Press.

Pagell. M. and Krause, D.R. (2004) 'Re-exploring the relationship between flexibility and the external environment, *Journal of Operations Management*, **21**: 629–49.

Panagiotou, G. (2007) 'Reference theory: strategic groups and competitive benchmarking', *Management Decision*, **45**(10): 1595–1609.

Quayle, M. (2003) 'A study of supply chain management practice in UK industrial SMEs', *Supply Chain Management: An International Journal*, **8**(1): 79–86.

Rahimifard, S. and Clegg, A.J. (2007) 'Aspects of sustainable design and manufacture', *International Journal of Production Research*, **45**(18–19): 4013–20.

Salamatov, Y. (1999) *TRIZ: The Right Solution at the Right Time*, The Netherlands: Insytec B.V.

Souza, D.E. and Williams, F.P. (2000) 'Towards taxonomy of manufacturing flexibility dimensions, *Journal of Operations Management*, **18**: 577–93.

Suarez, F., Cusumano, M. and Fine, C. (1995) 'The empirical study of flexibility in manufacturing', *Sloan Management Review*, Fall: 25–32.

Szwejczewski, M. and Cousens, A. (2007) 'Increasing flexibility – what are your options?', *Control*, **33**(1): 21–4.

ng an Operations Strategy
gy

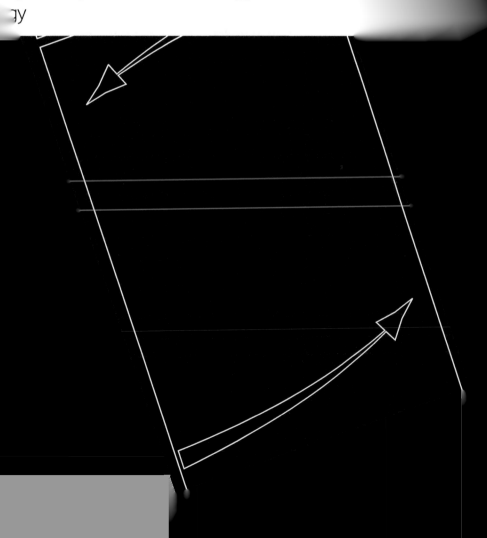

Summary

- Operations strategies can be market-driven, market-driving or both.

- Businesses must analyse markets before they can develop an operations strategy. They need to agree the current and future markets in which to compete and determine the known or anticipated order-winners and qualifiers within these markets.

- Customer needs can only be determined by analysing how they behave rather than listening to what they say they want.

- The most important orders are those a business turns away as these define who they are and the market in which they compete.

- Analysing markets starts with understanding executive opinion of market order-winners and qualifiers and then testing them with data showing actual demands for different customers, orders and products.

- Once market order-winners and qualifiers are known, operations can determine its key strategic tasks, review current performance against these tasks and identify areas for improvement. Typical analyses and improvements are described in the chapter.

- Successful strategy development and execution concerns balancing gut feel with in-depth analysis so that action is not delayed, but also focuses on areas of maximum impact, given the investment funds available.

- Generic strategies such as low cost or differentiation promise much, but deliver little. Successful strategies are tailored to the specific needs of a business.

The last two chapters introduced the concepts and principles of developing an operations strategy and the key strategic task of understanding how a company competes. This chapter addresses the question of how to develop an operations strategy.

Functions manage, control and develop the resources for which they are operationally and strategically responsible. The operational tasks concern managing and controlling the day-to-day, short-term aspects of a business. The strategic tasks concern investing in and developing those capabilities to provide the qualifiers and order-winners necessary to compete in agreed current and future markets. Exhibit 4.1 shows the steps involved in analysing markets and developing an operations strategy to support them.

Analyse markets

Agree markets	Determine market order-winners and qualifiers
Agree current and future markets in which to compete	Determine the order-winners and qualifiers for these markets

Analysing markets and developing an operations strategy

Develop an operations strategy

Identify key strategic task	Review current performance and identify improvements	Prioritize investments and developments
Identify key order-winners and qualifiers supported by operations and translate them into strategic tasks	Assess how well operations currently supports these strategic tasks and identify areas for improvement	Prioritize the investments and developments to improve support of strategic tasks

Generic strategies: the search for the alchemist's stone

Academics, consultants and other third-party advisers search for generic strategies in much the same way as those who sought to change base metal into gold. Firms themselves perpetuate this by seeking simplistic solutions to their complex problems. Perhaps this quest will only be set aside when firms realize that the diverse and dynamic needs of their markets cannot be met with the selection and application of one or more generic options.

Niche, low cost, differentiation and core competence are seductive offerings, but the uniformity they promise does not reflect the nature of business. Instead, organizations must recognize differences across their markets and develop multi-strategies to address these separate needs. Strategy is not a process leading to generalizations. It's a distillation process that identifies the very essence and purpose of a business before building the capability to achieve this.[1]

Strategy sets the direction of a business and points it at the market

All functions within an organization must face the same direction to ensure it competes effectively. They must all point at the market as this is where the company competes. Thus knowing how a firm competes in relevant markets is a prerequisite for sound strategy development. Without it, functions may pursue good practice but not necessarily sound strategy. They will, in terms of strategic direction, be simply working in the dark. That today's markets are different rather than similar has been stressed through these early chapters. Companies must identify these differences to establish the context and direction as a basis for developing functional strategies.

Most companies acknowledge the need to support their markets, but few truly understand what this means. A detailed and comprehensive review of a company's current and future markets is the first step in developing a strategy, but is often omitted. Why does this happen? Most companies work with general reviews of markets that typically provide descriptions, but this gives insufficient understanding of customer needs. For example, customers may be segmented using industrial codes into, say, aerospace, industrial and automotive segments. But, such segmentation does not identify the important competitive factors necessary to retain and grow market share with customers in each segment.

Strategy development is an iterative process

Markets are dynamic and the business direction must be reviewed and adjusted if it is to remain aligned with the market. This does not imply that firms should follow an approach that is largely without direction at the start and gradually evolve a strategy as one emerges. Firms need to have a direction, but be willing to adjust it as markets change and opportunities or threats emerge. It is important, therefore, that markets are discussed, checked and agreed on a continuous basis.

Strategy can be market-driven or market-driving

Operations strategy can be either market-driven, market-driving or both. Market-driven strategies develop capabilities to meet existing market requirements whereas market-driving strategies develop capabilities to meet anticipated market needs that do not currently exist. Either way, businesses must analyse markets before they can develop an operations strategy. Market-driving strategies tend to take a longer time to pay off as a new market or segment needs to be created and customers may not be ready for it. However, once they have been created, then the level of competition tends to be lower and profits higher. Organizations need to balance the risk and return of these two approaches.

Aspects to consider when analysing markets

Markets must be analysed in depth and on an ongoing basis. Companies need to allocate adequate time, attention and resources to do this. Developing and executing strategy is hard work and needs senior management's full attention. Without this commitment, firms take risks, especially in difficult environments. However, businesses often fail to recognize this and, consequently, do not develop and execute strategy well.

Analyse customer behaviour not customer voice

Customer needs must be analysed by reviewing customer orders (behaviour) rather than asking them what they want (voice). Regardless of what a customer says they want, the true reality of doing business with them is only known once they start placing orders. Often a business needs to satisfy the voice of the customer to win the business and the behaviour of the customer to retain the business. The role of sales and marketing is to appeal to the customer's voice, whereas operations has to then meet its behaviour. This often leads to differing functional perspectives of the same customer that need to be understood when analysing markets.

Example market reviews

The three example market reviews shown in *Exhibits 4.2, 4.3* and *4.4* highlight a number of important points to bear in mind when developing an operations strategy:

1 **Customers demand different order-winners and qualifiers** – the order-winners and qualifiers demanded by customers vary in terms of the criteria themselves and their level of importance. These differences must be identified before functional strategies can be developed to support them.

2 **Order-winners and qualifiers within a market change over time** – hence, functional strategies are both time- and market-specific.

3 **Analyse multifunctional perspectives of the market** – all functions interact with customers in different ways and, therefore, have different perspectives of their needs. The process of identifying order-winners and qualifiers must involve all business functions and opinions must be analysed and tested against data. Only by

sound, in-depth discussions will the essential characteristics of a company's markets be revealed.

4 **Determine the order-winners and qualifiers to be supported by operations** – when developing an operations strategy, it is important to understand operations perspective of the market. Marketing segments markets by identifying differences in customer buying behaviour, but this is not an appropriate segmentation for operations. *Exhibits 4.2, 4.3* and *4.4* illustrate how different order-winners and qualifiers may be present within a given marketing segment. Identifying and understanding these differences is an essential first step in developing an operations strategy.

The key to all these points is that in-depth discussion needs to take place. Only by statement, explanation, analysis and re-explanation will more accurate and better understood strategic shared insights be reached. Without this, companies revert to functionally based strategies that typically pull a business in different directions.

Order-winners and qualifiers for customers supplied by a US graphics company

Exhibit 4.2 shows the significant difference between the order-winners and qualifiers for two customers served by a US graphics company in one of this company's markets. At the time of the analysis, the sales revenue derived from Customer A was four times that of Customer B. As you will guess, the company supplies to a whole range of customers that, in turn, are in different markets themselves. The market review, therefore, would need to establish the order-winners and qualifiers for all customers in all markets. Typically, some customers will have similar order-winners and qualifiers and other customers will have other order-winners and qualifiers, a fact that must be clearly established as part of the analysis. The grouping together of customers with similar order-winners and qualifiers is then completed at the next stage. Assumptions on the similarity of segments must be avoided. Analysis will establish the level of similarity or difference that exists in a company's markets, and approaches to strategy formulation based on analysis and verification need to replace the broadbrush overviews that characterize current practice. Customers A and B represent two such clusters.

Criteria		Customer A			Customer B		
		CY	CY + 1	CY + 2	CY	CY + 1	CY + 2
Design (product specification)		40	40	40	30	40	50
Price		Q	Q	Q	40	20	Q
Delivery	– reliability	QQ	QQ	QQ	QQ	QQ	QQ
	– speed	30	20	Q	30	20	Q
Quality conformance		QQ	QQ	QQ	QQ	QQ	QQ
R&D support services		30	40	60	–	20	50

NOTE: Q denotes qualifier, QQ denotes an order-losing sensitive qualifier, CY denotes current year.

EXHIBIT 4.2 US graphics company: order-winners and qualifiers for two customers

Product design, delivery speed and technical support are currently important order-winners for Customer A. However, over the next two years, technical support will become more important as delivery speed becomes a qualifier. This is not a price-sensitive customer and the high margins provide the funds to keep investing in the business's product design and technical support capabilities. Delivery reliability and quality conformance are also both qualifiers and if they are not met, future business will be lost.

By contrast, Customer B is currently much more price sensitive and technical support is not important. However, the company intends to change Customer B's order-winners and qualifiers to bring them in line with Customer A. It is, therefore, trying to drive the market and capitalize on the technical support capability it has developed for Customer A. In this way, the company is moving from a market-driven to a market-driving strategy.

Order-winners and qualifiers for products supplied by a European cable-making company

Exhibit 4.3 shows the order-winners and qualifiers for two products supplied by a European cable-making company. Often companies assume that similar types of products (such as batteries) win orders in similar ways, but this is not always the case. For example, Product 1/80 is much more price sensitive than Product 8/25 whereas product design and quality conformance are less important. However, as competitors match the 8/25 product design over the next two years, price is expected to become an increasingly important order-winner. Delivery speed and reliability are of similar importance for both products.

Criteria		Product: Marine (1/80)			Product: Mining (8/25)		
		CY	CY + 2	CY + 4	CY	CY + 2	CY + 4
Design		45	35	25	50	45	40
Quality conformance		Q	Q	Q	30	20	Q
Delivery	– reliability	QQ	QQ	QQ	QQ	QQ	QQ
	– speed	40	35	30	20	20	20
Price		15	30	45	Q	15	40

NOTE: Q denotes qualifier, QQ denotes an order-losing sensitive qualifier, CY denotes current year.

EXHIBIT 4.3 European cable-making company: order-winners and qualifiers for two products

Order-winners and qualifiers by customers supplied by a European engineered sealing systems company

This company supplies engineered sealing systems to a range of customers throughout the world. The analysis shown in Exhibit 4.4 again illustrates how customers can differ from each other. The company wins orders from its customers in very different and sometimes opposing ways. Currently, price ranges from a qualifier for Customer C to the dominant order-winner for Customer B. By contrast, product design is more important for Customer C than A or B, delivery speed is important in winning orders from all customers, but more so for Customer A than B or C. Meanwhile, the criteria of delivery reliability, quality conformance, technical support and brand name are more similar to all three customers.

Criteria		Customer A (France)		Customer B (UK)		Customer C (Germany)	
		CY	CY + 3	CY	CY + 3	CY	CY + 3
Price		25	40	50	60	Q	20
Delivery	– reliability	QQ	QQ	QQ	QQ	Q	QQ
	– speed	35	40	20	20	15	25
Quality conformance		QQ	QQ	QQ	QQ	QQ	QQ
Design		Q	Q	Q	Q	30	25
Technical support		25	20	30	20	30	15
Brand name		15	Q	Q	Q	25	15

NOTE: Q denotes qualifier, QQ denotes an order-losing sensitive qualifier, CY denotes current year.

EXHIBIT 4.4 European engineered sealing systems company: order-winners and qualifiers for three customers

Agree markets

The first step in analysing markets is to agree in which ones the business wishes to compete today and in the future. Once markets and their characteristics are agreed, a company starts to gain control of its strategy. Then it is able to judge whether a piece of business fits its strategic direction.

The most important orders are the ones to which you say 'no'

These mark the boundaries by declaring the market in which a company decides to compete. Without this level of clarity, all orders are deemed to be equally attractive. This cannot be the case, but without a mechanism for knowing how to judge orders received, appropriate decisions cannot be made.

Determine market order-winners and qualifiers

Discussion and debate to determine market order-winners and qualifiers needs to be structured and data used to test views and opinions. The objective is to distinguish essential differences within a company's chosen markets. To facilitate the strategy debate, it is necessary to start with some stated view of the market as a focal point for discussion. The best place to start is to seek the views of marketing. This view is then tested against other functional perspectives and with data showing how customers actually behave.

Determine marketing's view of the market

To determine marketing's view of the market, it should be asked to:

- Segment the market from a marketing point of view and choose products or customers that represent each chosen segment.

- Establish for each segment appropriate future planning horizons that reflect the relevant timescales involved. Normally, this is given as two future time periods similar to the examples in *Exhibits 4.2* and *4.3*.

- Select and weight the order-winners and qualifiers for each segment for both current and future time periods, using the products and customers that represent each segment as part of this step.

Test marketing's view with other functional perspectives of the market

Marketing's view of the market then forms the basis for discussion and is challenged by the opinions of other functions. Using the initial views of marketing, other functions express opinions, ask questions and seek clarification of why segments work the way marketing suggests. This leads to an improved understanding between functions and a revised understanding of the markets in which a company competes. This may alter the weightings attributed to particular order-winners and qualifiers or change them altogether.

Throughout, it is important to use functional opinions within the strategy debate, not as sets of arguments and counter-arguments but as a means of directing analysis. When functional views are raised, the question to follow should be: 'what data need to be provided to check whether this view holds?' Only in this way can companies move to a level of debate that provides the essential quality and yields the necessary insights on which to make sound strategic decisions.

At all times, the business must remember that the purpose of the market debate is to:

- Improve a company's understanding of its markets

- Allow it to review its markets or parts of them

- Change its decisions on the relative importance of these parts

- Form the basis of functional strategies by prioritizing investments and developments.

Test executive opinion of order-winners and qualifiers with data

Data must then be collected and analysed to replace opinions with facts. This ensures that conclusions are not unduly swayed by the forceful arguments of individual functions. The discussion also seeks to identify any further analysis necessary to continuously verify these conclusions.

Example analyses to test opinions about market order-winners and qualifiers are now described. When completing them, it is important to bear in mind that the analyses will:

- Not be of equal value in all situations. Some may be difficult to undertake due to data availability, while others will not identify differences that would yield further insights.

- Sometimes overlap. Thus undertaking a customer-related review may duplicate (in part) the analysis involved in one of the operations-related checks.

- Test the subjective views of executives with the reality of the orders placed by customers and the demands they make on the business.

- Be based on representative customer orders or contracts selected and verified by the executives involved. Seeking their knowledge of what is representative is essential in order to ensure that the findings are relevant and usable.

Many companies confine their review of markets to the perspectives held by marketing and consequently limit their analysis to customer surveys, competitor analyses, SWOT reviews[2] and other classic marketing-oriented approaches. The purpose of these analyses is to review markets based on how customers actually behave.

Price

When price is considered to be an order-winner or qualifier, companies need to review the actual costs and margins for those customer orders. Contribution should be low if it is an order-winner and high if it is a qualifier. In many instances, companies use their own form of standard costs as the basis for reviewing margins. However, these cost calculations are invariably inaccurate. It is essential, therefore, that companies analyse the actual costs incurred in completing the orders under review. These figures must include as many direct costs as possible. Using these actual costs, businesses must test executive opinion of order-winners and qualifiers and the market segmentation proposed. In many instances, executive opinions will be proved wrong and the market resegmented.

Shop-floor records are often kept outside the formal system. These records need to be sought and, if they do not exist, a once-off arrangement needs to be made to capture the actual labour, materials and other direct costs incurred in completing an order or making a quantity of products. Using these figures, actual costs can then be compared with the selling price of the product.

Test estimated contribution with actual contribution

Exhibit 4.5 compares the estimated contribution (based on standard costs) against the actual contribution recorded for a representative sample of orders. The reason for this variance is that standard production times and material costs are generated as part of an initial costing exercise, but then rarely updated during the life of a product. During this period, many aspects change that can greatly affect the cost of producing it, such as working methods or typical batch sizes produced. This is why actual costs need to be determined before an accurate contribution figure can be calculated.

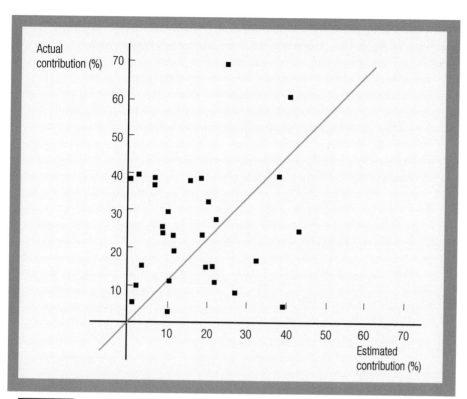

EXHIBIT 4.5 Actual versus estimated contribution for a number of representative products

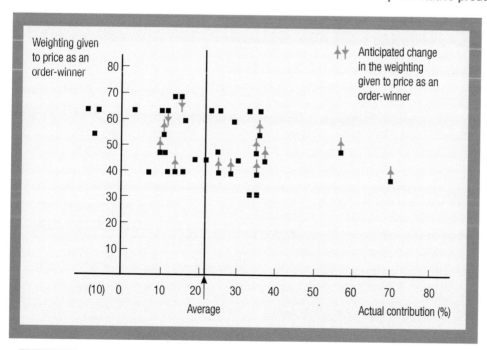

EXHIBIT 4.6 A comparison of actual contribution for a group of representative products to the order-winner weighting given to price

Test executive opinion of price as an order-winner or qualifier with actual contribution

Exhibit 4.6 analyses a group of products where executives believed price to be an order-winner. It shows the difference between the perceived importance of price and the actual contribution made on these products, and highlights the need to check opinion with fact. Based on this analysis, the order-winner weighting or selling price of the product must be reviewed. Either the weighting is too high for high contribution products, too low for low contribution products or the selling price too low for low weighting products.

Use as many direct costs as possible to calculate actual contribution

To improve the accuracy of the actual contribution calculation, companies must identify as many direct costs as possible. For example, delivery charges where a direct delivery service is provided.

Test actual contribution with actual contribution per machine hour

Contribution as a percentage of the selling price does not give the best insight into the relative value of orders, as it assumes that all other non-direct factors involved are of the same relative importance. If different orders are processed on the same equipment, and where this is a scarce resource, an additional calculation should be made to identify the contribution earned per machine hour. *Exhibit 4.7* shows how contribution per machine hour gives a clearer understanding of the true profitability of a product.

Order reference	Price (£)	Direct costs (£)	Contribution		Machine hours	Contribution per machine hour (£)
			(£)	(%)		
631	220	44	176	80	1.5	117
205	568	114	454	80	3.9	116
216	1,246	269	977	78	11.2	87
470	244	56	188	77	4.0	47
298	1,960	462	1,496	77	9.3	161
607	3,612	830	2,782	77	13.3	209
512	134	32	102	76	1.5	66
483	4,010	1,004	3,006	75	21.5	140
658	166	42	124	75	0.7	107
313	1,134	306	828	73	5.7	145
284	864	246	618	72	2.1	294
182	724	65	159	71	4.7	14
573	1,066	320	746	70	3.1	240
417	3,345	1,140	2,205	66	7.9	279

NOTE: All data are actuals.

EXHIBIT 4.7 Comparison of contribution percentage and contribution per machine hour for representative orders

Test executive opinion of market segments with actual contribution of customers in that segment

The initial view of the market from marketing's perspective will identify segments and assume that all customers and orders in that segment are similar. This assumption needs to be tested with data. *Exhibit 4.8* shows how customers believed to be within a segment actually have markedly different levels of contribution from one another.[3] From a marketing perspective, it may make sense to cluster these customers together, but they need to be resegmented when operations is considering how to develop the capability to support them.

Customer	Actual contribution		Customer	Actual contribution	
	% sales	Per machine hour		% sales	Per machine hour
Segment 1			Segment 2		
Hulton	41.8	918	Prelpac	14.0	243
Avis Robins	24.6	431	JRR	8.6	186
MKC	8.6	288	Sheuks	16.1	115
Clairelle	12.4	152	Dells	(1.0)	(64)
Artiste	30.7	714	Avenols	22.3	408

NOTE: Customer data are the average for a representative sample of orders.

EXHIBIT 4.8 Contribution percentage of sales and contribution per machine hour for representative orders for two segments

Quality conformance

Quality conformance needs to be reviewed for products, orders or customers where it is believed to be an order-winner or qualifier. Such analyses will also build into the direct material dimension of costs addressed in the last section. This helps a business to understand the importance of this criterion within its markets and also the current ability of operations to support it. Typically, this measure is calculated for the overall business rather than for a product, order or customer. As such, the true cost or customer impact is unknown.

Delivery reliability

The definition of on-time delivery is not always simple. Customers' needs may range from an hourly slot on a stated day to any day within a given week. Some may not want delivery before a given time but will accept delivery any time thereafter, within stated limits. Others may require all line items on the order at the correct quantities before it can be considered delivered. The dimensions of on time, order fill accuracy and being error free also affect the level of overall delivery reliability. For example, being 95 per cent on time with an order fill rate of 90 per cent and an error-free rate of 98 per cent could result in an overall delivery performance of less than 84 per cent.

Before measuring delivery reliability, on time needs to be defined. As with quality conformance, delivery reliability tends to be measured for the business rather than for a specific product, order or customer. Not only does this fail to distinguish the importance of individual customers, it also fails to identify the differing delivery needs of customers. Delivery reliability needs to be measured for customers and segments to test its perceived role in winning orders. In most companies, delivery reliability is a qualifier rather than an order-winner; in many, it is an order-losing sensitive qualifier. Once companies determine what to measure, then actual orders can be recorded and analysed.

Delivery speed

The delivery speed requirement of a customer is analysed by comparing the date and time a customer places an order with the date and time of requested delivery. Sometimes customers will pull forward the requested delivery after the order has been placed. It is therefore important to analyse order amendments as well as the original order placed. Customers who request short delivery lead times must also be contacted to confirm that this is their actual requirement. In some cases, this may not reflect when they actually need the product but may result from their current working practices, such as order generated using inaccurate standard lead times in their computer system or nervousness caused by previous poor delivery performance.

Product range

The number or product types and dates they were requested must be reviewed for an appropriate time period for customer and product groups to show the ranges that are being supplied. A new type must be used for each product variant to reflect changes such as size, colour or packaging. It is then possible to assess how ranges have increased or decreased over an appropriate time period for products and customers.

Demand fluctuations

It is necessary to analyse both the date and volume of orders placed, and the date and volume of products requested. This highlights if demand fluctuations occur in either the order entry or fulfilment processes. As with other analyses, this must be performed for specific products or customers to highlight differences between them.

Other market order-winners and qualifiers

There are many different order-winners and qualifiers besides those discussed above. Once again, it is important to test executive opinion with how customers actually behave by analysing a representative sample of customer orders and requirements. Without this analysis, companies will not fully understand how they win and qualify for orders in their markets.

Test executive opinion of customers and products within a market segment with data

The process of testing order-winners and qualifiers often shows that the initial grouping of products, ranges of products and customers into market segments is inaccurate. Orders from the same customer often have significantly different order-winners and qualifiers from each other depending on factors such as the stage in their life cycle and the nature of the markets their customers serve.

Exhibit 4.9 shows how the products supplied to a customer can vary in terms of their gross margin, quality conformance and inventory held to meet delivery speed requirements, while *Exhibit 4.10* illustrates how the lead time demanded by customers believed to be in a market segment can vary. Both exhibits highlight the importance of reviewing the range of products supplied to a customer and the range of customers within a segment. As with previous analysis, it also shows the importance of checking 'customer's behaviour' rather than only listening to 'customer's voice'.

Aspect	Products	
	All	Top 17 by annual sales value
Parts supplied	94	10
Total annual quantity for all products supplied (000s units)	1,300	600
Average gross margin (%)	10	3
Level of quality conformance – customer demerits awarded:		
number of parts given one or more demerits	23	2
total demerits awarded	102	21
% total inventory holding for Customer A's products	100	31

NOTE: The higher the number of demerits, the worse the performance on meeting the agreed product specification.

EXHIBIT 4.9 Analysis of the order mix received from a customer regarding gross margin percentage, quality conformance levels and associated inventory levels for alternative products

Company	Lead times (days) – # stock-keeping units											Total
	Current day minus				Current day	Current day plus						
	11+	7–10	4–6	1–3		1–3	4–6	7–10	11–20	21–30	31+	
A	–	1	1	–	2	2	1	9	–	2	52	70
B	–	–	–	25	–	–	18	–	51	40	112	246
C	–	4	–	6	5	–	12	–	–	–	24	51

NOTES
1 The review was taken at a specific point in time and includes all orders waiting to go into production and already in work-in-progress. Calculations for the latter were based on the original receipt date of the order or schedule.
2 A stock-keeping unit (SKU) is a distinct product with a unique reference number.
3 The figures also include where a customer reschedules delivery dates. Here the original lead time was taken out of the sample (the order date no longer being relevant) and the new requirement was added to the review.
4 The lead time calculations are based on the date the order or schedule was received (for telephoned orders, the date used was that of the telephone call and not that of the confirmation order) compared to the date of the required delivery.
5 Current day minus figures mean that the date the order or schedule was received was one or more days after the required delivery date specified on the paperwork.

EXHIBIT 4.10 Review of customers believed to be in a segment showing the varying delivery lead times requested

Outcomes of debating and testing market order-winners and qualifiers

Debating and testing order-winners and qualifiers improves market understanding, helps to align functional strategies within an organization and forms the basis for developing an operations strategy, as well as other functional strategies:

- **Improves market understanding** – debating and testing markets enable key distinctions between customers, orders and products to be understood. In this way, a company's view of its markets is improved and based on shared functional agreement.

- **Helps to align functional strategies** – functions typically develop strategies independently of one another. Debating and testing markets allow essential differences and perspectives to be exposed and explored. This creates a cross-functional perspective of markets that, in turn, aligns functional strategies.

- **Forms the basis for developing an operations strategy** – the order-winners and qualifiers within a company's markets must be supported by operations and, therefore, define the capabilities that it needs to develop.

Developing an operations strategy

The process of agreeing the markets to be served by a company and the order-winners and qualifiers that need to be supported have been explained. The next steps are to identify the order-winners and qualifiers to be supported by operations, test its support of these and prioritize future investments and developments. This is not just a one-off activity, but an ongoing debate involving market analysis and capability development.

Identify key strategic task

The first step in developing an operations strategy is to identify the key order-winners and qualifiers it must support from the market review. These can then be translated into strategic tasks. For example, if price is a key order-winner, costs must be reduced throughout all aspects of the operation; if quality conformance is a key qualifier, errors must be reduced and quality built into the process rather than checks after the event.

Review current performance and identify improvements

Current operations performance must then be reviewed against these key strategic tasks. *Exhibit 4.11* gives examples of how to check current performance against order-winners or qualifiers and the typical improvements to improve their support.

Order-winner or qualifier	Review current performance	Typical improvements
Price	• Review actual material, direct labour and overhead costs • Map current manufacturing process and identify areas of material and labour waste • Review mix of production volumes in an operation • Review annual production volumes within a product range • Review production run lengths • Review contribution per machine hour • Review product pricing	• Reduce large areas of costs – materials and overheads are typically 70–90 per cent of total cost • Reduce material and labour waste • Reduce process changeover and set-up times • Reallocate products across operations • Focus operations on markets or resources
Quality conformance	• Review quality conformance levels for products, orders, customers and market segments	• Reduce quality conformance errors • Build quality into the process rather than checking conformance after the event
Delivery reliability	• Review delivery performance for products, orders, customers and market segments • Analyse and compare customer requested and operations actual delivery lead times • Compare actual processing with overall operations lead time	• Improve scheduling of activities • Improve process reliability • Hold inventory at varying stages in the process
Delivery speed	• Analyse and compare customer requested and operations actual delivery lead times • Compare actual processing with overall operations lead time • Map actual operations process and identify areas of material and labour waste	• Eliminate waiting time between process steps • Reducing lead time of process steps • Eliminate wasteful activities
Product range	• Review the process capability to meet required current and future product range	• Develop process capability to cope with product range • Develop employee skill levels • Reduce changeover and set-up times
Demand fluctuations	• Assess ability of capacity to respond to known or anticipated demand changes	• Invest in capacity or inventory
Speed of new product development	• Map new product development process and identify areas of waste • Determine length of activities and their dependency on other activities or key resources • Identify activities for which operations has responsibility	• Eliminate wasteful activities • Increase capacity of constraining resources • Reschedule activities so they are completed in parallel (rather than in sequence) with other parts of the process

EXHIBIT 4.11 Examples of how to review performance and typical improvements to meet alternative order-winners and qualifiers

Price

Operations must check its current performance on a number of aspects to understand if price is being supported. Example analyses that give further insight into current or potential problems and highlight areas for improvement are now discussed.

Review actual material, direct labour and overhead costs

All aspects of cost must be reviewed to identify significant elements. Materials and overheads are typically 70–90 per cent of total cost and the areas of focus. Trends should be reviewed to understand historical and forecasted changes. In some instances, companies may wish to stabilize cost fluctuations by putting in place supplier or employee agreements.

Map activities and identify areas of waste

As well as splitting costs by type, companies must also separate them into different activities. To do this, the entire business process from customer order placement through to customer payment must be mapped. Waste such as unnecessary process steps, movement, inventory, paperwork or inspection can then be eliminated, and working practices for the remaining value-adding activities improved. Both these actions will reduce cost.

Review mix of production volumes in an operation

Cost-efficient operations typically focus on a narrow range of high-volume products. However, as markets mature, product ranges expand and production volumes decrease. Businesses must review the product and volume mix within operations if they are to remain focused. *Exhibit 4.12* is a review of product and volume mix across four North American pharmaceutical operations and shows how Operation 4 is starting to become unfocused. Based on these findings, the business moved the low-volume products from Operation 4 to Operations 2 and 3. This reduced Operation 4's operating costs and improved the support of its price-sensitive markets.

Dimensions	Operation			
	1	2	3	4
Annual units (in millions)	55	128	47	91
Number of SKUs	316	1,642	852	260
Annual units per SKU (in thousands)	175	78	56	351
Number of active compounds	25	72	45	28

EXHIBIT 4.12 A review of product and volume mix across four North American pharmaceutical operations

Review mix of production run lengths in an operation

As well as reviewing the mix of production volumes, it is important to assess the mix of production run lengths of an operation. As products mature, their typical production run size (in hours) reduces, more set-ups are incurred and net output per hour reduces (see *Exhibit 4.13*). Production costs and inventory holdings will increase unless process changeovers and set-up times are reduced. For example, a review by a US consumer goods manufacturer of a process used to make one of its high-volume, price-sensitive products showed reducing volumes of other products supplied using this process. This meant that average production run size (in hours) for the process had fallen 38 per cent over the last six years. It therefore reduced process changeover and set-up times to meet the cost targets required to support its price-sensitive markets.

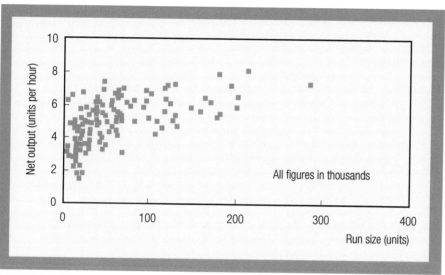

EXHIBIT 4.13 Correlation between the size (units) of a production run and the net output (units) per hour

Review actual contribution per machine hour

Low contribution products identify areas for cost reduction. For example, *Exhibit 4.14* showed an organization that contribution per machine hour was actually highest for its high-volume, price-sensitive markets and lowest for its low-volume, non-price-sensitive markets. As a result, it modified its support for the low-volume products by reducing process set-up times that, in turn, increased the contribution of these products.

Product	Production volume	Key order-winner	Contribution per machine hour ($)
A	Very high	Price	625
B	High	Price	415
C	Low	Delivery speed	593
D	Low	Non-price	380

NOTE: When the key order-winner is 'non-price', then orders are won predominantly on non-operations criteria.

EXHIBIT 4.14 Production volume, key market order-winner and actual contribution per machine hour for four products

Review product pricing

The significant differences in contribution between one product or customer and another are not always due to varying operations costs. They often result from how the products are priced. Standard costing methods are often used to price products and the basic assumptions and formulas in the model reflect some products, but not others. Also, once the product price is set, it is rarely reviewed and increased or decreased to reflect production volume, material cost and transport cost changes. Once low actual contribution products are identified, then improvements and developments must be made to reduce production costs, but price increases also need to be negotiated with customers.

Review quality conformance

Quality conformance levels must be reviewed for products, orders and customers to assess how well markets are being supported. General reviews are useful, but specific reviews identify improvement areas.

Review delivery reliability

Collecting and analysing delivery performance data are important to understand how delivery reliability varies for products, orders or customers. Comparing this with aspects such as order size, customer lead times (including schedule changes), process lead times and material deliveries help to identify causes of above- or below-average delivery performance and highlight improvement areas and actions.

Review delivery speed

To review current delivery speed performance, companies should:

- Analyse the total customer lead time from receipt of order to point of payment

- Map actual operations process to determine all the process steps

- Analyse operations actual delivery lead time and break it down into the relevant elements of order processing, material or component purchasing, material or component delivery, operations, assembly, packing and shipping

- Compare customer requested delivery lead time with operations actual delivery lead time

- Identify areas of material and labour waste by comparing lead time for each process step with actual processing time and changeover or set-up time.[4]

These analyses will identify current areas and causes of poor performance and start to identify where improvements need to be made within the business.

THE MOST TELLING ORDERS ARE THE ONES YOU TURN AWAY

Understanding markets is **DIFFICULT**

Identifying actions is **EASY**

Making it happen is **DIFFICULT**

Other market order-winners and qualifiers

There are many different order-winners and qualifiers besides those discussed above. In all instances, current operations performance must then be reviewed against order-winners or qualifiers to understand if they are supported. For example:

- **Product range** – review the capability of all the steps in the operations process to meet the required current and future product ranges. This should be completed for all process steps

- **Demand fluctuations** – assess the ability of the current process capacity to respond to known or anticipated demand changes

- **Speed of new product development** – map the current new product development process and identify areas of waste. Determine the length of activities and their dependency on other activities or key resources and identify the activities for which operations has responsibility.

Prioritize investments and developments

Once improvement and development areas have been identified, they need to be prioritized before action can be taken. Assessing each improvement using three criteria can do this:

- **Cost of implementing the improvement** – the cost of making the change, the amount of cash that will be tied up by this change and the ongoing cost of operating differently

- **Ease of implementing the improvement** – the time and resource required for implementation. This will reflect the type and number of stakeholders involved and if they will agree on the course of action suggested

- **Impact of making the improvement** – how much cash will be released, the ongoing cost of operating differently and the result of improved market support such as increased sales and profits.

Initially, a gut feel assessment of these three criteria should be made by simply rating them out of 5, where 5 is low cost, high impact and easy to implement, and adding the total scored for each action together. The total scores identify areas of focus and improvement and teams can then be set up to look at each of them in more detail. Once a more detailed analysis has been completed and the cost, ease and impact are better known for each action, then the business can decide which improvements to make. There are two aspects that help to create focus when prioritizing actions and allocating resources to implementing them:

- **Impact of doing nothing** – how much cash will be tied up, the ongoing cost of the current operation and the result of current market support such as reduced sales and profits

- **Speeding up implementation** – how many resources are required and how can these be used to implement the improvements in less time.

Successful strategy execution concerns balancing gut feel with analysis so that action is not delayed, but also focuses on actions with maximum impact, given the investment funds available.

Reflections

Operations strategy can be market-driven, market-driving or both. Market-driven strategies develop capabilities to meet existing market requirements, whereas market-driving strategies develop capabilities to meet anticipated market needs that do not currently exist. Either way, businesses must analyse markets before they can develop an operations strategy. They must agree the current and future markets in which they wish to compete and determine the known or anticipated order-winners and qualifiers within these markets. Based on these order-winners and qualifiers, operations can identify its key strategic task, review current performance, determine areas for improvement and prioritize investments and developments. This is an iterative process rather than a series of steps as markets change and executive insights develop and grow.

Customer needs are only known by analysing how they behave rather than what they say they want. Analysing markets starts with understanding executive opinion of markets before testing them with data showing actual demands for different customers, orders and products. This process of debating and testing markets enables key distinctions between customers, orders and products to be understood. The result is an improved market understanding, better alignment between functional strategies and the basis for developing an operations strategy.

Operations must identify the key order-winners and qualifiers it must support in agreed current and future markets and translate them into key strategic tasks. For example, if price is a key order-winner, costs must be reduced throughout all aspects of the operation. It must then review current performance against these tasks and identify areas for improvement. Comparing the cost and ease of implementation with the impact of making them is used to rank improvement areas. This starts with a gut feel assessment to highlight areas of focus for a more detailed analysis. Action is only taken once the true cost, ease and impact are known.

Successful strategy development and execution concern balancing gut feel with in-depth analysis so that action is not delayed, but also focuses on areas of minimum cost and ease and maximum impact, given the investment funds available. Generic strategies promise much, but deliver little. Successful strategies are tailored to the specific needs of a business. It is important to know actual customer demands and their importance to current and future business sales, profits and strategies. Typically, companies end up replacing some 10 per cent of existing sales revenue with 'better' margin business. This has a dramatic impact on profit.

Customers, products and orders must be analysed within the overall context of the business. It is essential to identify their relative importance in terms of current and future total corporate profit/contribution. Supporting below-average customers today in the belief that they will become above-average customers tomorrow is good business sense, but checks must be in place to ensure that this happens.

The following chapters show how a company can respond to meet the ever-changing demands of today's dynamic and highly competitive markets. These responses, however, need to be within the context of agreed markets with clearly understood order-winners and qualifiers.

Discussion questions

1 'Operations strategies can be market-driven, market-driving or both.' Explain this statement using examples other than those described in this chapter. How do the alternative approaches to strategy development vary? What are the implications of each approach?

2 What steps are involved in developing an operations strategy? Use examples (other than any shown in this chapter) to illustrate the steps involved and the key issues at each step.

3 How should a business analyse its markets? Use examples (other than any shown in this chapter) to illustrate the steps involved and the key issues at each step.

4 'Successful strategy development and execution concerns balancing gut feel with in-depth analysis.' Explain this statement using examples other than those described in this chapter.

5 Why should all functions within a company, including operations, participate in business-level strategic planning?

6 Many companies fail to appreciate that the most critical orders are the ones to which a company says 'no'. Explain.

7 Why do companies use generic strategies? Explain the problems associated with this approach and how they can be overcome.

Notes and references

1 Taken from Hill, T. (1998) *The Strategy Quest*, Bristol: AMD Publishing, pp. vi and vii. This book, written in the form of a novel, addresses the issues in this chapter as well as those in Chapters 7 and 8 on focus.

2 A SWOT analysis determines the strengths, weaknesses, opportunities and threats relating to a company in its chosen markets. The limitations of SWOT analysis are brought into question by Hill, T.J. and Westwood R.K. (1997) 'SWOT analysis: it's time for a product recall', *Long Range Planning*, **30**(1): 46–52.

3 Further analyses can also be completed that test the level of consistency within a customer's portfolio of orders.

4 Several books and articles are available on the topic of business re-engineering. They include Davenport, T.H. and Short, J.E. (1990) 'The new industrial engineering: information technology and business process redesign', *Sloan Management Review*, **31**(4): 11–26; Davenport, T.H. (1993) *Process Innovation: Reengineering Work through Information Technology*, Cambridge, MA: Harvard Business School Press; Hammer, M. and Champy, J. (1993) *Reengineering the Corporation: A Manifesto for Business Revolution*, New York: Harper Business; Johansson, H.J., McHugh, P., Pendlebury, J. and Wheeler, W.A. III (1993) *Business Process Reengineering*, New York: John Wiley; Morris, D.C. and Brandon, J.S. (1993) *Reengineering your Business*, New York: McGraw-Hill; Obeng, E. and Crainer, S. (1994) *Making Re-engineering Happen*, London, Pitman; and Champy, J. (1995) *Reengineering Management: the Mandate for New Leadership*, New York: HarperCollins.

Exploring further

Champy, J. (1995) *Reengineering Management: the Mandate for New Leadership*, New York: HarperCollins.

Cobb, J.C., Samuels, C.J. and Sexton, M.W. (1998) 'Alignment and strategic change: a challenge for marketing and human resources', *Leadership & Organization Development Journal*, **19**(1): 32–43.

Davenport, T.H. (1993) *Process Innovation: Reengineering Work through Information Technology*, Cambridge, MA: Harvard Business School Press.

Davenport, T.H. and Short, J.E. (1990) 'The new industrial engineering: information technology and business process redesign', *Sloan Management Review*, **31**(4): 11–26.

Hammer, M. and Champy, J. (1993) *Reengineering the Corporation: A Manifesto for Business Revolution*, New York: Harper Business.

Hill, A. and Brown, S. (2007) ''Strategic profiling: a visual representation of internal strategic fit in service organisations', *International Journal of Operations & Production Management,* **27**(12): 1333–61.

Hill, T.J. (1998) *The Strategy Quest*, Bristol: AMD Publishing.

Hill, T.J. and Westwood, R.K. (1997) 'SWOT analysis: it's time for a product recall', *Long Range Planning*, **30**(1): 46–52.

Hughes, M. Hughes, P. and Morgan, R.E. (2007) 'Exploitative learning and entrepreneurial orientation alignment in emerging young firms: implications for market and response performance', *British Journal of Management*, **18**(4): 359–75.

Johansson, H.J., McHugh, P., Pendlebury J. and Wheeler W.A. III (1993) *Business Process Reengineering*, New York: John Wiley.

Kaplan, R.S. and Norton, D.P. (2004) 'Measuring the strategic readiness of intangible assets', *Harvard Business Review*, **82**(2): 52–63.

Kaplan, R.S. and Norton, D.P. (2007) 'Using the balanced scorecard as a strategic management system', *Harvard Business Review*, July–August, pp. 150–61.

Leisen, B., Lilly, B. and Winsor, R.D. (2002) 'The effects of organisational culture and market orientation on the effectiveness of strategic marketing alliances', *Journal of Services Marketing*, **16**(3): 201–22.

Morris, D.C. and Brandon, J.S. (1993) *Reengineering your Business*, New York: McGraw-Hill.

Obeng, E. and Crainer, S. (1994) *Making Re-engineering Happen*, London: Pitman.

Ulrich, D. and Smallwood, N. (2004) 'Capitalizing on capabilities', *Harvard Business Review*, **82**(6): 119–27.

Ulrich, D. and Smallwood, N. (2005) 'HR's new ROI: return on intangibles', *Human Resource Management*, 44(2): 137–42.

Ulrich, D., Smallwood, N. and Sandholtz, K. (2006) 'Making intangibles tangible', *Strategic Finance*, **88**(6): 9–12.

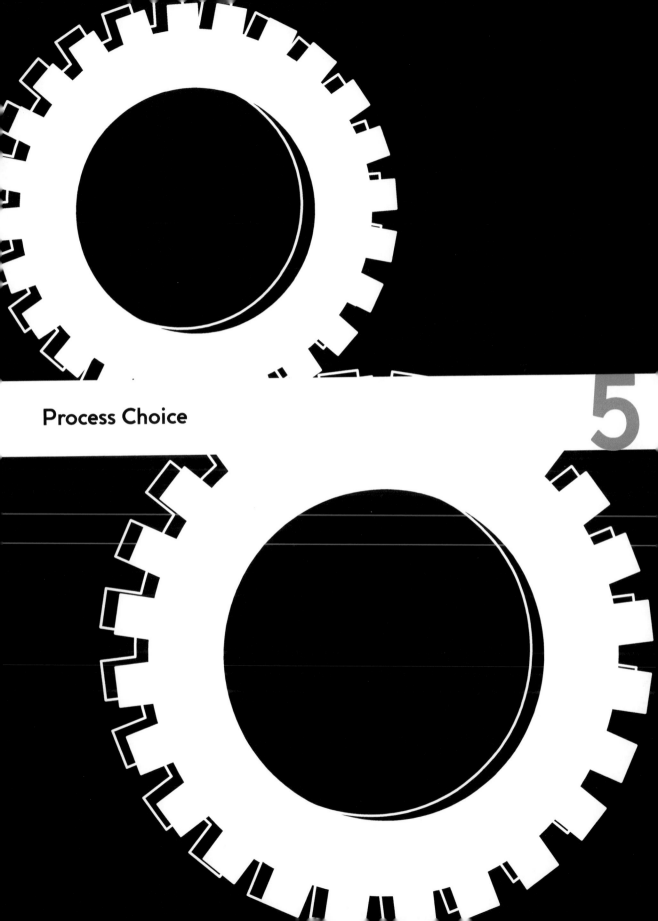

Process Choice

5

Summary

The most significant decisions a manufacturing company has to make concern customers, products and the processes by which to make them. This chapter covers the task of deciding which operations process to use and addresses the following issues:

- Factors involved in making products – the category or type of product, the product complexity and the volumes involved are key factors in the task of making products.

- Types of manufacturing process – there are five generic types of manufacturing process – project, jobbing, batch, line and continuous processing. Each is distinct from the other. While project and continuous processing are product/industry-type specific, the other three choices provide alternatives to a range of industries. Which one fits depends on the level of volume and repetition involved.

- Business implications of process choice – products have both a technical and business dimension. The former relates to the design, material and similar aspects, while the latter defines the business aspects (for example volumes, order-winners and qualifiers). Operations concerns providing the business specification of its products and selecting the most appropriate process to provide these dimensions.

- Hybrid processes – to gain a better fit between the business requirements and process characteristics, companies may choose a hybrid process (a mix of two generic types) as the best way. Hybrids may or may not be IT based.

- Technology strategy – advances in computer control have afforded fresh opportunities to compete in the manufacturing sector.

In addressing the key decision of which operations processes to use, many executives believe the choice should predominantly be based on the dimension of technology. As a consequence, they typically leave this decision to engineering/ process specialists on the assumption that they – the custodians of technological understanding – are best able to draw the fine distinctions that need to be made. The designation of these specialists as the appropriate people to make such decisions creates a situation in which the important operations and business perspectives are at best given inadequate weight and, in many instances, omitted all together.

Operations is not an engineering- or technology-related function. It is a business-related function. Although products need to be made according to their technical specifications, they also have to be supplied in ways that win orders in the marketplace. This business dimension is the concern of operations. When making process investment decisions, therefore, companies need to satisfy both the technical and business perspectives. The former is the concern of engineering, the latter is the concern of operations.

This chapter describes the operations and business implications of process choice and highlights the importance of these issues when making investment decisions. In this way, it helps to broaden the view of operations currently held by senior executives[1] and provides a way of reviewing the operations implications of marketing decisions, hence facilitating the operations input into corporate strategy. This ensures that the necessary marketing/operations interface is made and that the strategies adopted are business rather than functionally led.

Process choice

When choosing the appropriate way in which to manufacture its products, a business will take the following steps:

1   Decide on how much to buy from outside the company, which in turn determines the make-in task or internal phase of the supply chain.

2   Identify the appropriate engineering/technology alternatives to make a product to its technical specification. This will concern bringing together the made-in components with the bought-out items to produce the final product specification at agreed levels of quality conformance.

3   Choose between alternative manufacturing approaches to complete the tasks embodied in providing the products involved. This will need to reflect the market in which a product competes and the volumes associated with those sales. The present processes in many existing factories are often not ideal. Purchased some time in the past, advances in technology on the one hand and changes in market volumes and requirements on the other often contribute to create this position. This and other known items will be dealt with later in the chapter, when the important insights into process choice have been covered.

The choice of process concerns step 3 in this procedure. It will need to embody the decisions made in the other two steps and recognize any constraints imposed by them. The task then is to choose the most appropriate way to manufacture, given the market and associated volumes involved. In that way, it addresses the internal phase of the supply chain, with the external phase (suppliers and distributors) being the subject of Chapter 9.

The operations function

The principal function of the operations process is to take inputs (materials, labour and energy) and convert them into outputs (products). To complete this, a business chooses between appropriate engineering/technology alternatives (step 2 above) and operations alternatives (step 3 above). The rationale for this latter decision concerns choosing a process that is best able to support a company competitively in its marketplace. Each choice of process will bring with it certain implications for a business in terms of response to its markets, operations characteristics, level of investment required, unit costs involved and the type of scheduling system and style of management that are appropriate. To help understand these, it is necessary to review the process choices available.

But first, let's look at the factors involved in making products that help to determine the decision on which process to use.

Factors involved in making products

Categories of product

Exhibit 5.1 clarifies products into three categories and reflects the differences that need to be taken into account when designing the operations process. For example, it is clear that the process suited to making a Formula One/Indy racing car is, and needs to be, different to that used in an automobile plant making a mid-range model of car, as volumes, level of variety and degree of customization will all differ significantly and will need to be catered for by the process.

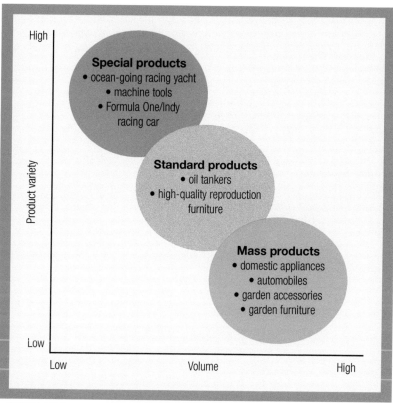

EXHIBIT 5.1 Categories of product

SOURCE: Adapted from Hill, T. (2005) *Operations Management*, 2nd edn, Basingstoke, Palgrave Macmillan

Product complexity

The complexity of a product varies. Compare engines for a lawn mower, automobile and aircraft and the differences are marked. As the product complexity increases, the number of steps and different processes involved will also increase, which, in turn, impacts process design.

Volumes

Exhibit 5.1 illustrates the important relationship between the three product categories and the levels of volume involved. The fundamental nature of this dimension is central to this chapter and the following section shows how it is reflected in the manufacturing process design.

Types of manufacturing process

There are five generic types of manufacturing process: project, jobbing, batch, line and continuous processing. However, in many situations, hybrids have been developed that blur the edges between one process and the next. What these hybrids are, how they relate to the classic types and what they mean for a business will also be discussed.

Before going on to describe the process choices involved, it is worth noting here that two of them (project and continuous processing) are associated with a particular product type (civil engineering and foods/liquids, respectively), a point addressed later in the chapter. A firm may find that in reality it has little option but to choose the one appropriate process (for instance oil refining and continuous processing are to all intents and purposes inextricably linked). However, a company must be aware of the business implications involved in the choice it is 'forced' to go along with and that the trade-offs associated with these dimensions are themselves fixed.

An important factor to note at this time is that companies do not invest then reinvest progressively as demand increases, for example when reflecting a product life cycle. It is simply too expensive. Neither will they wish to reinvest as demand decreases later in the cycle. Companies invest to reflect anticipated demand levels, a factor that relates to product profiling and focus, dealt with in Chapters 6 and 7 respectively.[2]

The generic types of process choice

Project

Companies that produce large-scale, one-off (that is, unique), complex products will normally provide these on a project basis. Examples include products involved in civil engineering contracts to build reservoir dams, tunnels and bridges, and aerospace programmes. A project process concerns the provision of a unique product requiring the coordination of large-scale inputs to achieve a customer's requirements. The resource inputs will normally be taken to where the product is to be built, since it is not feasible to move it once completed. All activities, including the necessary support functions, will usually be controlled by a total system for the duration of the project. Resources allocated to the project will be reallocated once their part of the task is complete or at the end of the project.

The selection of project as the appropriate process is based on two features. First, the product is a one-off, customer-specified requirement; second, it is too large to be moved or simply cannot be moved once completed. The second criterion is such an overwhelming facet of this decision that products of this nature will always be made using the project process. However, businesses will also be concerned with determining how much of the product to make away from site and how best to provide the parts or sections that go into the structures made on site. Making on site is not an efficient way of working, as resources have to be moved to and from the job as it progresses. This incurs costs and militates against achieving efficiencies. Hence, companies try to produce as much as possible of the product off site, which allows a more efficient process to be used. These parts of the total job will, in turn, be produced using a process other than project. Such decisions need to be based on other criteria, which will become clear in the descriptions of these other choices that follow.

Some confusion arises in the use of the word 'project'. It commonly refers to a one-off complex task and/or the managerial style used to control such an event. This needs to be distinguished from its use here, which identifies a distinct process of making a product, the characteristics of which (for example moving resources to and from a site) are detailed in *Exhibit 5.2*.

Products	Made or provided on site as it is too large or difficult to move after completion. Examples include building reservoir dams, tunnels, roads, bridges and houses
Process	Resources to make the product are brought to the site, allocated for the duration of the project and then reallocated once their part of the task is complete or at the end of the job

SOURCE: Hill, T. (2005) *Operations Management,* 2nd edn, Basingstoke, Palgrave Macmillan

EXHIBIT 5.2 Project: key characteristics

Jobbing

Once products are transportable, companies look to another process to make them. The jobbing[3] process is designed to meet the one-off (that is, unique) requirements of customers where the product involved is of an individual nature and tends to be of a smaller size (and, therefore, transportable) than those produced using a project process. Product examples include ocean-going racing yachts, a purpose-built piece of equipment (for example injection moulding tools), handmade, built-in furniture, customer-designed and specified control units and hand-crafted shoes and clothing. Such products require a supplier to interpret a customer's needs and/or design specification and apply relatively high-level skills in the conversion process. A large degree of this interpretation will normally be made by skilled employees, whose experience in this type of work is an essential facet of the process. Once the design has been specified, one skilled person – or possibly a small number of them, if the task is time-consuming – is assigned the task and is responsible for deciding how best to complete and carry it out. This may also include a level of responsibility for scheduling, liaison with other functions and some involvement with arrangements for the subcontracted phases, where necessary.

This one-off provision means that the product will not be required again in its exact form, or, if it is, the demand will tend to be irregular, with long time periods between orders. For this reason, investment in the operations process (for example in jigs, fixtures and specialist equipment) will not normally be warranted. *Exhibit 5.3* provides a summary of the key characteristics of jobbing.

Products	Special (that is, will not be repeated) products. Examples include the design and installation of a control system, purpose-built piece of equipment, handmade, built-in furniture and hand-crafted shoes and clothing
Process	One person or a small group of skilled people do everything, including interpreting the product specification, clarifying issues with the customer and ensuring that what is delivered meets the specification

SOURCE: Hill, T. (2005) *Operations Management,* 2nd edn, Basingstoke, Palgrave Macmillan

EXHIBIT 5.3 Jobbing: key characteristics

Jobbing versus job shop

It is worth noting here that confusion often arises around the terms 'jobbing' and 'job shop'. While the former refers to the choice of process explained above, the latter is a commercial description of a type of business. For example, a small printing business may often be referred to as a 'job shop' or even a 'jobbing printer'. This is intended to convey the nature of the business involved or market served, that is, the printer undertakes work, typically low volume in nature, that meets the specific needs of a whole range of customers. However, printing is in fact a classic example of a batch process, which is explained in the next section. Thus, from a commercial standpoint, such a firm takes on low-volume orders (hence the term 'job') from its customers but, from an operations perspective, uses a batch process to meet these requirements.

Special versus customized versus standard products

Finally, it is also important to distinguish between special, customized and standard products. The word 'special' is used to describe the one-off provision referred to earlier in this section – that is, the product will not be required again in its exact form or, if it is, the demand will be irregular, with long time periods between orders. The phrase 'standard product' means the opposite – the demand for the product is repeated (or the single customer order is of such a large volume nature) and thus warrants investment.

The word 'customized' refers to a product made to a customer's specification. However, the demand for a customized product can be either special (that is, not repeated) or standard (that is, repeated). An example of the latter is a container of a particular shape and size, as determined by a customer. Although customized, the demand for such a container (for example Coca-Cola or other soft drink products) will be high and of a repeat nature. The appropriate choice of process will, therefore, be determined by volume and not the customized nature of the product.

Furthermore, by their very nature, some businesses are the producers of customized products. The earlier example of the printing firm is such a case. Here products normally will be customized, in that the printed material may include the logo, company name, product name and other details of the customer in question. However, a printer will find a significant level of similarity between the demands placed on operations by the different customer orders. In fact, the differences will be in the plate containing the specific images and writing and the ink colours and paper size in question. To operations, therefore, the customized jobs are not specials (as defined earlier) but standards. Thus, it will select a process other than jobbing to meet the requirements of the markets it serves. In the printing example, this would be batch and the rationale for this and what is involved become clear in the next section.

Batch

A company decides to manufacture using batch processes because it is providing similar items on a repeat basis and usually in larger volumes (quantity × work content) than associated with jobbing.[4] This type of process is chosen to cover a wide range of volumes, as represented in *Exhibit 5.4* by the elongated shape of batch, compared to other processes. At the low-volume end, the repeat orders will be small and infrequent. In fact, some companies producing very large, one-off items will adopt a batch rather than a jobbing process for their manufacture. When this happens, the work content involved will be high in jobbing terms, while the order quantity is for a small number of the same but unique items. At the high-volume end, the order quantities may involve many hours, shifts, or even weeks of work for the same product at one or more stages in its designated manufacturing route.

The reason the batch process divides the operations task into a series of appropriate steps is simply to determine the most effective manufacturing route, so that the low-cost requirements of repeat, higher volume markets can be best achieved. At this stage, suitable jigs, fixtures and equipment will typically be identified to help reduce the processing times involved, the investment in which is justified by the total product output over time.

When using a batch process, the first step is to divide the job into a number of steps. How many steps will depend, in part, on the complexity of the product involved. A product may be completed by a single batch process, with more complex products being completed using a number of steps. An example of such a multi-step batch process is shown in Exhibit 5.5.

Each order quantity is manufactured by setting up that step of the process necessary to complete the first operation for a particular product. The whole order quantity is completed at this stage. Then, the next operation in the process is made ready, the total order quantity is completed and so on, until all stages required to make a product are completed. Meanwhile, the process used to complete the first operation for the product is then reset to complete an operation for another product and so on. Thus capacity at each stage in the process is used and reused to meet the different requirements of different orders.

A further illustration to the printing example given in Exhibit 5.3 is moulding. Here the mould to produce an item is put into a machine. The order for that component or product is then produced, the mould is taken off, the raw materials may have to be changed, a mould for another product is put into the machine and so on. Similarly in metal machining processes, a machine is set to complete the necessary metal cutting operation for a product and the whole order quantity is processed. When finished, the machine in question is reset to do the required metal cutting work on another item, while the order quantity of the first product goes on to its next stage, which is completed in another part of the process. At times, an order quantity may have more than one stage completed on the same machine. Here the same principle applies, with the process reset to perform the next operation through which the whole order quantity will be passed. Exhibit 5.6 provides a summary of the key characteristics of batch.

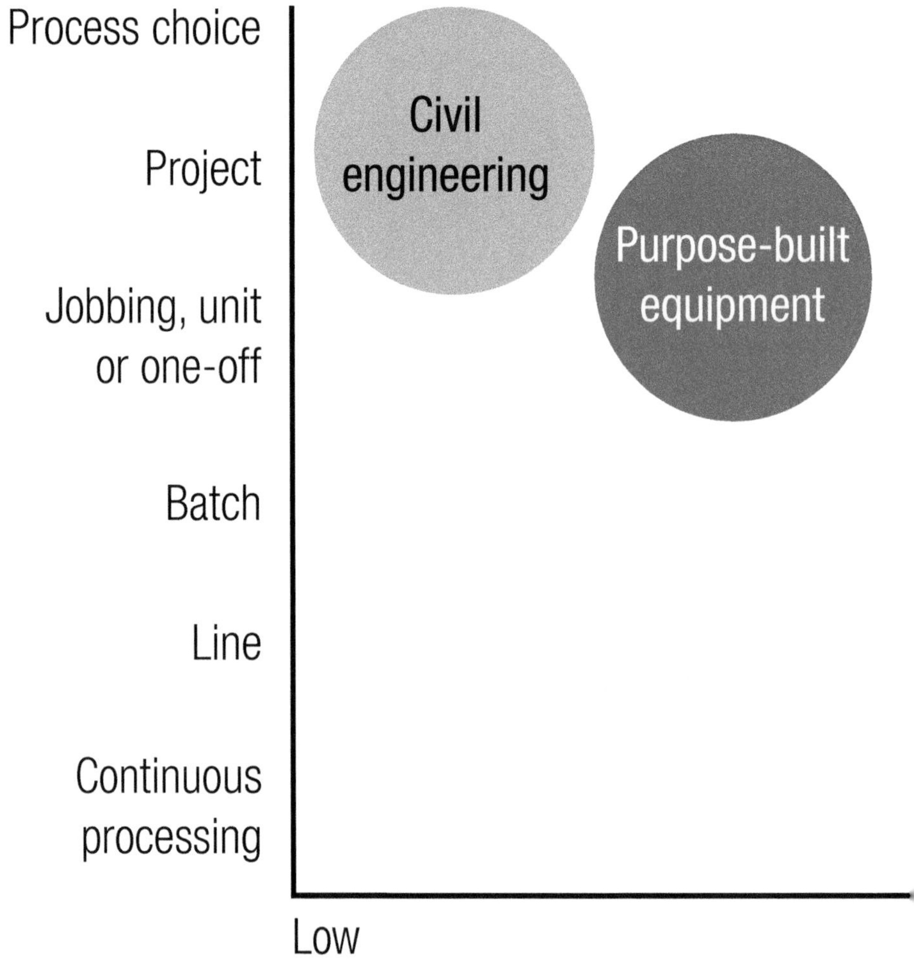

Process choice

Project

Jobbing, unit
or one-off

Batch

Line

Continuous
processing

Civil
engineering

Purpose-built
equipment

Low

NOTE: Volume refers to order quantity size.

Exhibit 5.4

Process choice related to volumes

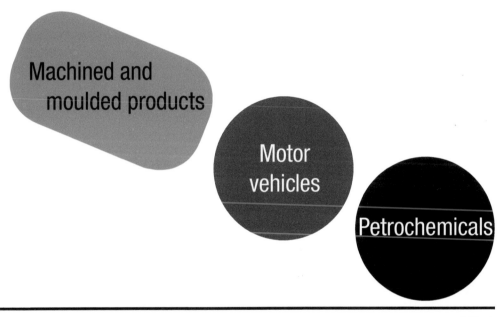

Machined and moulded products

Motor vehicles

Petrochemicals

High

Volume (quantity x work content)

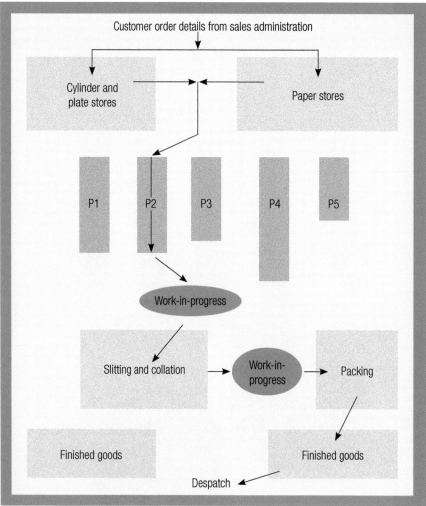

NOTES
1 P1–P5 are printing machines.
2 Arrows indicate the movement of a typical order.

EXHIBIT 5.5 Printing: a multi-step batch process

SOURCE: Hill, T. (2005) *Operations Management,* 2nd edn, Basingstoke, Palgrave Macmillan

Products	Standard, repeat products, the volume demand for which justifies the process investment. Examples include machined parts, injection mouldings and printing
Process	Having broken down the products into different operations, the order quantity is taken to the process where the first operation is to be undertaken. The process is made ready/set up and the whole order quantity is completed. The part-made product typically goes into work-in-progress inventory awaiting the next process that will complete the second operation. When available, the process is made ready, the whole order quantity is processed and so on or until the whole product is completed

SOURCE: Hill, T. (2005) *Operations Management,* 2nd edn, Basingstoke, Palgrave Macmillan

EXHIBIT 5.6 Batch: key characteristics

Line

With further increases in volumes (quantity × work content), investment is made to provide a process dedicated to the needs of a single product or a given range of products. The cumulative volume of the product range underpins this investment, with the width of the product range being determined at the time of the investment. In a line process, products are passed through the same sequence of operations. The standard nature of the products allows for this. As shown in *Exhibit 5.7*, the process transfers the product from one step to the next. Workers or equipment complete the designated tasks at that stage of the process and then move the product on to the next step, and so on until the product is completed. However, changes outside the prescribed range of options (which can be very wide, for example with motor vehicles) cannot be accommodated on the line itself.

EXHIBIT 5.7 Different stages on the Land Rover vehicle assembly line

SOURCE: Hill, T. (2005) *Operations Management*, 2nd edn, Basingstoke, Palgrave Macmillan

As explained in a later section, it is important to recognize the fundamental differences in what constitutes volume. In a car assembly plant, for instance, customer order quantities are normally small. The eventual owner of a car orders in units of one, which a dealership passes on to the assembly plant as an order for a single car or cumulates it with one or more other orders for single units. In operations terms, however, all orders for single cars are handled by the production process as being the same product. Hence the order quantity of a car assembly plant comprises the cumulative volume of all orders over a given period. This constitutes the high-volume nature of this business, making line the appropriate process.

Normally, the wider the product range, the higher the investment required in the process to provide the degree of flexibility necessary to make these products. Where the options provided are very wide and the products involved are costly or bulky, the company is more likely to make them to order. For example, a customer will normally have to wait longer for delivery when purchasing an automobile (especially if several options are specified)[5] than, say, a domestic appliance. The underlying reason is the different degree of product standardization involved. The automobile will be made against a specific customer order and the domestic appliance to stock.

In summary, in a line process all products (irrespective of the options involved) are perceived to be standard. Thus the process does not have to be stopped and reset to meet the requirements of the range of products made on a line. However, in order to accommodate another product using a batch process (which, for example, may only involve a different colour), the process has to be stopped and reset. *Exhibit 5.8* provides a summary of the key characteristics of the line process.

Products	Standard, repeat, high-volume, mass products. Examples include motor vehicles and domestic appliances. Not widely found in manufacturing today, as the required volumes to justify the investment are not typical of current markets
Process	Products are separated into different operations. These are met by a series of sequential processes through which all items in a selected range pass. To the process, all the products are the same and, therefore, the line does not have to be stopped and reset to accommodate a change in requirement. However, the line can only cope with the predetermined range for which the process has been designed. To widen the existing range would require additional investment

SOURCE: Hill, T. (2005) *Operations Management,* 2nd edn, Basingstoke, Palgrave Macmillan

EXHIBIT 5.8 Line: key characteristics

Continuous processing

With continuous processing, a basic material is passed through successive stages or operations and refined or processed into one or more products. Petrochemicals is an example. This choice of process is based on two features. The first is very high-volume demand; the second is that the materials involved can be moved easily from one part of the process to another, for example fluids and gases.

The high volumes justify the very high investment involved. The processes are designed to run all day and every day with minimum shutdowns, due to the high (often prohibitive) costs of starting up and closing down. Normally the product range is narrow and often the products offered are purposely restricted in order to enhance volumes of all the products in the range. For example, oil companies have systematically restricted the range of fuel octanes offered and hence increased the volumes of all those grades provided. Another feature in continuous processing is the nature of the materials being processed. Whereas in line there are manual inputs into the manufacture of the products as they pass along, in continuous processing the materials will be transferred automatically from one part of the process to the next, with the process monitoring and often self-adjusting flow and quality conformance levels. The labour tasks in these situations predominantly involve monitoring, checking and some adjusting of the system but typically do not involve manual inputs into the process as they would on a line. *Exhibit 5.9* gives an example of continuous processing. To close down and restart the plant would take several days, due to the complex process and safety requirements involved. *Exhibit 5.10* summarizes the key characteristics of continuous processing.

EXHIBIT 5.9 ExxonMobil's ethylene cracking plant, Fife, Scotland

SOURCE: Hill, T. (2005) *Operations Management*, 2nd edn, Basingstoke, Palgrave Macmillan

Products	Standard, very high-volume (mass) products. Examples include oil refining and some petrochemicals
Process	Materials are processed through successive stages, with automatic transfer of the product from stage to stage. The costs of stopping and restarting are typically so high that the process is not stopped, hence the name continuous processing

SOURCE: Hill, T. (2005) *Operations Management*, 2nd edn, Basingstoke, Palgrave Macmillan

EXHIBIT 5.10 Continuous processing: key characteristics

Product categories and production processes reflections

Exhibit 5.11 summarizes the last section and also relates the different processes to the product categories introduced in *Exhibit 5.1*. You will see from this that the transition from special through to mass products given in *Exhibit 5.1* relates, in general, to the types of process used. This section now reflects on this link between product type, process type and volumes.

1   **Project for special and standard products** – as shown in *Exhibit 5.11*, both special and standard products may choose project as the appropriate process. For example, a new estate of 120 houses comprising six designs would, for a builder, be a standard offering – that is, the house specifications would be known, the method of build would be decided ahead of time and any possible options to the basic design would be fixed. However, the houses would need to be built on site as they cannot be moved. On the other hand, a large country house built to a unique design, although a special, would need to be built on site.

2   **Project and continuous processing are specific to certain product types** – typically, project would only be used when a product has to be built on site. Setting up and dismantling a site, moving equipment and people to and from a site increase costs and make the management task more difficult compared to making a product in-house. As a consequence, project is typically only used where the product has to be made in situ.

Similarly, the use of continuous processing is limited. The products best suited to this process would be high volume, with the physical characteristics that allowed them to be moved from step to step in the process using pipework, such as the refining of oil and the production of petrochemicals.

So, the appropriate use of project and continuous processing is restricted (as shown in *Exhibit 5.12*) and most organizations choose from jobbing, batch and line for their business needs.

Process type	Product		Process description
	Category	Examples	
Project	Special	• Sydney Opera House • Oresund bridge connecting Denmark and Sweden • San Gottardo Tunnel in the Alps	Products that cannot be physically moved once completed use a project process. Here resources (materials, equipment and people) are brought to the site where the product is to be built. These resources are allocated for the duration of the job and will be reallocated once their part of the task is completed or at the end of the job
	Standard	• Estate housing • Prefabricated industrial and warehouse units	
Jobbing	Special	• Ocean-going racing yacht • Injection moulding tools • Formula One and Indy racing cars • The design and installation of a process control system	Once a product can be moved, companies will choose to make it in house and then despatch it to the customer. Jobbing is the name of the process that is used for special (that is, unique) products that will typically not be repeated. Here, one person or a small group of skilled people will complete all the product. Often the task requires the provider to install and commission the product as part of the job
Batch	Standard ↓ Mass	• Business cards • Golf tees • Packaging • Plastic bottles	The repeat and higher volume nature of standard products requires a process designed to take advantage of these characteristics. Batch, line and continuous processing are the alternatives. Which one to use depends on the volumes involved and the nature of the products. Batch can be appropriately used for low through to high (mass) volumes. As how to make the product is known, the steps involved are predetermined and products move from step to step until complete. Batch is chosen for standard products with volumes insufficient to dedicate processes. Thus, different products share the same processes by setting and resetting each time. Consequences of this include waiting between steps and the prioritizing of jobs using the same process
Line	Mass	• Domestic appliances • Cans of Coca-Cola • Automobiles • Pet food • Mobile phones	Higher volumes mean that processes can be dedicated to the needs of a given range of products. Whereas in batch a process has to be reset each time a new product is to be made, in line the process does not have to stop as it has been designed to make the range of products required without being reset. As with batch, the products are standard. The steps to make them are sequentially laid out in line and a product goes from step to step until completed. Although the range of products will vary, to the process they can be made without stopping and resetting the line
Continuous processing	Mass	• Petrochemicals • Oil refineries • Some chemical plants	For some products, the high volumes involved are best handled by continuous processing. In addition to high volume, these products will need to be transferable through piping or in liquid form. Continuous processing is similar to line in that it handles mass products without being stopped and reset. Its distinguishing feature is, however, that to stop and restart the process is lengthy and expensive and consequently it is designed to be run continuously

SOURCE: Hill, T. (2005) *Operations Management*, 2nd edn, Basingstoke, Palgrave Macmillan

EXHIBIT 5.11 Manufacturing processes and their relationship to the product categories in Exhibit 5.1

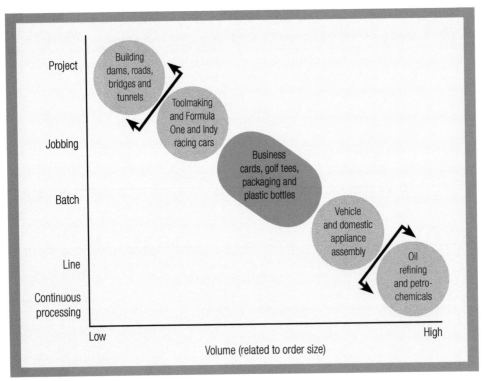

EXHIBIT 5.12 Process choice

SOURCE: Hill, T. (2005) *Operations Management*, 2nd edn, Basingstoke, Palgrave Macmillan

3   **Combinations of processes** – often companies will use more than one process type
to meet the overall needs of their business. The reason is that one process best
meets the different needs of a product or parts of a product. For example, building
the 120 new houses in point 1 above would use a combination of processes:

   • **project** to meet the overall requirements of bringing resources to and from the site,
     with one person having the overall management responsibility to undertake this
     task in line with the effective use of the resources and cost budgets involved.
   • **batch** would typically be used to meet several phases of the work. For example,
     once the footings had been completed on a number of houses, the concreting of
     the ground floor areas for these houses would be completed consecutively. In
     this way, one phase would be completed on one house and this same phase
     would be completed on the next house and so on until this task was completed
     for a number of houses. Other phases in the building of several houses would be
     cumulated by completing them one after another (for example roofing, glazing,
     electrics, plastering, bathroom fitting and kitchen installation). In this way, a
     builder would take advantage of the increased volume associated with the repeat
     nature of each phase by looking to reduce costs and make the management task
     easier. So, all roofing tiles for several houses would be delivered to site at the
     same time, as well as the materials for the glazing, electrics and other phases.
     Also, contractors to complete each phase would be less costly as they would
     undertake several consecutive days (even weeks) of work which, in turn, reduces
     their set-up costs on a job.

- **jobbing** – where specific alterations or additions to a standard design were requested and agreed, they would be completed using jobbing as the appropriate process. Here, skilled staff such as bricklayers and joiners would receive drawings, interpret these and be fully responsible for fulfilling the specification(s) and checking the results.

4 **Jobbing, batch and line** – these are the processes from which most companies choose and, again, they often choose more than one to best meet their needs, as illustrated in *Exhibit 5.13*. This shows that typically companies make components or parts in batch processes, while using line to assemble products. For example, the body panels for a Honda Civic will be made on a press. This will be set to make the left body panel, stopped and reset to make the right body panel and so on. However, Honda uses line to assemble the car.

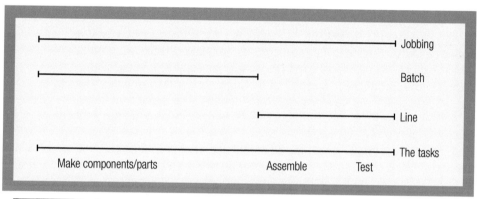

EXHIBIT 5.13 Tasks undertaken by jobbing, batch and line processes

SOURCE: Hill, T. (2005) *Operations Management,* 2nd edn, Basingstoke, Palgrave Macmillan

5 **What comprises volume?** – as volume is one of the fundamental factors in choosing appropriate processes, it is important to clarify the meaning. When choosing an appropriate process, the following dimensions of volume are involved:
- order quantity, that is, how many products are to be made at one time on the process. As jobbing typically involves making an order quantity of one for each product ordered, the order quantity volumes are low, whereas line is high volume because the order quantity comprises the total volume made during the life of the process. In vehicle production, the order quantity is the total number of automobiles processed over the length of time the assembly line is in place. The order quantity, in reality, is the combined volumes over that time period.
- volume is a combination of order quantity × unit time. The time taken to make the left body panel of the car is far less than to assemble the car itself, and so, although the quantity of panels and cars is the same, the panel is lower volume than the car and hence more suited to batch.

6 **Widening the product range to increase volumes** – several factors in today's markets have eroded demand for individual products and with it the volume to be processed by operations. Foremost among these factors is overcapacity within market sectors and

the increasing difference rather than increasing similarity of today's markets. One result is that companies have had to rethink process configurations, both in terms of the overall capacity (how many products in total a facility can produce) and the range of products that a process can make (the product range dimension of flexibility).

7   **The dimensions of flexibility** – one recent trend is to describe process capability as 'flexible' and 'agile'. Although these words capture the essence of the overall process capability dimension being described, such descriptions embody several important distinctions. It is better, therefore, to set aside these single-word descriptions and replace it with one that reflects the specific dimensions of process capability involved. As you will see from the list below, the dimensions differ markedly one from another, both in terms of their strategic relevance (the aspect of market advantage to which they relate) and how the investment spend would be directed. To achieve an improvement in any of the following aspects will result in more investment, so knowing the cost/benefit mix involved is an essential part of the decision.

In each of these dimensions of flexibility, companies need to assess how well a process can, and needs to, respond to the aspect of change involved, while recognizing that the flexibility factor will typically have both process and people skill implications:

- **Introduction of new products** – this aspect of flexibility concerns the ability of the operations process to handle new product introductions. These are vital to the long-term success of any business and operations is one of the functions that plays a key role in this overall process.
- **Handling a range of volumes** – as explained earlier, the level of volume required to justify the dedication of processes to a given range of products is typically not available. For this reason, batch is the most commonly used process as it is designed to be used and reused by a range of products. One key feature that results is the ease (that is, how long it takes) with which a process can cope with different levels of volume. The volume requirements of products will not only differ from one to the next but will also often differ for the same products in different time periods. How quickly a process can be changed from one product to another will directly impact the loss of output while the process change is taking place – the shorter the changeovers, the more flexible the process.
- **Handling a range of products** – most, if not all, companies produce a range of products and product options. Even Ford, with its Model T car and 'any colour as long as it's black' approach of the 1920s, was soon replaced by General Motors and its willingness to provide choice. The process flexibility to handle these dimensions is, in most markets, a key factor in the successful growth of a business as it reflects the nature of today's demand profile. One key feature that results is the ease (that is, how long it takes) with which a process can cope with a range of products – the shorter the time to complete a changeover, the more flexible the process.
- **Meeting demand peaks** – the demand for many products has a seasonality dimension. This aspect of flexibility concerns how easily the process can be ramped up to cope with sudden increases in demand.

Finally, other non-process dimensions of being responsive (such as meeting changes in customer delivery schedules) are accomplished not through process investment but, in this example, through developing a system that can handle the rescheduling of delivery dates.

The key factors in managing the need for flexibility are:

- Specify what dimension is involved – it brings clarity in analysis and prevents confusion in communication through a business.
- Identify where the investment needs to be made. This helps to ensure that the investment is appropriate to the need and that unnecessary investment is minimized.

8   **The use of batch to best meet the requirements of most companies** – as explained in points 2 and 4, for most companies the choice is between jobbing, batch and line and, of the three, batch is the most commonly used process. The reason is the nature of today's markets. Special products (using jobbing) and mass products (using line) are not commonplace. Demand for specials is limited, while the increasing level of difference required in today's markets has eroded volumes. For these reasons, batch is most suitable as the majority of companies make standard products but not in volumes that would justify investing in line. Instead, companies invest in and develop processes that can be used and reused by a range of products. In this way, they are able to make a range of products whose volumes vary.

Finally, it is useful here to explain that as the process is stopped and reset for each different product, the use of the process capacity is categorized in three ways:

- **unproductive time** – the utilization of the capacity is unproductive in nature. A classic example of this category is a machine breakdown.
- **non-saleable productive time** – the capacity is being used in a productive way but the outcome is non-saleable. Examples here include making samples and resetting the process for the next product. The time spent on samples is a productive use of the resource but the output cannot be sold. Similarly, setting up a process for another product is productive (it has to be done) but again the outcome does not result in saleable output.
- **saleable productive time** – completed products that will be sold to customers.

The non-saleable productive time element of this mix of outputs is a characteristic of batch as the process will need to be reset for each different product. Keeping the ratio between non-saleable and saleable productive time in balance is most important for a business. If the non-saleable percentage increases, saleable output goes down, which will have an adverse effect on sales and profits.

Markets and product volumes

As emphasized throughout the preceding sections, the underlying factor in choosing which of the five processes is most appropriate to manufacturing a product is volume (that is, quantity × work content). The link between the demand for a product and the investment in processes to complete this task is fundamental to this decision. It is important, therefore, to distinguish what is meant by volume.

Although companies express forecast sales in terms of a period (typically a year), operations does not make annual volumes – it makes order quantities. Thus contracts, based on agreed total sales in a given period, but not the size of actual orders (or call-offs), can be very misleading. On the other hand, in order to enhance volume, operations often cumulates orders from different customers (using order backlog/forward load principles) or decides to make products for finished goods inventory to be sold in the future. The choice is restricted by the degree of customization of the product and factors such as current forward load, seasonality of sales and lead times in supplying customers' requirements. Hence, the horizontal axis in *Exhibit 5.4* above concerns order quantities placed on operations. In project and jobbing, products are only made to customer order. In batch, decisions to cumulate demand, or make to stock, relate to appropriate volumes for the process investments in place and the actual sales order volumes required.

As explained earlier, the term 'flexibility' is used to describe several different requirements. One concerns the ability of a process to manufacture different levels of volume at required levels of cost. In turn, the latter concerns the relationship between set-up and process time. Thus, where a company experiences reducing order volumes but has already invested in a high-volume process designed to manufacture products at fast output speeds, it will need appropriate investment to ensure that it can keep set-up times sufficiently short to maintain the order quantity (hours) and set-up time (hours) ratio at an acceptable level. Current research work in many manufacturing companies provides numerous illustrations of where annual sales for a product may be similar to those in the past but actual order quantities (or call-offs) have reduced significantly. The link between this section and the previous one is fundamental in terms of process investment.

Technical specification versus business specification

As volumes increase, the justification for investing in processes dedicated to make that product increases. High utilization of plant underpins this investment rationale. Similarly, if processes will not be highly utilized by one product, they need to be chosen so that they can meet the operations and business needs of other products. Therefore, when choosing processes, firms need to distinguish between the technology required to make a product and the way the product is manufactured to meet the needs of their markets. On the one hand, the process technology choice concerns the engineering dimension of providing a process that will form, shape, cut and so forth a product to the size and tolerances required (the technical specification). On the other hand, the operations dimension concerns determining the best way to make a product. This decision needs to be based on volumes and relevant order-winners and qualifiers (the business specification) – see *Exhibit 5.14*. As volumes rise, the appropriate choice will change, as illustrated in *Exhibit 5.4* above.

Specification	Responsible function
Technical specification The fundamental requirements of a product including its physical dimensions	Research and development or engineering
Business specification The order quantities and relevant order-winners and qualifiers of the markets in which it competes	Operations

EXHIBIT 5.14 The constituents of customer orders when choosing processes and the function responsible for their provision

THE MOST
IMPORTANT BUSINESS
DECISIONS ARE
THE PRODUCTS TO SELL,
WHO TO SELL THEM TO
AND **HOW TO**
MAKE THEM

When companies invest in processes, they typically specify the technical requirements. This is recognized as fundamental, and appropriately so. On the other hand, they typically fail to specify the business requirements that the process investment has to meet, a factor crucial to the success of a firm. In the past, operations has failed to develop these critical, strategic arguments and insights, in part because it failed to recognize its role. The consequences for many companies have been serious, leading to premature reinvestment of a considerable size or even the closing down of parts of its business. Evaluating the choice of these investments against the single dimension of the technical specification has led to inappropriate decisions, based on the narrow base of technology. Operations management's failure to realize that it is the custodian of these decisions has indirectly supported this approach.

The choice of process needs to be understood, not in engineering terms (the technical specification), but in terms of operations constraints and other dimensions of the business specification. Understanding how well a process can support the order-winners of a product, the implications of the process for a company's infrastructure and other relevant investments are fundamental to this strategic decision. These issues are dealt with in the following section.

Business implications of process choice

It has already been explained that market characteristics (order-winners and qualifiers) and product volumes are underlying factors in choosing the appropriate process. In addition, the nature of the product is also a factor in the decision regarding project and continuous processing, as shown earlier in *Exhibit 5.11*.

With this in mind, let's now review the procedure to follow when selecting the appropriate manufacturing process:

1   The initial step reviews the technology/engineering alternatives to meet the technical requirements of the product.

2   However, at this juncture, the technology/engineering dimension finishes and the operations/business dimensions starts. Phase 1 of the second step is to assess the market/volume dimension. This then forms the basis for choosing which process is appropriate to best meet the essential needs of the business. Using *Exhibit 5.15* as an example, Phase 1 links volumes to the choice of process, while Phase 2 introduces the corresponding operations and business implications of the many dimensions given in *Exhibit 5.16*, which are represented on the vertical axis. *Exhibit 5.15* shows alternative volumes A1 and B1, the appropriate process choice and their corresponding points on the operations and business implications, dimensions A2 and B2.

3   The final step is an iterative process that assesses the sets of dimensions and any constraints involved when deciding on the appropriate manufacturing process to use.

However, while companies incorporate the technical dimensions, most do not include the operations and business dimensions in such decisions. Engineering proposals currently underpin the major part of process investment decisions, which, in turn, are based on the forecast market volumes that form part of the corporate marketing strategy. The operations and business implications embodied in a proposal are typically given scant recognition. But it is these issues that bind operations and regulate its ability to respond to the needs of markets and customers. Once the investment is made, not only are the processes fixed but also the whole of the operations infrastructure. The result is that this decision dictates the extent to which operations can support the needs of the marketplace – an essential factor in the short- and long-term success of a business.

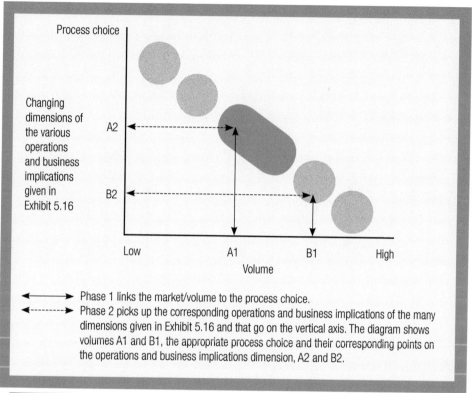

EXHIBIT 5.15 The operations and business dimension phases involved in process choice

When Phase 1 in *Exhibit 5.15* is completed, the choice of process is designated, while it stipulates the position on the vertical dimensions that will accrue as a result. Hence Phase 2 is inextricably tied to Phase 1. For this fundamental reason, decisions in Phase 1 cannot be taken in isolation. The choice has to embrace both Phase 1 and Phase 2. Only in this way will an organization avoid falling into the Cyclopean trap from which it may take years to extricate itself. Only in this way will a business take into account the short- and long-term implications that emanate from the decision to manufacture using one choice of process as opposed to another.

To help explain the business implications of process choice, in *Exhibit 5.16* the perspectives involved have been placed into four categories – products and markets, operations, investment and cost, and infrastructure. Furthermore, the issues for illustration and discussion have been chosen on the basis of their overall business importance. However, there are many other issues equally important to understand, and these have distinct operational rather than strategic overtones.[6]

Typical characteristics of process choice

Aspects	Project	Jobbing	Batch	Line	Continuous processing
Products and markets					
Type of product	Specials/small range of standards	Specials	→	Standard products	Standard products
Product range	Wide	Wide	→	Narrow	Very narrow
Customer order size	Small	Small	→	Large	Very large
Level of product change required	High	High	→	Low and within agreed options	None
Rate of new product introductions	High	High	→	Low	Very low
What does a company sell?	Capability	Capability	→	Standard products/commodities	Standard products/commodities
How are orders won?					
Order-winners	Delivery speed/unique capability	Delivery speed/unique capability/repeat business	→	Price	Price
Qualifiers	Price/on-time delivery/quality conformance	Price/on-time delivery/quality conformance	On-time delivery/quality conformance	On-time delivery/quality conformance	On-time delivery/quality conformance
Operations					
Nature of the process	Oriented towards general purpose	General purpose	→	Dedicated	Highly dedicated
Process flexibility	High	High	→	Low	Inflexible
Operations volumes	Low	Low	→	High	Very high
Dominant utilization	Mixed	Labour	→	Plant	Plant
Changes in capacity	Incremental	Incremental	→	Stepped change	New facility
Key operations task	To meet specification/delivery schedules	Responsive to changes in specification/delivery date requirements and changes	→	Low-cost operations	Low-cost operations

Aspects	Typical characteristics of process choice				
	Project	**Jobbing**	**Batch**	**Line**	**Continuous processing**
Investment and cost					
Level of capital investment	Variable	Low	→	High	Very high
Level of inventory					
Components/raw materials	As required	As required/low	Often medium	Planned with buffer stocks/low	Planned with buffer stocks
Work-in-progress	High[1]	High[1]	Very high	Low	Low
Finished goods	Low	Low	→	High[2]	High[3]
Percentage of total costs					
Direct labour	Low	High	→	Very low	Very low
Direct materials	High	Low	→	Very high	Very high
Site/plant overheads	Low	Low	→	High	High
Infrastructure					
Appropriate organizational					
Control	Decentralized/centralized	Decentralized	→	Centralized	Centralized
Style	Entrepreneurial	Entrepreneurial	→	Bureaucratic	Bureaucratic
Most important operations management perspective	Technical know-how	Technical know-how	→	Business	Technology
Level of specialist support to operations	High	Low	→	High	Very high

NOTES

1 This would depend on stage payment arrangements.

2 However, many businesses here only make against customer schedules or on receipt of a customer order.

3 The finished goods inventory in, for instance, oil refining is stored in the postprocessing stages of distribution and at the point of sale.

EXHIBIT 5.16 Selected business implications of process choice

The critical issue embodied in *Exhibit 5.16* is how each perspective reviewed changes between one choice of process and another. Thus when a company decides to invest in a process, it will also have determined the corresponding point on each dimension within these four categories. It is necessary for companies to understand this and be aware of the trade-offs embodied in that choice.

Exhibit 5.16 contains many generalized statements that are intended to relate the usual requirements of one type of process to the other four. The reason for this approach is to help explain the implications of these choices and examine the consequences that normally will follow. In almost all instances, there is an arrow between jobbing and line. This is intended to indicate that as a process moves from jobbing to low-volume batch to high-volume batch through to line, the particular characteristic will gradually change from one dimension to the other.

Companies selling products typically made using the project process will need to make decisions on how much is made away from the site and transported in. Today, for instance, many parts of a civil engineering structure are made off site by jobbing, batch or line processes, then brought in as required. Similarly, products with the fluid, semifluid or gaseous characteristics necessary to avail themselves of continuous processing may also be made on a batch process basis. Thus, the changing business characteristics displayed in *Exhibit 5.16* illustrate the sets of alternatives embodied in these choices as well.

Finally, *Exhibit 5.16* has been arranged to illustrate the linked relationship between jobbing, batch and line choices as opposed to the more distinct process–product relationship existing in project and continuous processing, described earlier. The section that follows adopts this division.

Selected business implications

This section further explains the implications of the dimensions provided in *Exhibit 5.16*. The four categories of products and markets, operations, investment and cost, and infrastructure are explained under each of the process choice headings, helping to link them. To emphasize the separate natures of project and continuous processing and the linked natures of jobbing, batch and line, the following sections discuss project first, followed by jobbing, batch and line in one general section, and then continuous processing at the end. Despite their link, jobbing, batch and line differ from each other and so each is discussed in a separate subsection. But since batch often links the change in dimensions between jobbing and line, the latter two processes are dealt with first to help to describe batch within this overall perspective.

Project

Products and markets

Companies choosing project processes sell capability. They sell their experience, know-how and skills to provide for a customer's individual needs. Hence they are in a market that will require a high level of product change and new product introductions. Its product range will be wide, with low unit sales volume. It will win orders on aspects such as unique capability or delivery speed, with price normally acting as a qualifier rather than an order-winner. Through the competitive nature of today's markets, criteria such as quality conformance and on-time delivery have typically changed from being order-winners to qualifiers, as signalled by their presence in all types of market.

Operations

Oriented towards general purpose equipment, with specialist plant to meet particular product, design or structural features, project processes are highly flexible in coping with the low product volumes of the market, together with the design changes that will occur during production. Changes in capacity mix, or in total, can be made incrementally, with the key tasks being on-time completion and meeting the specification as laid down by the customer.

Investment and cost

The capital investment in plant and other processes will tend to be low, but there will be some high-cost items that may be purchased or hired, depending on their potential usage, availability, costs and similar factors. Due to the opportunity to schedule materials, the inventory at this stage will be on an as-required basis. Work-in-progress levels will be high but normally much of this will be passed on to customers through stage payment agreements. In a make-to-order situation, finished goods are small, with immediate delivery on completion. The key cost will normally be materials, and sound purchasing arrangements, material usage and work-in-progress control are essential.

Infrastructure

Due to the uncertainties in the process and the need to respond quickly to any customer-derived changes, the organizational control should be decentralized and supported by an entrepreneurial, rather than a bureaucratic, style. In addition, once the business grows, the company must centrally control the key items of plant, internal specialist/engineering skills and other outsourced commodities or skills to ensure they are effectively scheduled by project and between projects. The operations manager must understand the relevant technology to appreciate and respond to unforeseen difficulties and problems, both technical and non-technical, and to use the local and centrally based specialist support effectively.

Jobbing

Products and markets

In essence, a jobbing business sells its capability to manufacture a customer's requirements. It is restricted only by the range of skills of its workforce or by its process capabilities. Thus it handles a wide product range, competing on aspects other than price. This does not mean that a business can charge any price it decides. But if the price is within what is reasonable for the market – and that includes provisions for post-contract changes such as shorter lead times and post-start modifications – then price is a qualifier rather than an order-winner.

Operations

As a consequence of the products it provides and markets it serves, the operations process must be flexible. Its major concern is the utilization of its labour skills, with processes equipment being purchased to facilitate the skilled operator to complete the task. Changes in capacity can be achieved incrementally. The order backlog position that exists in make-to-order markets will allow operations to undertake any foreseen adjustments in capacity ahead of time. The key operations task is to complete the item to specification and on time, since normally this one-off item forms an integral part of some greater business whole, as far as the customer is concerned.

Investment and cost

Although some of the equipment used in jobbing can be very expensive, generally this investment is low compared to batch and line. In addition, material will tend to be purchased only when an order has been received, with material delivery forming part of the total lead time. Work-in-progress inventory will be high, with jobs typically involving long process lead times, while the make-to-order nature of its business means that products are dispatched once completed. There will tend to be few specialist and other support functions, which leads to a relatively lower plant/site overhead cost. These specialist tasks will be largely part of the skilled worker's role, which, together with the high labour content, normally makes this the highest portion of total costs. Material costs will tend to be low; any expensive materials involved will invariably be on a customer-supplied basis.

Infrastructure

Organizational control and style need to be decentralized and entrepreneurial in nature, so as to respond quickly and effectively to meet the inherent response to change requirements of this market. For this reason, operations executives have to understand the technology involved, as this forms an important part of their contribution to business decisions (for example in accepting an order, agreeing estimated costs and resulting prices, confirming a delivery quotation or providing part of the specialist inputs into a business or agreeing customer-derived changes while estimating the additional costs and lead times involved).

Line

Products and markets

A line process reflects the other end of the spectrum to jobbing. The business sells standard products, which, to be successful, are typically sold on price and are associated with large customer orders or many orders for the same products. The level of product change afforded to a customer is usually prescribed within a list of options; outside this, the product is not normally available. Product design and quality conformance are determined at the outset to meet the perceived needs of the customer, with on-time delivery a qualifier in today's markets.

Operations

To provide low operations costs, the process is dedicated to a predetermined range of products. It is not geared to be flexible outside this range, due to the high costs of change. This provides the opportunity to maintain the necessary quality conformance levels throughout the process. Operations volumes need to be high to achieve the level of plant utilization necessary to justify the investment and to underpin the cost structures involved. As explained earlier, it is the cumulative volume of products made within the period that constitutes the volume dimension justifying investments. Output changes are more difficult to arrange, due to the stepped change nature of capacity alterations.

Investment and cost

The key to low operations costs is high process investment, which goes hand in hand with line. The volumes involved allow schedules of raw materials and components to be planned with associated buffer stocks to cover the uncertainty of supply. Work-in-progress inventory will be low. Although finished goods will tend to be high, many businesses, as part of a decision to keep inventory investment as low as possible, will only make standard products against customer schedules or on receipt of an order. Also, products offering many optional extras (such as motor vehicles) will tend to have a policy of only making to a specific order. Hence, even in times of relatively low sales, if the new car selected includes an unusual set of options and consequently is unlikely to have been built in anticipation of an early sale, delivery will be delayed. Finally, the high areas of cost tend to be in materials, bought-out components and site/plant overheads, with direct labour a relatively small part of the total.

Infrastructure

Since the choice of a line process represents a high-volume business, then a more centralized organization, controlled by systems, is more appropriate. On the operations side, the key production executive task concerns the business aspects of the job, with specialist support providing the technical know-how for products and processes.

Batch

Products and markets

Between jobbing and line, comes batch. This is chosen to cover a very wide range of volumes, as illustrated by the elongated shape depicted in *Exhibits 5.4*, *5.12* and *5.15*. Batch links the low-/high-volume, special/standard products and make-to-order/make-to-stock businesses. In most instances, the choice of batch, rather than jobbing, as the appropriate way to manufacture products signals that operations volumes (that is, quantity × work content) have increased and are of a repeat nature but insufficient to dedicate processes solely to them, as would be the case in line. Some unique high-volume orders may also be done on a batch basis.

At the low-volume end of batch, the processes are able to cope with a high degree of product change and a high level of new product introductions. Here, the business is oriented towards selling capability, with price starting to become a more important order-winner, due to the volume and repeat nature of the products. At the high-volume end of batch, products have become increasingly standard, order sizes larger and product change lower, all of which illustrate the shift in product market characteristics towards line. As mentioned earlier, market pressures typically have changed quality conformance and on-time delivery from order-winners to qualifiers.

Operations

It can be deduced from the product market features that batch processes usually have to cope with a wide range of products and operations volumes. To handle this task, these processes must be of a general nature, offering a high degree of flexibility. With some items of equipment, the utilization will be low; with others, equipment will have been purchased to meet the needs of a product or to offer distinct process advantages (for example numerical control machines, machining centres and flexible manufacturing systems, each of which will be described in a later section). In these cases, high investment will be justified normally on a usage basis and the aim will be to utilize the capacity to the fullest.

To help underpin the total process investment, many companies adopt a deliberate policy of increasing the utilization of equipment in three ways:

1   Putting a wide range of products through the same set of processes.

2   Manufacturing many of the same products in a single order quantity or batch quantity (hence the name). In this way, the number of set-ups is reduced, which decreases the setting costs and increases effective capacity and saleable productive time.

3   Making products wait for processes to become available. This policy, together with the order quantity decisions above, leads to a work-in-progress inventory investment that, in relation to the size of the business, tends to be very high compared to jobbing and, particularly, line.

Investment and cost

To be competitive in markets moving towards the high-volume end, a business will increasingly invest in its batch processes to achieve the low operations cost requirement of these markets. Many companies exploit this still further by putting more products through the same processes, thus increasing overall utilization. However, the major trade-off associated with this policy is the very high investment in work-in-progress inventory. The raw materials, components and finished goods inventory levels will in turn be associated with the make-to-order or make-to-stock decision adopted by the business. As with all companies in these mid-volume markets, the nearer it is to a make-to-order situation, the more the characteristics of that market will prevail and vice versa. The make-up of total costs is no exception.

Infrastructure

As a business moves away from the low-volume end of the continuum, centralized controls and a bureaucratic style become more appropriate. The increasing complexity of this growth will change the nature of the specialist functions, with design and production engineering becoming an ever-important support to operations. The operations manager's role will be bound up with appreciating and recognizing the critical business issues involved, providing coordination throughout and spearheading the development of manufacturing systems.

At the low-volume end of batch, in many situations the characteristics, although not the same, will be more akin to those in jobbing. It is important, therefore, to recognize the extent and trends in these changes and make the necessary adjustments.

Continuous processing

Products and markets

At the other end of the volume spectrum, companies that choose continuous processing will sell a narrow range of standard products in markets where product change and the rate of product introductions are low. The company will sell standard products rather than capability and large customer orders will be won principally on price.

Operations

In a price-sensitive market, the key operations task will be low-cost production. To help keep costs low, processes will be highly dedicated, with the cost structure based on high operations volumes, leading to a need to achieve high plant utilization. The fixed nature of capacity also creates restrictions when increases or decreases in output are required, with the decision based on whether or not to build a new facility on the one hand or how often to run the plant (known as 'campaigning') on the other.

Investment and cost

The high plant investment and high-volume output associated with continuous processing offer the opportunity to keep raw material inventory on a planned usage basis, with built-in buffer stocks to cover uncertainties. Work-in-progress will be relatively low, with inventory in finished goods high, as a way of maintaining output levels at all times against fluctuating sales patterns. In many cases, however, finished goods are held in the extensive distribution system of a business and sometimes at its own retail outlets (for example petrol stations).

Owing to the high process investment, direct labour costs are small, with the highest cost usually in materials. Site/plant overheads in this process will be sizable owing to the need to support the process and handle the high output levels involved.

Infrastructure

The high-volume nature of these businesses lends itself to a centralized, bureaucratic organization control and style. Operations performance is measured against budgets, variance analysis is the order of the day and investment proposals are centrally monitored. An understanding of the process and product technology is important when running a production unit, together with the ability to coordinate the high level of specialist support provided for operations.

An overview of process choice

To help clarify the issues involved in process choice, an overview of how these alternatives link to one another is now provided. The first important fact to stress is that each of the choices embodies a totally different approach to manufacturing a product. Although described in some detail in the chapter, a short explanation of these differences will serve to reinforce this important point:

- **Project** – this is used for one-off products that have to be built on site because it is difficult or impossible to move them once they have been made. Consequently, the resources involved need to be brought to the site and released for reuse elsewhere when they are no longer needed.

- **Jobbing** – for one-off products that can be moved once completed, jobbing is normally the preferred process. The responsibility for making the product is typically given to a skilled person (or group of skilled people), who decides how best to make it and then completes all or most of the operations involved, including checking quality conformance at each stage.

- **Batch** – with an increase in volumes and the repeat nature of products, companies select batch as the effective way to meet the requirements involved. Because the products are repeated, with a corresponding increase in volumes, companies can now invest at each of the operations steps. This includes engineering time to decide how best to make a product, jigs and fixtures to facilitate the completion of certain operations and equipment purchased with an eye to making these and other products with similar characteristics. However, the volumes involved do not warrant the purchase of dedicated equipment. The operations necessary to complete a product are, therefore, not linked and are said to be 'decoupled'.

- **Line** – when demand is sufficient to justify dedicating equipment solely to making a specified range of products, a line process is normally chosen. The operations necessary to complete a specified range of products are linked together so that each product goes from one operation directly to the next and so on. The operations necessary to complete a product in this instance are said to be 'coupled'. The operators involved will physically take part in assembling the products.

- **Continuous processing** – when the demand for a product is such that the volume required necessitates a process being used all day and every day, further investment is justified. Restricted to the products whose characteristics enable them to be moved between processes, the equipment in this instance is designed to automatically transfer the product from one stage to the next, check the quality conformance within the process and make adjustments where necessary. The investment associated with this is warranted by the volumes involved.

To emphasize these distinctions, *Exhibit 5.17* shows the gap between the five choices. It also makes the point that whereas there will sometimes be a transition from jobbing to low-volume batch, from low-volume to high-volume batch, from high-volume batch to line or from high-volume batch to continuous processing, the same will not apply between project and jobbing or from line to continuous processing. Similarly, when volumes reduce towards the end of a product's life cycle, the reverse movement may take place, but again it would only go as illustrated in *Exhibit 5.17*.

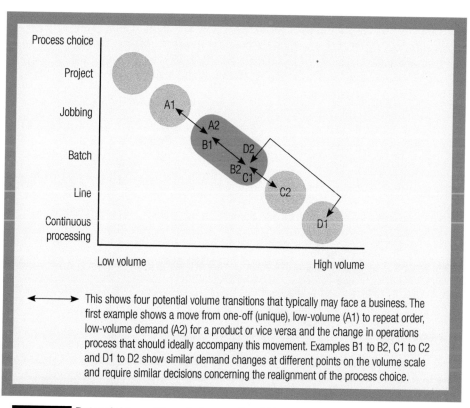

EXHIBIT 5.17 Potential transitions between the different choices of process

Some comments on *Exhibit 5.17* may help to clarify. Transition refers to the fact that, as volumes increase or decrease, a business should ideally change its choice of operations to realign its process to the new levels of volume. The degree of transition is limited, as many companies find themselves unable, or unwilling, to commit the fresh investment necessary to complete this realignment.[7] Thus, a motor vehicle manufacturer will use a jobbing process at the prototyping stage of product development but will invest just once to meet the commercial volumes of mainstream production. In the same way, a manufacturer of products that lend themselves to being produced using continuous processing (for example fluids and gases), but with insufficient volumes to justify the high investment associated with this choice, will handle these requirements by using a high-volume batch process. Similarly, when demand falls for products currently made by continuous processing, the system will be managed on a high-volume batch basis by, say, running the process for three months, stopping it for three months, running it for three months and so on. This is known as 'campaigning' and is illustrated by the D1 to D2 movement in *Exhibit 5.17*.

Hybrid processes

As mentioned earlier, many companies have developed hybrid processes to enable them to better support the characteristics of their markets. Some comprise a mix of two of the five generic processes, while others are developments within an existing process type, often based on the use of numerical control (NC) machines. Some of the more important hybrid developments are now explained, and to help position these in relation to the generic processes, they are included together in *Exhibit 5.18*. However, the list includes some (for example machining centres) that have been generally applied and are provided as standard items[8] from a supplier's catalogue.

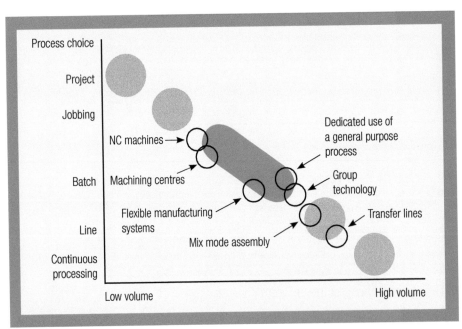

EXHIBIT 5.18 The position of some hybrid processes in relation to the five generic choices of process

As with all hybrids, there is a root stock. Thus, although each hybrid format will comprise a mix of two process types, it will still be classified as belonging to one or the other. This phenomenon is highlighted by the headings of 'batch-related' and 'line-related' in the sections that follow. These hybrids have batch and line roots, respectively. What happens is that they alter some of the trade-offs described in *Exhibit 5.16*. Some will improve and some will worsen. What a company seeks is an overall set of trade-offs that are better for the business as a whole than those provided by the current process(es) provision.

Batch-related hybrids

Numerical control (NC) machines

An NC system[9] is a process that automatically performs the required operations according to a detailed set of coded instructions. Since mathematical information is the base used, the system is called 'numerical control'. The first applications were to metal cutting processes such as milling, boring, turning, grinding and sawing, but in recent years the range of NC applications includes tube bending, shearing and different forms of cutting. The operation of machine tools is from numerical data stored on paper or magnetic tapes, tabulating cards, computer storage or direct information. Compared with conventional equipment, NC machines offer increased accuracy, consistency and flexibility to meet specification changes, even with the need to meet very complex manufacturing requirements. Thus design changes and modifications require only a change in instruction, nothing more.

In reality, an NC machine is a development of a batch process; it is also low volume in nature. It is batch because the machine stops at the end of one process and is reset for a new job or stopped while a new program is being loaded. It is low volume in nature because the set-up times are short, hence providing an acceptable ratio between set-up times and the length of the run before the next set-up. The position of NC machines on *Exhibit 5.18* illustrates this.

However, the trade-off against conventional plant and equipment is the increased investment associated with NC processes. In addition, the introduction of the new technology and associated changes can create problems for operators, setters and supervisors in terms of their roles, the level of specialist support and changing skill requirements.

Machining centres

Machining centres combine NC operations previously provided by different machines into one machine centre. With tool changing automatically controlled by coded instructions and carousels holding up to 200 or more tools, the underlying rationale for this development is to maximize the combination of operations completed at a single location.

A machining centre typically embraces several metal cutting facilities (for example milling, boring and drilling) that are applied to a given piece of work in a predetermined sequence reflected in the NC program. The relevant range of tools is stored in a magazine. The appropriate tool is then selected and the particular operation completed. The hybrid nature of this process is that several operations are completed before the item of work is removed. Thus a machining centre completes many operations in sequence, without removing the item from the process. This reflects aspects of line within what is, in reality, still a batch process. (That is, the process stops and resets itself not only between operations but between one item and the next.)

In this way, a machining centre changes the pattern of work-in-progress inventory associated with the generic process that could be adopted as an alternative, namely batch. Just as in line, a part now goes through a number of operations in sequence and thus changes the process design from functional to product layout. However, in most companies, the pre- and postmachining operations are performed on another process choice (for example batch). This use of a combination of processes would change the relevant point on the dimensions shown in *Exhibit 5.18*. Machining centres, like all NC-based processes, increase volume flexibility (for example reduced set-ups and the resulting ability to meet, say, the low-volume requirements of products) in relation to an alternative non-NC process, due to the nature and level of the capital investment involved. This is reflected in *Exhibit 5.18*.

Thus, machining centres are a hybrid between batch and line; as a consequence, the position on some trade-offs (see *Exhibit 5.16*) changes. For instance, work-in-progress inventory within the machining centre will decrease compared to completing the same operations at individual and unconnected work stations. Similarly, the relative level of investment will increase. As you will note, both these changes are more towards a line process, but the root process is still batch.

Flexible manufacturing systems

Whereas a machining centre is best suited to low volumes, a flexible manufacturing system (FMS) is appropriate to mid-volume requirements – see *Exhibit 5.18*. This too is designed to complete a given number of operations on an item before it leaves the system. However, rather than the item being contained in a single centre, in an FMS, the workpiece is automatically transferred from one process to the next. Besides volume differences, the physical dimensions of the items to be machined are typically much larger than those completed by machining centres.

Flexible manufacturing systems are a combination of standard and special NC machines, automated materials handling, and computer control in the form of direct numerical control (DNC)[10] for the purposes of extending the benefits of NC to mid-volume manufacturing situations.[11] Whereas NC equipment and particularly machining centres accommodate relatively low-volume demand, much less attention has been given to improving manufacturing's approach to mid-volume, mid-variety products, although this accounts for a large part of the products that would fall into the batch range of volumes.

FMSs are designed around families of parts. The increased volumes associated with bringing together the individual requirements of a range of products and treating these as one volume justify the investment. This, combined with the inherent flexibility of the NC equipment, creates the rationale for using FMSs in the mid-volume segment of demand. Classic families of products are:

1   **By assembly** – grouping parts together that would be required to make a single assembly (such as an engine). The system would be designed to allow the user to order against an assembly requirement, rather than scheduling order quantities for each part through an appropriate series of functionally laid-out processes.

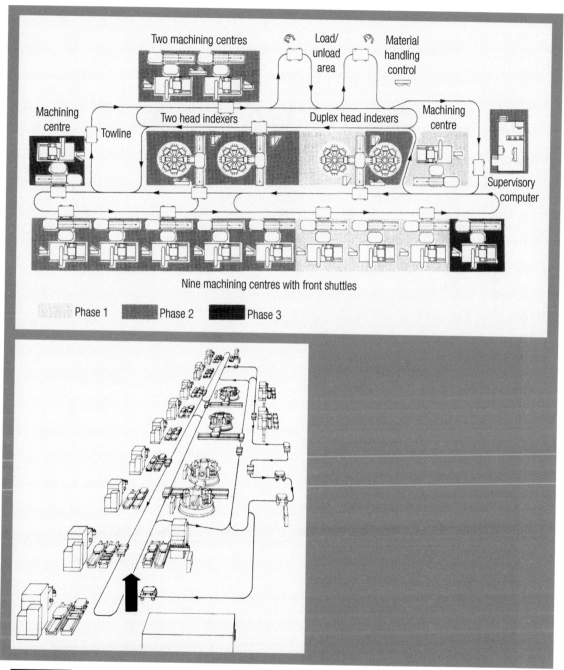

EXHIBIT 5.19 An example of a 15-station random FMS provided as a three-stage installation

SOURCE: Kearney & Trecker Corp. (1980) *KT's World of Advanced Manufacturing Technologies*, 2nd edn, Milwaukee, WI

2 **By type** – categorizing parts by type for a range of similar products. This would relieve higher volume production processes of the low-to-mid-volume components and thus reduce the number of changeovers involved. This aggregate family demand justifies the capital

investment, with the inherent flexibility within the FMS allowing a relatively wide range of products to be considered and facilitating the balancing and rebalancing of the workload as product mix and volumes change.

3   **By size and similar operations** – here the specification of the FMS reflects the physical size of the parts and the particular operations that need to be completed. Again, the flexibility within the system extends the range of work with which it can cope and allows high utilization owing to its ability to handle product mix and volume changes.

A typical series of events in processing a part in FMS (see *Exhibit 5.19*) is as follows:

* A DNC system directs a cart carrying an empty fixture to a load station and also advises the loader which part is to be loaded.

* On completion, the loader signals that it is ready; the computer directs the part to the first operation, selecting, if available, the lowest backlog potential.

* The part is automatically unloaded, the appropriate NC program selected, and the work completed.

* This procedure will be followed until the part is finished, goes to the unloading area and out of the system.

The hybrid nature of FMS is based on logic similar to machining centres in that it maximizes the combination of operations completed at a single location. The additional capital investment will bring with it both lower cost and lower work-in-progress inventory advantages, trade-offs more akin to line. However, the root process is still batch.

Cells

The first set of hybrids used NC equipment as the basis of process change. However, alternative hybrids can be adopted that use conventional or non-NC equipment. These are described here, the first of which is a batch-line hybrid known as 'cellular manufacture', or 'cells'.

A cell is a hybrid process. Although still batch in origin (the processes will have to be stopped and reset to handle a product change), they are in fact a mix of batch and line processes, offering changes on some key variables (see *Exhibit 5.16*). These include reduced lead times and lower work-in-progress inventory on the one hand and less flexible processes (it is more difficult to reuse any capacity that would become available if future demand were to reduce) and lower overall utilization of processes on the other.

Exhibit 5.20 shows the process or functional layout of the batch process (similar processes are grouped together in the same geographical area). The rationale underpinning cells is that grouping products together and treating them as being the same leads to an increase in volume (the volumes of all the products under consideration are added together and the aggregate is viewed as a whole) and hence justifies the allocation of processes to these products for their sole use. What happens, therefore, in cells is that the necessary processes, both in terms of capability and capacity, are allocated to the sole use of these products, with the 'dedication' being justified by the enhanced level of volume that results.

Type of process	Layout format	Type of layout
Batch	■ ■ ▲▲▲▲ ● ●● ● ■ ■ ■ ■ ■ ▲▲▲▲ ●●● ●●● ■ ■ ■ ■ ▲▲▲▲ ●●●● ●●●● ■ ■ ■ ■ ▲▲▲▲ ●●●● ●●●● ■ ■ Lathe　　Milling　　Drilling　　Grinding shop　　section　　section　　section All products take their own operation sequence through the different sets of capacities	Process or function
Cells	● ●●●● ■ ■ ● ●●● ●●●●●●● ■ ■ ▲ ●●● ■ ■ ■ ■ ▲ ▲ ■ ▲ ▲ ▲ ■ Group 1　　Group 2　　Group 3　　Group 4 All operations to make each product within the family are completed within a group of processes	Cellular
Line	►■—■—■—■—■—■—■► Series of work stations in operational sequence to complete a given range of products	Product

EXHIBIT 5.20 Cellular layout and the transition from a functional (batch) to product (line) layout

The approach involves separating out those processes that do not lend themselves to the application of cells because of factors such as the level of investment (where processes, in addition to those already available, would have to be purchased) and health considerations (for example noise or process waste/fumes). The next step is to group together families of like products. The criteria for this selection are similar to those outlined for FMS. However, note that the process flexibility inherent in cells is not of the same order as in FMS.

The third step is to determine the process configuration necessary to manufacture each product family involved and to lay out the cell to reflect the required manufacturing routings. The final stage is to complete a tooling analysis within each family, with a twofold aim. The first is to group together those parts within the family that can use the same tooling. This forms the basis for scheduling to reduce setting time. The second is to include this feature as part of the design prerequisites for future products.[12]

Cellular manufacture (cells) has its origin in group technology. The generic term 'cells' is now used to cover a range of alternative approaches that change the basis of process configuration from one based on process or function to a regrouping based on product.

Nagare production system

The Nagare production system was developed within the disc brake division of Sumitomo Electric. The layout is a derivation of cells and, in the same way, provides an alternative to the process layout used in batch, as illustrated in *Exhibit 5.21*. The key differences between this system and cells are:

- The sequence of steps reflects the flow of materials in making the product.

- Operators move the part from step to step and hence complete a whole product.

- Operators typically produce to a JIT system using a kanban-type arrangement (this and JIT systems are explained fully in Chapter 10).

- The quantity of products produced at any one time is relatively small.

- The Nagare production system is ideally suited to making products that are similar to one another. This helps keep the level of change involved low and hence set-up times are reduced.

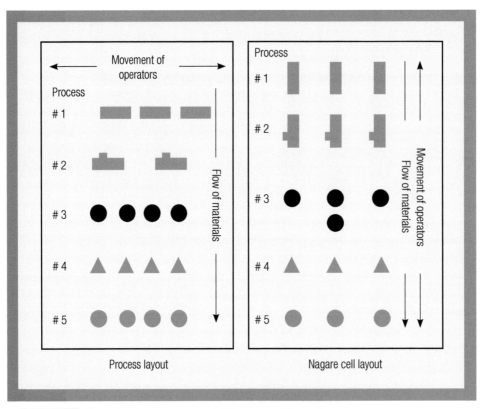

EXHIBIT 5.21 Changing from process to Nagare cell layout

SOURCE: Hill, T. (2005) *Operations Management*, 2nd edn, Basingstoke, Palgrave Macmillan

Linked batch

As with most of the developments discussed in this section, linked batch is a hybrid of batch and line. However, linked batch does not need to encompass a large number of processes, which is more typical in the examples given earlier. In some instances, only two or three sequential processes may be linked; in others, for example food packing, the whole of the filling and packing processes may be linked. Whereas in the other illustrations the investment decisions are typically made as part of a complete process review, linked batch is undertaken on a more piecemeal basis, as only two or three processes may be linked. The sequential processes, although physically laid out in line (that is, one operation follows another), are run as a batch process (that is, when a product change is required, all the linked operations have to be stopped and reset to accommodate this change). Irrespective of the length of the set-up changes, the fact that the process has to be stopped and reset makes it a batch process.

Dedicated use of general purpose equipment

Where the volume of a specific part is sufficient, operations can justify the allocation of a process to its sole use. This dedication is not in the plant itself but in the use of a general purpose process. Thus, the potential flexibility and other characteristics illustrated in *Exhibit 5.16* of a general purpose process are retained and they will be reclaimed when volumes reduce. Characteristically, the process is not altered. Hence the process is still batch and, therefore, general purpose in nature.

Thus the hybrid stems from a change in use to reflect the high-volume demand for a product and not a physical change to the process itself. It remains a batch process, even though during the period in which its use is dedicated to the manufacture of a given product, it may (for example for colour changes) or may not be reset.

Line-related hybrids

Just as the last section discussed developments and hybrids rooted in batch processes, this section reviews hybrids related to line.

Mix mode assembly lines

A line process can cope with a broad range of products without stopping, and, in reality, companies determine the product range to be handled when they make the process investment. However, the term 'mix mode' has been used to reflect processes in which companies have made systematic and purposeful investments to increase the product range involved. Typically this entails programming the line to make small quantities of different products in a predetermined sequence.

The origins of mix mode assembly lines are twofold. On the one hand, a reduction in demand for existing products releases capacity, which a company may wish to reuse. This, in turn, can lead to the adaptation of an existing line process to accommodate other products. On the other hand, a mix mode assembly line may be developed to handle a number of products currently completed in other ways (for example using linked-batch processes).

What makes the root here a line process is that it does not have to be stopped and reset to accommodate the next product.

Mix mode assembly lines are designed to cope with a range of products in any scheduled combination. This is achieved by the use of computer-controlled flow lines that schedule work according to overall operations requirements and the short-term workloads at the various stations. The increased range of products that can be accommodated increases volumes and justifies the investment necessary to provide this dimension of flexibility. In this way, a mix mode assembly line is an alternative process to using batch processes to meet the required level of volume of the products in question.

As can be deduced from this explanation, a mix mode assembly line is not technically a hybrid, in that the characteristics of another process have not been combined with those of line. Instead, it is a line process that can accommodate the requirements of a wider range of products than can typically be made on a classic line process. It has been included here to illustrate how process investment can change certain relevant trade-offs in a business.

Transfer lines

The last hybrid process to be discussed is transfer lines. Where the volume demand for products is very high, further investment is justified. Transfer line is a hybrid between line and continuous processing. However, its root process is still line because it can be stopped without major cost. The position of transfer lines on *Exhibit 5.18* illustrates the features of this process. High volumes justify investment designed to reduce the manual inputs associated with a line process and to move more towards a process that automatically transfers a part from one station to the next, positions it, completes the task and checks for quality conformance. Furthermore, deviations from the specified tolerances will be registered and automatic tooling adjustments and replacements will often be part of the procedure. To achieve this, the process is numerically controlled in part or in full, which provides the systems control afforded, in part at least, by the operator in the line process.

Review of the use of numerical control (NC) in hybrid processes

Whereas linked batch, cells and the dedicated use of a general purpose process are derived from alternative uses of conventional, non-NC processes, the other four hybrid processes are based on the concept of numerical control in one form or another.[13]

The last section explained, and *Exhibit 5.18* illustrated, that the basis for the choice between one NC hybrid process and another is volume. As with the choices between the five generic processes outlined in *Exhibit 5.16*, the implications for these choices have to be understood and taken into account at the time of their selection (see *Exhibit 5.22*). The NC base of these processes brings with it a level of flexibility that is far greater than that inherent with non-NC alternatives. This means that the process is more able to cope with a wider range of products and to handle product mix changes over time. However, dedication in these alternatives starts to be introduced when processes are brought together to meet the needs of a given range/family of products. In order to reuse these thereafter, further and often substantial investment will have to be made to relocate, adapt or change existing processes and their configuration to meet the needs of other products. This change is illustrated by the gap between machining centres and FMS. As the choice moves to the other end of the spectrum, the implications of dedication will begin to take hold.

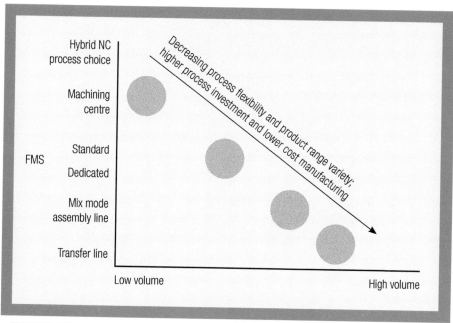

EXHIBIT 5.22 Hybrid NC process choice related to volume

Exhibit 5.22 illustrates the rationalized use of NC-based processes as they relate to volume. As with the generic processes described earlier, while volume is the basis for choice, two other equally important dimensions must form part of this decision. The first is the change in volume expected over time. The second is the host of implications to the business that must be understood and taken into account when arriving at this decision. Some of these are shown in *Exhibit 5.22*, but *Exhibit 5.16* earlier provided a more complete list.[14]

Operations responses to similar markets

Different approaches are used in the same industry. Companies making similar products may choose similar processes yet manage the total operations task in significantly different ways. But, process choice, as shown in *Exhibit 2.10*, is only part of operations' strategic response. For example, providing support for the criterion of delivery speed necessitates reducing lead times throughout the supply chain and not just in the process elements of lead time (see *Exhibit 5.23*).

As explained earlier, Japanese car makers typically schedule their plants in accordance with sales forecasts and work on make-to-stock rather than on order backlog, make-to-order principles. Furthermore, given little order backlog, these companies are now offering to make and deliver a car to a customer's specifications in a much shorter time.

Steps in the internal phase of the supply chain	Typical activities to reduce lead times
Customer order processing	Shorten administrative procedures
Material lead times	Purchasing-based negotiations to reduce lead times including consignment inventory arrangements
Order backlog/forward load	Adjusting short-term capacity to reduce the length of the order backlog or forward load
Process	Decreasing lead time through a combination of: • reducing set-ups • shortening process times • holding inventory to move increasingly towards an assemble-to-order and make-to-stock position
Postprocess tasks	Reducing the overall time it takes to complete: • testing • packaging • despatch arrangements/documentation • delivery

EXHIBIT 5.23 Elements of operations lead time and typical actions to reduce the length of time involved

As stressed throughout, coherence between the many elements involved results in an integrated strategy. By raising the car specification, a company keeps options low and thereby reduces customer choice. This in turn leads to fewer schedule adjustments. In many instances, the automobile specified may be already planned or even in stock. Similarly, reducing lead times in all parts of the process is a significant factor (see *Exhibit 5.23*) in helping to achieve this difference.[15] Thus, recognizing the order-winners and qualifiers in relevant markets becomes the focus of activity and facilitates coherent functional support for key criteria.

Technology strategy

Advances in computer control have brought fresh opportunities for the US and other Western manufacturers. The potential for innovation in operations is greater now than it has ever been. Advanced manufacturing technologies (AMT) have provided a viable option to sourcing manufactured components and products from other parts of the world. There is no doubt about the potential, and applications such as robotics and computer-aided design (CAD) are growing at up to 30 per cent per year.[16]

The approach to the use of technology and ensuring the suitability of its application create the most concern. Tripping over engineering white elephants in the past should make companies understandably wary, not of technology improvements themselves, but of approaches that lead to sizable investments in inappropriate technologies. However, the preoccupation with the search for panaceas may well lead companies to duplicate yesterday's mistakes. Indeed, the case for a technology strategy in itself should sound warning bells. For the most part, articles advocating a technology strategy provide descriptions of the technologies and illustrations of specific applications and resulting improvements.

But they fail to explain how to select those technological investments that best support a business. Without this conceptual base, companies are unable to make assessments and draw distinctions. As a result, they have to fall back on hunches, or support the judgement of specialists, who are devotees of technological innovation and advantage, rather than business-oriented executives trying to ensure fit with the market and viewing process investment in a supportive role.

To some extent, the emerging call for companies to develop technology strategies has its roots in recent process innovations and computer applications in operations. Historically, the clear link between operations and the marketplace, which developed in the postwar growth years, led to a well-understood operations strategy that was appropriately reflected in the activities and developments within the engineering functions. Not only was the status of engineering clearly reinforced but it also evolved that engineers were perceived to be the custodians of determining appropriate process and relevant elements of infrastructure investments.

This postwar role also led to, or reinforced, the low status of operations management, with the attendant difficulties discussed in Chapter 2. These role characteristics in operations were established in relations with other specialist functions, with similar consequences, some of which are discussed in later chapters on process positioning, infrastructure and accounting.

Flexibility: a strategic cop-out?

For many businesses, past investments in dedicated processes have proved inappropriate for current markets. New investment requirements have been brought about, in part, by pressures of competition. But the response has often been to purchase new equipment with sufficient flexibility for a wide range of products and to cope with low order quantity requirements. However, decisions that are not based on assessments of the marketplace and evaluations of alternatives are tantamount to strategic cop-outs. 'If in doubt, resolve the doubt' has become 'if in doubt, buy flexibility'.

One company, after witnessing an overall decline in volumes throughout the parent group, committed itself to the purchase of flexible processes to cope with an environment of change. An analysis of processes, product life cycles and order-winners clearly showed that the purchase, in part, of dedicated plant would best meet these requirements. This eliminated a $0.25m investment on unnecessary flexibility. As another illustration, three companies, each manufacturing in different segments of engineering, were using expensive NC machines primarily on high-volume products. Discussions revealed failures in the companies to separate comparisons of process capability of holding tight tolerances (current technology versus 15–20-year-old machining) and the business needs of the process (low cost based on high volumes).

Technology push versus pull strategies

Process investments can be used for either technology push or pull strategies. In a push strategy, the rationale for process investments comes from technology-based arguments; pull strategies reflect technology investments based on defined market needs. It is critical that companies with push strategies see arguments concerning the corporate potential to sell the spin-offs from the proposed technology investments as being only part of the evaluation. They must also be sure to evaluate such investments on their own merits.

Operations strategy and technological opportunities

Current process innovations present an important opportunity for companies to compete effectively in world markets. However, committing scarce resources to investments based primarily on the perspectives of specialists or in search of a panacea to update and realign operations presents enormous and unnecessary risks. It is essential that technology alternatives form part of operations strategy developments, as discussed in this and the previous chapter. A business must link investments with a well-argued understanding of its markets if it is to avoid inappropriate major capital expenditure.

Reflections

Assessing the level of mismatch between its current processes and current business, determining the adjustment it must or is able to achieve and making the appropriate choice of process for future products are difficult and critical operations management tasks – difficult, in that the decision is complex, and critical, in that the process investment will be substantial and changes will be expensive and time-consuming to implement.[17]

The nature of markets and operations

One of the core problems facing companies is that markets are inherently dynamic and operations is inherently fixed. Markets are continually changing in response to internal initiatives and external pressures, while operations remains fixed in terms of the trade-offs embodied in its investments at a given point in time. Thus, whereas market change is an inherent outcome of time, operations will not change unless a conscious decision is made and additional investment is committed. A company that fails to regularly undertake these reviews and then commit to the outcomes will have an operations function less able to support its chosen markets.

Operations' strategic response

Companies have always recognized the need to embrace the engineering/technology dimension when choosing their operations processes. But this is only part of the decision. The engineering input concerns providing alternative technical options that will enable the product to be manufactured. However, the choice of process concerns how the operations task is then completed to meet the needs of the markets served. Such choices need to involve the product/market, operations, investment/cost and infrastructure dimensions that have been examined in this chapter.

Engineering prescriptions, technology solutions seeking problems or the belief that panaceas are on hand have been instrumental, in part, for the uncompetitive position in which many manufacturing companies currently find themselves. Couple this with a marketing-led strategy in some businesses that have overreached themselves or the more universal impact of incremental marketing changes that, over time, have altered the business without companies recognizing the strategic consequences involved and the result has been the erosion of large, traditional markets by overseas competitors. Other companies, persuaded by the apparent desirability of new markets or the short-term solution to get out of tough manufacturing industries, have also left the way clear in these high-volume, established markets. However, there is no long-term future in easy operations tasks. The short run may appear attractive but learning and relearning how to be competitive is essential to the long-term wellbeing of companies and nations.

Successful manufacturing nations have been systematically picking off many of the existing markets of long-established industrial nations by a combined marketing/operations strategy, thus creating, at the expense of its competitors, a sound industrial base essential to a nation's long-term prosperity and growth. The Japanese have, in fact, built their manufacturing base on traditional smokestack industries. And, more recently, the emerging nations of China, India and Taiwan are now doing the same.

Discussion questions

1 What steps should a business take in choosing the appropriate way to manufacture its products?

2 What is the difference between a technical and business specification? How do they combine to form the total decisions facing a company?

3 What are the five generic types of process? Define each and explain the key differences.

4 What comprises volume?

5 Project and continuous processing are specific to certain product types. Explain.

6 What are the several dimensions of flexibility? Illustrate your answers.

7 Why does the batch process best meet the requirements of most companies?

8 Select three product/market business implications and discuss how and why they differ across the generic processes.

9 Select three operations business implications and discuss how and why they differ across the generic processes.

10 Select three investment and cost business implications and discuss how and why they differ across the generic processes.

11 Select three infrastructure business implications and discuss how and why they differ across the generic processes.

12 What is a hybrid process? Select two and explain how they work and when they could be appropriate.

Notes and references

1. One of the reasons for operations' reactive role in corporate strategy was discussed in Chapter 2.

2. This issue is specifically addressed by Hill, T.J., Menda, R. and Dilts, D.M. (1998) 'Using product profiling to illustrate manufacturing/marketing misalignment', *Interfaces*, 28(4): 42–63.

3. Also sometimes called unit or one-off.

4. Companies do manufacture order quantities of one on a batch basis. In this instance, what underlies their process decision is the repeat nature of a product, not the size of an order quantity.

5. Whereas this is typically the case in Western motor vehicle plants, Japanese car makers typically schedule their manufacturing plants on the bases of sales forecasts and make-to-stock rather than order backlog, make-to-order principles.

6. Many of these additional issues are illustrated and discussed in Hill, T. (2005) *Operations Management*, 2nd edn, Basingstoke: Palgrave Macmillan, Ch. 6.

7. A point examined in detail in Hill et al.'s *Interfaces* article, note 2.

8. In reality, some customization may be offered but the substance of this equipment is standard.

9. NC systems use computer-based numerical control (CNC), which replaced the hard-wired control unit of the NC system with a stored program using a dedicated minicomputer. The memory storage makes the process more reliable and more flexible in program changes. Direct numerical control (DNC) systems consist of a number of NC and/or CNC machines connected to a centralized computer. The centralized sources of information provided by DNC help in the control of manufacturing. Flexible manufacturing systems (FMS) combine the DNC principle together with the other features described in a later section.

10. See note 9.

11. Haas, P.R. (1973) 'Flexible manufacturing systems: a solution for the mid-volume, mid-variety parts manufacture', 2SME Technical Conference, Detroit, April; Hughes, J.J. et al. (1975) 'Flexible manufacturing systems for improved mid-volume productivity', Proceedings of the Third Annual AIEE Systems Engineering Conference, November.

12. A fuller explanation is given in Hill, T. (2005) *Operations Management*, 2nd edn, Basingstoke: Palgrave Macmillan, Ch. 6. Also refer to Edwards, G.A.B. (1971) *Readings in Group Technology*, Machinery Publishing Company; and Burbidge, J.L. (1975) *The Introduction of Group Technology*, Portsmouth, NH: Heinemann.

13. NC refers to the operation of machine tools from numerical data stored on paper or magnetic tape, punched cards, computer storage or direct information. The development of machining centres results from the concepts of NC. In a machining centre, a range of operations is provided using a carousel with up to 200 tools or more (that is, embodied in the centre) from which the program will select as required, with some taking place simultaneously as necessary. Consequently, a machining centre is not only able to cope with a wide range of product requirements, it can also be scheduled to complete one-offs in any sequence desired. More advanced NC systems include computer numerical control (CNC) systems using a dedicated minicomputer to perform NC functions and direct numerical control (DNC), which refers to a system having a computer controlling more than one machine tool. A DNC system includes both the hardware and software required to drive more than one NC machine simultaneously. To do this, DNC uses a computer, which may be a minicomputer, several minicomputers linked together, a minicomputer linked to a large computer, or a large computer on its own.

14. See note 6.

15. The lead time taken by typical US car makers from receipt of a dealer's order to the start of the manufacturing process is three times longer than the time taken by Toyota.

16 Small, H. (2007) 'Planning, justifying and installing advanced manufacturing technology: a managerial framework', *Journal of Manufacturing Technology*, **18**(5): 513–37.

17 This issue is further highlighted in the pharmaceutical industry where the gamble on plant investment not only concerns the potential level of demand but also whether a drug will be accepted by the relevant drug authorities and which formulae will eventually be best received in the market.

Exploring further

Blois, K.J. (1980) 'Market concentration: challenge to corporate planning', *Long Range Planning*, **13**: 56–62.

Bolwijn, P.T., Boorsma, J., van Breukelen, Q.H. et al. (1986) *Flexible Manufacturing: Integrating Technical and Social Innovations*, Amsterdam: Elsevier.

Burbridge, J.L. (1980) 'The simplification of material flow systems', *International Journal of Production Research*, **20**: 339–47.

Chakravorty, S.S. and Hales, D.N. (2004) 'Implications of cell design implementation: a case study and analysis', *European Journal of Operations Research*, **152**: 602–614.

Fraser, K., Harris, H. and Luong, L. (2007) 'Improving the implementation effectiveness of cellular manufacturing: a comprehensive framework for practitioners', *International Journal of Production Research*, **45**(24): 5835–56.

Hyer, N.L. and Wemmerlöv, U. (2002) *Reorganising the Factory: Competing through Cellular Mmanufacturing*, Portland, OR: Productivity Press.

Johnson, D.J. and Wemmerlöv, U. (2004) 'Why does cell implementation stop? Factors influencing cell penetration in manufacturing plants', *Production and Operations Management*, **13**(3): 272–89.

Park, J. and Simpson, T.W. (2008) 'Towards an activity-based costing system for product families and product platforms in the early stages of development', *International Journal of Production Research*, **46**(1): 99–130.

Sohal, A.S., Fitzpatrick, P. and Power, D. (2001) 'A longitudinal study of flexible manufacturing cell operation', *Integrated Manufacturing Systems*, **12**(4): 236–45.

Wang, H., Xu, X. and Tedford, J.D. (2007) 'An adaptable CNC system based on STEP-NC and function blocks', *International Journal of Production Research*, **45**(17): 3809–29.

Wemmerlöv, U. and Johnson, D.J. (1997) 'Cellular manufacturing at 46 user plants: implementation experiences and performance improvements', *International Journal of Introduction Research*, **35**(1): 29–49.

Yauch, C.A. and Steudel, H.J. (2002) 'Cellular manufacturing for small businesses: key cultural factors that impact the conversion process', *Journal of Operations Management*, **20**(5): 593–617.

Product Profiling

6

Summary

With markets as the agenda and functions investing and managing in line with their strategic roles, a company needs to assess the level of fit between needs and provision or check the future level of fit in the light of changes. Product profiling provides such a check and covers the following issues:

- The need to expand operations strategy's language base – to ensure that it makes an appropriate and full contribution to the business strategy debate and resolution, operations needs to explain its perspectives in such a way that other functions can relate and in the context of the overall business.

- Product profiling – selecting relevant market and operations dimensions, products/customers/markets can then be assessed in terms of where they fit. The key here is to keep the number of dimensions small so that the role of providing a way to discuss the level of fit between market requirements and operations characteristics is maintained.

- Using product profiling – the outcomes of profiles are part of the way companies can assess current levels of alignment, the origins of any deterioration of fit or alert companies to alignment issues in the future.

For operations, the size of process and infrastructure investments and the timescales necessary to bring about change are such that companies need to be aware of deteriorating alignment ahead of time. Chapter 5 discussed the implications of process choice, provided insights and, consequently, outlined some of the blocks on which to build operations' strategic decisions. Assessing how well existing processes fit an organization's current market requirements and making appropriate choices of process to meet future needs are critical operations responsibilities, owing to the high investment and timescales associated with the outcomes of these decisions.

When investing in processes and infrastructure, companies need to appreciate the business trade-offs embodied in these decisions (see *Exhibit 5.16*). Product profiling enables a company to test the current or anticipated level of fit between the requirements of its market(s) and the characteristics of its existing or proposed processes and infrastructure investments – the components of operations strategy (see *Exhibit 2.10*). The purpose of this assessment is twofold. First, it provides a way to evaluate and, where necessary, improve the fit between the way in which a company qualifies and wins orders in its markets and operations' ability to support these criteria (that is, operations' strategic response). Second, it helps a company move away from classic strategy building characterized by functional perspectives separately agreed, without adequate attempts to test the fit or reconcile different opinions of what is best for the business as a whole (as illustrated in *Exhibits 2.4* and *2.5*).

In many instances though, companies will be unable or unwilling to take the necessary steps to provide the degree of fit desired because of the level of investment, executive energy and timescales involved. However, sound strategy is not a case of having every facet correctly in place. It concerns improving the level of consciousness a company brings to bear on its corporate decisions. Living with existing mismatches or allowing the level of fit to deteriorate can be strategically sound if a company is aware of its position and makes these choices knowingly. Reality can constrain strategic decisions. In such circumstances, product profiling will help to increase corporate awareness and allow a conscious choice between alternatives. In the past, many companies have not aspired to this level of strategic alertness.

The need to expand operations strategy's language base

Operations has had difficulty expressing important perspectives in a manner that provides for corporate insight and discussion. Unless it can do this, other business functions will find difficulty in embracing the operations issues and choices on hand and, in turn, be party to their resolution. Intuition, experience and gut feeling must give way to business-related concepts and explanations. This is not to imply that the former are of little value. On the contrary, they form an integral part of sound management practice. However, at the strategic level, they need to be explained in a way that other executives can understand, so allowing them to become part of the ongoing corporate debate and strategic outcomes. In fact, one of the key tests for the usefulness of management theory is whether or not it crystallizes the intuitive insights of experienced executives. In this way it contributes to the essential intellectual nature of the management debate – intellectual not in the sense of theory but reflecting the complex and applied nature of the management task.

Each business will require its own approach and resolution. The examples described in the following sections met the specific needs of those businesses to which they relate. They should not be considered universally applicable. The conceptual base on which these analyses rest, however, can be transferred to other corporate scenarios and used to prepare similar analyses that will yield their own profiles.

Product profiling

Inconsistency between the market and the capability of the operations process and infrastructure to support the business specification of its products can be induced by changes in the market or process/infrastructure investment decisions or a combination of both. In all instances, the mismatch results from the fact that while operations investments are inherently large and fixed (once a company has purchased them, it will typically have to live with them for better or for worse for many years), markets are inherently dynamic. In addition, marketing decisions can often be relatively transient should a business so decide. The inherently changing nature of markets and a company's ability to alter the marketing function's perspectives to allow for change and repositioning are in opposition to operations decisions that bind a business for years ahead. A company must reconcile this but to do so requires strategic awareness, recognition and action.

Product profiling is a way to ascertain the level of fit between the process and infrastructure investments that have been or are proposed to be made and the order-winners and qualifiers of the product(s) or customers under review. The sections that follow describe situations and, to some extent, different dimensions of the same problem.

Levels of application

Product profiling can be undertaken at either the level of the company or level of a process. Company-based applications provide an overview of the degree of fit between all or the significant parts of a business and existing operations facilities (processes and/or infrastructure) or proposed operations investments and developments. Process-based applications provide a check of the fit between the products that the equipment under review is to provide.

Procedure

The procedure used in product profiling is outlined below. This explains the basic steps to follow but the essential direction of the analysis needs to reflect the match/mismatch issues within the whole or parts of a business. Remember, the purpose of profiling is to draw a picture to help to identify the current or potential problem, allowing discussion of and agreement on what steps should be taken to improve a company's strategic position.

1   Select relevant aspects of products/markets, operations, investment/cost and infrastructure as outlined in *Exhibit 5.16*. This choice must meet two overriding requirements:
    - the criteria selected must relate to the issues on hand and reflect the strategic dimensions of relevant markets. Thus dimensions other than those given in *Exhibit 5.16* will often be selected, as the examples that follow illustrate.
    - the number of criteria selected must be kept small enough to allow the picture illustrating the issues to show through. Choosing too large a list will blur the essential clarity required and detract from the facilitating role that this approach plays within strategic discussion and formulation.

2   Display the trade-offs of process choice that would be typical for each criterion chosen in 1 above. This provides the backdrop against which the product(s) or customer(s) can be profiled.

3   The purpose of profiling is to provide comparison. The next step is to profile the products, product groups, customers or companies involved. This is done by positioning the selected product(s), group(s) of products or companies on each criterion selected. Remember, this is a comparative technique; therefore you are looking to show the relationship of one product or customer to another, to compare a company today with what it was (or would be) in a selected earlier (or later) period or to review one business with another. The purpose is to test the correlation between market requirements and operations' current or proposed response to their provision. Thus profiling (the position on each chosen dimension where what is being reviewed is placed) is to display a comparative picture and should not become an issue or concern of exactness.

4   The resulting profile illustrates the degree of consistency between the characteristics of the market(s) and the relative position of the processes and infrastructure within operations. The more consistency that exists, the straighter the profile will be. Inconsistencies between the market and operations' inherent ability to meet these needs will result in a dogleg-shaped profile.

Remember throughout that the purpose of a profile is to display the issues relevant to a business and enable a company to review the degree of alignment that exists. This pictorial representation of those dimensions relevant to a business allows the executives responsible for strategic decisions to recognize the issues, their origins and the corrective action to take.

The examples that follow illustrate the points above and afford the opportunity to discuss particular applications.

Inducing mismatch with process investments

As emphasized in the last chapter, all process choices include fixed business trade-offs that can be changed only by further investment or development. Thus, a company investing in a process that embodies trade-offs inconsistent with part or all of its markets would induce a mismatch. The degree of the mismatch so caused would correspond to the relative size and importance of the process(es) involved and the associated level of reinvestment.

A company producing a range of cartons, for example, decided to invest $6m in part of its processes. These processes were core to a range of its products that accounted for some 30 per cent of total sales revenue. Based on the current level of activity, the investment had a payback of 5.5 years. However, to meet the parent group's return on investment, four-year norms, the company needed to increase the sales (and therefore the output) of these products by about 50 per cent.

For some time, the company's marketing strategy had been to position itself in the higher margin end of all its markets. However, to gain the larger volumes necessary to justify this process investment, the company had to seek business won on price. Soon the company had almost 15 per cent of its total business with distinct low-cost needs, while having to meet the schedule change needs of a further 30 per cent of sales. The consequences were significant and the ramifications substantial. Within a short space of time, the process investment had introduced operations conflict in a large part of its total business.

Product profiling can highlight these sorts of mismatches by graphically representing key marketing and operations differences that the single set of processes had to accommodate (see *Exhibit 6.1*).

In this example, the $6m process investment was, in terms of its point on the jobbing-batch-line continuum in *Exhibit 6.1*, consistent with its existing processes and chosen to support its existing business. However, the additional price-sensitive business required different process and infrastructure support. The straight line and dogleg relationships in the exhibit reflect this.

Applying the same operations strategy to two different markets

The last example concerned the impact of a process investment on the fit between a company's market and its operations capability. Without a well-developed operations strategy, the company was unconsciously driven by other functional (in this instance, financial) norms and arguments into an inappropriate major investment. Failure to recognize that investment decisions need to be based on strategy, and not functional perspectives and prerequisites, is a common contributor to poor corporate performance.

However, an equally important source of inappropriate investment decisions is the assumption that to meet different corporate requirements, a similar operations strategy approach can be applied. Typically, this happens where specialists' views form the basis

Some relevant aspects			Typical characteristics of process choice		
			Jobbing	**Batch**	**Line**
Products and markets	Product range		wide		narrow
	# of customer orders		few		many
	Level of schedule changes required		high		low
	Order-winners		delivery speed/ unique capability		price
Operations	Process	technology	general purpose		dedicated
		flexibility	high		low
	Operations volumes		low		high
	Key operations task		response to specification and lead time change		low-cost operations

●◐ Position of exisiting products on each of the chosen dimensions and the resulting profile

○◑ Position of new products on each of the chosen dimensions and the resulting profile

Exhibit 6.1

A product profile illustrating mismatch between the market and operations induced by process investment of initiatives, rather than an operations strategy formulated to the requirements of individual markets. Again, product profiling can provide a graphic description of the resulting mismatch to help explain these differences.

Faced with a decline in markets and profits, a company undertook a major internal review of its two manufacturing plants. To provide orientation for its business, it decided to manufacture different products at each of its two sites; each plant then manufactured distinct products and associated volumes. Four or five years later, the number of product types handled by Plant B was eight times as many as Plant A, and, as one would expect, product volume changes were reflected in this position. While in Plant A, average volumes for individual products rose by 60 per cent, in Plant B they decreased by 40 per cent. In addition, to redress the decline in profits, the company also embarked on major operations investments at each plant, comprising identical process investments and infrastructure changes. *Exhibit 6.2* illustrates how these changes fitted Plant A's markets, while they led to a significant mismatch for Plant B.

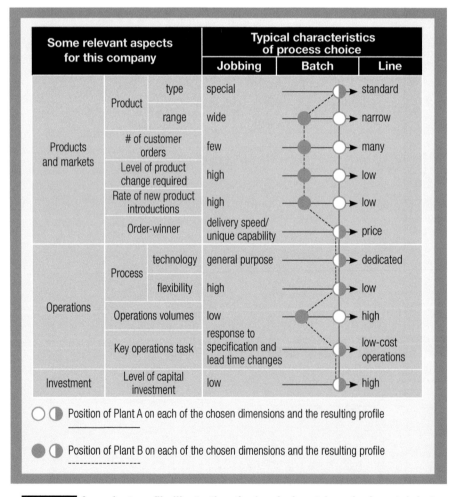

EXHIBIT 6.2 A product profile illustrating the level of match and mismatch between two plants and their respective markets induced by applying the same operations strategy to both plants

The procedure followed is similar to the one outlined in the previous section. The first step is to describe, in conceptual terms, the characteristics of product/markets, operations, investment/cost and infrastructure features pertinent to the business. The dimensions selected for these two plants are detailed in *Exhibit 6.2*. First, the characteristics that reflect the change between jobbing, batch and line need to be described. Thus, the product range associated with jobbing is wide and becomes increasingly narrow as it moves through to line, whereas the number of customer orders is few in jobbing and becomes increasingly more as it moves through the line, and so on. These dimensions represent the classic characteristics of the trade-offs embodied in process choice. Plant A's profile shows a straight-line relationship between the products and markets and the operations and infrastructure provision. However, Plant B's profile shows a dogleg shape due to the difference in markets compared to the similar process and infrastructure investments made in both plants.

Based on *Exhibit 6.2*, *Exhibit 6.3* provides a further illustration and additional insights into the extent of the mismatch brought about by applying the same operations strategy to Plants A and B described here. Whereas Plant A had appropriate process investments in line with its product volumes, Plant B did not (referred to as 'Profile mismatch 1' on *Exhibit 6.3*). As a consequence, whereas Plant A was appropriately positioned on each dimension on the vertical axis (see *Exhibits 6.2* and *6.3*), again Plant B was not (referred to as 'Profile mismatch 2' on *Exhibit 6.3*).

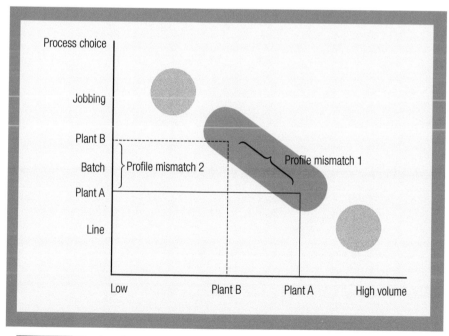

EXHIBIT 6.3 The level of inconsistency on all points of the dimensions on the vertical axis

Incremental marketing decisions resulting in a mismatch

For many companies, changes in market requirements happen over time. The incremental nature of these changes often results in them being unnoticed and in turn becoming the source of mismatches in businesses. Product profiling provides a way of describing the resulting mismatch (shown by the dogleg profile in Exhibit 6.4) and its overall impact on a company.

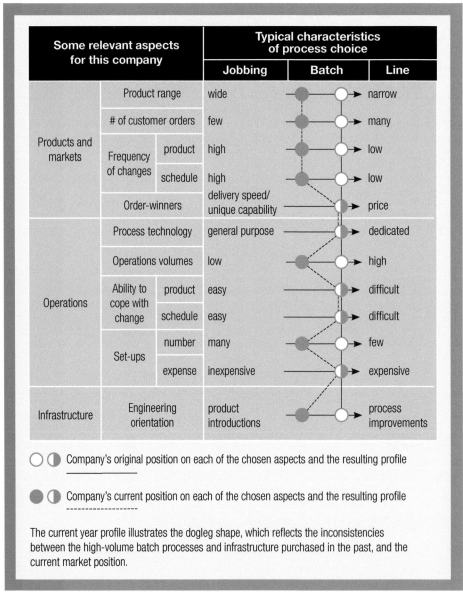

Company's original position on each of the chosen aspects and the resulting profile

Company's current position on each of the chosen aspects and the resulting profile

The current year profile illustrates the dogleg shape, which reflects the inconsistencies between the high-volume batch processes and infrastructure purchased in the past, and the current market position.

EXHIBIT 6.4 A product profile of a company's mainstream products to illustrate the impact of incremental marketing decisions

As highlighted earlier, while markets are inherently dynamic, operations is inherently fixed. This is not, however, a result of attitude or preference – markets will simply change over time whether or not a company so desires, whereas the operations investments will stay as they are unless deliberately changed by development or further investment.

Product profiling is a way of mapping the fit between the requirements of current markets and the characteristics of existing processes. The key to identifying these differences lies in a recognition that while the needs of the market may have changed, the characteristics of operations processes and infrastructure will not change without additional investment.

To illustrate, let us consider a US-based business that was under pressure from its parent company to grow sales and profits. Its response was to adopt a marketing strategy to broaden its product range. Process investments had already been updated and there was excess capacity over and above current sales levels. Supporting the required sales growth would consequently not require significant investment. As the strategy developed, the product range widened, while overall the trend saw a decrease in customer order size and an increase in the number of production schedule changes. Several years into their marketing strategy, the company experienced problems in terms of operations' ability to support current markets and provide profit at required levels. To explain the causes of this problem it is necessary to compare the current year with the year in which the operations process and infrastructure investments were made. This is because when a company invests in processes or infrastructure, it does so to reflect the characteristics of its markets as perceived at that time. As shown in *Exhibit 6.4*, at the time prior to the marketing strategy change, there is a match between the characteristics of the company's products and markets and the characteristics of its operations and infrastructure investments. The incremental marketing changes in the ensuing period had the cumulative effect of moving the company's position to the left on several, relevant product/market dimensions. The implications for operations of the incremental marketing changes in these years are revealed when drawing the equivalent profile for the current year. Again, the profile mismatch illustrates that operations had become increasingly less able to support the changing marketing trends, which the dogleg profile in *Exhibit 6.4* illustrates.

Reallocation of products due to downsizing

Companies faced with a reduction in overall demand often decide to downsize total operations capacity as a way of meeting future profit expectations. This decision typically involves the reallocation of products from one plant to another, thereby enabling one plant to downsize or close while improving current equipment utilization in the other. Decisions of this kind are typically evaluated against two criteria:

- A technical fit between the products to be made and the processes available to ensure that the processes on which there is spare capacity can physically make the product specifications to be transferred.

- The financial implications of the alternative decisions.

Often, however, companies fail to check whether the business specifications of the products to be transferred match the processes. Without this, companies can make decisions that, almost overnight, create alignment problems within a plant. The resulting profile is similar to that in *Exhibit 6.4* but is due to stepped rather than incremental changes. It results from the failure to recognize that different units of capacity, although meeting similar technical specifications, do not have the same business specifications (see *Exhibit 5.14*).

Internal sourcing decisions based on unit costs

Within a group of companies the same product may be manufactured in two or more locations. Executives with profit responsibility for a region will understandably look to sourcing products as a major factor in profit performance. Where two or more plants make the same product, differences in unit price will attract some sister companies within the group to place their business with the least cost company. For example, a North American multinational was under pressure to maintain its record of profit performance; the various parts of the business were required to match or even improve on their own performance. The result was that executives switched their internal source of products on the basis of lowest cost as one way of maintaining or improving individual profit performance. Within a short time, however, the least cost plant found that it could no longer maintain its previous cost levels. Attracting volumes of differing (often lower) levels and required to meet different market needs led to this 'once best' plant grossly underperforming. A product profile showed why, with reasons similar to those described in the last two examples, although with different origins.

Process-based profiles

Company-based profiles help reflect changes at the corporate level and identify the varying degrees of match or mismatch that exist or will exist if market needs and requirements are not reflected in operations. Process-based profiles provide similar insights but concern the review of a single process (or group of similar processes) in relation to the products produced on it (them). There can be more than one process-based profile completed within a single plant.

A prime reason why mismatches develop is that as demand for a product(s) changes, capacity is released. Typically, companies will see this as an opportunity to allocate other products to that process so as to use the spare capacity that now exists. The evaluation that is undertaken, however, is invariably restricted to a technical specification check with the equally essential business specification check neither recognized nor considered and hence not undertaken. The new products under review may be either new products or derivations of products already made on that process. In both cases the product range widens, overall individual order quantities decrease and the process stops and starts more often.

Consequently, a process will increasingly be required to support the business specification of products that have order-winners or other market characteristics different from one another. Profiles based on a format similar to those given earlier will help explain this to a business so that decisions are changed or expectations realigned.

A US-based pharmaceutical company located the manufacture of a major new product in its Kansas City plant. The initial sales of this product justified forecasts, and following this initial success, the company introduced new products and new variants to maximize total sales revenue – these variants took the form of dosage, package size and labels/leaflets in several languages. Sales continued to grow, and the company purchased further packaging equipment, similar to existing processes, to meet increased requirements. New products and variants continued and so did total sales growth. Although not competing on price (brand name and product patents were important factors for these products in winning orders), margins though high deteriorated. Furthermore, as competing products entered the market and price levels were revised, overall profit levels fell short of expectations.

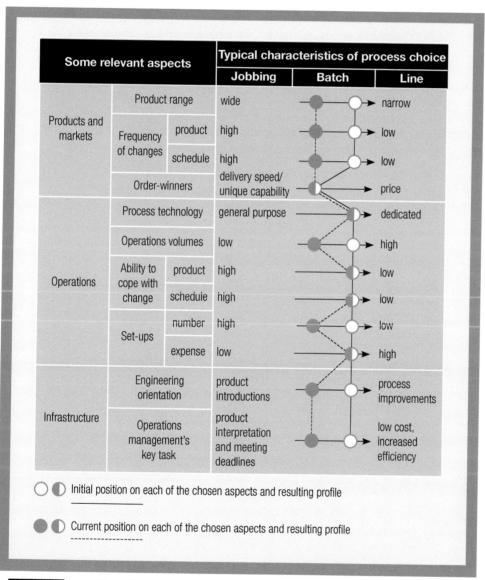

Some relevant aspects			Typical characteristics of process choice		
			Jobbing	Batch	Line
Products and markets	Product range		wide		narrow
	Frequency of changes	product	high		low
		schedule	high		low
	Order-winners		delivery speed/ unique capability		price
Operations	Process technology		general purpose		dedicated
	Operations volumes		low		high
	Ability to cope with change	product	high		low
		schedule	high		low
	Set-ups	number	high		low
		expense	low		high
Infrastructure	Engineering orientation		product introductions		process improvements
	Operations management's key task		product interpretation and meeting deadlines		low cost, increased efficiency

○ ◑ Initial position on each of the chosen aspects and resulting profile
_____

● ◑ Current position on each of the chosen aspects and resulting profile
- - - - - - - - - - -

EXHIBIT 6.5 A profile of the product variants packed on a number of similar packaging lines

The profile in *Exhibit 6.5* explains why. A mismatch between market requirements and operations characteristics resulted as the engineering and operations task shifted away from exploiting the potential cost advantages associated with volumes towards that of handling the introduction of new products and new variants. The existing process and infrastructure investments in operations become increasingly misaligned to the needs of the market as the growth into lower volume products continued. As a result, profit margins fell short of the level necessary to support the high R&D expenditure essential to secure future growth and market penetration in pharmaceutical markets.

Using product profiling

The examples given in the previous sections illustrate the role product profiling can play in helping a company to check its existing product and process choice relationship and allow, where relevant, comparisons to be made between similar applications or to measure trends over time. Although the illustrations given here were based on hindsight and not on the essential forward-looking characteristic of strategy, product profiling is similarly useful to illustrate current positions and future alternatives, as it helps to discuss options and determine which strategic direction best meets the needs of the business.

Companies that are, for whatever reason, experiencing a mismatch between their current market needs and existing operations processes and infrastructure face the following choices:

1   Live with the mismatch.

2   Redress the profile mismatch by altering the marketing strategy.

3   Redress the profile mismatch by investing in and changing operations processes and/or infrastructure.

4   A combination of 2 and 3.

Living with the mismatch would be appropriate where the trade-offs involved provided the best strategic option. Such a decision would result in a company's expectations being brought more in line with reality by making it aware of the real costs of being in different markets and raising the level of corporate consciousness about the overall consequences of continuing to be misaligned now and potentially being even more out of alignment in the future. Furthermore, future decisions concerning new products or switching existing products into other plants or onto other processes are now able to incorporate these essential perspectives. Such decisions would also help to reconcile the diverse functional perspectives on such key strategic issues under the mantle of what is best for the business overall.

Alternatives 2 and 3 concern ways of straightening or consciously avoiding widening existing mismatches or creating new ones and may be taken independently or in unison. Alternative 2 involves influencing policy through changes or modifications to existing or proposed marketing strategies. In this way, the implications of marketing decisions for operations are addressed and included as an integral part of the business strategy debate. Thus, operations is able to move from the reactive stance it typically adopts to a proactive mode, so essential to sound policy decisions.

DON'T **RE-INVENT** THE WHEEL, JUST **RE-ALIGN** IT

Anthony J. D'Angelo,
The College Blue Book

Alternative 3 involves a company's decision to invest in the processes and infrastructure of its business, either to enable operations to become more effective in providing relevant order-winners/qualifiers and hence better support the market for existing products or to establish the required level of support for future products in a market-driving scenario. As with alternative 2, this enables operations to switch from a reactive to a proactive response. By receiving pertinent inputs at the strategic level, the business is made more aware of the implications involved and is able to arrive at options based on the relevant and comprehensive inputs necessary to make sound strategic decisions.

Reflections

The reasons companies fail to incorporate operations perspectives into the strategy debate are many. For one, operations is traditionally seen as a predominantly technical- or engineering-related function. This not only creates barriers to discussion, but also misrepresents the key operations perspectives that a company needs to recognize and incorporate in its strategy-making process. A major thrust within operations strategy, therefore, is to reorient its contribution from being technical/engineering related to being business related. This widens the debate by introducing and highlighting the contribution made by operations in winning and retaining customers. This links operations with other functions by using the market as the common denominator. The result is business-based discussions leading to essential strategic outcomes.

Product profiling is one such development. By translating process investments into business issues, companies are able to assess the fit between these major resources and the markets they are required to support. In addition, being able to explain trends, mismatches and options in picture form enhances the power of the message and increases its role in corporate understanding and debate. It leads to sound strategy developments by enabling functions to explain themselves in corporate terms and provides a language to enhance essential discussion and agreement at the level of the business rather than at the level of functions.

Discussion questions

1 Why is it necessary to check alignment between market requirements and operations characteristics?

2 What are the steps to take in product profiling?

3 What situations/circumstances can induce a mismatch between market requirements and operations investments?

4 How can a company use product profiling as part of its strategic response?

Focus
Principles and Concepts

7

Summary

- The complexity of managing operations results from the size of its management and strategic task.

- The management task comes from the number and interrelated nature of the tasks involved and the strategic task reflects the level of fit between its strategic objectives and process and infrastructure capability.

- Focus creates a limited and consistent set of management and strategic tasks within an operation that enable it to better align processes and infrastructure to business and market needs.

- Focus moves away from the principles of economies of scale and control through specialists that have expanded product ranges, increased facility sizes and created unclear strategic tasks.

- Businesses can choose to focus their operation around resources, markets or a combination of the two using six alternative approaches: process, volume, variety, geography, products, markets or order-winners.

- Businesses must consider the cost, management and strategic implications before focusing operations. A movement away from economies of scale brings management benefit, but potentially some cost disadvantages.

- Order-winner focus is the only approach with strategic benefits. However, this is often the second step for organizations as it is a more difficult concept to understand and implement.

- It is not necessary to focus all products and processes. Equally, the advantages and disadvantages of each approach mean a combination may be most appropriate.

- Organizations can use an operation-within-an-operation arrangement to overcome the lower equipment utilization and investment costs that focus can create.

- Maintaining focus must be a conscious strategic decision. Focus does not occur naturally. In fact, corporate neglect and traditional views of what is best for a business tend to prevent it. The range of products supplied, markets served and processes used must be continually reviewed to ensure that a single consistent strategic task is present in each unit.

Operations is a complex function and managing this complexity is a key strategic task. Complexity does not come from the nature of the individual tasks of the job, but rather the number of aspects and issues involved, the interrelated nature of these and the level of fit between the strategic task and the operations process and infrastructure capability. In all but highly technical, special product market segments, it is not difficult to cope with the technology of the product or process. In most situations, the process technology involved has been purchased from outside, with appropriate engineering and technical support provided for operations. In a similar way, product design and the associated technology is provided by the customer and/or the design function. As such, neither process nor product technologies are generally difficult for operations to understand or manage.

The complexity in operations results from the size of the management and strategic task it faces. The management task comes from the number and interrelated nature of the tasks and issues involved.[1] The strategic task reflects the level of the fit between the strategic objectives and the operations process and infrastructure capability. Focus is one approach to organizing operations so the size of its management and strategic task is reduced.

Focus concerns linking operations to the appropriate competitive factors of its business(es), so that it can gain greater control of its competitive position. One of the most difficult tasks in managing operations is responding to the different market demands made on its facilities. This is due to the wide and diverse market demands to be met and the challenge of coordinating operations to meet them. Companies using focus to reduce the demands placed on their operations often find it easier to manage those operations and, as a result, their performance improves.

When explaining focus, the words 'narrow' or 'narrowing' are often used. For example, Skinner, who was the first to talk about the benefits of focused plants, argues that 'a factory that focuses on a narrow product mix for a particular market niche will outperform the conventional plant, which attempts a broader mission'.[2] However, taken at face value, this argument can be misleading. Many companies do not have the 'narrow product mix' alternative referred to here. The issue of focus, therefore, is more accurately explained in Skinner's fuller definition:

- **Management task** – learning to focus each plant on a limited, concise, manageable set of products, technologies, volumes and markets.

- **Strategic task** – learning to structure basic policies and supporting services so that they focus on one explicit strategic task, instead of on many inconsistent, conflicting, implicit tasks.[3]

The emphasis here is on a limited and consistent set of management and strategy tasks, which is often far from the layman's definition of narrow. So, to avoid confusion, the dimension of narrow should be omitted. It is the homogeneity of tasks and the repetition and experience involved in completing these that form the basis of focus. Thus, focusing the demands placed on operations enables resources, efforts and attention to be concentrated on a defined and homogeneous set of activities, which allows management to prioritize the key tasks necessary to achieve better performance. In most operations, however, focus is rarely understood, let alone achieved. The factors that cause this are now discussed.

Applying the principle of economies of scale in today's markets

For many years it has been (and still is) argued that the principle of economies of scale is a sound and appropriate way of organizing and managing businesses. As an underlying approach, it is highly attractive. However, for most organizations today this approach no longer works well. The advantages that can accrue from applying economies of scale are no longer being realized because the markets and the necessary corporate response to and support for them have changed. While markets in the past were characterized by similarity, today's markets are characterized by difference.

Economies of scale are most appropriate for and best applied to high-volume, steady state markets (where similarity is the hallmark). However, for most companies these conditions no longer reflect the nature of their businesses. For many, these prerequisites are far from reality. In fact, if anything, the opposite applies. Their markets are low volume and dynamic in nature (where difference is the hallmark). The key reasons why the conditions have changed are now discussed.

Expanding product ranges

Marketing-led strategies are typically based on principles of growth through extending the product range. Invariably, new products (even those requiring new technologies) are produced, partly at least, on existing processes and almost always within the same infrastructure. The logic for this is based on the principle of the economies derived from using an existing cost base to deliver increased sales. However, over time, the incremental nature of these marketing changes will invariably alter operations strategic task. The result is complexity, confusion and, worst of all, an organization that, because it is spun out in all directions by a kind of centrifugal force, lacks focus and an achievable strategic task.[4]

Increasing facility size

Faced with a shortage of capacity, companies find the attractions of on-site expansion irresistible. The tangible arguments of cost and overhead advantages, plus the provision of a better hedge against future uncertainty, provide the basis against which companies measure the alternatives. However, they rarely take into account the costs of the associated uplift in complexity and the bureaucracy that develops as facilities try to cope. These changes are further hidden or disguised by their piecemeal or incremental nature, as Schmenner concludes:

> Big plants usually have formidable bureaucratic structures. Relationships inevitably become formal, and the worker is separated from the top executives by many layers of management. All too often, managers are shuffling the paperwork that formal systems have spawned ... Although there has to be some formality in plant operations, too much can wipe out the many informal procedures that keep plants nimble and able to adapt to change.[5]

Unclear strategic task

As well as the increased management task from the larger facility, in these circumstances operations will rarely have a clearly defined strategic task. It will be required to meet multiple performance objectives that often change from one day to the next with the varying pressures placed on the business. The result is that operations, without an agreed strategy, will respond as best it can, independently deciding on the best corporate compromises or trade-offs involved. Invariably the result is reduced performance and lack of fit with overall business objectives and the market it serves.

Utilizing equipment and facilities

Embodied in the principle of economies of scale is the argument for continually increasing equipment and facility utilization. As capacity is released due to a fall-off in demand for a product(s), companies typically reutilize the spare capacity by introducing new products. There is constant pressure on operations to fully utilize existing process capacity before any new investment can be made, and the justification for purchasing new equipment will be partly based on future production volumes. However, when evaluating the suitability of processes for a product, companies invariably only check that technical specifications are met. They rarely check the consistency of the business requirement (its strategic task) for each of the new products involved. Furthermore, this check is necessary not just for current requirements; it must be made over time as products go through their life cycles and the relevant order-winners change.

Managing businesses using specialists

Businesses typically organize themselves into functional specialisms and appoint the individual with the highest specialist knowledge to manage each department:

> These professionals, quite naturally, seek to maximize their contributions and justify their positions. They have conventional views of success in each of their particular fields. Of course, these objectives are generally in conflict.[6]

This conflict often means that the close functional cooperation and understanding required to manage the business is missing. The failure of companies clearly to define the focus of their business exacerbates this problem. Without this direction, there is insufficient shared understanding of what is required. The result is that support systems, controls, information provision and other features of infrastructure are developed out of line with the appropriate and agreed corporate needs. The advantages and disadvantages of alternative strategies cannot be compared against a shared understanding of the business. Instead, they are assessed on the fragmented and uncoordinated specialist views based on what seems best at the time, rather than on an agreed strategic direction.

Looking for panaceas

Too often, strategy development is solution based rather than problem based. The belief is that success lies in simply finding the right solution, rather than understanding the problem a business faces and then developing an appropriate strategy to address this. The result is that many firms spend their time searching for which of the many three-letter acronyms holds the key to success (see *Exhibit 7.1*). Most companies can recall their own redundant solutions. The latest example of a long line in operations is exhorting businesses to adopt the best Japanese system rather than analysing their own organization and developing their own approach. Although such formulaic developments can contribute substantially to business success, they need to be derived from strategic discussion and in line with appropriate and agreed direction.

EXHIBIT 7.1 In pursuit of a panacea: which three-letter acronym next?

SOURCE: Operations Institute, Johnson & Johnson, with permission

For strategic initiatives to be successful, they must fit the needs of the market and there must be sufficient time to develop and implement them. The Japanese systems such as just-in-time (JIT) and total quality management (TQM) were developed in response to requirements placed on their business, and took some 30 years to perfect and carefully adapt these approaches to the needs of their business. Western companies often take the ideas of these initiatives in a prescriptive form and expect to implement them in only a few months. This approach results in inappropriate applications, unrealistic expectations and unsustainable developments. Worst of all, by continually searching for and trying to implement panacea approaches, managers are not only distracted from understanding and evaluating their own business requirements, but also feel that there is no longer any need to be concerned. They believe that everything will be solved by the latest philosophy they have discovered.

Alternative approaches to focus

Businesses can choose to focus their operations around resources, markets or a combination of the two. Six alternative approaches are now discussed and the orientation of their focus is shown in *Exhibit 7.2*.

Process

Products that are delivered using similar processes are grouped together and each allocated to alternative process-focused units. The principal rationale for this strategy is to gain advantages such as concentrated expertise and improved process utilization. Its application is most suitable when an operations resource is constrained either by the level of capacity available or the investment cost required to duplicate it. The creation of process-

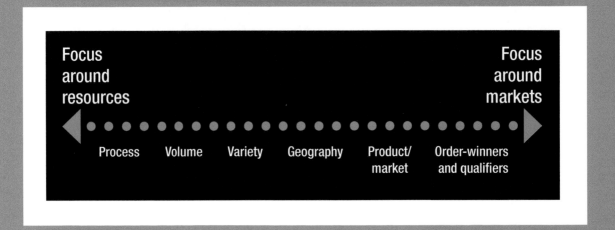

Focus around resources — Process — Volume — Variety — Geography — Product/market — Order-winners and qualifiers — Focus around markets

Exhibit 7.2
Focusing operations around resources or markets

focused units allows these constrained resources to be exploited through better management and control.

Volume

Products are split into units based on how many are produced in a typical operations order. This approach allows the processes and infrastructure in each unit to be better aligned to the needs of the products it supplies. For example, the emphasis on standardization and repetition in high-volume production typically requires different process technologies, labour skills and planning and control systems to lower volume products.

Variety

Alternatively, operations may choose to create units that have differing levels of product variety. For example, one unit may concentrate on a relatively low variety of standardized products, while another supplies a high variety of customized products. This approach has similar advantages to volume focus as the standardized and repetitive nature of the low variety unit is similar to that of high volume, and requires different processes and infrastructure to higher variety products.

Geography

Operations can also be split into the geographical markets it supplies. This approach is a move away from the more resource-based focus of process, volume and variety to one around markets. This method tends to occur where market characteristics vary significantly by geographical location, products are specific to certain geographical areas, the customer is heavily involved in the design or delivery of the product or there is a significant speed requirement for delivering products.

Product/market

Focused units are created that either supply a generic group of products, or support a particular group of customers. This approach involves focusing around markets, rather than processes, and typically occurs where the business wishes to either develop or exploit product or market knowledge. For example, using a product unit to develop a set of skills and capabilities or using a unit to support and exploit a certain market sector. In some cases, a customer may demand a focused unit so that they know there are processes and infrastructure dedicated to their needs.

Order-winners and qualifiers

Products are allocated to a particular unit on the basis of different order-winners and qualifiers demanded in their markets that operations supports. This approach is the one most based on markets as it creates a single, coherent strategic task in each unit that reflects the needs of the markets it serves. In some instances, orders for the same product may be won in different ways and therefore supplied using different units. For example, a product may compete on 'price' in one market and 'delivery speed' in another. The 'delivery speed' unit may hold stock or excess capacity to ensure customer lead times are met and provide a delivery tracking service for urgent requirements. However, the cost of providing this service will need to be reflected in higher prices charged for supplying this product.

	Advantages and disadvantages	Economies of scale	Focus by					
			Process	Volume	Variety	Geography	Product/ market	Order-winner and qualifier
Advantages								
Cost	High equipment utilization	•						
Cost	Minimal investment							
Cost	Minimal overhead costs	•						
Management	Less products		•	•	•	•	•	•
Management	Less operatives		•	•	•	•	•	•
Management	Smaller area		•	•	•	•	•	•
Management	Better communication		•	•	•	•	•	•
Management	Easier to control		•	•	•	•	•	•
Management	Reduced range of: – production technology		•					•
Management	– production volumes			•	•		•	•
Strategic	Single, coherent task							•
Strategic	High internal fit							•
Strategic	High external fit							•
Disadvantages								
Cost	Lower equipment utilization			•	•	•	•	•
Cost	Increased investment: – more overheads		•	•	•	•	•	•
Cost	– process duplication			•	•	•	•	•
Management	More products	•						
Management	More operatives	•						
Management	Larger area	•						
Management	Poor communication	•	•			•	•	
Management	Conflicting production volumes	•						
Strategic	Multiple, conflicting tasks	•	•	•	•	•	•	
Strategic	Lower internal fit	•	•	•	•	•	•	
Strategic	Lower external fit	•	•	•	•	•	•	

EXHIBIT 7.3 The advantages and disadvantages of alternative approaches to organizing operations

Focus advantages and disadvantages

Each alternative approach to organizing operations has advantages and disadvantages as shown in *Exhibit 7.3*. When deciding on the most appropriate approach, companies must consider the cost, management and strategic implications of their decision. The traditional approach of economies of scale has some cost benefit in terms of the high equipment utilization, minimal investment and minimal overhead necessary. However, this arrangement is more difficult to manage and has multiple, conflicting strategic tasks that create low fit within its operation and with its markets. A move to focus brings benefits from the reduction in size of the operation such as less products, less operatives, smaller area and reduced range of production technologies and volumes. These smaller units are easier to manage and control, but there are also cost disadvantages from the reduced equipment utilization and increased investment in overheads and equipment typically necessary to create the units. In the case of order-winner and qualifier focus, there are also strategic benefits from the increased level of internal and external strategic fit and the single, coherent task within each unit.

Strategic benefit only from order-winner and qualifier approach

As *Exhibit 7.3* shows, all focus approaches have management benefits that result from the reduction in size. However, there are still multiple, conflicting strategic tasks within each unit. Only the order-winner and qualifier approach creates a single coherent task and high fit within its operation (internal) and with its market (external). As such, it creates higher simplicity than other focus approaches. For example, a business choosing to split by market might find that each unit still produces high price-sensitive, low price-sensitive and rapid response products. So, although some management advantages are obtained through a reduction in the size of each operations unit, conflicting demands are still being placed on the same facilities. A move to split by order-winner and qualifier would create a price-sensitive unit and delivery speed unit. The single, coherent strategic task in each unit aligns the processes and infrastructure with each other and with the market it serves, thereby creating high internal and external strategic fit.

Order-winner and qualifier approach most difficult to understand

The concept of focusing facilities by order-winners and qualifiers seems more difficult to grasp than the other approaches. This may be because the market into which a product is sold, where it is sold, volume of sales, variety of sales and the process used in its manufacture can be more easily visualized than how a product competes within a market. For example, products in an organization are often referred to as 'aerospace', or 'automotive', but never, for example, as 'price-sensitive' or 'delivery speed products' even when those are its agreed competitive criteria. One consequence of this is that organizations tend to more readily split their facilities by process, volume, variety, geography or product/market.

Order-winner and qualifier focus is often the second step

Because organizations tend to more readily split their operations by process, volume, variety, geography or product/market, this is typically the first move away from economies of scale. The management benefits of these approaches can be seen and, with this, the strategic demands placed on operations become clearer as managers start to understand the markets they serve. The impact of the multiple, conflicting strategic tasks can be seen and only at this point is the strategic benefit of order-winner and qualifier focus understood. Thus, the first split leads to a second split by order-winner and qualifier.

Achieving focus

Not necessary to focus all products or processes

Each approach to organizing resources has different sets of advantages and disadvantages. As such, it may not be appropriate to focus all the products or processes within an organization and sometimes certain processes or products should be arranged using economies of scale. For example, a business supplies eight product groups where price is the major order-winner for only Group A. Here it would be appropriate to create a separate product-focused unit for Group A, while supplying the other seven product groups together in a facility organized using the principles of economies of scale. Although it only focuses a single product group, there will be improvement throughout the whole business. The business is able to create a dedicated unit focused on Group A's requirements, and also simplify the production of the other seven groups by removing the conflicting demands of Group A from the main site.

Equally, in some circumstances, the investment required to duplicate a certain process may be too great to justify this decision. In this instance, the process can remain centrally managed while being used to supply the other processes that have been split into focused units. Again, the management benefits of focusing some processes create an improvement throughout the whole business.

Use a combination of approaches

The varying advantages and disadvantages of alternative approaches also mean that many businesses are best served by adopting a combination of approaches when focusing operations. For example, process focus may be used where resources need to be exploited as they are either scarce, costly to duplicate or require specialist knowledge to manage that is not readily available. Equally, in other parts of the business, an order-winner and qualifier approach may be used to exploit certain markets. By adopting a variety of approaches, organizations are best able to organize their resources to meet the cost, management and strategic needs of their business.

Operation-within-an-operation arrangement

As shown in *Exhibit 7.3*, the main disadvantage of focus concerns the cost of lower equipment utilization and increased investment. A way to overcome this is to create a plant-within-a-plant (PWP) arrangement as this spreads overhead costs across a number of focused facilities. As many companies own existing sites, with sizable investments in bricks and mortar, utilities, plant, offices and other facilities, creating new facilities is often not financially viable. Equally, as businesses change, there is a real danger that the operations complexity associated with a lack of focus could gradually permeate some of the plants. Where rearrangement is constrained by the size of initial plants, their geographical location and the distribution difficulties involved, process and infrastructure support considerations and so on, the flexibility of overall size (the larger the factory, the greater the permutations available) can often be to a company's advantage. Although this second aspect may not be a major issue for many companies, the first is.

The way to provide focus in these situations (as implied in the earlier example of the vehicle supplier) is to adopt a PWP configuration. This involves physically dividing sites (often using partitions, different entrances and other facilities) into 'separate' operations focused on different business needs. Each unit is more manageable and strategically aligned to its markets than when the business tries to meet all these needs with a single operation.

Although there are cost disadvantages from the apparent loss of economies of scale, PWP provides an opportunity to review the overheads allocated to each unit. The improved clarity between business needs, direction and overhead requirements often makes this review easier. By splitting overheads down, the business is able to see clearly where they are required and their contribution to supporting the market. As such, the true profitability of products/services and the level of support given by alternative functions are better understood.

Maintaining focus

Progression or regression in focus

A single operations process will always be able to perform one task better than another. Every facility supplies a variety of products to a number of markets that place differing demands on its operations. As product/market variety increases or decreases, so does the management and strategic task to be met. The need to meet changing tasks causes the operation to become unfocused unless steps are taken. Equally, as processes develop, so does their ability to meet certain tasks. The range of products supplied, markets served and processes used must be continually reviewed to ensure a single, consistent task is present in each unit.

Focus and the product life cycle

Exhibit 7.4 shows how production volumes and strategic task change during a product's life cycle and the appropriate focus approach to each stage is outlined in *Exhibit 7.5*. In the early stages of growth, operations faces less predictable sales volumes, product and process modifications, customer orientation and varying levels of delivery speed. Process focus is usually most appropriate as it is flexible and technically capable to cope with these changes. As the product matures, sales volume increases, product and process technology are established and price becomes more sensitive. The narrow product range and product-dedicated processes of product focus allow it to concentrate on reducing cost. As the product goes into decline, operations volumes decrease, become less stable and delivery speed tends to be more important. A process-focused unit is better able to meet these demands.

Telecommunications switchgears have evolved over a number of years from mechanical to electromechanical and then electronic technology. A company has developed products to match this change that essentially perform the same task, but in a slightly more sophisticated manner. Each product was launched before the end of the life of the previous one. As a result, original equipment and spares for various products are currently supplied. In order to establish its operations task, the company reviewed its market to understand the requirements and issues involved.

Product A is based on a mechanical technology and sales are restricted to spares or replacement equipment for existing installations. The processes required to make this product were specific to this range and cannot be used to supply electronic technology products. Product B is also no longer sold as part of a new contract and has been superseded by Products C and D. These two products were introduced shortly after Product B due to a rapid advance in product technology. The company chose to organize operations using a process-focused approach where Product A is supplied from one unit and Products B, C and D from another. The reasons for this are to:

- Develop products within an existing facility and so avoid the need to use a new facility for each stage of a product's life

- Minimize total operating costs by spreading overhead costs across all products

- Manage demand fluctuations by having a wide range of products supplied by a single facility.

Everything was working well until sales started to increase for Products C and D as they entered the mature phase of their life. Table 1 shows the resulting change in production volume and strategic task across the four products.

Varying strategic tasks mean the process-focused approach meets the delivery speed requirements of Product A and B, but not the cost reduction needs of C and D. Here, a product-focused approach with a narrow product range and product-dedicated processes would allow it to concentrate on reducing cost to meet the increasingly price-sensitive nature of their markets.

Aspect		Product			
		A	**B**	**C**	**D**
Production volume	Current	Low	Low	High	Low/medium
	In 2–3 years	Stable	Decreasing	Decreasing	Increasing
Key strategic task	Current	Delivery speed	Delivery speed	Cost reduction	Quality conformance and on-time delivery
	In 2–3 years	Delivery speed	Delivery speed	Cost reduction	Cost reduction

TABLE 1 Changes over time in production volumes and strategic task

EXHIBIT 7.4 Production volumes and strategic tasks change in a product's life cycle

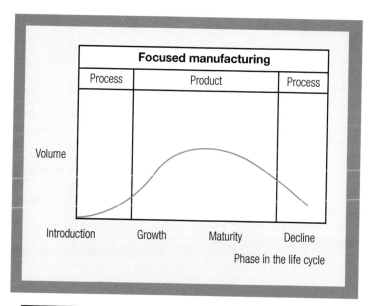

EXHIBIT 7.5 A typical product life cycle and its relationship to focus

Functional pressure to regress

Achieving and maintaining focus must be a conscious strategic decision. Focus does not occur naturally. In fact, corporate neglect or traditional views of what is best for a business often tend to prevent it:

FOCUS

REDESIGNS

A BUSINESS

Focus **clarifies** and **simplifies** a business

- **Marketing** often stimulates the desire to create and maintain a broad product line. This is usually an integral part of its strategy and an important measure of its performance.

- **Sales** understandably believe it is easier to sell a broad product line. They argue that a wide product range creates broader market appeal and smooths out seasonal or cyclical demand. The use of sales value-based (£s) commission schemes reinforces this.

- **Operations** may resist focus because of work practice union agreements, high cost of purchasing or moving processes and uncertain benefits.

- **Accounting and finance** often emphasize short-term earnings and, therefore, restrict capital investment. Also,w the practices used to monitor and evaluate operating costs can distort reality. For example, allocating overhead costs across a wide range of products often means that the actual profit for a single product and the actual financial impact of producing a wide product range are both unknown.

- **Corporate divisions** are typically organized into specialist areas with a single function dominant in strategy development. The trend stems largely from divisions between specialists and executives within management and the predominance, at different times, of a single function in formulating strategy. The background and perspectives brought to strategy discussions are therefore often imbalanced and too narrow. They may resist including operations in corporate strategy development and be reluctant to increase interaction between marketing and operations.

Reflections

Supporting markets with differing requirements

Businesses create problems by failing to understand how well their delivery system and infrastructure support their current and future needs. By blindly using economies of scale as a rationale for their organization, companies find they are not able to compete in today's markets. However, simply substituting economies of scale with focus is not the answer. Businesses must choose the approach to best exploit their resources and market opportunities. Markets are becoming increasingly different from one another and firms must learn to compete effectively in several markets at once. Selecting the right approach to organizing resources is a key strategic decision. Each method has varying cost, managerial and strategic advantages and disadvantages. The appropriate approach for an organization will reflect the resources it possesses and the requirements of its current and future markets.

Being able to fashion operations facilities and supporting activities to the needs of various markets enables companies to compete effectively. An approach based on reducing or eliminating diversity within corporate portfolios is often a weak strategy. Advocates of these policies are turning their backs on the reality of business today and the opportunities it provides. Companies must learn to compete in different types of markets and focus is an approach to achieve this.

Halting the drift into unfocus

Focus does not occur naturally. In fact, there are pressures from marketing, sales, finance and even operations itself to become unfocused. They result from strategic decisions made in isolation from other functions or based on reducing cost rather than supporting markets. As markets change and evolve, so do its customer characteristics, customer preferences and order-winners. Companies respond to this by expanding product ranges, increasing facility size, reusing equipment, reducing cost, focusing on short-term profit and restricting capital investment. These are often responses to market changes rather than strategic decisions and tend to occur as a set of independent actions. Cross-functional strategic debate, development and implementation must occur to prevent this from happening and the business becoming unfocused. Whether strategy is planned or emergent and market led or resource based, it must be built around key elements. The starting point is to identify the existing core of the business, in which it has a clear competitive advantage. Once this is understood, then a business can identify its current and future markets and how it will compete. The appropriate corporate and functional strategies can then be developed and implemented. In this way, functions will point in the same strategic direction and meet the overall corporate objectives. Financial decisions must be based on short-term and long-term strategic objectives and the reporting systems modified to provide data giving insight into these objectives and monitoring if they are being met. This is not a one-off exercise, but an ongoing process. Markets must be continually assessed to ensure changes are identified and understood so they can be appropriately reflected in products, processes and infrastructure. Even if the business chooses not to respond to changes, this must be a conscious, cross-functional strategic decision based on and supported by appropriate analysis.

Discussion questions

1 Explain why the complexity of managing operations results from the size of its management and strategic task. Use examples other than those described in this chapter.

2 What has been the historical rationale for organizing operations using the principles of economies of scale and control through specialists? What has been the impact of these decisions?

3 Explain how focus moves away from the principles of economies of scale and control through specialists. What are the advantages and disadvantages of the approaches to organizing operations?

4 'Businesses can choose to focus their operation around resources or markets.' Explain this statement using examples other than those described in this chapter. What are the advantages and disadvantages of alternative focus approaches?

5 'Order-winner focus is the only approach with strategic benefits.' Explain this statement using examples other than those described in this chapter.

6 Once focus has been achieved, what steps need to be taken to maintain it?

Notes and references

1 Brought to prominence in Schumacher, E.F. (1975) *Small is Beautiful: Economics as if People Mattered*, New York: Harper & Row.

2 Skinner, W. (1974) 'The focused factory', *Harvard Business Review*, May–Jun, pp. 113–21.

3 Based on Skinner, 'The focused factory', p. 114.

4 Skinner, 'The focused factory', p. 118.

5 Schmenner, W. (1983) 'Every factory has a life cycle', *Harvard Business Review*, Mar–Apr, p. 123.

6 Skinner, 'The focused factory', p. 115.

Exploring further

Berry, W., Bozarth, C., Hill, T. and Klompmaker, J. (1991) 'Factory focus: segmenting markets from an operations perspective', *Journal of Operations Management*, 10(3): 363–88.

Bozarth, C.C. (1993) 'A conceptual model of manufacturing focus', *International Journal of Operations & Production Management*, 13(1): 81–92.

Bozarth, C.C. and Edwards, S. (1997) 'The impact of market requirements focus and manufacturing characteristics focus on plant performance', *Journal of Operations Management*, 15(3): 161–80.

Brush, T.H. and Karnani, A. (1996) 'Impact of plant size and focus on productivity: an empirical study', *Management Science*, 42(7): 1065–81.

Casalino, L.P., Devers, K.J. and Brewster, L.R. (2003) 'Focused factories? Physician-owned specialty facilities', *Health Affairs*, 22(6): 56–61.

Davidow, W.H. and Uttal, B. (1989) 'Service companies: focus or falter?' *Harvard Business Review*, July–August, pp. 77–85.

Devers, K.J., Brewster, L.R. and Ginsburg, P.B. (2003) 'Specialty hospitals: focused factories or cream skimmers?' Washington: Center for Studying Health System Change.

Hayes, R.H. and Schmenner, R.W. (1978) 'How should you organise manufacturing?', *Harvard Business Review*, 56(1): 105–19.

Hayes, R.H., Pisano, G.P., Upton, D.M. and Wheelwright, S.C. (2005) *Operations, Strategy, and Technology: Pursuing the Competitive Edge*, New York: Wiley.

Hill, A. (2007) 'How to organise operations: focusing or splitting?', *International Journal of Production Economics*, doi:10.1016/j.ijpe.2007.06.002.

Ketokivi, M. and Jokinen, M. (2006) 'Strategy, uncertainty and the focused factory in international process manufacturing', *Journal of Operations Management*, 24(3): 250–70.

Kimes, S.E. and Johnston, R. (1990) 'The application of focused manufacturing in the hospitality sector', Proceedings of the Manufacturing Strategy Conference of the Operations Management Association UK, University of Warwick.

New, C.C. and Szwejczewski, M. (1995) 'Performance measurement and the focused factory: empirical evidence', *International Journal of Operations & Production Management*, 15(4): 63–79.

Pesch, M.J. (1996) 'Defining and understanding the focused factory: a Delphi survey', *Production and Inventory Management Journal*, 38(2): 32–6.

Pesch, M.J. and Schroeder, R.G. (1996) 'Measuring factory focus: an empirical study', *Production and Operations Management*, **5**(3): 234–54.

Shafer, S.M and Oswald, S.L. (1996) 'Product-focused manufacturing for strategic advantage', *Business Horizons*, **39**(6): 24–9.

Skinner, W. (1974) 'The focused factory', *Harvard Business Review*, May–June, pp. 113–21.

Skinner, W. (1996) 'Manufacturing strategy on the 'S' curve', *Production and Operations Management*, **5**(1): 3–14.

Van der Vaart, T. and Van Donk, D.P. (2004) 'Buyer focus: evaluation of a new concept for supply chain integration', *International Journal of Production Economics*, **92**: 21–30.

Van der Vaart, T. and Wijngaard, J. (2007) 'The contribution of focus in collaborative planning for make-to-order production situation with large set-up times', *International Journal of Production Economics*, doi:10.1016/j.ijpe.2006.12.053.

Van Dierdonck, R. and Brandt, G. (1988) 'The focused factory in service industry', *International Journal of Operations & Production Management*, **8**(3): 31–8.

Vokurka, R.J. and Davis, R.A. (2000) 'Focused factories: empirical study of structural and performance differences', *Production and Inventory Management Journal*, **41**(1): 44–55.

Focus
Methodology

8

Summary

- Operations tended to be arranged on the principles of economies of scale and control through specialists. Facilities are usually large, with similar processes grouped together and infrastructure centralized into specialist functions.

- When focusing operations, companies must understand their business and market requirements and use a combination of approaches. It is not necessary to focus all products or processes. The optimal solution often involves a combination of focus approaches and all products or processes may not be focused.

- Focus should only be applied if it meets business and market requirements.

- Focus involves six main steps that tend to be iterative in nature. Initially, it must review processes to identify any that are too expensive to duplicate. Market order-winners and qualifiers must then be identified. Based on these two reviews, a focus approach is selected for products and customer orders. Products and customer orders are then grouped using the focus approach selected. Processes and infrastructure are allocated and physically moved to each unit to meet their capacity and capability requirements.

- Maintaining focus is a conscious strategic decision. Businesses will become naturally unfocused over time as markets are dynamic and operations capabilities relatively fixed. The range of products supplied, markets served and processes used must be continually reviewed to ensure a single consistent strategic task is present in each unit.

The principles and concepts underpinning focus were outlined in the last chapter. We now turn our attention to the steps to take when focusing operations.[1]

The markets that businesses compete in have different needs to each other. Operations must therefore cope with the differing requirements placed on them. Increasingly, operations is using focused facilities or plant-within-a-plant configurations to meet these varying demands. However, before discussing the steps to achieve focus, we should consider the origins of existing facilities, how they are arranged and the reasons for these decisions.

Origins of existing approaches to organizing operations

Driven by the concepts of economies of scale and control through specialists, operations facilities are usually large, with similar processes grouped together and centralized infrastructures organized into functions. A typical outcome of this is shown in *Exhibit 8.1*.

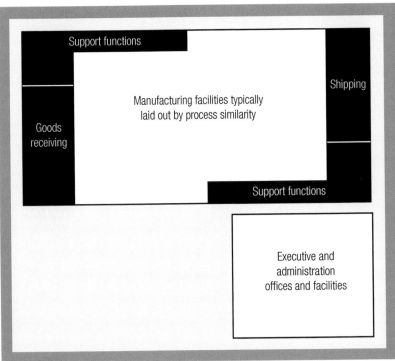

EXHIBIT 8.1 Typical layout of existing plants based on economies of scale principles (not to scale)

Processes are arranged so products share available capacity and equipment utilization is maximized. Similarly, a firm's organization structure is based on line/executive functions (such as sales and operations) with appropriate specialists undertaking advisory and support roles. The underlying rationale for this is economies of scale where skills and resources are grouped together to ensure they are best utilized and operating costs are minimized. Although there are sometimes cost benefits, this approach has managerial and strategic disadvantages, as shown in *Exhibit 7.3*. In fact, the additional resource required to overcome these management disadvantages, or the missed strategic opportunities, often mean the cost benefits are eroded.

Approach to focusing operations

The last chapter explained the concept of focus and the alternative approaches to achieve it. The idea is to arrange operations so there is a single consistent strategic task within each unit. Before outlining the steps to focus facilities, it is important to bear in mind the following:

- **Understand business and market requirements** – focus should not be seen as the preferred dogma on which to base operations arrangements. Replacing one dogma with another will lead to inappropriate investments or future situations of misalignment through neglect or lack of knowing what to do and how to do it.

- **Use a combination of approaches** – in reality, companies will typically use two or more approaches when focusing plants. Some developments will combine economies of scale principles with those of focus. Others will use a combination of the approaches to focus explained in the last chapter, such as products/markets, processes and market order-winners. Since combinations often yield the best overall results, companies must be pragmatic rather than dogmatic.

- **Not necessary to focus all products or processes** – very often, focus will not be appropriate for all parts of a business. When applying chosen approaches, companies may find that they are left with parts of the whole with which they can do little. Although requiring improvement, it can be difficult if not impossible to develop these remnants within the concept of focus because of insufficient similarity within the markets and strategic task.

- **Improving business and market support** – the principle of applying focus is to improve on what currently exists. Focusing parts of a business not only leads to gains within these parts but also simplifies that which remains unchanged, thus facilitating developments throughout.

- **Make incremental changes** – it is often best to rearrange a business one part at a time and enlarge the scope of change one phase at a time. Choosing areas where the rationale is clearest helps to improve the rate of success, reduce the size of the task, maintain acceptable timescales and allow everyone to learn.

The underlying theme when focusing a business must be pragmatism. Thus, if focus does not bring an overall cost, managerial or strategic benefit, it should not be applied. In most businesses, a combination of approaches will often result in the best overall improvement. Companies must have the desire to change and overcome the inertia and resistance that exists in most organizations. Furthermore, the process of change needs to be ongoing. As markets continually change, so must operations' response. In the past, many companies failed to question existing approaches because there has not been a viable, well-argued and well-articulated alternative. Focus provides another approach to organizing arrangements to better exploit its resources or market opportunities.

Focusing operations

This section outlines the steps to be followed when focusing operations *(Exhibit 8.2)*. As with most strategy developments, it is iterative in nature and needs adequate time to work through the issues involved.

1 Review processes

The first task is to review the existing operations to identify any processes that are too expensive to duplicate.[2] Examples of these differ from one business or industry to another and include heat treatment, clean room, coating or a specific technical process. These processes will either be managed centrally using economies of scale or process focus so their resources can be best exploited. Processes that are not too expensive to duplicate will be arranged to exploit market opportunities. In some companies, products are tied to given processes. Any rearrangement would therefore lead directly to process duplication, with potentially high additional investment. Upstream processes will often fall into this category. Downstream processes (for example packing) are normally less likely to be affected by this constraint because of the lower levels of investment typically involved.

2 Identify market order-winners and qualifiers

The next step is to identify the operations-related order-winners and qualifiers for the customer orders and products supplied. These will determine how best to arrange resources, given the constraints identified in the process review. It may be that some products have different order-winners depending on the nature of the order received. For example, an automotive component may be supplied to an original equipment manufacturer where orders are won on price. However, spares orders are also supplied and here delivery speed is more important.

3 Select focus approach for products and customer orders

The focus approach that creates the most advantages and least disadvantages must be identified. The process and market review in the previous two steps will highlight the cost, management and strategic advantages and disadvantages associated with alternative approaches for different products and customer orders. Order-winner focus is typically the best alternative, but sometimes the cost disadvantages associated with this are too great and other approaches are best used for certain customer orders, products or processes. Equally, as outlined in the previous chapter, focusing by order-winners may be a difficult concept for managers to grasp. In many instances, companies initially split by process, volume, variety, geography or product/market and then move to an order-winner focus at a later stage.

4 Group products and customer orders using focus approach selected

For example, if an order-winner focus approach is selected, products and customer orders should be grouped based on the order-winners and qualifiers identified in step 2. In some cases, it may make sense for a product to be supplied by two alternative units depending on the nature of the order received. Taking the example used in step 2, the business might decide to set up a price-focused unit and delivery speed-focused unit to meet the different order-winners of its markets. In this case, the same component may be supplied from two different units depending on the requirement of the customer order received.

Exhibit 8.2

Methodology: the six steps

Ideally, a similar set of order-winners and qualifiers within each customer order group should be created and therefore a single, coherent strategic task in each unit. However, the constraints of reality and what is best for the business need to be considered when making this decision. Once the split into customer order groups is agreed, then processes, products and infrastructure can be allocated to each unit.

5 Allocate processes

Once product and customer order groups have been agreed, processes are allocated and physically moved to each unit to meet their capability and capacity requirements. As identified in step 1, some processes may remain central, as they are too expensive to duplicate. These would be managed using economies of scale or process focus to serve the varying needs of each unit.

6 Rearrange infrastructure

The final step is to review and allocate the infrastructure required by each unit. As with allocating processes, it is important to review activities and assess if they should be allocated to a unit or remain central, serving all the units. Significant benefits can often be achieved because:

- Overheads are typically a large part of the cost and capability base of an organization. Aligning them to support the varying needs of its markets will ensure it is more competitive. The total overhead cost across the business is also often reduced as the appropriate level of resource to support each market is more clearly understood.

- Reshaping and repositioning overheads is usually not restricted by the same issues as processes, such as investment. Therefore, there is often more opportunity and gains to be made than in allocating processes.

Function	Activities typically best allocated to a	
	Central function	**Focused unit**
Quality	Quality assurance – agreeing sampling routines, laboratory testing and establishing checking procedures	Quality control – undertaking quality conformance checking procedures such as inspection
Operations planning control and scheduling	Long-term tasks such as capacity planning	Day-to-day scheduling and control of operations
Purchasing	Vendor selection and negotiating supply contracts	Arranging for call-offs of bought-out materials, components and other items in line with the operations schedule

EXHIBIT 8.3 Examples of the activities typically best allocated to a central function or focused unit

In reviewing and allocating infrastructure, two key principles must be considered:

- **Review activities not functions** – identify those activities that are better allocated to a unit and those which should remain central. In many instances, this will involve splitting existing functional activities, as shown in *Exhibit 8.3*.

- **Locate activities in the unit** – the overhead resources must be physically allocated to a unit and moved to the relevant site. This ensures that the unit is responsible for the level of resources required and how it should be managed. In this way, their prime interests and drivers are focused on the operational and strategic tasks of the unit.

Maintaining focus

As markets are inherently dynamic (they will change whether or not you want them to) and operations is inherently fixed (it will not change unless you deliberately change it), businesses will naturally become unfocused over time. Focusing operations is, therefore, not a one-off task and companies must continually review their markets and align operations to support their needs. A product's order-winners and qualifiers will change over time as it goes through its life cycle and the nature of the market in which it competes will also change. Very often the best response is to move the product to another unit that is oriented to its new strategic task, but new units may need to be developed.

Maintaining focus in maturing markets

A major supplier of components and products to the private, commercial and off-highway vehicle markets was reviewing one of its operations facilities. Product range increases, volume changes and the growing original equipment/spares mix in recent years had created a very complex operation. As a result, the facility was difficult to manage, had high work-in-progress inventory and was increasingly unable to meet customers' delivery needs or earn a satisfactory level of return on its investment.

To reduce the management task of the operation, it decided to create several product/market-focused units. It hoped these would better reflect customers' needs and reduce work-in-progress inventory. To test the validity of the approach, the company initially took the smallest manufacturing unit within the product/market split and relocated its processes and infrastructure to an unused part of the existing site. A review of this decision showed a series of gains resulting from the smaller units being easier to manage. However, more testing showed that market support had not been improved. The order-winners demanded were still not being met. The company had merely created smaller versions of the original facility with the same strategic problems. The high-volume original equipment and low-volume spares demanded different order-winning criteria. The appropriate split would have been to create order-winner-focused units. By aligning operations with its markets, it would create both management and strategic benefits.

Refocusing as products mature and diversify

A US-based pharmaceutical company reviewed its European operations in order to reduce cost and better align them to the markets they serve. At the time, the company had five product-focused units that supported all sales in Europe as well as the Middle East and Africa. Operations 1 and 2 were much larger than the other three and supplied a range of products at varying stages in their life cycles. Thus there were some high-volume products as well as low-volume demand from smaller countries and for products in the latter stages of their life cycle. Operations 3 and 4 also had similar mixed volumes, while all the products supplied by Operation 5 were low volume and at the end of their life cycle. The review identified excess capacity across the five facilities and so it decided to close Operations 1 and 2, and refocus the three remaining facilities. A market review showed that as price was not an order-winner, the key strategic task for operations was ensuring products are available to customers. Not meeting this requirement had previously resulted in lost sales and customers moving their loyalty to other brands. The decision was made to focus Operations 3 and 4 on the high-volume end of product demand and Operation 5 on low-volume products. This allowed Operations 3 and 4 to orient their priorities around process throughput speeds, meeting growing customer demand and always delivering on time, while Operation 5 prioritized reducing set-up times and developing a fast response capability for urgent orders. The overall result was a cost saving from the closure of the two facilities and a strategic benefit from the improved alignment of the three remaining facilities with its markets.

Focus examples

This section provides examples of alternative focus approaches and how they meet different business needs.

Strategic review resulting from increased demand for a product group

A large European electronics manufacturer was deciding where to locate its thick-film operation. It had two facilities in geographically separate sites but it needed to double its overall capacity in the near future to meet the anticipated growth in thick-film application. The alternatives were either to meet the increase using existing spare capacity in both sites or review existing demand in both facilities and move work to create room in one site. An assessment of the situation identified two issues. There was an increased quality conformance demand in the new market and increased engineering and development infrastructure support would be required.

A review of the market order-winners and qualifiers of its products showed they fell into two groups. One group has exacting product specifications, low volumes, requires a high level of development activity and a high calibre of engineering and specialist support. The other group has a lower product specification and higher volumes. The decision was made to create two order-winner-focused units to support these two groups. The availability and likelihood of attracting highly skilled engineering and specialist staff was higher at one facility than the other. This was therefore chosen for the low-volume products with the exacting specification and the thick-film operation was installed here.

The increase in demand for a product group had therefore initiated a strategic review of the whole business. There was no management benefit from the restructure as the units were still the same size as before, but there was strategic benefit from the improved alignment between operations and the markets it serves.

Benefits of allocating infrastructure

A large food company grew from its beginnings at the same operations site. The facility was sufficiently large to meet the increased demand and well placed to access the local labour pool and relevant distribution channels. Although the company enjoyed good profits and steady sales growth, it continually questioned its cost base and the appropriateness of its organizational structure. While it had managed to keep up with demand, its overheads had grown significantly. It decided to review them to see if they could be reduced and better aligned to its markets.

The first step was to review its processes. The technical requirements of product groups meant they could only be made on certain processes. This prevented any opportunity to cross-link different products by markets or order-winners, and meant the investment required to duplicate equipment could not be justified. However, it then reviewed its infrastructure and found that the centralized specialist and other overhead functions were not aware of the differences within its markets and their varying strategic tasks.

The result was that supporting activities were misaligned with market requirements. To rectify this, it chose to reallocate support staff to the separate manufacturing units. This allowed the company to provide support tailored to the particular needs of its various markets. The outcome was a significant reduction in overhead cost through the removal of unnecessary duplication of procedures, systems and excess support staff. There was also strategic benefit as the remaining overhead resource was better aligned to its markets.

Creating an operation-within-an-operation arrangement

A multinational packaging company has several operations in Europe and North America covering a wide range of packing from labels through to injection moulding. A strategic review in one of its Canadian facilities concluded that the most appropriate way to support its diverse markets was to move to an operation-within-an-operation arrangement[3] where each unit supports a different set of market needs. Before the change, the processes and infrastructure were functionally organized similar to that shown in *Exhibit 8.1*. The new layout is shown in *Exhibit 8.4*. Each of the three units contains the necessary capability and capacity of processes and infrastructure to support the needs of its market. However, some activities remained central such as vendor selection, negotiating supply contracts, goods receiving and shipping. It found that allocating some activities to the unit and keeping others central enabled it to better serve its markets without increasing operating costs.

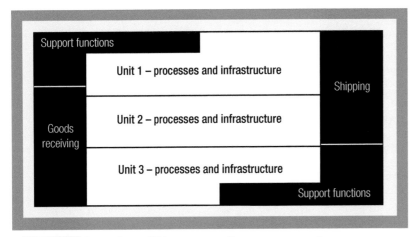

EXHIBIT 8.4 Operation-within-an-operation arrangement

Reflections

Focusing operations using individual units or plant-within-a-plant configurations can offer cost, management and strategic benefits that justify the investment involved. Markets are becoming increasingly different and operations must develop varying capabilities to support them. Using a functional approach to organizing operations can lead to a 'one size fits all' strategy where markets are supported using a single capability. The lack of market alignment, complex operations and resource required to manage this have led businesses to question traditional ideas and search for new solutions.

Focus is an alternative method for organizing operations where often the best results come from a mix of approaches. Companies must understand their markets before restructuring their businesses. Developments should be prioritized based on the cost, management and strategic benefit they create compared with the time and money required to make them.

Many companies need to review their manufacturing provision with some urgency. Splitting out those parts of a business that more readily lend themselves to focus is the place to start. However, avoiding the dogmatic use of these approaches is essential in order to gain substantial and lasting benefit. The dynamics of markets will necessitate continuous review and revision in order to avoid becoming unfocused.

Discussion questions

1　'When focusing operations, the optimal solution often involves a combination of approaches and all products and processes may not be focused.' Explain this statement using examples other than those described in this chapter.

2　Outline the main steps involved in focusing operations. Why do these tend to be iterative in nature? What are the main issues to consider at each stage? Give examples of how companies can overcome these issues.

3　Explain why maintaining focus needs to be a conscious strategic decision.

FOCUS
DOES NOT
OCCUR
NATURALLY

Businesses
NATURALLY
become
misaligned

Notes and references

1   In his book *The Strategy Quest* (1998) AMD Publishing, Bristol, Terry Hill depicts the procedures and concerns that characterize the development of a plant-within-a-plant business. Written as a novel, it is intended to help overcome the marked and understandable misgivings and questions raised when this issue is considered by any organization. While the style of the book is unusual, the issues addressed and debates pursued are commonplace.

2   In some instances, there may be other factors, for example space constraints, but often these also constitute cost-related reasons for not duplicating existing capabilities.

3   This is described in detail in *The Strategy Quest*, 1998.

▪ Exploring further

Berry, W., Bozarth, C., Hill, T. and Klompmaker, J. (1991) 'Factory focus: segmenting markets from an operations perspective', *Journal of Operations Management*, **10**(3): 363–88.

Bozarth, C.C. (1993) 'A conceptual model of manufacturing focus', *International Journal of Operations & Production Management*, **13**(1): 81–92.

Bozarth, C.C. and Edwards, S. (1997) 'The impact of market requirements focus and manufacturing characteristics focus on plant performance', *Journal of Operations Management*, **15**(3): 161–80.

Brush, T.H. and Karnani, A. (1996) 'Impact of plant size and focus on productivity: an empirical study', *Management Science*, **42**(7): 1065–81.

Casalino, L.P., Devers, K.J. and Brewster, L.R. (2003) 'Focused factories? Physician-owned specialty facilities', *Health Affairs*, **22**(6): 56–61.

Davidow, W.H. and Uttal, B. (1989) 'Service companies: focus or falter?', *Harvard Business Review*, July–August, pp. 77–85.

Devers, K.J., Brewster, L.R. and Ginsburg, P.B. (2003) 'Specialty hospitals: focused factories or cream skimmers?' Washington: Center for Studying Health System Change.

Hayes, R.H. and Schemenner, R.W. (1978) 'How should you organise manufacturing?', *Harvard Business Review*, **56**(1): 105–19.

Hayes, R.H., Pisano, G.P., Upton, D.M. and Wheelwright, S.C. (2005) *Operations, Strategy, and Technology: Pursuing the Competitive Edge*, Wiley: New York.

Hill, A. (2007) 'How to organise operations: focusing or splitting?', *International Journal of Production Economics*, doi:10.1016/j.ijpe.2007.06.002.

Ketokivi, M. and Jokinen, M. (2006) 'Strategy, uncertainty and the focused factory in international process manufacturing', *Journal of Operations Management*, **24**(3): 250–70.

Kimes, S.E. and Johnston, R. (1990) 'The application of focused manufacturing in the hospitality sector', Proceedings of the Manufacturing Strategy Conference of the Operations Management Association UK, University of Warwick.

New, C.C. and Szwejczewski, M. (1995) 'Performance measurement and the focused factory: empirical evidence', *International Journal of Operations & Production Management*, **15**(4): 63–79.

Pesch, M.J. (1996) 'Defining and understanding the focused factory: a Delphi survey', *Production and Inventory Management Journal*, **38**(2): 32–6.

Pesch, M.J. and Schroeder, R.G. (1996) 'Measuring factory focus: an empirical study', *Production and Operations Management*, **5**(3): 234–54.

Shafer, S.M. and Oswald, S.L. (1996) 'Product-focused manufacturing for strategic advantage', *Business Horizons*, **39**(6): 24–9.

Skinner, W. (1974) 'The focused factory', *Harvard Business Review*, May–June, pp. 113–21.

Skinner, W. (1996) 'Manufacturing strategy on the 'S' curve', *Production and Operations Management*, **5**(1): 3–14.

Van der Vaart, T. and Van Donk, D.P. (2004) 'Buyer focus: evaluation of a new concept for supply chain integration', *International Journal of Production Economics*, **92**: 21–30.

Van der Vaart, T. and Wijngaard, J. (2007) 'The contribution of focus in collaborative planning for make-to-order production situation with large set-up times', *International Journal of Production Economics*, doi:10.1016/j.ijpe.2006.12.053.

Van Dierdonck, R. and Brandt, G. (1988) 'The focused factory in service industry', *International Journal of Operations & Production Management*, **8**(3): 31–8.

Vokurka, R.J. and Davis, R.A. (2000) 'Focused factories: empirical study of structural and performance differences', *Production and Inventory Management Journal*, **41**(1): 44–55.

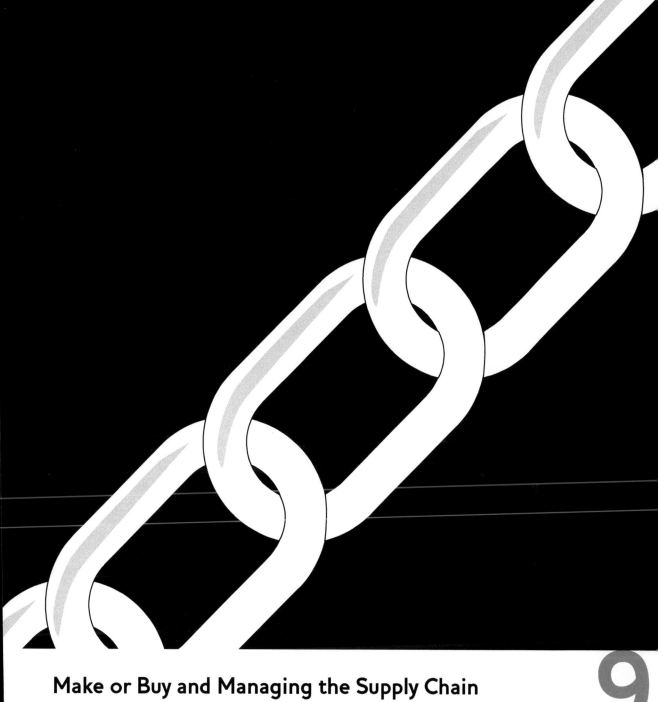

Make or Buy and Managing the Supply Chain

9

Summary

The increasing move by companies to outsourcing has increased the key decision area of make or buy and the task of managing the supply chain that results. Key areas within this aspect of operations are discussed:

- What is a supply chain? – the mix of internal and external phases of a supply chain need to be recognized and their joint roles in providing products need to be well managed.

- Make or buy? – choosing whether to make or buy is a key decision and various considerations need to be taken into account, including the retention of core technology, strategic factors and the supply chain management issues involved.

- Deciding what and how much to make in-house – the mix of benefits derived from making in-house and those derived from outsourcing offer different outcomes. These include compound market and technological intelligence, increased control over aspects of a firm's competitive environment, the provision of low-cost opportunities, more ability to differentiate products with in-house provision compared to freeing resources, reducing operating costs, access to world-class capabilities and increased focus on a company's own core tasks that come with outsourcing.

- Alternatives to making in-house – rather than making in-house, companies can choose from a range of halfway positions including joint ventures and non-equity-based collaborations.

- Domestic versus offshore sourcing options – the decision whether to outsource using domestic or offshore providers needs to be based on the level of strategic fit. Recent research shows that with low-cost alternatives is a reluctance to respond to changes in either product or lead time requirements.

- E-procurement – the increasing role of e-procurement needs to be considered as part of the supply chain provision.

- Managing the supply chain – a range of issues needs to form part of the task of managing the supply chain including managing uncertainty, level of customer/supplier dependence, the role of supply clusters and the ways to cushion the supply chain from the inherent instability of the market.

Companies rarely, if ever, own the resources, facilities and activities necessary to make a product from start to finish including delivery to customers. The decision on what to make in-house and what to buy and the task of managing the supply chain that results are key strategic issues within a company and ones that fall within the remit of operations. They concern the width of the internal phase of the supply chain (how much of a product is made in-house), the degree and direction of vertical integration alternatives and the links and relationships at either end of the spectrum with suppliers, distributors and customers (the external phase of the supply chain).

Both the make-or-buy decision and the task of managing the supply chain have major ramifications for a business. They impact growth and level of success and are crucial to survival. The corporate stance and response on both these key issues need to be the result of business-based discussions set in appropriate strategic context and involving sufficient recognition of the integrated nature of the resources and capabilities that forge a company's ability to compete.

What a company decides to make or buy will impact its potential to be successful in its current markets, while restricting or facilitating its ability to change direction in the future. Having made the decision, a company needs to appreciate that the various elements involved will invariably impact many of the order-winners and qualifiers in its own markets. Traditional corporate approaches, however, typically fail to recognize the integrated nature of the whole and the need to proactively manage all elements in line with its own market needs. Developing cooperation and improving coordination are not just good things to do but are essential if a company is to compete successfully now and in the future. In the past, the activities comprising the supply of materials through to the distribution of products to customers, although financially significant, were considered strategically peripheral. Now companies are recognizing that the ownership of activities and capabilities is not what matters but rather the ability to manage these in support of their markets.

What is a supply chain?

The series of steps between the origin of a product and its use or consumption is known as a 'supply chain'. Organizations will undertake some of these steps themselves – known as the level of vertical integration and the internal phase of the supply chain – while buying in earlier steps in the form of materials and services and contracting other organizations to undertake the later stages, for example distribution – known as outsourcing and the external phase(s) of the supply chain. There will be a varying number of tiers of suppliers and customers depending on the complexity of the product, and a varying number of suppliers and customers in each tier, reflecting not only the complexity factor but also how much of a product is provided in the internal phase, how much is bought in from outside and the steps in the route to market, as illustrated in *Exhibit 9.1*.

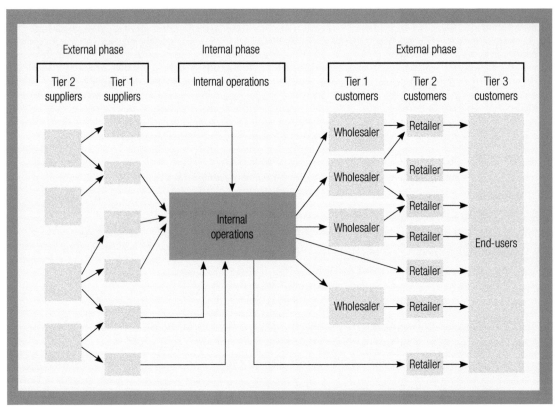

NOTE: The number of suppliers and customers is illustrative (not to scale).

EXHIBIT 9.1 Supply chain for a pharmaceutical company

Choosing whether to make or buy

Although in theory every item can be made or bought, in reality the choice is far more restricted. In some instances, companies may have no alternative other than to subcontract the making of a material, component, subassembly or even final assembly due to

technical, financial or other barriers to entry. Similarly, while making an initial buy decision or changing from a make to a buy decision are not, in theory, once and for all in
nature, in reality they often are. The difficulties of reversing such decisions at a future date
can be overwhelming due to the barriers to entry that have evolved. However, when they
consider their current make-or-buy positions, few businesses find that they have been
reached according to a well-considered and consistent set of criteria initially developed
and readdressed over time.

For well over a century, companies competed on the basis of the assets and resources
they owned. Being vertically integrated was the underlying philosophy on how best to
become and remain competitive. Since the 1980s, many, if not most, companies have
reconsidered their competitive position and increasingly migrated from the vertically integrated model. For instance, a recent survey of large and medium-sized companies reports
that 82 per cent of large firms in Europe, Asia and North America have outsourcing
arrangements of some kind and 51 per cent use offshore providers.[1] Similarly, in 2004, the
100 biggest US manufacturers spent 48 per cent out of every dollar of sales to buy materials and components compared with 43 cents in 1996.[2]

Given these trends, this section discusses the factors to be considered when deciding
whether to make or buy, while highlighting some of the actual reasons that underpin such
decisions and some alternatives to be considered.

Retaining core technology

Most companies choose to keep in-house those processes that represent the core technology elements of their business. For instance, a company that manufactures its own
finished items will invariably retain the assembly-onward end of the operations process.
The reasons include the wish to retain immediate control of product identity, design security, final product quality (conformance to design specification) and the ultimate link with
its customers.

In the same way, companies will seek to protect aspects of their products that reflect
advantage. Design security has already been highlighted and, in the same way, retaining
control over process technology developments will invariably lead to that stage being
retained in-house.

Strategy considerations

Make-or-buy decisions need to be made within the strategic context of a business and take
into account both the short and longer term competitive environment in which a company
will need to compete. In the short and medium term, the order-winners and qualifiers that
relate to a company's markets and that make-or-buy decisions affect need to be reflected
in such choices and their outcomes. In the longer term, such decisions must be set within
the scenario of future markets and the competitive forces that will likely prevail. For
example, in its early years, Dell Computer Corporation's ability to assemble personal
computers quickly in response to customers' orders was constrained by components
suppliers' long lead times.

However, other companies alert to key market-related issues incorporate these into their make-or-buy and sourcing decisions. For example, Lego, the Danish manufacturer of building kits and other toys, has concentrated its production in Europe and the US, arguing that this best satisfies its design and quality conformance requirements. And Lego is not alone in basing decisions on strategic rather than cost-alone factors. The apparel design and manufacturing companies', Benetton and Zara, decision not to source garments in Asia Pacific or Eastern Europe but to retain local (Italian and Spanish respectively) suppliers, who would meet the fast response needs of the supply chain support for their fashion-based marketplaces, are further examples of strategy-based make-or-buy decisions.[3]

Overall though, there has been a growing trend in many sectors towards outsourcing and away from making in-house. For example, the roll-out of the first Boeing 787 in July 2007 marked a strategic success for the company and its decision to build a fuel-saving, medium-sized passenger jet rather than going head to head with Airbus's giant A380. But the 787 is remarkable in another way – the degree to which Boeing (the giant US aircraft company) has outsourced production around the globe. This was for a number of strategic reasons, including the ability to tap into technical expertise and capacity elsewhere in the world and thereby avail itself of state-of-the-art technology while securing essential lead times and also reducing costs. The outcome is that Boeing itself is now only responsible for about 10 per cent by value of the 787 – the tail fin and final assembly. The rest is done by 40 partners. For example, the wings are built in Japan, the carbon composite fuselage in Italy and the landing gear in France This is in marked contrast to the past when, in the 1950s, only about 2 per cent of the Boeing 707 was built outside the US. Also in this sector, Embraer, the Brazilian aircraft maker, already uses a global manufacturing system and Airbus will follow Boeing's lead when building the A350, closing plants in Europe and outsourcing work to China and elsewhere.

Similar scenarios have been evolving in many, if not most, other sectors and not only fuelled by the attraction of lower cost labour, as in the cases, for example, of textiles, footwear and white goods. The continuing development of technical capability and accompanying skills has widened the opportunity to outsource in sectors ranging from heavy industries such as steel and shipbuilding through to pharmaceuticals and semiconductors while, in turn, the activities being relocated range from design through to final assembly. Couple this with government subsidies and the attraction to relocate and associated lower costs are both substantial and available. For example, in 2007 the Indian government announced a package of measures to attract chip and electronic factories and create 10 million additional jobs by 2012, with demand for semiconductors in India estimated to increase to $36bn by 2015 from $3.25bn in 2006, due to an expanding electronics goods manufacturing sector. These measures include interest-free loans and subsidies up to as much as 25 per cent of the capital needed where companies invest a minimum of $25bn in semiconductor plants and $250m for plants manufacturing other products. Similarly, China offers preferential tax rates if companies locate factories within a technology park or special economic zone.

As the examples below illustrate, the combination of lower costs coupled with technical capability offers a sound strategic option which many companies are choosing:

- **2005** – Advanced Micro Devices, the world's second biggest maker of PC processors, agreed a joint venture with SemIndia and the Indian government to build a $3bn factory in India to make chips for wireless phones and computers

- 2006 – Advanced Micro Devices began building its first plant in India

- 2006 – STMicroelectronics, Europe's largest semiconductor manufacturer, began building first plant in China

- 2007 – STMicroelectronics launched its first designed-in-India chip and announced plans to double its workforce in India to 3,000 by 2010 to take advantage of lower salaries, estimated to be as little as one-sixth of those in the US

- 2007 – Infineon Technologies, one of Europe's largest makers of semiconductors, licensed Hindustan Semiconductor Manufacturing to make products in two plants by 2009, involving a $4.5bn investment.

Whether or not a company makes in-house, supply chain performance regarding relevant order-winners and qualifiers in its markets will directly impact a company's ability to retain customers, grow share and make money. The issues involved will be addressed in detail in the later section on managing the supply chain, where the fundamental nature of this decision is clearly highlighted, fully discussed and appropriately illustrated.

Product/process technology and the internal phase of the supply chain

An earlier section highlighted make-or-buy positions that reflected a company's decision to retain relevant product and process technologies. In situations where there is a significant stepped change in product or process technology, the very opposite can happen. Take the case where a company applies new technology developments to its existing products or on the introduction of new, if similar, products into its current range and finds itself without the in-house process capability to meet all the new and more complex product technology requirements. One option is to buy in the technology as components. Normally, this narrowing of the internal phase of the supply chain takes place in the upstream stages of a process, where the new technology developments are the most radical; the later downstream processes are kept in-house because the technology associated with these is more in line with existing operations expertise and is also closer to the final product itself.

The IT sector provides a classic example of this. With the rapid rate of component development, IT companies often have no alternative other than to buy in the technology from outside in the form of chips and other parts in order to keep pace with competition and changing technical developments – the earlier examples of semiconductor and chip plants illustrate this trend. As *Exhibit 9.2* illustrates, although such companies may have had a wider internal span of process for their earlier products, with technology developments, this is correspondingly reduced.

In *Exhibit 9.2*, when producing only product range A, a company had developed in-house much of the process technology to make the products involved. The advent of product range B and, later, product range C heralded a distinct technology change. Not having the operations process capabilities to provide these new requirements, the company bought them in from outside in the form of components.

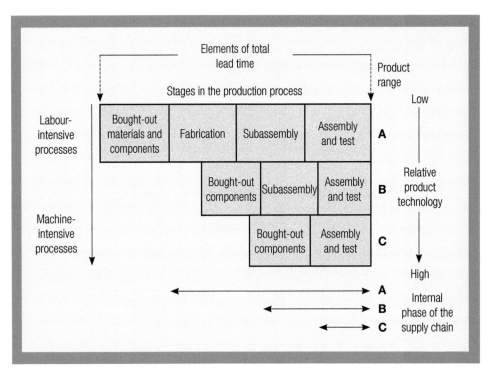

EXHIBIT 9.2 The reduction in the internal phase of the supply chain where more advanced technology is incorporated into a product (not to scale)

In such situations, when and by how much to widen the internal phase of the supply chain, after the initial narrowing, is a significant strategic decision, which in practice is often treated as an operational issue. A classic example of this was provided in the 1970s in the hand-held calculator market. Bowmar, one-time market leader, failed to integrate backwards into integrated circuit production and eventually withdrew from the business, while Texas Instruments (TI) successfully integrated forwards into calculators and took over the market leadership. One major reason for TI eventually displacing Bowmar was that its comparative process position gave it more opportunity to reduce costs and exploit potential experience curve gains, and that is what it did. Bowmar, restricted to assembly cost gains, was constrained by its suppliers' price reductions for a large part of its costs. TI, on the other hand, had no such limitations.

In the past two decades, the dominance of the Intel Corporation in PC design and the supply of chips, such as microprocessors, has redressed, if not revised, the supplier/ customer relations within the IT sector. Intel's increasingly powerful position as a supplier of chips has strengthened its opening position vis-à-vis customers and greatly changed the nature and results of subsequent negotiations within the board sector of the IT industry.

Product volumes

Companies faced with the different tasks involved with manufacturing high and low volumes can adopt a plant-within-a-plant alternative, as reviewed in Chapter 7. A company may also consider buying out those products with a low-volume demand. Examples of such decisions are typical in component-making companies in the automobile, truck and aero industries, among others. When the low-volume spares demand phase is reached in a product's life cycle, companies increasingly subcontract the manufacturing of these components and, in that way, keep the operations task within agreed bounds.

The reality of make-or-buy decisions

The previous section identified some of the principal reasons that may form the basis of make-or-buy decisions. In reality, many companies approach this critical task and base the strategic decision involved on reasons that are less rational and seldom sound. The more common of these are now discussed.

Continuing yesterday's decisions

Make-or-buy decisions taken at one moment in time are often not reconsidered at a later date. Inertia, a reluctance to add additional executive tasks and avoiding possible short-term problems militate against taking appropriate reviews. Once made, make-or-buy decisions often remain unchallenged.

Over the past three or four decades, a reduction in product life cycles, rapid changes in product and process technologies and growing world competition have increased the size and difficulty of the management task. One result has been that executives, while responding to changes that demand immediate attention, have deferred addressing other key, longer term issues. In some areas, this has resulted in companies taking their eye off the ball and failing to undertake periodic reviews regularly and within reasonable timescales. In key areas such as the make-or-buy decision, the corporate impact, especially in times of accelerating change, can be irreparable.

The dominance of cost and technology arguments

The format used to address the question whether to make or buy typically centres around issues of technology and cost. The initial consideration is whether or not a company has the process technology to make a component or product. Where the technical capability is not already in-house, to buy from outside is often an automatic response.

Where process technology is not a barrier, the next consideration is the cost of provision. While a most important dimension in itself, decision's made on this dimension alone and without addressing the requirements of markets and relevant order-winners and qualifiers (such as delivery speed, quality conformance, ability to ramp up and delivery on time) will invariably lead to inappropriate decisions, with a potentially damaging impact on a firm's short-term let alone long-term strategic position, as illustrated in *Exhibit 9.3*.

Part of a large US-based conglomerate, Rawlins Industries (RI) manufactures and assembles pumps to meet a wide range of industrial requirements including within the chemical, oil refining and mining sectors. Three years ago RI split its UK-based facility into a number of focused units to reflect the industries in which its customers competed. Since that time the company has arrested the decline in overall sales by increasing its market share in all sectors. Each focused unit is responsible for sourcing its own material requirements including castings, motors, seals and shafts.

The Group had set up a casting plant in Asia to avail itself of lower unit costs. All Group subsidiaries were encouraged to avail themselves of this opportunity and 12 months ago the focused units with RI made the switch. However, while previously its casting supplier provided a 4-week lead time, the Group's Asian casting plant offered lead times of between 16 and 20 weeks using fixed production schedules as a prerequisite to reducing manufacturing costs. With its own customers looking for lead times of 6 weeks, RI found itself no longer able to meet these requirements. In order to avoid losing sales, RI decided to hold casting inventories and also guarantee placing orders with its casting supplier equivalent to an agreed level of capacity with which it could decide on the actual castings it required. In this way, it brought its own operations lead time to 6 weeks and was now able to meet its customers on timescales.

However, RI now faces Group pressure to reduce its inventory levels.

EXHIBIT 9.3 The dominance of the cost argument

Shedding difficult operations tasks

Over recent years companies have tended to shed difficult operations tasks by subcontracting or divestment. Many firms approach this decision with an eye more on the difficulties embodied in the task, which may range from technical advances similar to those highlighted in the last section, reinvestments to update processes due to wear and tear, or enhancing staff capabilities. Short-term gains, taken on their own and without giving adequate weight to appropriate strategic issues, look most attractive and are easier to make. Surrendering ownership of costs, lead times, response to growth and issues around quality conformance, however, are key strategic issues. The accompanying loss of skill, operations' know-how and other factors that form the essential infrastructure from which to launch future changes in direction can limit future options. Such business decisions need to be based on more than the analysis of short-term figures, by taking account of the long-term consequences affecting a company's future options.

The accompanying loss of skill, essential operations know-how and infrastructure may limit a company's ability to respond in the future. A maxim to bear in mind is: 'if the operations task is easy, any company can do it.' The key to operations' success is to resolve the difficult operations issues, for this is where high margins are to be made.

Furthermore, in the evaluation of these decisions, some companies omit related costs and investments and so distort the picture. For example, a large manufacturing company established an offshore operations capability to avail itself of the low-cost opportunities inherent in that decision. In its subsequent assessment, the company failed to recognize that the costing and financial procedures did not allocate appropriate costs and inventory investment to the offshore site. Consequently, all rework costs and pipeline inventory were charged against the home-based plant. These distorted figures reinforced the buy decision that had been taken, encouraging similar decisions in the future. However, when the accounting rules were changed, future options became less attractive.

Political pressure

Within the context of the continuing movement of jobs to lower cost countries, some companies face growing pressure from workers to stem or even reverse this trend. One such recent example is Volkswagen. In 2007, VW factories had been running at about 70 per cent capacity for some time. As part of its restructuring agreement with IG Metall, the trade union representing 97 per cent of VW workers, employees' hours increased from 28.8 to 33 hours a week for the same pay (representing a reduction in labour costs per hour of almost 15 per cent), for which VW agreed to certain minimum production levels. The outcome was that VW plans to cut thousands of jobs at its Spanish, Portuguese and Belgium factories. With labour costs per hour at VW's Portuguese plants a third that for the company's West German factories, the restructuring gains will be more than cancelled out. In the long term, 'you can still argue [that] this is a company with too much production in Germany and too many decisions made by Germans', reflects one VW executive.[4]

General issues involved in make-or-buy decisions

Until recently, changes in make-or-buy decisions were associated principally with widening the internal phase of the supply chain. Faced with growing world capacity in the manufacturing sector with the advent of countries such as India and China, companies in more developed economies have, possibly for the first time in their recent histories, been confronted with the necessity to narrow the internal phase of their supply chain and often on many major business fronts. Well-received arguments about identifying core competencies and shedding other investments and process capabilities have further accelerated such moves.

The numbers

When repositioning the internal/external phases of a supply chain, a business must fully assess the issues involved. In particular, it needs to ensure that the estimated process and infrastructure costs, investments and savings are realistic. All too often the benefits fail to measure up to expectations. Additional sizable investments are often incurred after the event, which, although not included in the original decision, form an integral part of securing the benefits on offer. Ensuring that the numbers underpinning such decisions are robust, while being obvious, is all too often undertaken with insufficient rigour. While estimates will remain estimates, analysing past decisions after the event enables companies to check assumptions (of benefits, as wells as costs) and leads to more realistic (and thereby accurate) numbers being used in the future. The increase or decrease in overhead costs provides a classic example of the difficulty of making estimates and the value of past analysis to check corporate perception (estimates) against corporate reality (actuals). While direct costs (those costs concerned with selling the product and the physical handling of materials through the process including material purchase) can be more accurately ascertained, some aspects of cost, although sizable, are more difficult to assess and quantify. These include:

- the costs of coordination between the supply, operations and distribution functions.

- the elimination of associated overhead tasks. With a decision to change from a make to buy provision, the overhead cost reduction typically claimed and included in the evaluation is invariably difficult to identify and even more difficult to bring about. Known as 'vertical slicing', *Exhibit 9.4* depicts these costs.

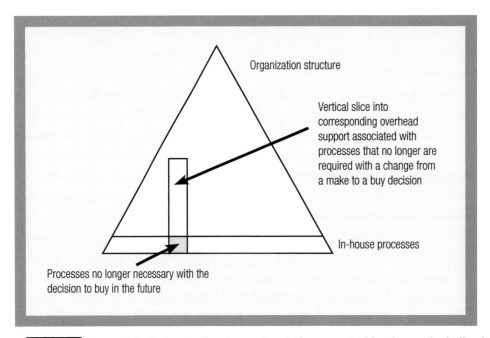

EXHIBIT 9.4 The anticipated reduction in overheads (represented by the vertical slice into organizational support and associated costs) that accompanies a decision to buy rather than make part of the operations requirement

- hardware, controls, procedures and other infrastructure requirements (such as training) to support the process investment. While the tangible costs of plant and equipment are readily identified and agreed in principle, the costs of less tangible areas that support such investments are not as apparent nor as easily quantified. Such decisions require careful judgement and so are often more closely examined by executives. As everyone has a view, these projected costs are scrutinized in great detail, invariably leading to lower estimates, even to the point that the existing infrastructure is believed to be able or just will have to cope. The numbers are made to look better at the time but, as reality has not changed, the costs may well resurface in the future, and the final tally can sometimes be in excess of that on which the initial strategic decision was based. Post-analysis will check what really happens and serve to inform future discussions and decisions.

Strategic factors

While make-or-buy decisions usually embody their own set of specific strategic issues, there are some important general factors that need to be taken into account:

- **Barriers to entry** – in industries where a wide internal phase of the supply chain creates distinct barriers to entry advantages, increasing the internal phase will heighten the financial and managerial resources required for a potential competitor to enter. Established firms may, therefore, raise the stakes, thus discouraging new entrants.

- **Supply assurance** – the supply of key materials may well be of such importance to a company that this gain alone would justify the associated investment. As with all forms of backward integration, whether or not a company decides to keep process capacity solely in balance with its internal needs raises its own set of advantages and disadvantages. It does, though, create uncertainty for customers, particularly regarding any planned future growth they may have.

- **Secured outlets** – as supply can be assured by integrating backwards, securing sales outlets can result from integrating forwards. Additional advantages also accrue with this move – improved customer feedback leads to a position of being more aware of demand changes and provides an opportunity to increase the accuracy of forecasts.

The management task

Changes in make-or-buy decisions invariably lead to changes in the management task within a business, for which many executives remain unprepared. What makes the task of managing a business complex is not the technical dimension as with, say, nuclear physics but the number of factors involved in the issues to be handled, that these factors all interrelate and are constantly changing. In the make-or-buy scenario, the complexity of the management task that accompanies the growing role of supply chains in meeting the day-to-day and strategic needs of companies changes the mix of issues to be understood and addressed and often outweighs any simplifying gains from shedding tasks. Such factors need to be part of any discussions on changing the make-or-buy status quo, while the changes in perspective and scope that follow then need to be embraced.

Width of internal phase of the supply chain: deciding what and how much to make in-house

The previous sections introduced important perspectives, issues and context concerning make-or-buy decisions. The following sections address alternative strategies. This first section concerns determining how much to make in-house, what is entailed and the benefits and disadvantages involved. The next flags up a growing problem for many industrialized nations: the hollowing of the manufacturing sector, and the final section discusses a company's alternatives to widening the internal phase of the supply chain.

Dimensions involved

The principal dimensions of deciding on the internal phase of the supply chain are the breadth and level of activity and the form it takes. Breadth addresses decisions on which of the principal activities a firm decides to undertake in-house. This involves functions such as design, operations and distribution. Closely linked to this is the decision on the amount, or level, of each activity to be undertaken in-house and how much will be subcontracted. Finally, the form concerns the level and type of ownership, trading partnership arrangements and other issues, outlined in a later section.

Benefits of making in-house

All make-or-buy decisions bring a mix of internal and external benefits and costs. For example, making in-house offers firms a range of potential advantages linked to greater knowledge of markets and technology, improved control over its environment and increased opportunity to support the characteristics of its markets. These include:

- **Support for markets in own hands** – having in-house the sets of processes and capabilities that directly support the order-winners and qualifiers within its markets results in corporate ownership of those aspects of a business essential to the successful application of its chosen strategy. In this way, the link between investment priorities and strategic needs is in one's own hands.

- **Improved market and technological intelligence** – increases the ability to more accurately forecast trends concerning key aspects of a business from demand patterns to technology and changes in the cost structure. Such awareness provides insights into current and future markets, which, in turn, strengthens a firm against known and opportunistic competitors.

- **More readily available technological innovations and options** – leads to a greater opportunity to share in the benefits from technology initiatives and their outcomes. Furthermore, it enables companies to transfer experience, so helping to reduce some areas of uncertainty.

- **Creates control over aspects of a firm's competitive environment** – these opportunities can take the form of backward integration to reduce dependency on suppliers and forward integration to help gain market penetration or acceptance; instances of the latter range from overcoming strong entry (even monopolistic) barriers, to gaining acceptance of new products. For example, St Gobain, a French glass-maker, purchased the UK-based glass processor and merchant, Solaglass, as a way of entering the UK glass market, which at the time was dominated by Pilkington Glass. Similarly, the advent of both aluminium and rayon provide examples of the way vertical integration facilitated the acceptance of the use of these new materials as substitutes in existing markets.

- **The provision of low-cost opportunities** – internal demand contributes to the high volumes that underpin low-cost manufacturing. For example, in the semi-conductor market, Japanese companies such as Fujitsu, Hitachi, Mitsubishi, NEC and Toshiba have progressively outcompeted their US rivals partly through the high level of integration that characterizes their businesses. Since the invention of semiconductors in the 1950s, accelerating growth has created a worldwide industry of over $130bn, more than four times what it was in the mid-1980s. However, the highly integrated Japanese semiconductor manufacturers are able to make their products at increasingly lower costs than their competitors throughout the rest of the world. A substantial part of this is the result of the high-volume base created by internal, corporate demand. Giant Japanese zaibatsus (conglomerates) make semiconductors along with everything else from robots to cars and satellites. The result is that Japan currently has over 50 per cent of the world semiconductor market.

- **More ability to differentiate products** – this occurs in all aspects of operations from product customization to the availability and use of new, alternative materials to meet a product's technical, cost and other requirements.

Benefits of outsourcing

On the flip side of this key decision are the benefits to be gained from outsourcing. These primarily concern cash, costs and technology and include the following:

- **Freed resources** – buy decisions reduce or more often eliminate the associated resources necessary to make the component, subassembly or final assembly. One outcome is that resources are freed, making funds available to be used elsewhere in a business.

- **Reduced operating costs** – with less being made internally, the process technology requirements and associated support are reduced together with the management and control tasks that typically accompany these aspects of operations.

- **Easier to control costs** – with buy decisions, the dimension of cost control is simplified to one of a supplier's unit price. Although contract negotiations demand their own set of skills, the task of cost control for the materials, components, subassemblies or assemblies involved is simplified.

- **Access to world-class capabilities** – purchasing from selected vendors creates the opportunity to source from potentially world-class capabilities. It gives access to the technologies and expertise that make up a provider's primary business.

- **Increased focus on own core tasks** – the reverse side of the last point, it allows a company to increase its attention, in terms of development time and investment, on its own primary business and associated core tasks – the underlying advantage of the strategy alternative known as 'core competence'.[5]

Disadvantages of outsourcing

To some extent, the disadvantages of outsourcing are the inverse of the benefits discussed above and supplement the section 'Benefits of making in-house'. They include:

- **May lose control of important capabilities** – outsourcing brings with it the possibility of losing control of key capabilities. For example, dimensions such as quality conformance, delivery speed and delivery reliability are now, in part, within the processes and systems of suppliers. Managing the whole supply chain, as discussed later, becomes increasingly important.

- **Control over the supply of key materials** – the decision to outsource brings with it less control over the supply of materials. While sound supplier relationships help to mitigate possible supply problems, exposure to potential material shortages goes hand in hand with the decision to outsource. For example, in late 2004, Nissan Motors was forced to stop production at three of its four car assembly plants in Japan for five working days after running out of steel, with the loss of 25,000 vehicles. It is expected that the growth of the manufacturing sectors in China, India and South Korea will continue to put Asian steel suppliers under pressure to meet the demand for steel in the decade to 2017. In the meantime, steel prices have risen sharply, bumping up companies' costs and eating into profits.

- **Control over intellectual property** – one concern for companies that outsource from offshore is how rigorous is the intellectual property rights protection regime within the countries where the suppliers are based, with China as the country where these concerns are currently highest. In 2005, General Motors and Honda both sued Chery Automobile in the Shanghai courts concerning unauthorized use of trade secrets and breaches of competition laws.[6]

- **Creating your own competition** – outsourcing, no matter what form it takes, presents a new risk to companies. Sensitive information needs to be shared on the one hand and providing the opportunity for new entrants to gain expertise presents a risk on the other. It is important for firms to look long and hard before turning to suppliers for engineering help. If the technical dimension in all its forms is part of a company's competitive advantage, giving it away means having less of an edge in the marketplace. In today's competitive environment, this could be a significant, long-term disadvantage. As illustrated in *Exhibit 9.5*, examples from the past illustrate the consequences, while more recent ones point to the potential involved.[7]

- **Reversability** – the decision to subcontract is invariably irreversible. This is due, in part, to a reluctance to reconsider and then change direction on previous outsourcing decisions, coupled with the stepped nature of such a change in terms of buying in technical capability and expertise from a zero base.

- **New management skills** – managing a supply chain requires different, and often more demanding, skills than those needed to handle in-house operations. Often, and particularly in the past, purchasing and related functions within a business have been allocated 'Cinderella' status, with corresponding levels of resource and management talent. Integrating the essential links within a supply network requires skills of a high order to secure the essential contribution to ensure the needs of a firm's markets are met.[10]

- In the 1960s, the then-dominant US television industry gave the technology to build picture tubes to low-cost Asian suppliers. Some time later, Asian companies began making entire TV sets and the US industry nearly went out of business.

- In an interview, Hisashi Sakamaki, who at the time oversaw all Canon's (the Japanese photo and printer giant) operations, recalled the important lessons learned from US companies' mistakes as described by the MIT Commission on Industrial Productivity.[8] He said: 'The key for us has been to figure out how to benefit from production overseas without losing our capacity to develop production at home. Most American firms rushed abroad and lost that knowledge.'[9]

- As described earlier, Boeing's outsourcing of some 90 per cent by value of the 787 provides a more recent example, with Airbus following suit in producing the A350. Critics of Boeing's decision argue that the company is giving away intellectual property in return for capital. In that way, it is helping suppliers in China and Japan to develop technology that they will use to make their own aircraft. Since the 1980s, Boeing has let Japanese suppliers get close to fuselage design practices on wide body jets. Boeing has long advocated partnerships as a way of controlling the Japanese but there is growing concern that such practices will help to stimulate an Asian aircraft industry. And, given Japanese engineering prowess in other sectors, aerospace is a ready-made extension of their current expertise.

- IBM essentially created the PC industry, but by 2008 the company's nameplate will no longer be seen on PCs as IBM leaves this sector except for its recently formed joint venture with Lenovo. Formed in 1984 as a distributor of IBM's and other companies' equipment in China, Lenovo now makes its own PCs and is the fourth largest PC manufacturer in the world. The same story is repeated with Sanmina-SCI who makes IBM's PCs and in 2005/6 acquired some of IBM's own factories. Originally distributors of well-known brand names, Lenovo and Sanmina moved into assembly and now design and engineer custom electronic products.

EXHIBIT 9.5 How to create your own competition

The rationale for outsourcing is well articulated but needs to be set within the strategic context of a business in terms of its own long-term position and how it needs to manage those relationships to ensure it controls the overall scenario to its own desired advantage. Reducing labour costs and freeing up capital on the one hand and allowing the original equipment manufacturer (OEM) to concentrate on its strengths – R&D, design, marketing and product launches – on the other have been well articulated in the past. However, such decisions are a two-edged sword. Access to an OEM's intellectual property, its exposure to developments in the range of companies it serves and its growing operations prowess provide sufficient advantages and strengths to integrate forward and bite the hand that feeds them. Taking the easy option of subcontracting the difficult operations tasks in support of thinning profit margins, on the one hand, and facilitating support for short product life cycles and speed to market of new products, on the other, looks good on paper and points to immediate success and a pain-free resolution of a company's immediate difficulties.

The counter-argument is that this is the way the world is, and without doubt this is a growing trend. Identifying what should be the preferred supply chain mix between the internal and external phases is one that companies need to address and readdress with care. Once the decision is made to outsource, the decision is virtually irreversible, and may result in losing out altogether. Lessons from history continue to be disregarded.

How much to make in-house

The final dimension concerns how much of the supply chain a firm chooses to undertake and the extent of each part of the supply chain it then fulfills. Four options exist:

1. At one extreme, firms may decide on a fully integrated strategy, where all their requirements for a given material, product or service are provided internally. In these instances, the supplying units are usually fully owned subsidiaries. This alternative works best where:
   - the level of price competition does not require companies to pursue the lowest cost alternatives to compete effectively in a market
   - the advantages derived from accessibility to scarce resources outweigh other factors
   - capacity increases are not stepped in nature, which can create investment obstacles in terms of changing demand and associated volumes.

2. At the other extreme, firms may decide to have their products completely made outside and may be only handling the finished goods warehousing phase themselves.

3. The classic option is one where companies determine what to make in-house and agree with chosen suppliers for them to provide the other parts of the supply chain.

4. An option within the last alternative is referred to as a 'taper-integrated strategy'.[11] With this, firms rely on outsiders to provide a portion of their requirements, which enables its own facilities to secure a high level of capacity utilization by alternating the make-or-buy decision to advantage. However, such strategies, especially when exercised to the full, incur a number of disadvantages, including:
   - alternating the make-or-buy decision to advantage militates against developing good customer/supplier relations. In the long run, it may alienate suppliers, as such strategies often do not provide them with adequate lead times to enable resources to be switched, capacity to be reduced or alternative sales to be secured
   - by definition, a taper-integrated strategy implies splitting volumes and dilutes those conditions that maximize low-cost opportunities
   - alert suppliers may charge a price premium where volumes are low and subject to fluctuations.

Judging what and how much to make in-house must be well thought through and fit the needs of the business. Where it has not, rationalization will often replace strategic rationale. The decision to make in-house is based on the assumption that the potential benefits are tangible and achievable. In some instances, companies may integrate because the opportunity to do so was available and timely. But it is essential to separate the action itself from the rationale underpinning that action, otherwise a firm may unknowingly incur significant disadvantages.

As emphasized earlier, determining the appropriate width of the internal phase of the supply chain needs to be based on sound data. Unless what is involved at each level is known, deciding where is best is not possible. A realistic assessment of costs and benefits is essential as well as the timescales involved in terms of current decisions and future changes.

The hollow corporation

There is an increasing recognition of and growing concern about a phenomenon referred to as the 'hollow corporation'. Where companies have considered the question of how operations should best be organized to meet the dynamics of their markets, many have shied away from addressing and incorporating the operations dimension within the debate concerning the appropriate short- and long-term strategy for a business. The attraction of low-cost opportunities in Asia Pacific, Eastern Europe and Mexico has lured many European and North American firms to subcontract substantial parts of their existing processes without regard for, adequate understanding of, or sufficient in-depth debate about the long-term implications of these critical and often irreversible decisions. The simplistic rationale of problem avoidance has such siren-like qualities as to make the decision difficult to argue against.

The long-term consequences of these decisions to companies and nations need to be fully recognized and adequately assessed. Such decisions bring the instant rewards of solution and profit. For many organizations, moving offshore becomes a last resort to offset sizable structural disadvantages. The alternative is to become competitive in the relevant dimensions such as design, price, quality conformance and delivery speed and on-time performance. The impact of this short-term thinking has to be fully assessed. To the nation as a whole, there is an increasing dependency on imports, compounded by a loss of technological know-how and ownership, which will invariably lead to being driven out of some businesses altogether. Companies pursuing this rationale rarely do so as a way of buying time to enable them to strategically regroup. For most, it is a comprehensive solution in its own right, with an apparent disregard for the long-term implications and inherent constraints imposed on future strategic options. Furthermore, the ripple effect means that for every $1bn of imports, there is a further substantial loss to a nation's economy as a whole.[12] In addition, as time goes on, these offshore plants will draw the service jobs that surround operations and at a company level, the effects are similar; once skills have been transferred out, that know-how will eventually be lost to that company.

The trend towards outsourcing on a larger scale has gathered momentum partly on the back of increased corporate moves towards downsizing that took a strong hold on business strategy direction from the mid-1980s. Bolstered by doctrines such as core competence, the benefits and rewards offered by solution-based approaches have a unique appeal to unquestioning recipients. The attraction of such offerings as fixed asset freedom, cash infusion, capital fund availability and lower overhead cost structures was and still is much heeded at the economic altar of financial markets.

The decision on whether or not to outsource is a sound one to address. What is of concern are the bandwagon consequences of panacea solutions, the failure to review the decisions within the context of the overall business and to assess the strategic impact over appropriate timescales. *Exhibit 9.6* humorously depicts one ultimate outcome, with the commentary, as always, aimed at exposing and questioning, in this instance, the potential folly of the underlying trend.

At the extreme, the postindustrial company could be vertically disaggregated, relying on other companies for operations and many essential business functions. They become industrial, corporate shells. And there are strong forces pushing companies this way. In the short term, these decisions offer fixed asset freedom and dynamic networking, both arguably suited to meeting the characteristics of today's markets. Such arrangements allow companies to respond quickly to exploit new markets and new technologies. The organizations become more agile, flexible and responsive. Typically, firms need less capital, carry lower overhead costs and can better tap into outside technology. In essence, they are more entrepreneurial.

One outcome of this is that manufacturing companies of a new kind are evolving – those that do little operations. They import components and assemble them or import the products themselves and sell them. The result is a hollowing of once-powerful manufacturing companies. Following a strategy of this kind, companies become trapped in a position where their ability to compete is increasingly undermined by their own and their competitors' actions. Unchecked, this will invariably lead to the abandonment of their status as strong industrial companies and the retardation of their capacity for innovation and productivity improvement. The erosion of a nation's wealth-creating activity is the aggregate effect of these policies, which in the end reduces the standard of living enjoyed by its people.

Alternatives to making in-house

The discussion so far has implied that the choices companies must make also involve an ownership or non-ownership option. Either a company invests in the process through ownership or it buys out its requirements from suppliers. In certain situations, many companies perceive that they have limited options or just Hobson's choice.[13] To them, being reliant on suppliers is not a feasible alternative.

Where greater control is necessary, alternatives to making in-house (widening the internal span of process) may be an option. The alternatives below are based on an appropriately high degree of liaison between those involved. Some involve legal agreements or arrangements of some kind. Others attempt to exploit opportunities with links that are beneficial to all concerned.

Joint ventures

Where companies have similar needs and both can benefit from combining, a joint venture is a sensible alternative. This is particularly the case in areas such as applied technology and research.

© Roger Beale

Exhibit 9.6

A hint of satire in this comment on the trend towards outsourcing by highlighting the potentially simplistic approach to these key strategic decisions

Joint ventures are separate entities sponsored by two or more actively involved firms. Because joint ventures draw on the strengths of their owners, they have the potential to tap the synergy inherent in such a relationship and the improved competitive abilities that should accrue. Since the late 1970s, joint ventures have increased substantially in Europe and the US, particularly in sectors such as communications systems, IT and services. As *Exhibit 9.7* shows, most companies see joint ventures as a viable alternative and one that, in most businesses, will increase.

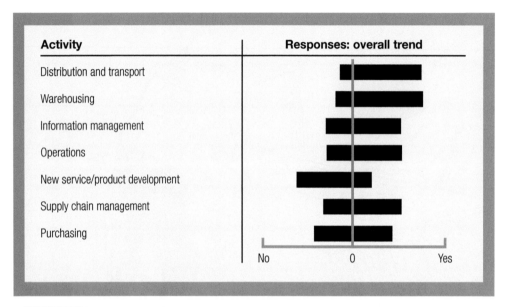

EXHIBIT 9.7 Responses to the question 'Are joint ventures a viable alternative?'

SOURCE: Hill, T. (2005) *Operations Management,* 2nd edn, Basingstoke, Palgrave Macmillan

Joint ventures have become an important way of improving the strengths and reducing the weaknesses of cooperating businesses. Companies willing to undertake the necessary high degree of commitment and cooperation can exploit opportunities from which they previously would have been debarred, due to investment or lead time barriers.

However, joint ventures should not be seen as a convenient means of hiding weaknesses. If used prudently, such arrangements can create internal strengths. They can be resource-aggregating and resource-sharing mechanisms, allowing sponsoring firms to concentrate resources where they possess the greatest strengths. *Exhibit 9.8* provides a comprehensive list of reasons for forming joint ventures, classified into operational and strategic uses.

Joint ventures, therefore, not only share investment but, often more importantly, provide direction and make fresh opportunities possible. Identifying the areas on which to focus attention, with the knowledge that the developments will have a commercial outlet, can give substance to such decisions. Reducing risk in this way while also limiting the investments required to bring the activity to fruition may provide an ideal solution. In this way, a joint venture is a sensible alternative to the owner/non-owner options.

Advantages		

Strategic	• Strengthens current strategic position by
	  – pioneering developments into new segments
	  – rationalizing existing segments
	  – reducing competitive volatility

	• Pre-empts competitors
	  – facilitates access to new markets and customers
	  – supports growth in market share
	  – strengthens negotiating position
	  – gains access to global markets

	• Augments strategic position
	  – creates and develops synergies
	  – technology and skill transfers

Operational	• Reduces uncertainty
	• Shares investment and risk

	• Process capacity sharing
	  – increases utilization
	  – avoids process duplication

	• Shares facilities in other parts of the supply chain, for example distribution channels

	• Increases technological know-how by
	  – facilitating information exchange
	  – potentially creating critical mass in areas such as research and development
	  – broadening expertise in, for instance, engineering and IT systems

	• Strengthens market intelligence

	• Helps retain key staff
	  – increased job scope
	  – better career opportunities

EXHIBIT 9.8 Reasons for forming joint ventures

Non-equity-based collaboration

Companies unwilling or unable to cope with joint venture arrangements can resort to an appropriate form of non-equity-based collaboration to meet their needs. These mechanisms provide the means of establishing cooperative working arrangements that need a long-term base if the collaboration is to yield meaningful and useful results. Such arrangements include:

• Research and development consortia to enhance innovation and the exploitation of results.

• Cross-marketing agreements to provide opportunities, such as utilizing by-products, widening product lines and sharing distribution channels.

• Cross-operations agreements to avoid duplication of facilities, provide vertical integration opportunities and transfer technology know-how.

- Joint purchasing activities to enhance buying power in terms of price gains and increased supplier allegiance.

Developing the supply chain

The goal of supply chain management is to link the market, distribution channel, operations process and supplier base such that customers' needs are better met at lower costs. While many companies began fixing their operations problems from the early to mid-1980s, few addressed the total cost of ownership. By the early 1990s, progressive companies had begun to realize the need to refocus from 'fixing' operations to addressing how to better manage their supply chains, a fact confirmed by a 1996 European-based survey. This identified that 88 per cent of the companies reviewed had been carrying out significant overhauls of supply chains and saw supply chain management as the focus for improvement in their overall performance.[14] But, we should have learned from history that little ever changes. In 1929, Ralph Borsodi observed that in the

> 50 years between 1870 and 1920 the cost of distributing necessities and luxuries had nearly trebled, while production costs had come down by one fifth … what we are saving in production we are losing in distribution.[15]

A similar scenario exists today.

Origins and evolution of supply chains

As emphasized earlier when discussing the concept of focus (Chapters 7 and 8), the origin of organizations in the 21st century is rooted in functional management and control, with the subsequent result of split responsibilities. The classic outcome was a fragmented supply chain emphasizing vertical rather than horizontal processes, as illustrated in *Exhibit 9.9*.

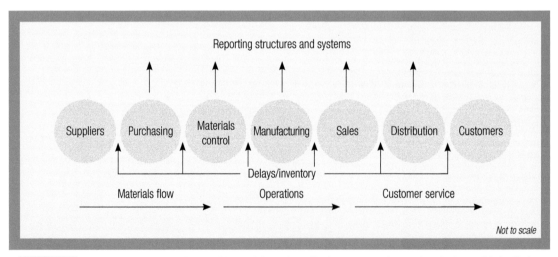

EXHIBIT 9.9 Phase 1: typical initial position of functionally fragmented supply chains with built-in delays/inventory, vertical reporting structures and systems and the separation of suppliers, operations and customers

For most companies, developing a supply change is a multiphase task. It starts with integrating the steps within the internal phase of the supply chain, as illustrated in *Exhibit 9.10*. This internal coordination emphasizes the horizontal nature of the processes inherent in the basic tasks of procurement through to finished goods provision and forges cooperation between the steps to create an integrated whole and the opportunity to reduce costs and delays on the one hand and improve responsiveness to customer needs on the other.

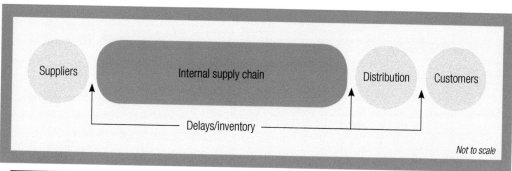

EXHIBIT 9.10 Phase 2: integration of the supply chain activities within a business

The next step concerns coordinating activities between businesses. As shown in *Exhibit 9.11*, this stage involves recognizing additional facets within the supply chain (for example tier 1 and tier 2 suppliers and stages in the distribution channel) in order to ensure that these form part of the collaborative development between supply chain partners.

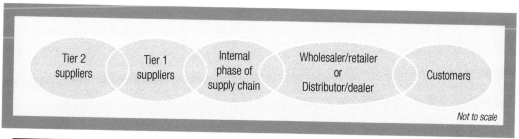

EXHIBIT 9.11 Phase 3: collaboration across the supply chain by coordinating activities between businesses

The final phase is to synchronize the planning and execution of activities across the supply chain, as shown in *Exhibit 9.12*. This requires partnership and strategic alliance arrangements that will include the transfer and access of data between businesses from design through to order fulfilment, call-offs and delivery schedules. Traditional roles and responsibilities will change dramatically, with suppliers at times taking responsibility for design through to the internal phase of the supply chain and deciding how much and when to ship goods to customers at other times.

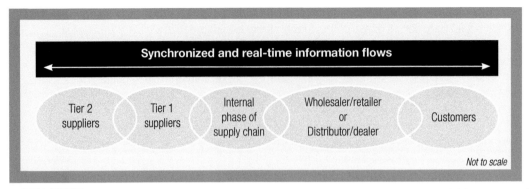

EXHIBIT 9.12 Phase 4: synchronized and real-time planning and execution of activities across the supply chain

The principles underlying these changes have their origins in a recognition that the whole, and not solely the internal phase, of a supply chain is the basis for today's competition. Given the extent and nature of the support for markets that is provided by operations, aligning the supply chain provision with the requirements of agreed markets needs to be a central feature of strategy implementation. Key issues that result include:

- **Overcoming the barriers to integration** – functions within organizations and organizations themselves create barriers to integration. Viewing the supply chain as a whole is a prerequisite for rethinking how best to provide market support through the entire supply chain and overcoming these inherent obstacles.

- **Responding to short lead time** – delivery speed is an order-winner or qualifier in many of today's markets. Customers are seeking to reduce lead times and the strategic response of suppliers needs to match these quick response demands. To do this reliably requires developing lean logistics and managing the supply chain as an integrated whole.

- **Eliminating costs** – an integrated approach lowers costs by reducing inventory, simplifying procedures, eliminating duplication and other non-value-added activities together with associated overheads. Viewing the supply chain as a whole enables processes and procedures to be structured with the associated gains of reduced time and cost.

- **Moving information, not inventory and delays** – non-integrated approaches have built-in delays comprising time and inventory. By moving information, delays are reduced and subsequent parts of the chain can match real-time needs rather than using inventory to provide against uncertainty and the unknown.

One parallel to lean supply chain management is provided by the revolutionary changes brought to high-peak climbing by Reinhold Messner. As *Exhibit 9.13* explains, the 'direct alpine approach' he introduced changed the 'conventional mountaineering strategy' (one based on 'massive amounts of support including extra oxygen') to one using 'little equipment and no oxygen support to reach the top'. Messner argued that under the conventional approach, the slowest man set the pace, whereas his goal was 'speed of execution' – the final assault was made 'by himself, or with one other person, in a single day'.

'Reinhold Messner, the Italian climber, is one of the great sports heroes of Europe. His claim to fame is not so much that he climbed all 14 of the world's highest peaks. Messner's primary achievement is that he introduced a totally new way of climbing – the direct alpine approach – which uses little equipment and no oxygen support to reach the top.

Conventional mountaineering strategy is based on massive amounts of support, including extra oxygen, thought essential for climbs over 25,000 feet. Men such as Sir Edmund Hillary and Chris Bonington relied on hundreds of guides who carried food, oxygen and other supplies; an American expedition to climb Everest in 1963 included 900 porters trudging up the mountain with 300 tons of equipment.

Messner argues that under this strategy, the slowest man sets the pace. His goal is speed of execution. Although assisted by guides up the base of a mountain, Messner usually makes the final assault by himself, or with one other person, in a single day. He scaled the north face of Everest solo, without oxygen – one of the most severe mountaineering challenges ever attempted.'[16]

When Hillary and Tenzing became the first mountaineers to climb Everest in 1953, they took seven weeks. On 22 May 2004, Pemba Dorji Shelpa took 8 hours and 10 minutes using the direct alpine approach.

EXHIBIT 9.13 Lean supply chain works elsewhere and brings similar benefits

Globalization

With trade barriers easing and markets opening up, the globalization of business activity has accelerated. Two key issues result from this – a widening choice of offshore suppliers and the need to manage the global supply chain that emerges.

The growing operations base of regions and countries such as Asia Pacific, Eastern Europe, Mexico and South America has received high exposure in part, if not exclusively, due to the low-cost manufacturing provision they offer. While for some companies low cost is consistent with their market needs, it is essential that market requirement and not unit cost drives choice. Low cost is often not the strategic priority for a business and companies are clearly beginning to recognize this. For example, developed countries typically take up to two-thirds of foreign direct investment inflows, while developing countries accounted for the remainder.

There is an increasing emphasis on global capability. In order to take full advantage of this opportunity, companies need to manage the processes and interfaces involved. It is essential to avoid the scenario of gaining advantage in one phase of a supply chain and losing the benefits in the next. Key to this is globalizing total customer support from design through logistics to the end user.

Domestic vs offshore sourcing options and strategic fit

As highlighted in the last section, companies across all sectors are taking advantage of lower priced goods and services offered by offshore suppliers. The advantage of lower labour costs means that they are able to undercut domestic competitors. But outsourcing decisions include a domestic as well as an offshore option. So, what are the trade-offs involved in this choice, particularly regarding strategic fit?

Retailer	Percentage of goods purchased over 12 months by location						
	Asia	Africa	Central America	Europe	North America	UK	Other
North America	20	3	24	1	52	0	0
Average discount (%) available	20–30	10–15	20–25	5–10	0	–	–
UK	36	2	0	24	3	34	1
Average discount (%) available	25–35	15–20	–	10–15	1–5	0	5–10

SOURCE: Based on Lowson, R.H. (2001) 'Offshore sourcing: an optimal operational strategy?', *Business Horizons*, November–December, pp. 61–6

EXHIBIT 9.14 Sourcing location, percentage of goods purchased and discounts available

Relative to start of the sales season	Sourcing region	Supplier latitude for change once order is placed					
		Order volume change (%)			Order mix change (%)		
		None	Some	Substantial	None	Some	Substantial
Before	Asia	66	22	12	70	19	11
	Africa	58	19	23	62	20	18
	Central America	41	38	21	46	34	20
	Europe	29	43	28	37	38	25
	North America	16	49	35	21	49	30
	UK	9	52	39	21	46	33
	Other	34	40	26	30	37	33
After	Asia	70	21	9	86	12	2
	Africa	66	16	18	73	8	19
	Central America	52	33	15	63	30	7
	Europe	35	38	27	41	35	24
	North America	39	33	28	47	29	24
	UK	19	46	35	28	39	33
	Other	32	42	26	39	37	24

SOURCE: Based on Lowson, R.H. (2001) 'Offshore sourcing: an optimal operational strategy?', Business Horizons, November–December, pp. 61–6

EXHIBIT 9.15 Suppliers' latitude for volume or mix change before and during the sales season, by geographical region

Recent research on retail companies in North America and the UK and the sourcing of goods from both domestic and overseas suppliers highlighted many of the trade-offs involved. As the results in *Exhibits 9.14* and *9.15* show, not only does the domestic versus offshore alternative differ but so does the offshore region involved. The trade-off between high discounts and low latitude for change is clearly evident for Central American and Asian suppliers versus alternatives. As the whole supply chain needs to support the needs of a company's chosen market, both the external and internal phases of the chain need to support the relevant order-winners and qualifiers of these markets, the concept of strategic fit.

Offshore manufacturing plants

Offshore manufacturing plants are typically established for the classic benefits of tariff and trade concessions, lower labour costs, subsidies and reduced logistic costs. As a consequence, they are often assigned a limited range of tasks and responsibilities that reflect the prime reason for which they were built. Companies are now reviewing this classic perspective and broadening their expectations of offshore plants and the way they manage and measure them (see *Exhibit 9.16*). It is important for companies to exploit these opportunities and *Exhibit 9.17*[17] lists some potential roles for offshore factories.

Company	Location	Tasks
Hewlett-Packard	Guadalajara (Mexico)	• Assembles computers • Designs memory boards
3M	Bangalore (India)	• Manufactures software • Writes software
Motorola	Singapore	• Manufactures pagers • Designs pagers

EXHIBIT 9.16 Examples of companies seeking and gaining additional roles from offshore plants

Development phase			Characteristics
1	Type of factory	Offshore	Established to manufacture specific items at low cost
			Technical and managerial investments kept to a minimum
			Level of local autonomy is typically not extensive
2		Server	Supplies specific national or regional markets
			Typically located to overcome tariff barriers, reduce taxes, minimize logistic costs or cushion the business from exposure to foreign exchange fluctuations
			Provides a base from which to launch products into a market (for example the European Union)
3		Contributor	Serves a specific national or regional market
			Responsibilities extend to product development and process engineering as well as the choice and development of suppliers
			Potential site as a testing ground for new products, process technologies and computer systems
4		Lead	Creates new products, processes and technologies for the company as a whole
			Responsible for tapping into and collecting local knowledge and technological resources in general and for use in developing new products and processes
			Key role with suppliers including choice and development
			Whole range of external relationships including customers, process technology suppliers and research centres
			Frequently initiates innovations

EXHIBIT 9.17 Progressive roles of offshore manufacturing plants

Logistics costs

It is estimated that US companies spend almost 11 per cent of GDP (about $1450bn in 2006) to wrap, bundle, load, unload, sort, reload and move goods around. By 2010, the estimated logistics bill in Europe will be approaching $250m. With figures like these, the cost of making products is not necessarily the area in which to seek savings. A typical box of cereals in the US is estimated to spend 140 days getting from factory to supermarket shelf. It goes through a procession of stages, each of which has a warehouse. The resulting inefficiencies and logistic costs are staggering.

When developing their supply chains, companies need to take into account location choices and associated costs. The lack of attention paid to supply chain development in the past and the growing size of logistics in terms of costs and lead times make the potential benefits attractive and should be high on most companies' priority list.

Aspects of change

Underpinning the developments set out in the last section are a number of changes that need to be secured if the desired supply chain benefits are to be realized. The most important of these are now discussed.

Effective consumer response

There is more to supply chain development than hard-nosed procurement and securing tight controls over inventory levels. While effective supply chains concern eliminating delays and reducing resources along the way, the orientation of such developments needs to be towards more effective consumer response where market requirements and not traditional dimensions such as cost reduction underpin priorities and direction.

More effective consumer response combines a company's own internal orientation with seeking changes in all the external elements of the supply chain. These range from suppliers shouldering some or all of the associated development costs to smaller, more frequent deliveries, necessitating suppliers to hold inventory or produce more often in smaller lot sizes. For most companies, there is little choice but to seek more from suppliers because their own customers are exacting the same pressure on short lead times and sharing risk.

The result fosters closer relations with fewer suppliers. The greatest challenge is developing both the internal and external phases of the chain in line with the needs of agreed markets. One key to making this happen is information, the topic of the next section.

Increasing use of IT

Since the early 1960s, four major IT developments have transformed the way that companies conduct business and each wave of technology has radically altered the supply chain that links suppliers through to end users:

1   The initial phase of IT application was based on mainframe computers. It began in the early 1960s and continued to be the dominant technology for the next 10–15 years. Business applications included material requirements planning and manufacturing resource planning (MRP and MRPII respectively). These enabled companies to standardize and systemize the day-to-day tasks in operations and parts of the supply chain. As a result, companies developed functional expertise supported by systems designed around the tasks of relevant functions.

2   The second phase was based on PCs and began in the 1970s and continued well into the 1980s. PC applications such as word processors, spreadsheets and presentation software facilitated communication across functional boundaries. PCs also put the power of computing into the hands of employees, and businesses built on this opportunity by focusing on the development of cross-functional processes that brought both functional and overall business benefits.

3   The third phase of IT applications was based on network computing. Starting in the mid-1980s, it continues to be a dominant influence on how companies are managed

and business is conducted. Network computing, customer/supplier applications, electronic data interchange (EDI), point-of-sale (POS) response and other forms of electronic mail are reducing the costs of handling information and transactions, while speeding up information exchange that allows real-time systems and responses to be developed at the same time as leveraging the efficiencies of functional expertise (phase 1) and cross-functional business processes (phase 2).

4   The fourth phase is based on the internet and the World Wide Web. Providing a universal infrastructure, the internet facilitates the interchange of information between businesses by not only reinforcing existing trends of cooperation but also helping companies to consider their supply chains as a whole and their role to manage and orchestrate process priorities and performance. By fostering better communication and interchange of information between companies, this phase enables fully integrated processes between businesses, not only customers to suppliers but also between suppliers.

One of the lasting effects of these technology applications is that they have facilitated the breakdown of barriers from cross-individuals to cross-corporations (see *Exhibit 9.18*).

Phase	Aspects of change
1 Cross-individuals	Broke down barriers between functional experts themselves and between this group and the executives responsible for managing core parts of a business, particularly operations
2 Cross-functions	Facilitated links between functions by requiring and helping the interchange between different parts of the same business
3 Cross-businesses	Impacted the way companies conducted business by removing barriers within an organization and between parts of the immediate supply chain
4 Cross-corporations	Continued the cross-corporate changes by facilitating cooperation of businesses within a supply chain including tier 2 suppliers

EXHIBIT 9.18 The evolving role of IT in managing a supply chain

The rapid growth of e-commerce has, however, brought with it some concerns that originate from both the delivery system that underpins the system and the speed of its use within commercial activities and transactions:

- **Fraud** – the Fraud Advisory Panel (the UK government's Serious Fraud Office) estimates that fraud could be costing £5bn a year and is likely to increase. US data from the National Consumers' League supported this trend. Its reports showed that in 1996 incidents of internet fraud were 689 and by 1999 these had increased to 10,660, at a value of $3.2m. The rise has continued, with 37,183 incidents by 2003, with a corresponding value of $20.5m.

  While *Exhibit 9.19* depicts the humorous side of fraud (but no doubt equally concerning if you were the parent), the implications are suitably highlighted.

EXHIBIT 9.19 One type of internet fraud

SOURCE: Hill, T. (2005) *Operations Management*, 2nd edn, Basingstoke, Palgrave Macmillan, © Roger Beale

EXHIBIT 9.20 A vulnerable side of the internet

SOURCE: Hill, T. (2005) *Operations Management,* 2nd edn, Basingstoke, Palgrave Macmillan, © Roger Beale

- **Vulnerability** – the level and nature of vulnerable outcomes inherent in the growing use of the internet are being highlighted in a series of incidents throughout the world, from bomb-making to arranging and managing gang violence. *Exhibit 9.20* provides a humorous exposition of the trend and possible outcomes.

Focusing on non-value-added activities

Increasingly companies have focused attention on minimizing non-value-added activities while providing information and communication tools that allow employees to focus on the value-added and strategic activities within the business. As firms reduce non-value-added activity, they redirect those newly released resources to the value-added and strategic dimensions of their business. For example, companies are increasingly using electronic intranet catalogues that enable office staff (the consumers) to order non-production goods (for example office supplies and computer software) directly from agreed suppliers. Not only does this break down barriers but it also eliminates non-value-added activities such as data re-entry and checking, thus allowing more time for purchasing staff to focus on their value-added activities such as developing supplier relations and contract negotiations.

E-procurement

Within these supply chain management developments is the role of e-procurement. While supply chain management addresses the core activities within a business, e-procurement extends electronic applications into the wide range of indirect goods and services that are bought by staff at all levels in an organization. As with the purchase of direct services and goods in the past, the procurement of indirect services and products has received little attention, while the size of spend is sizable. For example, in the UK government, procurement accounts for some 4.5 per cent of the country's GDP. Similarly, at the corporate level, it is estimated that companies can spend up to 15–20 per cent of sales revenue on indirect services and products.

While the IT investment required to move to e-procurement systems has to be made, the change is more cultural than technological. Many organizations have already taken on board electronic catalogues but the necessary cultural changes do not stop there. Online procurement is not a new tool for the purchasing function but a new way of working for the whole organization. With e-purchasing, everyone in the organization is now empowered to buy online. For this transition to take place, a leap of faith is required. Gone is the system based on forms, counter-forms and authorizations. This is replaced by checks and controls embodied in the software. It is not a case of computerizing the old manual process but of re-engineering the system itself. Now repetitive ordering can be devolved through the organization in a controlled manner.

As illustrated in *Exhibit 9.21*, electronic catalogues are at the heart of this development. These can be managed by the purchasing company or a third party such as British Telecommunications Group and Commerce One, a US-based provider. Goods are purchased by anyone in the organization by completing an electronic purchasing application. The system checks the specification, searches, visualizes the requirements, offers checks on price and delivery dates and then places the order. Progress of an order is then monitored electronically. The electronic catalogue is updated by supplier information and the growing needs of the organization. Estimates suggest that companies can save up to 11 per cent of indirect purchasing costs by introducing e-purchasing systems for dealing with the procurement of indirect services and products.

Online procurement has arrived and the challenge for companies is how to turn its potential to best organizational advantage. The principal benefits awaiting these developments include:

1 **Increase in contract compliance** – typically this benefit comprises the largest element of the e-procurement development, bringing with it:
   - increased use of preferred suppliers
   - reduced off-contract spending
   - reduced processing errors.

2 **Leveraging the purchasing spend** – e-procurement brings together the disparate transactions that characterize most organizations' traditional approach to purchasing indirect services and products. In so doing it allows companies to improve the potential leverage of these purchases through:
   - providing greater oversight of the purchasing spending
   - recording details of the actual spend by supplier and service/product category
   - allowing full purchasing power to be leveraged when negotiating discounts, with more goods ultimately purchased at lower prices.

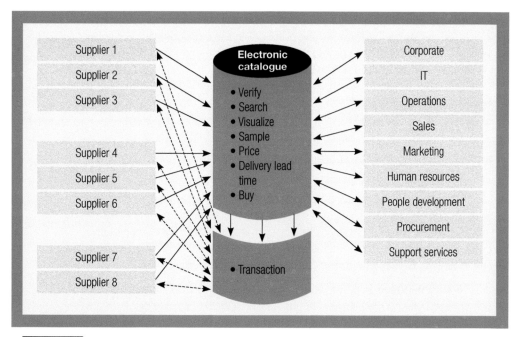

EXHIBIT 9.21 E-procurement system

SOURCE: Hill, T. (2005) *Operations Management,* 2nd edn, Basingstoke, Palgrave Macmillan

3   **Lower processing costs** – the business, staff and system costs involved in procurement will be reduced as a result of several factors including:
   • faster processing times
   • lower number of fax/telephone calls
   • reduced error rates.
   Cisco Systems, for example, has reduced the cost of procurement from an average of $130 to $40 per order – its target is to lower the cost to $25 per order.

4   **Increased involvement of people** – being able to purchase online takes delays out of the procurement process. The result is that staff feel more involved, with an increased sense of responsibility for their own sphere of work. The controls built into the system are further enhanced by an individual's ability to seek alternatives and the increased personalization of the system, both of which enhance the search for good value.

5   **Optimizing corporate tax savings** – locating the purchasing function in a low tax economy can enable a company to attribute cost savings (that is, profit) there.

6   **Offers a sure route to an early e-business success** – the low-risk nature of these developments in what are non-business critical systems make these developments a good place to start. Furthermore, the measurable objectives of e-procurement investment proposals result in a clear and persuasive business case, offering a short financial payback.

Online procurement offers the opportunity to break down departmental and intercompany trading barriers that opens the way to reducing costs and time in the purchase of indirect goods and services. The organization-wide nature of these changes requires a top-down process in order for an organization to grasp the potential of the e-procurement opportunity. While the technology base of these developments is not in itself complex, the cultural change within the organization should not be underestimated.

Managing the supply chain

The make-or-buy decision is not only critical in itself but it also governs the mix between the internal and external phases of the supply chain and thereby the nature of the operations task in managing these resources.

Whether a company makes or buys, effectively managing the whole supply chain has increasingly been recognized as a key executive role and one that directly impacts a company's ability to compete in its chosen markets. The task of managing the in-house or internal phase of the chain is addressed throughout this book. This section deals with the key issues and approaches that relate to managing the external phase(s) of a supply chain.

The concept of a totally integrated supply chain – from material producer through to end customer – is bringing great changes to the way businesses operate. Increasingly, companies no longer compete just with each other but rather they compete through their supply chains (see *Exhibit 9.22*). To bring this about, companies need a supply chain that is managed as an integrated whole in line with market needs and corporate objectives and underpinned by responsive and adaptive systems and procedures. This, in turn, requires meaningful collaboration and fuller relationships with suppliers to provide the essential basis for cooperation and joint developments.

Period	Basis of competition
Yesterday	Manufacturing company versus manufacturing company
Today	Manufacturing company's supply chain versus manufacturing company's supply chain

EXHIBIT 9.22 The changing basis of competition

Supply chain management issues

In the 1980s, companies turned their attention to fixing their operations problems but few addressed total supply chain costs. By the early 1990s, firms started to realize the need to shift emphasis. With shortening product life cycles, more customer choice and reducing lead times set within the context of growing world competition, it became essential to review the whole supply chain, identify opportunities and manage these requirements. As most companies have been outsourcing more and more in recent years and future trends point the same way, the need to manage the supply chain effectively should continue to be high on the corporate agenda. Whether you make or buy, the responsibility for managing the whole chain can no longer be ignored as it was in the past. Some of the key management issues involved are now discussed.

Changes in attitude

Relationships with suppliers have a history where cooperation was not the way in which most customers behaved. Pitting suppliers against each other and ruling by threat and fear are being abandoned in favour of long-term relationships often with single suppliers. Companies are also bringing suppliers on board much earlier in the design process, seeking technical help and contributions and even inviting suppliers to help in identifying future products.

To underpin these changes, customers are reviewing the way they handle suppliers and the level of cooperation involved. The trend towards greater cooperation goes hand in hand with a more proactive style, as illustrated in *Exhibit 9.23*.

Changing customer attitudes to suppliers	
Threat and fear	Traditional stance. Perceptions based upon: • customer dominates the relationship with suppliers • suppliers respond to demands • suppliers pitted against each other • underpinned by the threat of purchase orders and contracts being given to other suppliers on the one hand and a supplier's fear of losing the business on the other
Reward	First step towards cooperation and moving from a reactive to a proactive stance. Characterized by elements such as: • fewer suppliers • award of long-term contracts • customer is proactive in building relationships with suppliers
Collaboration	Progressive move towards fuller and more cooperative relationships, the pace of which is set predominantly by the customer. Evolution through a series of steps such as a customer: • identifies improvements that a supplier can make • provides support and resources (for example technical capability) to undertake supplier improvements • gives actual help to improve suppliers including training a supplier's staff • starts to take into account the processes of its suppliers when designing products so as to help them improve their level of support • focuses attention on tier 2 suppliers as a source of improving tier 1 suppliers' support (see *Exhibit 9.11*)
Integration and synchronization	The final step is to integrate activities achieving benefits typically associated with ownership – the concept of virtual ownership. Based upon mutual respect and trust these include suppliers access to real-time information with customers harmonizing their suppliers' work and synchronizing their support. These changes include: • access to design-related information and responsibility for product design • suppliers responsibility for deciding when and how much to deliver

EXHIBIT 9.23 Phases in changing customer attitudes to suppliers

Reflecting on the earlier section 'Creating your own competition', whatever the type of relationship a company has with its suppliers, proactive collaboration on all aspects of supplier relations needs to underpin its supply chain management style. While content and level of trust need to reflect the company's short- and long-term strategy, the style used to manage suppliers needs to be driven by the recognition that they form an integral part of the total capability essential to remaining competitive in today's markets.

Incorporating uncertainty

Today's markets are characterized by shortening product life cycles and stiffening requirements for all aspects of customer service. Against this background, large manufacturing companies are characterized by complexity, as clearly illustrated by a review of the material flows for typical products. Multiple suppliers provide materials, parts and subassemblies to manufacturing sites with varying regularity. These are processed through a number of stages that, in turn, are characterized by uncertainty. Finished products then go to a range of customers, often with varying sets of demands. These patterns are further confused by the range of transportation options to meet the spread of customers around the world.

The real management problem within this complex network is, however, the uncertainty that characterizes it. But many companies still treat this task as if it were predictable. The planning and scheduling systems inadequately take account of demand uncertainty. They are designed as if certainty rather than uncertainty was the reality with which they had to cope. And, as the situation today is increasingly less predictable than in the past, this leads to circumstances of unnecessary inventory and high obsolescence.

Furthermore, all this is in the context, on the one hand, of IT developments such as electronic POS scanners that provide up-to-the-minute data on customer buying patterns and, on the other hand, operations improvements concerning the production of smaller order sizes. At the same time, the drive to meet customer requirements has dramatically widened product ranges, even in industries that traditionally have not been considered fashion driven. But new product introductions have two adverse side effects:

- average life cycles are reduced. This, in turn, shortens the relative duration of the more stable phase of demand in relation to the less certain initial and end phases.

- total demand is spread over more stock-keeping units (SKUs).[18] The more items on offer, the more difficult the task of forecasting sales.

Overall, the result is a growing unpredictability that increases the need to manage each phase of the supply chain and the interface between them. As highlighted earlier, Dell, having shortened its own assembly lead times in response to the delivery speed requirements of its customers, found itself constrained from meeting these needs by the long lead times of its component suppliers.

Customer/supplier dependence

The relationship between customers and suppliers is influenced by the level of dependency of the one on the other – see *Exhibit 9.24*. Where customers and suppliers are positioned will impact potential relationship options, as explained in the next section.

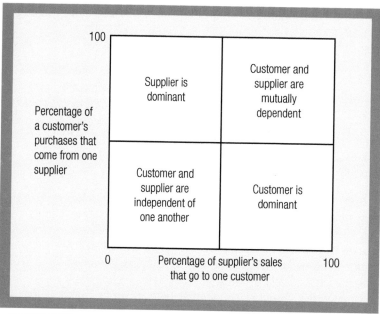

EXHIBIT 9.24 Customer/supplier dependence

Types of supplier relations

Part of managing the make-or-buy decision is how best to structure relationships with suppliers. Customers can position themselves in a number of ways within the constraints of dimensions such as the 'dependence factor' introduced above. The characteristics of these different types of supplier relationships are now reviewed. Which one a company should choose needs to reflect the characteristics of the materials or components involved and the marketplace in which a company operates:

- **Trawling the market** – here suppliers are held at arm's length with a growing amount of business completed using computerized interaction. For example, General Electric (GE) in the US increasingly purchases components over the internet where it posts details of parts and prequalified vendors then quote for the contract. Here, there is little face-to-face interaction and the key order-winner is price. Delivery on time and quality conformance are qualifiers and form part of the listing prerequisites. Benefits also include reduced processing costs, for example GE quotes a 90 per cent reduction compared to traditional paperwork procedures. Finally, this phase may entail placing a significant amount of business with competitors.

- **Ongoing relationships** – these involve establishing medium-term contracts with suppliers, developing relations in terms of information sharing and require sound management by customers.

- **Partnerships** – involve long-term contracts characterized by the extensive sharing of information and increased trust. For example, since 1988 the US car maker Chrysler's average contract length with suppliers has more than doubled.

- **Strategic alliances** – the trend in sourcing is towards strategic alliances that are characterized by the increased depth and breadth of the whole customer/supplier relationship. A prerequisite of more cooperative relationships is a dramatic reduction in the supplier base and a recognition by customers of the fact that their costs, quality conformance levels and lead times are partly within the processes of their supplier. For example, Xerox has reduced its suppliers from over 5,000 to about 400, while Chrysler has saved more than $0.5bn from supplier-generated ideas.

In Japan, key automotive suppliers are incentivized to acquire organizational capabilities from their customers' organizations. Long-term supplier relations encourage investment in relationship-specific skills,[19] a joint problem-solving approach and a clear set of rules for sharing gains between those involved. Key to this is the long-term relationship developed by the customer. For example, Toyota's purchasing philosophy is embedded in its 1939 Purchasing Rules,[20] which state that once nominated as a Toyota supplier, they should be treated as part of Toyota, that Toyota shall do business with these suppliers and not switch to others and that Toyota will seek to raise supplier performance.

End customer	Customer/supplier developments
Hitachi (VCR equipment)	• Six-monthly supplier meetings where Hitachi's CEO provides details of aggregate plans and policies to suppliers' top executives • Suppliers arranged into groups by categories of parts – cosmetic, electronic, mechanical and assembly. Each group has bimonthly two-day meetings to resolve quality conformance, technical and delivery reliability issues
Volvo (cars)	• 75 per cent of every car is made outside Sweden • Volvo collects parts from suppliers and ships them to Gothenburg • Suppliers required to maintain two to four weeks of stock • Pallets of parts not opened until moved to the assembly area, necessitating a guarantee on quality conformance and quantity • Volvo provides a 12-month forecast: first six weeks are firm, next 12 weeks can vary but Volvo accepts responsibility for materials and work-in-progress inventory
Boeing (passenger aircraft)	• Design-build teams used on the 777 passenger airliner • First plane off the assembly line – parts were so accurate that the nose-to-tail measurement was less than 23/1000 of an inch (0.6 mm) from design specification • Success built on computer-based design and the design-build teams used that included suppliers. Core to this success was the mutual respect and trust built up within the teams
UK-based motor manufacturers	• Forum established comprising experts from General Motors, Honda, Nissan, Toyota and Volkswagen • Purpose is for these major competitors to cooperate in educating and improving tier 2 supplier base to the auto industry
Canon (photocopiers and printers)	• Sent own engineers to Daisho Denshi (a $0.25bn maker of circuit boards and other parts) at a time when it was on the verge of bankruptcy • Improvements in efficiency, quality conformance and on-time delivery resulted • Led to Daisho Denshi cutting prices to Canon by 10 per cent

EXHIBIT 9.25 Examples of customer/supplier relationship developments in a range of industrial sectors

Strategic alliances are marked by long timescales, extensive sharing of information, increased trust, joint development of products and processes and the intent to work together over an extended period. Boeing has strategic alliances with GE and Rolls-Royce, partly to reduce the financial risk of new aeroplane programmes and partly to cope with the complex technical interfaces between engines and airframes that have to be designed in conjunction with each other.

- **Backward integration** – the final step is to change from relationship to ownership. This leads to the full sharing of information and the transfer of goals and culture. To illustrate the nature and extent of partnering arrangements and supplier developments, *Exhibit 9.25* provides examples of relationship developments in a range of industries.

Strategic partnering

Building on from the last section, the need to be more competitive has led some companies to partner others in the supply chain. As highlighted earlier, customer/supplier relations continue to undergo major changes where the goal is to synchronize activities to the point where virtual integration is achieved (see *Exhibit 9.21*).

Strategic partnering involves a

> long-term relationship between (an) organization and its suppliers. It is designed to leverage the strategic and operational capabilities of individual participating organizations to help them advance significant, ongoing benefits.[21]

Such developments concern the extent to which critical and even proprietary information is communicated within the partnership.

The extent to which this can be secured is not only constrained by the parties involved but also by the stage in a sector's evolution. For example, in the early days of the computing industry, the major players had no option but to build the infrastructure to produce all the components and parts a computer needed. They had little choice. As the industry grew, more specialized companies developed to produce specific components. This allowed new entrants a choice. As Michael Dell (founder of Dell Computers) explained:

> As a new start-up, Dell couldn't afford to create every piece of the value chain. But more to the point, why should we want to? We concluded we'd be better off leveraging the investments others have made and focusing on delivering solutions and systems to customers ... It's a pretty simple strategy ... but at the time it went against the dominant 'engineering-centric' view of the industry. Companies such as IBM, Compaq and HP subscribed to a 'we-have-to-develop-everything' view of the world. If you weren't doing component assembly, you weren't a real computer company.[22]

Strategic partnering is based on a conscious decision that sees its ultimate goal as virtual integration. This seeks to incorporate other parts of the supply chain as if they are part of one's own business – a long way from the not uncommon stance of outsourcing parts of a business that were, in fact, problem areas that a company could not fix.

On the delivery end of the chain, companies work with their customers to better understand their needs. In some partnerships, retail stores are sharing POS data to help suppliers better meet market trends and changes. On the sourcing end of the chain, suppliers are delivering more frequently, keeping consignment stock in a customer's warehouse (and only invoicing on use) and managing the replenishment cycle to reflect usage while helping to optimize their own schedules. While the customer frees up resources, the supplier has longer term customer commitment, a barrier from competition that reduces sales and marketing effort and firm data on which to plan and schedule operations and its own suppliers.

However, a partnership must deliver value and should not be entered into for its own sake. They are costly to implement, require additional management costs to develop, coordinate and maintain together with an attendant increase in the level of risk-sharing. They can only be justified if they yield substantially better results than a firm would achieve without partnering, with the added check that the results could not be achieved without a partnership in place.[23]

Supply clusters

At the heart of Toyota's supply chain lies the concept of clustering. Of Toyota's 15 plants in Japan, 12 (along with the manufacturing facilities of most of its suppliers) are located around Toyota City (the once mill town of Koromo), situated less than an hour's drive from Nagoya. This organizational arrangement in the sourcing and manufacturing phases of a supply network is called a 'supply cluster' – a geographically close group of interconnected companies and associated businesses in a particular sector(s) including end product manufacturers, component suppliers and supporting firms.[24] Senior executives in Toyota 'believe that the cluster not only has allowed the company to use its just-in-time system but has also shaped Toyota's culture. They plan to create similar clusters overseas.[25]

While the above example relates to a corporate cluster, industrial clusters represent a collection of many interrelated supply chains (or supply networks). These industrial clusters comprise many levels of independent suppliers and manufacturers, with different companies possibly supplying the same manufacturers and different manufacturers ordering from the same supplier.[26] This supply cluster concept, for example, forms the basic structure by which almost all manufacturing in China is conducted.

There are two principal types of supply clusters used in China.[27] The first is known as 'hub and spoke'. Here a large manufacturer (often a state-owned enterprise or joint venture) is surrounded by many suppliers and support firms. The hub company is typically highly regulated and limited to certain capital-intensive industries such as chemicals, energy and steel. The second type of cluster comprises a large number of small and medium enterprises (SMEs) that have developed into the equivalent of large revenue-generating conglomerates, which again are surrounded by many related suppliers and support firms. The companies making up these clusters are a mix of domestic and foreign owned. Between 2000 and 2003, it is estimated that 66,000 new foreign-owned factories opened in China.[28]

In 2006, there were well over 1,000 such supply clusters covering almost all major export products, with most of these configurations located in China's more developed economic regions including the eastern provinces of Guangdong, Fujian, Zhejiang and Jiangsu and large metropolitan areas such as Shanghai, Beijing and Tranjin. Examples include:

- The Nanhai district of Foshan in Guangdong province comprises some 18 townships, each specializing in an aspect of operations such as ceramics, textiles, ferrous metal

EVEREST
CLIMBED
IN **7 WEEKS**
IN 1953

Everest
climbed in
8 hours
10 minutes
in 2004

processing, electric appliances, underwear and toys. The township of Dali, for instance, accounts for 40 per cent of China's output of aluminium products by volume.

- The Donman township in Guangdong province has 13 factories employing 18,000 workers producing cell phones, game consoles, PCs and other electric hardware. Within two hours of these factories are thousands of suppliers, resulting in component costs that are less than 20 per cent for similar products made in the US.[29]

- In Zhejiang province, there are hundreds of industrial clusters each generating annual sales revenues of between $150m and $2.5bn. For example, some 5,000 companies in the Zhili township produce children's garments while the combined annual output of companies in the Datang township exceeds six billion pairs of socks.

The impact of clustering enhances supply chain performance for both customers and suppliers and is derived from a range of benefits including:

1 **Material and component supply**
   - facilitates the sourcing of material and components
   - increased purchasing power for raw materials and components lowers costs
   - simplifies the flow of inventories, facilitating just-in-time provision

2 **Capacity-related benefits**
   - capacity pooling to better handle uncertain demand including outsourcing customer orders in times of high demand and supplementing the level of activity of another supplier experiencing a short-term dip in sales
   - spreading the investment costs of facilities that can be shared, for example treatment plants for the dying and printing sectors and warehousing

3 **Operational costs**
   - lowers costs for both inbound and outbound transportation
   - spreads infrastructure development investment
   - shares process improvements and technical know-how
   - increased purchasing power for support services and equipment lowers costs

4 **Information-related benefits**
   - sharing of hardware and software facilities and capabilities in information transmission. Many SMEs do not have the means (investment and skilled staff) to develop and maintain effective IT systems on their own
   - facilitates the collection and flow of market, technical and competitive information

5 **Working relationships**
   - helps create and maintain personal relationships, strengthen community ties and fosters trust in working relationships between suppliers and between suppliers and customers

6 **Regional benefits**
   - regions develop a reputation for expertise in a particular sector, so helping to maintain current and increase future levels of activity with existing customers while attracting new business
   - arranging joint marketing activities such as trade fairs

– creates local competition so enhancing the drive for continuous improvement and helping a cluster remain competitive.

Managing stability in the internal phase of the supply chain

In most companies, operations is responsible for managing the major portion of costs and investments to maximize profit and cash flow. Stabilizing delivery systems is an essential element of achieving this, especially given the increasing reliance on suppliers due to companies outsourcing more goods and services and the task of better managing the external phase of the supply chain that results. Various researchers[30] have highlighted the role of inventory, order backlog and capacity in managing the variation between an operations delivery system and its markets. Their findings support Hopp and Spearman's conclusion that 'while there is no question that variability will degrade performance, we have a choice of how it will do so. Different strategies for coping with variability make sense in different business environments.'[31, 32]

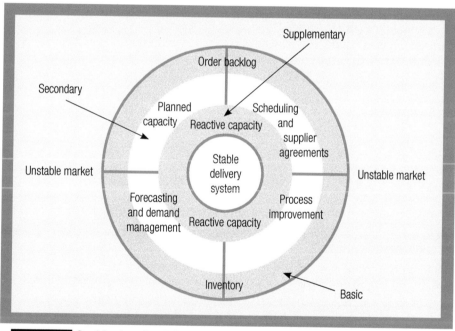

EXHIBIT 9.26 Cushioning the delivery system categories and options

Just as the concepts underpinning the process choice respond to different market characteristics and mix of qualifiers and order-winners (see Chapter 5), the underlying characteristics of supply chains will need to exhibit similar characteristics and appropriate outputs.

While markets are inherently unstable, an operations delivery system needs to be kept as stable as possible to help control costs and schedules. Consequently, a company must decide how best to cushion its delivery system from the instability inherent in its markets.

As shown in *Exhibit 9.26*, there are three categories of mechanisms (and choices within each category) by which to cushion the operations delivery system and these are now outlined.

Basic category

One fundamental decision that companies make concerns whether to make to order (resulting in a backlog of orders waiting to be processed) or make to stock (making ahead of demand with customer orders met from finished goods inventory) or a combination of the two approaches by assembling to order (completing products from the work-in-progress stage on receipt of an order). Some companies use a mix of the first two options by initially building up a backlog of orders and then making sufficient products to meet all outstanding orders plus a quantity that goes into finished goods inventory. Future orders are then met from this finished goods stock and when the inventory is used up, further orders go into order backlog and the cycle repeats.

Alternatively, companies that experience seasonal demand may decide to make inventory in low demand periods, thereby absorbing capacity in one time period and transferring it forward to be sold in a future time period. Where this occurs, companies may choose to make work-in-progress or finished goods inventory, taking into account future demand forecasts and the labour hour to value of inventory ratio.

Strategically, these alternatives embody trade-offs concerning operations lead time and delivery speed requirements versus cost and cash flow.

Secondary category

Companies can also choose from a range of secondary mechanisms to help provide the cushioning role. As illustrated in *Exhibit 9.26*, these include demand management, forecasting, scheduling, supplier agreements and process improvement. You will see from these that while the first two help make demand more stable, the latter three help the operations delivery system to better meet demand with the actual capacity on hand.

Within this category there is also the mechanism of 'planned capacity'. This provision can take several forms including planned overtime or additional shifts in peak demand periods, employing temporary versus permanent staff, annualized hours and including an element of non-direct activity in the work mix of direct employees which can be switched into direct activity should the need arise. Such decisions as these need to be assessed and made well ahead of time and will form a more permanent element in the capacity provision within operations.

Supplementary category

The final category of cushioning mechanisms available to a business is the option of providing additional capacity through overtime working. Such a capacity increase is short term and arranged on an as-needed basis. Referred to as 'reactive capacity' (to distinguish it from planned capacity mentioned earlier), it is an option used somewhat as a last resort.

Managing stability in the external phase of the supply chain

A key aspect of managing a supply chain is to recognize that a company's suppliers also wish to cushion their own delivery systems and do so by choosing from the same options within the basic, secondary and supplementary categories described above and overviewed in *Exhibit 9.27*. Helping suppliers handle this requirement becomes an integral part of a company's approach to managing its supply chain. Key to a company understanding the task and helping suppliers are the following factors:

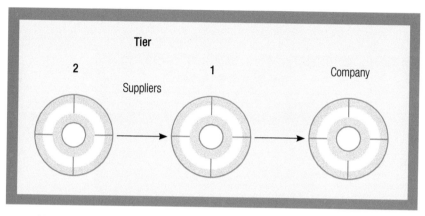

NOTE: The company is Tier 1 supplier's customer.

EXHIBIT 9.27 The cushioning requirements at each step in a supply chain

1   The instability of a company's suppliers' markets is generated by the company itself.

2   A supplier's choice of basic mechanisms is in response to the company's own behaviours. Uncertainty of demand will be met by a make-to-order response, associated order backlog and a corresponding increase in a supplier's operations lead time.

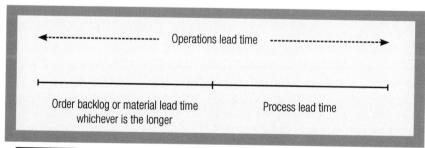

EXHIBIT 9.28 Components of operations lead time

3   As a supplier's operations lead time comprises the same elements as its customer's (see *Exhibit 9.28*), the key to help to shorten a supplier's lead time response is to change its own behaviour so as to remove or reduce the cushioning mechanisms that a supplier uses which have a lead time element. A look at *Exhibit 9.28* shows that two of the dimensions making up a supplier's operations lead time are in response to customer behaviour and hence fall within the scope of a customer's ability to shorten material lead time and order backlog. Material lead time in that suppliers are typically unprepared to hold materials inventory because of cash flow and uncertainty of future sales. Similarly, uncertainty of customer demand will be met by a make-to-order response and associated order backlog lead time.

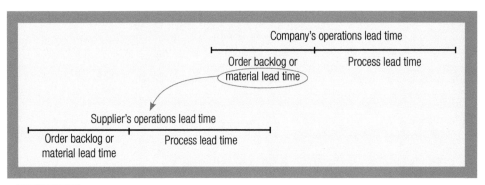

EXHIBIT 9.29 A company's material lead time equates to a supplier's operations lead time

4   Customers can directly help shorten a supplier's lead time by guaranteeing future orders equivalent to an agreed level of capacity within a supplier's delivery system, or eliminate the element of material lead time by guaranteeing usage (or payment if material inventory is unused) of an agreed amount of material, or both. In this way a supplier's operations lead time could be so reduced as to comprise only the process lead time element. Shorter material lead times from suppliers will, in turn, reduce this element in a customer's own operations lead time (see *Exhibit 9.29*). In this way, companies can begin to better manage their supply chains to create a more responsive operations system of their own, while helping suppliers to better manage this own delivery systems.

Summary benefits

While some supply chain developments attract specific sets of gains, there are several benefits that are invariably present, in full or part, in all such developments. This section summarizes these sets of general gains as a way of reflecting on the issues discussed in the last sections, while highlighting the potential benefits involved.

Reducing costs

Companies are becoming increasingly aware of an obvious truth, at least in hindsight –

the maker of a part should be more able to design and make it at a lower cost than its customer. The expertise base, the experience curve benefits associated with cumulative volume (Chapter 3) and continuing transfer of ideas from one solution to another should always lead to lower cost applications.

Johnson Controls

In its research centre in Detroit, Johnson Controls Inc. (a major supplier of automotive seats) designs and tests seats for the principal car makers in the US and Europe. Different teams are allocated to meet the seating needs of a range of competing companies. As a supplier that sells parts to an entire industry, the system is a way of transferring new techniques from one manufacturer to another, with the result that as a maker of a part, Johnson Controls is able to conceive a new seating requirement more cheaply than a final assembler responsible for the whole product.

Airbus

In 2006/7, Airbus, the European aircraft maker, outlined plans to shed more than four-fifths of its suppliers as part of a cost-cutting programme. At the time, Airbus had been badly hit by costly delays to its A380 superjumbo and announced its decision to reduce the number of suppliers from 3,000 to 500 as part of its drive to cut €350m from its annual costs by 2010. It hopes that by whittling down its supplier base it can force down the price by buying in greater bulk.

A.T. Kearney Inc., a Chicago consulting firm, estimates that where manufacturers properly incorporate suppliers into their product development process, they can cut their purchased parts and services costs by as much as 30 per cent. Working with suppliers can lead to cost reductions other than from more traditional sources. Encouraging suppliers to come up with cost-cutting ideas and design innovations can lead to potentially large savings.

Accessing technical expertise

The cost gains associated with cumulative volume can similarly be secured on the dimension of expertise. The application of a supplier's technical capabilities to similar design requirements together with the transfer of solutions to and from other applications enhances technical insights and accelerates design improvements. Many companies recognize these benefits and such gains can drive supplier choice. For example, Dell, the world's largest PC maker, recently announced its decision to increase its manufacturing contract suppliers in Taiwan. In 2006, it increased its procurement spend to US$12.5bn up from the US$8bn and US$10bn spend in 2004 and 2005 respectively. But, explained Dell, the main requirement of its partners was that they could deliver the 'newest, greatest technology'.[33]

The major Japanese car companies Honda and Toyota do not source much from low-wage countries. To them, their suppliers' technical capabilities are more important than their wage costs. While Western companies are turning more and more to China and India,

Toyota and Honda purchase little there, as these countries only offer them wage savings, which is not enough for them, as they value suppliers' innovation capabilities far more.

Shortening lead times

The importance of recognizing the value-creating potential of the supply chain is central to successful strategies into today's competitive environment. For many companies, this translates into the opportunities available in each phase – suppliers, internal supply chain, logistics and customers – and their roles in bringing about these gains. One key competitive dimension is lead time reduction.

IKEA, the Swedish home furnishings retailer, has more than 100 stores and 1,800 suppliers in over 50 countries. The company's insistence on low cost from its suppliers has two key implications. First, the sourcing is widely dispersed and parts of finished items may be purchased from different locations. Second, items must be bought in large volumes. Both factors require an efficient system for ordering parts, integrating them into products and delivering them to stores, while keeping inventory levels low and meeting demand quickly. This is achieved by building on long-term supplier relations and a sophisticated logistics system, the centrepiece of which is IKEA's network of warehouses. Point-of-sale information at each retail outlet provides online sales data to the nearest warehouse and the operational head office in Almhult where information systems analyse sales patterns worldwide. In turn, the warehouses act as logistic control points and consolidate requirements. As transit hubs, they work with retail stores to anticipate demand and eliminate shortages while keeping inventory (and corresponding floor space) low. Underpinning all this is the need for short lead time provision. Working with suppliers as well as in-house supply chain developments have enabled IKEA to meet the delivery speed needs of the fashion market is serves.

Reducing lead times has also been at the centre of the supply strategy of A.W. Chesterton Co. (a family-owned seal, pump and packing manufacturer in Massachusetts). Key to the substantial but essential improvements has been the company's management of its supply chain. This is well illustrated by the reduction in suppliers from 1,300 to 125 and allocating delivery reliability, short lead times and quality conformance twice as much importance as price when evaluating which suppliers to partner. For Chesterton, the demands of its own markets require putting pressure on its own suppliers. A decade ago, delivery time for mechanical seal parts was 12–16 weeks. Today, it is down to days or even hours. To facilitate this, the company has installed computer systems that allow customers to transmit drawings and engineering specifications directly to the plant floor where new process investments reduce process lead times.

But the lead times of other aspects of a business are equally critical to overall success. The emphasis is on getting suppliers to become more than just parts' providers. One key area is to participate in and contribute to new designs, particularly with regard to cutting costs and reducing development lead time. Dana Corporation, a major supplier of truck axles, has an entire 60-engineer laboratory near Toledo dedicated to U-joints. Using a computer-aided design (CAD) system, Dana can design new products cheaply and quickly – in fact, prototypes for customers can be built in a few hours.

The Taiwanese Acer Corporation, with other PC makers, has had to reduce lead times in line with the short product life cycles of its market. The company works on a ten-month product life cycle, with three months allowed for product development and modifications, six months for sales of the product and one month to sell old inventory before the next cycle begins.

Lower inventories

The classic, uncoordinated approach to managing a supply chain typically results in each stage having enough material (or its equivalent) inventory not to run out and sufficient finished goods (or its equivalent) to ensure that customers would not be caught short. One result of each stage adopting these positions is excess inventory; and the longer the lead time, the greater the likelihood of these inefficiencies occurring in the process. Managing the supply chain as a whole means stitching together an entire business, with external providers being treated as partners as if they were inside the company. *Exhibit 9.30* provides a simple illustration of the 'one-firm concept' designed to eliminate the interfaces between the external and internal phases of the supply chain that results in an integrated system. Some examples of how lower inventories result now follow.

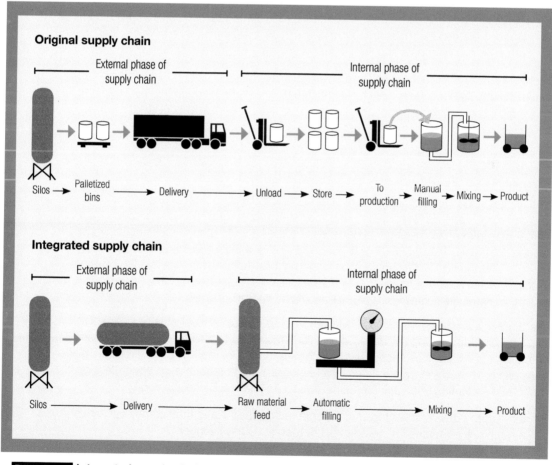

EXHIBIT 9.30 Integrated supply chain: the one-firm concept

Eastman Chemical's processes call for 1,500 different raw materials provided by 850 suppliers. To make sure that as little inventory as possible sat idle, Eastman devised what it calls 'stream inventory management'. This requires treating the whole supply chain as a pipeline. 'When an order comes in from the customer, we take one pound of product out of the tail end, with the raw material function working with the supplier to put another pound in on the other end. We want to achieve continuous flow' is how Eastman describes its approach.[34] And stream inventory management has paid off. Eastman can now monitor inventory while at its suppliers which, combined with more accurate production forecasts, means that there is no longer the need to hold excess inventory that sits idle, just in case. Examples of the dramatic inventory reductions that have been achieved include:

- wood pulp stock down from three months' supply to nine days with the next target set at four days.

- 20 years ago the company kept 18 million pounds of paraxylene, a material for polyethylene terephthalate (PET) plastic soda bottles, to support 520 million pounds a year of PET production in the US. Today, Eastman holds only 14 million pounds of paraxylene to support three times the volume of PET production.

- company-wide, the company's inventories as a percentage of sales had almost halved in the decade from the late 1980s. In 2006, total inventory had fallen to 9 per cent, with raw materials and supplies at less than 2 per cent of sales.

Michael Dell began in 1984 with a simple business insight: to sell direct to customers and make to order. Thus, in one swoop, he eliminated the reseller's mark-up and the costs and risks associated with finished goods inventory. The 'direct business model', as it is known, gave Dell Computer a substantial cost advantage and directly contributed to growing a $60bn company by 2007.

To achieve this, Dell uses technologies and information to blur the traditional boundaries in the supply chain from suppliers through to customers. In so doing, Dell is moving towards 'virtual integration' (as Michael Dell describes it) that combines individual strategies such as customer focus, supplier partnerships and just-in-time operations into a coordinated whole. Virtual integration harnesses the economies of scale benefits of two traditional business models. On the one hand, it taps into the benefits of a coordinated supply chain traditionally only available through vertical integration while, on the other hand, it taps into the benefits of specialization where companies (in Dell's case, its suppliers) focus on what they are good at with the associated gains from volumes and technology investment.

There are many challenges facing Dell Computer to realize this potential and establish these collaborations. One key driver to do this is monitoring low inventories. In the fast-changing technology business, inventory carries more risk than in other sectors. The dimensions of risk in computing concern response time to launching product developments and protection from falling material prices. As Michael Dell explained:[35]

- if I've got 11 days of inventory and my competitor has 80, and Intel comes out with a new chip, that means I'm going to get to market 69 days sooner.

- if the cost of materials goes down 50 per cent a year and you have two or three months of inventory versus 11 days, you've got a big cost disadvantage. And you're vulnerable to product transitions, when you can get stuck with obsolete inventory.

For these reasons, Dell works closely with its suppliers to keep reducing inventory and increasing speed, as its arrangements with Sony exemplify. With Sony (considered a reliable supplier with defect rates on monitors of less than two per million), Dell now collects monitors daily in the quantities needed to meet its own customer orders and then ships direct. The result is reduced lead times and no finished monitor inventory. Similarly, Dell has agreed with Airborne Express and United Parcel Services (UPS) to collect, say, 12,500 computers a day and the same quantity of monitors from Sony's plant in Mexico. Then they match the one with the other and deliver them directly to Dell's customers. To do this, Dell has developed real-time information on its own demand profile and links this into its suppliers, sometimes every few hours. With this insight and certainty, suppliers can meet Dell's five or six days of lead time. 'The greatest challenge in working with suppliers is getting them in sync with the fast pace we have to maintain. The key to making it work is information', explained Kevin Rollins, vice-chairman of Dell Computer Corporation.[36]

The outcome of all this was that in 1998, inventory at Dell was $223m to support $12.5bn of sales, while by 2007 inventory was as little as $660m to support $57.4bn of sales.[37]

Efficient customer response (ECR) is a relation of just-in-time and partnership sourcing. Its central doctrine is that many practices that make good business sense to individual parts of the supply chain add cost and complexity from the perspective of the chain as a whole. One central theme of ECR is co-managed inventory. Instead of sending out orders to suppliers as stock gets low, customers hand over to suppliers the task of generating orders. Both parties agree forecasts and suppliers take over the responsibility for replenishment using up-to-date sales information from the customer.

VOAC, the Swedish-based division of the US manufacturer Parker Hannifin, makes mobile hydraulic equipment. Originally the company had its head office and factories in Sweden and eight sales offices across Europe. All had their own warehouses and distribution set-ups. Inventories were high, the level of customer delivery performance was variable, lead times were long and logistics costs were substantial. Its partner in changing the logistics organization was UPS Worldwide Logistics. It now has one European distribution centre in the Netherlands, online connections for all offices and direct order input. Electronically processed orders are then tracked from beginning to end, with UPS providing vendor-managed inventory facilities that take into account future demand forecasts, operations lead times and existing inventory levels. Improved supply chain management has extended the customer order cut-off point during a working day from 3 pm to 6 pm and resulted in shorter delivery lead times and inventory reductions of 60 per cent.

Reflections

Whether to make or buy needs careful assessment and the factors that substantiate these decisions need to be clearly understood. In the past, carried on the winds of growth and believing that they could manufacture anything, as a matter of course, many companies decided to make rather than to buy without an adequate understanding of strategic fit and the tactical consequences involved. On the other hand, early entrants into new technology markets such as IT had little option at the time but to make the components involved. In recent times, subcontracting is in vogue. What often characterizes these trends is flavour of the month rather than issues of strategic fit. It is essential when deciding whether to make or buy that companies undertake strategic and tactical analyses while being careful to avoid the lure of short-term gains without considering long-term outcomes.

When changing make-or-buy decisions, companies need to establish the true extent of the costs and benefits involved. Understatement of costs and overstatement of benefits are all too often the basis on which companies make decisions and evaluate outcomes. But, such make-or-buy decisions are not only substantial but often final, at least within commercial timescales – when a company closes a plant, it will never reopen it. The make-or-buy decision invariably commits a company for years ahead and consequentially is critical to the strategic positioning of a company.

Make or buy is the first part of a two-phased task. The second is that once the make-or-buy decision is made, companies have to recognize the need to manage both the internal and external phases of the supply chain. And this typically requires a company to make a fundamental shift in approach and thinking, as summarized in *Exhibit 9.31*.

Dimensions		Approach	
		From	To
Customers and suppliers		Contractual relationships	Harness the power of partnerships
Basis for competition		Manufacturer	Supply chain
Organisation relationships		Functional/corporate orientation	Cooperation
Focus		Individual contract	Relationship
Communication		Primarily one way	Two way and balanced
Performance measures	Focus	Individual parties	Partnership
	Development	Independently	Jointly
	Results	Might be shared	Joint performance
Risk/reward evaluation		By transaction	Over the life of the relationship

EXHIBIT 9.31 Changing approach to managing supply chains

The format of the joint cooperation that is core feature of strategic alliance developments is moving at a pace, as the following illustrations highlight.

Volkswagen

Components account for some 60 per cent of the cost of a new car. Yet the component makers have traditionally shared relatively few of the risks of a new launch. The car makers, on the other hand, have to meet large fixed investments, such as factories and capital equipment, in what are increasingly uncertain markets. Part of the move to strategic alliances is now based on shared costs and shared uncertainty. At Volkswagen's bus and truck plant in Resende (some 150 km from Rio de Janeiro, Brazil), about 35 per cent of the fixed costs have been met by component suppliers. Resende in also co-managed by VW and its suppliers under a profit-sharing consortium.

Mercedes-Benz

The Hambach plant in eastern France, which builds the two-seater Mercedes-Benz sports car, provides another example of the changing relationships within strategic alliance developments. Ten suppliers preassemble important sections. For example, steel bodies come from Magna International, the Canadian group; VDO, the German automotive electronics maker, builds fully assembled cockpits, including the instruments; while Ymos (the German component specialist) makes complete door assemblies, including trim, window winders and glass. But that is not all. The ten suppliers invested almost $300m in the project.

Skoda

The assembly plant for Skoda's Octavia saloon is designed with six zones adjacent to the production line. The zones are also positioned on an outside wall so that the suppliers involved have direct truck access. The component suppliers are responsible for supporting the production schedule that includes the preassembly of parts just before they are required to go on to the car.

Other examples serve to illustrate the developments in supplier/customer relations that are changing the mindsets of those involved. In 1999, TNT (Europe's biggest freight and logistics company) launched its internet service known as Quickshipper to enable its customers to track orders from beginning to end directly through the TNT website. After planning their order, customers can then use the site to follow its progress to delivery. Quicker order processing also means faster deliveries.

As response time becomes a more important factor than low labour costs in keeping major customers, offshore manufacturers of everything from PCs to garments need to embrace e-commerce developments. Take Lite-on Technology Corporation, the Taiwanese manufacturer of computer hardware. In the late 1990s, it typically had a month to execute orders from IBM, Compaq Computer and other overseas customers. Since then the required lead times have shrunk dramatically (see *Exhibit 9.32*).

Item	Lead time to fill a US order
Colour monitors	2 days
Notebook computers	1 day
CD-ROM drives	4 hours

EXHIBIT 9.32 The short lead time requirements of customers

Lite-on achieves this by integrating its customers, factories, warehouses, accounting functions and parts suppliers into a single digital supply chain. This cuts lead times in all phases of the procedure from order taking, operations scheduling, suppliers' deliveries and shipping.

With today's markets becoming more global and competitive in nature, companies need to rethink their response. As support for many order-winners and qualifiers is the responsibility of the operations function, how it manages these responses is a key strategic task. But to do this effectively, it needs to manage the internal phase of the supply chain as well as the external elements including a proactive relationship with customers. In this way, a coordinated response that harnesses the potential of the whole supply chain will be looked for, identified and delivered. Without it, strategic advantage will be surrendered and the growth and prosperity of a company will be undermined.

Discussion questions

1 What factors should be taken into account when choosing whether to make or buy?

2 What are the principal benefits of making in-house?

3 What are the principal benefits of outsourcing?

4 What are the principal disadvantages of outsourcing?

5 What is meant by a hollow corporation? What is the significance of this phenomenon?

6 What are the key factors to assess when deciding whether to source from domestic or offshore providers?

7 What is e-procurement? Explain its increasing use in companies.

8 What types of supplier relations can be used?

9 What is strategic partnering?

10 What are supply clusters? Explain their evolution and the benefits that may accrue.

11 How can companies cushion the operations process/delivery system from the inherent instability of its markets? How do these approaches extend into the management of the supply chain?

Notes and references

1   Gottfredson, M., Puryear, R. and Philips, S. (2005) 'Strategic sourcing: from periphery to core', *Harvard Business Review*, **83**(2): 132-9.

2   Institute for Supply Management (formerly US National Association of Purchasing Management), Tempe AZ, US.

3   Also see Tait, N. (1997) 'Handling the sourcing decisions: lowest cost is not always the answer', *Financial Times*, 15 Oct., p. 13.

4   Milne, R. (2006) 'Volkswagen chooses to swim against the current', *Financial Times*, 7 Oct., p. 28.

5   Hamel, G. and Prahalad, C. (1994) *Competing for the Future*, Boston, MA: Harvard Business School Press.

6   For example, see Norman, P.M. (2001) 'Are your secrets safe? Knowledge protection in strategic alliances', *Business Horizons*, **44**(6): 51–60.

7   For example, see Arruñada, B. and Vázquez, X.H. (2006) 'When your contract manufacturer becomes your competitor', *Harvard Business Review*, **84**(9): 135–59.

8   Desmond, E.W. (1998) 'Can Canon keep kicking?', *Fortune*, 2 Feb., pp. 58–64.

9   Desmond, 'Can Canon keep kicking?'

10 For example, see Slone, R.E., Mentzer, J.T. and Dittmann, J.P. (2007) 'Are you the weakest link in your company's supply chain?', *Harvard Business Review*, September, pp. 116–27.

11 Harrigan, K.R. (1983) *Strategies for Vertical Integration*, Lexington, MA: Lexington Books, discusses these alternatives and offers frameworks to help in their selection.

12 It is estimated that for each $1bn of foreign-made consumables, up to a further 50 per cent is the total cost to a nation including other manufacturing, wholesale and retail margins, transportation, plant construction, other new materials, mining, financial and insurance.

13 Thomas Hobson, a Cambridge carrier, had a policy of letting out his horses in rotation, without allowing his customers to choose among them. Hence they had to take or leave the one on offer.

14 Economist Intelligence Unit and KPMG management consultants 1996 report entitled *Supply Chain Management: Europe's New Competitive Battleground*.

15 Borsodi, R. (1929) *The Distribution Age*, New York: D. Appleton & Co.

16 Blecke, J.A. (1989) 'Peak strategies', *McKinsey Quarterly*, Spring.

17 Adapted from Ferdows, K. (1997) 'Making the most of foreign factories', *Harvard Business Review*, March–April, pp. 73–88.

18 Products that are different to any other product in any way (including, for example, the number of units in an outer packing case) will have a unique company code number and are referred to as stock-keeping units (SKUs).

19 Asanuma, B. (1989) 'Manufacture–supplier relationships in Japan and the concept of relation-specific skill', *Journal of Japanese and International Economies*, **3**: 1–30.

20 Toyota Motor Corporation (1988) 'Toyota: A history of the first 50 years', Toyota City: TMC.

21 Li, S., Ragu-Nathan, B., Ragu-Nathan, T. and Subba, S. (2006) 'The impact of supply chain management practices on competitive advantage and organisational performance', *OMEGA, International Journal of Management Science*, **34**: 110.

22 Margretta, J. (1998) 'The power of virtual integration: an interview with Dell Computer's Michael Dell', *Harvard Business Review*, March–April, pp. 72–83.

23 Lambert, D.M. and Knemeyer, A.M. (2004) 'We're in this together', *Harvard Business Review*, December, pp. 114–22.

24 Porter, M. (1988) 'Clusters and the new economics of competition', *Harvard Business Review*, Nov–Dec, pp. 77–90.

25 Stewart, T. and Raman, A. (2007) 'The HBR interview with Katsuaki Watanabe: lessons from Toyota's long drive', *Harvard Business Review*, Jul–Aug, pp. 74–83.

26 Wu, L., Yue, X. and Sim, T. (2006) 'Supply clusters; a key to China's cost advantage', *Supply Chain Management Review*, March, pp. 46–51.

27 Wu et al., 'Supply clusters', p. 48.

28 As reported in *The Economist* (2004) 'A world of work: a survey of outsourcing', 11 Nov.

29 Wu et al., 'Supply clusters', p. 49.

30 For example, Newman, W., Hanna, R. and Maffei, M.J. (1993) 'Dealing with the uncertainties of manufacturing, flexibility, buffers and integration', *International Journal of Operations & Production Management*, **13**(1): 19–34; and Caputo, M. (1996) 'Uncertainty, flexibility and buffers in the management of a firm's operating system', *Production Planning and Control*, **7**(5): 518–28.

31 Hopp, W.J. and Spearman, M.L. (2000) *Factory Physics: Foundations of Manufacturing Management*, 2nd edn, Burr Ridge, IL: Irwin/McGraw-Hill.

32 See also Fisher, M., Hammond, J., Obermeyer, W. and Raman, A. (1997) 'Configuring a supply chain to reduce the cost of uncertainty', *Production and Operations Management*, **6**(3): 211–25. In this, they highlight the different supply chain requirements for innovative and 'functional' products, which they term 'responsive' and 'efficient' respectively.

33 Hille, K. (2006) 'Dell to add to Taiwan suppliers', *Financial Times*, 9 May, p. 25.

34 Brown, E. (1997) 'The push to streamline supply chains', *Fortune*, 3 March.

35 Margretta, 'The power of virtual integration', p. 76.

36 Margretta, 'The power of virtual integration', p. 81.

37 Dell Inc. company data, February 2007.

Exploring further

Arnold, D. (2000) 'Seven rules of international distribution', *Harvard Business Review*, November–December, pp. 131–7.

Barnes-Schuster, D., Bassock, Y. and Anupindi, R. (2002) 'Coordination and flexibility in supply contracts with options', *Manufacturing and Service Operations Management*, **4**(3): 171–207.

Blois, K.J. (1972) 'Vertical quasi-integration', *Journal of Industrial Economics*, **20**(3): 253–72.

Buzznell, R.D. (1983) 'Is vertical integration profitable?', *Harvard Business Review*, January–February, pp. 92–102. This offers an analysis based on the profit impact of market strategies (PIMS) data to assess a number of relationships, including vertical integration and profitability, vertical integration, investment intensity and return on investments, and vertical integration, relative market share and profitability.

Carranza Torres, O.A. and Villegas Moràn, F.A. (eds) (2006) *The Bullwhip Effect in Supply Chains: A Review of Methods, Components and Cases*, Basingstoke: Palgrave Macmillan.

Child, J. and Faulkner, D. (1998) *Strategies for Cooperation: Managing Alliances, Networks and Joint Ventures*, Oxford: Oxford University Press.

Childerhouse, P. and Towill, D.R. (2003) 'Simplified material flow holds the key to supply chain management', OMEGA, *International Journal of Management Science*, **31**(1): 17–27.

Childerhouse, P., Aitken, J. and Towill, D.R. (2002) 'Analysis and design of focused demand chains', *Journal of Operations Management*, **20**(6): 675–89.

Childerhouse, P., Hermiz, R., Mason-Jones, R., Popp, A. and Towill, D.R. (2003) 'Information flows in automobile supply chains: present industrial practice', *Industrial Management and Data Systems*, **103**(3): 137–49.

Choi, T.Y. and Hong, Y. (2002) 'Unveiling the structure of supply networks: case studies in Honda, Acura and DaimlerChrysler', *Journal of Operations Management*, **20**(5): 469–93.

Cigolini, R., Cozzi, M. and Perona, M. (2004) 'A new framework for supply chain management: a conceptual model and empirical test', *International Journal of Operations Management*, **24**(1): 7–41.

Croom, S.R. (2000) 'The impact of web-based procurement on the management of operating resources supply', *Journal of Supply Chain Management*, **36**(1): 4–13.

DTI and Society of Motor Manufacturers and Traders (1994) 'A review of the relationships between vehicle manufacturers and suppliers', February.

Fisher, M. (1997) 'What is the right supply chain for your product?', *Harvard Business Review*, March–April, pp. 105–16.

Fisher, M., Hammond, J., Obermeyer, W. and Raman, A. (1997) 'Configuring supply chain to reduce the cost of demand uncertainty', *Production and Operations Management*, **6**(3): 211–25.

Frohlich, M.T. and Westbrook, R. (2001) 'Arcs of integration: an international study of supply chain strategies', *Journal of Operations Management*, **19**(2): 185–200.

Gattorna, J. (ed.) (1998) *Strategic Supply Chain Alignment: Best Practice in Supply Chain Management*, Aldershot: Gower.

Groucutt, J. and Griseri, P. (2004) *Mastering e-business*, Basingstoke: Palgrave Macmillan.

Hagel, J. III and Brown, J.S. (2005) 'Productive friction: how difficult business partnerships can accelerate innovation', *Harvard Business Review*, February, pp. 83–91.

Handfield, R.B. and Krause, D.R. (2000) 'Avoiding the pitfalls in supplier development', *Sloan Management Review*, **41**(2): 37–50.

Harland, C.M., Lamming, R.C., Zheng, J. and Johnsen, T.E. (2001) 'A taxonomy of supply networks', *Journal of Supply Chain Management*, **37**(4): 21–7.

Lamming, R.C. (1993) *Beyond Partnership: Strategies for Innovation and Lean Supply*, Prentice Hall: New York.

Lamming, R.C., Johnsen, T., Zheng, J. and Harland, C. (2000) 'An initial clarification of supply networks', *International Journal of Production & Operations Management*, **20**(6): 675–91.

Lancioni, R.A., Smith, M.F. and Oliva, T.A. (2000) 'The role of the internet in supply chain management', *Industrial Marketing Management*, **29**(1): 45–56.

Lee, H.L. (2002) 'Aligning supply chain strategies with product uncertainties', *California Management Review*, **44**(3): 105–19.

Liker, J.K. and Wu, Y.-C. (2000) 'Japanese automakers, US suppliers and supply chain superiority', *Sloan Management Review*, **42**(1): 81–93.

Lowson, R.H. (2003) 'How supply network operations strategies evolve: composition, competitive priorities and customisation', *International Journal of Physical Distribution and Logistics Management*, **33**(1): 75–91.

Mason-Jones, R. and Towill, D.R. (1997) 'Information enrichment: designing the supply chain for competitive advantage, *Journal of Supply Chain Management*, **24**(7): 17–23.

Nassimbeni, G. and Sartor, M. (2006) *Sourcing in China: Strategies, Methods and Experiences*, Basingstoke: Palgrave Macmillan.

Rudberg, M. and Olhager, J. (2003) 'Manufacturing networks and supply chains: an operations strategy perspective', OMEGA, *The International Journal of Management Science*, **31**: 29–39.

Salvador, F., Forza, C., Rungtusanatham, M. and Choi, T.Y. (2001) 'Supply chain interactions and time-related performance: an operations management perspective', *International Journal of Operations & Production Management*, **21**(4): 461–75.

Smeltzer, L.R. and Carr, A. (2002) 'Reverse auctions in industrial marketing and buying', *Business Horizons*, March–April, pp. 47–52.

Tan, K.C., Lyman, S.B. and Wisner, J.D. (2002) 'Supply chain management: a strategic perspective', *International Journal of Production & Operations Management*, **22**(6): 614–31.

Vickery, S., Calantone, R. and Droge, C. (1999) 'Supply chain flexibility: an empirical study', *Journal of Supply Chain Management*, **35**(3): 16–24.

Wu, Y.C. (2003) 'Lean manufacturing: a perspective of lean suppliers', *International Journal of Operations & Production Management*, **23**(11): 1349–76.

Infrastructure Choice

10

Summary

- Infrastructure is used to manage processes and support markets.

- It comprises a number of complex interacting elements that must be aligned to business and market needs. Some examples of the aspects involved are functional support, operations planning and control systems, systems engineering, clerical procedures, payment and reward systems, work structuring and organizational structure.

- Infrastructure is typically managed in functional areas where there is little strategic debate between functions. This often leads to unconnected, uncoordinated, functionally biased and reactive developments.

- Functions resist infrastructure developments as they challenge their size, roles, responsibilities and activities. To overcome this, decisions must be based on data or evidence of actual current and future market requirements.

- Businesses must make incremental infrastructure developments based on continual market reviews. Step changes should be avoided wherever possible, as they are costly, disruptive, difficult to get right and difficult to change once made.

- Cross-functional teams must be empowered to identify improvement areas with high return, compare alternative developments, consider all elements and make incremental changes.

- Many organizations make inappropriate infrastructure decisions. Examples of these are managing through specialist functions, creating functional silos, supporting delivery systems from a distance, paying and rewarding inappropriately, creating too many management layers and reducing line roles and responsibilities.

- To overcome these problems, businesses must redefine functional objectives based on a cross-functional market review supported with data. They must challenge existing management structures, redefine roles and responsibilities, pay and reward based on skills and performance, reduce overheads, flatten management structures and set up cross-functional improvement teams.

- Once the appropriate infrastructure has been developed, it must be managed to support business and market needs. Three critical areas of management focus are quality conformance, inventory and operations planning and control systems.

Once companies identify the processes to best support market order-winners and qualifiers, they must choose the appropriate infrastructure to manage these processes. As illustrated in *Exhibit 10.1*, businesses must develop processes and infrastructure that are aligned with market order-winners and qualifiers. Infrastructure developments involve high investment levels that are difficult to change and set operations performance parameters. Thus the need to align infrastructure to markets is as critical as processes and, for some companies, more so.

Corporate objectives	Marketing strategy	How do you qualify and win orders?	Operations strategy	
			Process choice	Infrastructure choice

• Sales revenue
• Survival
• Profit
• Return on investment
• Other financial measures
• Environmental targets
	• Product/service markets and segments
	• Range
	• Mix
	• Volumes
	• Standardization versus customization
	• Innovation level
	• Leader versus follower
		• Price
		• Quality conformance
		• Delivery
		  –Speed
		  –Reliability
		• Demand increases
		• Product/service range
		• Design leadership
		• Technical support
		• Brand name
		• New products and services – time to market
			• Process choice
			• Trade-offs embodied in these choices
			• Make or buy
			• Capacity
			  –Size
			  –Timing
			  –Location
			• Role of inventory in the process
				• Functional support
				• Operations planning and control systems
				• Systems engineering
				• Clerical procedures
				• Payment and reward systems
				• Work structuring
				• Organizational structure

NOTES
1 Although the steps to be followed are given as finite points in a stated procedure, in reality the process will involve statement and restatement, for several of these aspects will impinge on each other.
2 Column 3 concerns identifying both the relevant order-winners and qualifiers.

EXHIBIT 10.1 Framework for reflecting operations strategy issues in corporate decisions

Markets are dynamic and constantly changing. Businesses must identify these changes and develop capabilities to support them (see *Exhibit 10.2*).[1] While the overall infrastructure investment is similar to that made in processes, it can be broken down into smaller elements, such as functional support, operations planning and control systems, quality assurance and control, systems engineering, clerical procedures, payment and reward systems, work structuring and organizational structure. Taken individually, each element is often easier and cheaper to modify than the processes used to deliver products and services. For this reason, businesses tend to meet market changes by modifying and realigning infrastructure. Only if market needs cannot be met through infrastructure developments will subsequent process investments be made.

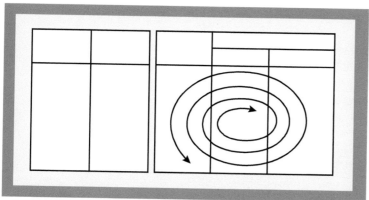

EXHIBIT 10.2 Strategic awareness ensures businesses identify market changes and develop the capability to support them

Issues to consider when developing infrastructure

It is important to consider a number of issues when developing infrastructure:

- **Complex and interacting elements** – operations infrastructure comprises a set of complex interacting factors. Modifying any element will impact other elements and the overall strategic capability of the operation.

- **Managed in functional areas** – Western companies traditionally manage this complexity by breaking it down into smaller parts. Technically similar activities are grouped into functions. The logic for this is creating economies of scale and control through specialists.

- **Little strategic debate between functions** – typically functional areas are managed separately and only work together on tactical or operational issues. There is very little strategic debate around current and future market requirements or how to develop the appropriate infrastructure to support them.

- **Unconnected and uncoordinated developments** – the lack of strategic debate means that infrastructure developments result from individual functions reacting to demands placed on them rather than cross-functional debate about how to support or drive current and future markets.

- **Functionally biased developments** – without a clear strategic focus based on a cross-functional perspective of markets and infrastructure, functions pursue their own objectives and pull the business in different directions. Equally, some functions have more power and influence over investment fund allocation.

- **Reactive developments** – developments are too often a reaction to changes that have already occurred. Instead businesses should continually review current and forecast future market needs and make proactive developments to support or drive markets in a desired direction.

- **Functional resistance to change** – infrastructure developments often involve changing functional size, responsibilities and activities. This can mean eliminating existing functional management structures and moving to cross-functional product or customer-based teams. Functional managers resist this change by presenting a strong case for maintaining the existing structure and arguing their case with great clarity and strength. It is important that these debates and discussions are based on how best to support markets rather than functional needs.

Infrastructure development

When developing infrastructure, businesses must ensure they:

- **Continually review markets** – to identify current and forecast future needs. This enables companies to make decisions about how best to develop infrastructure to support or drive current and future markets.

- **Continually develop infrastructure** – infrastructure needs to be continually developed to ensure that changing current and future market needs are met. As markets are continually changing, operations become misaligned with them once developments stop.

- **Make incremental changes** – if markets are continually reviewed, then infrastructure can be incrementally developed to support or drive them. Structures, controls, systems and procedures can be modified, simplified or eliminated on an ongoing basis. Step change is only required when infrastructure has become significantly misaligned with market needs. This may result from a significant market change, but is typically due to lack of development or market awareness over a long period of time.

- **Avoid step changes** – by making incremental changes, companies can often avoid step changes. Step changes are costly, disruptive, difficult to get right and difficult to change once made. Also, the need to make them implies that the market has not been supported for a period of time.

- **Empower employees to make changes** – continuous incremental development is easier to bring about with local responsibility for improvement identification and implementation.

- **Use cross-functional teams** – to review and develop infrastructure. This happens more readily in organizations with order-winner, product or customer-based teams. In functionally structured organizations, cross-functional teams must be established to identify and implement improvements.

- **Focus on areas of high return** – identify the areas with highest strategic impact to ensure that businesses get the best return from their resources; 80 per cent of benefits typically come from 20 per cent of developments.

- **Compare alternative developments** – identify and select developments based on their benefits and costs.

- **Consider all elements** – as they are complex and interact with each other.

DEVELOPMENTS MUST BE BASED ON DATA OR EVIDENCE OF **ACTUAL MARKET REQUIREMENTS**

Business must **BREAK DOWN** functional silos

Infrastructure is critical to the effectiveness and efficiency of an operation. Choosing the right infrastructure is key to supporting markets and it is expensive to develop, run and maintain. However, many organizations make inappropriate infrastructure choices that result in a number of issues. Some of these are now discussed, although the relevance and importance of each aspect varies depending on the markets served and processes supported.

Managing through specialist functions

Most organizations create specialist support functions to supply advice and guidance to their line functions. By doing this, companies hope to maximize the utilization of their skills and resources under the principle of economies of scale. This is true for high-volume, steady state markets, but most companies now operate in low-volume, dynamic markets where the principles of economies of scale no longer apply (see Chapter 7 on focus for a more detailed explanation). Consequently, companies managing their business through specialist functions tend to experience major difficulties:

- **Differing functional perspectives** – line and support functions view market and business needs very differently. As a result, delivery systems are often not supported. To redress this issue, support functions have developed user-oriented, user-sensitive and user-friendly approaches. However, the attitudes and perspectives creating the mismatch are taking time to change.

- **Differing functional objectives** – differing functional market and business perspectives result in differing functional priorities and objectives. Although each function is clear about what they need to do, this is often not consistent with other functions.

- **Unclear roles and responsibilities** – the roles and responsibilities of line and support functions are often not clear. This leads to confusion and may even create resentment from functions feeling unsupported by others. For example, line managers typically seek specialist support to improve weaknesses within their operation either as a reaction to a recent event or as part of a long-term strategy. Reactive demands are urgent and often not planned into specialist budget and resource allocation. Equally, line managers can focus too much on day-to-day activities and end up delaying long-term strategic decisions until they become urgent. Both situations create problems unless there are clear roles and responsibilities within line and support functions. Without these, misunderstandings and criticism result that can lead to bitterness and disdain between functions.

- **Functions not aligned with each other** – differing functional perspectives and objectives mean that they point in different directions and focus on different goals. The organization becomes less effective and efficient.

- **Markets are not supported** – functional rather than market needs drive the business. This eventually leads to loss in market share and future sales and profits.

Given these difficulties, companies need to review if control through specialists is appropriate for their business and market needs. This must be a systematic evaluation rather than a 0–100 management[2] response that characterizes many changes made. A mix of control through specialists and other approaches such as order-winner, product or customer-based teams will probably be most appropriate. Distinguishing those tasks that are clearly specialist in nature from those that are operational will start the process of reconsidering what tasks should go where.

Creating functional silos

The decision to manage through specialist functions often results in silos. Functions work independently from each other and only make cross-functional decisions at senior organizational levels. There is a lack of line support as specialists pursue their own objectives and goals rather than helping delivery systems to support markets.

Exhibit 10.3 shows the growth of specialist roles and responsibilities in recent years. This often comes from a desire for 'organizational neatness' rather than a review of how best to support markets. Activities that were once integrated into line functions have been moved into specialist areas (Phase 1) and an independent reporting structure then evolves (Phase 2). Once businesses decide to do this, it is difficult to reintegrate support and line activities.

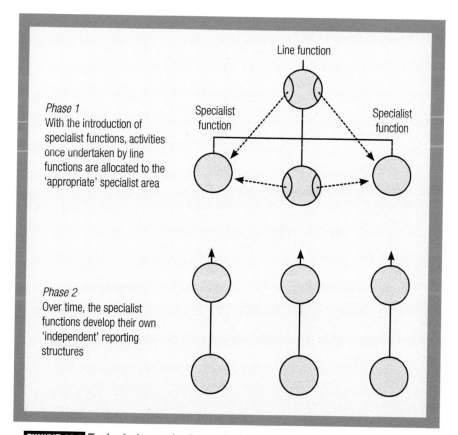

EXHIBIT 10.3 Typical phases in the evolution of specialist functions in an organization

Supporting delivery systems from a distance

As activities move from line to support functions and grow in size, they are often moved away from the line into a central location. Delivery systems are now managed and controlled from a distance using performance measures, financial analyses and reporting systems. This is not the best way to support line activities or markets. Executives believe they can manage effectively from a distance using controls and systems. However, this only gives one type of insight; it is also important to see and feel how an operation is working. Some support activities are most effective when located in or next to the line.

Paying and rewarding inappropriately

Companies must recognize and reward executives on their relative importance and contribution to a business. People need to be attracted into key jobs and rewarded on their direct business effect. Instead, salary structures and promotion opportunities reflect a perceived employee scarcity, assumed contribution and market rates. Consequently, people are attracted to support functions away from the line activities so critical to business success. Equally, payment and reward systems tend to be based around jobs rather than individuals. Such approaches create inflexibility and barriers to change.

Creating too many management layers

Layers of middle management build up in head office and local operations as organizations grow. The principles of economies of large scale and control through specialists contribute to this problem. As Steward of McKinsey & Co. warned in 1981:

> ever since the 1960s, when we started to believe that a professional manager can manage everything, we've been on the wrong track. [As we hire] new managers, unfamiliar with the businesses they were expected to run, [they hire new] staff to advise them. When they moved on, a new manager comes and repeats the cycle … The problem was compounded when companies started going international.[3]

As Peters and Waterman comment:

> Along with bigness comes complexity … And, most big companies respond to complexity in kind, by designing complex systems and structures. They then hire more staff to keep track of all this complexity.[4]

Exhibit 10.4 shows how the number of levels within a typical organization increased fourfold between 1900 and 1960. This trend is now starting to be reversed as companies are cutting out the fat. For example, during the 1980s, DuPont's Maitland plant in Ontario, Canada reduced its management layers from 11 to 6 and shed 700 employees including many highly paid middle managers. These employees performed well, but their roles did not add value and slowed down decisions and actions. Before the change, a production manager supervised 90 workers through 6 foremen, whereas today he has 40 workers and no foremen. Workers now order tools directly from suppliers when they need them without waiting for authorization from senior managers. Also, customers now telephone the plant directly to discuss orders, rather than having to go through DuPont's head office in Toronto and four layers of bureaucracy. There is now better support for line activities and markets.[5]

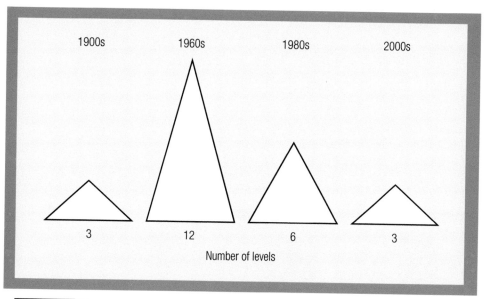

EXHIBIT 10.4 The number of levels within a typical organization at different times

Although there are obvious benefits of reducing management layers, it is too often done in a haphazard fashion. Workforces are cut, perceived frills dispensed with and overheads reduced in an unstructured way. For example, all managers are often asked to reduce staff levels by the same percentage without considering the resultant market support. Corporate or central functions are often left intact as they direct the restructure and do not question their own role. As result, organizations become even more sluggish, top heavy, less effective and less profitable.

Existing business structures do not support delivery systems or markets. Similar across-the-board changes will not work. The organization must be reshaped to become more effective and efficient. This requires careful surgery of both line and support staff based on an assessment of current and future market needs. Only then can appropriate functions and staff levels be determined.

Reducing line roles and responsibilities

As companies create support functions, they split out planning and evaluating activities from the 'doing' aspect of a job. *Exhibit 10.5*[6] shows this separation. Operators become focused on 'making' or 'assembling' products and are not involved in the planning or evaluating aspects of the job. This leads to a number of problems:

- **Lack of responsibility** – operators are less responsible for planning and evaluating activities. For example, product quality conformance is seen as quality control's responsibility rather than the person making the product.

- **Lack of empowerment** – operators are not able to make changes or improvements. Their job is simply to make products. However, often the best improvement ideas come from the person doing the job.

- **Lack of motivation** – as power and responsibility is taken away from employees, they become demotivated.

- **Inflexible capacity** – when 'doing' activities are not required in a period, employees cannot be moved onto planning or evaluating functions. Therefore shop-floor supervisors either have to record labour excess or make inventory. The pressure to meet resource utilization targets means that inventory is often created.

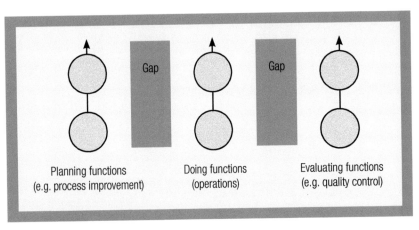

EXHIBIT 10.5 The separation between planning, doing and evaluating created by organizational structure

To rectify these problems, companies must recombine planning and evaluating with doing activities. This often occurs as part of reducing management layers and restructuring roles and responsibilities to empower line staff to make key decisions. Support functions advise them, but the final responsibility rests with the line manager. For example, the human resource function would advise the line on how to select staff and negotiate industrial relations, but it is the line manager's responsibility to make these decisions. As with all developments, decisions must be made around how best to support markets.

Developing infrastructure

Existing infrastructure is designed for high-volume, stable markets, whereas businesses today face low-volume, unstable markets with increasing competition and overcapacity. To compete effectively, firms must develop infrastructure that reflects current market needs and can adapt to future changes. *Exhibit 10.6* shows a number of developments that overcome the organizational issues outlined in the last section and help businesses to create better infrastructure support for processes and markets.

Aspect	Issue	Development
Organizational structure	Managing through specialist functions can result in differing functional perspectives, differing functional objectives and unclear roles and responsibilities	Set functional objectives, roles and responsibilities using cross-functional perspective of market order-winners and qualifiers (developed in Chapter 3)
	Functional silos are created where functions work independently from each other and only make cross-functional decisions at senior levels in the organization	Create cross-functional teams
	Too many management layers	Reduce overheads and flatten organizations by pushing responsibility as far down the organization as possible
Functional support	There is a lack of specialist support for line functions as they pursue their own goals and objectives rather than helping the delivery system to support the market	Create cross-functional teams and restructure roles and responsibilities to recombine planning, doing and evaluating aspects of a job
	Delivery systems are supported from a distance as support activities are moved away from the line	Relocate support activities next to the line
Payment and reward systems	These do not reflect relative executive importance and contribution to the business	Pay and reward staff based on skills and performance measures that reflect market needs and can be influenced by the individual
Operations planning and control	Businesses split out planning, doing and evaluating aspects of the job. Line staff, in doing roles, have a lack of responsibility, lack of empowerment and lack of motivation and thus capacity becomes inflexible	Restructure roles and responsibilities to recombine planning, doing and evaluating aspects of a job. Set up improvement teams

EXHIBIT 10.6 Indication of how developments can be used to address infrastructure issues

Define functional objectives

Functional objectives must reflect how best to support the current and future market order-winners and qualifiers established in Chapter 3. This cross-functional market view clearly outlines the capabilities to be developed and, therefore, all the functional objectives. Discussing how to support markets means that objectives reflect customer rather than individual functional perspectives. Clearer objectives are developed that are aligned to markets. Functional roles, responsibilities, performance measures and reward systems can then be developed using these objectives.

Challenge existing management structures

Companies must determine if managing through specialist functions is appropriate for their delivery systems and markets. Some support activities may still remain central such as supplier contract negotiation, but others can be allocated to cross-functional order-winner, product or customer teams. This starts to move specialist functions back into the line and enables them to work more closely together. Although overall specialist staff levels often reduce, gaps are also identified and staff levels may increase in certain areas.

To reshape overheads, organizations must challenge current structures, attitudes and expectations. Functionally driven businesses can become top heavy, unresponsive and unable to utilize employee capabilities. Creating cross-functional teams can make them more efficient and effective, but only if markets are better supported.

Restructure roles and responsibilities

Organizations must recombine appropriate planning, doing and evaluating tasks to increase the responsibility, empowerment and motivation of line functions. *Exhibit 10.7* shows how roles and responsibilities increase for line functions and decrease in support areas. Operators become more motivated as they take responsibility for tasks such as process improvement, equipment maintenance and quality control.[7] Equally, specialists are released from non-specialist work and activities become easier to coordinate.[8] Although these changes bring small returns in themselves, the cumulative effect can be enormous.

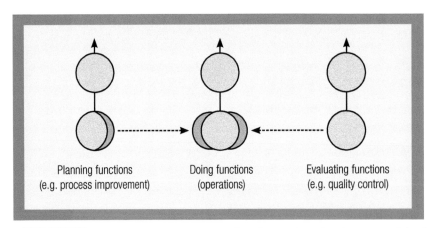

Planning functions
(e.g. process improvement)

Doing functions
(operations)

Evaluating functions
(e.g. quality control)

EXHIBIT 10.7 Incorporating appropriate planning and evaluating steps into the doing tasks

As discussed above, DuPont's Maitland plant significantly changed roles and responsibilities when it reduced management layers from 11 to 6 and shed 700 employees. Previously, customer quality conformance complaints were handled by head office, but now the operator who made the product goes to see the customer and decides how to correct the problem. Problems are cleared more quickly and customers are happier. Operators were also trained in computer technology and now maintain their own computers and develop new systems as required.[9]

Pay and reward based on skills and performance

Payment and reward systems must reflect relative employee importance and contribution. They need to attract people into key jobs and reward them based on their business contribution. Skills and performance-based systems start to do this and move away from systems based on jobs to ones based around individuals. It is critical to use performance measures that reflect market needs and can be influenced by individuals. Otherwise they can create further ineffectiveness and demotivation.

Reduce overheads and flatten organizations

Overheads will be reduced and organizations flattened as businesses challenge existing management structures and redefine roles and responsibilities. Companies must push planning and evaluating responsibilities as far down the organization as possible by investing and developing the people involved in doing activities. This will reduce overhead costs while increasing staff flexibility, resource utilization, decision-making effectiveness and employee motivation. Making a business more effective and efficient requires careful pruning of both line and support staff. Organizations must look at their business and market needs before reducing their management layers.

Set up improvement teams

Improvement teams tap into employee ideas and empower them to make the incremental changes necessary to keep businesses aligned with markets. Quality circles emerged in postwar Japan when they were struggling to meet quality conformance targets. Since then, similar teams have been used by organizations to improve other performance aspects such as cost or delivery speed. Quality circles illustrate how performance can be enhanced by systematically involving workers in improvement activities.

Improvement teams are key to the performance of many Japanese companies. Consequently, businesses in other countries have adopted this approach in an attempt to achieve the same returns. However, too often managers introduce these initiatives because they are fashionable rather than as part of a strategy to improve support for current and future markets. Without a clear strategic focus, these initiatives do not have business support or direction and become discontinued.

European and US manufacturing companies often fail to recognize the potential shop-floor business contribution. Improvement teams tap into the most underdeveloped asset of many companies – the ideas and contributions of their workers. *Exhibit 10.8* shows how world-class automotive component operations use operators to suggest and implement improvements more than other organizations.[10] To do this, managers must genuinely commit to continuous improvement principles and work with their employees. A participative management style must be used to support improvement activities without interfering with their nature.

Aspect	Operation classification	
	World-class	Other
Percentage participation	80	54
Meetings per month	4	3
Suggestions per employees	17	12
Percentage suggestions accepted	79	13

EXHIBIT 10.8 Shop-floor workers are significantly more involved in world-class operations

Managing infrastructure

Once appropriate infrastructure has been developed, businesses must ensure that it is managed to support business and market needs. This concerns a wide range of aspects that cannot be covered in a single chapter. This section looks at three important aspects of managing infrastructure: quality conformance because it is usually either a market order-winner or qualifier; inventory because it is typically a substantial asset on the company's balance sheet; and operations planning and control systems because they are a significant investment and set the performance parameters of an operation.

Managing quality conformance

Quality conformance is either an order-winner or qualifier in most markets and probably impacts market share more than any other factor. Japanese companies have systematically increased the quality conformance levels and fundamentally changed customer expectations in many sectors. By targeting markets where quality conformance was a qualifier, they delivered products with significantly less defects and made it into an order-winner. Unable to meet the higher quality levels, other companies started to lose share. They set about improving their quality and, in most markets, are now able to meet the increased customer expectations. Thus quality conformance is now a qualifier in most markets, but it is still critical to get onto customer shortlists and compete for orders.

Task and responsibility

Managing quality conformance concerns the task of measuring levels and responsibility for meeting targets. The allocation of tasks and responsibilities varies for different types of processes. In some they are combined with doing activities, whereas in others they are kept separate. *Exhibit 10.9* shows how, in project and jobbing processes, the task and responsibility for quality conformance rests with the person delivering the product or service. In continuous processing, quality checks are built into the process itself. However, in batch and line, the doing and evaluating tasks and responsibilities are often separate and conformance levels tend to drop – businesses need to consider how they recombine the doing and evaluating activities. As mentioned earlier, challenging existing management structures, redefining roles and responsibilities and setting up improvement teams are ways to achieve this.

Process type	Quality conformance	
	Task	**Responsibility**
Project and jobbing	Highly skilled people deliver the product or service and ensure conformance levels are met	The person delivering the product or service is also responsible for quality conformance
Batch and line	Doing and evaluating tasks are separated to deskill the doing aspect of the job and reduce labour costs. Inspection and quality control functions evaluate if conformance levels are met	Inspection and quality control functions are primarily responsible for quality conformance
Continuous processing	Quality specification is set and checked by the process itself. Operators may check and monitor the process to ensure conformance levels are met	Conformance levels are controlled by the process itself. Operators may be responsible for ensuring conformance levels are met

EXHIBIT 10.9 Varying quality conformance tasks and responsibilities by process choice

Select approach to managing quality

Once tasks and responsibilities are established, businesses must decide to take a reactive or proactive approach to managing quality:

- **Reactive approach** – products and services are checked during delivery to see if they meet target conformance levels. If levels are not met, changes to the process are made.

- **Proactive approach** – processes are continually monitored and redesigned to ensure poor quality products or services are never delivered. This ensures minimal cost of rectification, scrap, returned products and non-repeat business.

The reactive approach tends to occur in batch or line processes where the doing and evaluating tasks are separate. However, this can be overcome by challenging management structures, redefining roles and responsibilities and setting up improvement teams.

Combine quality assurance and control

Just as companies separate doing and evaluating activities, they also divide quality assurance and control tasks. Quality assurance develops quality management structures, determines roles and responsibilities and establishes procedures to ensure that quality target levels are met; whereas quality control ensures that specifications are met. As with splitting the doing and evaluating tasks, this separation of roles can lead to a lack of responsibility, empowerment and motivation. To overcome this, companies must recombine assurance and control aspects and start to merge them with doing tasks. Challenging existing management structures, redefining roles and responsibilities and setting up improvement teams will help facilitate this.

Develop quality improvement culture

Businesses must recombine quality assurance and control tasks and reintegrate them with doing activities. The Malcolm Baldrige Quality Award[11] found that although respondents in Europe and the US identified quality as their number one competitive priority, they still kept doing and evaluating activities separate. Baldrige examiners (using the categories in *Exhibit 10.10*) found senior managers committed to quality, but were

> surprised to find they come up short at the other end of the organizational chart. Many companies with high-profile reputations for quality have been told to do more to empower their employees as well as their upper ranks.[12]

Category	Points
Information and analysis	85
Strategic planning	85
Leadership	125
Human resource focus	85
Information and analysis	85
Process management	85
Business results	450
Total	1000

EXHIBIT 10.10 Baldrige Award (points allocation by category)

Reallocating the task and responsibility for quality and moving to a proactive approach leads to significant cost, customer and employee benefits.[13] However, it will not happen overnight as cultures and traditions are difficult to change. It is interesting that while Western manufacturing companies consider product quality as their number one competitive priority, Japanese respondents in the same survey placed it fourth. They are apparently now looking at other priorities to give them a competitive edge. Unless radical changes are made, Western companies will always be playing 'catch up' with their Japanese counterparts.

Inventory

Inventory is a mechanism used to cushion stable delivery systems from unstable markets. Other such mechanisms include order backlog, proactive capacity, forecasting, scheduling, process improvement, demand management and capacity management, as shown in *Exhibit 10.11*.

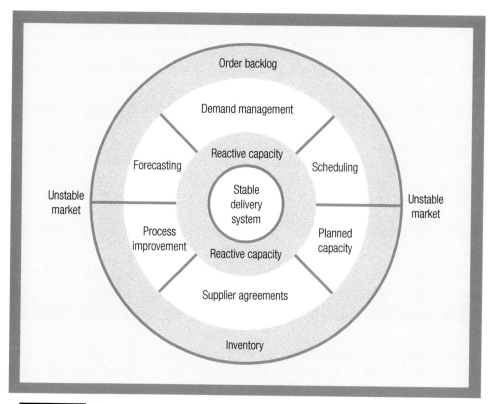

EXHIBIT 10.11 Three levels of mechanisms to cushion delivery systems from unstable markets (see Exhibit 9.26 and accompanying narrative)

Issues with current management practices

In most manufacturing companies, inventory accounts for 30–40 per cent of its total assets. While other funding decisions such as plant and equipment are carefully monitored, the effort and attention to inventory control is generally too little and too late. Issues with current inventory management practices are:

- **Uncontrolled increases** – operational activities often increase inventory. These increases are not controlled or managed until after they have happened.

- **Infrequent stock counts** – many companies take few complete physical stock counts, often as little as twice a year to coincide with financial accounting periods.

- **Inaccurate stock counts** – as the stocktaking date approaches, companies hold off purchases and physically move existing inventory to other parts of the business to show a more favourable financial position.

- **Stocktaking seen as a chore** – companies often look at stocktaking as a chore rather than an opportunity to collect valuable data allowing it to be better controlled.

- **Only analyse for accounting purposes** – inventory is usually analysed by its process stage such as raw material, work-in-progress or finished goods. This is to enable its value to be calculated for the profit and loss account and balance sheet. Thus, stock takes are seen to provide accounting information rather than data for controlling inventory.

- **Inventory levels do not reflect market needs** – as *Exhibit 10.11* shows, the purpose of having inventory is to provide a set of advantages that reflect a business's needs. Depending on what constitutes the needs in the marketplace and the agreed manufacturing requirements within the business, the size and spread of inventory will differ. Effective control is based on an understanding of why inventory is held, where it is and what functions it provides. Currently, however, many companies attempt to control inventory by global, across-the-board mandates over short time periods. This approach neither reflects real control nor time dimensions.

Two illustrations of poor inventory management are outlined below.

Analyse markets using cross-functional perspectives supported with data

The marketing function within a US company believed its construction, mining and steel customers wanted products to be supplied in two days. It therefore chose to put in finished goods and work-in-progress for all its products to reduce the operations lead time. However, sales did not increase as forecasted and the business was left with high levels of slow-moving stock. An operations strategy review highlighted the inventory and questioned if the two-day lead time was actually required by customers. In-depth customer discussions and analysis of the orders they placed on the business showed that less than 15 per cent of orders were required in two days. Inventory could therefore be reduced or eliminated for most products. This reduced inventory by 46 per cent, releasing a significant amount of cash and reducing costs while maintaining market support.

Do not issue across-the-board inventory reduction directives

A company decided to reduce inventory by 15 per cent to 20 per cent across all its operations. However, one plant supplied optional features for vehicles to customers wanting to have them off the road for a minimum length of time. To meet the short lead time requested by customers, operations has to hold raw material and subassembly inventory so it can assemble the final product to order within two days. Reducing inventory would mean it could not support its market and would lose future sales and profits. After significant discussion and debate, the corporate directive was finally rescinded.

Categories and types of inventory

Inventory is used by different functions for a number of reasons. Some categories and types of inventory are:

- **Corporate** – safety stock to safeguard against supply uncertainty such as national or international strikes

- **Sales and marketing** – meet demand uncertainty, customer agreement to hold stock or launch a new product

- **Purchasing** – bulk buying to achieve quantity discounts

- **Operations** – decouple processes so they can be run independently from each other (decoupling), allow processes to produce different batch sizes (cycle), outsource processes (pipeline), meet demand fluctuations (capacity) or buffer against demand or supply uncertainty (buffer).

Benefits of using inventory

Category	Type	Benefit
Corporate	Safety	Safeguards against supply uncertainties such as national or international strikes
Sales and marketing	Demand uncertainty	Ensures demand is met even if demand forecasts are inaccurate
	Customer agreement	Meets customer requirement such as holding safety stock on a customer site to ensure demand is met and lead time reduced
	Product launch	Allows demand spike to be met when product is launched
Purchasing	Quantity discounts	Supports price order-winner by reducing material cost through bulk buying
Operations	Decoupling	Separates one process from the next so they can be run independently of each other and used more efficiently
	Cycle	Allows process to run different batch sizes to each other to reflect set-up times, customer order sizes and call-off patterns. Increasing production run lengths reduces set-up costs and increases capacity utilization
	Pipeline	Allows the company to outsource one or more processes and utilize capability and capacity not present in-house
	Capacity related	Meet anticipated future sales by making inventory in low sales periods and selling in the high sales periods. This stabilizes demand and increases capacity utilization
	Buffer	Protects against unpredictable changes in demand or supply to ensure service levels are maintained. Note that inventory levels above this requirement are corporate safety stocks

EXHIBIT 10.12 Benefits of using inventory by category and type

Exhibit 10.12 shows the benefits of different inventory categories and types. When choosing to invest in inventory, businesses must be aware of why they are doing this and the benefit they hope to achieve. They must also consider the other alternatives available to them, as shown in *Exhibit 10.11*. Different cushioning mechanisms are more appropriate for certain markets. Essentially, the main benefits of using inventory are:

- **Reduce raw material cost** – achieving quantity discounts by bulk buying products

- **Reduce production cost** – by levelling production schedules and increasing capacity utilization

- **Reduce operations lead time** – by eliminating lead time of raw material or certain process stages

- **Improve delivery performance** – by buffering against demand and supply uncertainty

- **Utilize capability or capacity elsewhere** – by outsourcing processes

- **Meet high demand levels** – such as buffering against demand and supply uncertainty or launching a new product

- **Meet customer-specific agreements** – for example holding consignment stock at a customer site.

Disadvantages of using inventory

While using inventory brings benefits, disadvantages are also involved:

- **Cash** – inventory ties up cash within a business that could be better invested in other areas such as equipment or planning and control systems.

- **Cost** – businesses incur costs by holding and managing inventory such as storage, heating, counting, monitoring and transporting.

Inventory is the most appropriate method to cushion delivery systems for certain businesses and markets. However, organizations may be better investing in forecasting, demand management, scheduling, proactive capacity, supplier agreement or process improvement. Each mechanism is better suited to varying order-winners and qualifiers, demand volume and certainty, and breadth of product range.

Managing inventory

To address the issues with current inventory management practices, companies must change a number of aspects:

- **Use inventory to support markets** – based on the market review outlined in Chapter 3, organizations can decide to use inventory to support markets. For example, bulk buying achieves quantity discounts and supports the order-winner of price.

- **Establish inventory targets and functional responsibilities** – once it is clear how inventory should be used to support markets, target holdings and functional responsibilities can be established, for example purchasing for bulk buying, sales for demand not meeting forecast or operations for outsourcing processes. Targets and responsibilities must be continually reviewed as markets are always changing.

- **Analyse and manage inventory by cause** – instead of analysing inventory by the stage in its process, businesses must understand why it was created using the categories and types outlined in *Exhibit 10.12*. Once targets and responsibilities are established, inventory levels can be monitored and managed by cause rather than process stage.

Reducing inventory

Organizations find that historical inventory mismanagement or market changes lead to excess inventory. Reducing this holding involves a number of steps:

1   **Identify large inventory holdings** – initially, this can be a rough assessment of current inventory holdings rather than a detailed stocktaking. From this, areas can be identified for the more detailed analysis of its process stage and cause.

2   **Analyse inventory process stage and cause** – determine the process the inventory has just left and the one it will go to next. Then identify why it has been created.

3   **Identify improvement areas** – a Pareto analysis[14] will almost certainly show that 20 per cent of the inventory items account for about 80 per cent of its total value. Companies can then focus on this 20 per cent and use simpler management controls for the other low value items.

4   **Use other cushioning mechanisms** – businesses must remember that inventory has been created for a reason. Using other cushioning mechanisms shown in *Exhibit 10.11* means inventory can be reduced and market support maintained. The cost and cash implications of investing in other mechanisms must be compared against the benefit of reducing inventory. Improving operations is always a balance between reducing cost, releasing cash or improving market support, as shown in *Exhibit 10.13*.

5   **Change inventory management rules and procedures** – to use up existing inventory and stop it recurring.

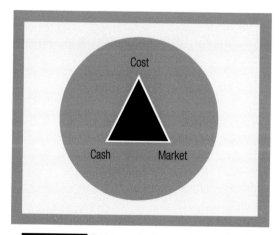

EXHIBIT 10.13 Balance between improving the cash, cost and market support of operations

Planning and control systems

Organizations use manual or computer-based systems to schedule, plan and control their operation in the following ways:

- **Schedule production** – determine the products to be made in a period of time based on either known or forecasted customer orders. Critical to this is the make-to-order, assemble-to-order or make-to-stock decision.

- **Plan materials** – using a bill of materials for each product, material requirements are calculated from the master production schedule. Planning how many materials to produce and when to produce them depends on whether the business uses a time-phased or rate-based approach.

- **Control shop-floor activities** – finally, shop-floor activities must be controlled to ensure that orders are delivered in line with customer requirements. Organizations can choose to either push or pull orders through the operation.

Issues with current planning and control systems

System investments are too often driven by a panacea approach rather than considering how best to support business and market needs. The high cost and fixed nature of these investments make them essential to securing short- and long-term prosperity and supporting dynamic markets. However, investments in systems such as material requirements planning (MRP), just-in-time (JIT) or optimized production technology (OPT) are often made without understanding business and market needs. As a result, many companies find these large, expensive and time-consuming investments fail to realize their full benefits.[15] Three illustrations of inappropriate investments are now discussed.

Computer system makes operation more expensive and less effective

A medium-sized US furniture company makes high-volume standard products using simple process technologies with few operations and little work-in-progress. Customer lead times are short and met using finished goods inventory. Production is controlled with central scheduling, manual shop-floor controls, visual checks and verbal communications between departments. To improve equipment utilization, productivity and shop-floor order tracking, the company decided to install a computer-based shop-floor control system with automated order tracking, queue control and capacity planned features. The system cost about $0.75m and was justified on increased sales from faster order fulfilment and tighter finished goods management. However, it was subsequently found that the computer system neither made the process faster nor better controlled. It only increased paperwork, increased overheads and diverted supervisors away from key management areas.

A European telecommunications company developed its technology by moving from electro-mechanical to electronic-based products. The decision was made to outsource the manufacturing and assembly for the new electronic-based components. Previously, operations managed and controlled a wide range of complex internal processes with high work-in-progress inventory. Now it manages a range of suppliers with high component inventory. However, it did not modify its existing MRP system to meet these significantly different business needs. The system was unable to manage and control the new operation and this resulted in increased cost, poor delivery performance and lost market share.

A UK aerospace company manufactures a wide range of products at varying stages in their life cycles. It chose to invest in a comprehensive, standard computer-based MRP system to manage and control all its products. Its varying product and customer requirements meant that the system was expensive to develop, install and maintain. System development, installation and training cost $8m and lasted for over two-and-a-half years. There were also high ongoing running and support costs. A review of the system after it was installed showed that it met the needs of its original equipment manufacturer (OEM) products, but not its spares business. Simpler master scheduling, materials planning and shop-floor controls would better support the spares business. There is no need for the order tracking, queue control and priority despatching features required by OEM products; 60 per cent of the development and installation investment cost was unnecessary.

Selecting the right planning and control system

As with all aspects of infrastructure, planning and control systems must be used to support business and market needs. Based on the cross-functional market review outlined in Chapter 3, the business must decide how to develop its master production schedule, plan its material and control its shop-floor activities. *Exhibits 10.14, 10.15* and *10.16* show the alternative approaches for different markets and some of the key points are now discussed:

- Make-to-order, assemble-to-order or make-to-stock production scheduling – a business should choose either one or a combination of these approaches to support its markets, as shown in *Exhibit 10.14*. The make-to-order approach suits markets with low-volume, wide-ranging special products. Operations uses a jobbing or low-volume batch process, manages changes in sales volume and product mix with order backlog and reschedules orders to meet delivery speed requirements. By contrast, a make-to-stock approach suits high-volume, standard products with a narrow range. Operations uses a high-volume batch or line process and holds finished goods inventory to meet demand changes and delivery requirements. An assemble-to-order approach is used when market characteristics fall between these two extremes. Here work-in-progress is used to reduce the process lead time and enables demand changes and delivery requirements to be met.

- **Time-phased or rate-based materials planning** – time-phased planning suits low-volume, special products with a wide range using a jobbing or low-volume batch process, as shown in *Exhibit 10.15*. No inventory is held and operations overheads are low as skilled operators plan and schedule activities themselves. The process is able to cope with product mix changes, but a long process lead time means delivery speed and schedule changes are difficult to meet. By contrast, a rate-based approach suits a narrow range of high-volume, standard products delivered using high-volume batch or line processes. Operational activities have been automated and deskilled to reduce labour cost, but this means it is less able to cope with product mix changes. Overheads are a higher cost percentage and finished goods are used to meet delivery requirements and schedule changes.

- **Push or pull shop-floor control** – in markets with high-volume, standard products, orders can be pulled through the shop floor using kanban systems to control material flows and finished goods to meet delivery requirements, as shown in *Exhibit 10.16*. By contrast, low-volume specials are manufactured by skilled operators who control the flow of orders as they are pushed through the shop floor. This is a complex task and there tend to be high changeover costs between jobs, but demand increases are more incremental and easier to meet.

Strategic variables			Master scheduling approach		
			Make to order	Assemble to order	Make to stock
Markets	Product	Type	Special	⟶	Standard
		Range	Wide	⟶	Narrow
	Individual product volume per period		Low	⟶	High
	Delivery	Speed	Difficult		Easy
		Reliability	Difficult	⟶	Easy
Operations	Process choice		Jobbing or low-volume batch	⟶	High-volume batch or line
	Managing volume and mix changes		Order backlog	Work-in-progress inventory	Finished goods inventory
	Meeting delivery speed requirements		Reschedule orders	Reduce process lead time	Eliminate process lead time

EXHIBIT 10.14 Linking the master scheduling approach to operations and market needs

Strategic variables			Material planning approach	
			Time phased	**Rate based**
Markets	Product	Type	Special	Standard
		Range	Wide	Narrow
	Individual product volume per period		Low	High
	Ability to cope with product mix changes		High	Limited
	Delivery	Speed	Difficult	Easy
		Schedule changes	Difficult	Easy
Operations	Process choice		Jobbing or low-volume batch	High-volume batch or line
	Cost reduction sources	Overheads	No	Yes
		Inventory	No	Yes

EXHIBIT 10.15 Linking materials planning approach to operations and market needs

Strategic variables			Shop-floor control approach	
			Push	**Pull**
Markets	Product	Type	Special	Standard
		Range	Wide	Narrow
	Individual product volume per period		Low	High
	Demand variability	Volume	Easy Incremental	Difficult Stepped
		Product mix	High	Low
	Delivery	Speed	Schedule change	Finished goods inventory
		Schedule changes	More difficult	Less difficult
Operations	Process choice		Jobbing or low-volume batch	High-volume batch or line
	Cost reduction sources	Overheads	No	Yes
		Inventory	No	Yes
	Changeover cost		High	Low
	Control	Key feature	Order status	Flow of materials
		Basis	Person or system	System
		Ease of task	Complex	Easy

NOTE: In jobbing, shop-floor control is handled by the skilled operator.

EXHIBIT 10.16 Linking shop-floor control systems to operations and market needs

Good practice examples

Exhibit 10.17 shows examples of how planning and control systems can be used to support markets with different needs. Company A supplies a wide range of customized low-volume products where orders are won on product design and delivery speed using raw material and work-in-progress inventory to reduce the process lead time. Products are delivered using low-volume batch process with high precision work undertaken by skilled operators. The key operations tasks are meeting high product design and quality specifications, controlling high labour costs and reducing long process lead times. It uses make-to-order and assemble-to-order approaches to schedule production, although the long process lead time means work often starts before orders have been confirmed. Material is planned using a time-phased approach against known or anticipated orders. Extra material is ordered to cover scrapped items and some raw material and work-in-progress inventory are held to reduce the operations lead time. Orders are pushed through the shop floor using skilled operators to manage delivery priorities. The company is very successful, as all aspects of its planning and control system are aligned to its markets.

By contrast, Company B competes on price and delivery speed for a narrow range of high-volume standard products. It uses a high-volume batch process and holds finished goods inventory at its distributors to meet seasonal demand changes and short customer lead times. The process is automated, has short set-up times and manufactures small batch sizes. As price is a key order-winner, operations continually reduces material, overhead and inventory costs. To fully utilize resources, products are made to stock using a fixed three-month production plan and capacity is finitely planned. Materials are planned using a rate-based approach against forecasts. Orders are pulled through the shop floor using a kanban and JIT approach to minimize raw material and work-in-progress inventory. This planning and control system successfully meets its price and delivery speed market requirements.

Reflections

Infrastructure comprises a complex set of interacting activities that must be aligned to processes and markets. However, organizations often split support activities into specialist areas and create functional silos. There is little strategic debate between functions and this leads to unconnected, uncoordinated, functionally biased and reactive developments. This has created a situation where many organizations support delivery systems from a distance, reduce line roles and responsibilities, pay and reward inappropriately and create too many management layers. To realign infrastructure to markets, businesses must redefine functional objectives based on a cross-functional market review supported with data. Using these objectives, businesses must challenge existing management structures, redefine roles and responsibilities, pay and reward employees based on their skill and performance, reduce overheads and flatten management structures. Changes must be made on an ongoing basis by cross-functional teams monitoring market needs, identifying improvement areas, comparing investment alternatives and developing infrastructure. Step changes should be avoided as they are costly, disruptive, difficult to get right and difficult to change once made.

Aspect			Company	
			A	**B**
Market	Characteristics		• Low-volume products • Customized products • Wide product range • Short product life • Customers give demand forecast and then call off order against it	• High-volume products • Standard products • Narrow product range • Seasonal demand • High level of new product introduction • Changing product mix
	Order-winners		• Product design • Delivery speed	• Price • Delivery speed
	Qualifiers		• Delivery reliability • Quality conformance • Price	• Quality conformance • Delivery reliability • Product design
Operations strategy	Operations	Features	• Low-volume batch process • Long process lead time • Use raw material and work-in-progress inventory to reduce process lead time • High precision work • High labour cost (60 per cent total) • Uncertain process and product	• High-volume batch process • Short set-up times • Small batch sizes • Use finished goods inventory held at distributors to meet demand changes • Low-cost manufacturing • Low labour cost • High material cost
		Task	• Meet product design and quality specification • Reduce process lead time • Control labour cost • Deliver on time	• Reduce material and overhead costs • Manage finished goods inventory • Reduce raw material and work-in-progress inventory
	Planning and control system	Master production scheduling	• Make to order and assemble to order • Manufacture to known and forecast customer orders • Rough cut capacity planning due to long process lead time	• Make to stock • Manufacture to forecast customer orders • Fixed three-month production plan • Finite capacity planning
		Material planning	• Time phased • Material purchased or manufactured for known and forecast orders • High product obsolescence risk • Extra material ordered to cover scrapped items • Raw material inventory held to reduce operations lead time	• Rate based • Material purchased or manufactured against forecast • Finished goods inventory held to eliminate operations lead time and meet seasonal demand
		Shop-floor control	• Push system • Skilled operators schedule and track orders • Despatch and production control staff liaise between customer and operators to manage delivery priorities • Capacity planned by work centre	• Pull system • Kanban system • Just-in-time material flow • Low raw material, component and work-in-progress inventory

EXHIBIT 10.17 The relevant manufacturing tasks and MPC system investments of two companies serving different markets

Panaceas don't work

Generic strategic solutions assume that businesses have similar characteristics and support markets with similar needs. This is not true. Organizations must develop their own solution based on their own business and market requirements. The Toyota Production System is an example of how to do this. It successfully manages the three major phases in its business – the before phase (its suppliers), the owned phase (its own processes) and the forward phase (the sale of cars through its networks). It stabilizes the before and owned phase by holding finished goods inventory in the forward phase of its business. This cushions operations from the market and allows Toyota to reduce raw material and work-in-progress in its own processes and those of its suppliers. This released cash that could be invested elsewhere in the business and reduced operating costs, creating profit that was also reinvested.

To achieve this, it recombined planning and evaluating with doing activities and empowered operators to identify and make improvements. As improvements were made, processes were simplified and so was the infrastructure used to manage them. Visual controls and kanbans replaced computer-based systems, making it easier for operators to plan and evaluate activities. There have been significant cash, cost, quality, delivery and product design improvements. Markets are better supported and have often been driven in a particular direction. The ongoing incremental nature of these developments means they are more efficient, effective and sustainable than a step change. Many Western companies trying to imitate this approach do not appreciate how developments are made and why they are successful.

Developments must be based on a clear strategy

A clear operations strategy enables infrastructure to be developed from a common base and in a common direction to meet a common requirement. Historical and personal views fall by the wayside and are replaced by clear strategic thinking. This ensures that current and future business and market needs are met. Without a strategy-based approach, developments are based on personal judgements, fixed ideas and specialist arguments about what they can provide rather than what the market requires.

Businesses must challenge existing approaches

Businesses must challenge their organizational structures and redefine roles, responsibilities, authorities, specialist functions and all other aspects of infrastructure. Konsuke Matsushita sums this up in a speech he made to a group of Western managers in 1985, entitled 'Why the West will lose', challenging them to rethink existing approaches. While some organizations have made changes and improvements over the past 20 years, others are still far behind. One thing is certain, to be successful in the future, companies must adapt to markets and effectively use all their resources.

Why the West will lose

We are going to win and the industrial West is going to lose: there is nothing much you can do about it, because the reasons for your failure are within yourselves.

Your firms are built on the Taylor model; even worse, so are your heads. With your bosses doing the thinking, while the workers wield the screwdrivers, you are convinced deep down that this is the right way to run a business.

For you, the essence of management is getting the ideas out of the heads of the bosses into the hands of labour.

We are beyond the Taylor model: business, we know, is now so complex and difficult, the survival of firms so hazardous in an environment increasingly unpredictable, competitive, and fraught with danger that their continued existence depends on the day-to-day mobilization of every ounce of intelligence.

For us, the core of management is precisely this art of mobilizing and pulling together the intellectual resources of all employees in the service of the firm. Because we have measured better than you the scope of the new technological and economic challenges, we know that the intelligence of a handful of technocrats, however brilliant and smart they may be, is no longer enough for a real chance of success.

Only by drawing on the combined brainpower of all its employees can a firm face up to the turbulence and constraints of today's environment.

This is why our large companies give their employees three to four times more training than yours; this is why they foster within the firm such intensive exchange and communication; this is why they seek constantly everybody's suggestions and why they demand from the educational system increasing numbers of graduates as well as bright and well-educated generalists, because these people are the lifeblood of industry.

Your 'socially-minded bosses', often full of good intentions, believe their duty is to protect the people in their firms. We, on the other hand, are realists and consider it our duty to get our own people to defend their firms, which will pay them back a hundredfold for their dedication. By doing this, we end up by being more 'social' than you.[16]

Discussion questions

1 'Infrastructure comprises a number of complex interacting elements that must be aligned to business and market needs.' Explain this statement using examples other than those described in this chapter.

2 Businesses can make either incremental or step change infrastructure developments. Explain the advantages and disadvantages of these two approaches using examples other than those described in this chapter.

3 Outline the reasons why many companies make inappropriate infrastructure decisions. What actions can be taken to rectify the problems caused by these decisions? How can they be prevented from reoccurring in the future?

4 'Cross-functional teams must be empowered to identify improvement areas with high return, compare alternative developments, consider all elements and make incremental changes.' Explain this statement using examples other than those described in this chapter.

5 Outline the three levels of mechanisms that can be used to cushion delivery systems from unstable markets. How can the different mechanisms be used? Explain why some are more suitable to certain circumstances than others.

6 Outline the advantages and disadvantages of using inventory. Describe how it should be managed by organizations using examples other than those described in this chapter.

Notes and references

1 Peters T.J. and Waterman, R.H. Jr (1982) *In Search of Excellence: Lessons from America's Best-run Companies*, New York: Harper & Row.

2 The expression '0–100 management' was developed to highlight the pendulum-like response to problems or disadvantages that typifies organizational action. Instead, companies need to reposition themselves on a gradual and continuous basis while clearly recognizing that the diverse nature of markets will require diverse responses.

3 'A new target: reducing staff and levels', *Business Week*, 21 December 1981, pp. 38–41.

4 Peters and Waterman, *In Search of Excellence*, p. 306.

5 Stoffman, D. (1998) 'Less is more', *Report on Business Magazine*, pp. 97–8.

6 This and some of the other concepts discussed here are taken from a set of well-developed work structuring principles that have been presented in various unpublished papers by P.C. Schumacher, Schumacher Projects, Godstone, Surrey, UK.

7 Examples of this are described in Senju, S. (ed.) (1992) *TQC and TQM*, Tokyo: Asian Productivity Organization, and Takahashi, Y. and Osada, T. (1990) *TPM: Total Production Maintenance*, Tokyo: Asian Productivity Organization.

8 A key feature of quality circles is that those involved not only implement their ideas but also evaluate the gains they yield.

9 Stoffman, 'Less is more', pp. 97–8.

10 Anderson Consulting (1993) *The Lean Enterprise Benchmark Project*, Cardiff Business School/University of Cambridge.

11 The Malcolm Baldrige National Quality Award is a US government industry venture but supported solely by the industry-funded Baldrige Award Foundation. Started in 1988, the programme entails assessment against the criteria given in Exhibit 10.10.

12 Burrows, P. (1990) 'Five lessons you learn from (Baldrige) Award entrants', *Electronic Business*, 15 October, pp. 22–4.

13 There are many references to the advantages to be gained and examples of the results of such decisions. These include Juran, J.M. (1981) 'Product quality: a prescription for the West', *Management Review*, June, pp. 9–20; Schonberger, R.J. (1982) *Japanese Manufacturing Techniques: Nine Hidden Lessons in Simplicity*, New York: Macmillan, pp. 47–82, 181–98; Garvin, D.A. (1983) 'Quality on the line', *Harvard Business Review*, September–October, pp. 65–75; Lorenz, C. (1983) 'A shocking indictment of American mediocrity', *Financial Times*, 17 October; Kona, T. (1984) *Strategy and Structure of Japanese Enterprises*, New York: Macmillan, pp. 194–6; Imai, M. (1986) *Kaizen: The Key to Japanese Competitive Success*, New York: Random House, Ch. 3; Gunn, T.G. (1987) *Manufacturing for Competitive Advantage: Being a World Class Manufacturer*, Cambridge, MA: Ballinger; Alston, J.P. (1989) *The American Sumurai*, Berlin: Walter de Gruyter; Dale, B.G. and Plunkett, J.J. (1990) *Managing Quality*, Hemel Hempstead: Philip Alan; Slack, N. (1991) *The Manufacturing Advantage*, London: Mercury; Stahl, M.J. and Bounds, G.M. (eds) (1991) *Competing Globally through Customer Value*, New York: Quorum Books.

14 A Pareto analysis orders the data from highest down to lowest. The list provided then helps to show the 80/20 relationship that exists between the data being reviewed.

15 Earlier research in the early 1980s alerted companies to the extent of this phenomenon. Schroeder, R.G. (1981) 'A study of MRP benefits and costs', *Journal of Operations Management*, 2(1): 1–10 , reported that 63 per cent of MRP applications studied cost as much as $5m, yet failed to realize their full benefits.

16 Matsushita, K. (1985) 'Why the West will lose: extracts from remarks made by Mr Konosu Matsushita of the Matsushita Electric Industrial Company (Japan) to a group of Western managers,' *Industrial Participation*, Spring, p. 8.

Exploring further

Alston, J.P. (1989) *The American Sumurai*, Berlin: Walter de Gruyter.

Berry, W.L. and Hill, T.J. (1992) 'Linking systems to strategy', *International Journal of Operations & Production Management*, **12**(10): 3–15.

Burrows, P. (1990) 'Five lessons you learn from (Baldrige) Award entrants', *Electronic Business*, 15 October, pp. 22–4.

Champy, J. (1995) *Reengineering Management: the Mandate for New Leadership*, New York: HarperCollins.

Cobb, J.C., Samuels, C.J. and M.W. Sexton (1998) 'Alignment and strategic change: a challenge for marketing and human resources', *Leadership & Organization Development Journal*, **19**(1): 32–43.

Dale, B.G. and Plunkett, J.J. (1990) *Managing Quality*, Hemel Hempstead: Philip Alan.

Davenport, T.H. (1993) *Process Innovation: Reengineering Work through Information Technology*, Cambridge, MA: Harvard Business School Press.

Davenport, T.H. and Short, J.E. (1990) 'The new industrial engineering: information technology and business process redesign', *Sloan Management Review*, **31**(4): 11–26.

Garvin, D.A. (1983) 'Quality on the line', *Harvard Business Review*, Sept–Oct, pp. 65–75.

Gunn, T.G. (1987) *Manufacturing for Competitive Advantage: Being a World Class Manufacturer*, Cambridge, MA: Ballinger.

Hammer, M. and Champy, J. (1993) *Reengineering the Corporation: A Manifesto for Business Revolution*, New York: Harper Business.

Hayes, R.H. and Wheelwright, S.C. (1984) *Restoring Our Competitive Edge: Competing through Manufacturing*, New York: John Wiley & Sons.

Hill, A. and Brown, S. (2007) 'Strategic profiling: a visual representation of internal strategic fit in service organisations', *International Journal of Operations & Production Management*, **27**(12): 1333–61.

Hill, T.J. (1998) *The Strategy Quest*, Bristol: AMD Publishing.

Hughes, M., Hughes, P. and Morgan, R.E. (2007) 'Exploitative learning and entrepreneurial orientation alignment in emerging young firms: implications for market and response performance', *British Journal of Management*, **18**(4): 359–75.

Imai, M. (1986) *Kaizen: The Key to Japanese Competitive Success*, New York: Random House.

Johansson, H.J., McHugh, P., Pendlebury J. and Wheeler W.A. III (1993) *Business Process Reengineering*, New York: John Wiley.

Juran, J.M. (1981) 'Product quality: a prescription for the West', *Management Review*, June, pp. 9–20.

Kaplan, R.S. and Norton, D.P. (2004) 'Measuring the strategic readiness of intangible assets', *Harvard Business Review*, February, pp. 52–63.

Kaplan, R.S. and Norton, D.P. (2007) 'Using the balanced scorecard as a strategic management system', *Harvard Business Review*, Jul–Aug, pp. 150–61.

Kona, T. (1984) *Strategy and Structure of Japanese Enterprises*, New York: Macmillan.

Leisen, B., Lilly, B. and Winsor, R.D. (2002) 'The effects of organisational culture and market orientation on the effectiveness of strategic marketing alliances', *Journal of Services Marketing*, **16**(3): 201–22.

Lorenz, C. (1983) 'A shocking indictment of American mediocrity', *Financial Times*, 17 October.

Matsushita, K. (1985) 'Why the West will lose: extracts from remarks made by Mr Konosu Matsushita of the Matsushita Electric Industrial Company (Japan) to a group of Western managers,' *Industrial Participation*, Spring, p. 8.

Morris, D.C. and Brandon, J.S. (1993) *Reengineering your Business*, New York: McGraw-Hill.

Obeng, E. and Crainer, S. (1994) *Making Re-engineering Happen*, London: Pitman.

Peters, T.J. and Waterman, R.H. Jr (1982) *In Search of Excellence: Lessons from America's Best-run Companies*, New York: Harper & Row.

Rayner, B.C.P. (1990) 'Market-driven quality: IBM's Six Sigma crusade', *Electronics Business*, 15 October, pp. 26–30.

Senju, S. (ed.) (1992) *TQC and TQM*, Tokyo: Asian Productivity Organization.

Stahl, M.J. and Bounds, G.M. (1991) *Competing Globally through Customer Value*, New York: Quorum Books.

Takahashi, Y. and Osada, T. (1990) *TPM: Total Production Maintenance*, Tokyo: Asian Productivity Organization.

Ulrich, D. and Smallwood, N. (2004) 'Capitalizing on capabilities', *Harvard Business Review*, June, pp. 119–27.

Ulrich, D. and Smallwood, N. (2005) 'HR's new ROI: return on intangibles', *Human Resource Management*, **44**(2): 137–42.

Accounting, Finance and Performance Measurement in the Context of Operations Strategy

11

Summary

This chapter provides some critical observations on the accounting and finance function's contribution within a business, the measures of performance used by companies and the impact on the operations function:

- Investment decisions – investment is the lifeblood of development. It is essential, therefore, that a business takes a strategic-based view when evaluating investment proposals and to separate those that are strategic and those that are operational in orientation.

- Strategic investments to be based on order-winners and qualifiers – where investments are strategic in nature, they need to address the order-winners and qualifiers within relevant markets.

- One reason to substantiate an investment – to bring clarity as to why an investment is being proposed, companies should seek to establish the one reason that substantiates the proposal.

- Quantify working capital and infrastructure investments – while the 'hardware' of a proposed investment is specified and acknowledged, additional investment in working capital and for infrastructure is often understated only to be eventually met in an after-the-event way.

- Post-investment audits – while the detail underpinning investment proposals is typically well explained and substantiated, most companies do not undertake post-investment audits to ascertain the actual benefits secured and to use this learning in assessing future proposals.

- Performance measurements – 'what gets measured gets done' holds true for most companies. Selecting what to measure, therefore, is the key first step. Dimensions such as avoiding long lists, establishing priorities, separating strategic from operational measures, holding regular reviews, looking forward as well as backwards and measuring all parts of a supply chain are key to sound management.

- Setting targets – key issues when setting targets include debating the assumptions on which targets are based and ensuring that the targets set are feasible.

The purpose of this chapter is to provide some critical observations on two fundamental aspects of managing businesses: the accounting and finance function's contribution in terms of data provision, processes, controls and insights; and the measures of performance used by companies. The observations reflect an operations executive's perspective and hence they may be seen as provocative when examined by others in an organization. If this causes debate between operations and the rest of the business, the purpose of the chapter has been well served.

With operations invariably tasked with meeting many of the financial targets and performance measures within organizations (and understandably so as it accounts for so much of the costs and investments), it is essential that the premise on which these targets and measures are built and the data used to calculate them are sound. Where this is not so, the extent of the potential inaccuracy (both data processes and insights) remains unexposed and is then built into corporate expectations. Being unaware, companies set aside these inherent deficiencies, base targets and measures on available data and consequently fail to evaluate performance on reality.

Accounting and finance

Two common denominators are used in manufacturing businesses as the basis for control and performance measurement. The first is the time base on which operations principally works. Product mix and volumes, capacity, efficiency, utilization and productivity are normally measured by time. The second common denominator is that of money. At the corporate level, forecasts, performance measures, levels of investment and similar activities use the money base. The importance of getting the correct links between the time-based and money-based measures is self-evident – correct not only in terms of being accurate, but also in reflecting the key perspectives associated with the business itself.

The money-based denominator issues addressed in this section are controlled by what, in many companies, is frequently one of the least developed functions: accounting and finance. Based on approaches established when business activities were very different, this area has not really faced up to resolving many of the important changes in business with appropriate developments. This section highlights a number of areas that need to be addressed from the point of view of both operations and overall strategy. It will link the area of operations and corporate strategy with accounting and finance and illustrate some of the key issues that need to be developed and the essential direction these improvements need to take. In addition, it will show the ways in which operations strategy will influence and, in some cases, facilitate some of these changes, while also drawing attention to the essential nature of operations' needs and the accounting and financial information provision.

The purpose of this section is to make a number of critical observations about the impact on operations of finance and accounting practices. Solutions to the issues addressed must be worked out in the context of a company's own corporate and operations strategies. Since the financial systems in a business can, and do, have a major impact on operations' ability to develop and maintain effective competitive strategies, one essential objective of the finance function must be to give operations the ability to measure and assess its performance accurately in relation to major competitors, the relative and actual contribution of products, customers and operations activity to overall profits and the competitive value of investment proposals. This section deals with two broad areas of interaction between finance and operations: first, the effect on operations strategy of investment appraisal methods; second, how management accounting systems critically affect the control and performance measurement of operations.

Investment decisions

The approach to developing an operations strategy was explained earlier. One important consideration highlighted in those explanations was the level of alternative investments associated with different decisions (see *Exhibit 11.1*). Many organizations, bounded by limited resources, need to commit these wisely. However, the criteria for assessing the level or nature of this critical corporate decision have rarely been arrived at with the care and in-depth analysis warranted. In many companies, investment decisions – initially chosen or stimulated by corporate competitive requirements – are finally evaluated solely by accounting measures and methods of appraisal. The effect of these financial measures on both strategy and the consequent investment decisions is illustrated by the framework introduced in Chapter 2. Accounting methods of investment appraisal are generally based on one important premise – the relative return on capital associated with each investment proposal under review. With capital investment often in limited supply and capital rationing a widespread consequence, the argument to invest predominantly on the basis of return is not only built into the appraisal system itself, but invariably is reinforced by the discussion and argument that will take place. In this way, the figures will unwittingly support investment return as the predominant or even exclusive measure on which these key corporate strategy decisions are assessed.

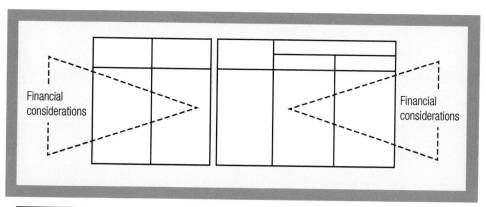

EXHIBIT 11.1 Restrictions imposed at both ends of the operations strategy process

The consequences of this undue weighting have been felt by many companies, and the ramifications within the manufacturing sector have been widespread. The necessity to question this view of investment decisions has stimulated a series of well-argued articles and papers that illustrate the simplistic nature of the accounting perspective and challenge its unevaluated application. As early as 1974, Dean declared that 'because of our obsessive concentration on short-term gains and profits, US technology is stalemated'.[1] Hayes and Abernathy's 1980 article said it all in the title, 'Managing our way to economic decline',[2] and Hayes and Garvin captured the essence of the issues in the article 'Managing as if tomorrow mattered'[3] in which they make, among other things, a concerted challenge on current accounting approaches to investment appraisal. They provide a detailed argument to support their view that companies have increasingly turned to sophisticated, analytical techniques to evaluate investment proposals. The long-term result has been that many of the managers involved have 'unintentionally jeopardized their companies' future'. As Hayes and Garvin conclude, 'investment decisions that discount the future may result in high present values, but bleak tomorrows'.

Since then, the basic criticisms have been taken on by others, particularly from the accounting profession. Of these, Kaplan well illustrates these growing concerns, as clearly shown in the title of his book with Johnson, *Relevance Lost: The Rise and Fall of Management Accounting*[4] and again with Cooper in the two articles, 'How cost accounting distorts product costs'[5] and 'Measure costs right: make the right decisions'.[6] Little has changed.

The need for a strategic view of investments

When evaluating investment proposals, companies need to make a strategy-based review. What constitutes a sound investment needs to be measured by its contribution to the agreed corporate strategy and not by how well it meets the criteria laid down by a set of accounting rules and evaluations. In one of several critiques of current management accounting, Simmonds observes that:

> the emphasis ... accounting and finance have placed on return on investment over the years has subtly transmuted into a widely and deeply held belief that return comes from the investments themselves ... The truth is much different. Sustained profit comes from the competitive market position. New production investment to expand sales must imply a change in competitive position, and it is this change that should be the focus of the investment review. Without it, the calculations must be a nonsense.[7]

This sleight of hand has been detected by all too few companies. Consequently, the key factor by which investment proposals have been assessed has increasingly swung away from strategy considerations towards levels of investment return per se. But return must be defined in terms of improved long-term competitiveness rather than just short-term measures.

Changing the basis of investment appraisal is complex and fraught with difficulties. It is one of those issues in which operations executives have traditionally felt relatively weak, while those who control the cash are professionally strong. The debate has, therefore, been one-sided, with operations the casualty by default. The argument that investments must provide a quick payback is financially, and emotionally, attractive. Furthermore, the difficulties inherent in strategy-based vis-à-vis return on investment-based investment decisions (from putting the case together, presenting the arguments and the ease of understanding alternatives) add weight to the current trend.

Decisions based on return oversimplify the investment issues at stake and fail to drive executives towards determining and analysing the fundamental components of competitive strategy. Falling back on investment appraisal by financial numbers becomes the easy and less risky option. It simplifies the task, avoids the need to agree the strategic issues involved and dilutes the link between decision-making and subsequent evaluation. As the overriding reason for going ahead is based on perspectives provided by a function that does not carry the executive responsibility for making it happen, this essential link is weakened.

A short section on investment can only begin to open up the debate from the operations perspective by providing some guidelines that operations can use to raise key questions. The hope is that finance executives will also use them to develop their own appreciation of the strategic issues involved in investment decisions. Eleven key contentions are made, each of which is expanded to give substance, but none is claimed to be comprehensively examined. They are:

- Strategic vis-à-vis operational investments

- Strategic investments must be based on order-winners and qualifiers

- Financial control systems need to be developed to meet the needs of the investment evaluation process

- Investment decisions are not separate but part of the corporate whole

- There can be only one given reason to substantiate an investment proposal

- Excessive use of return on investment (ROI) distorts strategy building

- Government grants are not necessarily golden handshakes

- Linking investment to product life cycles reduces risks

- Operations must test the process implications of product life cycle forecasts

- Investment decisions must quantify working capital and infrastructure requirements

- Post-investment audits capture learning and improve future decisions.

Strategic vis-à-vis operational investments

Companies invest in processes and infrastructure for strategic and operational (day-to-day) reasons. Both are sound but separating which dimension of operations' business contribution is being served is essential. For example, investing in processes or systems that will reduce costs can have either a strategic or operational rationale. Where the cost reductions that result are used to lower price, the underlying rationale is strategic. Where the cost reductions that result are used to increase profits, the underlying rationale is operational. Where the cost reduction outcomes are used in part to lower price and in part to increase profits, the investment serves a dual purpose.

It is essential for companies to clarify the orientation of their investments in order that the purpose and intent of these critical decisions are understood. Knowing why an investment is being made and the outcomes it is intended to provide help to sharpen the strategic debate, clarify the underlying rationale and establish the expectations that should result. Which alternative, therefore, needs to form part of the proposal and decision.

Strategic investments must be based on order-winners and qualifiers

The impact of investment policies and appraisal methods on operations strategy's contribution to the competitiveness of a business is clearly significant. If high hurdle rates are imposed, capital investment will invariably decrease. In times of capital rationing, the argument put forward in support of high ROI thresholds is that they motivate a company to cream off the more attractive investment proposals and hence use available funds for the best opportunities. But this line of argument fails to assess the relevance of investment proposals in the context of an agreed corporate strategy. The result, at best, is a hit-and-miss alignment of essential investments with operations' strategic contribution; at worst, the investments essential for operations to contribute to market objectives are not even made. For instance, delays in appropriate investment would lead to costs not declining as expected. Hence, achieved experience curve gains would fall off and if the delay itself and extent of the investment requirement were large, loss of market share would eventually follow.

Operations strategy arguments for process investment to meet order-winners and qualifiers, other than price and the associated low-cost operations task, come up against the difficulties of accounting and finance-based rationale. Proposals, for instance, to invest in processes that increase operations' ability to provide, say, customized products and/or short lead times when these are the key order-winners will be difficult to prepare in an appraisal system where ROI is paramount. Similar forces will also work against facilities focus, irrespective of the importance of its role within operations' support of business needs. As explained in Chapter 7, focus will sometimes require process duplication. However, investment appraisal systems typically fail to incorporate, as part of the evaluation procedure, the need to orient facilities to better meet the order-winners and qualifiers of different markets. This, by implication, gives undue weight to ROI or capacity utilization and will militate against the concept of focus.

Other accounting and financial perspectives will also work against the pursuit of focus in operations. The accounting function's desire and argument to manage revenues and cash flows by smoothing cyclical business swings carries substantial corporate weight. However, focused operations requires greater interaction between operations and sales/marketing, which leads to a higher level of shared dependence between these two prime functions of a business. This argues against smoothing, with the dynamics of sustaining and improving market share becoming more significant and carrying more weight than the accounting and finance argument for smoothing.

In a reflective mood, Drucker pinpoints a belief in their own accounting figures as one of the common mistakes made by companies, which always leads to trouble:

> The conventions are very inadequate, inappropriate … It gives [companies] the wrong information. They don't know what the real savings are … Cost accounting gives you information on the cost of doing, but not on the cost of not doing – which is increasingly the bigger cost. Quality [conformance] and downtime are neither of them in the model.[8]

In developing a sound understanding of their need to compete effectively in different market segments, companies will recognize the importance of relevant order-winners and qualifiers. With these established and reflected in the evaluation of operations performance, companies can assess their importance and take them into account when judging appropriate investments. Until then, companies will continue to use apparently 'hard' data as the predominant, or even sole, arbiter. Thus, in developing operations strategy, companies must recognize the role of order-winners and qualifiers in the evaluation procedure and ensure that they reflect the business and not accounting conventions.

An assessment of current and future markets in terms of order-winners and qualifiers is essential in a company's investment proposal procedure, especially when investments are based on a forecast increase in sales. This will include a review of the way that the existing and proposed capacity support the relevant criteria. In particular, it should identify levels of match or mismatch with an eye towards changing the way a company will win current and future orders.

Financial control systems must meet the needs of the investment evaluation process

Financial control systems tend to be designed to meet the needs of accountants; consequently, they are usually structured around a network of expense codes or account numbers, clinically constructed to facilitate electronic processing and the consolidation of final accounts and budget reports. From the accountant's viewpoint, this is a reasonable and sensible way of handling what are often complex sets of analysis. The result is that business transactions are then analysed on the basis of the account codes available and squeezed through a straitjacket of top-down apportionment to provide accountants with a view of expenditure and its relationship to business activity.

Taking such an approach, many financial control systems seek to trace actual expenditure to points of authorization and compare it to planned expenditure. The authorization provides the link on which to establish explanation and the formulation of corrective action. As highlighted in the last section, these evaluation procedures create major problems for a manufacturing company seeking to update its technology in response to relevant order-winners and qualifiers. These criteria may be one of two types:

- Product oriented, for example quality conformance or lowest cost supply.

- Process oriented, for example short lead times, widening product range or reducing customer order size.

Existing financial control systems tend not to provide management with a realistic basis for analysis against these criteria, while in some instances existing systems can be misleading.

Exhibit 11.2 provides a summary of some of the key differences between traditional financial analysis (geared to a steady state, low variety, high-volume and slowly changing business environment) and the approaches to analysis required by the highly competitive nature of today's business environment.

Dimension	Financial control system provision	Investment evaluation process requirement
Direction	Backward – examine expected historical trading performance	Forward – project future performance
Orientation	Internal – examine and report on current business performance	External – evaluate current and future markets and competitors
Timescale	Short-term – review performance monthly	Long-term – examine expected performance over a given period
Expenditure base	Revenue expenditure – trace performance on the evaluation of revenue	Capital expenditure – evaluate investment in facilities to incorporate risk
Control base	Return on investment – assess return in respect of the net capital employed	Cash flow control – relate expected cash flows to initial cash outlays

EXHIBIT 11.2 Typical financial control system provision versus investment evaluation requirement

Investments decisions: not separate but part of the corporate whole

Companies with more than one site, particularly multinationals, need to review investments within the context of total corporate markets and total operations provision. Investments are often taken as a series of separate decisions. While companies may identify overlaps, they need to review marketing and operations strategies for the whole business. Having companies everywhere may give a company global reach but it does not necessarily follow that it will compete on a global basis. Outcomes include excess capacity, uncoordinated strategic responses and a failure to capitalize on corporate size and worldwide presence.

Given the increasingly competitive nature of global markets, companies need to move towards total reviews of their many businesses in order to assess within and between geographical regions. Only in this way can operations' response be continuously reshaped. This will not only improve the fit between existing capacity, capabilities and chosen markets, it will also provide an overall view of existing operations capabilities for current and future markets, the necessary investments and the appropriate location of these within the total business.

A cable maker decided to integrate backwards into wire-drawing. The opportunity to purchase an existing factory some distance away from the main cable-making facility had financial and practical advantages over expanding on the main site. The justification for the investment was reduced costs. Calculations based on well-established and publicly available drawn wire prices pointed to an acceptable return on investment.

In reality, while the calculations were based on drawn wire purchase prices, the supplier's costs were based on the high-volume nature of its total business. Supplying solely to meet its parent company's cable-making demand, the wire-drawing schedule resulted in short runs over the wide range of drawn wire sizes required. The resulting high costs due to increased set-ups, lower throughput rates, lower effective capacity and resulting overtime working, higher waste and more frequent deliveries led to 18 months of losses before the new facility broke even.

There can be only one reason to substantiate an investment proposal

Investment appraisals typically include an extensive list of arguments and reasons for supporting a particular proposal. In many companies, the appraisal procedure has developed into an art form. Not only are the numbers massaged but also the rationale underpinning the investment typically encompasses a long list of arguments, in the belief that the cumulative weight of these will win the day. Consequently, the essential clarity that should pervade these critical proposals is neither recognized as being essential nor required in the evaluating decision procedure.

Two major disadvantages result:

- **Stated reasons do not always reflect reality** – In many instances, proposals reflect the corporate norms and expectations recognized as being prerequisites for consideration let alone success. As *Exhibit 11.3* shows,[9] key decisions are often taken for undisclosed reasons and the essential control of investments and agreement on their underlying support for a business is thus obviated.

- **The essential argument distilling investment issues and insights is not considered necessary** – If investment proposals do not require a distinction to be drawn between prime and other reasons, the essential argument distilling the key issues is not an inherent part of the procedure. Hence, the rigour necessary for sound strategic argument is typically not applied. Furthermore, with the passage of time, the real reasons for investments are lost and post-investment evaluations, if undertaken at all, are set against incorrect strategic dimensions. The outcome is that before and after evaluations are typically not recognized as key steps in investment proposal procedures.

Purchase reasons	Documented	Perceived
Cost reduction	50[1]	19[2]
Update/introduce new technology	37	55
Increase throughput/productivity	37	17
Increase capacity	37	27
Part of a reorganization	28	34
Improve quality	25	16
Process dedication requirement	25	21
Reduce changeover times	21	–
Improve product flexibility	20	–
New process/existing technology	18	1
Reduce supervisory costs	16	12
Purchase of available machine	15	17
Improve material control	10	–
Reduce lead times	6	–
Process modernization	5	22
Automate process	4	–

NOTES
1 In 50 per cent of the cases cost reduction was documented as a reason for investment.
2 In 19 per cent of the cases, cost reduction was perceived to be a reason for investment. Perceived reasons were reached sometimes after the investment had been made.

EXHIBIT 11.3 Documented and perceived reasons for all investments over a 30-month period, UK manufacturing company

Companies should, therefore, adopt the maxim that there can be only one given reason to substantiate an investment proposal. The logic may appear to be simplistic but the rationale is sound. If one reason alone cannot support an investment, the substance and focus of the arguments need to be questioned. While such a procedure does not disallow listing secondary reasons, it will force strategic debate and clarify the essential rationale underpinning these key decisions.

Excessive use of ROI distorts strategy building

Companies in developed economies, highly sensitive to the shareholders' view of short-term declines in profits, have become all the more prone to adopting a short payback posture. Furthermore, in times of low profit performance, pressure invariably increases to effect short-term recovery programmes as a way of demonstrating improvement and management action. In turn, the argument to set high thresholds can win the day when inadequate strategic direction and agreement have been reached or when the real need for investment has not been identified. Like drowning men clutching at straws, companies are attracted by the promise of higher returns. But investments in operations processes and infrastructure taken out of their strategic context can commit a company for years ahead in an inappropriate direction. Although procedures require potential benefits to be clearly explained before investments are made, few companies rigorously assess the actual level of benefits achieved to determine the extent to which reality measured up to proposal and to identify why any significant disparities arise. A UK survey verified this practice. It found that while 96 per cent of respondents reported a requirement to demonstrate quantifiable future benefits from capital investment, only 58 per cent validated these after the fact.[10] While hindsight is no substitute for foresight, such assessments provide a review of the effectiveness of these critical decisions in terms of the assumptions made and data used. Such analyses not only identify the actual level of return but also enable a company to measure the extent to which past investments have supported its corporate strategic requirements.

The approach to investment appraisal in Japan and Germany has a different basis. When they invest they are often prepared to sacrifice the short term for longer term profits that accrue from market share and increased volumes. In this way, they demonstrate two important differences in approach. First, they avoid the delusion that, in an imprecise environment, numbers are precise and thereby reliable, that is, they understand that the use of numbers does not reduce risk. Second, they accept that to run a successful business, risks must be taken.

Ohmae summarizes the clear difference in approach between Western and Japanese businessmen. Discussing the investments made by two Japanese companies, he concludes that

> in neither case ... is any attention given to return on investment (ROI) or payback period, let alone to discounted cash flow. In both, the dominant investment criterion is whether the new business is good for the corporation as a whole.[11]

Ohmae illustrates these differences by posing the following questions:

> How many contemporary US corporations relying on ROI yardsticks would have embarked on the development of a business that required a twenty-year incubation period, as did Nippon Electric Company with its computer and semiconductor businesses? . . . Would Honda have so obstinately persisted in using its motorbike profits to bring its clean-engine

vehicle to market if it were a corporation that measured the ROI of each product line and made its decisions accordingly? In fact, would any manufacturers be entering the four-wheel vehicle market in today's environment if ROI were the investment criterion?[12]

Similar questions and observations hold true today.

In many companies, a by-product of emphasizing ROI in the corporate evaluation of investments has been an increasing tendency to view these proposals as a series of one-off, unrelated events and not, as they invariably are, characterized by strategic sequence. Only when companies review investment decisions in the light of their corporate strategies and, in turn, their marketing and operations strategies will the essential cohesion be established. Until this happens, companies will be in danger of investing in ways that will not give them the necessary synergistic gains of strategic coherence. An example of what happens is provided by a company involved in the manufacture of office equipment and supplies. Over the years, the company had added capacity in a piecemeal way. It eventually had seven manufacturing units in the same road, only two of which were interconnected. On paper, buying new sites as they were required made better ROI scores than resiting the business. However, the costs of handling and transportation between units added complexity and duplicated overheads. The position was only assessed when a new chief executive called a halt to the proposal to add another part to the 'rabbit warren'.

Perhaps the ultimate illustration of the excessive use of ROI and the distortion it brings is provided by Stephen Roach, Morgan Stanley's influential chief economist and the guru of downsizing (the cult of corporate shrinking that wiped out millions of jobs around the world in the name of efficiency and ROI). After a decade of arguing for and influencing businesses to pursue downsizing as a prerequisite to corporate, long-term success, he decided that he had got it wrong. He then declared that 'relentless cost cutting was bad for business. If you compete by building, you have a future, if you compete by cost cutting, you don't.' Carlin's article[13] commented on Roach's own reflections on his complete turn-around following a decade of advocating downsizing as the only path to follow. Roach observed that it had been 'a powerful learning experience for him and the debate had been a healthy one', to which Carlin's response was that even by the standard of a modern guru such a change was 'breathtaking'. Carlin continued:

> So there we are, this is the Age of Exoneration by Amazing Unforeseen Circumstances. No-one could have foreseen the effects of deforestation, artificially stimulated overproduction or leaking water pipes.

Government grants are not necessarily golden handshakes

With disproportionately high unemployment rates in parts of many Western countries and the impact of declining primary and secondary sectors of the economy, most governments have, understandably, pursued policies to attract manufacturing and other activities to these areas to redress regional imbalances. In a similar way, they have persuaded organizations to take on ailing companies or parts of companies to avert significant instances of primary and secondary redundancy. In addition, at plant level, governments have attempted to stimulate or support investment in manufacturing companies to help increase their competitiveness in world markets. In each instance, the carrot has been a generous system of grants and other awards. Many companies, attracted by the size of the handouts and the cash and ROI gains they represent, have decided to take up the offer and relocate or establish all or parts of their business in one of a number of distressed areas, take on a relatively large piece of manufacturing capacity at one go or invest in state-of-the-art equipment to improve their operations process capability. Companies that have not established clear strategic parameters and have evaluated proposals largely in terms of return or cash injection have all too often rued the decision. They are often bound by a minimum period of residence, the relative size of the investments involved or the desire to save face, at least in the short term or while the custodians of the decision still have responsibility for the business concerned. Examples are numerous.

A carpet company integrated vertically into yarn production instead of continuing its policy of buying from a number of yarn suppliers. The mill selected was in a remote area and some 100 miles away from the parent company's carpet plants. The deal included sizable government grants and incentives as part of its regional policy and job creation and retention schemes. These investment benefits made the resulting ROI calculations highly attractive.

Besides the difficulties associated with recruitment at all levels in the mill and the distances involved in what was a linked process, the decision incurred one additional and fundamental problem. The rationale to split yarn and carpet manufacturing was made on the basis that it was a natural break in the processes involved. However, the company had established its niche in the quality end of the market. Separating the business at the natural break between the sets of processes involved had satisfied the investment-oriented arguments but, at the same time, the essential quality control link had been broken between yarn spinning and carpet manufacture, both of which were now a corporate responsibility. Thus, an operations split based on processes had ignored the essential qualifier – that of meeting the design specification of top of the range carpets. The quick feedback and opportunity for close liaison were not easy to exploit. In the early months, top management was preoccupied with justifying the investment from both parts of the total business. Reality, however, proved more difficult to handle than formulating the integration proposals.

A medium-sized company decided to establish a subcontract machining facility. The company abandoned its first choice of industrial site for one some 25 miles away. The carrot offered was that the latter had a development classification attracting a high level of grant and expenditure exemptions. This alternative proved significantly more attractive to the executives, banks and other financial institutions, who all developed a fixation on the impact it made on ROI, profit and cash flows. However, when the order-winner of delivery speed was introduced into the debate, these accrued financial advantages paled into insignificance. Without the sales, the calculations had no foundation.

A large manufacturing company that had great difficulty in achieving adequate profit margins was persuaded to absorb part of another group of companies. The cash injection offered as part of the government proposal to avert job losses swung the balance. The difficulties of absorbing such a large addition to operations capacity, matching systems, controls and other parts of the infrastructure, besides the production processes involved, added to the company's already difficult task. The rationalization that ensued cast serious questions on the fit between the decision and the strategic needs and direction of the existing business. The outcome was added problems, less time and attention given to managing the base task of unacceptable profit levels and an overall deterioration in its financial performance during the next two years.

Linking investment to product life cycles reduces risk

Many companies entering markets for replacement or new products need to make decisions on which processes to buy. A key factor in these decisions is the forecast sales at each stage in the life cycle. However, as explained in Chapter 5, products rarely move from jobbing to batch to line levels of volume over their life cycles. The decision facing companies, therefore, is which level of volume becomes the basis for the choice of process. Clearly, it typically does not make sense for them to invest in, say, a low-volume batch process to meet one level of sales then reinvest in, say, a high-volume batch or line process in response to life cycle sales growth. The difficulty inherent in these decisions is the judgemental nature of predicting the future. Where a high level of certainty exists, there is less difficulty in matching the process investment to eventual product volumes. For many companies, however, the future is uncertain and given the typical ways of appraising investments and evaluating alternatives, companies invariably place themselves in a yes/no situation. Long delivery times for equipment further aggravate this position. Commitments have to be made months, sometimes years, in advance of the scheduled launch.

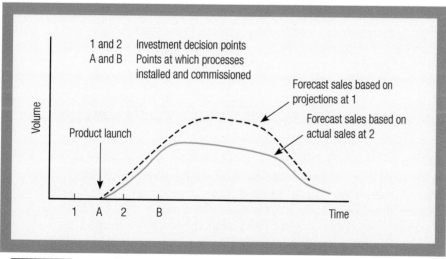

EXHIBIT 11.4 Alternative approaches to investment decisions

An alternative to this can be used in many situations. Consider *Exhibit 11.4*, which shows a projected life cycle for a product. At 1, process investment decisions would have to be made and purchase orders raised for the equipment to be installed and commissioned to meet the intended product launch at A. An alternative approach is to delay the process investment decision until 2, allowing sales forecasts to be amended in line with the actual sales to date. The choice of process made at 2 would probably be more in line with actual life cycle sales simply due to improved data being available. The trade-off to be made concerns whether existing processes could cope with the operations task to point B plus the likelihood that associated operations costs would be higher in the period A to B, yielding lower margins. The potential loss of profit in the period between A and B and the risk of inappropriate investments being made is the trade-off to be assessed.

Operations must test the process implications of product life cycle forecasts

Investment proposals rarely cover each main phase of a product's life cycle. Yet operations' task is to produce products over each phase of their life cycles and respond to the consequent variations in volumes, qualifiers and order-winners. However, not only does production engineering, for instance, typically ignore the change in the operations task towards the end of a product's life cycle but also the potential process investment requirements associated with this change are omitted from the overall product launch decision. The result is that processes become unaligned with the needs of the market, such as companies retaining high-volume processes to meet low-volume requirements (see Chapter 6). Faced with this mismatch, operations does the best it can. Unless businesses recognize the need to look at alternative approaches, operations will unilaterally choose the solution that makes most sense in light of the difficulties and constraints it faces and the measures by which its performance is assessed. Given that the order-winners and qualifiers associated with the volumes involved at each stage are invariably different (see *Exhibit 11.5*), the appropriate process choice would require realignment if operations is to be able to meet these different requirements.

What needs to happen is a corporate recognition of the changing nature of operations' strategic task throughout a product life cycle and, for each phase, to ascertain the associated investments or adjust expectations on how well operations can meet market requirements and then build these into the corporate strategy decision.

Investment decisions must quantify working capital and infrastructure requirements

Many investment decisions are distorted in two ways. On the one hand, they ignore intangible, difficult-to-evaluate reductions or benefits that accrue from the investment itself.[14] On the other, they underestimate the working capital needs associated with each proposal and often ignore altogether the infrastructure costs involved. The tangible nature of the investments associated with the equipment, plant and support services involved in a process lead to a clear identification of the costs involved. However, many areas of investment directly associated with the proposed capital expenditure are overlooked, understated or assumed to be unnecessary. As those who prepare the proposals are often not the people responsible for either the control of operations or achieving the required levels of performance, an oversimplified review of infrastructure requirements is often taken. Companies, therefore, need to recognize increases in complexity and not assume that the existing systems, controls and structures are either appropriate or adequate. Such assumptions about levels of infrastructure lead to an incremental deterioration in operations executives' ability to control and manage the function, resulting in the eventual reappraisal of one or more parts of its infrastructure with attendant additional costs.

A company starting with a greenfield site on which to make a single product will usually take full account of the investment needs for the principal services, systems and controls. However, most companies are more complex and are generally investing in existing plants or introducing products to be made in already up-and-running facilities. Investment considerations when introducing a product are usually more akin to the following examples:

- The decision to enter a market brings with it a recognition of the need to invest in the process capability to manufacture the products in question. However, these new products will be assumed to use existing site services, support systems and overheads. Such an assumption belies reality. It ignores the increase in complexity and corresponding demands placed on the non-process aspects of operations that go hand in hand with the decision. Deterioration in the effectiveness of existing systems and structures results.

- Most product introductions use parts of existing operations processes. Such additions impact the status quo and typically result in more inventory, longer lead times and more complexity to manage due to more products and their associated demands sharing the use of existing processes and infrastructure and the interplay between them.

- The importance of customers is viewed in terms of revenue generated. Querying the position of low-volume sales to a customer is typically brushed aside under the auspices of quid pro quo arguments – 'we support low-volume requirements to get the high volumes accompanying them'. However, customers need to be evaluated on total contribution/profit generated as well as other relevant aspects such as associated inventory holding and lead time demands.

Post-investment audits capture learning and improve future decisions

Investment proposals detail the tasks involved and the benefits to be gained. By definition, the proposal comprises estimates and projections, most of which will change when events unfold. As many of these are core to the evaluation and projected outcomes of the proposals, post-implementation checks not only provide an audit but, more importantly, are a source of refining future estimates and assumptions by testing them against what actually happens. In this way, reality checks capture the learning, increase the accuracy of projections and thereby improve future decisions.

Companies need to undertake audits as an integral part of their investment appraisal procedures. The detail demanded in the appraisal phase of an investment is extensive and often in marked contrast to that undertaken after the event. In such situations, the learning that could be transferred to future decisions is ignored. Meeting financial hurdles

Volume

High-volume phase:
Typical order-winners of price requiring low-cost operations processes

Exhibit 11.5

Product life cycles, order-winning criteria and process investment interact

Low-volume phase:
Typical order-winners of delivery speed and delivery reliability requiring flexible operations processes to cope with low volumes and wide product range

Price would typically be a qualifier

Process investment considerations

becomes the important area of attention, while the key issue of making sound and better future investment decisions is, at best, relegated to a secondary activity.

The simplistic nature of accounting information

To assess current performance, a company needs control information that reflects the key aspects of the task. Although much information is collected and recorded, many companies fail to separate clearly the difference between records and controls.[15] Furthermore:

> the development of the marketing orientation [in many companies] has led to an increase in the amount of market-based information available to management. In contrast, the paucity and limited availability of relevant internal information is striking.[16]

One key problem area is that of management accounting. Although money is used as the common denominator to assess current and future corporate performance, this function is often lacking in relevance and sensitivity towards changing circumstances.

The accounting information provided in most companies can be characterized in a number of ways (also refer to *Exhibit 11.2*). First, it is historically based. Although this is an inherent part of cost information, accountants, and thus the business, do not consider it to be of paramount importance to provide information that is relevant and close to reality. Second, invariably the information provided is primarily focused on management accounting which relates to the business as a whole rather than the management control of operations. One outcome is the inadequate provision of critical information by which management can assess performances and make future decisions.

In broad terms, accountants work primarily on the basis of norms. They choose averages to simplify the measurement task. The procedure is then to compare each part of the business to a norm. However, the broad-based nature of these comparisons hides the key to control. Failing to go back to the information from which the average has been drawn obscures the level of performance achieved. An average is a compilation of many parts but it is important to be able to assess the level of performance within each. The argument put forward in defence of the averaging approach is that to collect and update data for all parts would be very time-consuming and expensive; therefore it is necessary to simplify the procedures and tasks involved to make some sense of reality and to be able to report within acceptable timescales.

Reality, however, is complex. The controls need to reflect and measure reality. The accountants' approach is to simplify reality by simplifying the data on which controls are based. In this way, they are able to account for all the parts and cope administratively with the task, that is, they meet the obligation of 'accounting for everything in a systematic way'. However, the basis for control in companies needs to reflect the complex business issues and not the tasks required by company law. Hence, the controls need to reflect the size and importance of the area (process, product or customer) concerned – detailed controls for the significant areas and simple, broadbrush controls for the insignificant areas.

Several general examples illustrate these points:

- Most companies use total sales revenue as a key performance indicator. Invariably within this evaluation, the contribution of individual products is not addressed nor does it form part of the assessment. In profit and loss account terms, the top line becomes the measure of the sales function's performance and the bottom line, the measure of the operations function's performance. What fails to be clearly distinguished is that these performances are inextricably linked. Without this additional dimension, the argument for the need to retain all products is not challenged. As the simple total sales revenue measure of marketing performance fails to distinguish the relative contribution of each product and/or customer, the conclusion that all sales are equally good business holds sway.

- It is usual for operations' task to be based on a proposed or forecast level of volumes. Invariably, the volumes experienced differ from period to period and over time. Rarely are costings provided for different volume levels, without which the costings appropriate to the actual levels experienced are unavailable. Having costings that reflect different volumes allows a company to assess a period's performance in a more accurate way and to form part of the checks to assess the level of achievement or lack of achievement recorded.

- Accounting systems should reflect the type of processes being used. As shown in *Exhibit 11.6*, the treatment of costs, pricing and the development of accounting procedures and controls should vary. The costing structure and performance reporting system needs to take account of these differences in order to distinguish between the provision of sensitive cost information and the measurement of performance.

Aspect		Type of process	
		General purpose	Dedicated
Overhead	Recovery	Process or product oriented	Blanket rate per standard hour
	Control	Complex control: needs to assess the impact of product mix and volume changes, alternative routings and other similar factors	Simple variance control, derived from comparing actual to standard unit volumes
Costs	Set-ups	Direct to product	Overhead rate based on machine utilization
	Process scrap	Specific to the process or product	Blanket allowance
	Quality	Direct to product	Overhead rate established
	Tooling	Direct to product	Overhead rate established
	Maintenance	Direct to process	Overhead rate established
Basis for pricing		Product cost basis	Contribution basis
Development of accounting procedures and controls		Bottom up	Top down

EXHIBIT 11.6 Some accounting approaches depending on the type of process

- Plant decisions constitute a big business risk due to the size of the investment, the uncertainty inherent in forecast sales on which the capacity decision is based and how well the chosen operations process can meet the actual demands (for example customer order size and rate of new product introductions) of the market. However, accounting policies on depreciation reinforce this risk when they are classified in relation to the type of plant rather than the life of the product for which the plant is to be purchased. Typically, the plant is depreciated by rule-of-thumb accounting classifications. For instance, one large manufacturing company used the rules in *Exhibit 11.7*, which were based on historical usage and precedents.

Item of plant		Typical length of depreciation in all parts of the company (in years)
Tool room equipment		25
Presses		20
Automatic lathes		15
Numerically controlled machines		10
Machining centres		5
Test	Dedicated	5
	General purpose	10

EXHIBIT 11.7 Rule-of-thumb accounting practices

The gains accrued from having common accounting procedures belie the simplistic nature of such policies. Consequently, these sizable assets become detached from their essential business orientation in order to accommodate the administrative requirements of the accounting function and policies involved.

The need for accounting system development

Demands to develop current accounting systems are not new. Criticisms levelled at existing approaches have become both increasingly vocal and more broadly based. So far these overtures have resulted in little progress other than some tinkering at the edges. Concerted pressure for improved accounting data has increased due to growing competition and the need to make informed strategic responses. To be able to assess options and alternative strategies, companies need insights and, in today's competitive climate, the pressure to make significant and speedy strategic responses has never been greater. However, accounting systems, even in their recording mode, do not provide information that helps the decision process. It is neither relevant nor timely. A far more fundamental question concerns accountants' perception of the role of accounting systems. Past history clearly marks them, at best, as being reactive, hence their bean-counter/record-keeper image. What is needed is an executive response, proactively developing systems that fulfil the needs of the decision-making processes necessary to meet the demands of today's markets and competitive threats.

Attempting to improve the competitive nature of their performance, many companies are paying greater attention to a whole range of improvements in quality conformance processes, inventory holdings and workforce policies – all essential developments to help meet these new challenges. Not only is the level and urgency of response high in these endeavours but the approaches challenge the very basis of previous practice. The same, however, cannot be said of accounting.

In markets characterized by increasing difference and rapid change, most companies still use the same cost accounting and management control systems developed decades ago for a competitive environment markedly different from that of today. When trying to assess the level of contribution provided by each product or customer as a prerequisite for judging what steps to take, many companies find the accounting information provided to be inadequate for the task. For example, while everyone knows that higher volumes decrease costs and product proliferation increases them, rarely are these essential trade-offs differentiated within accounting procedures. Companies need appropriate information to assess sensibly the trade-offs associated with product breadth and focus. The accounting procedure of averaging costs across a product range obscures true costs, disguises the relative profitability of products and/or customers and distorts decision-making. The impact on business competitiveness can be significant.

Working on the left side of the decimal point

Information used in companies is not accurate and accounting and finance data are no exception. As accounting information is rarely, if ever, exact, plus or minus 10 per cent is a good rule of thumb when using the data. What these numbers offer is a 'feel' for the financial dimensions of various activities, opportunities and decisions.

The typical presentation of accounting information implies a level of accuracy that is not present. Figures to one or two decimal points give a spurious level of accuracy. All the system does is refine inaccurate data. Accounting functions need to remind those using the information that it is not as accurate as it may appear.

Working only on the left side of the decimal point, although a symbolic statement, also has a practical dimension. It highlights the need to use data as a guide by emphasizing the need to understand all the issues and to ensure that all relevant perspectives are considered in the decision process.

Assessing current performance

One basic procedure used by companies to help control their business is comparisons between actuals and plans. At different periods, a company will have a strategic plan (usually agreed the previous year), budgets based on the plan and actual levels of sales revenue, costs and other activities.

Companies then compare actual performance with the original budget as the principal way of reviewing corporate performance.[17] As plans and targets often do not match forecasts, such comparisons will not provide insights into actual performance. Performance needs to be measured against revised plans as this will enable actual performance to be set against reality. Analysing budget changes resulting from adjustments to strategic plans serves a different purpose. It helps to assess the robustness of the planning procedure, the reasons for change and the impact of revisions on corporate expectations.

Allocate, not absorb overheads

Overheads comprise a large proportion (in most manufacturing companies, they are between 25 and 50 per cent) of total costs and are usually increasing both in themselves and in terms of their relative size. Yet all too often the bulk of these are absorbed. A review of one manufacturing company revealed that close on 80 per cent of overhead costs were absorbed and as these costs accounted for over 40 per cent of the total, the implications were significant. The principal reason that overhead costs are predominantly absorbed is because it involves less administrative work and system maintenance than alternatives. Many accountants abuse this principle still further, by using one overhead absorption rate for several parts of the same business as well as across businesses and often absorb on a single basis rather than the several necessary to reflect the business diversity involved. One business within a group of manufacturing companies had seven sites with a variety of activities including holding and distributing raw materials, spares and low-volume operations, high-volume operations and the distribution of finished goods. Overheads for all seven sites were pooled and absorbed at one common rate for each site based on the single factor of direct labour hours. Faced with declining profits, the group executive turned to the basic performance evaluation of each site. The data gave few answers. To decide how to redress the decline required financial information that was site specific and also reflected the products and their cost structure within each site.

To provide information that gives greater accuracy and insights, one key step is for accounting functions to adopt the policy of allocating overheads wherever possible.[18] As a general rule, a minimum target of allocating 80 per cent of total overheads should be the initial aim. The consequences would be that only a relatively small portion of total costs would then need to be spread on an absorption basis.

Information that provides more accurate insights is a prerequisite for making sound management decisions. This is particularly so regarding:

- **Products** – decisions concerning pricing and the impact on margins, sales and growth potential are at the very core of commercial activity and will significantly influence the financial performance of a company.

- **Opportunities for cost reduction** – when the sources and extent of costs are more clearly identified, the opportunity to reduce costs is improved. This opportunity is particularly enhanced by developments in activity-based costing, addressed in the next section.

Activity-based costing

Activity-based costing (ABC) identifies and bases costs on activities rather than functions. Using the latter approach, the need to disperse these groups of cost (that is, the cost of each function) results in using allocation/absorption procedures. Identifying costs on the basis of activity eliminates the need for such a two-stage procedure.

In ABC, activities/transactions are the focus of the costing system as they, not products, cause costs to be incurred. While products consume direct materials and direct labour, activities consume overhead resources, with products, in turn, consuming these activities.

Thus ABC is concerned with understanding the cost of activities and their relationship to products and services. The approach to follow is as follows:

- Identify the major activities.

- Determine the underlying factors that cause the activity to occur – known as 'cost drivers'.

- Create cost pools to collect activity costs that have the same cost driver. The major activities must constitute a homogeneous set of tasks and costs such that cost variations in any pool can be explained by a single cause.

- Attribute the costs of the activities gathered in each cost pool to the products/ services based on cost drivers (that is, how much of the activity has been used by the product/service in question).

In this way, ABC is a more sophisticated absorption/allocation system resulting in a more accurate identification of costs. There are two important but distinct ways to use the information provided by ABC – product decisions and identifying opportunities to reduce costs.

Product-related decisions

Analysis of the cost structure of overhead activities enables a full review of products/services, customers, markets and profitability. It is used to support key decisions about

- product pricing

- growth, decline, renegotiation or exiting market segments, customers and/or products.

Reducing or reshaping non-value-added activities

Once a company's key activities have been agreed, ABC identifies non-value-added activities. It determines if types of activity are necessary in part or at all and whether each is efficiently provided. In this way it ensures that the cost of non-value-added activities is visible, so enabling management to review the size and shape of overhead costs as part of its operational decision-making process.

Whereas companies investing in ABC systems always use the new information in product-related decisions, many do not use it to review non-value-added activity itself. In fact, organizations that have not systematically reduced overhead costs as a direct result of introducing ABC can be considered to have failed to fully use this approach. Many businesses still fall into this category and thereby miss many of the real opportunities for overall improvement.

Use actual not standard costs to make decisions

Even with the more recent developments such as ABC systems, the data provided by accounting procedures are still based on averages. While average costs are appropriate for the accounting function's task of providing period statements for the whole business such as profit and loss accounts and balance sheets, they are a most inappropriate basis on which to make decisions. To evaluate which products to retain, which customers with which to grow and which prices to charge, average costs are of little value. Standard costing data were never intended to be the basis on which to evaluate such options and make such key decisions. Actual data need to be collected and used in order to provide the necessary insights to enable evaluations to be provided and appropriate decisions to be made.

Focused operations helps to identify overhead costs

A significant reason why accounting functions have been unable to provide adequate costing system developments is that the problem has become too complex to handle by a single solution. However, unless companies find ways to drive out costs and arrive at sound product decisions, they will find it difficult to compete effectively in today's tough market conditions.

Adopting the principle of focus and plant-within-plant configurations (see Chapter 7) will help facilitate the provision of more accurate cost information. These approaches enable companies to more easily identify the overheads associated with each part of operations and to assess the contribution provided by each part to the whole business. This change brings with it a shift from the principle of accounting for overheads on a functional basis to that of direct overhead allocation. Instead of summarizing the costs involved in providing a support function as a total for that function, it accounts for those overheads that are dedicated to or are directly associated with a part of operations. In this way, a part of each relevant overhead function and associated costs are assigned to a focused unit. This negates the need to absorb these overhead costs and enables companies to verify that the current overhead costs are indeed necessary. Furthermore, when overhead costs are clearly identified with a particular part of operations, the level and nature of support can be agreed not only to meet current needs but also to accommodate changes in the future.

A further refinement to these changes involves making overhead functions into business units. This moves a business away from the position where accounting procedures arbitrarily spread unallocated overheads to make the books balance to one where each part of a business declares a budget for the amount it intends to purchase from each overhead function. The gains are obvious. Beware, however, of two possible developments:

- The counter-argument put forward by accountants is that these changes are difficult to accomplish and lack a high degree of accuracy. These changes will, in fact, enhance the relevance and accuracy of this information in the light of business needs.

- Attaining accuracy as an end in itself. The corporate gain is providing information to help prioritize product decisions and cost reduction activities.

Create business-related financial information

The key role of business-related financial information has been highlighted in the sections concerning cost system developments. As an essential input into developing both a marketing and operations strategy, accounting information is rarely designed specifically to provide analyses that would form an integral part of the formulation of either functions' strategic statement. Examples of key marketing information include:

- **customer sales and profitability** – an assessment of both the sales and total costs associated with selling to, and support for, major customers enables a company to establish the true worth of these relationships

- **market share and profitability** – identifying the value of sales in each market, its relative size, associated costs to promote and support relevant activities and the level of profitability for each market segment are essential inputs into formulating marketing plans.

For the operations side of the business, information that is rarely provided by existing accounting systems but would offer invaluable insights in the strategy formulation includes:

- costs of operations at varying levels of throughput

- capacity analyses identifying any bottleneck or limiting factor in the manufacture of each product (known as 'analysis of contribution by limiting factor'). This enables companies to assess proposals to increase capacity and decide how best to allocate existing capacity in the meantime (see Chapter 4)

- costs for supplying items outside the normal product range.

Finally, the need to separate out those costs incurred by operations but not induced by operations decisions is seldom reflected in the control statements provided by the accounting system. Excess operations costs incurred as a result of a change in schedule to meet a sales or customer request, for instance, are usually not shown under their own separate headings (for example 'operations excess cost due to customer schedule change') but are recorded as part of the total operations cost.

Provide performance-related financial information

The final area of development concerns the provision of accurate performance-related information. As the measurement of actual performance, the subject of the next section, needs to be set against targets that reflect reality, so levels of performance within a business will differ from one part to another. Not all products can be expected to achieve the same performance standards during each and every year of their lives. Therefore, why should products in different stages of their life cycles be expected to meet the same performance standards as one another? For this to be appropriate would require a portfolio made up solely of products all in the same stage of their life cycles.

Once performance expectations have been resolved, the next issue concerns the level of expected activity. Budgets, by definition, are out of date by the time they are completed. It is necessary, therefore, to review budget figures by using the latest information. In this way, the basis for establishing and assessing levels of performance is changed from a budget to a latest estimate basis. One clear example of this is the use of flexible budgeting which changes the cost base in line with actual volumes and alters the basis for related cost information (for example overhead absorption either by traditional or ABC systems).

A final illustration concerns the distortions that businesses experience as a result of the way in which they calculate inventory values. Inventory can desensitize cost information by becoming a cost buffer. Most accounting systems assume that the value of work-in-progress inventory is calculated by the system. Often, accumulated cost excesses or undervaluations are discovered when inventory is physically counted at the end of period stocktaking and then recorded as an inventory or stocktaking loss/profit. Since many firms physically count inventory only twice a year, control or responsibility is not easy to establish.

Performance measurement

This part of the chapter looks at how organizations measure the performance of functions in terms of their role and contribution to the success of a business.

The maxim 'what gets measured gets done' holds true for most, if not all, organizations. Consequently, great care needs to be exercised when selecting the aspects of performance to measure. The purpose of this section is not to comment on which performance measures to use and what insights different measures provide but to highlight key factors in their use as part of the management of functions. What follows are key points to bear in mind which have been further categorized into 'selecting measures', 'setting targets' and 'using measures'.

Selecting measures

This section highlights some key considerations when selecting which measures to use:

- **Avoid long lists** – the purpose of measuring the performance of functions is to highlight those activities central to their operational (day-to-day) roles within an organization and also the key contributions they make to the overall success of the business in terms of retaining and growing market share (their strategic role). Failure to identify these will dilute appropriate emphasis in terms of resource allocation, direction of purpose and priority of action. Without this as the starting point, the tendency is for the number of measures to grow. This upward drift in the length of the list results from several factors, including adding to the list is the easy option, requires less judgement and attracts less potential questions or criticism.

    Examples illustrating the long list phenomenon are plentiful. One such is provided in *Exhibit 11.8*.[19] While Company 1 distorts the overall average of 57 measures per function, the average figure, excluding Company 1, is still 27, with even the lowest average of 16 per function (Company 4) still well on the high side.

- **Separate measures into different levels of priority** – as part of the move away from long lists, organizations need to separate measures into different levels of priority. This facilitates review, helps in reducing the overall list and focuses executive attention on the critical few.

More recent developments such as the balanced scorecard[20] have invariably added to the number of measures used by companies. The question that executives need to address is not one of balance but one of relevance.

Company		Number of		Average measures per function
		Functions	Measures	
1		3	591	197
2		2	113	56
3		2	79	39
4		7	114	16
5		3	71	24
Total	all	17	968	57
	excluding company 1	14	377	27

EXHIBIT 11.8 Number of measures used by 17 functions in 5 companies

- **Separate strategic and operational measures** – supplementing the last point, it is essential that the measures used are also separated into those concerned with the strategic role of a function and those that reflect the key day-to-day tasks. In this way, the 'why' as well as the 'what' are identified even in those instances where one measure is on both lists.

- **Check relevance of same measure/target for different businesses or parts of the same business** – the appeal of league tables is self-evident. Comparisons offer effective ways to evaluate the performance of different parts of a business or different businesses one with another. However, the premise of using the same measures and/or targets assumes that they are equally relevant and the performance that can be expected should be similar. With difference being the hallmark of most businesses, this typically is not so.

- **Regularly review chosen measures** – part of undertaking the last four points is the need to regularly review the chosen measures and categories. In this way, the focus of attention is maintained and the key management task of regularly testing the relevance and importance of what is measured is highlighted and stays at the forefront of executives' attention.

- **Look forward as well as back** – traditional business measures are indicators that look back at past information and performance. This creates a gap between where an organization is currently and where it will need to be in the future. To identify where an organization needs to be necessitates identifying measures that reflect growth opportunities as well as markets under pressure. As a result, companies become aware of where change is needed and are more able to adapt and react to future needs. Organizations will thus create greater transparency on where and why to focus time and money as looking forward helps to identify problems, spot opportunities and make more informed choices.

- **Include the external as well as internal phases of the supply chain** – given the increased use of suppliers within the provision of products, measuring how well suppliers contribute to meeting the needs of a company's own markets needs to be integral with what is to be measured. In addition to this strategic information, measurement provides the basis for comparison and helps to demonstrate the need and scope for supplier improvements; for example, Nissan's 'capability enhancement activity' emphasizes evaluation and diagnosis. Without measures, Nissan would be less able to provide effective assistance and convince suppliers of the need to improve.

Setting targets

This section highlights some key factors to be taken into account when setting targets:

- **Debate assumptions not targets** – in many companies the targets set are the result of a negotiated settlement. While functional executives seek to keep targets within manageable boundaries, top executives press for higher levels of achievement. To avoid target setting becoming largely a political process embedded in concerns over performance evaluation and executive compensation, discussion needs to focus 'on the assumptions that drive performance'[21] and not on the targets or forecasts themselves. Once the assumptions are understood, realistic yet demanding targets can be set.

- **Stretch targets not guess targets** – the idea of asking for a little more in performance is sound in itself. But whereas stretch targets are fine in theory, they need to be realistic in application. Unless executives understand the various businesses they manage, the multi-markets in which they compete and how well functions and businesses are currently performing, then selecting appropriate targets (stretched or otherwise) is corporate guesswork. Recent research shows that 'less than 15 per cent of companies make it a regular practice to go back and compare business results with performance forecasts'.[22] Where such checks are not made, the opportunity to verify assumptions, so as to better understand what is possible and viable and also to ascertain what prevents targets being met, is lost.

Setting targets is not a difficult task in itself. The key dimensions are understanding and realism. If targets are known to be achievable with effort, control is retained. If targets are recognized as being unachievable, control is lost.

- **Meeting targets** – recent research found that on average performance loss due to failures in the planning and execution process averaged 37 per cent.[23] The broad categories of loss are provided in *Exhibit 11.9*. Performance loss needs to be investigated and the outcomes addressed. Understanding the relevant measures to use, the achievable (including stretch) targets to set and reasons for performance loss are prerequisites to building successful businesses. Executive insight, time and attention underpin all these factors.

Category of performance loss	%
Lack of clarity of action and accountability	14
Organizational constraints – resources and culture	11
Leadership and monitoring failures	8
Other	4
Total	37

EXHIBIT 11.9 Categories of performance loss

Using measures

With measures selected and set, the next step is to use them to help provide direction, create consistency of purpose and motivate staff throughout the organization:

- **Broaden the use** – most organizations use as little as 20 per cent of the data they collect and share them with less than 10 per cent of the people who could use it.[24] When used throughout an organization, measures provide part of the business information that can help evaluate performance, monitor what is going on, understand what has happened, identify direction, highlight key issues, prioritize activities, motivate people, help formulate what needs to be done and adjust future strategy.

- **Remove organizational barriers** – since the 1980s, one stated aim within most businesses has been to roll measures down through the organization. Thirty years on, progress is well behind the talk, with few organizations having made significant moves forward.

  While each function has its own set of objectives, they need to be an integral part of the business whole. Performance measures that help to integrate the parts are a prerequisite for linking overall business strategy with individual execution by helping to monitor and analyse results, compare actions to the plan and pinpoint remedial action. Significant untapped potential is available to make better use of measures and supporting information to identify direction, improve performance and create competitive advantage. However, while organizational barriers persist, fulfilling potential is not easy.

- **Create a proactive mindset** – as highlighted above, traditional measures look principally at past performance. While knowing where you are is an important way to evaluate current and past performance, measures also need to reflect future growth opportunities, take account of new challenges in existing markets or anticipate moves by competitors and/or new entrants. In this way, all levels of an organization are alerted to the need to change and the direction to take.

INVESTMENT DECISIONS **MUST** BE BASED ON HOW BEST TO SUPPORT ORDER-WINNERS

Working on the **left-hand side** of the decimal point

Stretch targets **NOT** guess targets

Echoing the structure of this chapter, this final section is provided in two parts. The first addresses the accounting and finance function and the second the performance measures used by companies.

Accounting and finance functions

The growing criticism of existing accounting systems and investment appraisal procedures is more than justified. The accounting profession in most Western countries is responsible for providing financial information. Unfortunately, accountants have generally been reactive in responding to the changing needs of business and have spent too much of their time keeping records rather than providing information for, and partaking in, the control and development of the business. The description of bean-counter sits well.

Two general misconceptions have contributed to this:

- management concerns developing not just maintaining existing procedures

- like most other functions, accountancy has failed to recognize that its role is subservient to that of the business. Its prime task is to respond to and meet the needs of a business, because functions do not exist in their own right but only in the context of the business as a whole. Evaluating a function's contribution, therefore, needs to be set within this frame.

The potential contribution of the accounting and finance functions is significant. The key insights and overall executive role they can bring to a business are considerable. To realize this level of effectiveness, companies must recognize changes in need and respond to them in an appropriate manner. This chapter has posed several issues that companies must address. Of these, three dimensions need to be at the forefront of accounting provision.

Markets are changing

The traditional perspective of productivity and the evaluation of investment decisions need to be modified in line with the needs of businesses in current, highly competitive world markets. The principle that should drive today's businesses is based on keeping existing customers and winning new ones, not just lowering labour costs. Cutting lead times, boosting quality conformance levels, improving delivery reliability, reducing inventories and supporting product range are factors that top the list in these endeavours. Accounting systems and financial reviews have to reflect this.

Businesses are characterized by difference, not similarity

Difference not similarity characterizes today's businesses. Rules and procedures need to reflect and embrace this. Levels of control, therefore, should be established to ensure that the more difficult and complex a proposal, the less formal and bureaucratic the approach. Investment proposals for relatively small sums are well served by laid-out procedures and predetermined hurdles. Major investments, on the other hand, are ill served by such approaches. Yet usually one set of rules applies, as characterized by the bureaucratic belief that the essence of control has its root in well-defined procedures.

Major investments need approaches that are the very opposite of current developments and executive behaviour. The maxim should be that the larger the investment, the more informal the approach and the lack of definition within the procedures used. Thus, major investments should be led by strategy and subject to open debate, ideally involving non-executive contributions to enhance neutrality. Putting forward functional proposals in line with agreed and structured procedures discourages strategic debate, stifles discussion and encourages rationalization – the very opposite of what is required to handle complex and fundamental strategic decisions.

Linking process investment decisions and the evaluation of control systems

In many companies, the link between process investment decisions and the need to provide supporting control systems is not appreciated. Decisions about processes are not only tangible, but they are also taken at a different phase in the decision sequence (see *Exhibit 11.10*). On the other hand, the sizable investments associated with operations process decisions of working capital and infrastructure are often obscured for exactly the opposite reasons – they are less tangible and occur in the operating phase of the installation.

Phase	Timescale	Features of the investment	Tangible nature	Features of evaluation and control
1	Preoperation	Fixed assets in the form of plant, equipment and associated installation costs	High	Constitutes taking one investment in isolation. Traditional investment appraisal techniques used, which are cash flow oriented
2	Operating	Supporting working capital in the form of inventory		The investment now becomes an integral part of the business summary. It reverts to revenue accounts that measure profit to investment as the basis of control or assessment.
3	Operating	The service and support overheads necessary to provide an appropriate level of infrastructure	Low	Control of individual investments now relatively loose – rarely have post-audits

EXHIBIT 11.10 The three phases in an investment programme

Furthermore, when a process investment is installed on the shop floor, a distinct accounting change takes place. At the preoperational stage highlighted in *Exhibit 11.10*, a process is singularly evaluated in great detail as part of the investment appraisal system and is cash flow oriented. But, once installed, this same process will no longer be treated as an individual item in accounting control terms. Instead, it will be controlled by a number of broadbrush accounting systems based on profit. It will become just part of a functionally based set of assets and costs comprising a range of investments that differ in usage, degree of dedication to the manufacture of specific products and support system requirements. The change in accounting treatment highlights the contrasts involved and the necessary high level of control in the preoperational phase compared with the lack of sensitivity in the global controls once the asset is being used.

Performance measures

The desire to measure performance is understandable and the rationale is sound. The issue facing executives is not one of desire or underpinning rationale but one of selecting measures that will provide appropriate insights to help manage and control a business and focus executive attention and help direct action.

In many organizations, the executive desire for control, the ready availability of data and the need for corporate staff to fulfil their support and advising roles have contributed to a situation of too many measures that give the appearance of control but the reality of bureaucracy and confusion of purpose. As with many dimensions of business management, the 80/20 rule again exercises its overriding logic. What executives need to determine is the 20 per cent of measures that provide the 80 per cent of insights that best help to manage and control the business. The role of managers is to determine which pictures to draw that yield appropriate insight, but this can only be achieved if sufficient executive time is allocated to undertaking this essential task. Inadequate understanding leads to inadequate insight and consequent lack of control. As highlighted earlier when discussing strategy development:

- defining the problem is difficult

- identifying the solution is easy

- implementing the solution is difficult.

Here the problem is 'which insights'.

Ways forward

What then are the ways forward? They involve changes at two levels in the organization. At the top, many executives have often become involved in, or even spearheaded, activities designed to generate earnings by financial transactions. This has the major drawback of diverting management effort and interest away from the core business activities as they become more distant from the prime profit-generating activities. They start to control from a distance. Without an understanding of each firm's strategies, they feel unable to contribute to the essential developments that must be made in the tough competitive climate that characterizes the manufacturing sector, including the evaluation of long-term alternatives. As a consequence, they exert pressure through short-term measures and assessments. Lower down the organization, plant-level executives being measured by the short-term success of the business often respond by adopting similar opportunistic patterns of behaviour such as reducing expenditure or withholding investments to increase short-term profits and improvements in cash flow. Similarly, groups of companies often monitor investments centrally against a common set of criteria but leave the post-installation assessment to be taken at the plant level. Seen as part of their role, the group executives' action reinforces the predominant use of financial measures when assessing investments and weakens the key responsibility link between the investment decision and its future evaluation. The need to decentralize these responsibilities could not be more strongly argued.

The way forward is through the emergence of strategy-based decisions and controls. Accounting and operations together need to determine the investment criteria and day-to-day accounting control provision that should be adopted. Not only will this orient operations towards its key tasks, it will also provide information that is both relevant and current. This growing awareness of the need for strategic management accounting must be accelerated if companies are to make sound operations and other strategy decisions.[25] It is most necessary, therefore, that firms stem the apparent drift away from their operations focus.

Perhaps a final lesson for Western European companies is that 'in Japan, perpetuation of the enterprise, not profit, is the driving force'. As Toshiba's Okano puts it: 'the company is forever'.[26] Although in no way implying that this should be adopted as the corporate value system, it highlights one essential difference. Strategy is the driving force; survival and success will only be achieved through a strategic orientation and this must become the pattern by which companies both give direction and assess current and future performance.

Discussion questions

1   What are the arguments for developing current accounting systems?
2   When does an investment have a strategic as opposed to operational purpose?
3   Why should strategic investments be based on the order-winners and qualifiers of relevant markets?
4   What is the rationale for the proposal that there should only be one reason to substantiate an investment?
5   How does excessive use of return on investment distort strategy building?
6   Why are post-investments essential?
7   Why should long lists be avoided when measuring performance?
8   What are the key things to take into account when selecting performance measures?

Notes

1   Dean, R.C. Jr (1974) 'The temporal mismatch: innovation's pace versus management's time horizon', *Research Management*, May, pp. 12–15.

2   Hayes, R.H. and Abernathy, J. (1980) 'Managing our way to economic decline', *Harvard Business Review*, July–August, pp. 66–77.

3   Hayes, R.H. and Garvin, D.A. (1982) 'Managing as if tomorrow mattered', *Harvard Business Review*, May–June, pp. 71–9.

4   Johnson, H.T. and Kaplan, R.S. (1987) *Relevance Lost: The Rise and Fall of Management Accounting*, Boston: Harvard Business School Press, includes important insights into accounting systems, for example Ch. 8.

5   Cooper, R. and Kaplan, R.S. (1985) 'How cost accounting distorts product costs', *Management Accounting*, April, pp. 20–7.

6   Cooper, R. and Kaplan R.S. (1988) 'Measure costs right: make the right decisions', *Harvard Business Review*, September–October, pp. 96–103.

7   Simmonds, K. (1988) 'Strategic management accounting', in R. Crowe (ed.) *Handbook of Management Accounting*, 2nd edn, Aldershot: Gower, pp. 25–48.

8   Foster, G. (1987) 'Drucker on the record', *Management Today*, September, pp. 58–9 and 110.

9   Parkinson, S., Hill T.J. and Walker, G. (1991) 'Diagnosing customer and competitor influences on manufacturing strategy', in F. Bradley (ed.) *Marketing Thought around the World*, Proceedings of the 20th Annual Conference of the European Marketing Academy, Dublin, May, pp. 741–55.

10 Davies, R., Downes C. and Sweeting, R. (1991) *UK Survey of Cost Management Techniques and Practices, 1990/91*, London: Price Waterhouse, p. 11.

11 Ohmae, K. (1982) 'Japan: from stereotypes to specifics', *McKinsey Quarterly*, Spring, pp. 2–33.

12 Ohmae, 'Japan', p. 3.

13 Carlin, J. (1996) 'Guru of downsizing admits he got it wrong', *Independent on Sunday*, 12 May, p. 1.

14 Davies et al., *UK Survey*, p. 11, confirmed this point. Although 96 per cent of respondents were required to demonstrate quantifiable future benefits, only 55 per cent regarded intangible benefits as playing an important role in the justification process.

15 Hill, T.J. and Woodcock, D.J. (1982) 'Dimensions of control', *Production Management and Control*, 10(2): 16–20.

16 Blois, K.J. (1980) 'The manufacturing/marketing orientation and its information needs', *European Journal of Marketing*, **14**(5/6): 354–64.

17 Davies et al., *UK Survey*, p. 11, reported that budget versus actual was employed by 98 per cent of respondents as a performance measure. However, only 35 per cent utilized flexible budgeting procedures.

18 Overhead allocation involves the allocation, apportionment or allotment of overhead costs to the appropriate cost centre or cost unit. Overhead absorption is achieved by dividing the costs involved on a suitable basis (for example standard labour hours, direct clocked hours, direct labour costs, material costs or floor space) and then spreading them on a pro rata basis in line with the common factor that has been chosen.

19 Based on research findings by Hill, A.J. and Hill, T.J. (2003) 'Seminar report: arguing functional strategies to the market/customer needs of a company', Templeton College, University of Oxford.

20 Kaplan, R.S. and Norton, D.P. (1992) 'The balanced scorecard: measures that drive performance', *Harvard Business Review*, Jan–Feb, pp. 71–80.

21 Mankins, M.C. and Steele, R. (2005) 'Turning great strategies into great performance', *Harvard Business Review*, July–Aug, p. 69.

22 Ibid., p. 66.

23 Ibid., p. 68.

24. Newing, R. (2007) 'Pervasive BI, persistent barriers', Business Intelligence Supplement, *The Times* (South Africa), 26 March, p. 2.

25. Simmonds, 'Strategic management accounting'.

26. Ohmae, 'Japan', p. 7.

Exploring further

Barber, F. and Strack, R. (2005) 'The surprising economics of a people business', *Harvard Business Review*, **83**(6): 80–90.

Briers, M. and Hirst, M. (1990) 'The role of budgetary information in performance evaluation', *Accounting, Organisations and Society*, **15**(4): 373–98.

Bryan, L.L. (2007) 'The new metrics of corporate performance: profit per employee', *McKinsey Quarterly*, **1**: 57–65.

Carr, L.P. (1992) 'Applying cost of quality to a service business', *Sloan Management Review*, **33**(4): 72–8.

Davidson, S. (1963) 'Old wine into new bottles', *Accounting Review*, **38**(2): 278–84.

Goldratt, E.M. (1983) 'Cost accounting is enemy number one of productivity', International Conference Proceedings, American Production and Inventory Control Society (October).

Hyland, P.W., Mellor, R. and Sloan, T. (2007) 'Performance measurement and continuous improvement: are they linked to manufacturing strategy?', *International Journal of Technology Management*, **37**(3/4): 237–53.

Kaplan, R.S. (1984) 'Yesterdays accounting undermines production', *Harvard Business Review*, July–August, pp. 95–101.

Olsen, E.O., Zhou, H., Lee, D.M.S. et al. (2007) 'Performance measurement system and relationships with performance results: a case analysis of a continuous improvement approach to PMS design', *International Journal of Productivity and Performance Management*, **56**(7): 559–73.

Roy, R. Souchoroukov, P. and Griggs, T. (2008) 'Function-based cost estimating', *International Journal of Production Research*, **46**(10): 2621–50.

Shank, J.K. (1989) 'Strategic cost management: new wine or just new bottles?' *Journal of Management Accounting Research*, **1**(1): 47–65.

Shank, J.K. and Govindarajan, V. (1993) *Strategic Cost Management*, New York: The Free Press.

CASE STUDY	Developing an operations strategy	Order-winners and qualifiers	Process choice	Product Profiling	Focused manufacturing	Make or buy and managing the supply chain	Manufacturing infrastructure development	Accounting, finance and performance measurement
IN THE BOOK								
Apple	●	●	●			●	●	●
B & W: The Great Nuclear Fizzle	●	●		●				
Dell	●	●	●		●	●	●	●
Fabritex	●	●	●		●			●
Hoffman Tobacco	●	●	●	●				
HQ Injection Moulding	●	●	●		●			
Jackson Precision Castings	●	●					●	●
Millstone Packaging	●	●	●					●
Peterson Carton Services	●	●	●					●
Precision Steel plc	●	●	●	●				●
Rumack Pharmaceuticals	●	●	●					
Sherpin	●	●			●	●	●	
Zara	●	●			●	●	●	
ON THE WEBSITE								
Aztec Holdings Inc.	●	●	●				●	
Franklin, Singleton and Cotton	●	●	●	●		●	●	●
Klein Products	●	●	●					●
Meta Products	●	●			●		●	
Nolan and Warner plc	●	●	●	●				●
Norex Printing Services	●	●	●	●				
Ontario Packaging	●	●	●	●				
Santal (SA)	●	●			●		●	
Shire Products	●	●			●		●	
Tama Electronics	●	●	●	●				●
Tyndall Furniture Company (A)	●	●	●					
Tyndall Furniture Company (B)	●	●	●					●
Tyndall Furniture Company (C)	●	●					●	●

1 Apple

" In 1985, Steve Jobs, CEO and co-founder of Apple Computers was fired for his highly opinionated and visionary approach to management and leadership only to return 12 years later and rescue it from dire straits', reflected the analyst Paul Keane. 'When he came back, he was still idealistic about design and technology, but his years in exile had made him more realistic and collaborative. As a result, he invited Microsoft to invest in Apple, developed iPod and iTunes products for Windows, fitted Macs with Intel chips, outsourced operations, developed supply chains and ventured into retailing. There is no doubt he has turned the business around, but the question is whether this is only a temporary 'up' in the 'up-and-down' story of Apple. Remember how sales suddenly slumped before he left last time, even though Macs were widely recognized as the best computers on the market. "

The story

Steve Jobs and Steve Wozniak founded Apple Computer Inc. in 1976 as a pair of twenty-something college dropouts building Apple I computer circuit boards in Jobs' family garage. They soon started working with Mike Markkula, a millionaire who retired from Intel at the age of 33, to raise venture capital and bring out an easy-to-use personal computer (PC). It was a good team with Markkula as the businessman, Wozniak the technical genius and Jobs the visionary wanting to change the world through technology. In 1978, they started a computing revolution by launching Apple II, a relatively simple PC that could be used straight out of the box. Three years later, the PC industry was worth

US\$1 billion and Apple was the industry leader with 16 per cent market share. But things suddenly changed when IBM entered the market in 1982 (see *Exhibit 1*). IBM computers had a less secure operating system (Microsoft's DOS), slower processors (Intel) and looked grey and bland, but were easier to clone than the Apple machines. As a result, other manufacturers started making cheap IBM-compatible computers and Apple's market share fell to 6 per cent by 1982. To try to gain back share, Apple launched the Macintosh (Mac) computer in 1984. It was a breakthrough in ease of use, technical capability and industrial design, but the lack of compatible software limited sales. As a result, Apple's market share fell even further and in 1985 the company was in crisis. Jobs was moved out of an operational role and left later that year to set up another company called NeXT Software.

John Sculley, who had been recruited two years earlier from Pepsi, was appointed CEO. He focused Apple on desktop publishing and education customers by designing products from scratch with unique chips, disk drives, monitors, unusually shaped computer chassis, its own proprietary operating system and application software. Customers loved the simple, user-friendly and integrated desktop solution and sales exploded and by 1990 Apple owned 8 per cent of the market. As Jamie Mayers, a senior analyst, commented: 'IBM-compatible users "put up" with their machines, but Apple customers "love" their Macs.'

Apple invested more in R&D than competitors and developed high-end, premium-priced products selling for as much as US\$10,000. Sculley wanted to grow the business and move it back into the mass

This case was prepared by Alex Hill (University of Kingston). It is intended for class discussion and not as an illustration of good or bad management. © AMD Publishing.

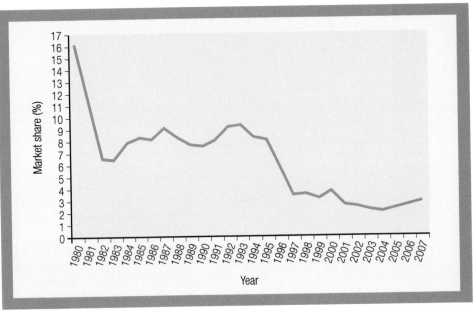

EXHIBIT 1 Apple's worldwide PC share, 1980–2007

market by becoming a low-cost producer launching new products every 6 to 12 months. As part of this strategy, he launched the Mac Classic in 1990, Apple's first lower end desktop and followed this with the PowerBook laptop later that year, achieving rave reviews and significant product sales. However, other product and software developments didn't take off and although Sculley continued to outsource manufacturing and drive down costs, Apple's profits fell to 34 per cent of sales in 1993 after averaging 48 per cent in the previous decade. Apple's board asked him to step down and Michael Spindler took over as CEO later that year. In an attempt to restore profits, he made 16 per cent of Apple's workforce redundant, slashed the R&D budget and licensed a handful of companies to make Mac clones. Despite this, Apple reported a US$69 million loss in 1996, announced further layoffs and two weeks later Gilbert Amelio replaced Spindler as CEO. Amelio refocused Apple on technically superior, premium-priced products, looking to grow sales in high-margin segments such as servers, internet access devices and personal digital assistants. He cancelled the development of the much-delayed operating system, acquired NeXT Software to use a product it was already working on and appointed the founder of NeXT, Steve Jobs, as a part-time adviser. Despite these

bold moves, Apple still lost US$1.6 billion in 1997 and its worldwide PC market share fell from 6 to 3 per cent. As a result, Steve Jobs replaced Amelio as CEO, 12 years after he had left.

Jobs quickly started to turn the business around. He immediately persuaded Microsoft to invest US$150 million in Apple and commit to developing core products such as Microsoft Office for the Mac. He ended the Mac cloning programme and consolidated its product range from 15 to 3 lines. The following year, the iMac was launched, with a distinctive translucent case available in a variety of colours and supporting a wide range of 'plug and play' Windows-based peripherals. It was a success and sold 6 million units over the next three years. He continued to restructure the business by outsourcing the manufacture of Mac products to Taiwanese contractors and revamping distribution by eliminating relationships with smaller retailers and expanding its presence in national chains. Inventory reduced significantly and R&D investment grew (see *Exhibit 2*). In November 1997, the Apple website was launched to sell products directly to consumers and it began promoting itself as a hip alternative to the other computer brands on the market.

Performance	1997	2000	2003	2004	2005	2006	2007
Gross margin (%)							
Apple	21	28	29	29	30	30	35
Dell	23	21	19	19	18	17	19
Hewlett-Packard (HP)	38	31	29	27	25	26	24
R&D/sales (%)							
Apple	12	5	8	6	4	4	4
Dell	1	2	1	1	1	1	1
Hewlett-Packard (HP)	7	5	5	4	3	3	3

EXHIBIT 2 Gross margin and R&D as a percentage of sales for Apple, Dell and HP, 1997–2007

Apple finally introduced its new operating system called Mac OSX in 2001, offering customers a more stable, secure and user-friendly environment than Windows. The same year, it launched the iPod, its first non-Mac product. Although sales were slow for the first couple of years, it now has 70 per cent of the portable media player market (see *Exhibit 3*). A number of different models are now available and every year a new generation of each model is launched that is typically lighter, has more features and costs less than the previous version (see *Exhibit 4*). Since then, it has introduced other non-Mac products such as iTunes, Apple TV and the iPhone (see *Exhibit 5*). In 2007, it began to use Intel chips in its Mac products to overcome problems with its existing chips that were blocking advances in laptop performance and preventing Macs from running Windows-based software. Alongside this product development, it continued to invest in software applications such as iLife (iPhoto, iTunes, iWeb, iMovie), video editing (Final Cut Pro) and the Safari web browser now also available for Windows.

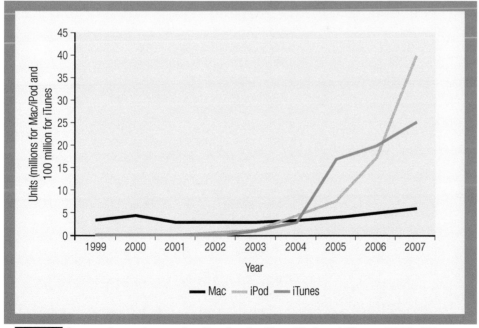

EXHIBIT 3 Comparison of annual unit sales for Mac, iPod and iTunes, 2001–07

Model and generation		Storage (Gigabyte)	Price (US$)	Battery life (Up to hrs)	Developments	Release date
Classic	1	5 10	399 499	10 audio	• New product · Mechanical scroll wheel	Oct 01
	2	10 20	399 499	10 audio	• Touch sensitive scroll wheel · Redesigned hold switch	Jul 02
	3	15 30 40	299 399 499	8 audio	• Touch sensitive buttons • Connector port	Apr 03
	4	30 60	349 449	12 audio	• Photo viewer · Buttons integrated into wheel • 'Click wheel' · Colour display	Jul 04
	5	30 80	249 349	20 audio 3 video	• Video player · Lyrics support • Slimmer design with · Dock included larger screen · Available in white and black	Oct 05
	6	80 160	249 349	40 audio 7 video	• New software interface • Anodized front plate in silver or black	Sep 07
		120	249	36 audio 6 video	• 120GB replaced 80 and · New software interface 160GB	Sep 08
Mini	1	4	249	8 audio	• New product · 'Click wheel' • Available in five colours	Jan 04
	2	4 6	199 249	18 audio	• Brighter colours • Longer battery life	Feb 05

Nano	1	1
		2
		4
			149
			199
			249
				14 audio	• New product succeeding · Flash memory
					  mini · Lyrics support
					• Slimmer design and
					  colour screen
						Sep 05

	2	2 4 8	149 199 249	24 audio	• Anodized aluminium · Longer battery life case in six colours · Music search function • Brighter screen	Sep 06
	3	4 8	149 199	24 audio 5 video	• Video player · New software interface • New product design with larger screen	Sep 07
	4	8 16	149 199	24 audio 4 video	• New product design with · Available in nine colours larger screen · New software interface • Built-in accelerometer	Sep 08
Shuffle	1	0.5 1	99 149	12 audio	• New product · Flash memory • No screen or 'click wheel'	Jan 05
	2	1	79	12 audio	• Smaller aluminium case · Available in multiple colours with built-in clip	Sep 06

Touch	1	8
		16
		32
			299
			399
			499
				22 audio
				5 video
					• New product in one · A variety of software
					  colour (silver) including: Safari web
					• Multi-touch interface with browser, Mail, Calendar,
					  built-in accelerometer Contacts, Google Maps,
					• Wi-Fi connectivity iTunes web store, YouTube,
					    Photos, Weather iPod
						Sep 07

	2	8
		16
		32
			229
			299
			399
				36 audio
				6 video
					• Modified product design: · Access to new third-party
					  slimmer, contoured back, software applications
					  volume controls and through iTunes app store
					  built-in speaker
						Sep 08

EXHIBIT 4 iPod model product development, 2001–08

NOTES
1 With each upgrade, the previous generation is discontinued.
2 The products still currently available are: Classic 6, Nano 3, Shuffle 2 and Touch 1.

Although Microsoft had announced in 2004 that it would no longer develop Internet Explorer for the Mac, it did agree to develop Office products for at least another five years. Meanwhile, Apple continued developing iWork (Pages, Number, Keynote) just to be safe.

Since Jobs' return in 1997, the make-up of the company has changed significantly. It has refocused itself on developing cutting-edge, easy-to-use products that are updated every 12–18 months (see *Exhibit 6*). As well as innovating products, it has also transformed its operations. The analyst

Product group	Development

iPod	• Launched in Nov 2001 to work with Macs and then in Aug 2002 for Windows
	• Now offers a full range of MP3 players from US$49 to US$399 including:
	  – iPod shuffle – randomly plays up to 240 songs
	  – iPod nano – stores up to 2,000 songs or 8 hours of video
	  – iPod classic – holds up to 40,000 songs or 200 hours of video
	  – iPod touch – stores up to 3,500 songs with a variety of features including touch screen, WiFi connectivity and a variety of applications
	• Its sleek design and simple functionality have made it a design icon
	• By Apr 2007, 100 million iPods had been sold and it owned 70 per cent of the MP3 player market
	• Competitors were getting fewer and fewer as rivals left the market
	• Estimates show that each iPod customer spends another 30 per cent of the iPod value on accessories

iTunes	• Launched in Apr 2003 for Macs and then in Oct 2003 for Windows-based PCs • Customers download songs for 99 cents from major and independent record labels • By Jun 2007, 500 million copies of Windows-based iTunes had been downloaded (it is installed on a Mac when you buy it) • By Feb 2008, iTunes had sold more than 4 billion songs, owned 70 per cent of the worldwide digital music market and was the third largest US music retailer behind Wal-Mart and Best Buy • Profits on sales very low (about 9 per cent), but iPod sales grew sevenfold when iTunes was first introduced in 2003. It also created specific standards in users' music libraries that locked them into using iPods
Apple TV	• Launched in 2005, it allowed customers to download TV shows (US$1.99 per episode) and movies (US$9.99 or more each) from iTunes and play them remotely through their TV • By Jan 2008, customers had downloaded 125 million TV shows and 7 million movies • Early in 2008, introduced movie rentals (US$2.99 to US$4.99 for 24 hours) • Launched a second version of Apple TV, allowing customers to access iTunes on the internet directly without having to go through their computers
iPhone	• Launched in Jun 2007, combined the iPod touch with a mobile smartphone with a variety of features including email, web access, text messaging, photos, video, camera, calendar, maps, visual voicemail, iTunes, WiFi, music store and address book • Instead of a keyboard, it has a multi-touch widescreen display • The entire system runs on a specially adapted version of Apple's OSX operating system • It costs between US$399 and US$499 to buy plus the cost of a contract with one of its mobile operator partners such as AT&T (US) or O2 (UK) • By Jan 2008, just 200 days after its launch, Apple had sold 4 million iPhones

EXHIBIT 5 Non-Mac product group development, 2001–08

Mac product group	Model	Generation	Introduced	Discontinued
Desktops	Power Mac	G4 Cube	Jul 00	Jul 01
		G4 Titanium	Jan 01	Sep 03
		G4 MDD	Aug 02	Jun 04
		G5	Jun 03	Jun 04
		G5 FX	Jun 04	Oct 05
		G5 Dual core	Oct 05	Aug 06
	eMac	eMac	Apr 02	Jul 06
	iMac	G4 15"	Jan 02	Aug 04
		G4 20"	Nov 03	Aug 04
		G5 17"	Aug 04	Jan 06
		G5 20"	Aug 04	Mar 06
		iMac	Jan 06	Sep 06
		iMac	Sep 06	Aug 07
		iMac	Aug 07	Current
	Mini	Mini	Oct 05	Feb 06
		Core Solo	Feb 06	Sep 06
		Core Duo	Feb 06	Aug 07
		Core 2 Duo	Aug 07	Current
	Mac Pro	Mac Pro	Aug 06	Jan 08
		Harpertown	Jan 08	Current
Portables	PowerBook	Prismo	Feb 00	Jan 01
		G4 Titanium (15")	Jan 01	Sep 03
		G4 Titanium (12")	Jan 03	May 06
		G4 Titanium (17")	Jan 03	Apr 06
		G4 Aluminium (15")	Sep 03	Feb 06
	iBook	Firewire	Sep 00	May 01
		G4 (12")	Oct 03	May 06
		G4 (14")	Oct 03	May 06
	MacBook	14"	May 06	Feb 08
		Penryn	Feb 08	Current
	MacBook Pro	15"	Sep 06	Feb 08
		17"	Apr 06	Feb 08
		Penryn	Feb 08	Current
	MacBook Air	MacBook Air	Jan 08	Current
Servers	Server	G4 Quicksilver	Jul 01	Aug 02
	Xserve	Xserve	May 02	Feb 03
		Slot loading	Feb 03	Jan 04
		Cluster node	Feb 03	Jan 04
		G5	Jun 04	Aug 06
		G5 Cluster node	Jun 04	Aug 06
		Xserve (Intel)	Aug 06	Jan 08
		Harpertown	Jan 08	Current
	Mac Server	G4 MDD	Aug 02	Jan 03

EXHIBIT 6 Mac product development, 2000–08

Paul Jones commented: 'Apple broke every rule of traditional retailing when it opened its first stores in 2001. They were much larger than necessary and encouraged customers to linger by offering free internet browsing and provided extensive product training rather than just sales help.' These stores showcase Apple products and create a fun and enjoyable experience. Each store has a simple, intuitive and logical layout and is split into four sections: products, music, photos and accessories. They also offer a number of free services such as the 'Genius Bar' to solve customer technical problems and the 'Design Studio' to help customers create photos and design graphics. Regular workshops and presentations are held in theatre-like sections of the store to train customers on aspects such as the Mac operating system, editing home movies and recording music. In 2003, the stores became profitable and by 2007 Apple was the fastest growing retailer in the world, with 197 stores drawing over 100 million visitors a year.

Four operations are used to supply products to the Apple retail stores, other resellers or directly to customers who have ordered online. Two are located in the US serving the Americas, one in Ireland for Europe, the Middle East and Africa and the fourth in Singapore for the Asian market. All operations have been outsourced apart from basic assembly to compile the products, peripherals, software, documentation and accessories necessary for each order. No products or materials are single sourced, but the number of suppliers has been significantly reduced in recent years and is now down to about 250. Long relationships are in place with key suppliers and Apple often accounts for 70–80 per cent of a supplier's total business. Sixty per cent of components tend to be locally sourced by each of the four Apple operations, while the other 40 per cent come from a number of global suppliers including Samsung, Wolfson Microelectronics, SigmaTel and Hitachi. Apple's global procurement function is split into product teams comprising buyers, engineers and designers who work collaboratively with suppliers to plan capacity and meet delivery schedules. Suppliers deliver against daily requirements, are expected to reduce costs over time and are measured against price, delivery reliability, quality conformance and technical support (listed in order of importance).

As well as managing this physical supply chain, Apple has also developed a digital supply chain for its iTunes products. This has proved to be a huge success and in 2008, AMR Research identified it as the best supply chain within Fortune 500 companies (see *Exhibit 7*). As the analyst Paul Jones commented:

Position	2004	2005	2007	2008
1	Dell	Dell	Nokia	Apple
2	Nokia	Procter & Gamble	Apple	Nokia
3	Procter & Gamble	IBM	Procter & Gamble	Dell
4	IBM	Nokia	IBM	Procter & Gamble
5	Wal-Mart	Toyota Motor	Toyota Motor	IBM
6	Toyota Motor	Johnson & Johnson	Wal-Mart	Wal-Mart
7	Johnson & Johnson	Samsung Electronics	Anheuser-Busch	Toyota
8	Johnson Controls	Wal-Mart	Tesco	Cisco Systems
9	Tesco	Tesco	Best Buy	Samsung Electronics
10	PepsiCo	Johnson Controls	Samsung Electronics	Anheuser-Busch

NOTES

1 Rating is based on peer opinion (20 per cent), research opinion (20 per cent), return on assets (25 per cent), inventory turns (25 per cent) and revenue growth (10 per cent).

2 Apple only became a Fortune 500 company in 2006.

EXHIBIT 7 Top 10 companies for supply chain management, 2004–08

66 *Apple have made significant supply chain developments and moved away from a 20th-century production efficiency mentality toward a new era of value, based on ideas, design, and content. In 2007, it delivered US$2 billion sales of zero-inventory iTunes products. Not only does this significantly improve cash flow, but it also creates a platform for selling its higher margin iPod and iPhone products. Rather than distributing through retailers, products such as music, movies, television shows, music videos, games and publications are delivered instantly and directly to customers through its online store. This has revolutionised not only the industries within which it competes, but also how we fundamentally think about supply chains. The number and types of products being supplied through iTunes is increasing all the time and the possibilities seem endless.* 99

The future

In early 2007, Apple changed its name from Apple Computer to Apple Inc. to signify its growing focus on consumer electronics rather than computers (see *Exhibit 8*). Some analysts feel its move into consumer electronics has made it more competitive as customers value its easy interface and simple design, but others feel that it is losing its focus. Paul Keane concluded:

66 *Apple is still essentially only a small player in the PC industry [see Exhibit 9] and diversification will only cause it problems. iPod sales are starting to level off and the recent iPhone launch has moved it into industries with fiercer competition. Companies such as Nokia, Motorola and Samsung are much bigger and more aggressive than its iPod competitors and are not going to give up without a fight. Continually developing products and moving into new markets puts huge stress on all parts of its business. I'm not sure if its operations and supply chains can keep up with this.* 99

Product group	Annual sales (US$M)					
	2002	2003	2004	2005	2006	2007
Desktops	2,828	2,475	2,373	3,436	3,319	4,020
Portables	1,706	2,016	2,550	2,839	4,056	6,294
Total Mac	4,534	4,491	4,923	6,275	7,375	10,314
iPod	143	345	1,306	4,540	7,676	8,305
iTunes and other music products	4	36	278	899	1,885	2,496
iPhone and related products	–	–	–	–	–	123
Peripherals and other hardware	527	691	951	1,126	1,100	1,260
Software, service and other	534	644	821	1,091	1,279	1,508
Total	5,742	6,207	8,279	13,931	19,315	24,006

NOTES
1 Desktops include iMac, eMac, Mac Mini, Mac Pro, Power Mac and Xserve products.
2 Portables include MacBook, iBook, MacBook Pro and PowerBook product lines.
3 iTunes and other music products include sales from iTunes Music Store, iPod-related services and accessories.
4 Peripherals and other hardware include Apple-branded and third-party displays, wireless connectivity and networking solutions and other hardware accessories.
5 Software, service and other include Apple-branded operating system, applications software, third-party software, AppleCare Services and internet services.

EXHIBIT 8 Annual sales revenue by product group, 2002–07

Vendor	Market share (% total unit sales)				
	1995	2001	2004	2006	2007
HP	4	7	16	17	19
Dell	3	13	18	18	15
Lenovo	–	–	2	6	8
Acer	–	–	4	5	8
Toshiba	3	3	3	4	4
Apple	8	3	2	2	3
Compaq	10	11	–	–	–
Fujitsu Siemens	5	5	6	–	–
IBM	6	6	6	–	–
Gateway	2	2	2	2	–
Other	59	50	41	46	43
Total (%)	100	100	100	100	100
Total (million units)	89	122	178	235	269

NOTES
1 HP acquired Compaq in 2002.
2 IBM sold its PC business to Lenovo in 2005.
3 Acer acquired Gateway in 2007.

EXHIBIT 9 Comparison of market share for major PC vendors, 1995–2007

THE GREAT NUCLEAR FIZZLE AT OLD

66 Everything went wrong when the venerable boil-ermakers turned to building pressure vessels for atomic reactors. The whole electric power industry felt the consequences. 99

The long-awaited transition for the US electric power industry into the nuclear age has been slowed by a number of factors, including technological difficulties and public resistance. But a specific and unexpected cause for delay has been one company's crucial failure to deliver a single vital component of nuclear power plants. The failure, basically, was a management failure, and on a scale that would be cause for concern even to a fly-by-night newcomer to the nuclear industry. The company, however, was no newcomer. It was proud old Babcock & Wilcox Co. (B & W), a pioneer of the steam generating business, whose boilers were used in one of the first central power plants ever built (in Philadelphia, in 1881). B & W had an impressive $648m in sales last year, making it 157th on *Fortune*'s list of 500 largest industrials, and it has been engaged in nuclear work in a major way for 15 years, producing, among other things, atomic power systems for Navy submarines.

Moreover, the corporation is one of only five that are engaged in building nuclear power plants in the USA. With consumption of electricity growing by nearly 10 per cent a year, the utilities are counting heavily on the new nuclear stations to avoid brownouts and power failures in the years ahead. Poor performance at B & W is thus one of those problems that could send ripples through the whole economy.

All of B & W's troubles involve a single product: nuclear pressure vessels. These are the huge steel pots – some are more than 70 feet long and weigh more than 700 tons – that contain atomic reactions. They must meet rigid specifications set by the Atomic Energy Commission (AEC), and B & W built a $25m plant at Mount Vernon, Indiana, just to fabricate them. Cockily sure that the Mount Vernon plant would operate as planned, B & W sold its entire projected output of pressure vessels for years ahead. But nothing seemed to go right at Mount Vernon. Plagued by labour shortages and malfunctioning machines, the plant produced just three pressure vessels in its first three years of operation. Late 1968, after the production snarl reached horrendous proportions, a vice-president responsible for the Mount Vernon operation committed suicide in a bizarre fashion.

Last May, B & W was forced to make a humiliating disclosure. Every one of the 28 nuclear pressure vessels then in the Mount Vernon Works was behind schedule, by as much as 17 months. For the utility industry, the news from B & W meant intolerable delays in bringing 28 badly needed nuclear plants into service, with all the added expense and problems that would be entailed. Philadelphia Electric Co. estimated that it would have to spend an extra $50,000 a day just to provide from other sources, such as high-cost gas turbines, the power that it had counted on getting from its delayed nuclear units.

Creating its own competition

With so much at stake, B & W's customers could not well afford to be patient. Twenty-one of the

This article was written by H. B. Meyers and published in Fortune, *November 1969. It is reprinted with permission by the publishers © 1969 Time Inc. All rights reserved.*

pressure vessels tied up in Mount Vernon Works were there on subcontracts from the two giants of the nuclear industry, General Electric (GE) and Westinghouse Electric. Both companies swiftly took the almost unprecedented step of forcing B & W to turn most of their partially completed vessels over to other manufacturers. When B & W, in an ill-conceived gambit, tried to hang on to two of the transferred vessels, Westinghouse took the case to court and won. In all, 14 GE and Westinghouse vessels – perhaps $40m worth – were taken out of B & W's shops. Some of the firms that got the business had never made a pressure vessel before for use in a US reactor; B & W had managed to create hungry new competitors in its own line of work. Only four GE and three Westinghouse vessels remain at Mount Vernon.

The company itself has barely begun to pay the high price of failure. Its earnings last year were still a robust $2.04 a share. In the first six months of this year, losses associated with nuclear work pushed earnings down to 22 cents a share (not even enough to cover the 34-cent quarterly dividend). From a 1969 high of 40.5 last January, B & W stock has sagged into the low 20s. At that price, the stock is hovering around book value.

The man in the middle of all these troubles is President George Zipf (pronounced Ziff), 49, a low-key executive who started with B & W in 1942 as a metallurgical engineer. But the man who bears the main onus of responsibility is Zipf's predecessor, Chairman Morris Neilson, 65, who chose Zipf for his present job a year ago, and handed him his present problems.

In trouble down by the Ohio

'All areas of the company were profitable in 1968 with the exception of automatic energy', President George Zipf told B & W stockholders, after taking over as chief executive officer from Chairman Morris Neilson in September 1968. Up to then, losses on nuclear work had never seemed particularly troublesome. They were regarded simply as the price of B & W's ticket into the automatic age; and B & W had been getting into, and prospering in, new technologies for a hundred years.

However, one segment of its nuclear venture has driven B & W into deep trouble. The plant that it built along the Ohio River at Mount Vernon, Indiana, to produce huge steel pressure vessels for atomic reactors, failed to function as expected, with all kinds of dire results. One especially unhappy result was that B & W had to give up some partially completed pressure vessels to competitors.

Bad boy from Blair, Nebraska

Neilson is a flamboyant leader, a big bluff man with bright blue eyes and a full head of grey-blonde hair, who has a gift for salty language. More than one secretary quit 'Doc' Neilson's employ because of his profanity, and more than one executive suffered a colourful tongue-lashing in the chairman's office.

Neilson got his nickname by virtue of being a doctor's son in Blair, Nebraska, where he was known as 'Young Doc'. That was as close to earning an academic degree as Neilson came. As a boy, he himself has said, he was 'incorrigible' and was kicked out of school 'for being a bad influence on the rest of the students'. He then enrolled in a Lincoln, Nebraska, high school and worked part-time as an embalmer.

❝ *I got into trouble in Lincoln, too', Neilson told an interviewer a few years ago. 'One night, I came home with my nose over and under my eye. I'd been in a fight and got hit with a pair of pliers. I woke up my old man and he looked at my nose, and said, "You're going to look like a goddamn syphilitic the rest of your life." My old man used to tell me that there were two steps ahead of me – first reform school and then the pen.* ❞

Instead, Young Doc became a steeplejack and ironworker and in 1924 joined the corporation he was later to head.

❝ *I came to B & W by accident', Neilson has recalled. 'I was working at American Bridge as an ironmonger on a job in Chicago, and another fellow and I got drunk. We got on the train and got off at Des Moines. We were walking past this construction job, and a fellow slid down a column and said, "You looking for work?" We figured we were.* ❞

It was a B & W job, erecting boilers for central station power plants, and from the start Doc Neilson felt at home in the two-fisted company. 'Those construction workers were goddamn rough people. They were hard drinkers, fighters, and lived by their wits.'

By the time the Second World War came along, Neilson was superintendent of marine erection. He supervised the installation of B & W boilers in 4,100 Navy and merchant-marine ships during the war. Later he headed the entire boiler division, including manufacturing, and in 1957 became president and chief executive officer.

When Neilson took charge of B & W the company was already deeply involved in nuclear work. Neilson's predecessor, Alfred Iddles, had recognized early that B & W would have to prepare for the day when the atom would challenge fossil fuels as a source of energy for central generating plants. Under Iddles, B & W attracted an outstanding stable of nuclear scientists and engineers and, in 1956, set up an extensive research facility at Lynchburg, Virginia. One of B & W's first important nuclear jobs was to build Consolidated Edison's Indian Point Plant. Another project was the reactor for the nuclear ship Savannah. B & W lost money on these jobs, but it gained the experience needed to secure a corporate toehold in the nuclear era.

Nuclear losses continued under Neilson, but he improved B & W's overall profitability dramatically. Iddles had run the company as a loose-knit grouping of semi-autonomous subsidiaries. Neilson centralized and systematized management. Every executive's areas of responsibility and authority were carefully spelled out in manuals that defined company policies and aims in all sectors of the business. Although sales stayed near or below the 1958 figure of $366m until 1963 – this was a low period in the utility buying cycle – earnings climbed year by year. Profits went from $13m in 1958 to $22m in 1963. At that point, sales also began to go up, rising by 71 per cent in the next five years. Profits peaked in 1967 at $33m, at $2.69 a share (compared to $1.05 a share in Neilson's first full year).

In view of his critics, who have lately become numerous, the seeds of B & W's present problems were planted in the years of Neilson's rich harvests. It can be seen, in retrospect, that he may have been too

successful in keeping B & W lean. His determination to keep down the fat sometimes 'had the effect of cutting into good red meat', says a former B & W executive. Experienced managers found themselves stretched too thin to cover all their areas of responsibility. Worse, they did not always feel that their authority matched their responsibility (that is, men in the field were held responsible for results they did not have the power to bring about).

The most biting criticism of Neilson's regime comes from men charged with nuclear assignments. In their eyes, Neilson's lack of formal education proved a serious handicap. Explains one former B & W executive: 'Neilson created an atmosphere in which engineers and technical people just didn't feel at home. Their ideas were not treated with respect. They felt that top management didn't understand technical problems, and didn't trust those who could understand them.'

A touch of corporate arrogance

From the start, B & W had foreseen a long wait before its nuclear work became profitable. Developing the necessary skills and technologies to compete in the nuclear industry has proved to be a slow and expensive process for every company that has tried it, including GE and Westinghouse. But what B & W had not expected was to lose money on its Mount Vernon Works. When the plant was planned in the early 1960s, Neilson appeared to believe that he had found a niche in the nuclear industry that offered a quick return. A nuclear pressure vessel, though huge and manufactured to demanding technical standards, is essentially just the kind of heavy steel unit that B & W was accustomed to fabricating with ease.

While the Mount Vernon plant was under construction, US utilities went on a nuclear-plant buying spree, starting in 1965. At the time, the surge in orders seemed like a lucky break for B & W. The Mount Vernon plant was designed to produce one completed pressure vessel a month, once it was in full operation, and there had been considerable doubt during the planning stages 'if we'd ever get enough work to fill the place', a former B & W executive recalls. Orders for pressure vessels poured in, faster than anyone had predicted, and the

Mount Vernon plant soon got loaded up with work. It is now clear that management made too little provision for the time it would take to get the new plant operating at full capacity. Says one B & W customer: 'I think you have to say that corporate arrogance was involved.'

The first delays at Mount Vernon were caused by suppliers falling far behind schedule in providing vital equipment. A linear accelerator, used to detect welding flaws, was not delivered until August 1966, 11 months late. Even worse, a highly automated, tape-controlled machine centre – the heart of the plant as originally conceived – arrived a full year behind schedule, in September 1967.

The lure of unspoiled labour

By then, the plant had been operating on a make-shift basis for almost two years. And it had already become apparent that B & W's century of demonstrated competence in the fabrication of heavy steel products had not protected the company from grievous error. A principal one was the site itself, a cornfield near the little farm town of Mount Vernon (population: 6,200) in south-western Indiana. The location had been chosen mainly because of its position on the Ohio River, safely above any known flood level, and yet reliably accessible for deep-water barges. This was an important advantage because nuclear pressure vessels are so immense that they can best be transported by water. B & W had owned the land for a number of years, and had set up a small plant there for making boiler parts.

What Mount Vernon did not have was a pool of skilled labour. This was a serious drawback because the AEC, for safety reasons, sets rigid standards for machine work and welding on nuclear projects. Late last year, a company memorandum reviewing the Mount Vernon fiasco observed: 'Production workers required a new level of knowledge, intelligence, and judgement to operate the machinery, perform operations, and maintain the very high quality standards.' At the outset, however, B & W took an optimistic view of its prospects and chose, according to that 1968 memorandum, to regard Mount Vernon as 'an unspoiled labour market'. Presumably, the company expected to find a more tractable group of workers there than it had at Barberton, Ohio, where B & W's power generator division had had its headquarters and principal manufacturing facilities for many years.

The company planned to overcome the obvious shortcomings of Mount Vernon's labour pool in two ways: first, through automation – using that sophisticated machining centre – and second, through a massive training programme that would entice farmers away from their cornfields and quickly turn them into skilled welders and machinists. In one year, B & W spent $1m just to train welders. But almost as fast as men reached the levels of skill required, they left B & W for jobs elsewhere. On 30 September 1968, only 514 of the 1,060 hourly employees hired in the preceding three years were still working for B & W; in other words, the company had hired three men for each one it retained. 'Turnover of the Mount Vernon workforce has been a particularly frustrating problem, and a major reason B & W has been unable to bring its full manufacturing capabilities to bear on the situation', the 1968 memorandum concluded. Some potential workers proved to be untrainable, others had a 'general negative attitude' towards heavy industry, and 'some were not able to adjust, and therefore returned to their farms'.

'It drove us out of our minds'

Workers who remained with B & W did not prove to be as unspoiled as the company had hoped. Even before the pressure vessel plant opened, it was organized by the Boilermakers Union (which also represents B & W workers at Barberton) amid charges of unfair labour practices against the management. The plant was closed by labour disputes on several occasions. The most serious occurred when the three-year contract expired in 1967, while equipment was still being installed. The Boilermakers went on strike over wages and work rules, and the plant was down for 40 days; unnecessarily long, in the view of President Thomas Ayers of Chicago's Commonwealth Edison, who had pressure vessels tied up at Mount Vernon.

From the standpoint of production, Neilson won a victory that amounted to overkill. Under the new contract, wages remained too low to stem the flow of workers away from B & W or to attract qualified workers from other areas. The B & W memo cites the 'noncompetitiveness of our wage scale' as a reason for the high turnover rate in the Mount Vernon workforce. Even for experienced workers, welding two pieces of eight-inch steel together is a demanding task, particularly in nuclear work, in which each weld is examined by X-ray. When an imperfection is found, the weld must be 'mined out' and done over again. In most plants, less than 10 per cent of the welds must be reworked, and a rework level of less than 1 per cent is sometimes achieved. But at Mount Vernon 70 per cent or more of the welds were rejected on being inspected. 'It drove us out of our damned minds', recalls Ayers, 'So costly! So time-consuming!' Ayers and other B & W customers say that they urged the company to increase the supervisory force – which regularly worked one-and-a-half to two shifts daily – so that a closer watch could be kept on the welds as they were built up.

In addition to its problems, B & W ran into unexpected trouble with equipment. The linear accelerator for X-raying welds was installed in mid-1966 but did not go into full operation until a year later. The tape-controlled machining centre was even more of a headache, and began functioning as planned only a few months ago. In this centre, huge vessel segments are positioned on optically aligned ways, and then moved a distance of 250 feet, while a series of precise machining operations are performed simultaneously, controlled by computer-prepared tape. The concept was a good one, since nuclear pressure vessels are custom jobs, each tailored to a customer's specifications. But 'debugging' of the machinery proved unexpectedly difficult. One problem was that the plant was not air-conditioned, and temperature changes threw off the many delicate adjustments that had to be made. In addition, an earthquake – fairly rare in Indiana – shook up the plant last year and it took nearly a week to reset the machine tools. Other start-up difficulties were simply incomprehensible. For example, a vital boring mill was put out of operation for several weeks when a tool broke. There was no spare on hand.

Death in a dry bathtub

The man directly responsible for the Mount Vernon plant was John Paul Craven, vice-president in charge of the power generation division at Barberton. As head of B & W's largest division, Craven was number three man in the company, and was paid $87 000 a year. At one time, there was speculation in the company that Craven might someday become president. A gentle, upright bachelor of 60, Craven was tall and distinguished looking. An engineer by training, he had been with B & W all his working life, and he had no interests outside his job. For a while, Craven had raised roses as a hobby, but after he was made vice-president he gave up roses in order to devote himself more fully to B & W. 'His work was his whole life', says an old friend.

As the bottleneck at Mount Vernon grew worse, Craven came to feel that neither his customers nor corporate headquarters in New York fully appreciated the difficulties of Mount Vernon's advanced machine tools. He did not believe that he was given the authority, the budget or the personnel that he needed to fulfil the plant's commitments. Says another of Craven's old friends: 'Paul couldn't bear to sit in Barberton and have all the shots called from New York – and then be expected to take responsibility for not producing.'

In September 1968, before the seriousness of the pressure-vessel crisis at Mount Vernon became generally known, Neilson stepped aside as chief executive in favour of George Zipf. For a man destined for the top at B & W, Zipf had an unusual background. All of his predecessors had been identified with boilers, but Zipf came from B & W's tubular products division at Beaver Falls, Pennsylvania, near Pittsburgh. This division, whose work is more akin to steel manufacturing than boilermaking, produces tubing for B & W's own use and for sale to other industrial customers; it accounts for roughly 30 per cent of B & W's total sales, and more than half its profits. When he transferred to New York as executive vice-president in 1966, Zipf had been at Beaver Falls for 20 years, ever since graduating from Lehigh University. He was a stranger to the problems of the power generation division, and to that division's big corporate customers.

Less than a month after taking over as chief executive from Neilson, Zipf scheduled a meeting at the Mount Vernon plant with Craven and Austin Fragomen, vice-president for manufacturing. The meeting was set for a Monday morning. During the preceding weekend Craven told friends that for the first time in his life he thought his job was getting beyond him. Sometime on the Sunday afternoon or evening before his scheduled meeting with Zipf, Craven took off his clothes and climbed into a dry bathtub in his $250-a-month apartment at Akron's luxurious Carlton House. Then he slashed his ankles, cut his throat and stabbed himself in the heart with the serrated eight-inch blade of a butcher's knife.

After Craven's death, George Zipf took personal charge of the power generation division, and of the Mount Vernon works in particular. Before long, both Austin Fragomen and the Mount Vernon plant manager, Norman Wagner, resigned. That left Zipf free to put a whole new team to work on the company's pressure-vessel debacle.

The chairman sells some stock

Beginning in 1967, both GE and Westinghouse, along with many of the utilities that were the ultimate customers for B & W pressure vessels, repeatedly expressed worry over the Mount Vernon plant's faltering operations. In the fall of 1968, B & W pacified GE to some extent by setting up a temporary welding shop on barges anchored at Madison, Indiana, where expert welders from the Louisville, Kentucky, labour pool could be obtained. But for the most part, B & W brushed aside its customers' worries with assurances that things at Mount Vernon were not really as bad as they seemed. Even after Craven's death, the B & W management continued to maintain that its optimistic scheduling, with some minor changes, would prove to be realistic.

Some utility executives who met with Zipf to express their concern left with the conviction that he did not appreciate just how serious the pressure-vessel delays had become. On some occasions, he seemed to regard his callers as bothersome intruders. 'He just sat there like a damned Budha [sic]', reported one customer after such a meeting.

Faced with such frustrations, GE and Westinghouse began to consider the drastic step of pulling some of their delayed pressure vessels out of the overloaded Mount Vernon shops. Both companies assigned teams to scout for other manufacturers that might be able to take over B & W vessels and complete them. There were not many potential candidates. Up to then, B & W and Combustion Engineering, Inc., had pretty much divided the US pressure-vessel business between them. Combustion Engineering had managed to keep close to schedule on its deliveries, and had been expanding its Chattanooga machine shops. It had unused capacity. In addition, Chicago Bridge & Iron Co., which had previously done only on-site fabrication, was setting up a pressure-vessel plant in Memphis. (On-site fabrication is a more expensive method of constructing pressure vessels, used only when it is extremely difficult to transport the massive units to a site intact.) The GE and Westinghouse teams also looked abroad for companies that might be able to take over some of the work.

In April, while B & W's biggest customers were searching for other suppliers, Doc Neilson – who was retiring on 1 May as an officer of the company, but keeping the title of chairman – quietly sold 15,000 of his 20,000 shares of B & W stock. The price at the time was about $33 a share. A couple of weeks later B & W stockholders got their first official hint of serious trouble ahead. George Zipf revealed at the annual meeting that he expected earnings to drop by 20 to 30 per cent in 1969 because of the company's losses on nuclear business. (The actual decline, of course, has since proved to be much greater than Zipf predicted.) Before long, the price of B & W's stock sank into the 20s.

Quick trip to court

On 14 May, less than a month after the annual meeting, B & W sent out telegrams brusquely letting customers know that the situation at Mount Vernon was even worse than they had suspected. Zipf and his new team had completed a gloomy re-evaluation of the plant's capabilities, and B & W was adding 2 to 12 months to earlier delivery schedules, some of which had already been stretched past the dates called for in B & W's original contracts.

On receiving this news, both GE and Westinghouse sought B & W's cooperation in transferring vessels to the other shops that they had scouted out. B & W agreed to subcontract some of its work to these plants. But an unexpected difficulty soon arose. Westinghouse had determined that Rotterdam Dockyard Co., a major shipbuilding and steel fabricating firm in the Netherlands, could take two vessels and improve on the B & W schedule, provided that the vessels were transferred promptly. Westinghouse located space on a ship that would be calling at New Orleans on the desired date and, by paying a premium, was able to arrange for the ship to cancel calls at other ports and proceed directly to the Netherlands. B & W agreed to put the two pressure vessels on barges and start them on their way to New Orleans, while it negotiated a subcontract with Rotterdam Dockyard. But negotiations broke down when B & W and Rotterdam could not come to terms. To the horror of Westinghouse officials, B & W ordered the barges back to Mount Vernon.

Westinghouse then decided to pay B & W for the work it had already done, and take over the vessels itself. But speed was required. If the barges did not continue down the river while these new arrangements were made they would miss the ship to Rotterdam. Now Westinghouse found itself at a strange impasse: it could not reach anyone at B & W who would rescind the order for the barges to return to Mount Vernon. Neilson was 'not available', and Zipf was 'out of the country'. Frustrated in its efforts to reach top management and work out an amicable settlement, Westinghouse reluctantly went into the US district court in Pittsburgh, and won a temporary restraining order to prevent B & W from taking the vessels back to Mount Vernon.

During the hearing, Federal Judge Wallace S. Gourley had a revealing exchange with John T. Black, B & W's manager for commercial nuclear components.

Judge Gourley: On this contract for $2,542,000, what would you say that you expect to make on this?'
Black: This specific contract?
Judge Gourley: Yes.
Black: I don't expect to make a profit.

Judge Gourley: You don't expect to make a profit?
Black: No, sir.
Judge Gourley: I don't know why you would want the material to work on. You are not in business to lose money for your stockholders.
Black: We do not expect to make it.
Judge Gourley: In other words, on this contract [for] $2,542,000, you don't expect to make a penny profit for your corporation, if you went ahead and finished it?
Black: No, sir.
Judge Gourley: How much on this other one [for] $2,304,789. What profit could you be reasonably expected to make on this contract, if you finished it?
Black: I would think that one probably [is] in the same condition.
Judge Gourley: If you went ahead and finished this, you wouldn't make a cent?
Black: I think on direct cost, we would cover our direct cost to labour and shop expenses.
Judge Gourley: I meant after everything, would you or would you not make any money on this?
Black: No.
Judge Gourley: I wouldn't think your stockholders would want you to finish. I certainly wouldn't.

Back on the track

After Westinghouse won possession of the two pressure vessels and sent them off to Rotterdam, B & W raised no further objections to transferring work out of its shop. Indeed, it actively cooperated with its customers to get the job done. Westinghouse sent five vessels to Combustion Engineering's Chattanooga shops and two to a French firm, Société des Forges et Ateliers du Creusot. GE turned three vessels over to Chicago Bridge & Iron and had B & W send two others to Japan's Ishikawajima-Harima Heavy Industries. In every case, these firms are expected to equal or better the delivery dates set in May by B & W.

With the load at Mount Vernon lightened, prospects look better for the 14 pressure vessels that remain there, including seven for nuclear plants that B & W itself is building. For example, the Sacramento Municipal Utility District has been notified that the vessel for its Rancho Seco nuclear plant, a B & W project, will be only a couple of months late, instead of the year that seemed likely in May. That means that the vessel for Sacramento is essentially on schedule again, since the delays now expected are no more than could be accounted for by the labour disputes and earthquake that Mount Vernon suffered.

To his utility customers, George Zipf remains very much a man on trial. But now that their pressure vessels are moving along again, some utility executives are convinced that he has quietly managed to put B & W back on the track. One move that has met their approval was the appointment in September of an experienced Westinghouse man as vice-president in charge of the power generation division (John Paul Craven's old job). Bringing in an outsider at such a level is something new for B & W, and one B & W customer believes that he knows what it means: 'I think George Zipf is really in command now.' If this is so, he will have a lot to do to restore the honoured old name of Babcock & Wilcox to its former lustre.

Technical note

Nuclear equipment, as stated earlier, is manufactured in a job-shop environment, while most of the fossil equipment is manufactured in a flow-shop environment. In fossil manufacturing operations, the work stations are usually arranged in proper sequence to allow materials to enter one end of the shop, and flow sequentially to completion. The normal work mix means that some work be performed at each work station, but seldom requires the product to pass over any of the work stations more than once. All jobs follow, essentially, the same path from one work station to another. Consequentially, it is relatively easy to 'line-up' or 'load' each shop with a high degree of certainty as to work content, schedule requirements and completion capabilities. Over the years, certain rules of thumb were developed, which allowed relatively accurate manufacturing planning decisions to be made for fossil manufacturing operations.

A shipping unit for a large fossil-fired boiler, such as used in power plants, differs greatly from a shipping unit for a nuclear plant. Fossil boilers are shipped as a large number of parts, which are assembled or erected at the job site. Nuclear equipment is mostly shop assembled, whereby a small number of large, assembled components are shipped to the site for installation. Complex planning is, therefore, required for the nuclear shop operations, which produce all detail parts fabricated into various levels of subassembled, and finally into large components.

Source: E. D. Thomas and D. P. Covelski, 'Planning Nuclear Equipment Manufacturing', *Interfaces*, 1975, **9**(3): 18–29.

In January 2007, Michael Dell was reinstated as CEO of Dell. The company he had lovingly built over the previous 25 years was in trouble and its shareholders were getting nervous. Market share had fallen and it was rapidly losing ground to Hewlett-Packard (HP), now the world's largest PC manufacturer. Analysts argued that Dell's business model no longer gave it a competitive edge. It didn't focus on product innovation or customer experience and its growing product line was becoming difficult to manage. As Marc Auerbach explained:

  ❝ *The traditional PC markets of the US, Europe, and Asia-Pacific are maturing and growth has shifted to emerging markets such as China, India, Indonesia, Brazil, Pakistan and Russia. Times are hard and three of the top ten PC manufacturers have already exited the market. Compaq sold to HP in 2002, IBM to Lenovo in 2005 and Gateway to Acer in 2007. Demand for desktop PCs is falling as notebooks and mobile devices become more popular. As product innovation grows, life cycles shorten and choice widens. Also customers increasingly want to touch a product and talk to someone about its features before buying it. Dell's current business model doesn't allow this.* **❞**

The evolution of Dell

In 1983, Michael Dell was studying at Texas University and upgrading PCs in his spare time. He soon realized that he could offer customers cost-effective computers by buying components, assembling them and selling to them directly. Three years later, he was running a company with $34 million annual

sales, 100 employees and a 3,000 sq. ft facility. In 1987, when Dell entered the UK market, sales doubled compared to the previous year and in 1988 Dell went public, issuing 3.5 million shares at $8.5 each. To meet the growing UK demand, an assembly plant was set up in Ireland and retail agreements established with CompUSA, Staples, BestBuy, Costco, Business Depot and PC World to serve small businesses and individual consumers. By 1992, annual sales were $2 billion, with a profit of $102 million. Everything seemed to be going from strength to strength, but then problems struck.

In 1994, inaccurate sales forecasts left the business with high inventories (55 days finished goods and 70 days components) and 17,000 notebooks had to be recalled for quality problems. It made a loss of $36 million in the year and had a cash deficit of $154 million. To rectify this situation, Dell went back to its roots by exiting the retail market and focusing on direct sales. Although retail sales were growing, profit margins were low and products couldn't be customized. Eliminating middlemen and distributors allowed Dell to better understand customer needs. Passing this information onto its suppliers reduced component inventory from 70 to 20 days and average lead time from 45 to 10 days. Finished goods inventory was eliminated as products were now assembled to order within five days after receipt of an order. The cash released by the stock reduction was invested in higher quality products to compete with Compaq and IBM.

This was a radical change, but the developments didn't stop there. In 1998, the website www.dell.com was launched and by the year 2000, customers could

This case was prepared by Alex Hill (University of Kingston). It is intended for class discussion and not as an illustration of good or bad management. © AMD Publishing.

select, price, purchase systems and check their order status online. Dell found that over half its sales were now through the internet and it increased its product line by selling refurbished PCs, notebooks, scanners and printers from companies who had recently upgraded their systems. It also expanded its product range beyond PCs, with serviced network servers, workstations and storage systems, while launching a series of digital entertainment products such as digital music players, TVs and personal organizers in collaboration with Lexmark, Fuji, Xerox, Samsung and Kodak. While PC sales continued to grow, Dell looked for other opportunities (see Exhibit 1).

Product group	% total annual sales			
	2004	2005	2006	2007
Desktop PCs	45	42	38	34
Notebooks	23	24	25	27
Software and peripherals	12	14	15	16
Servers and networking	10	10	10	10
Enhanced services	7	8	9	9
Storage	3	3	3	4
Total	100	100	100	100

EXHIBIT 1 Percentage total sales by product group, 2004–07

A year later, it became the largest PC manufacturer in the world, with annual sales of $32 billion, of which 72 per cent were in North and South America, 20 per cent in Europe and 8 per cent in Asia Pacific. The company grew from strength to strength and in 2004 it broke the worldwide industry record by shipping 8 million PC units in the first quarter. At the same time, Michael Dell stepped down as CEO to become chairman of the board. The current organization activities is shown as Exhibit 2.

Driving success

Dell's operations strategy turned the business around in 1994 and grew it in subsequent years (see Exhibit 3). Exhibit 4 summarizes its operating model from product selection through to distribution. It continually focuses on inventory reduction and turned it over 107 times in 2006 compared with 8.5 times at HP and 17.5 times at IBM. This gives Dell a competitive advantage as products do not become obsolete, having then to be sold at a discount while new product lead time is almost two months shorter than competitors because existing component inventory does not have to be sold beforehand. The direct client interface guarantees precise knowledge of their needs and this information drives product and service innovation. Eliminating retailers also focuses the sales force on end users rather than distributors and makes it possible to offer very competitive prices.

Function	Description
Headquarters	• Corporate headquarters based in US (Texas) and also serves as the regional headquarters for US, Canada, South America and Latin America • Regional headquarters for Europe, Middle East and Africa based in England and Singapore for Pacific Rim

Operations	• Manufacturing – six facilities in US (including Texas, Nashville and North Carolina), Brazil (Eldorado do Sul), Ireland (Limerick), Malaysia (Penang) and China (Xiamen)
	• Purchasing activities are split into:
	  – Global procurement team in US (Texas) – contracting activities such as cost negotiation, contract terms and sourcing of major components
	  – Local manufacturing units – commerce-related activities such as purchase order release, delivery management, payment and sourcing of consumables

Sales	• Products are sold in 170 countries through sales offices in 34 countries
New product development	• New products are developed in US (Texas) • These are then customized by the regional offices to meet requirements such as local power supplies, language specific keyboards and documentation

EXHIBIT 2 Current organization activities

$ millions	1999	2000	2001	2002	2003	2004	2005	2006	2007
Revenues	18,243	25,265	31,888	31,168	35,404	41,444	49,205	55,908	57,420
Costs	14,137	20,047	25,445	25,661	29,055	33,892	40,190	45,958	47,904
Gross profit	4,106	5,218	6,443	5,507	6,349	7,552	9,015	9,950	9,516
Operating income	2,046	2,263	2,663	1,789	2,844	3,544	4,254	4,347	3,070
Net income	38	188	531	(58)	183	180	191	227	275

EXHIBIT 3 Financial performance, 1990–2007

Key to Dell's success is how it manages its supply chain. Products and information flow through a variety of relationships and partnerships (*Exhibit 5*) and across a number of regions (*Exhibit 6*). It collaborates closely with suppliers and bases procurement decisions on four criteria: cost (30 per cent weighting), quality conformance, service and flexibility (70 per cent weighting). Kevin Kettler, chief technology officer at Dell, explained that:

66 *Product features, functions and performance are important, but we also need to know if suppliers can hit our quality and volume requirements. They must be able to quickly diagnose and respond to any customer-related issue and, if necessary, trace it back to component-level. We have to work together to ensure we are both successful.* 99

Dell separates procurement activities, with cost negotiation, contract terms and sourcing of major components managed by the global team in Texas, and purchase order release, delivery management, payment and sourcing of consumables managed within the local manufacturing units. All suppliers must have a warehouse called a supplier logistics centre (SLC) located within a few miles of each Dell factory to reduce transport costs and lead times. In fact, some small component suppliers actually have premises within the Dell factory next to the production line. Several suppliers typically share an SLC and use it to either produce or stock components. Dell schedules its production lines every two hours and the SLC then supplies components to meet these requirements. Suppliers have to maintain 8–10 days of inventory for each component and

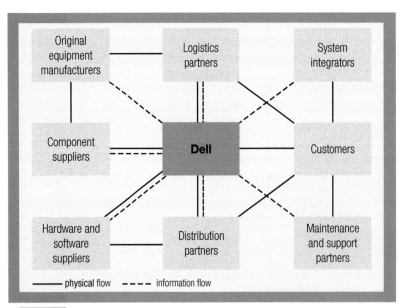

EXHIBIT 5 Supply chain

Aspect	Description

Product selection	• The website caters for different market segments: individuals, home office computers, small business, medium business, large business and public sector customers (government, educational and healthcare institutions)
	• Customers customize their order on the website by selecting:
	  – *Features*, such as processors, operating system, display screen, memory, hard drive, video card and audio card
	  – *Accessories*, such as printers, power options, TV tuner, batteries and carrying case
	  – *Software*, such as Microsoft Office
	  – *Services*, such as warranty, installation and internet
	• At every step, customers are warned if their shipping date could be delayed due to components unavailability

Sales order processing	• Orders are received by telephone, email or downloaded from internet every 15 minutes (on average 50 per cent are received through the internet) • Customer credit and order configuration is checked • Orders are sent to the order management system, which reviews component inventory, generates material requests and sends these to the relevant suppliers
Production planning	• All products are assembled to order • Once all components are available for an order, a barcode is printed and attached to the necessary components • Production lines in all factories around the world are rescheduled every two hours • Dell only assumes ownership of the components when they reach the assembly line • Once the production plan has been established, a message is sent to the relevant supplier logistics centre(s) telling it the components to deliver and which delivery dock they should go to • Suppliers are given 90 minutes to deliver components to the delivery dock and Dell has 30 minutes to move them from here to the assembly line before the next production cycle starts • Production is planned on a first-in-first-out basis • All orders are planned to be fulfilled within five days after receiving the customer order • All factories have flexible assembly lines that can be used for desktop PCs, notebooks or servers • Activities within a factory are rescheduled if defective units need to be replaced or if there is a large corporate order

Assembly	• Once all the components for an order are received at the delivery dock, the barcode is scanned and parts are sent on a conveyor belt to the assembly line
	• The assembly process consists of a number of steps:
	  1 Required computer system is assembled by a single worker in a single location
	  2 Necessary software is loaded onto it
	  3 Authenticity labels such as Intel and Microsoft are added
	  4 System is cleaned and placed into a box
	  5 Inspection is completed on a random selection of 10 per cent of the systems
	  6 A separate box containing the keyboard, documentation and mouse (all supplied by one subcontractor) is added to the existing box
	  7 The order is packaged and sent to distribution

Distribution	• Using the barcode on the box, orders are sorted depending on their final destination • Products are then shipped to the relevant distribution hub before travelling on to the final customer
After-sales service	• All subsequent technical and after-sales services is handled by Dell through its call centres

EXHIBIT 4 Examples of Dell's operating model

most suppliers replenish the SLC stock three times a week. In 2005, radio frequency identification (RFID) was installed in some facilities and some suppliers to allow tagged component kits to be routed through the production, ensuring the correct type of customization occurs and software is installed. This greatly reduced production stops, order cancellations and incorrect product shipping.

Region	Located in countries		% total supplier spend
US and Latin America	United States Mexico	Costa Rica Brazil	27
Europe	Germany Ireland	Italy Spain	1
Asia	China Indonesia Japan Korea Malaysia	Philippines Singapore Taiwan Thailand	72

EXHIBIT 6 Location of suppliers and level of spend

Dell maintains close supplier relationships and shares information regarding inventory levels, demand expectations and long-term plans. In turn, suppliers share information on capacity and new technology drivers. With some suppliers, Dell has purchase agreements in place to ensure there is adequate supply in high demand periods. Dell holds monthly sales and production planning meetings to review changing product strategies, competitive factors and constraints. Dell's marketing department generates 75 per cent accurate sales forecasts based on new product developments, purchasing patterns, budget cycles and seasonality trends, such as the end of a government department financial year, beginning of the academic year or the Christmas holiday period. Commodity teams break down the forecast to component level and create six-month forecasts that are updated every week and passed onto suppliers with a firm commitment for the following week's order. Suppliers immediately confirm their ability to meet this forecast and real-time requirements are placed on suppliers through the extranet site: valuechain.dell.com.

Dell holds a weekly lead time meeting with sales, marketing and supply chain executives to interpret demand trends, resolve supply issues and manage delivery lead times to customers. If component lead times increase, then orders are expedited, additional suppliers are brought in or customers are encouraged to buy substitute products. Within hours, the marketing team creates advertisements for computers with abundant components, which are then posted on the Dell and other popular websites. Similarly, if component inventory accumulates, then customers are provided with incentives to buy those products. Pricing is changed from week to week to reflect the balance between demand and supply, and lead times are updated on a daily basis.

Daily performance figures for each supplier against price, quality conformance, delivery speed and delivery reliability are posted on valuechain.dell.com to show a comparison within each component sector. Performance feedback and future expectations are outlined at quarterly supplier meetings. Based on their performance, suppliers are awarded a percentage of Dell's purchases for the next quarter. Thirty of its 250 suppliers are used to meet 75 per cent of the demand for its 3,500 components and, based on the previous year's performance, 'Best Supplier' awards are given at the annual supplier conference. Supplier engineers often work with Dell's new product development teams to understand customer requirements, develop products and solve problems. Collaborative supplier projects are also used to raise awareness of working hours, health and safety and environmental issues and improve business processes.

Competitive pressures

By 2006, Dell had been successful for a number of years and it couldn't seem to put a foot wrong. Its worldwide PC shipments had grown threefold in the previous seven years to 38 million units for the year (*Exhibit 7*). Then suddenly competitive pressures caused market share to drop (*Exhibit 8*). HP took over as number one with a very different strategy to Dell by focusing on product innovation (*Exhibit 9*), outsourcing product assembly and selling both directly and through retailers. Customers could order products through HP's

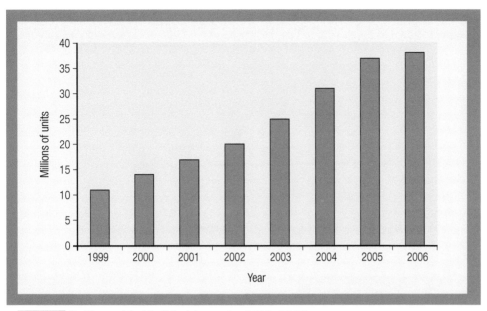

EXHIBIT 7 Dell's worldwide PC shipments, 1999–2006

internet site, but the majority of orders come from retailers through its extranet site. Both types of order are assembled and delivered by one of its manufacturing partners within five days. Retail partners forecast their own demand, manage their own stock and provide a variety of technical and after-sales services. HP develops long relationships with a few suppliers, selected for their performance against price, quality conformance, security, service, capacity and technology. In order to get competitive prices, it has more than one supplier for each product, but 85 per cent of components come from only 35 suppliers. HP buys components centrally to achieve economies of scale and then sells them on to its manufacturing partners at a slightly higher price.

HP's success meant that many analysts were now questioning Dell's strategy. Matt Raine explains:

66 *Although Dell has low inventory and distribution costs, it has high support costs to service customer requests, queries and orders. Its competitors have offloaded these tasks to their distribution partners and retailers and they are now also benefiting from falling component prices and automated manufacturing. Customers increasingly want to touch and feel a product, buy it and then walk away with it.*

You can't do this with a Dell product. On top of this, Dell's wide product range results in diseconomies of scale while the product features aren't innovative and there are no after-sales service centres. 99

Vendor	1995	2001	2004	2006	2007
HP	4	7	16	17	19
Dell	3	13	18	18	15
Lenovo	–	–	2	6	8
Acer	–	–	4	5	8
Toshiba	3	3	3	4	4
Apple	8	3	2	2	3
Compaq	10	11	–	–	–
Fujitsu Siemens	5	5	6	–	–
IBM	6	6	6	–	–
Gateway	2	2	2	2	–
Other	59	50	41	46	43
Total (million units)	89	122	178	235	269

NOTES
1 HP acquired Compaq in 2002.
2 IBM sold its PC business to Lenovo in 2005.
3 Acer acquired Gateway in 2007.

EXHIBIT 8 Comparison of market share for major PC vendors, 1995–2007

Performance	1997	2000	2003	2004	2005	2006	2007
Gross margin (%)							
Apple	21	28	29	29	30	30	35
Dell	23	21	19	19	18	17	19
Hewlett-Packard (HP)	38	31	29	27	25	26	24
R&D/sales (%)							
Apple	12	5	8	6	4	4	4
Dell	1	2	1	1	1	1	1
Hewlett-Packard (HP)	7	5	5	4	3	3	3

NOTE: Based on data from company financial reports.

EXHIBIT 9 Gross margin and R&D as a percentage of sales for Apple, Dell and HP, 1997–2007

New direction

Shortly after being reappointed as CEO in 2007, Michael Dell put in place a new executive team and brought in Michael Cannon as head of global operations organization to consolidate manufacturing, procurement and supply chain activities. He immediately started to integrate supply chains, eliminate overlapping activities, laid off 1,000 employees in existing factories and set up new plants in India, Poland and Brazil. Dell also started to move away from its direct-only model by opening retail stores in Dallas, New York and Russia and launched a 'PartnerDirect' programme with a number of 'value added resellers' in North America (Wal-Mart, Sam's Club and Macy's), Europe (Carphone Warehouse, Carrefour, BestBuy and Staples), Asia (Bic Camera Inc. and Gartner Group) and online (Shoplet.com). Customers can see products, touch them and place orders, but cannot take them away as no inventory is actually held here. However, some resellers will assemble products themselves and install software to ensure they are delivered in five days.

Dell's new strategy received a mixed response. Matt Raine explains:

❝ For years Dell didn't have to change because it was so successful, but it is now finally listening to its customers. Indeed the market responded well in the last quarter of 2007 as PC shipments grew for the first time in a year. ❞

However, others feel Dell is taking a big risk by moving away from the strategy that has made it so successful in the past. As Marc Auerbach comments:

❝ This represents a significant change and I'm not sure its supply chain is geared up for it. Inventories need to be managed differently and its cost advantage is weakened. Any company jumping from a direct to a channel-based model cannot expect a soft landing. This model caused so many problems for Dell in the early 1990s, why should it be any different now? Partnering with retailers that have strong established strategic relationships with its competitors – and remember the problems caused when Dell backed out last time – doesn't seem like a good idea to me. A recent online poll found 45 per cent of retailers were most profitable by partnering with HP, 15 per cent with IBM and only 13 per cent with Dell. It doesn't take a genius to work out what's going to happen. ❞

FABRItex

The room bore all the hallmarks of a long meeting. The Fabritex management team relaxed in their chairs. Empty coffee cups patterned the boardroom table. Not for the first time Charles Franklin, the company CEO, reflected on the quality of the business-based discussions and the noticeable financial improvements over the last 18 months.

✨ *Well I think we're agreed. Next year we'll target Pearlwear as one of our major areas for sales growth.' Charles glanced around and got the nods of approval he was anticipating.*

Good. However, before we finish for today, let us review the issues around how we will grow our share of the Pearlwear business.

Charles looked towards his sales and marketing director. 'Perhaps you can start us off, John. ✨

Background

Fabritex is part of the Wardman Group which manufactures a range of textiles for a wide variety of fashion and industrial applications, as well as having interests in engineering, furniture and finishings. Because of intense competition from Southeast Asia, particularly on price, the UK textile industry had undergone major reorganization and much of the overcapacity in the sector had now been squeezed out.

Fabritex focuses on knitted fabrics for garment manufacturers, mainly for lingerie. These customers in turn sell either to major retailers or through independent outlets. Some of the garment manu-

facturers sell under their own brand name but many are making products to retailers' specifications to be sold under a retailer's own name.

Much of the development of new fabrics is done by manufacturers like Fabritex or even prompted by suggestions from raw material suppliers. Fabritex believes its strength lies in developing innovative fabrics that look good and perform well technically. Even when cus

tomers like a supplier's new fabric design, this does not guarantee that supplier all its business, particularly over the longer term. It is common for customers to show designs to their other suppliers, with the intention of dual or triple sourcing, a commercial practice accepted within the industry.

The life of a particular fabric can vary widely from a few months to several years. It all depends on the popularity of the material with the final consumer. As part of the fashion industry, the search for a new and different feel or look is a constant task, essential to a company's future growth and prosperity.

After a struggle in the early days to become profitable, Fabritex has increased profits to the point where it is above average for the Group. Sales at £45 million have grown rapidly in the last two years and similar growth levels are forecast over the next few years. The management team believes that the basic operations capability is in place which will underpin the continued sales growth. This view has the support of the Group but funds for investment are limited and Fabritex still has to demon-

This case was prepared by Terry Hill (University of Oxford) and R. Lily. It is intended for class discussion and not as an illustration of good or bad management. © AMD Publishing.

strate that it can outperform its competition rather than just hold its own.

Marketing

Fabritex regards its market as a number of distinct segments that reflect differences in product, geography and type of customer. Customers are described as 'branded', selling under their own product name, or 'nonbranded'. Customers are also grouped by garment type and divided into lingerie and outerwear (see *Exhibit 1*) and they can appear in several segments. The product distinction relates to the way the fabric is knitted, either warp or weft.

Many segments have a degree of seasonality associated with the type of garment in which the fabric is used. If a garment is well received, repeat orders for fabrics may come very quickly. Consequently, forward demand is not easy to predict, particularly for new fabrics.

Segment		Current year forecast (£m)		Next year forecast (£m)	
			Sub-total		Sub-total
UK lingerie warp knit	Branded	12.3	15.9	15.9	19.5
	Non-branded	3.6		3.6	
UK lingerie weft knit	Branded	15.3	16.2	15.6	16.5
	Non-branded	0.9		0.9	
Export lingerie warp knit	Branded	5.4	5.4	6.3	6.3
	Non-branded	0.0		0.0	
Export lingerie weft knit	Branded	0.9	2.1	1.2	2.4
	Non-branded	1.2		1.2	
UK outerwear	Branded	0.9	4.2	0.9	4.2
	Non-branded	3.3		3.3	
Export outerwear	Branded	0.6	2.1	1.2	2.7
	Non-branded	1.5		1.5	
Total			45.9		51.6

EXHIBIT 1 Sales forecast by segment

Responding to Charles Franklin's request, John Watson (the sales and marketing director) pulled himself forward, shuffled through the pile of papers in front of him and began:

66 *The segment in which we have chosen to grow is UK lingerie warp knit which currently generates £15.9 million sales, about 35 per cent of our total sales revenue. Within this segment Pearlwear sales total £4.2 million. As you are aware, Pearlwear is a premium company with an internationally recognized brand name with manufacturing plants in Europe and Southeast Asia. Pearlwear sales and its share of its markets are both growing. Where it places those additional sales and grows capacity is in part, as you would expect, related to the performance of its manufacturing plants. Initially we intend to grow our share with Pearlwear's UK factory, which we estimate to place purchase orders to the value of some £30 million, of which we have only £4.2 million, or 14 per cent. The opportunity to grow is, therefore, realistic.*

The Pearlwear brand name is key in selling its products and that has implications for us. We have to remain competitive on price to avoid losing share but the name of the game is conformance quality.

If we have any significant problems with meeting the specification of our fabrics, then Pearlwear will take its business elsewhere.

So far our two companies have worked well together over a number of years and we appear to have a good understanding of its requirements. Also, the management team at Pearlwear's UK plant is committed to developing sound customer–supplier relations. And this is by no means a lip service statement. Pearlwear is keen to discuss problems and has, on a number of occasions, cooperated on changes that have affected the way both companies work. If we are proactive in those developments, we will undoubtedly be able to grow our share next year.

Pearlwear currently splits its business between three or four main suppliers. Some fabrics are allocated to only one company for the life of the fabric and some are ordered from two or more suppliers. Pearlwear seems to be happy with its current suppliers and overall share has not changed much, even though demand from the UK plant has increased significantly over the last five years. We continue, however, to be very much the minority supplier, taking about 14 per cent of Pearlwear's total business.

Where we are the sole supplier for a fabric, Pearlwear is absolutely dependent on us. The annual sales from these 'sole supplier' fabrics are £2.7 million and should grow by about 10 per cent next year. Responding to short lead times on sales orders is important but even more crucial is meeting our promises on delivery. Nothing gets Pearlwear more upset than having to reorganize its production schedules due to missing agreed delivery promises. **"**

John paused for a sip of cold coffee and noticed the wry look from Mike Stewart, the operations director, after his last comment. Mike said:

" We do recognize the delivery issue, John, but from an operations point of view the pattern of orders is very unpredictable. Some of these fabrics have regular orders. Demand for other fabrics keeps going over time but we never know when we will see the next order. This affects our response, for example on raw material inventory. And short runs do reduce our capacity due to changeover losses. **"**

John Watson nodded and continued:

" When Pearlwear sources a fabric from two or more suppliers, the company that wins the lion's share is usually the one that can supply to the shortest promise date for an initial order. Of course, thereafter a supplier must hit its delivery promises consistently. Failure to deliver on time can affect our share of jointly sourced products. Mike's point about a mix of regular and irregular orders applies to these fabrics as well, although probably to a lesser extent.

Price can also influence the volume split when a fabric is running regularly with joint suppliers. At the moment I estimate Pearlwear's total purchases of fabrics that are shared by two or more suppliers are £5.1 million per annum and we have 30 per cent of this. The spend should grow by 10 per cent next year.

The fabrics that are only sourced from one of our competitors constitute the biggest part of Pearlwear's annual purchases at £22.2 million. Some of these fabrics are reaching the end of their life cycle and I think purchases in this category will decline next year, perhaps to £20.4 million. If we are selective there may be opportunities on the higher volume fabrics to become a second supplier. The attraction to Pearlwear would be to gain more insurance on obtaining short delivery lead times. The usual reason we do not have a share is that we have not provided the design and performance characteristics of particular fabrics for which Pearlwear is looking. On occasions we believe we can but we have not been close enough to Pearlwear's designers to convince them that we have the technical know-how. Designers have their favourite suppliers, for whatever reason, so cultivating that relationship is important. So, the way forward is to carefully target some fabrics and get our technical people working closely with theirs.

Also, we may have to sweeten our move a bit on price to get them through the hassle of approving us. My initial assessment suggests that next year, if we really go for it, we could gain perhaps 7 per cent of the sales that currently go solely to one of our competitors. But it will mean allocating a special team in the technical department to this end. Finally we need to consider new fabrics. Next year about £1.2 million of Pearlwear's purchases will come from fabrics currently under development. The value of these fabrics can grow substantially in later years if they include some real winners. To get our slice of this business (we should be looking at half), the criteria are the same as those we have just considered. First, the fabrics must look good and perform well. Second, if the designer is sympathetic to Fabritex and works with us on the development, clearly we have a better chance of supplying a production fabric. And on some, attractive prices can then help tip the balance. **"**

John paused and looked round his colleagues.

66 *If we can achieve all those objectives, we will take a quarter of the Pearlwear business in the UK lingerie warp knit segment. And that accounts for most of the growth required in our overall business forecast.* 99

Charles Franklin thanked John for his clear overview of the position and asked him to circulate a statement to everyone. He then turned to his operations director:

66 *Also, Mike, I would like you to tell us how we are performing against the operations issues raised. After that we can start to review the technical situation.* 99

Operations

The basic manufacturing task is knitting the fabric and then dyeing it. There are two knitting processes known as warp and weft. They use different machine types, giving different fabric characteristics. The dyeing is done at another plant in the group located 12 miles away. Part of the dye plant is dedicated to Fabritex's requirements, with the remaining capacity being used to process fabric from other customers outside the Wardman Group.

A fabric is described by the specification that identifies the knitted fabric and the 'shade' that results from dyeing.

Knitting times for fabrics vary substantially. Some typical knitting times for Pearlwear orders are shown in *Exhibit 2*. The knitting machines require skilled staff support to complete a set-up on a fabric change. Set-up or changeover times for warp knitting average four hours. (A set-up or changeover is where the required quantity for one fabric is completed, the machine is stopped and then reset to make the next fabric. During this set-up or changeover, no saleable output is produced.) The knitting machines are manned over three shifts covering 24 hours per day, five days per week. Overtime at weekends is commonly worked to supplement capacity.

Order #	Specification[1]	Quantity (metres)	Knitting time (hours)[2]
43651	PN503	250	140.8
43600	PN522	500	289.9
43360	PN523	200	96.4
44754	PN704	1200	578.3
43671	PN713	450	236.8
43900	SA12	1100	354.8
44826	SA9	400	190.5
44849	SK24	900	371.1
44852	SK28	400	142.9
46096	SK33	2600	298.9
44347	SK51	74	41.1
44784	TD468	700	53.5

NOTES
1 The term 'specification' identifies the knitted fabric before dyeing.
2 The knitting time includes an allowance for set-up.

EXHIBIT 2 Sample of knitting times for Pearlwear fabrics

Knitted fabric is called greige and is held in store until the required batch size for dyeing has been reached. No two knitting machines produce exactly the same fabric so dye batches unique to a knitting machine are usually accumulated before dyeing is commenced. The dyeing process determines the shade of a fabric. Setting up the process consists of loading the greige onto beams, which is done offline, and loading the beams onto the machine which only takes about 20 minutes. Some colour sequences require the dyeing machine to be cleaned before use which takes another two hours. Typical dye times are seven hours for white and nine hours for coloured shades but about 10 per cent of dyed fabrics are unsatisfactory and have to be redyed. These times include an overall allowance for cleaning where necessary. The dye plant works a basic 24 hours per day for four days per week. Four dyeing units are used solely for Fabritex work.

The dyed fabric is shipped back to the knitting plant where it is inspected and finished before delivery to the customer. On average this takes about six days. For new or difficult fabrics the customer may require a sample of the fabric before approval is given for delivery.

Fabrics are normally made to order. On receipt of a customer enquiry a promise date is given based on knowledge of the fabric, raw material availability and current knitting loads. The scheduling system is based on actual times for completing past orders. When a customer places an order, it is scheduled on the system. Losses in the knitting and dyeing processes can be high and unpredictable, and the volume of the final fabric is unlikely to match exactly the order quantity.

Some key customers place orders for greige stock prior to orders for final fabrics. Marketing is also allowed to place orders for greige stock to cover special situations agreed by the management team. An example would be in anticipation of a large order where the required knitting capacity would mean an unacceptably long lead time to the customer. If marketing misread the situation, Fabritex can end up with unwanted greige stock to be gradually disposed of at lower prices.

The way forward

Charles Franklin was determined to give his team a strong lead at what he saw as a crucial stage in Fabritex's development.

I have a lot of confidence in the group of people sitting round this table and in the people out there working for us. We have done well in recent years in growing the business. Now is the time to be ambitious. Now is the time to build on our success and deliver a further big increase in sales revenue. We can show the Wardman Group that Fabritex is the place in which to invest for the future. Pearlwear is a major customer and represents a big opportunity. Our two companies have developed together over a number of years. We know the people in Pearlwear and the way they like to do business.

Competition for the Pearlwear business is and will continue to be tough. But it is time we moved from being a minority supplier. Our target must be to secure half the Pearlwear business. We have to do this by improving our communications at all levels and by fast and reliable response to their orders. We currently have the manufacturing capacity to respond. This way we can drive the sales revenue from the current £4m to something close to £15m.

Following the meeting Mike Stewart set about collecting some information for his operations analysis which is given in *Exhibits 3–6*.

Specification	Estimated share of Pearlwear spend (per cent total)	Specification	Estimated share of Pearlwear spend (per cent total)
PN503	1002	SA42	0
PN522	21	SA45	0
PN523	100	SK24	42
PN640	0	SK28	29
PN704	100	SK33	100
PN713	100	SK51	100
SA12	100	TD680	0
SA9	100	TD468	32

NOTES
1 The table shows the sales and marketing director's estimates of Fabritex's share of the Pearlwear spend on a selection of fabrics.
2 100 per cent of the total means Fabritex is the sole supplier and 0 per cent of the total means Fabritex does not supply the fabric.

EXHIBIT 5 Fabritex share of Pearlwear spend by fabric[1]

Fabrics ordered on an irregular basis	Fabrics ordered on a regular basis
PN503	SK51
PN523	PN522
SA9	PN704
SK28	PN713
SK33	SA12
	SK24
	SK51
	TD468

NOTE: The classification of Pearlwear fabrics was made by the Fabritex operations planner and will change over time.

EXHIBIT 6 Regularity of Pearlwear orders

Order #	Specification	Shade	Quantity (metres)	Order value (£s)	Date order received		Customer required delivery	
					Week #	Day #	Week #	Day #
42322	SK28	Black 1	424	1823	10	3	15	2
43360	PN523	Beige	200	736	16	4	33	1
43600	PN522	White 0	500	2600	13	2	18	3
43651	PN503	Beige 4	250	920	2	2	7	4
43671	PN713	Beige 4	450	1665	21	2	29	4
43893	PN522	White 0	600	3120	19	3	25	1
43900	SA12	White 0	1100	5280	7	4	16	1
43904	SK28	Black 1	600	2844	4	3	15	3
43906	SK28	Champagne 73	400	1896	18	1	29	1
43924	SA9	White 0	330	1584	10	1	13	1
43985	PN704	White 0	700	2499	4	4	8	1
44207	PN522	White 0	1600	8320	25	4	33	4
44212	SA12	Black 1	300	1482	16	4	23	2
44213	SK24	White 0	800	3680	22	3	27	4
44214	SK24	Black 1	750	3555	22	2	31	2
44224	SA9	Black 1	300	1482	36	3	42	1
44347	SK51	Beige 4	74	204	16	4	21	3
44354	SK33	White 0	555	1487	15	3	28	1
44643	SK51	White 0	778	2085	15	4	22	1
44649	SK51	White 0	178	477	33	3	38	2
44650	SK51	White 0	709	1900	23	2	30	1
44662	SK33	White 0	709	1900	14	3	20	4
44663	SK33	White 0	140	375	28	3	32	1
44674	SK51	White 0	555	1487	33	1	37	3
44687	SK51	White 0	1993	5341	18	3	23	4
44754	PN704	White 0	1200	4284	13	2	23	1
44755	PN704	Black 1	100	368	18	2	28	1
44784	TD468	White 0	700	5054	22	3	24	4
44825	SA12	White 0	1000	4800	19	1	22	4
44826	SA9	Champagne 73	400	1976	23	1	34	1
44827	SA9	Black 1	500	2470	30	4	34	2
44832	SA12	Black 1	400	1976	34	3	38	1
44849	SK24	White 0	900	4140	14	4	20	2
44852	SK28	Champagne 73	400	1720	28	4	34	2
44935	SA12	Champagne 73	500	2470	31	5	35	3

cont'd

Order #	Specification	Shade	Quantity (metres)	Order value (£s)	Date order received		Customer required delivery	
					Week #	Day #	Week #	Day #
44952	SK33	White 0	1993	5341	5	4	16	1
44976	SA12	Champagne 73	300	1482	32	5	40	1
45060	TD468	Black 1	150	1116	35	1	39	1
45074	SA9	Champagne 73	150	741	17	1	23	3
45075	SK24	Black 1	200	948	19	1	21	3
45175	SK24	White 0	400	1840	34	4	41	1
46096	SK33	White 0	2600	6968	8	4	19	1
2611	SK51	White 0	2400	6432	22	2	27	1
2612	SK51	White 0	2400	6432	13	1	19	2
2613	SK51	White 0	2400	6432	20	4	28	2
2614	SK51	White 0	2800	7504	29	4	38	4
2669	SK33	White 0	1400	3752	15	2	19	4
	SK24	Black 1	500	2370	13	2	18	4
	SK24	New Black	700	3318	28	3	34	4
	PN503	Beige 4	200	736	4	2	15	3
	SA12	Black 1	1050	5187	18	1	26	2
	SA12	Champagne 73	350	1729	23	3	32	2
	PN704	White 0	300	1071	20	1	29	2
	PN522	Black 1	500	2675	16	1	20	3
	TD468	White 0	700	5054	28	3	35	1
	SA12	White 0	1000	4800	12	4	17	3

NOTE: Fabritex uses week numbers 1 to 52 and day numbers 1 to 5 only.

EXHIBIT 3 Sample of Pearlwear orders showing required delivery times

Order #	Quality	Shade	Fabritex promised delivery		Fabritex actual delivery	
			Week #	Day #	Week #	Day #
42322	SK28	Black 1	18	1	20	1
43360	PN523	Beige	39	1	44	3
43600	PN522	White 0	22	3	26	1
43651	PN503	Beige 4	12	3	23	1
43671	PN713	Beige 4	39	2	43	4
43893	PN522	White 0	25	1	29	1
43900	SA12	White 0	18	4	24	2
43904	SK28	Black 1	18	1	20	3
43906	SK28	Champagne 73	29	1	32	2
43924	SA9	White 0	16	2	21	2
43985	PN704	White 0	9	3	21	3
44207	PN522	White 0	38	1	43	1
44212	SA12	Black 1	26	4	25	4
44213	SK24	White 0	32	3	33	4
44214	SK24	Black 1	35	3	35	1
44224	SA9	Black 1	44	2	42	5
44347	SK51	Beige 4	21	3	22	1
44354	SK33	White 0	29	3	33	4
44643	SK51	White 0	22	1	25	1
44649	SK51	White 0	39	1	42	2
44650	SK51	White 0	30	1	29	4
44662	SK33	White 0	22	1	23	4
44663	SK33	White 0	34	4	34	3
44674	SK51	White 0	38	4	41	4
44687	SK51	White 0	23	4	27	2
44754	PN704	White 0	23	1	22	1
44755	PN704	Black 1	28	1	27	1
44784	TD468	White 0	26	1	32	1
44825	SA12	White 0	25	3	28	1
44826	SA9	Champagne 73	34	1	41	3
44827	SA9	Black 1	38	3	37	1
44832	SA12	Black 1	42	2	40	5
44849	SK24	White 0	24	3	24	1
44852	SK28	Champagne 73	37	3	37	4
44935	SA12	Champagne 73	35	3	33	5
44952	SK33	White 0	17	2	22	1

cont'd

Order #	Quality	Shade	Fabritex promised delivery		Fabritex actual delivery	
			Week #	Day #	Week #	Day #
44976	SA12	Champagne 73	42	4	40	3
45060	TD468	Black 1	38	4	38	4
45074	SA9	Champagne 73	23	3	26	2
45075	SK24	Black 1	22	1	28	3
45175	SK24	White 0	40	4	40	2
46096	SK33	White 0	20	2	26	4
2611	SK51	White 0	27	1	29	5
2612	SK51	White 0	19	2	23	2
2613	SK51	White 0	28	2	30	3
2614	SK51	White 0	38	4	40	5
2669	SK33	White 0	25	2	23	1
42302/1	SK24	Black 1	28	1	30	5
43231/1	SK24	New Black	34	1	38	2
43651/1	PN503	Beige 4	15	4	25	1
43901/2	SA12	Black 1	31	3	32	2
43902/1	SA12	Champagne 73	32	2	36	5
43985/2	PN704	White 0	31	1	34	5
44075/1	PN522	Black 1	25	2	31	3
44784/1	TD468	White 0	36	5	35	5
44825/1	SA12	White 0	22	3	23	2

NOTES

1 Fabritex uses week numbers 1 to 52 and day numbers 1 to 5 only.

2 The orders above are typical Pearlwear orders over a sample period.

EXHIBIT 4 Sample of Pearlwear orders showing promised and actual delivery times

Curt Muller sat back. He had just finished analysing last month's performance summary for the two manufacturing units, a review that confirmed the significant disparity between their results. After discussions, initiatives and promises, the Norwich plant's performance was still well short of target. In addition, this was in marked contrast to the Edinburgh plant, which seemed to go from strength to strength. The reasons for this difference were not at all apparent. In fact, the similarity of investments and approaches undertaken at each site made comparisons easier to make and contrasts easier to conclude. The problem was to identify the fundamental nature of this difference, which was marked in itself and difficult to understand given the circumstances involved.

Background

Hoffmann Tobacco is a wholly owned subsidiary of Teison Industries, Inc., a North American holding company with interests in papermaking, printing and textiles, besides the tobacco industry. With its head office based in Virginia, the Teison Group has subsidiaries throughout North America, Europe and Australasia. Hoffmann Tobacco (HT) has two manufacturing plants within the UK (besides others in continental Europe) that produce cigarettes for both domestic and overseas markets. It was recognized that while imported cigarettes would have some appeal in overseas markets, they would inevitably lose out to other brands (particularly local products) on the basis of price. In addition, a climate of reducing demand for cigarettes

in the UK and other traditional markets added to the pressure for HT to offer a wider range of products and also to reduce costs wherever possible.

Marketing

Due to the growing recognition of the harmful effects of smoking on a person's health, the level of cigarette sales in many countries had fallen appreciably. The tobacco industry, therefore, had been forced to rethink its strategy in order to adjust for the loss of sales revenue and profit that had resulted.

In addition, the move from short to king-size cigarettes, the introduction of cut-price cigarettes from R. J. Reynolds, Philip Morris, manufacturers in Germany and own-brand labels added to the pressures for additional investment to meet new brand requirements and essential reductions in cost.

HT's marketing strategy was to increase market share at home (in an attempt to maintain current sales revenue in what was recognized to be a declining market) while increasing exports abroad. The principal target areas for growth in export sales were the Middle East, Africa, Asia and the European duty-free segments.

In broad terms, HT's marketing strategy had three principal features:

1 **Product quality:** to ensure that the product was manufactured and presented at the highest level of quality, in terms of tobacco

This case study was written by Terry Hill (University of Oxford). It is intended for class discussion and not as an example of good or bad management. © AMD Publishing.

blend, the feel and look of the cigarette itself and packaging, as a way of maintaining its position.

2 **Price:** the decline in sales had resulted in surplus manufacturing capacity within the UK cigarette industry as a whole which, together with the low-priced European cigarette imports mentioned earlier, had placed significant emphasis on the need for cost reduction. In addition, export sales had similar pressures on price due to the nature of these markets and the low-priced alternatives manufactured domestically in each of the countries or regions in question.

3 **Product range:** in response to the fact that while cigarettes were bought for many reasons, one of those clearly identified was image. Although this was in part related to product quality, the need to offer a wide range of products was a most important way of increasing both HT's share of the UK market and sales in current and future export markets.

One further feature of the UK market also emphasized many of the changes taking place. The continued growth in sales to multiple retailers (such as Tesco and Sainsbury) at the expense of the small retail outlets meant an increasing squeeze on prices similar to that which these retailers had successfully applied to food and other products in the past. This factor further emphasized the need to reduce costs in order for HT to remain competitive within its markets.

Operations

One part of the total response to declining cigarette sales and increasing competition had been a productivity improvement drive in the key manufacturing areas. In this context, the company and the Tobacco Workers Union (TWU) agreed a whole series of changes that needed both worker cooperation and substantial capital investment. The aim of the programme was to help the company survive in a competitive market while maintaining real corporate earnings, especially in future years. The changes were a combination of restructuring, process investments and changes in working methods and manning levels.

Restructuring

In the context of declining sales for cigarettes, the need to improve the links between the marketing and operations functions was well appreciated. The previous structure had formalized the separation of these two parts of the business and was recognized as an important source of liaison, communication and coordination problems.

In order to improve these important links within the business, a policy decision was taken to allocate those products to be made at each plant in such a way as to achieve greater product identity within the business as a whole. This orientation also needed to reflect the capacity requirements at each plant and was undertaken over a period of three years, as shown in *Exhibit 1*. Completed last year, it was agreed by all the principal functions concerned to have brought a significant improvement to the working relations, particularly between the marketing and operations functions.

Process investment

Multifunctional task forces were established in both plants to undertake a review of the manufacturing and distribution activities. Their broad terms of reference were to recommend the best process mix, manning levels and working practices to achieve the required production levels with associated lower costs. Considerable work was undertaken to identify the technical suitability of available processes that incorporated the latest designs and controls and offered significant improvements in terms of throughput speeds.

The principal investment proposals concerned the secondary stage of the manufacturing process, that involved the making and packing of the cigarettes themselves. The primary stage was concerned with preparation and blending, which were completed prior to the secondary stages: see *Exhibit 2* 'An overview of the cigarette-making process'. The throughput speeds of cigarette-making and packing machines had increased considerably since the late 1960s. The new generation of Protos could now run at speeds of 8,000 cigarettes per minute (cpm) compared to the current Molins makers, which worked at speeds of 5,000 cpm. In addition, the Molins HLP4 and the GD packers gave corresponding uplifts in throughput speeds. Finally, the proposals also called for the introduction of a number of conveyor/reservoir systems with elevator arrangements that were designed to link a maker and packer together. With reservoir capacity giving storage space in excess of 50,000 cigarettes, the system comprised an automatically controlled conveyor that linked the two parts of the process together (see *Exhibit 2*, which gives a brief description of the cigarette-making process). As cigarette makers have much higher throughput speeds than packers, then the basic concept of linking one maker to one packer can be extended by additional conveyors enabling the linking together of machines of different speeds in order to achieve desired levels of matching and the resulting improved overall use of the capital investments involved.

Factory location	Brand type		Percentage product by volume each year		
			1	2	3[4]
Edinburgh	Virginia Mild	UK	33	47	61
		Europe duty free[1]	10	21	32
	Hoffmann Special		20	14	7
	Hoffmann Special (plain)		25	15	–
	Other brands[2]		12	3	–
	Total		100	100	100
Norwich	Virginia Mild	UK	35	17	10
		Europe duty free[1]	18	10	–
	Hoffmann Special 10s		15	18	19
	Hoffmann Special		16	15	17
	Hoffmann Special 50s		3	4	3
	Gold Tip		6	10	14
	Hoffmann Mild[3]		–	3	3
	Hoffmann Special (plain)		–	9	16
	Mild leaf		–	3	4
	Other brands[2]		7	11	14
	Total		100	100	100

NOTES
1 Europe duty free is packed in both 200s and 300s.
2 The 'other brands' category at Edinburgh totalled 6 brand types in year 1. This category at Norwich totalled 6 brand types in year 1 and 17 brand types by year 3.
3 The Hoffmann Mild brand is produced as both a plain and tipped cigarette.
4 Year 3 is the current year to which the case study relates.

EXHIBIT 1 Volume of production by brand type at each factory over the three-year transition period

Growing the tobacco leaf

Tobacco plants are grown in five main areas of the world: Asia, North America, Europe, South America and Africa. There are three principal varieties of tobacco (Virginia, Burley and Oriental) which are harvested differently. With both Virginia and Oriental plants, the leaves are picked selectively, starting from the bottom upward. This allows each leaf to ripen fully on the plant. The Burley plant, however, is harvested as a whole so leaves higher on the plant have less ripening time than the lower leaves. Cigarette companies take a mix of different tobaccos and blend them to meet their own product specifications in line with particular market segments. HT's recipes can use over 50 different grades of leaf, from all varieties of tobacco, to formulate a single blend, and leaves from up to three different crop years will be blended to even out any variabilities in flavour.

Primary processing

When the blender believes the tobacco samples are ready for processing, the matured crop is brought into a cigarette-making plant (such as HT's Edinburgh and Norwich plants discussed in this case study). The primary processes comprise a number of steps. The dried and compressed leaves are first conditioned (to make them pliable) by steam moisturizing, then mixed in appropriate blend proportions in a long blending bin. The blended leaves (or lamina) then go to a compressing chamber, where they are sliced into finely cut tobacco and dried once more. The tobacco leaf stem is separately processed, being blended in a similar manner to, but cut more finely than, the leaf. After drying, lamina and stem are then blended together in precise quantities. Flavouring (such as menthol) may be added at this point in the process. The cut tobacco is now ready.

Secondary processing

The cut tobacco, paper, filters, tipping paper and packaging are all controlled by very advanced production systems. Correct amounts of tobacco blend pass into the machines through airlocks and are combined and spread onto moving belts. The tobacco is sucked into a continuous rod, meets the paper and is sealed into shape and printed with the repeated blend name in line with the desired length of the eventual cigarette. Electronic weighing heads ensure that every cigarette contains its precise weight of tobacco. The continuous length is then cut into individual lengths, two of which are then joined to a double length filter and fused together with tipping paper for a fraction of a second. Cutters then halve the filter, and pairs of cigarettes are conveyed to the end of the line, with faulty cigarettes being eliminated by automatic scanners. Here they are loaded onto trolleys for taking to the packing area (see *Exhibit 3*). It is this transfer to the packing units that part of the new investments at Edinburgh and Norwich are designed to overcome. With these changes, cigarettes are conveyed directly to the packing units through the reservoir arrangement described in the case study narrative. *Exhibit 3* provides an outline of the process for cigarette making. The link to packing machines would be made at the end of the process shown in this outline diagram.

As some 85 per cent of all cigarettes made are filter tip, the filter-making process is an integral part of the second processing unit. The material is processed from a bulk feed to achieve specified filter consistency. The long tube of filter is then cut into rods equal to the requirement for two cigarettes in line with particular specifications. These are then transferred to the cigarette maker, as shown in *Exhibit 3*, and fused to the cigarettes as described earlier.

The final stage is packing, where cigarettes are automatically packed, foil-wrapped and cartoned for delivery.

EXHIBIT 2 An overview of the cigarette-making process

The process investments centred around the provision of two major savings:

- high-speed makers and packers that would reduce the number of machines required for a given production volume and hence reduce the direct operator, indirect support and overhead requirements throughout

- secondary process investments to allow further reductions in direct and indirect employees by mechanizing certain tasks and reducing the manning levels involved in taking part-finished products from one process stage to the next.

Exhibit 4 summarizes the present product-mix characteristics at both plants, while *Exhibits 5* and *6* list the current secondary equipment in use at Edinburgh and Norwich, the advantages to be gained and the anticipated reduction in costs.

Current position

By involving the employees and trade union representatives at an early stage and continuing this high level of involvement throughout, the necessary reorganization and manpower reductions that had ensued were completed without any signs of animosity or disagreement from those involved. The overt and genuine wish to involve those concerned in the rationale for the proposed changes was built on many years of increasing openness displayed within the company. The result was that the relatively complex sets of arrangements were duly completed on time and the expected reductions in factory-based staff (in excess of 500) were achieved.

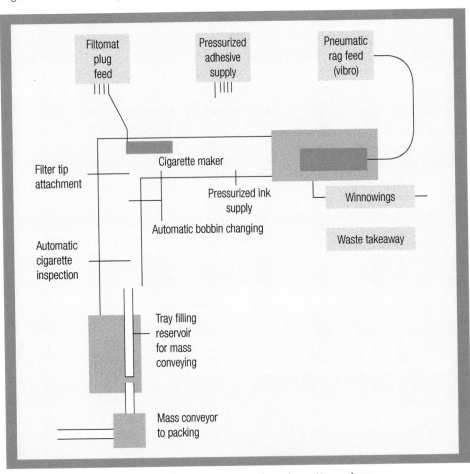

EXHIBIT 3 The layout for a typical new generation cigarette maker

HT's current range of products reflects its need to increase the number of cigarette types as part of its competitive response in both home and export markets. In the normal way, a product code is allocated wherever there is a difference in blend, brand, length of cigarette or packing specification from one requirement to another.

Thus export orders often require packing and insert changes, the number of cigarettes per pack differ to facilitate the use of slot machines,[1] and different packs are used to meet the perceived needs of customers. Below is a summary of the differences currently required at each plant.

Number of specifications used in a typical month		Edinburgh	Norwich
Average	Blends	3	12
	Brands	3	25
	Product codes	65	560
Number of different packings per cigarette size (in mm)[2]	70	–	4
	80	–	2
	84	1	5
	95	–	2
	100	–	2

NOTES
1 Slot machines refer to the coin-operated dispensing machines increasingly used in clubs, restaurants, airports and other public places. Customers serve themselves through inserting the appropriate amount of cash required.
2. The different packings used included hinged lid, shell and slide, soft cup, box and drum.

EXHIBIT 4 Overview of current blends, brands, packing sizes and product codes at each factory location

Equipment category		Edinburgh		Norwich	
		Before	After[3]	Before	After[3]
Filter rod makers[1]		6	6	6	6
Free-standing plain[2]	Makers	2	–	4	6
	Packers	2	–	4	6
Free-standing filter	Makers	30	8	34	7
	Packers	40	10	42	8
Linked makers and packers (filter)		–	15	–	20

NOTES
1 Filter rod makers are the machines used to make the filter tips (see *Exhibit 2*).
2 The equipment for making and packing plain (or non-filter tip) cigarettes that was originally sited in the Edinburgh plant was transferred to Norwich when these products were also resited.
3 The investments involved in making these changes (new equipment, reorganizations and compensation payments) totalled £40m for both plants. About 80 per cent of this was spent on new equipment and the reorganization of existing equipment (including linking the making and packing processes) both within and between the two plants.

EXHIBIT 5 Principal secondary equipment at the Edinburgh and Norwich plants before and after the capital investments had taken place

The rationale supporting the capital investments in both plants was principally as follows.

The linking of a maker and packer required a conveyor and reservoir facility which provided an automatic feeding system from one process to the next. Previously (and currently with free-standing equipment) indirect labour was used to transport cigarettes from the makers to the packers. This would necessitate the movement of cigarettes loaded onto trolleys often from one floor to another and usually involving lengthy distances.

In order to decouple the maker from the packer the total holding of made cigarettes in a conveyor and reservoir system was in excess of 50,000. Thus, this afforded the two processes a practical level of independence within the linked system.

The advantages offered concerned a significant reduction in indirect labour together with small (but significant in terms of actual costs) savings on direct materials, particularly tobacco and is explained in more detail below.

The principal gains which accrued from these changes were:

(a) direct labour cost reduction: the introduction of higher speed makers and packers, together with the increased efficiency of the new equipment,[1] resulted in a reduction in direct labour requirements;

(b) direct material cost reduction: the new equipment and concept of linked processes resulted in a reduction in material loss/waste from lower levels of rejects and damaged product in the process;

(c) indirect labour reduction: the linked process concept reduced the need for indirect support in several ways, including movement of product, storage, administrative support and maintenance/technical support for the equipment.

The expected results of these improvements were a 20 per cent reduction in factory-related staff and an anticipated 1 per cent reduction in material costs. Over 90 per cent of this planned labour reduction was achieved by the introduction of linked processes in the two plants.

NOTE

1 Efficiency in this context refers to actual output achieved compared to the expressed or standard output and came from reduced downtime and the greater level of attainment of expected throughput rates.

EXHIBIT 6 Rationale supporting the capital investments summarized in *Exhibit 4* and the resulting reductions in labour

However, although the planned labour reduction had been accomplished within the set timescales, the anticipated profit improvements had only been achieved at the Edinburgh plant. Given the similarity of investments made and the gains in labour cost reductions that accrued, it was difficult, at least from a distance, to understand the success of one application and the relative failure of the other.

Brent Murdoch (plant manager, Norwich) was currently completing an in-depth review of the reasons behind this underperformance. He explained:

❝ Over the last three years the market has changed. Customer lead times are now much shorter, and as many of our products are now customized at least in terms of packing, then there is increased pressure on meeting agreed delivery dates. This is particularly so in export markets and the lower volume end of our business, which we tend to support. We estimate that ideally we need between three and five weeks to meet a delivery, depending upon the degree of customization involved. As higher volume items are normally met from finished goods inventory, then the total lead times estimated above [the lead times of three to five weeks quoted here comprise material lead time plus process lead time] are for customized products, including larger volume orders of an infrequent nature from some less developed countries. At our last review, about 65 per cent of all orders received were for delivery in less than five weeks, while almost 35 per cent were for less than three weeks. But, this pattern is increasingly common through businesses and certainly is mirrored in our Edinburgh plant. In addition, whereas our overall sales (both in terms of revenue [£s] and number of cigarettes sold) has slightly increased, since the decision to orient different products to the two plants the order size for our products has, if anything, declined. About half the orders received are for 100,000 cigarettes or less, with over 75 per cent for up to 500,000. Although many of these are for our higher volume products and are, therefore, cumulated within the production scheduling system, there are also those brands of cigarettes that experience a more intermittent pattern of demand as you would anticipate with lower volume products. Certainly this mix of work embodies a wider range and spread of volumes than before and particularly compared to Edinburgh. However, overall, the planned investments are achieving the desired labour cost reductions we anticipated. It has been a long haul, but through good working relationships we have negotiated the necessary changes and implemented them in line with the plan. On the new equipment itself we have experienced some problems [see Exhibit 7], which we are in the process of investigating. Certainly, however, the new high-speed makers and packers have made a sizable impact on our capacity needs (and subsequent manning levels), and the concept of linking makers with packers has reduced the work-in-progress inventory and associated labour support in a most dramatic fashion. All that's left is to get Norwich's performance up to plan and on a par with that being achieved in Edinburgh. 99

Reasons for stoppage		Downtime as a percentage of total observations
Making machine[1]		
Related directly to linked process	Conveyor/reservoir fault	2.1
	Reservoir full	3.3
	Need to empty reservoir on a changeover/end of shift	9.4
	Other	3.8
	Total	18.6
Unrelated to linked process	Maker fault	14.2
	Other	2.5
	Total	16.7
Total for the making machine		35.3
Packing machine[1]		
Related directly to linked process	Conveyor/reservoir fault	2.7
	Reservoir empty/waiting on a changeover/start of a shift	12.9
	Other	2.1
	Total	17.7
Unrelated to linked process	Packer fault	16.1
	Other	2.8
	Total	18.9
Total for the packing machine		36.6

NOTE

1 The conveyor/reservoir faults given for both the makers and packers are independent of each other, as they are related to the feed into and out of the reservoir.

EXHIBIT 7 Downtime analysis experienced on the linked processes at the Norwich plant

6 HQ
INJECTION
MOULDING

If we are to adhere to product launch sched-ules, we must try every mould on receipt, then bring in the mould maker to modify it as required, regardless of whether we can then go ahead and produce initial launch quantities', said George Brett, the manufacturing director. *'If we leave mould testing until we are ready for a production run there is a risk that the need for substantial mould modification will cause us to miss launch dates.*

HQ Injection Moulding had been a major compo-nents supplier to the domestic appliance industry prior to its acquisition by one of its customers. It also, at the time, had its own range of homeware products and supplied components to other indus-tries. Some 10 years ago, the group was restruc-tured and notice was given that the group requirements on the company would be phased out over the following two years. At that time, the parent company accounted for over 50 per cent of existing capacity (*Exhibit 1* shows the make-up of machine sizes).

This was not the only problem. The company's homeware range also faced competition from small firms who were able to compete effectively in this sector of the market.

The consumer saw our homeware products as plastic first and homeware second', said Graham Brown, the managing director. 'The traditional image of plastic as a cheap and transient material dominated, and we competed in the marketplace on price, rather than on the basis of our products. We had to rethink how we were to compete.

The company evolved a marketing strategy to design, manufacture and sell a range of high-quality products. This would enable it to compete in a different sector of the market where price was not the dominant order-winner. Over the years, the company designed several ranges of new products and the mould intro-ductions associated with this are summarized as *Exhibit 2*.

Operations

A brief outline of the process is shown as *Exhibit 3*. Starting with raw materials, a moulded prod-uct is produced. Certain subsequent operations (such as removing the sprue – that is, excess plastic from the mould passageways – by hand, knife or drill, checking the quality of the mould-ing and first packing operations) are all completed at the machine. The products are then transported in containers to the work-in-progress stores. From there, they are withdrawn as required by the assembly department, who complete any subassembly operations (such as glueing or welding components), assemble (for example, fit lids to bases and attach labels) and finally pack into inner and outer cartons, prior to transportation to the finished goods warehouse. With many of the products from the original product ranges the assembly and packing was completed during the moulding process, as the work content was relatively small due to the bulk style of packaging involved.

This case study was written by Terry Hill (University of Oxford). It is intended for class discussion and not as an example of good or bad management. © AMD Publishing.

Details of the number of machines available in each machine group defined by the company

| Machine group | Number of machines | | |
| | Current year minus: | | New |
	8	1	
1	29	1	–
2	15	11	5
3	5	8	6
4	2	2	1
Total	51	22	12

Details of the 'new' machines in each group

| Machine group | Year of purchase/new machines | | | | | | | Total |
| | Current year minus: | | | | | | | |
	7	6	5	4	3	2	1	
2	–	–	–	–	3	2	–	5
3	2	1	1	1	–	1	–	6
4	–	–	–	–	–	–	1	1

Details of a typical machine

| Machine group | Features of an average machine | | |
	Cost (£000s)[1]	Shot weight (ozs)	Locking pressure (tonnes)
1	116	10	200
2	276	45	450
3	333	60	600
4	360	150	600

NOTE
1 Cost includes the purchase price of the machine and installation costs at current year prices.

EXHIBIT 1 Details of injection moulding machines

Raw materials

The advent of the new range of products brought with it a significant increase in raw material types and colours. In order to support the new product concept, more expensive materials were introduced and the colour range was widened. Also the old products had tended to be moulded where close colour matching was not required and material specification was less critical. Moreover, the new products were clustered around a 'matching' range of products as a strategy to enhance sales, with the purchaser who has bought one item for the home being more likely to buy another item of the set when next purchasing. This meant that it was necessary to maintain colour matches over a long period of time.

Product range[2,3]	Number of moulds[1]							Current year
	Current year minus:							
	7	6	5	4	3	2	1	
A	–	–	1	5	–	–	–	–
B	–	4	1	1	4	4	2	–
C	19	8	10	8	3	1	–	–
D	4	20	–	6	1	2	12	–
E	4	19	–	26	9	14	15	30
F	–	–	–	–	–	2	–	–

NOTES

1 The number of moulds indicates the number of different products within each range. However, in many instances, one mould will have two or more impressions on it, so that in every moulding cycle one, two or more products would be made depending on the number of impressions on that mould.

2 Product ranges A and B belong to the original (pre-change) designs, while C to F were of the revised (post-change) designs. Further details are given in *Exhibit 5*, under the column headed 'Product'.

3 The dimensional sizes of old and new products vary across the different product ranges but, in overall terms, tend to be similar.

EXHIBIT 2 Summary of the moulds introduced or planned in the past seven years

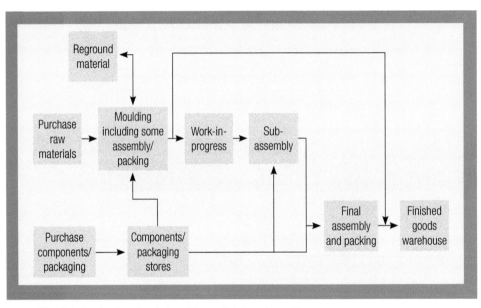

NOTE: All products do not go through each stage of the manufacturing and assembly process.

EXHIBIT 3 An outline of the manufacturing and assembly process

Toolroom

Nine skilled men (including three apprentices) work days, while one skilled man provides a breakdown service for the mould shop covering the period 22.00 to 07.00 hours. About 15–20 per cent of their time is spent on new moulds and the remainder on modification and repair.

Design

Over the years, design had expanded to become a separate function with a manager and four staff. Their job was to liaise with customers (often large department stores), agree on design detail then complete the drawings. The manager of the toolroom then undertook to make or subcontract the moulds and get them into production. The tool-room always had one draughtsperson, who dealt with mould modifications.

Technical services

The technical support to the mould shop is provided by John Burton, the technical manager. John has extensive knowledge of injection moulding and provides specialist help on the shopfloor. The work varies and includes:

1 Contributing to the design of a mould at the start of the mould-making process

2 Getting new moulds to a production state and establishing the settings and adjustments to be made in all future runs

3 Fine tuning a mould at the start of its production run (very important in terms of productivity)

4 Helping to determine the necessary modifications to a mould.

Before the switch in product concept, John would spend most of his day on task 3, but increasingly, due to the new product strategy, John and his staff of three technicians spend the majority of their time on the other three tasks.

66 *Until six or seven years ago, we concentrated on thinning product wall thickness and reducing cycle times because, particularly with the long production runs associated with the old-type products, this kept the cost down. The mould was made as cheaply as possible and we used black plastic where we could so that we could use reground plastic of mixed colours. And, of course, we would use contrasting colours for lids and bases, to avoid the need to colour match.*

The new products changed this. We increased wall thickness to give products greater rigidity and substance, colour match became critical, lids and bases were the same colour, quality took precedence over cycle times, packaging became far more important and quality became the order of the day. The repercussions of this on the shopfloor were considerable. A new team had to be trained and premoulding treatment of material

became necessary to achieve the necessary colour and quality standards.

Many existing machines were old and often unable to meet or maintain the new product specifications. Until new machines could be justified, sanctioned and installed, many preliminary operations were necessary to overcome the inadequacies of the old machines. As an estimate, only some 25 per cent of the machines were originally up to meeting the new technical specifications required, due to wear and tear.

On the technical side, our existing fitters had to be retrained to set up moulds with complicated water circuits, heating subsystems, temperature controls and complex core-pull and ejection systems. A new class of staff, the technician, became necessary. Recruitment from outside proved fruitless, and our best setters took on this role, with the best operators replacing them as setters.

The proposed range of moulds appears bigger and more sophisticated. Overall, machine setting is now more difficult and the machine adjustment controls are inadequate for the fine level of tuning required. When several new product ranges are introduced within a short period, everyone is under pressure. The new machines due this year will have microprocessor controls, with the set-up reductions they bring justifying the 15 per cent increase in capital cost. Although we expect this margin to decrease over the next year or two, persuading top management that this additional expenditure is necessary as standard policy is a different matter. These three new machines will be groups 2, 3 and 4, with locking pressures of 450, 600 and 600 respectively. 99

Maintenance

According to Phil Stokes, the maintenance manager:

66 *Many of the old machines weren't up to the quality specifications required by the change of product mix. For this reason, new machines were bought and the worst of the old machines sold. Now, besides the high-volume, low-margin products, we also make low-volume products. Our revenue and profits have both increased. For my department, this has meant fewer machines and fewer problems.* 99

Exhibit 4 gives the financial information for the company for the past seven years.

	Current year minus:						
	7	**6**	**5**	**4**	**3**	**2**	**1**
Fixed assets							
Plant	561	552	399	420	612	838	980
Moulds	102	130	170	180	320	584	620
Total	663	682	569	600	932	1,422	1,600
Current assets							
Inventory	262	532	1,029	1,259	1,559	2,243	2,567
Debtors	483	798	842	817	1,321	963	1,373
Total	745	1,330	1,871	2,076	2,880	3,206	3,940
Current liabilities							
Creditors	626	532	628	1,134	1,774	1,744	1,765
Overdraft	2	480	412	42	38	284	575
Total	628	1,012	1,040	1,176	1,812	2,028	2,340
Working capital[1]	117	318	831	900	1,068	1,178	1,600
Net assets employed[2]	780	1,000	1,400	1,500	2,000	2,600	3,200
Financed by							
Share capital	50	50	50	50	50	50	50
Retained profit[3]	280	420	530	570	830	1,760	2,660
Total	330	470	580	620	880	1,810	2,710
Group indebtedness	450	530	820	880	1,120	790	490
Net capital employed	780	1,000	1,400	1,500	2,000	2,600	3,200
Net sales	2,552	2,872	4,212	4,466	5,810	5,394	8,021
Net profit before tax[3]	146	185	274	362	564	708	1,050

NOTES
1 Working capital = current assets − current liabilities.
2 Net assets employed = fixed assets + working capital.
3 Any difference between the net profit for any year and the increase of retained profits is due to a transfer of profit to the group.

EXHIBIT 4 Some financial management information for the past seven years (year ended 31 December, all figures in £000s)

Mould shop

'We are now in a totally different manufacturing situation than we were previously', was George Brett's opening comment when discussing the present situation. At the beginning of the change-over, he explained, there were several technical difficulties that had not been foreseen. These ranged from the inadequacies of many old machines to do the job, through to the moulding properties of the new materials.

He recalled how jobs had often to be allocated to a larger machine in order to achieve the required product specification (for instance, an increased locking pressure was needed to keep a mould closed during the machine cycle to avoid 'flashing'). Also, there were great difficulties experienced with colour matching, especially in the 'bright, modern' colours now being used.

“*We even had to rethink our mould design, in some cases, from one that minimized the cycle time by injecting in the centre of the mould (that is, the shortest distance for the material to flow) to injecting so as to minimize the sprue mark, which lengthens the time cycle[1] and complicates the moulding process. Since then, we have overcome these initial difficulties and many more besides. But, in doing so, it has resulted in a lot of pressure, effort and cost. At times we can have seven or eight of the machines working on new products, which effectively means no production, and a complete loss of productive standard hours from some 30 per cent of our capacity. The problems of trying to complete the tasks of a development unit and a production unit under the same roof, and calling on the same capacities and skills, are enormous. The pressure of achieving deadlines, particularly when little or no slack time has been allowed in the plan (the design/customer agreement phase always absorbs whatever slack there is), requires all our attention so that normal production has to look after itself.*”

As shown in *Exhibit 1*, the available production capacity had shifted towards larger machines, sometimes in actual numbers, but markedly as a percentage of the total capacity available. Trying to keep moulding costs down supported the argument for multi-impression moulds, whereby every cycle produced a 'shot' with each of the impressions in the formed state (for example two lids or two bodies, or two lids and two bodies and so on). Of course, multi-impression moulds always become much larger and much more sophisticated. These, in turn, require larger machines and accounted, in part, for the drift away from the earlier mix of machines. In addition, mould changes and set-ups take longer and details of a representative sample of products throughout the current range is given as *Exhibit 5*. Besides the cost advantages inherent in multipurpose moulding, particularly with high-volume production runs, another advantage gained is that it facilitates the moulding of a product that has more than one component and where colour matching is essential.

Part of the production management's job was to consider ways of reducing costs throughout the process wherever possible. Some of these suggestions come from marketing pressure in addition to the continuous flow of ideas from manufacturing itself, with the aid of support services such as industrial engineering, toolroom and design. *Exhibit 6* gives cost breakdowns for some representative products from across the current ranges.

Assembly

The assembly department undertakes sub-assembly, final assembly and packing, and is located away from the mould shop in a 50,000 square foot warehouse, which also contains work-in-progress and some of the finished goods inventory. The work of this department has increased with the need for packing and presentation that accompanied the new products. At the other extreme, any assembly or packing of the industrial products is mainly carried out at the machine. There are, at present, some 17 assembly benches and three subassembly locations, with 27 full-time and 16 part-time packers and an indirect staff of three.

Finished goods warehouse

Although the product quantities have decreased since the early 1970s, the requirement for warehousing is considerably higher. Reasons for this include:

1 subcontract industrial work for the group was moulded on a contract basis and shipped daily to the various companies

2 the traditional homewares and industrial products were (and still are) packed several together, inside a box or polyethylene bag

3 components required to assemble the new ranges of products are greater

4 the emphasis on quality means that components have to be stacked with greater care

5 the new products are packed individually in inner boxes, increasing the space requirement at the finished goods stage.

| Product[1] | Machine group | Number of | | Number of components[3] | When last moulded | |
		impressions[2]	colours		Months ago	Colour changes
1132 Tray	2	2	1	3	27	1
2225 Bowl[8]	2	1	8	2	1	3
1138 Bucket	3	1	8	2	6	3
1386 Jug	2	1	1	3	2	1
1263 Tray[8]	2	1	8	5	5	4
2687 Tidy	3	1	2	4	1	2
2241 Bin	3	2	6	7	1	5
2366 Bin	3	1	1	2	–	1
1393 Box	2	2	2	2	1	1
1267 Tub	3	1	1	1	5	1
8282 Bowl[9]	3	4	6	3	2	6
(B) Industrial Mouldings: Original Product Concept						
6900 Board	2	1	2	1	8	2
6908 Basin	4	2	1	2	2	1
6074 Lid	2	1	1	2	3	1
6010 Tray	4	2	1	–	50	1
6085 Knob	1	2	5	1	16	2
6990 Frame	3	1	1	4	2	1
6491 Cap	1	6	1	1	6	1
6209 Case	2	1	1	5	4	1
8860 Tray[10]	4	1	12	1	–	1
8009 Case	3	2	2	1	8	2
8010 Tray	3	1	2	1	4	1
(C) General Homewares: Revised Product Concept						
3910 Container	3	1	10	5	1	3
3941 Rollholder	2	1	3	8	10	3
3995 Container	3	1	10	5	30	4
6115 No. 4	3	4	6	5	14	5
6110 No. 9	2	1	9	4	20	1
6246 No. 28	4	2	12	4	1	5
6151 Jug	2	1	4	3	20	3
6313 Box	1	1	4	6	30	1
6332 Rack	4	1	6	3	3	3
6846 Shelf	4	2	2	9	4	2
6463 Clock	3	1	4	10	14	3

Production run (hours)		Production runs past 12 months	Hours to change[6]		Annual sales (units)	Finished goods[7]		Outstanding orders	
Last[4]	Average[5]		Mould	Colour		Units	Colours	Units	Colours
1,700	1,700	–	2(½)	–	20,686	67,159	1	–	–
192	248	6	2(1)	2	159,120	33,769	8	–	–
138	138	1	3(1½)	2	13,236	5,829	5	–	–
190	147	3	3(1)	–	44,237	34,618	1	–	–
70	120	4	2½(1)	1½	48,162	15,050	8	–	–
124	82	7	7(3)	2	50,400	8,280	2	–	–
103	100	4	13(5)	2	47,646	3,642	5	195	1
156	120	6	7(1)	1	11,779	–	–	288	1
190	83	6	2½(1)	1½	22,405	3,987	2	–	–
44	44	1	2½(1½)	1½	13,465	734	1	–	–
220	250	2	10(4)	2	57,840	480	6	–	–
144	144	1	1(–)	½	6,735	–	–	–	–
62	62	1	22(10)	–	–	–	–	–	–
45	45	1	3(1)	–	–	–	–	–	–
106	106	–	3(1)	–	–	–	–	–	–
125	125	–	2(½)	½	–	–	–	–	–
163	163	1	24(10)	–	–	–	–	–	–
110	511	6	2½(1)	–	533,318	–	–	48,703	1
95	83	7	7(3)	–	65,159	1,152	1	–	–
2,400	371	10	9(3)	½	159,489	4,804	6	19,835	1
60	54	1	11(5)	½	5,443	3,650	2	–	–
90	36	2	11(5)	½	2,741	717	1	–	–
134	87	9	4(2)	3	35,238	520	2	7,917	3
55	55	1	13(3)	3	3,312	610	2	432	1
77	77	–	3½(2)	1½	157	108	2	–	–
20	20	–	9(1)	6	13,814	28,225	6	–	–
24	24	–	3(1)	2	1,242	6,660	8	–	–
81	39	9	7(3)	4	14,472	6,485	12	–	–
102	102	–	9(2)	2	3,284	1,035	2	209	2
24	24	–	3½(2)	2	405	6,294	3	–	–
106	106	1	10(4)	3	18,453	2,489	5	–	–
42	92	2	8(4)	2	10,598	2,003	2	–	–
78	78	–	2½(1)	1½	6,393	1,749	4	–	–

cont'd

Product[1]	Machine group	Number of		Number of components[3]	When last moulded	
		impressions[2]	colours		Months ago	Colour changes
D) Bathroom Ranges: Revised Product Concept						
5426 Holder	3	2	10	7	–	2
5229 Dish	4	2	9	6	–	2
5624 Holder[11]	2	1	10	8	–	3
5315 Dish[11]	2	1	5	7	–	3
6213 Hook	2	2	10	6	17	2
6420 Mirror	4	2	11	9	1	1
6428 Holder	1	2	13	5	1	2
6606 Beaker	3	4	5	6	1	2
6397 Caddy	3	1	4	8	1	2
6309 Mirror	4	1	4	8	1	3
(E) Kitchen Ranges: Revised Product Concept						
4141 Bowl	4	2	4	4	2	2
8284 Large sieve[12]	3	2	4	7	1	3
4150 Small sieve[12]	2	2	4	7	1	3
4151 Large spoon[13]	3	2	4	4	3	4
4156 Small spoon[13]	3	2	4	4	3	4
4161 Scraper[13]	4	4	4	4	3	4
4159 Jug	2	1	4	4	3	3
4219 Cutter[14]	2	8	4	4	3	4
8424 Mould[14]	2	8	4	4	2	3
4213 Holder	2	1	4	6	5	3
(F) General: Revised Product Concept						
2849 Hanger	3	12	6	3	–	5
6049 Bracelet	2	4	6	2	22	4

NOTES

1 In the case of several of these products there is more than one moulding involved (for example a body and a lid); here the principal moulding (for example the body) has been analysed as representative.

2 If a product involves only one moulding, but there are (say) two or four impressions on the relevant mould, this means that such moulds have been designed to make the product concerned in (say) multiples of two or four, each time the moulding cycle is completed (the exception to this is given in Note 1).

3 Number of components refers to the number of different components used in assembling a product. The components will usually be purchased, and typically are metal fittings and other non-plastic parts.

4 If no production runs in the past 12 months, the last order has been taken as average.

5 Average production run has been taken over the past 12 months (see above).

6 Hours to change a mould includes changing the mould, then the time taken to get the mould working to production and quality requirements, which is shown in brackets. For example, Tray 1132 2(½) means 2 hours to change the mould and get it working to production and quality requirements. Of this 2 hours, the adjustment process to get it working to production and quality requirements after the mould change takes ½ hour.

| Production run (hours) | | Production runs past 12 months | Hours to change[6] | | Annual sales (units) | Finished goods[7] | | Outstanding orders | |
Last[4]	Average[5]		Mould	Colour		Units	Colours	Units	Colours
67	155	14	4(2)	2	119,367	–	–	12,816	8
45	110	7	4(2)	2	40,819	966	4	4,196	4
40	40	1	14(2)	2	–	3,240	3	3,240	3
20	20	1	14(2)	2	–	1,080	3	1,050	3
47	47	–	4(2)	1½	2,018	12,725	8	–	–
39	39	5	5(2)	1½	11,768	15,283	7	–	–
35	35	5	2½(1)	1	16,913	21,392	10	–	–
33	50	3	5(2)	1½	24,244	18,785	4	3,000	1
95	34	3	8(4)	1½	10,752	11,167	4	–	–
43	32	4	4(2)	1½	9,720	3,994	3	1,500	1
60	80	8	3(1)	1½	58,850	12,280	4	–	–
100	35	8 ⎫	3(1) ⎫	1½	39,638	96	1	8,222	3
100	63	8 ⎭	⎭		35,450	233	1	1,607	2
367	117	4 ⎫	⎫		74,020	49,017	3	–	–
367	140	4 ⎬	6(3) ⎬	1½	98,828	4,961	2	608	1
367	144	4 ⎭	⎭		119,765	26,666	3	–	–
143	72	7	9(4)	1½	54,022	4,764	4	–	–
90	47	5	4(2)	1½	162,492	188,261	4	–	–
108	26	6	5(2)	1½	122,472	95,994	4	–	–
142	36	6	4(1)	1½	19,128	34,178	4	–	–
183	50	9	11(3)	2	540,615	58,333		–	–
74	74	–	2(1)	1	–	–		–	–

7 The colours in stock are not the same as those required for outstanding orders.
8 The colour range of these products was increased from 3 to 8 as part of extending the 'revised product concept' to products of the 'original concept'.
9 This product was in fact packed in assorted colours and held in finished stock as such.
10 The range of colours for this item was due to the fact that customers tended to prefer their own colour for reasons of brand image, recognition and so on.
11 New product range (outstanding orders represent initial launch).
12 Both these products are on the same mould.
13 These three products are on the same mould.
14 Impressions are of different shapes: two sets of shapes x 4 impressions.
15 The products shown here are considered to be representative of both their own and the total product range.

EXHIBIT 5 Production, sales and inventory details on several products[15]

Work-in-progress and finished goods warehousing capacity has been increased significantly, as shown in *Exhibit 7*.

Operations control

66 *The new range of products presents a set of operations control problems, that are different from those of the old products'*, said Geoff Sissons, the operations controller. *'The number of components and the assembly and packing requirements have increased the complexity of the process.* 99 *Exhibit 5* illustrates this.

66 *In addition, the uncertainty inherent in the mould-testing process, the procedure for agreeing packaging and the launch dates have added factors which made planning and control far more difficult.*

Then, the marketing department often requires additional colours in order to increase sales in existing markets or break into new markets [an example of such a request is shown as Exhibit 8]. These short runs and special colours often have target dates which necessitate fitting them in at all stages of the process at the expense of normal production runs. It is difficult to balance these two sets of priorities. 99

Marketing

The marketing department is split into product areas and subdivided into home and export. Each subdivision has a sales manager who reports to Mark Williams, the marketing director. Mark, who has been with the company for 12 months, confirmed that the change in product direction had enabled the company to compete successfully in a new sector of the market. 'Before I joined, the company had already achieved recognition as a front runner in this section, manufacturing high-quality, well-designed products. Frankly, this was one of the reasons I took the job.'

As Mark explained, the markets for the two products the company currently manufactured and sold were very different.

66 *Sales of the old product are normally negotiated on a large-volume contract, with call-offs to meet*

the agreed customer deliveries. In the new markets, retail outlets hold our ranges, but the mix of products and colours means that we often need to be able to supply orders within a few days. While this is not always possible, we have a good reputation with our customers for the level of support we provide. For, as they emphasize, if the exact product wanted by their customers is not available at the required time, then often the sale is lost as they spend their money on something else altogether. 99

Mark explained that he had continued to push this policy and had been instrumental in bringing out several new ranges since joining the company. The latest was due to be launched quite soon, with another due out early this year. 'This redirection has also had a few spin-offs in the older homeware range, where we have redesigned some packaging and increased and improved the colour range.'

Corporate policy

'We have come a long way since those days of change', said Graham Brown, managing director.

66 *My predecessor had the foresight to rethink corporate policy when the group restructuring created the substantial excess moulding capacity. For the past two years, I have reinforced this sound strategy. The marked increase in sales is anticipated to continue, and home and export sales support this forecast. The lower volume products have allowed us to gradually decrease our overall moulding capacity. It is now important that we use this capacity efficiently and, in making the budgets for the coming year, we have taken account of the anticipated non-productive demands on the manufacturing facilities. But although these new product launches make large demands on the system, they are our future lifeblood. We must keep costs down, and so look at all areas of costs. Our decision to go towards multi-impression moulds is one way of staying competitive [see Exhibit 9]. Our recent and future product ranges reflect this perspective.* 99

| Product details | | Cost details (pence per 12)[1] | | | | | | | |
| Range[2] | Item | Raw materials[3] | Labour | | Packaging and components | Mould depreciation[5] | Overheads | | Total |
			Moulding[4]	Assembly[4]			Moulding[6]	General[7]	
A	2225 Bowl	254	35	–	38	25	179	148	679
A	2687 Tidy	409	56	–	78	40	303	242	1,128
A	2366 Bin	2,103	142	–	272	160	787	957	4,421
A	8282 Bowl	44	6	8	11	4	32	25	130
B	6491 Cap	9	–	–	1	1	15	8	34
B	8860 Tray	1,621	88	–	668	116	491	695	3,679
B	8009 Case	1,093	73	–	515	83	406	496	2,666
C	6246 No. 28	1,799	110	103	435	280	609	839	4,175
C	6846 Shelf	457	79	106	764	108	438	324	2,276
D	5426 Holder	288	105	69	311	100	508	300	1,681
D	5624 Holder	163	92	88	272	77	440	232	1,364
D	6420 Mirror	1,942	139	334	2,469	317	773	951	6,925
D	6428 Holder	578	165	78	786	173	812	518	3,110
D	6606 Beaker	237	91	73	298	82	411	246	1,438
E	8284 Large sieve	250	48	49	409	20	112	61	949
E	8424 Mould	21	6	10	17	6	29	19	108
F	2849 Hanger	54	4	8	18	4	21	25	134

NOTES

1 'Pence' – one penny = one hundredth of a £.
2 The product range abbreviations A to F are detailed in *Exhibit 5*.
3 Raw material costs are normally adjusted twice a year.
4 Moulding and assembly labour costs are based on calculated standard times.
5 Mould depreciation is a fixed percentage of the first stage costs, which comprises raw materials, moulding overheads, mould depreciation and moulding labour.

6 Moulding overheads are based on the machine size cost below:

Group	1	2	3	4
Moulding overhead allocation (£ p)	19.48	22.95	24.60	24.60

If a product is to be moulded on a machine in Group 1, then the moulding overhead allocation will be based on £19.48 and so on. These allocations include indirect moulding labour, production staff, development, site, utilities, plant depreciation, blocks, dies and plant repairs.
7 General overheads are calculated as a fixed percentage of first stage cost.

EXHIBIT 6 Cost details of representative products

Warehousing	Current year minus:	Size (square feet)	Distance (miles)	Total (square feet)
Components/packing	7	5,000	–	
	4	5,000	–	10,000
Work-in-progress	7	9,000	–	
	3	9,000	–	18,000
Finished goods	7	27,000	–	
	6	10,000	20	
	4	40,000	1	
	3	(10,000)	20	
	1	20,000	3	87,000

EXHIBIT 7 Changes in components/packing, work-in-progress and finished goods warehousing over the past seven years

Product	Colour requests (units)					Actual time taken per product (minutes)[1]		Allowed moulding standard time per product (minutes)[3]
	Beige	Brown	Blue	Green	Total	Moulding	Colour change[2]	
4012 Dish	24	42	24	42	132	405	65	156
4013 Holder	20	42	24	42	128	550	100	152
4014 Beaker	24	42	24	42	132	480	60	111
4018 Holder	24	42	24	42	132	260	60	129
4019 Holder	24	42	24	42	132	670	110	132
4020 Sticks	40	42	30	42	154	270	60	137
4021 Ring	60	60	36	36	192	390	95	200
4023 Rack	20	36	20	24	100	1,140	220	175
4028 Rail	24	42	24	42	132	445	60	139
4029 Frame	24	42	26	42	134	530	120	137
Total	284	432	256	396	1,368	5,120	950	1,468

NOTES
1 'Actual time taken per product' is the number of standard minutes taken to mould the quantity of the product.
2 Colour change time is the total time taken to change from one colour to another in this production run. It is in addition to the actual moulding time given here.
3 'Allowed moulding standard time per product' is the number of standard minutes calculated to mould the quantity of the product.

EXHIBIT 8 Details for marketing samples in new colours

Multi-impression moulds

An important design decision to be made concerns the number of impressions to be built into a mould. A single impression would mean that with every shot only one moulding is produced. With multi-impression moulding, two or more products (depending upon the number of impressions) are made with every shot, thus giving a significant decrease in moulding time to complete an order quantity. This could be a lid or base of the same product, two lids and two bases of the same product, two or more identical products (such as trays), or two or more products that are not identical (such as a set of spoons to be sold as a set), or two or more different products to be sold as different products in the marketplace.

- Normally the number of impressions are even-numbered to retain balance in the mould.

- The capital cost of a two-impression mould is more than twice the cost of a single-impression mould of the same item due to the increased complexity of the mould design.

- The more impressions per mould then the larger the mould size (that is, physical dimensions) and the longer it takes to set up and colour change.

Moulding machine

With wear and tear over time, moulding machines increasingly find it more difficult to achieve the upper limits of their specification. One common problem is that when the raw material is injected into the mould under pressure, the machine is less and less able to exert the locking pressure necessary to keep the two halves of a mould together. If it does not, then flashing will become apparent. If flashing does appear, with a low-quality item it can be trimmed off, with a high-quality item, this would normally make it a reject.

Moulding

A mould can go on to any machine, providing that the machine is physically large enough to take the physical dimensions of the mould, has the shot weight to fill the mould and hence produce a complete moulding and has the locking pressure to keep the two halves of the mould closed during the machining cycle.

Hence the division of moulding machines into four groups reflects the fact that machines are in a range of 'sizes' (that is, physical dimensions, such as the opening to take the mould, shot weight and locking pressure). Moulds, therefore, are loaded according to the appropriate machine size. There is little opportunity to sensibly transfer one mould to another machine group.

Finally, the size of a mould is primarily a factor of the dimensional size of the product (that is, height and diameter). Similarly, the moulding cycle time (how long it takes a machine to inject material into the cavity of the mould) is a factor of product size, the wall thickness of a product and, to a much lesser extent, the condition of the machine (that is, the effects of wear and tear).

EXHIBIT 9 Technical note

Note

1   Cycle time is the length of time it takes for the machine to close the mould, inject the material, initial cooling, open the mould and present the moulded part for the operator to remove from the mould. In many instances, a mould is so designed as to complete this last operation on a part or wholly automatic basis.

JACKSON
PRECISION CASTINGS

Matt Boyd, the Group CEO of Jackson Engineering (JE), was reviewing a proposal from Jackson Precision Castings (JPC), one of the businesses which reported to him, and he looked pleased.

The remarks followed an initial decision on the proposals outlining the reasons for introducing the recent continuous improvement programme (CIP) and a revised incentive scheme proposal. The others involved were Paul Farmer (CEO of JPC), Dave Jenkins (V-P Manufacturing, JPC) and Michael Jacques, a senior partner from an international consultancy company that had been advising parts of JE over the past eighteen months. The two intitiatives which had met with such solid approval had been put forward by Paul Farmer and concerned JPC, the business for which he had responsibility. They were based on recommendations from the consultants.

'Yes', concluded Matt Boyd, 'these proposals have my full support. Let's get on with it, Paul.'

As the meeting finished and Paul, Dave and Michael made for the door, Matt called out 'And Paul, I am expecting to see the signs of an upturn in sales and profits. Soon!'

Background

JE is a long-established, UK-based company. After growing in a haphazard fashion over many years to an annual sales revenue of some £150m, it was acquired by a US-based industrial conglomerate, AK Industrials (AKI). Over the past five to six years, AKI had been expanding its European operations, particularly in the industrial sector, and JE fitted well into AKI's portfolio which included automotive, precision and general engineering, injection and rubber mouldings and other general industrial companies. Matt Boyd was brought in as CEO to improve the overall profitability of the three companies within JE. One of his first actions was to decentralize the company into three autonomous businesses. There are now two larger units, each with annual sales of a little over £30m and JPC with a sales revenue of £19.8m.

The market for die castings has contracted in the UK and the rest of Europe in recent years, resulting in the closure of many small companies. Although JPC had improved its market share it still experienced reducing sales revenues over the past five years. Tight control on internal costs has kept JPC profitable, in fact above not only JE's but also AKI's corporate average. Importantly, JPC also generates a positive cash flow even though over a period of years there has been regular investment to update plant and equipment. Certainly before the change in ownership obtaining investment had not been a problem given JPC's profit and cash flow performance.

Matt Boyd's second major initiative was to ask consultants to work with each business in JE and formulate plans to improve profitability. Last year's business plan from JPC had been rejected by Matt Boyd. The reasons he gave were the company's contracting market and uncertainty about future sales revenue. The consultants were then asked to get involved in JPC with a clear instruction from Matt Boyd to start with a review of the market.

The consultants spent several months of interviewing and analysis both inside the business and talking with major customers. The market review led to a proposed strategy for growing precision casting sales.

The review was followed by an assessment of internal issues. The consultants concluded that workforce involvement had to be improved as a major factor in the overall success of the unit. They suggested the introduction of a continuous improvement programme (CIP). This was launched six weeks ago after providing relevant training for those involved. While carrying out their initial analysis the consultants examined the existing incentive scheme and concluded that it needed a major overhaul. During the period since it was introduced, the scheme had become 'loose'.[1] Paul Farmer, while agreeing with the conclusions about the current incentive scheme, felt strongly that a good, well-directed incentive scheme was an important element in achieving the projected sales and profit growth goals set within JPC's business plans.

Market review

The market review was organized and managed by the consultants. Michael Jacques kept an eye on the work and attended the internal meetings to discuss progress but a specialist marketing consultant, Jonathan Clarke, was brought in to work on the day-to-day analysis.

The consultants suggested visiting major customers to understand what they wanted from suppliers like JPC. The selection of customers was made by Paul Farmer to match the guidelines drawn up by the consultants. The guidelines

suggested visiting enough large customers to cover over half the business's current sales revenue. Four important UK customers were selected and an export customer in France. These five companies accounted for 56 per cent of the current sales revenue. The remaining 44 per cent came from over 70 customers which were usually small companies. The chosen customers were then visited by Jim Wilson (V-P Marketing, JPC) and Jonathan Clarke.

Where possible, the team spoke with the top executives of each customer and the interviews lasted between two and four hours, depending on the availability of those involved.

The stated objectives of these visits were to:

- determine how well JPC was performing

- understand the customers' own plans for growth

- establish the basis on which customers placed their casting business, either with JPC or competitors.

Prior to the visits the consultants drew up a list of questions and this was used as a script for the interview. *Exhibit 1* shows the customers, their spend on castings, the expected growth or decline in spend and the share of the current spend placed with JPC.

The main conclusions drawn from the market review were:

- as capacity for die casting had reduced throughout Europe and was now more in line with demand, the market had become less price sensitive

- JPC should aim to grow share in its well-established UK market

- the European foothold should be expanded. Target customers should be identified. As a start, companies that already transacted business with other parts of JE should be on the priority list.

In fact, the French company included in the market review had been introduced through an initiative from AK1 and in 12 months had become JPC's fifth largest (£s) customer.

Customer	Customer		JPC		
Customer	Annual die casting spend (£m)	Expected growth or decline of die casting spend	Current share of annual customer spend		Share of own current sales (%)
			£m	%	
Wilson Automotive Components	16.6	slow growth[1]	3.0	18	15
Gagnard Freres	3.8	static	1.1	26	6
Gordon Stoves	4.2	steady decline	2.4	57	12
Hardy-Belmont Engineering — standard products / special products	6.4	slow decline / erratic growth	1.4	22	7
Anscombe Products	7.4	slow decline	3.2	43	16
Total	38.4	–	11.1	29	56

NOTE
1 However, the potential for a rapid increase in sales is available if current decisions on Wilson Automotive Components supplying European car plants are changed.

EXHIBIT 1 Market review – size of customer die casting spend and current JPC share

In addition to recommendations on the future direction of the precision castings business, the output from the review included an assessment of the factors each customer considered important when selecting suppliers for die castings (see *Exhibits 2* to *6*).

On the basis of the market review a new business plan was constructed. This showed that the sales growth would come from increasing share with current, major UK customers and increasing sales in Europe. The plan also proposed the introduction of continuous improvement groups and a new incentive scheme within the early part of that year. The plan had been accepted.

Operations

JPC makes zinc and aluminium die castings and aluminium gravity die castings. Secondary operations after casting are carried out on some parts. In addition, other parts are sent out for painting before despatch to the customer. A brief explanation of die casting is provided in *Exhibit 7*.

The basic layout of the factory is by groups of similar machines. The die casting equipment is generally modern reflecting the history of regular investment. Some of the machines for the secondary operations are many years old but well maintained. There is also a small toolroom that carries out basic tool maintenance. All tools are inspected after running a part and before being stored. New tools are subcontracted using two external local suppliers who have invested heavily in modern tool-making equipment. Frequent checks are made on alternative tool markets in Europe and elsewhere in the world. To date, the local suppliers have proved very competitive on price and particularly in terms of offering short lead times.

The factory is tidy and the machines are well maintained and kept clean. Breakdowns are few and quality conformance issues with customers are infrequent. The die casting machines are normally manned for a double day shift with a much smaller night shift operating a limited number of machines. The secondary operation machines and the toolroom are manned on a single day shift basis.

Background

Wilson Automotive Components (WAC) was a small independent manufacturing company until four years ago when it was purchased by a large automotive components group. Through the parent company's involvement it has become a supplier to two major automotive vehicle manufacturers in the UK. It supplies two main product families, each with variants, to these customers in the form of assemblies. It also supplies a variety of smaller niche manufacturers involved in both automotive and industrial applications.

In addition to original equipment sales, WAC sells spares, both components and assemblies, through its original equipment customers and independent dealers.

JPC have supplied WAC for many years.

Location

The WAC factory is a 45-minute drive from the JPC plant.

Growth

The company is shedding some of its smaller customers in order to focus on the large-volume vehicle manufacturers. Growth is based on these customers and to date has been slow, in line with a sluggish automotive market. Currently, it only supplies the UK plants of its major customers. Any move to supply other European plants would lead to large volume increases. In recent months, this is now being actively considered.

Requirements of suppliers

The components purchased are high-precision parts.

1 Quality conformance

'Our automotive customers are teaching us about quality' was WAC's opening comment on quality conformance. Consequently, WAC now expects its suppliers to deliver defect-free parts. No internal inspection is carried out on parts from JPC prior to use. If problems are found with parts when they are used on assembly then JPC is charged the cost of the lost assembly time, which is much higher than the cost of the part supplied.

WAC also carries out annual, on-site audits of the quality systems of all major suppliers, including JPC.

2 Delivery reliability and delivery speed

WAC places weekly schedules on major suppliers. The schedules for the main running original equipment parts give a fixed four-week lead time. It regards delivery reliabiliy for these parts as essential.

WAC is planning to move to JIT and is already reducing inventory levels. At the moment, buffer stock is held against suppliers' failure to deliver but within 12 months this will all be removed.

For spares orders, WAC is often in competition with other suppliers who make functional replacements for WAC products. Availability usually determines who gets the order. Therefore, WAC are looking for a fast response from suppliers.

3 Price

All qualified suppliers have to quote against a selection of parts on an annual basis. Competitiveness on price affects share for the following year. Spare parts are rarely sourced from a company other than an established supplier.

EXHIBIT 2 Consultant's market review report – Wilson Automotive Components

Background

Hardy-Belmont Engineering (HBE) manufactures two types of products. Its staple product has been a range of standard motors for industrial applications. More recently it has started supplying expensive, customized motors for a variety of companies involved in large projects. Many of the projects are in the Middle East. These customers typically develop the specifications for ancillary products such as motors late in a project and being able to meet the lead times required becomes an important factor in HBE's choice of suppliers.

HBE classifies its castings as standards or specials depending on which of the two types of products they are used for.

Location

The company is located near Glasgow, Scotland.

Growth

While sales of the HBE standard range of motors has been increasing steadily throughout Europe, the demand for castings has been reducing as castings have increasingly been substituted by other technologies. The special products have led the company into a new growth area and these products will certainly use castings for at least the next five years.

Requirements of suppliers

HBE has always tended to source from a group of four or five castings suppliers with a strong accent on price.

For its standard parts HBE places annual, indicative orders with call-offs on fortnightly schedules to a four-week lead time. Their project work is, however, much more unpredictable and an important factor in winning this business is the ability to meet shorter delivery times than competitors. Because the castings are product specific no inventory is held while delivery promises must be met. For each project so far, HBE has asked all its regular suppliers to quote but recently it declared its intention to work with only one, or possibly two, suppliers on project work in order to cut down the time involved.

So far, JPC has supplied about 30 per cent of the parts for special projects.

EXHIBIT 3 Consultant's market review report – Hardy-Belmont Engineering

Background

Anscombe Products (AP) is a small engineering company which is part of a larger group. AP makes assemblies used in medical equipment. All the products are supplied to other parts of the group.

Location

AP is located about two hours' drive from the JPC plant.

Growth

AP is growing but the spend on castings is declining due to design changes in the end product.

Requirements of suppliers

Although it is a small company, AP is very efficient in its manufacturing and planning activities. It has been progressively reducing inventories and lead times over the past two to three years.

AP also has a supplier reduction programme and sets its suppliers annual targets to reduce lead times and improve delivery reliability performance. Deliveries have to be made within nominated periods on the required day.

AP is not particularly price sensitive.

EXHIBIT 4 Consultant's market review report – Anscombe Products

Background

Gagnard Freres (GF) is a privately owned group. It has done business for many years with a machining company in France which is owned by AKI. The machining company was drilling and grinding castings purchased in France by GF and suggested getting quotations from JPC. This led to GF placing orders with JPC initially for one simple, high-volume part. This has now built up to three parts which make up over a quarter of GF's spend on castings. All the parts are of low complexity and involve product specifications that are not difficult to meet.

GF makes standard products for industrial applications. The demand for its products is uneven but it prefers to order from JPC in large quantities to minimize transport costs.

Location

GF is based in Lyon, France.

Growth

The market for the company's products is static.

Requirements of suppliers

Because the parts are so straightforward, quality conformance has not been an issue.

For GF, to source parts outside France was an important departure from its previous policy. It appears to be pleased with the results and stated that it was getting good, on-time delivery service from the UK and if this continued to be the case it would be prepared to switch more high-volume parts to JPC. However, given the variable element in its own demand, GF needs to be confident of having short response time support especially where suppliers are not close at hand.

GF seem to be happy with the prices it is paying.

EXHIBIT 5 Consultant's market review report – Gagnard Freres

Background

Gordon Stoves (GS) is one of JPC's oldest customers. It manufactures gas cookers for domestic use. Over the years it has seen its market share decline in the UK, which is its only market.

There is a lot of variety in its products and some order quantities are small.

Location

GS is situated approximately three hours' driving time from the JPC plant.

Growth

Due to a major reorganization of distribution channels, over which GS has no control, there is a lot of uncer-

tainty about its future prospects. Over the past five years GS sales have dropped by a third.

Requirements of suppliers

The components purchased are a mix of simple and complex parts but with fairly straightforward tolerances. GS is very insistent that its parts must be delivered to specification and in a clean condition.

The issue of price is usually raised at an annual negotiation. Purchasing is not a strong department in GS and price pressure has never been high. Because of high product variety GS has always held large finished-goods inventory. However, financial pressures are leading GS to reduce working capital (including inventory) and it has notified major suppliers that, in future, it wants them to operate to much shorter lead times.

EXHIBIT 6 Consultant's market review report – Gordon Stoves

Die casting is a process in which molten metal is forced by pressure into a metal mould known as a die. Because the metal solidifies under pressure, the casting conforms to the die cavity in both shape and surface finish.

The size is so accurately controlled that little or no subsequent machining is necessary. This is particularly so when zinc alloys are used. The process also eliminates such machining operations as drilling and certain types of threading.

One of the limitations of die casting is the high cost of the equipment and dies. This is not an important factor in high-volume production applications but it does limit its use in short-run jobs.

For large or complex mouldings, a single-cavity mould is used. If the quantity of castings to be produced is large and they are relatively small in size, a multiple-cavity die can then be used.

EXHIBIT 7 Brief explanation of die casting

The load on manufacturing fluctuates considerably. The work content of different orders varies significantly and smaller customers tend to be erratic in their requirements making forward planning difficult. Many parts can only be made to order because of the irregularity of demand. Paul Farmer's intention is to hold finished goods inventory of more regular components for larger customers but to date this has happened only to a very limited extent because of problems of keeping up with overall demand. One of the next stages of the consultant's involvement is to assess inventory policy and opportunities for reducing work-in-progress. An initial analysis of customers' orders has started and a representative sample of orders for the customers interviewed in the market review is shown in *Exhibits 8* and *9*.

Continuous improvement programme

In the early part of the continuous improvement programme (CIP), four key areas to review were agreed. These, together with other details of the activities so far, are explained in the following sections with details given in *Exhibit 10*.

Manufacturing methods continuous improvement team

The objective agreed for this team was to seek opportunities for improving manufacturing methods particularly in the die casting areas. Details of the initial meetings and agreed actions are given in *Exhibit 10*.

Systems continuous improvement team

The objectives agreed for this team were to ensure that the company has appropriate systems in place, particularly in the areas of estimating, costing and sales documentation. Also, to evaluate the current production scheduling and control systems and to identify a future outline plan of action to implement any agreed improvements. Details of the initial meetings are given in *Exhibit 10*.

Set-up reduction continuous improvement team

The objective of this team was to reduce the time taken to make ready and set up (change over) the die casting machines. Details of the initial meetings are given in *Exhibit 10*.

Customer	Customer order details			Order contribution (£s)	Date order received		Delivery promised to customer	
	Order number	Part number	Order value (£s)		Week	Day	Week	Day
Gordon Stoves	2568	2445A	650	156	10	5	12	5
		2445B	750	195	10	5	19	3
		7643	1,840	644	10	5	13	5
		7643C	140	57	10	5	16	5
		8904	800	224	10	5	20	5
	2889	2445A	650	156	11	4	14	4
		7643	1,200	420	11	4	15	2
		7643C	90	37	11	4	17	4
		9456	280	90	11	4	15	4
	4675	2445A	600	144	12	5	16	5
		2445B	400	104	12	5	16	5
		7643	880	308	12	5	16	2
		7643C	120	49	12	5	18	5
Gagnard Freres	1224	6748	2,600	832	10	4	16	5
		6749	2,800	784	10	4	16	5
		6750	1,250	425	10	4	16	5
	1225	6748	2,900	928	14	2	19	2
		6749	2,800	784	14	2	19	2
		6750	1,150	391	14	2	19	2
	1226	6748	3,100	992	16	1	23	1
		6749	2,800	784	16	1	23	1
		6750	1,200	408	16	1	23	1
	1227	6748	3,100	992	16	1	28	3
		6749	2,800	784	22	1	28	3
	1228	6748	2,600	832	26	1	32	1
		6749	2,400	672	26	1	32	1
		6750	1,400	476	26	1	32	1
Anscombe Products	25013	12445	650	156	14	1	16	1
		17643	80	33	14	1	20	1
		18904	700	196	14	1	24	1
		1945	360	115	14	1	17	1
		1988	630	170	14	1	20	1
	25089	12445	650	156	14	5	18	2
		12460	850	221	14	5	18	5
		17645	1,320	462	14	5	18	5
		1945	620	198	14	5	19	5
		1988	240	65	14	5	20	5
		19885	150	54	14	5	20	5

cont'd

Customer	Customer order details			Order contribution (£s)	Date order received		Delivery promised to customer	
	Order number	Part number	Order value (£s)		Week	Day	Week	Day
Wilson Automotive Components	3674	264405	6,840	1,231	10	2	13	4
		288114	4,860	778	10	2	13	4
	7610	11702	280	129	10	2	11	1
		11468	258	103	10	2	13	1
		21744	85	45	10	2	12	1
	3744	264405	6,250	1,125	11	2	14	4
		288114	4,380	701	11	2	14	4
	7643	11949	285	134	11	2	12	3
	3821	264405	8,600	1,548	12	2	15	4
		288114	4,630	741	12	2	15	4
	7689	11702	485	223	12	2	14	2
		11468	35	14	12	2	13	1
	3927	264405	8,400	1,512	13	2	16	4
		288114	4,820	771	13	2	16	4
	7705	11702	470	216	13	2	14	3
Hardy-Belmont Engineering	2300	76609	800	120	10	1	14	1
		76682	300	66	10	1	14	1
		76698	400	72	10	1	14	1
		X4220	2,500	750	10	1	13	4
	2400	76609	800	120	12	2	16	2
		76682	300	66	12	2	16	2
		76698	600	108	12	2	16	2
	2500	76609	800	120	14	1	18	1
		76682	200	44	14	1	18	1
		76698	400	72	14	1	18	1
	2600	76609	600	90	16	1	20	1
		76682	600	132	16	1	20	1
		76698	600	108	16	1	20	1
		X4220	3,400	1,088	16	1	19	1

NOTES
1 The period for the sample varies by customer and not all orders for the period are shown. The orders are typical for each customer.
2 The total order value by customer will not necessarily reflect the annual split by customer or the total annual revenue.
3 For Wilson Automotive Components six digit part numbers are original equipment, five digit part numbers are spares.
4 Hardy-Belmont Engineering components for special products have an X prefix on the part number.
5 The order contribution was calculated by the consultants as order value minus manufacturing cost. Manufacturing cost includes direct material, direct labour and an allocation of indirect costs such as supervision, maintenance, depreciation, rent and rates.

EXHIBIT 8 Representative sample of customer orders

Customer	Customer order details						
	Order number	Part number	Customer required delivery		Actual delivery to customer		
			Week	Day	Week	Day	
Gordon Stoves	2568	2445A	12	5	13	2	
		2445B	14	5	19	5	
		7643	13	5	14	5	
		7643C	16	5	17	3	
		8904	18	5	22	4	
	2889	2445A	14	4	14	4	
		7643	14	4	16	1	
		7643C	17	4	18	2	
		9456	15	4	15	4	
	4675	2445A	15	3	17	2	
		2445B	15	5	17	1	
		7643	16	2	16	2	
		7643C	17	5	19	2	
Gagnard Freres	1224	6748	16	5	16	5	
		6749	16	5	16	5	
		6750	16	5	16	5	
	1225	6748	19	2	19	2	
		6749	19	2	19	2	
		6750	19	2	19	2	
	1226	6748	23	1	23	1	
		6749	23	1	23	1	
		6750	23	1	23	1	
	1227	6748	27	1	28	3	
		6749	27	1	28	3	
	1228	6748	32	1	32	2	
		6749	32	1	32	2	
		6750	32	1	32	2	
Anscombe Products	25013	12445	16	1	16	3	
		17643	19	1	20	1	
		18904	23	1	28	1	
		1945	16	1	16	4	
		1988	19	1	20	1	
	25089	12445	17	5	18	1	
		12460	16	5	20	2	
		17645	18	5	19	2	
		1945	19	5	20	4	
		1988	20	5	22	3	
		19885	20	5	23	2	

cont'd

| Customer | Customer order details | | | | | |
| | Order number | Part number | Customer required delivery | | Actual delivery to customer | |
			Week	Day	Week	Day
Wilson Automotive Components	3674	264405	13	4	15	1
		288114	13	4	14	5
	7610	11702	11	1	11	1
		11468	11	4	18	4
		21744	11	3	16	3
	3744	264405	14	4	15	5
		288114	14	4	15	5
	7643	11949	12	3	12	3
	3821	264405	15	4	16	4
		288114	15	4	16	5
	7689	11702	13	4	16	3
		11468	12	5	13	5
	3927	264405	16	4	17	5
		288114	16	4	17	4
	7705	11702	14	3	15	3
Hardy-Belmont Engineering	2300	76609	14	1	14	3
		76682	14	1	14	3
		76698	14	1	14	1
		X4220	12	5	14	4
	2400	76609	16	2	16	4
		76682	16	2	16	1
		76698	16	2	16	1
	2500	76609	18	1	18	1
		76682	18	1	18	1
		76698	18	1	19	2
	2600	76609	20	1	20	4
		76682	20	1	19	5
		76698	20	1	20	4
		X4220	19	1	19	5

NOTE: The orders are a representative sample of JPC's performance on delivery.

EXHIBIT 9 Representative sample of customer orders

A Manufacturing methods continuous improvement team

The following tasks were identified at the team's initial meetings and are numbered sequentially.

1　Introduce a rotary table for post-casting operations for high-volume jobs in order to reduce handling and associated labour costs.

2　Identify any excessive operations on existing methods in all stages of casting and secondary operations.

3　Check if untrimmed castings can go directly to the deburring and polishing area thus eliminating the cast trimming operation currently undertaken.

4　Install a drill and tap slide for high-volume work to reduce handling operations at the casting stage.

5　Establish three designated storage areas for pallets to reduce time looking for pallets by machine operators.

6　Check current cycle time on the ten highest-volume jobs loaded each week. Establish lowest times and update all records including the cost information sheets.

7　Assess reasons for casting flash. Draw up a programme of mould refurbishment to reduce post-casting operations and associated tasks.

8　Reduce energy costs in the foundry:
- replace lids on the aluminium holding furnaces
- pre-heat dies.

B Systems continuous improvement team

1　Verify existing roles and responsibilities in the manufacturing planning and control system.

2　Review the foundry and machine shop loading system.

3　Introduce shop-floor visual loading charts for each section.

4　Review machine capabilities in the die casting areas.

5　Improve shop-floor documentation.

6　Review the current estimating system:
- responsibilities

- synthetic data used
- pricing arrangements.

7　Detail the current sales entry and production control procedures to reduce the steps involved and associated costs.

C Set-up reduction continuous improvement team

1　Reduce set-up times on zinc and aluminium die casting machines:
- agree priority machines and dies
- analyse using video recordings.

2　Assess availability of tools necessary for completing set-ups and consider a machine-specific tool set throughout the die casting areas.

3　Overview oil and water hose couplings as an immediate general step. Consult with coupling suppliers.

4　Check lubrication arrangements for all die casting areas as a general step.

5　Review pre-heating arrangements on break times and times between shifts.

6　Review pre-heating die arrangements on changeovers.

D Quality continuous improvement team

1　Identify top five products with highest reject rates. Investigate extent and cause of rejects.

2　Give additional training to setters and operators on product specifications and quality conformance.

3　Review all rejects at the final view stage of the process. Identify cause of rejects and report back on bi-weekly basis.

4　Review all rejects by customers. Identify cause of rejects and report back on a bi-weekly basis.

5　Check each operator's ability to undertake the necessary quality conformance checks. Agree and implement a training programme to bring all operators to required levels.

6　Identify areas for cost-effective, corrective action to reduce rejects.

EXHIBIT 10 Details of the four teams' activities in the continuous improvement programme – initial meetings, tasks identified and actions to be taken

Quality continuous improvement team

The objective of this team was to promote and engender a 'quality-right-first-time' culture throughout the company. Details of the initial meetings are given in *Exhibit 10*. Dave Jenkins (V-P manufacturing) summed up the progress so far:

❝ *The introduction of the continuous improvement programme has been an excellent way of formalizing employee contributions to improving key areas of the firm. Although improvement has always been a major facet of our overall activity in manufacturing, the programme has sharpened our orientation, highlighted the contributions of those involved within the organization as a whole, placed the activity within a corporate context and given a general boost to manufacturing in general and this part of our activity in particular. It's going well. The results to date have been encouraging and, as I agreed with Paul, manufacturing's role in supporting the corporate strategy of JPC has always been recognized and this continuous improvement programme will be one key element in delivering the necessary results.* **❞**

The incentive pay scheme

The basis of the current incentive scheme was a measurement of standard hours produced against actual hours worked for each employee. The standard hours were based upon an agreed time for each operation completed (for example casting) and each employee was paid an individual bonus. When the consultants examined the agreed standard times in use, they found that many had:

- not been checked for changes in work content due, for example, to alterations in methods in the past two years
- been negotiated between supervisor and the operators and the estimated times agreed had not subsequently been checked and an agreed standard time introduced.

The consultants undertook an exercise which timed a sample of jobs. This showed that many agreed times fell outside any logical pattern. It was also found that times were adjusted on occasions depending on the employee carrying out the work in order to reflect some sort of 'experience' factor and maintain pay differentials.

It was concluded that the current scheme was no longer providing a consistent incentive in terms of reflecting different levels of effort and rewarding the productivity associated with each operator's performance.

An analysis of two years' history of output was gathered by the consultants to test how the level of bonus payments varied depending on the principles of alternative schemes before a new scheme was devised. The new scheme also proposes payment based on standard hours produced compared to actual hours worked but the scheme differs from the old one in a number of important respects.

First, the scheme is a group scheme. All employees in production and associated services are paid a standard group bonus. To do this the existing scheme will have to be 'bought out'. Part of the current pay differentials between employees associated with the existing scheme are to be incorporated into their basic pay. The cost of this will be a substantial, one-off cost to the business.

Second, the standard hours achieved are calculated by a formula which allocates time based on total output. Initially the formula suggested a link with the number of components sold. However, when the formula was applied to the past two years' history of output, it was obvious that, because the parts vary in size and complexity, the number of parts produced in different periods varied substantially. This led to large fluctuations in bonus payments when the principle of number of components sold was applied to past output levels. The formula was then revised to calculate the standard hours produced on the basis of a combination of the number and weight of parts produced. The output is converted into an index figure which determines the level of bonus. The basis of the calculation is shown in *Exhibit 11*. To further smooth out fluctuations, the scheme would make bonus payments based on the average of the actual output achieved for the two preceding months.

The scheme is linear with a cut-off point. The bonus rises exactly in line with the increase in the index. When the bonus hits 28 per cent of basic pay, any further increase in the index is not rewarded. Part of the agreement with employees is to review the formula every three months.

Finally, to encourage what Paul Farmer calls 'a quality mentality', the number and weight of parts returned from customers each month are deducted from the output achieved. To emphasize the importance of quality, the return figures are multiplied by a factor of two before being deducted from the 'output achieved' in the period under review.

During the development of the scheme a series of discussions with employee representatives was held. Their support was obtained to run the scheme on a trial basis for two months in parallel with the old scheme. This is planned to take place after approval of the scheme by the Group CEO.

---

1 The scheme is a group incentive scheme covering all shopfloor employees. The scheme calculates a single performance figure and pays a uniform rate of bonus to each participant.

2 Performance is calculated for each calendar month by comparing the allowed hours for the total number and weight of castings recorded on the sales report with the total number of clocked hours for that month.

3 The allowed hours total is calculated by multiplying the volume figures by the standard allowed times as follows:

- 0.85 allowed standard minutes for each casting

- 4.65 allowed standard minutes for each kilogram of castings.

4 The performance level is the total number of allowed hours as a percentage of the total number of clocked hours. This scheme starts to pay a bonus at a performance level of 70.[2] The bonus rises linearly with increases in the index.

5 To smooth out large fluctuations, performance will be calculated on a two-month, rolling average basis.

6 The scheme will be capped when the bonus is equal to 28 per cent of average pay for the group.

EXHIBIT 11 The incentive scheme proposal

Notes

1 The description 'loose' implies that the values and measures against which performance is evaluated had not been updated as changes occurred. The result is that individual performance targets are no longer consistent with each other and that achievement and reward are no longer linked. The outcome is anomalies within the scheme and unfairness in the payments made.

2 Work ratings and perfomance levels are based on the 0–100 British Standard Institute (BSI) scale.

MILLSTONE
PACKAGING

❝ *The competitive nature of our markets is demanding on several dimensions'*, explained Steve Bishop, chief executive officer of Millstone Packaging.

Our response had, therefore, been on many fronts, and much of our sustained performance is a direct result of these actions. One aspect that is a key criterion in most of our markets is that of delivery – both speed (relating to lead times) and reliability (relating to its on-time nature). In fact, our current target on delivery reliability is 98.5 per cent on all job orders.

To help achieve greater control over and also reduce lead times within our total process, we have systematically invested in several areas of our pre-press (that is, pre-printing) operations. This has brought improvements in many areas including quality conformance and costs. A review of relevant aspects of our pre-press activities is underway, and early insights and analyses are now available. Our task is to continue improving in this and the other aspects of our total process in order to keep ahead and maintain our good performance and sound growth record of the past few years. ❞

Steve Bishop was commenting on the rationale and importance for completing the analysis within the pre-press (that is, pre-printing) areas so that the necessary discussion and subsequent decisions could proceed.

Background

Millstone Packaging is a subsidiary of Kingsbury Holdings Inc., a US conglomerate based in New Jersey with interests in food, tobacco, toiletries and domestic products. Millstone was one of eight packaging companies Kingsbury recently purchased, as part of a much larger deal, from a European-based multinational. Three of the companies (including Millstone Packaging) were based in the UK. Of the other five, one was located in France and two each in Italy and Germany. Recognizing the synergy between packaging and its other subsidiaries, Kingsbury saw this move as part of its consolidation strategy within Europe.

Marketing

❝ *As with most companies'*, explained Marco Angeli, vice-president marketing of Millstone, *'we are continuously reviewing our markets in order to track developments and reposition ourselves to maximize opportunities for profitable sales growth'*. Marco continued:

Many of these initiatives are market segment and/or customer oriented in that we identify specific developments or opportunities and plan accordingly. Less often we make decisions concerning much broader issues. One example of the latter was identified almost two years ago and concerned reducing our dependence on line flexographic [used for designs that only comprise solid colours and text, whereas process flexographic is used where the designs include photographic

This case study was written by Terry Hill (University of Oxford). It is intended for class discussion and not as an illustration of good or bad management. © AMD Publishing.

or illustrated elements] *work. Developments have now enabled process flexographic processes to meet the higher demands of designs that until then could only be achieved using gravure processes.*[1] *During the past two years, we have achieved a threefold increase in sales of process flexographic work so that it now accounts for over 20 per cent of total sales revenue. Process flexographic work has brought more sophisticated designs within the budget of more customers for lower priced products, and there is no doubt that this trend will continue both in these and other similar products.*

Today, meeting the design specification in process flexographic work is the key order-winner. In the future, as more companies will be able to meet these design specifications, this will decline in importance as line flexographic work currently has [see Exhibit 1]. However, this will not happen for a few years, and our increasing ability to meet the design specification for process flexographic work will continue to be the most important factor in these markets.

Delivery performance is also an increasingly important criterion in our markets. The need to respond quickly to reducing customer lead times is already important and is generally becoming more so, while failure to deliver on time will lose business quickly. Our customers use fast-throughput, high-speed processes, and if we don't get the packaging there on time then feathers fly. Similarly, an enforced change in our customers' schedules for one of a number of reasons will trigger off the need for a relatively fast response on our part. **99**

Marco continued to describe the nature of the company's markets. While most (72 per cent) of the orders were for repeat items (that is, designs for which the artwork and flexographic plates were already available), the remainder were for amendments to existing (10 per cent) or new designs (18 per cent) (see *Exhibit 2*, Note 2).

66 *Some amended and new designs can take many months to progress. The decision to introduce such a change is typically signalled some months ahead of time. A launch date will be agreed at this time and then a series of discus-*

sions will take place, centred on a customer's decision process to agree the final design. Very often the final outcome is rushed, so by the time we get customer clearance, the expected delivery date gives manufacturing little leeway. Our investment in origination over the past two years is aimed at gaining more control over the total process as well as the lead times in the operations process itself. Support for customers in this aspect of their requirements is most important in itself as well as for repeat orders. **99**

Criteria	Flexographic	
	Line	**Process**
Quality conformance	20↓	60↓
Delivery reliability	QQ	QQ
Delivery speed	30↓	30↑
Price	20↓	Q
Sales/technical support	30	10

NOTE: Q denotes a qualifying criterion; QQ, an order-losing sensitive qualifier.

EXHIBIT 1 Order-winners and qualifiers: current weightings and trends

Operations

Printing is relatively simple in operations terms, as the number of manufacturing processes through which a job passes is at most two or three. Although typically using high-volume batch processes, the nature of printing work demands highly skilled staff. One outcome of this is that the responsibility for all aspects of quality conformance, work scheduling and set-ups has always been part of an operator's job.

Jim Moeller, vice-president operations, explained that the company had systematically invested in machines, in part to do with supporting sales growth and also to keep abreast of process technology developments, that included customer demands for an increased number of colours within packing designs. 'In operations there is pressure on a number of dimensions. Cost reduction and quality conformance have been with us for many years', explained Jim.

Customer	Design type[1,2]	Quantity (000s)	Order dates		
			Customer placement	Delivery	
				Agreed	Actual
Browns	R	500	14 Oct	10 Jan	10 Jan
Aztec	R	1,000	11 Nov	18 Jan	18 Jan
Cottons	N	200	15 Jan	6 Apr	16 Apr
Solent Bar	A	400	7 Oct	23 Mar	25 Mar
Hartstone	A	700	6 Jan	18 Mar	18 Mar
A. J. Foods	R	5,000	2 Dec	17 Feb	17 Feb
Browns	N	4,660	2 Dec	18 Mar	18 Mar
Mirror Foods	R	850	17 Jan	30 Mar	29 Mar
Homewood	A	700	3 Feb	27 Mar	29 Mar
Abbey	R	450	3 Feb	13 Mar	12 Mar
F-lite	A	500	10 Jan	20 Mar	28 Mar
Cottons	N	750	8 Dec	10 Mar	18 Mar
Cottons	R	3,500	30 Oct	20 Jan	20 Jan
Hartstone	A	1,800	8 Jan	16 Mar	24 Mar
Browns	N	250	10 Dec	8 Mar	8 Mar
Abbey	R	3,000	21 Nov	10 Jan	8 Jan
Hartstone	N	500	17 Dec	21 Mar	30 Mar
A. J. Foods	A	1,500	4 Jan	8 Feb	8 Feb
A. J. Foods	N	600	29 Nov	7 Feb	7 Feb
Farnells	R	800	10 Nov	8 Jan	8 Jan
Alexon	A	850	14 Dec	10 Feb	11 Mar
A. J. Foods	N	1,200	4 Jan	28 Mar	28 Mar
Homewood	R	400	6 Jan	25 Mar	25 Mar
Cowies	N	300	14 Feb	28 Mar	30 Mar
Browns	A	900	10 Nov	12 Jan	19 Jan
J. B. Foods	R	1,200	30 Oct	7 Jan	7 Jan
Alexon	N	650	11 Nov	1 Feb	22 Feb
F-lite	A	750	17 Dec	18 Jan	16 Feb
A. J. Foods	N	450	6 Feb	10 Mar	22 Mar
Shelleys	R	800	10 Nov	10 Feb	10 Feb
Lakewood	A	300	18 Oct	7 Jan	16 Jan
F-lite	N	1,500	25 Nov	1 Mar	14 Mar
Farnells	A	600	7 Jan	16 Feb	16 Feb
Marcos	R	200	1 Dec	19 Mar	19 Mar

cont'd

Customer	Design type[1,2]	Quantity (000s)	Order dates		
			Customer placement	Delivery	
				Agreed	Actual
Richards	A	1,000	10 Oct	12 Jan	21 Jan
JBK	A	900	17 Dec	21 Jan	21 Jan
F-lite	R	1,200	12 Jan	30 Mar	30 Mar
A. J. Foods	N	850	4 Dec	21 Feb	1 Mar
Hartstone	N	600	8 Nov	30 Mar	18 Apr
Abbey	R	1,000	28 Oct	18 Dec	18 Dec
Shelleys	A	900	14 Dec	29 Jan	29 Jan
Alexon	N	400	16 Nov	8 Feb	16 Feb

NOTES
1 R = repeat design; A = amended design; N = new design.
2 The above sample gives 14 orders for each design type. However, of the orders processed in the first three months of the year, the actual breakdown between design types was: repeat, 72 per cent; amended, 10 per cent; and new, 18 per cent. In all other ways, however, the sample given is representative.

EXHIBIT 2 Sample of completed customer orders for all design types

Customers upgrading their own processes in order to increase throughput speeds has resulted in the need for tighter packaging specifications. This has put even more pressure on quality conformance as well as contributing to the growing importance of on-time delivery. The advent of developments in process flexographics has also allowed customers to increase the features of their packaging design, a factor that has always been an important part of a customer's own product offering. Furthermore, the company has systematically invested in pre-press activities such as origination and platemaking in order to increase its overall control and reduction of lead times and to strengthen ties with customers, a move that makes a lot of sense. In addition, we have achieved the substantial cost savings in all the pre-press areas that the investment proposals identified.

He went on to explain that the company had also moved from rubber mats to polymer plates as the medium for print transfer. Although the actual plate costs for polymer are twice that of rubber due to material costs, the former are reusable up to five or six times, whereas rubber mats could only be used once, which suited the changing mixture of the company's business to smaller, repeat orders.

Our markets are also increasingly characterized by shorter lead times', explained Jim.

Our scheduling rules call for lead times to be in the order of 10 days to allow for all manufacturing needs to be met. Given the importance of delivery reliability, breaking into schedules may put some orders at risk in terms of delivery and will undoubtedly increase costs and invariably lead to losses in machine capacity. In fact, machines are sometimes held waiting for a job to be ready to run.

Origination

Three years ago', explained Tom Herbert, 'the company decided to invest in an origination capability.

The reasons were several. The improvements in process flexographics enabled customers to undertake pack designs that previously, because they could only be completed by gravure, could not have been justified on cost grounds. We recognized that we needed to be in at the start of these developments and build on our technical capability and the strong technical image we enjoyed in the marketplace. At that time our mix of orders for line and process work was 93 and 7 per cent, respectively. Today it is 78 and 22 per cent, respectively.

Similarly, three years ago we bought in all our origination work. The artwork and customer liaison was, at that time, managed within the company, but the actual artwork and negative preparation was subcontracted. From the negatives, we make plates to go on to the machines and we have, for many years, completed this in-house. The real change has been in the preparation of artwork and the production of negatives. To be at the forefront of these changes and to offer a more complete service to our customers, we decided to undertake these tasks and have moved from a position three years ago where we bought all these services from

outside to today where 82 per cent of all our needs are provided in-house. 99

He went on to explain that the trend in work mix towards process flexographics would continue as customers sought to improve their packaging designs as a way of enhancing sales of their own products. The rationale for investing in origination was that it offered increased control over the new design procedures, better response times, a more integrated liaison with customers and reduction of origination costs. The aim by next year was to complete almost all jobs in-house. A short synopsis of origination procedures is provided in *Exhibit 3* and information relating to the department is given in *Exhibit 4*.

When an order is received that requires either a new design or an amendment to an existing design, it goes to a planner within the origination department. The planner then allocates it to a buyer, taking into account existing workloads and also customer knowledge where this has relevance to the smooth running of a job. A buyer then prepares the customer brief and passes it to the studio for the artwork to be completed. Currently, there are five staff members[1] working in the studio and they select the priority for completing jobs in line with customer delivery requirements. Including customer liaison, there are nine steps in the procedure before the negatives are sent to manufacturing, which then makes the plates and prints the job.

The length of time it takes to approve initial designs or subsequent changes varies with each customer. For planning purposes, the total lead times allowed were 21 days for an amended design and 22 and 25 days for a new design (for line and process, respectively). Many of these steps were, in fact, allocated one day in terms of overall planning, yet took only a few hours to complete. Also, 10 days were allocated to the artwork

task in the studio even though the average time was only four hours. The 10 days were allocated in order that a realistic allowance would be made to include the backlog position in this part of the procedure.

The most difficult dimension in planning origination schedules was caused by customer delays in approving artwork and subsequent modifications. Customer placement dates recognized the lengthy lead times in this stage of the total procedure (see *Exhibit 2*). However, very often customer approvals were delayed until the point that delivery dates of the printed packaging were put at risk. Then all efforts had to be made to ensure that the agreed deliveries were met, which often was linked to a customer's own product launch date.

Currently, the marketing/sales team is responsible for customer liaison. The customers discuss orders of all types with the relevant sales personnel, who are the prime contacts throughout all stages of the job. The exception is distribution, as direct discussion/confirmation of delivery details are made with the customer by the distribution function.

NOTE

1 Of the five staff members in the studio, one is a trainee. The company has found that studio staff of the necessary experience and capability are hard to come by and can command high salaries. For these reasons it decided to train its own staff within this area.

EXHIBIT 3 Origination department procedures

Customer	Line/process[1]	Agreed delivery date	Design type[2]
Abbey	L	30 Jun	N
Browns	L	15 Jul	A
Shelleys	P	27 May	N
Hartstone	L	4 Apr	A
Aztec	P	11 Jun	A
Oaks	P	27 Mar	A
A. J. Foods	L	3 Jul	N
Aztec	L	18 Apr	A
F-lite	L	20 Mar	N
Texet	L	2 Aug	A
Radcliffes	P	4 Jun	N
Coles	P	10 Mar	N
Texet	L	10 Jul	A
Hartstone	L	31 Mar	A
A. J. Foods	P	13 Apr	A
J. B. Foods	L	18 Jun	N
Abbey	L	21 Jun	N
Cowies	L	21 Mar	A
JBK	P	20 May	A
Browns	L	6 Sep	N
Alexon	P	16 Mar	N
Crystal	L	21 Aug	N
Oaks	P	16 Apr	A
Marcos	L	29 Mar	N
Solent	L	18 Jun	A
Hartstone	P	2 Apr	N
Crystal	L	8 May	A
Shelleys	L	10 Apr	N
Abbey	L	2 Apr	A
F-lite	L	4 Apr	N
Radcliffes	P	1 May	A
Marcos	L	16 Sep	N
Shelleys	L	30 Aug	N

NOTES
1 L = line; P = process.
2 A = amendment; N = new.

EXHIBIT 4 Representative sample of the 491 jobs in progress in the origination department on 31 March

The future

Steve Bishop concluded:

❝ *Our decision to move into origination has given us much of what we hoped. It gets us closer to our customers and means that we can respond more quickly to changes in their needs. The investments involved were not large, but the cost advantages we have secured have yielded a good return. Overall our business is growing and this has been one contribution to our improved position. Certainly we feel we have the potential to gain more control over more of the process and at least afford ourselves the opportunity of reviewing lead times with the intention of reducing them and thereby supporting the key delivery-related criteria, which are a growing part of our markets.* ❞

Note

1. Lower priced consumer products, such as potato chips or potato crisps, could not justify designs that could only previously be met using gravure processes. The lower costs of flexographic processes now enabled more sophisticated designs to be used on those types of product.

PETERSON
CARTON SERVICES

9

"*Well, Jim'*, concluded Gerry Townsend, '*I do not understand why the downward trend in our financial performance is still continuing and particularly why last month does not show the improvement we expected.'* Gerry Townsend, managing director of Peterson Carton Services, was discussing the management accounts for February with Jim Redman, the financial director.

With the increase in sales and manufacturing activity achieved since this time last year, the expected performance improvement has not materialized. In fact, the very opposite has happened. The financial position has now become very worrying. Well, by the end of next week we need to have prepared a summary of events and review of the actions we intend to take in order to bring about the necessary improvements. So far, the group board of directors has been patient, but at next week's meeting I am sure they will demand a clear statement of why this has happened and the

steps we intend to take to turn the position around. We have to know how we are going to achieve our annual budgeted profit, having made losses in the first two months of this year amounting to £46,000 and £54,000, respectively [see Exhibit 1]."

Background

Peterson Carton Services (PCS) is situated in Lancaster, the county town of Lancashire in the north-west of England. Established in 1948, it was taken over in the late 1980s by Stebro Industries plc, a diverse group of companies involved in food processing, civil engineering, steel fabrication, general engineering, distribution, waste disposal, paper and carton making. PCS currently employs about 200 people and processes approximately 3,000 tons of cardboard (referred to as *board* within the carton industry)

Aspect	Accounting period results and current year budget							
	Current year minus			Last year		Current year		
	4	3	2	Jan–June	July–Dec	Jan	Feb	Budget
Sales revenue (£000s)	6,292	6,266	5,505	3,060	3,745	581	563	6,800
Trading profit (£000s)	283	135	(151)	79	(321)	(46)	(54)	236
Percentage of sales margin	4.5	2.2	(2.7)	2.5	(8.5)	(7.9)	(9.6)	3.5
Percentage of return on investment	2.8	2.5	(4.6)	1.4	(12.6)	(11.8)	(14.2)	8.0
Net working capital as percentage of sales revenue	14.1	14.4	13.2	14.2	18.1	18.2	18.1	10.7

EXHIBIT 1 Summary of trading results and current year's budget

This case study was written by Terry Hill (University of Oxford) and S. H. Chambers (University of Warwick). It is intended for class discussion and not as an example of good or bad management practice. © AMD Publishing.

a year, making it one of the top 30 carton manufacturers in the UK. The carton-making industry is highly fragmented, due principally to the costs of distribution, with some 250 companies serving the country. Most of these produce a wide range of general cartons for most market applications, with some companies also making speciality products to meet the particular needs of customers. PCS uses lithographic ('litho') printing and other traditional processes (see *Exhibits 2A* and *B*) to make its 'general' cartons (see *Exhibits 3A* and *B*) but has also developed specialized processes to make 'windowed' cartons at high speed and high quality. In addition, PCS also makes a non-carton product range of drip mats for breweries and distributors of imported wines. Also known as coasters, drip mats are sold for distribution to hotels, taverns and wine bars, where they are used to protect the surface of tables and bars. The shape and print details are customer-specified for each order.

Three years ago, the company had brought on to its main site a smaller carton business, which it had purchased some years earlier. As part of a rationalization plan, it was anticipated that this would lead to higher profits in the longer term, due to the estimated reduction in manufacturing and overhead costs resulting from this consolidation. Although cost savings did result, lower prices for existing products brought about by higher levels of competition led to a decline in profits for that year. When in the following year sales revenue also declined by 12 per cent, the company went into a loss situation (see *Exhibit 1*). In order to try to identify those market segments in which there was the greatest potential for sales growth, PCS completed a major

EXHIBIT 2a Five-colour, offset lithographic printing machine
SOURCE: Peterson Carton Services

EXHIBIT 2b A cut and crease machine
SOURCE: Peterson Carton Services

EXHIBIT 3a Completed cartons waiting to be despatched
SOURCE: Peterson Carton Services

EXHIBIT 3b A typical carton
SOURCE: Peterson Carton Services

market analysis, with the help of a large firm of marketing strategy consultants. This exercise reviewed the potential for sales growth in each of the main segments in which PCS operated. As a result, the consultants recommended a strategy for the company to concentrate its major sales effort in the beverages, food and 'windowed products' segments, which they identified as having the greatest potential for the rapid increase in volume necessary to sustain the required level of recovery in sales revenue and profit. The report argued that growth in these segments would be the best way to compensate for the sales revenue decline experienced in some other market segments. The reason for the sales decline in these areas was believed to be the result of intensive competition from carton companies beginning to specialize in supplying the needs of particular industries

Marketing

By the middle of last year, most of the consultant's recommendations had been actioned, and the increased understanding of the market was found to be useful in establishing sales revenue budgets for this year (*Exhibit 4*). As a direct result of the market-

Market segment	Customer	Last year's actual	Current year's forecast
Beverages	Maister Teas[1]	335	610
	ARD Coffees	270	230
	Tea Specialty Packers	225	260
	Others	41	50
	Total	871	1150
Industrial products	Agroparts[2]	178	100
	NY Equipment[2]	174	50
	Rotabearings	156	150
	F C Bruce	104	90
	Others	10	10
	Total	622	400
Food	Maister Cakes[3]	256	475
	McPhee Foods[4]	208	250
	Country Cuisine[4]	20	60
	Others	82	35
	Total	566	820
Pharmaceuticals	Pharmex	228	230
	AB Products	157	160
	HMR	103	120
	Others	40	40
	Total	528	550
Drip mats	Pride Ales[5]	309	145
	Hop Products	128	95
	Korolla Cola	31	30
	Others	42	30
	Total	510	300

cont'd

Market segment	Customer	Last year's actual	Current year's forecast
Toiletries (non-luxury ranges)	Prince & Haywood	224	220
	SC Packers (Export)	187	185
	Others	75	75
	Total	486	480
Confectionery	Elizabeth Ross	181	150
	Others	105	100
	Total	286	250
Small electrical items[6]	GRA Electrical	168	100
	Domelex	62	50
	Others	50	30
	Total	280	180
Sundry[6]	Various general cartons	1,025	870
	Total	1,025	870
Group[7]	Various general cartons	430	400
	Total	430	400
Windowed products[8]	Various	1,064	1,300
	Group[7,9]	137	200
	Total	1,201	1,500
Grand total		6,805	6,900

NOTES
1 The first order for Maister Teas was placed in May for delivery in July of last year.
2 The sales representative serving Agroparts and NY Equipment left PCS in September last year and joined a competitor. He is known to be arranging trial orders for these customers and is offering four-week delivery for any new orders. Given the examples in the case study narrative of what has happened in these circumstances in the past, current year budget figures reflect the position which PCS forecasts will result.
3 The first order for Maister Cakes was placed in July for delivery in October last year.
4 Both McPhee Foods and Country Cuisine are introducing just-in-time (JIT) programmes. This will require its suppliers to provide a weekly delivery of all their range of cartons. However, as part of this change to JIT, both customers are intending to reduce the number of suppliers they currently use.
5 Marketing has decided (with appropriate corporate approval) not to renew the annual contract, which is due for signature in the next two months. Contract work was not undertaken prior to last year.
6 Many of the small electrical items/sundry accounts are under severe competitive pressure from small carton manufacturers offering short lead times.
7 'Group' refers to sales to companies within the carton division of Stebro Industries plc.
8 The major marketing initiatives commenced this January, and are now leading to improvements in sales revenues. However, reports from the field are indicating difficulties caused by PCS's current long lead times.
9 To help boost sales in this segment PCS is encouraging other companies within the Carton Division to seek suitable work, where it could provide the subcontractor windowing capacity.

EXHIBIT 4 Summary of actual sales revenue for last year and sales budgets for this year (£000s)

ing thrust, sales revenue rose by 22 per cent in the second half of last year (see *Exhibit 1*). Details for the main segments served by PCS are given in *Exhibit 4*.

Beverages

The long-established relationships with ARD Coffee and Tea Specialty Packers (two of PCS's main customers) are expected to be maintained. This is largely due to the company's reputation for high levels of product quality conformance and delivery reliability and also because of the support given by its design function to help develop new products giving greater added value (for instance, by incorporating gold-leaf designs). All beverage cartons are printed in four or five colours and are normally delivered on completion.

The account with Maister Teas began with a small order first placed in May of last year for delivery in July. Since then, the business has grown. In fact, actual sales are substantially higher than the original forecasts given to the company. The potential for large sales with this customer is considerable for two reasons. First, its annual expenditure on cartons is significant; second, it is moving to a position of developing long-term relationships with a smaller number of highly competent suppliers to provide all its needs. All Maister's contracts are for high-quality, five-colour products, and the company expects its suppliers to operate strict internal quality control procedures. Orders are generally very large, but delivery is to weekly call-offs over a three-month period. In discussions on the future, Maister's buyers have stated that they wish to reduce further their own in-house carton inventory and intend to move gradually during the current year to twice-weekly deliveries on most cartons. While sales margins are low compared to general carton work, this is normal for high-volume contracts because, with considerable overcapacity existing in the carton-making industry at this time, there is strong competition for high-volume work.

Food

Before last year, this segment was considered to comprise general carton work, with many small to medium orders being processed for a variety of customers. The marketing strategy report, however, highlighted the potential to acquire more regular, high-volume work in this segment. This was actively pursued last year, resulting in an early contract for McPhee Foods. In addition, the developing relationship with Maister Teas resulted in an introduction to Maister Cakes, another division of the same company from whom a first order was received in July of last year. The order characteristics of this work are very similar to those of Maister Teas. The only significant difference is that cartons for Maister Cakes are physically larger. As with the tea division, orders soon increased and sales levels for this account are expected to continue to grow in the current year. Last November, an order from Maister Cakes was delivered five working days late. This was due to a quality conformance problem

requiring sorting to remove below-standard cartons, This late delivery brought a serious complaint from Maister Cakes and a claim for compensation to cover disruption to, and loss of output from, their own factories.

Drip mats

Following the marketing strategy report and corporate discussions on PCS's business as a whole, it has recently been decided to reduce the company's sales efforts in this market in order to allow the business to develop other segments deemed to be more in line with the company's needs. Keith Bowyer, sales/marketing director, explained:

" *There are several factors that make this segment unattractive. Margins are generally low and the total market is declining. Although contract-type business for large, nationally based brewers (for example, Pride Ales) is ordered on an annual basis with regular call-offs, other ('promotional') orders (accounting for about 25 per cent of their business) are required relatively quickly, resulting in the need for some schedule changes to the litho print programme. These promotional drip mats are very often of a five-colour design and considerably more demanding in quality requirements. This necessitates slower running on the presses, and higher levels of rejects are typically experienced. In addition, because they form part of a one-off brand sales promotion, it is always critical that orders are delivered on time.*

Predominantly two- and four-colour work, drip mats are made out of thicker and lower quality board and use the same litho printing and die-cutting/creasing (but not glueing) processes as cartons. However, the final stripping, separating and packing processes use specialized equipment dedicated to these products. This product range accounted for 7 per cent of last year's total sales revenue and current year budgets reflect the downward trend agreed for this segment in our strategy [see Exhibit 4]. The irregular nature of orders often leads to an imbalance in departmental workloads. This is particularly so in glueing, as drip mats do not require this process, whereas most other products do. A high level of drip mat business, therefore, results in less work for some of the subsequent sections, such as glueing.

These factors have all contributed to our decision not to pursue growth in this segment and not to defend existing accounts against competitors' price reductions. **99**

Windowed cartons

There is a very large number of customers for windowed cartons, each placing irregular orders, often for small quantities. Most orders are for four- or five-colour printing, generally of high-quality artwork or photographs. The function of a windowed carton is to give the eventual customer sight of the product it contains, without opening the packaging. Often quite ordinary products (such as car accessories) are packed in this way and are usually bought as gifts (for example at Christmas).

The marketing review highlighted the considerable growth potential for this product, a fact reflected in this year's budget. It is known that very few compet-

itors possess the necessary equipment and skills to produce high-quality windowed cartons. Of particular importance is the need for a supplier to be able to work with customers in the development of suitable designs, that would enhance their products in the desired manner. This was normally achieved by a combination of sales representatives' visits and subsequent design and prototype development by PCS's design department. Many customers use this form of packaging as a one-off marketing exercise, and hence most designs were produced once and are not subsequently reordered.

Other carton manufacturers within the Stebro Industries group do not possess windowing capacity. Therefore they will sometimes use PCS as a subcontractor to provide this service but complete all the other operations needed to make a windowed carton within their own factories. When quoting for windowing work in the group, PCS produces an

Works order number	Customer	Invoiced sales (£)	Actual variable costs (£)			
			Material[1]	Processing	Delivery	Windowing machine hours
16862	Group[2]	9,320	1,306	2,795	50	124.0
16893	Panda Pottery	12,436	2,140	1,806	90	56.5
16897	Electronica	17,008	3,670	2,385	165	121.5
16912	Group	2,451	625	541	25	24.5
16935	Durham Foods	8,250	1,710	902	60	26.0
16939	Stafpots	4,241	787	447	25	19.5
16956	Group	6,895	1,651	1,668	45	74.0
16974	Giftware Enterprises	7,908	1,367	945	35	24.0
16987	AG Camm	4,266	934	759	28	9.5
17007	Photo-X	6,121	1,452	792	40	33.5
17016	Group	3,549	770	721	30	32.0
17089	Ceramica	14,733	2,748	2,368	210	51.0
17091	Essex Confectionery	12,236	2,960	2,129	185	46.0
17115	Carac Gifts	17,450	4,976	2,903	305	16.0
17144	Group	6,982	2,041	1,499	55	66.5

NOTES

1 In the case of products processed for the group, material costs only include the windowing materials (PVC), adhesives and packaging used (for example corrugated cardboard boxes and shrinkwrap film). Processing costs normally only relate to the windowing machine, as this process also carries out any necessary glueing.

2 The term group refers to another company in the carton division for which a windowing subcontract service is provided by PCS, as explained in the narrative.

EXHIBIT 5 A representative sample of windowed cartons produced in the period July to September, last year

estimate of the cost of this operation based on material, transport and processing costs. The latter are calculated using the normal hourly estimating rate for windowing machines. The carton division as a whole has recognized the potential for this product. Consequently, a similar sales effort in the other carton companies has been made and rapid growth is anticipated. *Exhibit 5* lists a representative sample of orders for windowed cartons.

Other market segments

The marketinng strategy recognized that while 'other market' business as a whole represents nearly half of PCS's sales revenue, much of this is average volume and comprises work that is of a technically undemanding nature which could be manufactured by most, if not all, carton producers. Much of this business was regular, repeat work, with only minor and infrequent design changes. Commenting on this segment, Keith Bowyer explained that it is probably retained by factors such as:

- customer inertia (packaging may be low on a buyer's list of priorities)

- goodwill developed by long and successful trading relationships

- customer satisfaction with the service provided by PCS (comprising a combination of quick delivery when necessary, delivery reliability and consistent quality conformance)

- good personal relationships between PCS's sale representatives and the purchasing function of its customers

- low prices for high-volume contracts.

He continued:

" Our current marketing approach recognizes that many of our customers' orders are potentially vulnerable to competition. An example of this is illustrated by the significant amount of business we lost when a salesman (specializing in handling agreements with a number of industrial customers) left our employment and joined a competitor. Unfortunately, with his knowledge of this aspect of our business, he was able to attract many orders away from us

to his new company. As we supplied nothing that could be considered unique, he was able to take many customers with him by offering a slight improvement on one or more factors, or even just offering to guarantee the same level of overall service he, and we, had provided in the past.

Our strategy is to improve our levels of service to these customers, and to defend our current business when necessary, by lowering prices. In the long term, it is intended to offset the inevitable decline in these segments by increasing sales in more profitable areas, such as windowed products – a fact that is central to the marketing review completed some 15 months ago. However, the decline in sales we experienced two years ago and the impact this had on our profit performance is a factor of which we are always mindful. "

Operations

Processes

All equipment is laid out on a functional basis. For example, there is a printing area in which all printing processes are located, a die-cutting/creasing area, containing all die-cutting and creasing processes and so on. See *Exhibit 2*, which shows examples of some of the plant used, and *Exhibit 6*, which summarizes the process capabilities and records of utilization.

In general, a machine can process any width of cardboard up to the maximum size stated (see *Exhibit 6*). But those responsible for planning orders aim to maximize the use of available machine widths by appropriate carton design layouts. Thus, for most products the 52-inch litho presses are capable of producing more cartons per sheet of cardboard than the 40-inch machines, resulting in lower processing costs and often less material waste per unit of output. (There is always some material waste built into sheet design, if only at the edges. This comment refers to the fact that this inherent waste would, on a 52-inch press, be spread over more carton designs than for a 40-inch press printing the same design.) The cost of tooling (litho plates and die-cutting dies) increases approximately in proportion to the area covered, but this is usually more than compensated for by the lower processing costs inherent in a wider press. Any litho press can print fewer colours than its capability (for example a five-colour litho printer can print four or fewer colours: see *Exhibit 7*, which gives a representative sample of orders completed on the five-colour printer).

All the machines, except L5 and the windowing processes, are over 10 years old and fully depreciated. More modern equipment would offer faster running speeds, marginally quicker set-ups and improved consistency of quality. However, the capital investment involved is very high. Because of the financial record of the company and current low market prices, replacement equipment has been difficult for PCS to justify in the past few years.

Process	Machine manning	Basic capability		Manned time as percentage of available time[1,2]				
		Maximum size	Maximum colours	Q1	Q2	Q3	Q4	Total year
Litho printing[3]	L1	40	2	97	77	73	61	77
	L2	40	4	99	98	93	99	97
	L3	52	2	62	56	63	67	62
	L4	52	4	101	94	97	107	100
	L5	52	5	78	93	113	127	103
Die cutting and creasing	C1	40	–	97	85	73	84	85
	C2	40	–	52	51	42	50	49
	C3	60	–	89	81	78	99	87
	C4	60	–	91	75	81	94	85
	C5	60	–	83	83	86	98	88
Glueing	G1	–	–	67	60	84	91	76
	G2	–	–	69	58	77	81	71
	G3	–	–	56	57	46	60	55
	G4	–	–	34	29	41	40	36
	G5	–	–	59	48	55	76	60
	G6	–	–	56	52	40	45	48
	G7	–	–	56	52	36	40	49
Drip mat punching	D1	–	–	20	41	40	25	31
Windowing	W1	–	–	64	52	120	70	77
	W2	–	–	64	70	125	71	83

NOTES
1 Manned time includes (a) all running time, including overtime, (b) all set-ups, and (c) short duration downtime (less than one hour), due to mechanical/electrical breakdowns, where it was not considered necessary to reallocate the operators involved.
2 Available time is taken as normal two-shift working (weekdays) and excludes shutdowns.
3 Any press can print fewer than its maximum number of colours; for example, L5 can print five-, four-, three-, two-, or one-colour work. Conversely, a two-colour press can print four-colour work, but this would require the cartons to be passed through a second time. Neither printing fewer colours nor passing a job through the same press twice makes sound commercial sense and it is only done as a last resort.

EXHIBIT 6 Analysis of average plant utilization

Completion date (printing)	Works order number	Customer	Total machine time set-up and running (hours)	Number of colours
January	16261	ARD Coffees	46	5
January	16301	Pride Ales	27	5
February	16326	Prince & Haywood	17	5
February	16349	Tea Specialty Packers	29	5
March	16407	Agroparts	41	4
March	16514	McPhee Foods	63	5
April	16527	GRA Electrical	21	5
April	16602	S C Packers (export)	36	4
May	16640	Barking & Hollis	32	5
May	16695	Pride Ales	11	3
May	16715	S C Packers (export)	24	4
June	16756	Country Cuisine	17	5
June	16809	Hop Products	22	5
July	16846	Prince & Haywood	55	5
July	16903	Wigan Breweries	22	4
August	16954	McPhee Foods	63	5
August	17001	Group	52	5
September	17063	Maister Cakes	10	5
September	17127	Tea Specialty Packers	62	5
October	17189	Korolla Cola	28	5
October	17231	Tea Specialty Packers	83	5
November	17277	Maister Tea	35	5
November	17336	Maister Cakes	41	5
December	17390	Elizabeth Ross	32	5
December	17426	Domelex	12	5

EXHIBIT 7 A representative sample of work printed on L5 during last year

Personnel

The plant is operated on two shifts of 7.5 hours per shift for five days a week, with varying levels of overtime throughout the year (see *Exhibit 8*). Manning levels for all the main processes are agreed nationally between the relevant trade unions and employers' federations. Thus there is an agreed manning level on a four-colour printing press and another on a five-colour printing press. Where an order specifies five colours, then it is more cost effective to print it on a five-colour press than to have to process it twice through a three- or four-colour press. PCS, as with most other businesses, conforms to these agreements, leaving only service areas (such as packing, materials handling, warehouse and quality control) where manning levels are determined by agreement between local management and the relevant trade union representatives. It is in these areas that reduction in labour could be achieved more easily by investment in equipment.

Month	Total overtime premium paid (£)[2]
January	5,460
February	2,100
March	3,246
April	3,672
May	6,256
June	4,107
July	5,363
August	11,718
September	19,869
October	26,207
November	32,111
December	17,006

NOTES

1 Overtime premium is the supplement paid to employees for working overtime and ranges from one-third of their hourly rate for short periods of weekday overtime to 100 per cent of hourly rate for Saturday afternoons and Sundays.

2 These figures do not include extra salaried costs (mainly supervisors).

EXHIBIT 8 Overtime premium costs for January to December, last year[1]

Operations and materials control

On receipt of a customer order, the sales administration department raises a works order, which is passed to the operations control department. (A works order is an internal document giving details of a customer order and providing the manufacturing function with the authorization to print a particular product in line with the volumes required. It would normally be accompanied by details of the design and the relevant litho printing plates.) At this stage, materials are ordered (board, any special inks and printing plates), and the order is scheduled using a bar chart for each machine. This procedure also shows the loading for each process.

Some excess board is always purchased to allow for both the tolerances (usually ± 10 per cent) of the manufacturer's actual supply of material and for the uncertain material yield from the processes. Customer orders are accepted on the basis of the carton industry's 'standard conditions of sale', that allow a tolerance on the quantity of cartons delivered (usually ± 10 per cent). Generally, orders are

planned to produce around 10 per cent more cartons than the quantity ordered. All good cartons produced can then be delivered and invoiced at the full price. All materials are usually received within three weeks of order but this lead time can be reduced if a supplier is notified that the particular item is urgent. In addition, most specifications of board can be obtained from stockists within 24 hours but such deliveries cost about 40 per cent more than supplies direct from the manufacturers.

The prinicipal objective of the operations control function is to ensure that the capacity of all processes is allocated effectively and supplies are obtained at the agreed level of quality and delivered on time to ensure that customers' orders are produced by the contracted date. However many changes in these schedules have to be catered for and are caused by factors such as:

- special customer orders are required to be produced in less than the normal lead time

- customer schedule changes to quantity and/or delivery dates

- cancelled orders

- machine breakdowns or manning problems

- quality control issues (such as faulty printing plates, inks and board), resulting in jobs being stopped and/or taken off the process until the problem can be resolved

- late deliveries from suppliers.

Furthermore, the operations control function is responsible for ensuring the most efficient utilization of the processes, by sequencing jobs in such a way as to minimize set-up times and levels of work-in-progress inventory. In addition, processes with a high level of utilization must be planned to keep levels of overtime within acceptable limits, while ensuring that order backlogs do not get too long, which would result in a potential loss of orders. (Order backlogs – also known as *forward load* – refer to the number of orders that, at any one time, are waiting to go into the manufacturing system. Promised delivery dates to customers, therefore, have to take into account not only the process lead time – the length of time a product takes to be completed – but also the number of agreed orders ahead of it in the queue of work.)

During the second half of last year, many changes in these factors were apparently brought about by the major alterations to the work mix resulting from the new strategy. *Exhibit 6* summarizes changes in utilization and *Exhibit 9* is a record of the order-backlog position for all main processes.

In addition, the operations control department maintains records of all material issued to production and the output of 'good' cartons. As job costing is not regularly carried out by the accounting function this information is only used by the materials planner as a guide for the purchasing and issue of board. Special analyses are sometimes carried out on new contracts to ensure that the actual material usage is in line with estimates; *Exhibit 10* summarizes the data for early orders from Maister Cakes. Because the relationship between the output and input of board is shown to be within only 1 per cent of the estimate, the estimating rates are considered to be satisfactory, as some improvements in material usage would normally be made as a result of producing a particular carton on a regular basis.

Quality control

For most customers, quality standards are established on initial production orders, usually in the presence of a customer's representative. Samples are selected that reflect the extremes of acceptable quality, and subsequent production and future repeat orders are controlled to fall within these agreed parameters. Quality is maintained by the process operatives, with random inspections by patrolling quality control staff and the final inspection of random samples undertaken by the packing section.

For Maister Teas and Maister Cakes, the procedure has to be much more rigorous. Production trials are conducted (at PCS's expense) and control samples are selected and authorized off-site by Maister's quality assurance function. Generally, the acceptable limits are very narrow (relative to other customers' orders), and Maister also lays down strict quality control procedures, that have to be followed during production and include the frequency of patrol inspections. In addition, a specified number of cartons from each pallet of finished goods must be kept aside for subsequent inspection and referenced to the relevant pallet. When

Process	Machine	Last year												Current	
		Q1			Q2			Q3			Q4			Q1	
		Jan	Feb	Mar	Apr	May	June	July	Aug	Sep	Oct	Nov	Dec	Jan	Feb
Litho printing	L1	4	5	2	2	2	3	4	2	2	1	1	1	2	2
	L3	2	6	3	3	5	4	4	3	4	6	4	3	4	5
	L3	3	3	4	3	4	4	2	4	3	3	4	6	4	4
	L4	5	6	5	4	4	4	5	6	6	8	6	9	9	8
	L5	2	3	5	4	4	4	6	7	8	9	9	10	9	8
Die cutting and creasing	C1, 2	2	2	0	1	1	1	2	1	2	1	1	2	1	1
	C3, 4, 5	3	2	1	1	0	1	1	1	2	3	3	3	2	2
Glueing	All	1	0	0	1	0	0	0	0	1	1	2	1	2	1
Windowing	All	5	5	4	4	5	12	10	7	4	3	2	0	2	9
Drip mat punching	–	0	0	1	1	0	0	0	0	1	0	0	0	0	0

NOTES
1 The information relates to the principal processes and is calculated to the nearest working week.
2 Order backlog is recorded on the last day of each month.

EXHIBIT 9 Order backlog for the principal operations processes (in weeks)[1,2]

these orders are being processed, the procedures described involve two quality inspectors on a full-time basis. Delivered goods are subject to further inspection by Maister personnel and deviations from quality limits may result in returns to PCS of complete carton deliveries.

Works order reference	Month completed	Quantity of cartons ordered		Number of cartons per board (number-up)[1]	Input: number of boards issued to operations[2]		Output: number of cartons delivered	
		Number (000)	Tolerance (±%)		Estimate	Actual	Estimate[3]	Actual
17063	September	150	10	12	22,000	20,050	165,000	188,850
17122		250	10	8	42,950	40,100	275,000	280,400
17181	October	200	10	12	25,800	22,950	220,000	215,600
17204		175	10	8	33,000	30,000	192,500	201,350
17212		1,000	7.5	12	95,800	99,750	1,075,000	1,053,300
17292	November	250	10	12	30,550	33,900	275,000	332,200
17336		1,500	5	12	139,000	142,500	1,575,000	1,550,950
17345		75	10	8	18,090	17,250	82,500	108,300
17372		175	10	6	38,500	38,200	192,500	190,925
17373		550	10	12	61,000	58,050	605,000	608,850
17390	December	450	10	12	50,000	50,000	495,000	508,800
17396		2,500	5	12	230,000	225,100	2,625,000	2,474,200
17411		100	10	6	25,820	26,250	110,000	120,450
17412		50	10	8	12,170	14,150	55,000	81,050
17440		1,100	7.5	8	156,400	166,000	1,182,500	1,160,650
Total					981,080	984,250	9,125,000	9,075,875
Variance percentage						+0.32		−0.54

NOTES
1 Boards are normally purchased from a supplier to suit the size and specification of individual works orders. Quantities received may vary by ±10 per cent from the ordered quantities. However, as with the final product, all quantities within this tolerance band would be paid for.
2 The number of boards issued is decided by the production control department and later adjusted by the materials controller. The production controller may plan quantities slightly greater than the estimate, if he is aware that Maister has low stocks and is thus critically dependent on receiving at least the ordered quantity. The materials controller may increase the input, if the quantity of board received from the suppliers exceeds the ordered quantity (see Note 1 above).
3 The estimated output for each order exceeds the ordered quantity by a tolerance. Because of the uncertainty of quantities received from the board mills, and because of variable process material yields, the standard conditions of sale which operate throughout the carton industry allow defined maximum percentages of under- and overproduction to be delivered and charged to customers.

EXHIBIT 10 An analysis of board usage and output of cartons for all orders from Maister Cakes during past year

Finance and accounting

The decline in performance of the company was highlighted by the summary of trading results given as *Exhibit 1*. It was clear that two factors had contributed to the worsening position: increasing levels of working capital and a decline in sales margin.

Working capital

At a management meeting in September last year, it was shown that the major item of working capital was inventory, and it was agreed that it must be reduced this year by at least 40 per cent. In order to achieve such a reduction, all categories of inventory would have to be cut on the following basis.

Raw materials
The buyer was instructed to adhere rigidly to the company policy of only purchasing for customers' orders. Inventory holdings of material for drip mats would be reduced and the buffer inventory of board for regular business, such as the industrial and food segments, would be eliminated.

Work-in-progress
Increasing levels of work-in-progress were attributed to unsatisfactory planning, resulting in occurrences such as the following:

1 Interruptions to long print or die-cutting/creasing runs (for example Maister Teas), in order to allow the production of short-run items, where there was pressure to deliver cartons soon after receipt of raw materials and in line with a customer's requirements. Output from the interrupted order would be held as work-in-progress awaiting its later completion

2 Overloading of certain downstream processes, resulting in work-in-progress queues

3 Failure to ensure that orders are progressed in the best sequence to minimize work-in-progress inventory.

Apart from identifying the need to improve production scheduling procedures, the finance department proposed the introduction of a computerized planning system. This would ensure that all planning decisions resulted in a forecast level of inventory being reported. In this way, the planners would not only have a means of improving their effectiveness but would also become more aware of the results of their decisions on inventory levels.

Finished goods
The main categories of finished goods inventory are:

1 overproduction (that is, output in excess of the agreed upper-tolerance level) held in anticipation of further orders

2 inventory held awaiting call-offs due to customers delaying deliveries

3 cartons produced to meet the whole of an order, although actual call-offs were scheduled for delivery over an extended period.

At the end of last year, 75 per cent of finished goods inventory was in the category of awaiting call-offs, where manufacturing had made the whole of an order, with specified scheduled deliveries over the following three months. From this January, planners were instructed to manufacture only for call-offs up to six weeks ahead, and this was expected to reduce finished goods inventory by approximately 30 per cent.

Sales margins

Currently, there is no job costing system but complete weekly records of process utilization are maintained. In addition, regular analyses are prepared, comparing actual and standard running speeds and set-up times for each process. It is believed that this approach highlights critical variances from standards and provides an adequate basis for management control.

Job costings are sometimes calculated on a sample basis for new orders but are found to be extremely time consuming. It has been calculated that to cost up to 1,000 orders each year would require additional staff and a substantial increase in overhead costs, which could not be justified at this time. On the suggestion of the group internal auditors, a one-off job costing exercise was undertaken in February, the results of which are shown in *Exhibit 11*.

Market/customer	Works order number	Invoiced sales (£s)[2]	Estimated contribution[1]		Actual costs (£s)				
			£s	% of order value	Board	Other material	Processing variable[3]	Delivery	Total
Beverages									
Maister Teas	17120	14,096	825	5.9	11,047	733	1,676	436	13,892
	17392	55,512	9,485	16.3	43,396	3,002	9,542	1,980	57,920
	17451	54,450	9,596	17.0	41,128	2,202	7,579	1,649	52,558
ARD Coffees	17186	2,836	1,203	42.7	401	188	1,025	21	1,635
	17347	30,206	3,672	12.7	17,483	2,756	5,541	1,354	27,134
	17369	15,542	6,946	45.4	3,162	2,091	3,098	245	8,596
Tea Specialty Packers	17242	4,519	2,333	52.0	646	381	1,130	29	2,186
	17301	2,374	1,002	42.2	356	286	705	25	1,372
	17405	9,799	4,889	50.5	1,496	1,585	1,808	121	5,010
Eastern Teas	17408	3,973	2,391	61.1	945	174	403	60	1,582
Industrial products									
Agroparts	17214	5,996	3,127	51.9	1,597	630	1,151	177	3,555
	17446	7,671	2,393	33.2	3,907	499	1,288	448	6,142
NY Equipment	17284	5,582	1,828	40.8	2,358	440	864	158	3,820
	17427	20,404	8,208	41.8	9,712	1,204	2,090	748	13,754
Rotabearings	17269	23,712	10,206	47.2	8,459	1,730	4,302	850	15,341
	17391	14,809	6,026	45.6	5,478	1,032	2,400	556	9,466
F C Bruce	17279	7,830	2,309	31.5	4,110	499	1,268	479	6,356
	17431	10,674	3,775	39.6	2,217	3,252	552	251	6,272
Food									
Maister Cakes	17122	15,346	1,571	10.8	11,423	1,190	2,563	677	15,853
	17212	53,366	8,164	13.9	40,062	3,963	10,224	1,712	55,961
	17440	59,971	9,541	15.4	44,606	2,953	11,994	1,838	61,391
McPhee	17190	4,403	1,641	41.8	1,728	147	1,191	123	3,189
	17320	4,766	1,299	31.0	1,888	387	1,519	125	3,919
	17448	6,397	4,053	63.4	1,205	883	2,738	249	5,075
Country Cuisine	17298	7,738	2,009	29.9	4,252	629	1,636	250	6,767
Pharmaceuticals									
Pharmex	17216	2,560	1,139	49.0	654	172	795	20	1,641
	17377	7,082	4,026	51.4	2,080	591	2,041	55	4,767
	17450	2,205	908	46.1	669	332	302	17	1,320

cont'd

Market/ customer	Works order number	Invoiced sales (£s)[2]	Estimated contribution[1]		Actual costs (£s)				
			£s	% of order value	Board	Other material	Processing variable[3]	Delivery	Total
AB Products	17323	1,052	469	55.7	156	52	262	11	481
	17436	6,016	2,339	43.1	1,180	1,379	666	78	3,303
HMR	17356	1,728	880	58.4	227	203	469	28	927
Drip Mats									
Pride Ales	17243[4]	1,950	164	10.8	968	189	784	71	2,012
	17311[4]	2,025	259	16.6	953	72	722	67	1,814
	17400	1,885	280	18.5	838	145	397	71	1,451
	17452	3,415	590	22.4	1,368	249	354	59	2,030
Hop Products	17261	5,337	1,974	52.8	1,191	197	505	85	1,978
	17439	18,333	7,827	41.4	8,529	1,120	2,760	657	13,066
Korolla Cola	17365	5,511	1,995	42.7	2,024	246	855	95	3,220
Toiletries									
Prince & Haywood	17276	29,289	14,143	47.1	10,498	2,523	4,304	903	18,228
	17308	32,868	11,133	38.4	12,655	3,307	5,599	895	22,456
	17415	20,227	6,840	39.0	7,277	2,150	3,466	524	13,417
SC Packers (exports)	17199	10,521	5,821	46.2	3,791	837	3,394	359	8,381
	17437	3,861	1,678	48.1	1,033	354	942	79	2,408
Soap Exports	17348	8,436	4,364	49.9	2,610	445	2,656	70	5,781
Confectionery									
Elizabeth Ross	17288	2,783	1,453	58.5	370	225	449	34	1,078
	17395	3,222	1,856	60.4	456	445	664	34	1,599
Prestar	17341	6,540	4,180	60.2	1,016	686	1,370	75	3,147
Small electrical appliances									
GRA Electrical	17208	12,396	7,033	52.3	5,908	1,135	3 680	332	11,055
	17398	12,064	5,044	45.9	3,482	1,342	3,539	270	8,633
Domelex	17423	6,019	2,821	48.2	1,165	1,058	1,741	78	4,042
Exit Fans	17257	3,584	1,574	52.0	774	301	736	40	1,851
Sundry									
Jones & Straw	17193	2,646	560	20.7	1,270	330	462	90	2,152
FJ Agrichem	17278	5,762	1,656	30.7	1,639	749	1,290	250	3,928
Electronica	17370	1,875	451	21.5	996	207	325	30	1,558
London Shirts	17454	2,179	379	17.2	1,206	355	278	45	1,884

cont'd

| Market/ customer | Works order number | Invoiced sales (£s)[2] | Estimated contribution[1] | | Actual costs (£s) | | | | |
			£s	% of order value	Board	Other material	Processing variable[3]	Delivery	Total
Group									
Companies in the carton division	17209	3,873	1,523	48.0	562	613	888	50	2,113
	17318	6,782	3,809	62.7	1,024	443	2 227	238	3,932
	17359	5,463	3,360	60.8	916	522	1,711	318	3,467
	17442	1,600	1,013	63.4	301	221	685	62	1,269
Windowed									
Panda Pottery	17246	3,672	1,912	70.7	394	741	574	18	1,727
Stafpots	17420	7,753	3,684	68.3	860	396	833	23	2,112
Electronica	17443	9,199	4,249	66.6	1,018	752	1,655	56	3,481
Windowed subcontract[5]									
Spa Cartons	17352	8,779	5,547	63.0	–	2,449	2,099	50	4,598
Stebro Packaging	17457	7,369	3,756	54.2	–	2,225	1,254	45	3,524

NOTES

1 Estimated contribution is the difference between the order value and the estimated variable costs of materials, processing and delivery.
2 Invoiced sales is the value of all the goods as delivered, but excludes any credit notes or returned goods.
3 Processing variable costs are calculated from the machine variable (hourly) cost rates which include:
  A direct labour with fringe benefits
  B energy costs
  C consumable materials
  D adjustments for average downtime, and
  E repairs and maintenance materials.
Typically, direct labour with fringe benefits accounts for less than 50 per cent of total processing variable costs.
4 These two orders are of a contract nature, as explained in the narrative. The other two orders for Pride Ales are of the promotional type.
5 This category refers to orders from other companies in the carton division, requiring only the 'windowed' process to be completed.

EXHIBIT 11 Costings for representative orders: October to December, last year

Estimating

Except for very regular work (contract drip mats for national brewing companies and high-volume work for Maister), an estimate is prepared for every enquiry. Two years ago, the standard estimating procedure was computerized. This has proved to be invaluable because there were nearly 6,500 enquiries processed last year and the computerized procedure has reduced the clerical staff requirement from six to three people.

The computer program allows estimators to enter details of the product specification and quantities, select the process route, enter their estimate of expected material wastage and specify delivery details. Fixed estimating data (machine throughput rates, processing costs per hour, set-up times, material costs and delivery charges) are reviewed by the accounting department every six months. The estimate provided by the computer is based on standard process running and set-up times. The estimator then applies a profit margin on the basis of advice from the salesman and sales manager, while taking into account any history of prices accepted by the customer. For large enquiries and contract renewals, the management team reviews all estimates before quotations are sent to the enquirer.

Precision Steel plc

Introduction

Although there are a few, small aspects of the report on which we could take issue, it seems to me that Bill Carey has, by and large, reflected the marketing changes we have been expressing and given some sound guidelines on where we must place our future energies. The emphasis given to increasing our share in all segments of the customized sections market and the need to continue to expand the customer-orientation strategy with Gambert Fabrique, one of our key accounts, seem to have struck a chord with us all, both in terms of past trends and our feel for these markets. What we now have is a strategic framework to give context and direction. This will help us to replace the more short-term response philosophy we have been using in our marketing decisions. Thanks, Bill, we have found your work helpful, and I am sure it will prove to be a document to which we will refer many times in the future.

Brian Finn, the chief executive of Precision Steel (PS) was addressing the board of directors, following a meeting to discuss a recent report titled 'Future Marketing Strategy Proposals', completed on behalf of the company. In addition to the board, Bill Carey (a senior executive from the strategic unit within the group central services, who had been responsible for preparing the report) had also attended the final part of this meeting in order to answer any queries not addressed earlier.

Background

PS sells high-quality steel sections in a wide range of standard steel specifications, together with customer-specified material requirements. PS is part of Harbridge Industries, a large group of companies with a wide range of interests including shipping, civil engineering, electronics, fabrication and engineering, as well as steel processing. PS was established in 1932 to roll precision steel sections for the electric motor industry.

Although many aspects of its activities have since changed, the rerolling of steel sections, using hot and cold processes, in a variety of steel specifications, and up to a maximum section height of 250 mm, still constitutes PS's principal business. Due to falling demand and subsequent plant closures, PS found itself, by the late 1970s (like many of its European counterparts) in a near-monopoly position, as it was now the only supplier based in the UK. However, similar businesses in Europe are always keen to export to the UK, particularly to high-volume (tonne) users.

PS's markets

PS buys steel sections from a limited number of suppliers (principally English Billets plc), then sells rerolled precision sections into three market segments with different characteristics. These are electric motors, stockist steel sections and customized sections, which are now described.

This case study was prepared by Terry Hill (University of Oxford) and S. H. Chambers (University of Warwick). It is intended for class discussion and not as an illustration of good or bad management. © AMD Publishing.

	Current year minus				Current year
	10	6	2	1	
Total sales (tonnes)	79,600	65,300	55,500	52,000	50,400
Average order quantity (tonnes)	286	205	235	220	190
Average number of sizes per order quantity	20	20	29	27	26

NOTES

1 There are now seven different specifications (that is, material properties) of steel raw materials (in a different range of sizes) required by this market. Each specification in all sizes is normally held in stock by PS. Ten years ago, there were only two specifications.

2 A typical order comprises several sizes of finished precision steel sections, but usually all of the same steel specification and finishing/heat treatment requirements. The various sizes will, however, be processed in separate hot mill programmes (see *Exhibit 7*). To explain, let's take an order from one customer for a total of 200 tonnes. If this order quantity comprised 20 sizes then, as far as manufacturing is concerned it would be similar to 20 different orders (that is, one order per size), as similar sizes (and not one customer order) are processed through manufacturing.

3 Typical delivery lead times are 6–8 weeks from receipt of an order.

EXHIBIT 1 Current and past sales (tonnes) of steel sections for the electric motor market

Electric motors

PS's traditional market was to provide steel sections for electric motors. While demand for this market has fallen in the past 15 years it still accounts for almost 50 per cent of PS's revenue (£s). Steel sections are rolled and subsequently precision machined by the customer. This accounts for some 50,000 tonnes per year, and details of current and past sales are given in *Exhibit 1*.

Stockist steel sections

Sales in this market are for a range of standard sizes and shapes, all rolled from the one internationally specified steel, known by the company as PS 2000. Both home and overseas customers, therefore, order from a standard catalogue, with items being differentiated only by size and shape.

In order to compensate for the falling sales experienced in the electric motor market, the stockist steel sections segment has been built up over the past 15 years. The annual volumes processed this year totalled 30,000 tonnes, and details of representative orders are given in *Exhibit 2*. PS was supplying five major UK stockists and about 50 stockists overseas. Last year, PS received a major contract from a French company, Gambert Fabrique (GF), which yielded orders totalling 8,000 tonnes in the following year. Apparently running at a substantial loss in its steel rerolling

	Current year minus				Current year
	10	6	2	1	
Total sales (tonnes)	15,100	17,700	19,400	28,900	29,700
Average order quantity (tonnes)	84	95	105	130	123
Average number of sizes per order quantity	17	20	24	25	23

NOTES

1 The steel specification for this market is PS 2000 only.

2 There are 140 international standard sizes in the stockists' range.

3 GF (France) orders once a month an average of 670 tonnes in 34 standard sizes (minimum 10 tonnes per size) for delivery 6–8 weeks from receipt of an order.

4 GF (UK and Denmark) each order twice a month an average of 35 tonnes each in nine sizes (minimum 3 tonnes per size) for delivery 4–6 weeks from receipt of an order.

5 Current delivery lead times for UK stockists are 6–8 weeks from receipt of an order.

EXHIBIT 2 Current and past sales of stockist steel sections

business, GF decided two years before to close its own rolling mill, and negotiated a contract for PS to supply its standard steel sections, using steel PS 2000. GF sells a wide range of products and is a large exporter of engineering supplies and metal sections (steel, brass and aluminium). It distributes these by a well-developed container service to its own depots and clients throughout the world.

The negotiations with GF resulted in agreed prices and terms for delivery by PS to its main distribution centre in Brest, an industrial port in northern France. *Exhibits 3* and *4* give brief details of these agreements, as compared to other products in this segment. Last year PS initiated discussions on the possibility of direct supply to some of GF's depots. John Breen, marketing director, explained the reason for this:

❝ *The GF contract is an important part of our customer portfolio. The annual volume is substantial, characterized by relatively large order quantities and stable schedules. But, the trade-off has been low prices. However, within a relatively short period of time, we saw the opportunity of supplying direct to GF's depots in one or more countries. The direct gains for Gambert were reduced distribution costs and for PS an increase in price. Our first successes early last year were the United Kingdom and Denmark, with each buying about 450 tonnes per year. Having received permission to negotiate directly with these two parts of the Gambert organization, we were able to satisfactorily agree higher prices than for similar products, due to the fact that GF passed on distribution costs to its customers (including parts of its own organization), as well as adding its own margin. We are now able, therefore, to take for ourselves some of that additional margin and still offer a favourable price for direct supply [see Exhibits 3 and 4]. Our policy is to encourage this, and the recent report on future marketing strategy highlights this development as one of the major planks on which we should build. We have now identified Brazil, Italy and Germany as the next areas, and early soundings seem to be favourable.*

In addition, we propose to consolidate our relationship with Gambert by setting up direct computer interface with Brest, which allows their buying office to link with our sales and production control systems. In this way we hope to lock them into a long-term dependence on PS. ❞

Markets	Billet size (mm)	£/tonne[1]
Electric motor: XR7 material	70	600
	110	500
	120	465
	140	420
	190	425
	250	430
Stockist steel: UK stockists	70	570
	100	490
	120	475
	140	465
	170	470
	250	450
Gambert Fabrique (France)	85	420
	110	340
	130	320
	150	300
	190	300
	250	300
Gambert Fabrique (UK)	85	480
	110	390
	130	360
	150	350
	190	340
	250	330
Customized section: MK 200 steel[2]	85	810
	120	680
	190	610
	210	610

NOTES
1 All prices are corrected to ex-works equivalents.
2 MK 200 is an expensive alloy steel.

EXHIBIT 3 Some examples of typical invoiced rates per tonne (current prices)

Markets	Tonnage	Input steel height (mm)					
		70–85	100–110	120–130	140–150	170–190	210–250
Electric motors (typical steel specification XR7)	5	490	411	385	350	355	360
	10	460	386	363	330	335	340
	20	445	376	350	320	330	335
Stockist steel (PS 2000 steel)	5	410	336	314	290	295	300
	10	380	316	298	280	285	290
	20	365	306	290	275	280	285
Customized sections	5	635	550	520	500	490	490
	10	600	525	500	480	470	470
	20	580	510	485	460	455	455

NOTE

1 Variable cost includes all direct labour, materials and other direct costs (for example variable energy costs) and an allowance for size changes between items on a programme. It also allows for average yield losses for the market category.

EXHIBIT 4 Summary of estimated variable cost[1] per tonne (£) in various markets, for different tonnages per size, based on current costs

Customized sections

The decline in overall sales had stimulated the need to increase sales in the customized sections segment of the market. Customized sections business refers to orders that cater for the specific needs of a wide range of manufacturing businesses, including automotive components (for example struts), agricultural machinery and oil rig fabrication, as well as general engineering. The growth was based on converting customers from using non-precision, standard steel sections requiring extensive and costly machining and heat treatment, to purpose-rolled sections to meet their specifications in terms of dimensional tolerance, steel specification and heat treatment requirements. PS's sales force had, over the past few years, developed a broader technical knowledge in order to help increase the company's penetration in these markets. Orders can, however, involve both standard and special steels, but size and shape will always be specified by, and therefore special to, each customer. Many customers, however, place repeat orders for the same product, often on a call-off or schedule basis. Most requirements can be met by the hot rolling process, and a representative sample of orders is given in *Exhibit 5*. (Hot rolling is a less expensive process than cold rolling, therefore products are designed, where possible, to be made in a hot-rolled format.)

Current year's sales in this market segment totalled 20,000 tonnes, 85 per cent of which went to UK companies, with the remainder sent to all parts of the world. An important element of this growth came from sales to the oil industry.

Operations

Steel sections pass through a series of processes, which are now briefly described. Orders differ and, whereas all products go through the hot rolling stage, requirements from then on vary in accordance with the specification. Individual customer orders are cumulated, wherever possible, by input height (often referred to as billet size) in order to maximize the tonnage processed through the high-volume hot mills. The task in the operations planning office, therefore, is to combine quantities of the same billet size (irrespective of material type) and programme these through the hot mills in order to minimize the numbers of major and minor changeovers (explained later) in line with customer delivery requirements. Following this initial stage through which all steel is processed, customer orders are then separated and follow the individual process requirements to completion.

	Current year minus				Current year
	10	6	2	1	
Total sales (tonnes)	4,200	9,600	18,200	18,600	20,400
Average order quantity (tonnes)	18.3	16.6	11.2	11.8	12.2
Average number of sizes per order quantity[1]	1.1	1.2	1.2	1.2	1.3

NOTES
1 Most orders are only for one size, but a few are for up to four different sizes.
2 Steel specification, finishing process and heat treatments are specified by each customer. Some high-usage steel specifications are held in raw material stock at PS either against known call-offs or in anticipation of future orders.
3 Call-offs or scheduled requirements (that is, orders for a number of deliveries spread over several months) are treated in this analysis (and by the planning office and within manufacturing) as individual orders.

EXHIBIT 5 Current and past sales of customized sections

Mill C

- Constructed 15 years ago.

- Maximum input section height: 250 mm.

- Maximum length of output: 5250 mm.

- Average output rate: 13.5 tonnes/gross hour.[1]

- Average size change time: 9 minutes within a programmed range.[2]

Mill D

- Constructed 10 years ago to provide efficient capacity for the high-volume electric motor sections market.

- Maximum input section height: 200 mm.

- Maximum length of output: 6000 mm.

- Average output rate: 20.3 tonnes/gross hour.[1]

- Average size change time: 10 minutes within a programmed range.[2]

- Estimated cost of upgrading to provide size capability of 250 mm sections: £550,000.

NOTES
1 The average output rates refer to the tonnes of processed steel averaged per hour, including any size changes made. It is known as the output rate/gross hour.
2 Although size change times within a programmed range are short (between 8.5 and 10 minutes), changeovers between one range of sizes and another are much longer. Consequently, planning establishes a programme which enables these short changes to take place (which amount to small adjustments in the process) before requiring a major size change to be made. These latter changes also vary in duration depending, in turn, on the extent of the changeover. If the size alteration is itself sequential (that is, to the next size range, whether larger or smaller) then the time taken is about 1.75 hours for Mill C and 2.15 hours for Mill D. However, if the size range alteration is not sequential, then the changeover is increased by up to a further 1.5 times. Thus, the hot mill programmes are planned to minimize downtime wherever possible, while maintaining order quantity levels within the delivery requirements of customers.
3 Output rates are not significantly affected by section width, as this is not a constraining factor.
4 Both mills currently operate on a two-shift basis, 40 hours per shift week, 46 weeks a year.
5 Furnace shut down, light up, and preparations for rolling each weekend cost approximately £3,000 per mill. Overnight idling of furnaces costs approximately £60 per hour (fuel and labour).
6 Company policy is to roll minimum tonnages of five tonnes per size, although authorized exceptions are allowed.

EXHIBIT 6 Characteristics of the hot rolling mills

Hot rolling

Currently, two hot rolling mills are in use. One was installed 15 years ago and the second 5 years later to replace earlier mill capacity that had gradually been phased out. While the basic layout for hot rolling is similar, the process capabilities are different. This difference concerns the height and length of steel sections that can be processed. *Exhibit 6* gives details.

Hot roll finishing

All products go through the hot roll finishing section. The processes are simple and the set-up times are short. After initial cooling, the steel sections are lifted by an overhead crane into the work-in-progress warehousing area. The crane is, however, limited to a maximum of a five-tonne lift, which means that many order quantities are split at this stage. From this warehousing area, all products follow their own specified routing, according to the process requirements involved.

Cold rolling

About one-third of all products are cold rolled. The orders are drawn from the work-in-progress inventory after hot roll finishing. These processes enable higher levels of accuracy to be achieved, particularly where the product specification calls for thinner sections. They all require very long set-up times and involve expensive tooling. The specialized tooling has a three-month lead time from the suppliers, and therefore needs very careful planning. In addition, there is a disproportionate amount of tool wear at the start of a production run, until fine adjustments can be achieved.

Other auxiliary processes

There are several additional processes involved, none of which have long set-up or process times. They include cold roll finishing, heat treatment, cutting to precise lengths and specified packing prior to despatch. Not all products go through all processes.

Lead-time calculations

The lead times used by sales in quotations are agreed annually by the sales and production directors, being occasionally adjusted as necessary by the production planning office, if overload situations seem to be arising. The following norms are currently used as a basis for calculating lead times on which delivery promises were then made: 10 weeks are allowed for the purchase of non-standard steel, 4 weeks for hot rolling, 1 week for standard heat treatment and finishing and 4 weeks for cold rolling. Non-standard finishing process lead times were calculated for each job on the basis of an assessment of the complexity involved

and the degree of overall delivery speed required by the potential customer.

In all markets where customers require quicker deliveries than the total based on the above norms, shorter lead times for customer quotations are agreed by the manager of the production planning office. This is achieved by identifying areas of process-time reduction, based on current and future loading, experience and judgement. In all cases, delivery is quoted as 'ex-works' (the standard practice for the industry) and does not, therefore, include delivery arrangements. See *Exhibits 7, 8*, and *9*, which give details of actual deliveries in a representative period.

Standard steels are assumed by the production planning office to be available from PS raw material stock holdings and thus no allowance is made in sales quotations involving standard steels to cover purchase lead time. (Most standard steels are kept in stock, as explained in the notes to *Exhibit 10*.) The inventory holding of each size and specification of standard steel is tightly controlled by the planning manager, using simple controls, based on average usage for the past three months, current stock and estimates of forward demand. Steel delivery is normally requested and acknowledged by suppliers as being 10 weeks from the order date. (See *Exhibits 10* and *11* for information on the delivery performance of PS's steel suppliers.)

Process yields

Process yield is defined as saleable output divided by the input of raw material and expressed as a percentage. The yields achieved by each different process are closely monitored every month and are reported by market category. Losses (some of which are unpredictable) arise from oxidation (scale losses), damage in the process plant, cutting losses in the finishing section and quality rejects (dimensional, surface finish and metallurgical). All losses are closely monitored and investigated. They are accounted for in the estimation procedure when calculating material requirements and order pricing. Yields currently used in these calculations are based on information gathered over the past 12 months, and average 92 per cent for the electric motor and stockist steel sections markets and about 85 per cent for customized sections.

Works order number		Tonnes ordered	Key dates (week numbers)		
			Works order raised	Required and acknowledged delivery	Actual delivery
Electric motor	M864	10.0	5	12	11
	M866	15.0	5	15	15
	M878	8.0	5	12	12
	M879	5.0	5	16	17
	M880	10.0	5	12	9
	M881	8.0	5	12	12
	M910	6.5	6	13	16
	M912	12.0	6	13	13
	M913	12.0	6	13	13
	M914	15.0	6	16	14
	M930	8.0	7	13	14
	M936	5.0	7	13	13
	M937	10.00	7	13	15
	M938	8.0	7	16	16
	M939	8.0	7	14	13
Stockist steel	S420	4.0	5	10	11
	S426	4.0	5	10	11
	S427	6.0	5	12	12
	S428	5.0	5	12	11
	S440	4.0	6	12	10
	S441	10.0	6	12	12
	S448	4.0	6	12	13
	S449	4.0	6	12	11
	S479	10.0	6	13	13
	S480	4.0	6	13	13
	S481	5.0	6	13	11
	S503	5.0	7	14	14
	S504	5.0	7	13	15
	S505	3.0	7	13	13

NOTES
1 A separate works order is raised for each size within a customer order.
2 Works order numbers M866, M879, M914 and M939 were also cold rolled.

EXHIBIT 7 A representative sample of orders for UK electric motor and UK stockist steel markets

Delivery to/ works order number		Tonnes ordered	Key dates (week numbers)		
			Works order raised	Required and acknowledged delivery	Actual delivery
France	S463	10.0	6	13	12
	S464	25.0	6	13	13
	S465	25.0	6	13	10
	S466	20.0	6	13	13
	S467	16.0	6	13	9
	S468	28.0	6	13	12
	S469	35.0	6	13	13
	S470	25.0	6	11	10
	S471	20.0	6	11	12
	S472	20.0	6	11	11
	S473	15.0	6	11	13
	S474	25.0	6	11	10
	S475	10.0	6	11	11
	S476	20.0	6	11	13
	S477	20.0	6	11	11
	S478	15.0	6	11	14
UK	S416	3.0	5	10	12
	S417	5.0	5	10	13
	S418	3.0	5	8	9
	S419	5.0	5	8	8
	S492	4.0	7	12	12
	S493	4.0	7	12	11
	S494	5.0	7	10	11
Denmark	S412	4.0	5	9	13
	S413	4.5	5	9	12
	S414	5.0	5	9	9
	S415	4.0	5	9	10
	S489	5.0	7	10	10
	S490	5.0	7	10	9
	S491	3.0	7	10	11

NOTES

1 A separate works order is raised for each size within a customer order.

2 Delivery promise for overseas destinations is acknowledged as the date the sections leave PS.

EXHIBIT 8 A representative sample of current orders from Gambert Fabrique

Works order number	Standard steel	Special steel	Ordered tonnes	Key dates (week numbers)			Total steel input (tonnes)	Total saleable output (tonnes)
				Works order raised	Required and acknowledged delivery	Actual delivery		
C026	✓		46.0	5	10	9	49.9	45.4
C052[1]	✓		7.5	5	15	16	8.0	7.3
C053		✓	3.0	5	19	22	5.1	4.6
C057		✓	6.0	5	20	20	7.9	6.4
C061	✓		10.0	5	12	10	11.0	9.6
C082		✓	8.5	5	19	20	8.7	6.9
C092		✓	3.0	5	18	26	7.5[2]	2.2
C094		✓	20.5	5	20	19	23.1	19.0
C099	✓		52.0	5	11	10	58.0	53.3
C121	✓		10.0	6	10	12	11.0	10.1
C126		✓	10.0	6	22	21	13.0	11.1
C128	✓		20.0	6	9	10	22.5	20.9
C132	✓		75.0	6	12	12	83.5	77.1
C136	✓		15.0	6	8	9	15.5	15.0
C150[1]	✓		20.0	7	18	20	22.5	19.4
C151		✓	3.0	7	21	21	4.0	3.2
C152	✓		15.0	7	12	11	17.0	15.3
C160		✓	3.0	7	24	21	4.9	4.2
C167		✓	10.0	7	26	29	22.0[2]	11.5
C169		✓	3.0	7	21	21	3.8	3.4
C182	✓		5.0	7	10	9	5.5	4.0
C186	✓		3.0	7	12	14	3.5	3.2
C187		✓	10.0	8	22	29	24.0[2]	12.5
C192		✓	12.5	8	25	23	14.0	13.4
C193	✓		3.0	8	12	12	3.5	2.6
C194[1]		✓	3.0	8	28	28	3.7	3.1
C204		✓	3.0	8	26	32	4.2	2.5
C207		✓	16.0	8	25	24	20.3	17.3
C222		✓	4.0	8	20	22	4.0	2.6
C231	✓		10.0	8	14	12	11.0	8.9

NOTES
1 These were also cold rolled.
2 Two separate rollings were necessary to achieve the required output (all or part of the first rolling was rejected by quality control).

EXHIBIT 9 A representative sample of current UK orders received for customized sections (hot rolled and standard finishing)

Steel specification	Billet size (mm)	Tonnes ordered[3]	Week number:		
			Ordered	Required	Received
PS 2000	100	250	25	36	44
PS 2000	120	105	25	36	34
PS 2000	130	85	25	36	38
PS 2000	150	80	25	36	35
PS 2000	190	130	25	36	34
PS 2000	250	270	25	36	32
XR 6	100	45	25	36	35
XR 7	110	45	27	37	38
XR 7	120	140	27	37	41
XR 7	140	150	27	37	40
XR 7	230	105	27	37	38
SA 270	70	55	27	37	38
SA 270	85	120	27	37	37
SA 270	100	80	27	37	34
SA 275x	70	40	27	37	42
SA 275x	100	20	27	37	41
SA 275x	120	20	27	37	40
PS 2000v	230	30	27	37	43
PS 2000x	250	35	27	37	41
PS 300	70	10	29	40	40
PS 300	100	40	29	40	38
PS 2000	70	115	29	40	42
PS 2000	85	60	30	40	42
PS 2000	170	40	30	40	43
PS 2000v	100	30	30	40	42
PS 2000v	120	35	30	40	40
XR 7	70	80	30	40	39
XR 7	85	90	30	40	41
XR 7	100	40	30	40	41

NOTES

1 English Billets plc is PS's principal raw material supplier.

2 A standard steel is classed as such by PS if it has been processed previously, irrespective of the quantity used. This distinction from special steels signals the fact that manufacturing will have processing experience of the material, which will, in turn, lead to a reduction in problems and differences associated with one-off specials. Thus, actual process lead times are more in keeping with the norms used in lead-time calculations.

3 Most (especially the high usage) standard steels are kept in stock by PS at levels which relate to annual usage. Orders on suppliers to replenish stocks are then made in the normal way based upon reorder levels.

EXHIBIT 10 A representative sample of deliveries from English Billets plc[1] for standard steel specification orders[2]

Steel specification	Billet size (mm)	Tonnes ordered[2]	Week number: Ordered	Required	Received	Received tonnage
5Y102	100	28	27	37	40	22.2
SD204	70	4	27	36	36	3.1
BS840	200	32	29	35	40	30.2
DX6DM	170	16	29	35	36	15.8
DN34B	85	4	29	39	36	4.2
DN36	140	32	29	35	39	31.9
Spec 2a	250	100	29	36	40	97.2
DN8	70	8	29	39	40	8.7
PS37	120	6	30	39	37	7.9
804/10	190	12	30	40	37	8.5
DL10	190	32	30	40	40	34.8
SA520	100	16	30	40	44	17.5
DL12	100	4	30	40	36	3.5
Spec 3b	250	16	30	40	38	14.9
DN8D	140	4	30	41	42	5.1
DN474	170	28	31	41	41	29.3
C2138	190	24	31	41	37	23.1
C2139	120	20	31	44	46	20.1
MK200	230	120	32	38	37	116.4
550B20	120	12	32	44	45	11.9
D142	210	4	32	42	40	3.7
820x	85	90	32	42	45	105.0
D1020	170	4	32	44	42	4.4
D1022	130	4	32	44	42	4.6
540C10	70	8	32	44	42	7.9
DN8D	210	16	33	44	45	15.5
DN36	100	4	33	44	43	4.4
SA862	100	4	33	44	43	2.8
DX6DM	210	16	33	44	40	19.6

NOTES

1 English Billets plc is PS's principal raw material supplier.
2 Special steels must be ordered in multiples of 4 tonnes up to 40 tonnes because of process restrictions (ingot sizes). The effective delivery tolerance on these orders is ± 1 tonne.

EXHIBIT 11 A representative sample of deliveries from English Billets plc[1] for special steels ordered for specific jobs

Planning procedures

Orders are received in the sales department, where they are recorded before being passed through to the production planning office. *Exhibits 12* and *13* provide information on this activity. Orders are then collated by input height (that is, billet size) required and loaded on to the hot mills within a four-week programme. Thus, works orders for the same size (input height) of steel (the material specification is not normally a factor to be taken into account when compiling hot mill programmes) are grouped together to provide as large a quantity to be rolled as possible. However, as volumes decline, programmed quantities in the same period will decline, especially where the delivery-speed element of a market is becoming important. In these latter situations, the steel will, of course, have to be programmed into the hot mills to meet the customer delivery date, rather than to meet the programming rules used in the planning department. This would lead to lower production volumes and/or more frequent mill changes. Furthermore, when cumulative orders for the same steel size have been rolled, the individual orders are then separated to follow their own routing through the remaining processes in line with each product specification.

- Customer orders are received by post, telephone, fax or email.

- They are passed to the administrative department specializing in either electric motor, stockist, or customized sections.

- They are then technically and commercially appraised by experienced sales staff.

- Works orders and acknowledgement copies are raised.

- These are finally approved by both the estimating and metallurgy departments.

- Works orders are then passed to the production planning office, where orders for special steel are raised (if appropriate) and all works orders are collated in order to prepare mill programmes.

NOTE: An analysis of a representative sample of orders is provided as *Exhibit 13*.

EXHIBIT 12 Customer order clerical processing procedures

Market	Average time elapsed (working days)		
	1	2	3
Electric motor	1.1	1.9	n.a.
Stockist steel	2.5	2.5	n.a.
Customized special steels	5.3	4.2	2.1
Customized stock steels	5.7	3.8	n.a.

NOTES

1 This information is based on a large sample of orders which are considered to be representative.

2 The sales administration office is responsible for the processing and interpretation of customers' orders and the provision of checked works orders for production.

3 The first part of this procedure is completed in the sales office and involves commercial appraisal and appropriate administrative tasks. The average time to complete these tasks is shown in column 1.

4 The second part of this procedure is completed in the metallurgy and estimating departments for technical verification of a works order. The average time to complete these tasks is shown in column 2.

5 The final part of this procedure is compleed by the production planning office, where orders for special steels are raised. Column 3 shows the delay between this office receiving order details and the time when the order is placed; n.a. = not applicable.

EXHIBIT 13 An analysis of customer order clerical processing times for a representative period

This results in steel sizes being processed once in each four-week cycle, so as to maintain agreed target levels of mill utilization. The procedure, therefore, is to sequence orders to minimize size of section changes and so reduce cumulative set-up times within a cycle. *Exhibit 14* shows a typical hot mill rolling programme, while *Exhibit 6* gives the key data for mills C and D regarding product range, output rates and changeover times on which these programmes will be established.

Date	Billet size: input steel height (mm)	
	Mill C	Mill D
March		
1	250	70
2	150	70
3	150	70
4	140	70
8	140	70
9	110	85
10	110	85
11	120	85
14	130	100
15	130	100
16	130	100
17	190	100
18	140	100
21	140	100
22	150	70
23	150	70
24	170	70
25	170	120
28	250	120
29	230	120
30	210	85
31	110	85

NOTE: Also refer to the details in *Exhibit 6*, which gives the characteristics of these two mills, including product range, throughput rates and changeover times.

EXHIBIT 14 Rolling programme, March, current year

After the rolling stage, each order will then be routed according to the necessary finishing process operations to be completed. Jobs in excess of five tonnes will have to be split down after hot rolling, due to the crane-lifting limitations detailed earlier. The result is that delays occur in later production stages, when supervisors from these sections have to regroup part orders prior to processing in order to avoid additional set-ups.

Corporate decisions and future markets

Brian Finn reflected:

    ❝ *Looking back over the past decade clearly illustrates an overall volume decline in some markets. But we're in no worse a position than anyone else in this industry. In fact, looking outside our business reveals that we are doing quite well. Current return on net assets is 26 per cent, which is well above average for the manufacturing companies within the Harbridge group. Our problem is deciding what to do in the future to maintain the business position and profit returns we currently enjoy and have done for the past three years.*

The key, we are certain, lies in getting our marketing strategy right. Bill Carey and his team's work in this matter is both opportune and supportive of our ideas. One advantage of being in a near monopoly position is that we work closely with our customers and hence get good feedback on our performance in the light of their needs.

Overall our quality seems about right. A recent analysis showed few complaints, although we have recognized the need to improve the state of cleanliness of finished products, and capital investment has been sanctioned to install the necessary processes.

On the delivery side, we get complaints from our customers, but I'm told it's not too bad. Mike Sotheby (the director of purchasing and planning) keeps me informed of likely areas for complaint as we are very aware that this is important to future business. We regularly get reports from the UK Stockists and Electric Motor Manufacturers Assoc-

iation. This allows us to compare our delivery performance with that of our European competitors. We certainly perform as well as they do. Our records show that we achieve about 95 per cent of ordered tonnage[1] delivered on time or early.

In addition, there is also a delivery-speed factor creeping into some of our markets. Companies need deliveries quickly, and if we can meet their demands then we get the business. In these markets, the customer requires delivery in less than the 'standard' lead-time calculations we use. These are becoming more frequent in the customized sections market, and it is most important that we succeed in this segment, as it is an essential part of our intended expansion in this market overall.

The final issue is that of price. While some of our markets are price sensitive (for example much of the stockist steel sections and in particular Gambert Fabrique), many are not.[2] This is especially so in the customized sections market. Achieving these high margins, therefore, is important to us in terms of current and future performance. This is why we see areas of high-margin businesses as an important part of our portfolio. Bill Carey has put his finger on two and they will certainly be where we will start. "

Notes

1. Note that in all markets, PS contracts to supply (for each size) a customer order within plus or minus 1 tonne of the quantity required for each size. Also, steel suppliers to PS work within this convention.
2. Typical invoiced prices (ex-works) are shown in *Exhibit 3*, and some estimates of typical variable costs in *Exhibit 4*.

RumackPharmaceuticals

❝ Of increasing concern is the difficulty we are having in meeting our schedules and the growing customer order backlog which is resulting. For many months now there has been pressure to maintain schedules and we have been trying hard to overcome these problems. But, it appears as though it may be a permanent feature needing a long-term solution. The part which is difficult to reconcile, however, is that on paper we should have more than sufficient packaging capacity to meet current sales levels. And, no doubt, the rest of the board will also have difficulty in understanding this apparent discrepancy. ❞

Pete Kovac, vice-president operations at Rumack Pharmaceuticals' plant in Bakersfield, California, was addressing the managers responsible for production, engineering and materials respectively (see *Exhibit 1*) at the weekly meeting to review current issues and progress on agreed developments.

Background

Nine years ago, Rumack Pharmaceuticals, needing to increase capacity, decided to build a new plant in Bakersfield, California to make and pack Restolvic, one of its successful stomach indigestion products. Within three years of making the decision, the plant was in full production and it now manufactures a wide range of derivatives under the Restolvic brand name together with some of its Hedanol products, one of Rumack's pain-killing preparations.

Marketing

❝ Restolvic has proven to be one of the most successful products we have developed in the past decade. This is certainly so given the systematic way in which we have developed relevant variants in order to exploit the obvious sales potential. When the plant opened we had two identical lines for packing our solid products. At this time, we had more capacity than we needed and our task, therefore, has been to identify new opportunities to increase sales and hence overall profits. Initially, we explored additional dosage forms which met the particular needs of consumers. Later recognizing the level of acceptance of Restolvic as a successful indigestion reliever for a wide cross-section of people, we decided to seek ways of capitalizing on the growing strength of its brand name. This led to adding further active ingredients in order to develop other OTC [over the counter] products and also prescription products such as Restolvic A (an anti-spasmodic preparation) and Restolvic E (an anti-emetic preparation). And the whole strategy has been highly successful. ❞

Jon Prynn, vice-president marketing, then gave further details of the way in which the product line extensions and derivatives had been built on the Restolvic image and, in turn, had added to the whole, thus leading to specific gains of both an 'individual and synergistic' nature.

❝ All products make very high margins. In fact, some of those which target specific markets will often attract a premium price and consequently even higher margins. All in all, we are a highly profitable business both in terms of total profit and as a per cent of sales. ❞

This case study was written by Terry Hill (University of Oxford) and R. Menda (University of Cape Town) as a basis for class discussion and not as an example of good or bad management. © AMD Publishing.

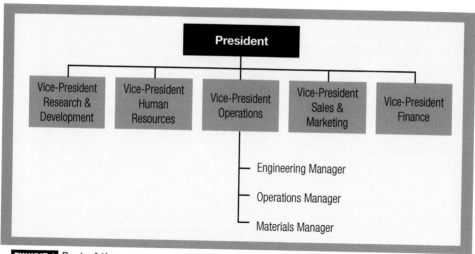

Part of the company's organization chart

Operations

❝ Since the opening of the plant some six years ago, we now make and pack OTC varieties of Restolvic, some Hedanol products and more recently prescription derivatives such as Restolvic A and Restolvic E. The latter were relocated here two years ago when the Rumack Group reassessed its overall capacity requirements in the USA and decided to close one of its plants. The outcome was that the prescription Restolvic products were relocated and are now made and packed here. ❞

Jim Lawson, operations manager, went on to explain that the manufacture of pharmaceutical dosage forms is divided into two major groups of activities – processing and packaging.

Processing concerns the conversion of powdered ingredients into bulk tablet or liquid preparations. Equipment is dedicated to a single operation such as granulation, blending, tablet compression, coating and liquid mixing. These products are manufactured in bulk normally in quantities dictated by the capacity of the particular piece of processing equipment.

Filling bulk tablets and liquids produced in the processing phase of manufacturing takes place in packaging. Here tablets and liquids are bottled according to a range of sizes and on the relevant processes.

There are now four packaging lines at the plant with specific products allocated to each line.

❝ When we opened up the plant, we installed the relevant processing capability and also packing Lines 1 and 2, with Line 3 scheduled to come on stream 12 to 15 months later. From the start, Lines 1 and 2 worked well and this confirmed our decision to invest in three identical processes. Staying with tried and tested equipment is a significant plus point as well as the benefits for engineering support and maintenance.

Jim continued: 'When the other US plant was closed, we transferred the prescription product range and the existing packaging equipment from that plant to here, then modified and added to the process in order to bring it up to the same specification as the other three lines. The prescription range is only made on Line 4. ❞

He added that when the Bakersfield plant was planned, sufficient floor space and facilities were allowed for in terms of future growth.

❝ The growth in demand for Restolvic has been rapid and this together with the transfer of products resulting from the plant closure has absorbed the excess floor space allowed for in the original plans.

The capacity problems we are experiencing do not concern the processing stage of manufacturing. Here we have sufficient capacity. The problems are in packaging. ❞

The discussion then turned to details on each of the packaging lines (see *Exhibit 2* for an outline of the steps involved and *Exhibit 3* for details of the four packaging lines).

The four packaging lines referred to in the case narrative have been developed to include both the filling and packaging stage of the process. The principal steps completed within a packaging line are outlined below:

1. Bottle unscrambling – bottles from outside suppliers are delivered and fed into a large hopper which unscrambles and delivers them correctly positioned onto the line.
2. Air cleaning – each bottle is cleaned in terms of dust by a jet of air.
3. Filling – the appropriate number of tablet/caplets are then put into each bottle.
4. Cotton insertion – a small quantity of cotton wool is placed into the empty head space of each bottle to prevent the tablets/caplets from moving. The amount of cotton reflects the space at the top of the bottle. This adjustment forms part of the set-up for each stock-keeping unit (SKU).
5. Capping – a cap is positioned and located on each bottle.
6. Induction sealing – the cap liner and bottle is then sealed, in part as a tamper-evident feature.
7. Labelling – the appropriate label is put on to the bottle.
8. Neck banding – a PVC band is heat shrunk around the neck/cap as a final seal and as another tamper-evident feature.
9. Cartoning – each bottle is placed into its own individual carton.
10. Packing – individual cartons are then placed in a case pack in predetermined quantities.

NOTE: Stock-keeping unit (SKU) is the phrase for any individual product specification that requires a manufacturing change including packaging.

EXHIBIT 2 Outline of the packaging process

Line 1 – This line fills and packs both Restolvic and Hedanol products. The selection of these products was made on the basis of bottle size. All products packed on this line use the same bottle. In this way, set-up or changeover times are reduced. Even so, they are still lengthy. Each product change means that the filler has to be stripped, cleaned and reassembled. Each line has a crew of seven, consisting of six operators and a mechanic. Three or four operators undertake the cleaning task which takes 3½ to 4 hours. The remainder work on carton and label changing which takes about the same time as the cleaning element of the changeover. So a typical change will take, at most, 4 hours. [Other details for this line are given in *Exhibits 4, 5* and *6*.]

Line 2 – This line is designed to accommodate three different bottle sizes.[1] Over the past two years engineering have redesigned the bottles so that the only dimension which changes is the height. This was selected as it is the easiest form of size adjustment to make on a changeover. Nevertheless, this increases the overall changeover to 5 hours. Without a bottle change then a product change would take between 3½ and 4 hours as with Line 1. Finally, all lines have the same crew make-up as explained for Line 1 and they all work on changeovers that do not require a bottle size change [see *Exhibit 6*].

Line 3 – This line was installed 12 months after the plant was opened. It handles all our liquid products for infants, children and adults. There are five bottle sizes here and each bottle size change takes some 8 hours. Engineering have this set-up reduction as a priority given the enormous benefits we have reaped from the improvements they made on Line 2 [see *Exhibit 6*]. Contamination factors and resulting set-up times restrict, for all practical reasons, the use of this line for packing non-liquid products. The result is that only liquid products are made on this line.

Line 4 – This line handles the 12 product types within the Restolvic prescription range. At present, there are five bottle sizes involved and typical set-up times for bottle and product changes are similar to those on Line 3. There is spare capacity, but if OTC products are to be packed on this line then they must meet the more exacting standards of prescription and associated costs. Furthermore, equipment will need to be added to provide the additional packaging formats which are required by OTC products.[2]

The current shift patterns allow us to run three lines for 24 hours a day throughout all seven days of the week. Priority is given, wherever possible, to Lines 1 and 2 as the products on these two lines have the highest demand and, therefore, require maximum capacity to allow us to meet current schedules. Lines 3 and 4 both have spare capacity and we can meet current demand by running these for two shifts and one shift per day respectively plus additional times when crews have completed their part of a changeover on another line but the mechanic has other work to do [see *Exhibit 7*].

Changeovers on Lines 3 and 4 are scheduled to be completed at times when the process is not manned.

NOTES
1 Bottle sizes differ, depending upon the two factors of tablet size and number of tablets involved.
2 Prescription products have simpler packaging specifications. For example, prescription products are bulk packed at the outer packaging stage where OTC products are individually packed. This additional equipment would require an investment of US$1.0m.

EXHIBIT 3 Details of the four packaging lines

Product[2]	Current year minus						Current year
	6	5	4	3	2	1	
AC Tablets (24)	1,148	1,755	1,906	2,773	3,844	3,896	4,597
AC Tablets (100)	631	907	1,179	1,053	1,180	1,304	1,666
AC Caplets (50)	145	163	402	210	326	409	341
AC Caplets (100)	226	127	172	277	306	440	498
IC Liquid (25 ml)	187	187	249	312	489	429	490
AC Liquid (75 ml)	262	112	158	234	325	294	388
CC Caplets (24)		232	674	977	1,038	1,356	1,457
AC Chewable (110)			438	485	281	480	509
IC Tablets (24)			109	145	254	331	265
CC Tablets (24)				151	151	165	127
IC Tablets (12)				504	432	720	832
CC Tablets (12)				138	311	248	204
AC Tablets (50)					208	256	243
AC Caplets (60)					96	240	262
AC Caplets (24)						65	470
Hedanol Tablets (24)						200	138
Hedanol Tablets (50)						150	42
Hedanol Caplets (24)						218	127
Chewable (20)							224
Chewable (12)							221
Total SKUs added[3]	17	20	22	35	37	45	51

NOTES

1 Annual volumes are in 000 bottles.

2 Other than the three Hedanol products, the remainder are Restolvic.

3 Total SKUs are the number of SKUs packed in each year given. Thus, currently the company packs 34 more products than it did 6 years ago. An SKU is the phrase used for any differently packed item.

EXHIBIT 4 Annual volumes[1] for a number of representative products packed on Lines 1, 2 and 3

Product	Number of production runs					Current year
	Current year minus					
	5	4	3	2	1	
AC Tablets (24)	10	17	24	33	35	41
CC Caplets (24)	4	10	16	20	22	24
IC Tablets (24)		4	6	9	10	10
CC Tablets (24)			7	6	7	7
CC Tablets (12)			6	9	8	8
AC Tablets (50)				8	9	8
AC Caplets (24)					3	12
Hedanol Tablets (50)					6	2
Hedanol Caplets (24)					4	5

NOTE: As explained in the case narrative, there are no bottle size changes on Line 1. Where the same product but not the same quantity of tablets is packed, padding is used as a filler.

EXHIBIT 5 Number of production runs for some representative products on Line 1

Products	Run size (bottles)	Average output (bottles/hour)
Chewable (24)	23,352	4,246
Chewable (24)	54,720	6,080
Chewable (12)	17,016	4,538
Chewable (12)	38,736	5,165
Chewable (24)	44,664	4,060
Chewable (24)	49,056	4,021
Chewable (24)	58,872	5,744
IC Caplets (24)	7,416	4,944
IC Caplets (24)	81,720	6,286
IC Tablets (30)	51,120	4,987
IC Tablets (30)	164,160	6,438
CC Tablets (12)	15,120	3,360
IC Tablets (24)	5,208	3,472
IC Tablets (24)	14,976	3,744
IC Tablets (24)	29,830	5,424
AC Caplets (24)	41,952	5,594
Hedanol Caplets (24)	31,176	4,454
Hedanol Tablets (50)	13,176	2,510
CC Caplets (24)	27,696	5,036
CC Caplets (24)	62,256	6,445
CC Caplets (24)	62,688	4,179
CC Caplets (24)	95,736	6,838
CC Caplets (24)	121,272	7,134
CC Caplets (50)	28,728	3,591
CC Caplets (50)	29,832	4,262
CC Tablets (24)	66,960	6,533
AC Tablets (24)	119,808	6,390
AC Tablets (24)	193,800	7,112
AC Tablets (24)	286,584	7,165
CC Tablets (24)	5,880	2,940
CC Tablets (24)	19,008	5,849
AC Tablets (30)	21,720	4,137

Engineering

The engineering manager, Rob Chow, explained how the priority for his support group was to accommodate the continued growth in the new product derivations.

❝ We launch line extensions and new products on a regular basis in order to capitalize on the Restolvic image and brand name. And it continues to be a very successful strategy. Our contribution is, therefore, to ensure that we can make those new products in line with the agreed launch dates. The trade-off is that we allocate little or no time to process improvements per se. Also of late, the need to work on rationalizing bottle sizes on Line 3 and working on set-ups in general has been put on a back burner. We are aware of the need to address these issues but, at the moment and for the foreseeable future, they will have to take a low priority. ❞

The future

Peter Kovac summed up:

❝ These are exciting times for our business. We have grown sales revenue and profits in line with, if not above, budget and the future looks equally promising. However, all this has been met only by making appropriate investments and the continued efforts of all concerned. The one issue of some concern is that of capacity in our packaging area. A new packaging line currently costs, including installation, some US$3.5m with a lead time of 12 months from the placement of the order before it is commissioned and up to speed. The rationale for such an investment and the case to support such a proposal will need to be carefully thought through and will understandably be questioned by the rest of the executive group given our existing capacity projections. ❞

NOTE: The above is a sample of the production order quantities packed on Line 1 in this period.

EXHIBIT 6 Run size and output data for a number of representative products packed on Line 1 during the past six months

The approach to completing the necessary set-ups/changeovers on the four packaging lines is explained below:

Line 1

As there are no bottle size changes on this line, the product changes are undertaken by the line crew and mechanic who are on the line at the time. A product change requires the filler to be stripped down, cleaned and reassembled. This takes about 3½ to 4 hours using four members of the team. The other members of the crew complete the labelling/carton changes with the mechanic providing support throughout. The whole change would take up to 4 hours.

Lines 2, 3 and 4

Product changes on these lines are undertaken in a way similar to that described for Line 1. However, where a bottle size change is also required then the packing crew would first complete the product change tasks, then move to another line which was ready but not being used. The mechanic would stay behind to complete the size change task. The length of time varies from line to line as shown below.

Line	Set-up (hours)		
	Product/ packaging changes	Bottle size changes	Total for both bottle and product/ packaging changes[1]
1	4	–	4[2]
2	4	5	5
3	4	8	8
4	4	8	8

NOTES
1 Size changes and product changes are completed concurrently.
2 No bottle changes take place on Line 1.

Further set-up reductions are constrained in two ways:

- The investment in a portable filling station and changes to existing lines to accommodate this arrangement total US$0.7m per station.

- These changes would also require additional floor space equal to 50 per cent of the existing floor space required for each packaging line. At this time floor space is at a premium.

EXHIBIT 7 Set-up/changeover arrangements

SHERPIN

12

❝ Growth opportunities we know to be substantial within our business overall', commented Matthew Jones, CEO of Northrop Industries. 'Given this and the profit margins we are currently able to maintain, then capitalizing on this opportunity is a corporate priority. Our concern, however, is whether manufacturing can support this future growth by meeting the needs of future customers while maintaining its support for the existing business. ❞

Background

Sherpin was established ten years ago as a strategic business unit within Northrop Industries, part of the Artne Group. It has grown through an ability to provide high-quality products to industries throughout the world, and today contributes just under 10 per cent of the company's overall sales revenue (see Exhibit 1).

Year	Northrop Industries annual sales (£m)	Sherpin		
		Annual sales (£m)	Number of employees	Gross margin (per cent sales)
1	65	1.6	40	19
2	70	2.8	40	22
3	76	4.0	36	28
4	85	5.2	44	33
5	94	6.4	44	36
6	105	7.4	44	47
7	118	8.6	44	50
8	130	11.1	60	50
9	140	14.7	64	58
10	162	17.2	84	54
11[1]	180	19.7[2]	90	52

NOTES
1 Year 11 is the current year and sales figures are based upon forecasts.
2 Sherpin's monthly sales (£000s) for last year were:

Jan	1,761	Jul	1,274
Feb	1,811	Aug	957
Mar	1,710	Sep	1,189
Apr	1,564	Oct	1,519
May	1,316	Nov	1,532
Jun	1,322	Dec	1,244

EXHIBIT 1 Actual annual sales, number of employees and gross margins for the past ten years and current year forecasts

This case was prepared by Terry Hill (University of Oxford) and Alex Hill (University of Kingston). It is intended for class discussion and not as an illustration of good or bad management. © AMD Publishing.

Markets

Sherpin competes in four distinct markets: aerospace, automotive, industrial and motor sport. The industrial market has always been core to the overall business in that the profits generated in this market have helped the company expand into other segments. However, as these segments have grown (see *Exhibit 2*), it has become apparent that there are different customer demands to be met within each. As Jim Heaton (sales manager) explains:

66 *Our overall strategy as a business is to use our technical expertise to provide solutions to problems. Every product we make is designed specifically to meet the technical requirements of a customer. It is this capability which initially wins an order at the prototype stage, and determines the product specification which manufacturing has to meet. Once this has been achieved, there are various other demands which then have to be met as a part moves into the subsequent original equipment manufacturer (OEM) and spares stages of its life cycle. These demands vary depending on the market sector within which a part competes and as explained in the next sections.* 99

Aerospace

66 *The aerospace market has historically had a traditional approach to undertaking business. This means that the relationships we initially forge and then maintain with customers are vitally important. Prototypes account for 5 per cent of total sales (£s). In this stage of a product's life cycle, new orders are won based on a combination of this relationship factor and the ability to meet the high design and quality conformance requirements within these applications. The price and delivery speed elements still play a role, but this concerns meeting norms rather than competing on price and delivery speed.[1]*

Year	Sales by market sector (£000s)			
	Aerospace	Automotive	Industrial	Motor sport
1	–	–	1,605	–
2	522	–	2,311	–
3	532	–	3,469	–
4	632	–	4,298	287
5	702	–	5,319	421
6	821	511	5,421	654
7	853	1,568	5,539	732
8	952	3,708	5,720	776
9	1,564	4,936	6,844	1,340
10	1,860	5,964	7,760	1,656
11[1,2]	2,636	6,808	8,636	1,616
12[2]	3,476	8,408	9,792	1,648
13[2]	3,276	11,824	13,624	1,684

NOTES
1 Year 11 is the current year.
2 Sales figures for years 11, 12 and 13 are based upon forecasts.

EXHIBIT 2 Historical and projected sales by market sector

However, once we move into the OEM phase the criteria change. Here price becomes more sensitive and it is necessary to be able to react quickly to a customer's short lead-time demands. In fact, at the spares stage in an aerospace product's life cycle, the requirement for fast and reliable delivery becomes vital, especially when an 'aircraft on the ground'[2] situation occurs. Due to the unpredictable nature of demand, it is often not possible to project future demand patterns in either the OEM or spares stages of a product's life. One-off orders are, therefore, placed by customers to meet their needs in both these phases of a typical product's life cycle. We tend to find that the remaining sales (£s) for products are split evenly between these two segments. **99**

Automotive

66 Sales (£s) in this sector are split into 10 per cent prototype, 60 per cent OEM and 30 per cent spares. In the initial prototype stage of production it is our design capability which initially wins an order, although the ability, as with aerospace customers, to meet price and delivery speed requirement norms is also required. As products move into the OEM phase of their life cycle they become more price sensitive, and there is often a need to demonstrate to major customers that the Sherpin production unit has the capability and capacity to meet the required future OEM and spares volumes.

Automotive customers typically use production lines in the OEM phase of a product's life. Their aim is to cut costs by creating lean production facilities often using a just-in-time philosophy to help reduce both costs and the level of inventory holding within their process.[3] To ensure that we can support this, products are purchased from us using a contract which normally gives a view into the future of some 12 or more weeks and typically also includes a material commitment for the same period.

The spares requirement for our products is not usually handled by the same customer as OEM orders. Thus, we find that price becomes slightly less sensitive, but demand is less predictable. However, the spares companies are experienced in this market and they tend to help our produc-

tion planning by using forecasting techniques to smooth their call-offs. This enables products to still be purchased using a contract with normally a 12-week commitment into the future. **99**

Industrial

66 Prototype work accounts for 10 per cent of industrial sales (£s), with the rest being divided equally between OEM and spares. Within the prototype stage of this market, orders are won primarily on our ability to react quickly to a customer enquiry. However, the proposal must also be able to meet price norms as in other markets, with design capability still an issue. Once the product moves into the next stage of its life cycle price becomes more sensitive and delivery speed less crucial, although these demands vary depending on whether orders for products are on a contract or one-off basis.

As with the automotive sector, some industrial customers use production lines and place purchasing contracts to help create the right environment for just-in-time manufacture in the OEM stage of a product's life. However, we find that they are not managed as effectively as in automotive, and thus there is still an element of delivery speed albeit of relatively low importance. This becomes even more apparent as a product moves into spares and wide fluctuations in demand can occur on a weekly basis. One outcome of this is that we need to be able to meet short lead times.

Unlike automotive, we find that both OEM and spares are handled by the same customer, and, due to the nature of our products, these two market segments are often supplied simultaneously. However, the spares demand is poorly managed and is merely 'front-end loaded' into the contract which gives us very little time to respond to an increase in demand. Also, because it is difficult to supply these two segments at a different price, we find that there is still a focus on price for the spares volume element of this business.

Other customers still purchase products from us using one-off orders rather than contracts in both the OEM and spares stages of their products' lives. This means that price is not as sensitive, but all other requirements remain the same. Collectively, these latter customers account for 20 per cent of total industrial sales. 》》

Motor sport

《《 The motor sport market is unique because customer requirements are the same throughout the life cycle of a product. One consequence is that price is always considered to be of very low importance. However, this is a very demanding industry and a high level of support is required within other market dimensions such as technical expertise, delivery speed, delivery reliability and quality conformance. For example, it is not unusual for us to receive a call from a customer asking for supply of a product to be used for a race in a few days' time.

In these circumstances, it is critical that we can respond to their needs, and deliver a high specification part to them on the exact date required. If there were to be any delivery reliability or quality conformance problems then we may lose the business altogether. Also, this continual focus by customers on design improvements means that modifications can occur at any stage in a product's life, and the relationship that exists between us and the customer always plays an important role in the development and maintenance of new business. 》》

Operations[4]

Compared with the rest of Northrop Industries, Sherpin's products require different materials and unique machining processes. Due to these factors, the decision was made to set up a facility solely dedicated to the manufacture of these parts. It comprises a number of functions including sales and marketing, commercial, design, production, purchasing and quality. Production and purchasing are now discussed in more detail.

Production

《《 Presently, all products are manufactured within a small plant using a number of batch processes',

explained Paul Davies. 'Components are purchased from external suppliers, and then processed in two or three days before being despatched to customers.

Operations is run on a one-shift basis and comprises goods inward, production and despatch functions. The production of a part is not complex, and normally involves two or three processes. The equipment used within these processes is inexpensive, with a new machine typically only costing between £5,000 and £10,000. The process equipment can typically be designed, manufactured and delivered in 6 to 8 weeks. However, the technical nature of these products means that the labour skill requirement is high. Thus, operators are extensively trained in the use of techniques such as statistical process control (SPC) to ensure that the quality standards are met.

The facilities are used to manufacture varying production order sizes. At one end of the scale, automotive customers tend to order weekly quantities of around 2,000 parts, which equates to somewhere between 2 and 3 days' production for one operator. Some industrial contract products are of a similar volume, but there are also one-off orders which come in sporadically and tend to comprise about 4 to 5 hours' work. Low volume parts are manufactured for aerospace and motor sport customers. Here, 2 hours' production is considered to be a large order. 》》

Purchasing

All products comprise a number of components which typically are purchased from several different suppliers. If any one of these components is not available, then the manufacture of a part is delayed. When suppliers fail to meet their promised delivery dates, there is often pressure to work overtime or employ temporary labour during the month end to meet sales targets and customer delivery requirements. As Bob Gilder (purchasing manager) explains:

《《 There is great pressure on me to ensure that Paul has all the components he requires for production. Without these our products cannot be made. In the past, the way that we achieved *this was to hold buffer and safety stocks on long-running jobs where we had a good view of future demand and knew that raw materials would not become obsolete. However, in recent years one of the priorities in the Group has been to reduce inventory levels. The outcome has been continued pressure to reduce these holdings. As a result, parts are now ordered from our suppliers as and when they are required. Safety stocks have now been removed and buffer stocks reduced to a minimum.* **99**

Order processing

Currently, orders received into the business unit are then processed by the commercial and operations functions through a number of stages, as explained below.

Commercial

Customer demands are received by the commercial department either as contracts,[5] or one-off[6] orders, and are immediately inputted into the computer system. Each customer has its own contact within the commercial department that processes and, when required, progresses work through operations. As Anne Ballow (commercial manager) explains:

66 *The idea is to create good customer relations at a personal level. By allocating a contact to each customer, we have been able to give them the service they require. This has proved a key feature for our large aerospace and motor sport accounts.* **99**

Operations

66 *Once orders have been received, they are processed in the following way',* explained Roy Price (SBU manager). *'Manufacturing and purchasing are run using an MRP-based computer system linked into the order processing database. This translates the customer order inputs made by the commercial department into demands for finished parts and raw materials. Orders are then raised in line with the operations standard lead times on the system.'*

When the initial quotation is made at the start of a product's life preferred suppliers for the different components are selected. If the contract is secured these companies then become the sole supplier of a given component(s). Standard lead times are keyed into the computer system in line with those quoted by suppliers, and can be anything up to fifty working days (see Exhibit 3). Using these standards, products are then purchased as and when required. For example, purchasing would receive a prompt to place an order for a product usually made by Supplier D twenty working days before it is required by manufacturing. This prompt is in the form of a material requirements list printed off the computer system on a daily basis, showing which products need to be ordered that day. Lead times are reviewed regularly to ensure that they reflect the delivery agreements we have with our suppliers.

Once components have been delivered, they are held in raw material stores before being issued to production. Even though products can be manufactured in three days or less, a standard two week production lead time has been set up for all parts. The reason for this is that historically suppliers have not been reliable, and so we have put in a buffer lead time to ensure that all of the relevant components are available when required for production. However, even with this buffer, we are still sometimes unable to produce a part due to component shortages.

A recent analysis of the business revealed that, on average, 40 per cent of all products are delayed going into manufacturing due to a lack of materials and components. One outcome is that when the outstanding components are finally received, we find ourselves working a high level of overtime to satisfy customers' delivery requirements and month end targets. As both of these requirements are key tasks for manufacturing then it sometimes means that we make products that are due for delivery in the next period in order to meet both these targets. **99**

Supplier reference[1]	Number of component types[2]	Lead time (number of working days)[3]
A	2	45
B	233	10
C	21	7
D	35	20
E	24	37
F	11	17
G	77	17
H	28	18
I	64	27
J	13	45
K	25	10
L	103	27

NOTES

1 In total there are 20 suppliers.
2 Each component type reflects a different stock-keeping unit.
3 Suppliers quote the same lead time for each component they manufacture.

EXHIBIT 3 Typical operations lead time of key suppliers

Exhibit 4 shows a typical month's production, Exhibit 5 presents delivery performance data and Exhibit 6 inventory holdings during the past year.

The future

66 *Although the Sherpin business unit is only 10 per cent of our sales, it has a key role in our overall profitability. With current margin levels and future market potential (see Exhibit 7), Sherpin plays and will play a key role in our overall strategy',* explained Matthew Jones.

The main opportunity for growth is in the automotive market. However, the price sensitivity of this sector means that we will be increasing sales within relatively low margin markets. Thus we must make sure that manufacturing can support this growth in terms of having sufficient capacity, and being able to support the relevant market needs, particularly re cost and delivery reliability.

In the other sectors, the growth potential is not as large, but there is scope particularly in some segments and markets. In addition, markets such as motor sport give excellent profit and keep our designers at the forefront of engineering and material technology. The requirements of markets differ markedly from one another and we need to recognize this in our developments. The challenge that faces us is how to expand successfully automotive sales, while continuing to support existing customers in other market segments. 99

Week	Sales orders received £000s	Production £000s	Despatches £000s	Labour hours worked[1]
1	370	222	209	1,254
2	350	347	180	1,272
3	355	383	229	1,308
4	365	567	831	1,758

NOTE

1 The basic labour hours worked averaged 1,218 per week in this typical month.

EXHIBIT 4 Sales, production, despatch and labour hours data for a typical month

Order number	Market sector[1]	Delivery date					
		Requested		Promised		Actual	
		Day	Week[2]	Day	Week[2]	Day	Week[2]
72614	Ae	4	13	5	13	2	14
85221	Au	3	14	3	14	3	14
64498	I	2	12	2	12	3	14
32987	MS	3	14	4	14	4	14
21589	I	5	15	5	15	5	14
55123	Ae	5	12	2	13	1	15
19985	Ae	2	14	1	15	1	15
18754	Au	4	14	4	14	2	15
54462	I	2	12	2	12	2	15
08956	I	3	15	3	15	4	15
12587	I	5	15	5	15	5	15
56147	Au	5	15	5	15	5	15
22932	Au	2	16	2	16	2	16
46511	I	2	16	2	16	2	16
55233	Au	5	15	5	15	4	16
67859	Ae	5	14	5	15	4	16
52315	MS	1	16	4	16	5	16
59521	Au	1	16	1	17	1	17
26691	Ae	2	17	2	17	1	17
11635	Au	2	17	2	17	2	17
11279	I	5	16	5	16	2	17
41246	Au	5	16	5	16	2	17
92137	Au	2	17	2	17	3	17
27561	MS	1	17	3	17	3	17
37249	I	3	17	3	17	3	17
21234	I	5	16	5	16	4	17
57943	MS	2	17	3	17	4	17
87613	Ae	5	15	5	16	5	17
81267	Ae	5	19	5	19	5	17
11237	Au	3	19	3	19	5	17

NOTES
1 Ae = aerospace; I = industrial; Au = automotive; MS = motor sport.
2 March is weeks 10 to 13, April is weeks 14 to 18 and May is weeks 19 to 23.

EXHIBIT 5 Requested, promised and actual delivery date for a representative sample of customer orders within a typical month

Month	Inventory (£000s)		
	Raw materials	Work-in-progress	Finished goods
Jan	473	53	101
Feb	412	58	103
Mar	388	24	102
Apr	361	30	75
May	336	29	87
Jun	347	14	73
Jul	354	9	133
Aug	378	4	93
Sep	367	10	79
Oct	355	45	58
Nov	372	25	77
Dec	414	81	78

EXHIBIT 6 Value of month end inventory holding for the past year

Sector	Market share (as a per cent total potential)[1]		
	UK	Other European	US
Aerospace	55	25	–
Automotive	10	7	2
Industrial	60	20	–
Motor sport	90	80	70

NOTE

1 Market share is based on last year's sales, and is estimated.

EXHIBIT 7 Market share by sector

Notes

1 Delivery speed refers to the dimension of short lead times.

2 An 'aircraft on the ground' is the term used to denote a situation where an aircraft is awaiting a spare part and, as a result, is unable to fly.

3 Within all markets, delivery reliability and quality conformance are expected by customers. However, if they are not supported for those using a just-in-time philosophy, production lines could be stopped and there is a potential to lose the business altogether.

4 The operations function comprises purchasing, production and despatch.

5 A contract is an order placed with a view into the future of normally 12 or more weeks. It typically includes a material commitment for the same period.

6 A one-off order is placed without a view to the future and is typically for an order quantity to be delivered on a specific date.

13 ZARA

The Zara boutique clothing store on Calle Real in the northern Spanish city of La Coruna is buzzing. Customers have made the journey here on a rainy Saturday morning to see what new exciting styles are available this week. The red tank tops and black blazers seem to be a hit, but they're also pining for beige ones and bright purple ones too. Faced with this problem, most fashion companies would normally have to spend months retooling and restocking their range. Not Zara, however. Each store manager is able to spot these changes in trends and type them into their Casio handheld computer on Saturday in the safe knowledge that they will arrive on Monday.

As Rosanna Padine, commercial director explains:

“ *There is a very strong link between the store managers and the central design team based at our head office in La Coruna in northern Spain. Each store is electronically linked back to head office so that we can view and assess sales on a real-time basis. This allows us to make sure that we can adapt quickly to customer wants and desires. An example of this happened last week with the new khaki skirt we initially just stocked in Spain to see how it would sell. In our La Coruna store, it was sold out after only having been on the shelves for a couple of hours. After speaking to our Barcelona outlet, it was apparent that sales were brisk there too. We decided that we should test it out elsewhere, so overnight we sent out 7,800 skirts to our 1,300-plus stores worldwide. The results were clear – the skirt was a hit and within the next few days our stores in Europe, Asia, North and South America were stocked with the khaki skirt.* ”

It is this mix of intelligence-gathering, fashion instinct and technological know-how that allows Zara to set in motion something unique in the clothing trade. The combination of being able to translate the latest trends into products in less than 15 days and delivering them to its stores twice a week means that it is able to catch fashion trends while they are hot, responding quickly to the fast-changing tastes of young urban consumers. As Keith Mortimer, European retail analyst, says:

“ *Nobody else can get new designs to stores as quickly. Unless you can do that, you won't be in business in ten years. Zara continuously analyses its value chain and seeks to achieve control on as many sections of it as possible. By focusing on reducing time between design and sale, it has developed a production cycle that is entirely different from fashion sector norms. The design team works throughout the season studying everything from the clothes worn in hit TV series to how clubbers dress. This means there is a continuous stream of new products that ensure customers keep coming back to see what's new. Its clothing has filled an untapped niche: Prada at moderate prices.* ”

Customers seem to love the results of this high-velocity operation. They are often known to queue in long lines at Zara's stores on designated delivery days, a phenomenon that has been dubbed 'Zaramania' in the press. And this popularity is generating tangible, bottom line results as well as admiration from the fashion world (see *Exhibit 1*). Over the past five years, it grew profitability at a 30 per cent average annual rate, which is 45 per cent faster than its four industry rivals during the same period.

This case was prepared by Alex Hill (University of Kingston). It is intended for class discussion and not as an illustration of good or bad management.© AMD Publishing.

Data	Annual value							
	2000	2001	2002	2003	2004	2005	2006	2007
Net store openings	53	60	85	95	97	129	174	186
Company-managed stores	382	435	487	587	649	770	1,077	1,231
Franchised stores	24	31	44	59	74	82	98	130
Selling area (000s sq. m)	408	480	562	888	811	962	1,138	1,290
Net sales (€m)	2,044	2,435	2,913	3,220	3,760	4,441	5,534	6,264
Operating income (€m)	327	440	540	478	654	712	911	1,116

EXHIBIT 1 Zara net store openings, number of company-managed and franchised stores, selling area, net sales and operating income, 2000–07

A global success

Founded in 1963 as a maker of ladies lingerie, Zara opened its first store in 1975 as a retail clothing company with a single location in La Coruna, north-west Spain. By 1989, the company had 98 retail shops and production facilities distributed around Spain and in the same year the company started its international expansion by opening a shop in Lisbon, Portugal. This was only the beginning of what has become a huge expansion plan across the world. It is now the largest and most profitable unit of Inditex SA, the Spanish clothes manufacturer and distributor, with over 1,300 stores distributed throughout Europe, the Middle East, Asia Pacific and the Americas (see *Exhibit 2*).

As Jonathon May, retail consultant comments:

66 *This rapid expansion has meant that Zara now has three characteristics that distinguish it from its competitors. First, it is the fastest growing retail business not only in Europe but also across the world. Second, it has been able to successfully export its formula at a time when many other clothing companies in the middle and lower middle markets have found it difficult. Next, for example, is a fantastic company, but has always struggled to export its particular format. And third, it has created a simple, singular message for all its customers. The shopping experience is upscale, while the product offering* is good quality, but not best quality, at a good price. It might well have sacrificed a little on technical quality but it has more than made up for it through product design in terms of fabrics, colours, patterns and styles. If you go into a store this immediately hits you and then when you look at a garment you will see that the price tags are big and colourful, emblazoned with the flags of a dozen countries, each accompanied by a local currency price that is the same for that item around the world, from Madrid to Riyadh to Tokyo. 99

Challenging the competition

In times when a combination of recession and some merchandising mistakes have forced Gap and comparable European stores like Sweden's H&M to retrench, Zara continues to expand. Much of the success is due to its unusual structure. For decades now, the majority of clothing retailers have outsourced their manufacturing to developing countries in the pursuit of lower costs and greater efficiencies. However, Zara bucked this trend and took a different stance. It felt that it would be better off developing a business that was able to respond quickly to shifts in consumer tastes and thus made the decision to set up a vertically integrated business model spanning design, just-in-time production, marketing and sales.

Region	Country	Number of stores
Europe	Andorra	1
	Austria	10
	Belgium	23
	Czech Republic	5
	Cyprus	4
	Denmark	4
	Finland	4
	France	109
	Germany	62
	Greece	48
	Hungary	4
	Iceland	2
	Ireland	8
	Italy	74
	Luxembourg	2
	Malta	1
	Monaco	1
	Norway	2
	Poland	18
	Portugal	73
	Romania	2
	Spain	491
	Sweden	9
	Switzerland	9
	The Netherlands	12
	Turkey	22
	United Kingdom	56
Middle East	Bahrain	1
	Israel	15
	Jordan	2
	Kuwait	5
	Lebanon	2
	Oman	1
	Qatar	2
	Saudi Arabia	18
	United Arab Emirates	5

Region	Country	Number of stores
Asia Pacific	China	12
	Indonesia	6
	Japan	29
	Malaysia	5
	Philippines	5
	Singapore	5
	Thailand	3
Americas	Argentina	7
	Brazil	22
	Canada	14
	Chile	6
	Costa Rica	2
	Columbia	4
	Dominican Republic	1
	El Salvador	2
	Guatemala	1
	Mexico	47
	Panama	2
	Puerto Rico	1
	United States	29
	Uruguay	2
	Venezuela	9
Other	Croatia	1
	Estonia	2
	Latvia	3
	Lithuania	4
	Morocco	3
	Russia	18
	Serbia	3
	Slovakia	1
	Slovenia	4
	Tunisia	1

EXHIBIT 2 Current number of Zara stores by region and country

As such, it now produces more than half its own clothes at its ultramodern factory in northern Spain rather than relying on a network of disparate and often slow-moving suppliers. H&M, for instance, has 900 suppliers and no factories, whereas Zara makes 40% of its own fabric and produces 60% of its merchandise in-house. David Johnston, a retail consultant in London, says: 'Vertical integration has gone out of fashion in the consumer economy. Zara is a spectacular exception to the rule.'

The result is that Zara has more flexibility than its rivals to respond to fickle fashion trends. It can make a new line from start to finish in three weeks, against an industry average of nine months. It is able to introduce 10,000 new designs into its stores each year – none of which stays there for over a month. This constant refreshment of the store offering creates a sense of excitement that attracts new shoppers and ensures that old ones return. It is also radically changing the way that people shop. As David Johnston explains:

66 If customers see a product that they like in the store, they know that it will only be there for four weeks, not four months, and that they will probably not be able to find it after that. It stimulates customers to buy now and creates a greater velocity of shopping. This is quite a different situation to the high streets of old and more and more retailers are finding it difficult to compete. For example, C&A chose to exit the UK market and the Japanese basics retailer Uniglo has closed all but five of its stores here. Boring, staple clothing is being killed off! 99

However, its not just the traditional high-street chains that have been affected. Even supermarket clothing retailer George at Asda has been inspired to react, by producing a collection called Fast Fashion.

Keeping up with fashion

According to Jose Maria Castellano, Inditex chief executive: 'Fashion expires, much the same way yogurt does. Being so quick allows us to reduce to a minimum the risk of making a mistake, and we do make mistakes, with our collections.' With this in mind, the designers at Zara work hard to constantly update, mix and match popular styles

rather than simply flooding the market with a single item, so that no product is available for more than a few weeks. As Rosanna Padine, commercial director, explains:

66 No one wants to dress like everybody else. It is important always to have fresh fashion. We have found that not only does our business model allow us to offer mid-market chic at downmarket prices, it also protects against slip-ups too. Whereas most retailers have already committed to 60 per cent of their production at the start of the season, at Zara the figure is only 15 per cent. This makes it easier to kill off a range that turns out to be unpopular and, like everyone else, this can happen. 99

Although mistakes can happen, Zara tries to minimize them by pushing its designers onto aeroplanes and sending them out in search of new trends. They spend their time looking through stacks of fashion magazines, attending fashion shows and frequenting fashionable cafes, restaurants and bars. Rosanna Padine says:

66 We find that it is particularly good to listen to our customers as they know better than anyone what they want. Our designers then act like sponges, soaking up information about fashion trends from all over the world and translating them into new ideas. The constant travel, catwalk shows and even music videos mean that a look seen on MTV can be in the stores within a month. Traditionally, fashion collections are designed only four times a year, but on average we will produce over 10,000 different designs each year. While the style and shape of the garments may not vary hugely each time, they are produced in a wide variety of different fabrics, colours and patterns.

From the beginning of our international expansion in 1989, we have always focused on developing products for the global market. We felt that it was important to capitalize on and exploit the many benefits of international product and brand uniformity, such as product development and manufacturing costs, logistics and inventory costs, plus a consistent product and brand image across all markets. The development of global products is the full responsibility of the design team at our head office in Spain. They consist of different types of people with fashion, marketing and retail experience. Drawing on each of their backgrounds and using information gathered through regular field research and computerized store data, the team then make all the decisions regarding developing and launching new products – for example which products, the timing of the launch, the quantity of the production run and how many should be shipped to each country. The result is that we have an international product line that can be found in all stores, the only difference being the proportion of items in each store.

However, these are not the only centralized decisions taken by the team. They are also responsible for pricing in each of the various countries. All our garments are displayed in stores with an international price tag showing the different prices in their respective countries. Prices are globalized, taking into account the difference in local market conditions, the problems of potential parallel imports, and in order to make sure we position the product uniformly. Once the team have decided on the type of product, the price and quantities to be held in each store, then we are ready to start the production process. **99**

The production and distribution system

For a fashion business, Zara is also unique in the way that it is driven by consumer feedback. As Mike Shearwood, Zara's UK managing director, explains:

66 Our store managers are the most important people in the Zara business. Selecting from over 10,000 lines a year, they are responsible for placing the orders with the factory and central office in Spain. These orders are placed twice a week and determine the type and quantity of products that will be stocked in their store. We rely on their ability to understand and monitor how well products are selling in order to ensure that we have the right stock at the right time in the right place. **99**

Each store manager receives information via a handheld computer showing images of the products that can be ordered. Based on sales over the past few days and trends that seem to be emerging in each of the local stores, they then decide which products and how many to order. In the head office

in Spain, there is a section dedicated to each country and the store manager will usually talk to them once or twice a day and three to five times on order days. The firm's commercial sections then liaise with the designers and factories to make sure that the products meet the needs of the local customers for each store. While there is an initial trend framework set up at the beginning of each season, modifications are continually made as required in response to the reaction of customers to each range.

As well as operating its own worldwide distribution network out of its facility in Spain, Zara also designs and manufactures products here too. Lead times for new designs average about four to six weeks, but may be as little as two. Zara achieves this by holding fabric in stock and then cutting and dyeing it at the last minute. With its team of commercials sniffing out new fashions while keeping in constant contact with store managers, the company can spot and react to trends quickly, including taking something stylish off a music video that has just been released. In contrast, other retailers need an average of six months to design a new collection and then another three months to manufacture it. A store manager will send in a new idea to La Coruna headquarters in Spain. The 200-plus designers decide if it is appealing, and then come up with specifications. The design is scanned into a computer and zapped to production computers in manufacturing, which cut and dye the material which is then assembled into clothes by outside workshops. The in-house manufacturing plant is futuristic, equipped with large clothes-cutting machines that are run by a handful of technicians in a laboratory-style computer control centre. The dyeing part of the process occurs in small units in another part of the factory. By dyeing products after they have been cut, they are able to minimize the quantities of dye used and help to control costs.

For most garments, the company owns all parts of the production process, apart from the sewing. Fabric comes from places including Spain, Southeast Asia, India, and Morocco and is cut and coloured at the company's state-of-the-art factory. Using information gathered from stores, production managers decide how many garments to make and which stores will get them. The fabric is then sewn together at 400 cooperatives run by local seamstresses before being shipped around the world. This combination of real-time information-sharing and internalized production means that Zara can work with almost zero stock and still have new designs in the stores twice a week, as opposed to the six months that it traditionally takes most competitors. The twice-weekly deliveries help to keep Zara stores looking fresh, and store clerks heighten the sense of rapid turnover by changing the location of key items.

Retail stores

In keeping with the philosophy of the rest of the business, the stores themselves are designed by an in-house team of architects with a 'white box' style that evolves as it goes along in terms of signage and lighting or, for example, the introduction of escalators. They are minimal in design and the way in which clothing is presented. However, the constant rapid turnover of products and changing location of key items results in keeping customers curious and keen to see the latest styles. They find that this in itself is sufficient to draw shoppers into the store. Again, unlike the majority of its competitors, Zara's approach to advertising is as minimal as its store interiors. It consists of only taking a full-page local newspaper advert twice a year, on the day before it has a sale.

As Mike Shearwood comments:

66 Our main media are the location of the stores and the shop windows. Our business model lends itself to the fact that our products are ones that customers want to buy, so we do not have to persuade them to buy products that we want to sell. Because of the short production and distribution lead times, there is less need to discount, except at those two sale periods each year. In fact, we do not really have to have a sale at all, but we find that it works well as a promotional tool. 99

The future

In terms of the future for Zara, Keith Mortimer, European retail analyst, reflects:

66 The question now is how far it can go with the concept of design-on-demand retailing, which it runs with almost no advertising outside its biannual storewide sales. While there is nothing wrong with it taking advantage of its rivals' weaknesses to grab market share, Zara's still entirely Spanish management team will have to be careful not to indulge in the overexpansion that has floored so many of its rivals. The further the Group gets from its heartland, where it has faced only modest competition, the more its model will be stretched. The chain is now well known in South America and Europe, but less so in the US where it is still establishing itself. Yet again this year, it will be pursuing a very aggressive expansion plan, claiming that the only restraining factor is the availability of suitable real estate. Given this, it will probably begin using the web to sell clothes as finding new store sites becomes more difficult. This may help to boost its low profile in the US as they have less reluctance to buy online than in its homeland of Southern Europe. 99

Note: Markets, operations strategy, order-winners and qualifiers are mentioned throughout the text, so in each case, the references given below are most relevant.

Printed and bound by CPI Group (UK) Ltd, Croydon, CR0 4YY